CUVEE DE RESERVE

2000 Champagnes

Richard Juhlin

Photography, graphics and production: Pelle Bergentz
Cover: Joel Berg Cover photos: Pål Allan
Editor: Peter Taggart-Holland
Translation: Keith Foster

For more information and the
most recent tastingnotes, please turn to
www.champagneclub.com

The Bubble Lounge has selected "2000 Champagnes" as the reference book for their champagne bars in New York and San Francisco. The Bubble Lounge is pleased to contribute to the enlightenment of the wines of champagne in the United States through this extraordinary book, and hope to continue to extend the pleasures of champagne to connoisseurs and novices alike.

Published in the USA by M.T. Train/Scala Books, 1999
Distributed by Antique Collectors'Club - Wappinger Falls - NY

Printed at
Milanostampa New Interlitho
Italy, 1999

ISBN 91-630-6260-7

A word of thanks

When I decided to write a book I had no idea how many different people were about to become involved. I'm so very grateful for all the help I've received in realising my dream of producing the first book about champagne to come from Scandinavia. Everywhere, both here and in France, people have been amazing, supporting me with information or some other form of assistance. Others among my personal circle of friends and loved ones, and who may not have been able to help in such an active fashion, have shown great understanding and patience with my introverted way of life these past three years.

The list would be much too long if I were to include the names of everyone who deserves my thanks. However, I would like to express my gratitude to all those I've met at the hundreds of champagne firms I've visited, and to Guillaume Bruneau and Marie-Pierre Locret at the C.I.V.C. who organised my trips to Champagne. Without their help this book would never have been published.

To Marketta, Stella and Mark Knopfler.

Foreword

The world of Champagne is in constant ferment. Vintages come and go but the yeasts work their special Champagne magic every second of the year. Every Champagne grower and every Champagne house works with one single appellation. Which is why we are all so different. Together, we form a mosaic of styles.

It takes a very perceptive outsider to create a coherent picture of this complex, ever-changing scene. Richard Juhlin, a young Swedish Champagne specialist, is just such a man. Widely noted for his prowess in blind tastings (he can pinpoint vintages and house styles with enviable ease) he has devoted countless hours exploring our region - its vineyards, producers, varieties, and wines.

To the world's most festive and light-hearted wine he has dedicated a work that contrives to be serious but not solemn. His book mirrors the fascination and complexity of Champagne. His effervescent prose leads us into a voyage of discovery of the region. Only a few enduring works exist on the subject of Champagne. This work is an addition to this body of literature. And it is noteworthy for being the first to emanate from Scandinavia.

If any truly universal language exists, it is the raising of a glass of Champagne. I do so now and the toast is Richard Juhlin.

Christian Pol-Roger

Christian Pol-Roger

Champagne is indeed a great wine. It is also the symbol of happiness.

When I read Richard Juhlin's book, I can feel he has achieved this perfect balanced "cuvée" of wine knowledge and pleasure.

Richard is one of the most dynamic champagne experts. His knowledge of the Champagne region, the soil, the climate, the grapes and the people who produce the wine is huge. Richard has also this slight touch of crazyness wich makes his book sparkle!

His first introduction to the Champagne region was when he tried to jump over the locked gates at Krug during an August week-end. (see page 6) This is just one example of how crazy he is about Champagne!

Since then, Richard visited Champagne many times and little by little collected the necessary information to build the great expertise that will make the reader dream about and long to open a bottle of champagne.

Henri Krug

Henri Krug

Contents

Introduction

When I first travelled to Champagne it wasn't so easy to get into the great houses. It took cunning - and no little strength!

For most people champagne is a drink associated with luxury, parties and important occasions, all of which has served to give champagne a very positive image. Sadly however, most people don't realise what a noble wine champagne is. Many don't even give a thought to whether the drink in their glass is a fine champagne or a cheap sparkling wine - so long as it bubbles they call it champagne. These preconceived ideas are so widespread that even experienced wine tasters forget their analytical thinking and well-rehearsed tasting rituals as soon as they get a glass of champagne in their hands. However, these attitudes are starting to change and there are now few wine journalists or sommeliers who question champagne's superiority over other sparkling wines.

Around 1,500 million bottles of sparkling wine are produced in the world every year, but only 200 million of these are genuine champagne. Only there, in the small, clearly-marked region in northern France, and nowhere else, may one use the term "champagne". This is because a series of circumstances have combined to make this by far the most suitable area in the world for the production of sparkling wines.

The wines became sparkling because of the area's chilly climate. It was only in the early 18th century that methods were developed to control the second fermentation in the bottle, which today creates around 47 million bubbles per bottle. The monk named Dom Pérignon - otherwise known as "the father of champagne" - was just one in a series of people who developed the process we now know as the "champagne method". This method is used more or less successfully in other parts of the world, but never with the same excellent results as in Champagne.

When the wines go through their special second fermentation in the bottle they are stored in huge chalk cellars many kilometres long under the streets of Champagne towns like Reims and Épernay. These chalk pits - Crayères - were dug by the Romans when they needed building materials for their homes.

The triumphant march of champagne across the world began when the major champagne houses were founded towards the end of the 18th century, and it continues to this day. In most countries the bubbly wine has almost always been drunk by the wealthier sections of society, but this need no longer be the case as a bottle of champagne is now cheaper than ever before.

I hope this book will give you an insight into the wonderful world of champagne so that you can go on to explore the many wines from the region in your own time. Perhaps you will discover that champagne can be a superb drink all by itself, but that it is also a perfect partner for any number of dishes. Once you've made the acquaintance of the wine of wines it probably won't be long before you decide to pay a trip to its home country. You may even play a part in inspiring more and more to become interested in the king of the sparkling wines!

The winegrowing regions of Champagne

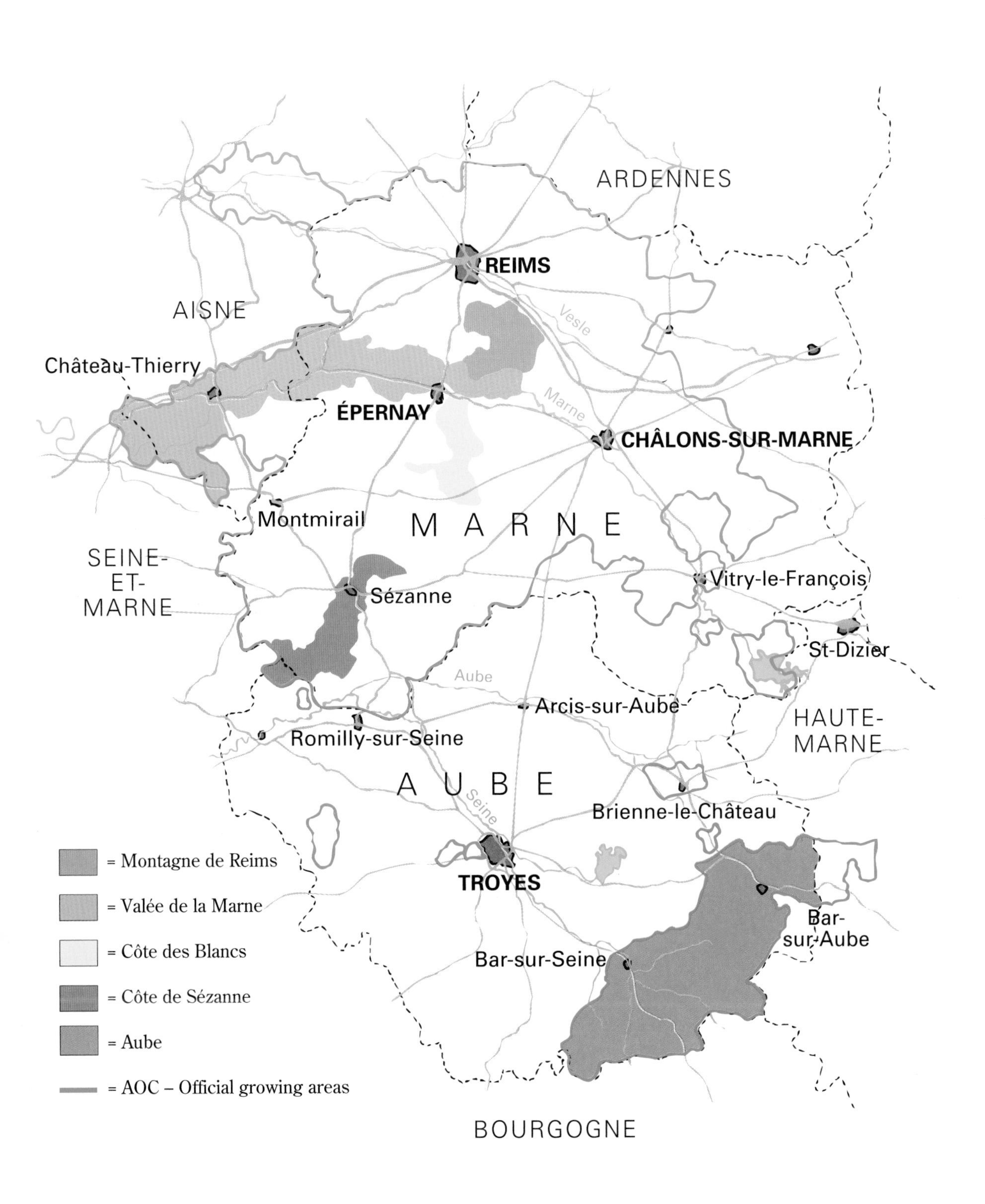

CHAMPAGNE

The history of champagne

Three regions - three meanings

Let us begin by stating that champagne is not just any old sparkling wine. Like Burgundy, Rioja or Mosel, Champagne is an individual geographically-defined district. How-ever, the name Champagne has three meanings:

— La Champagne (the province)

— Champagne Viticole (the wine-producing area)

— Le champagne (the wine).

Champagne literally means "open landscape", which is a good description of this area of long, gently-sloping hills, surrounded by a flat, broad expanse of farming land. The Champagne province is divided up into four "départements": Ardennes, Marne, Aube and Haute-Marne. From north to south the province is some 320 kilometres long and almost 150 kilometres wide, an area which almost equals that of Belgium.
Geologically the province has three distinct sections:

The province Champagnes geographical place in France.

— **Champagne Humide** has its geological origins in the eastern part of an inland sea called the Paris basin. This inland sea dried up some 70 million years ago, leaving behind it a layer of clay. The area stretches from the Ardennes to the French/Belgian border, the southeast pointing towards Burgundy. The soil is extremely fertile and is well-suited to growing crops of different kinds. On the other hand, a great sparkling wine needs a lean, meagre soil, so with that in mind Champagne Humide's earth is quite inappropriate.

— To the west of Humide runs another, equally narrow, geological strip called **Champagne Pouilleuse**. Here are deep layers of chalk covered by a thin top of clay, which is unable to retain the rainwater at root level. For that reason, vine cultivation is an unsuitable occupation here too.

— The only region that has the right to grow the true grapes for the champagne wines is **Champagne Viticole**. During the tertiary period, some 30 million years ago, the centre of the Paris basin was subjected to a series of tremors which raised the sea bed. Twenty million years later came more violent movements of the earth, raising the land by about 150 metres and building a chain of relatively steep chalk hills. As time went by, the hills were rounded off and covered with a thin surface of earth, and these mounds are today called Les Falaises de Champagne. Their unique cultivational qualities have made it possible to create the world's most perfect sparkling wine. The height, slope and soil of the hills, together with the climate, are one of nature's greatest gifts to mankind.

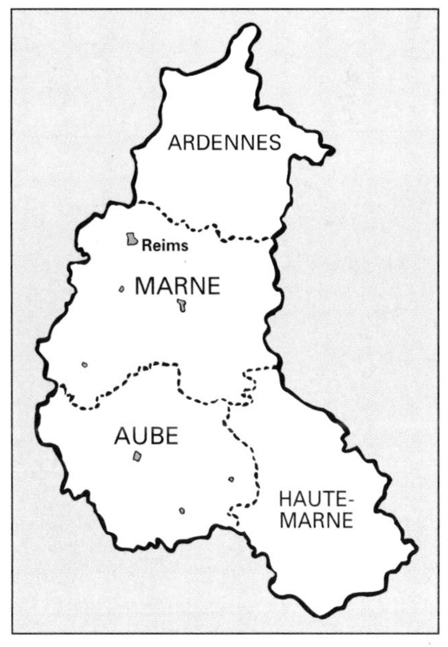

Champagnes four "départements": Aube, Marne, Ardennes and Haute-Marne.

Sunset over Aÿ.

Belimnite chalk - champagne's soil

The chalk that has shown itself to be the most suited to vine cultivation — Belimnita quadrata (Bq) — does not exist to the same degree anywhere other than the slopes of the heart of Champagne. The chalk gained its name from the Belimnite mollusc, which lived in the so-called Paris basin and left a rich supply of fossils after it. They contained large amounts of calcium, which slowly changed into chalk.

Opinions are divided as to whether Belimnita quadrata is superior to the second type of chalk - Micraster chalks - or not. My own opinion is that the unique tones of top-class, mineral-rich champagne can best be achieved from grapes that have grown in Belimnite-based soil. Most of the Grand cru areas are dominated by Bq and some of the best Premier cru locations rest securely on the mollusc's creation. It is said that this type of chalk releases more calcium, gives the grapes a greater oxygen content, has a positive effect on the plant's photosynthesis and prevents chlorosis, which can yellow the plant's leaves. Bq also gives perfect drainage, which is good for the vines as they don't like getting "wet feet". Another plus is the way all chalk has the ability to retain a constant temperature year-round. As the vine's roots go deep in their search for water, the mineral content of the grapes is high, giving a good champagne its characteristic taste.

The white chalklayer. In certain places almost 300 metres thick.

Early interest in wine production

Before the Romans captured Champagne it was part of a loosely-defined area called Gaul. You remember — the home of Asterix and Obelix. Some say that the Gauls grew vines here, but the most prevalent view is that it was the Romans who planted the first vines in Champagne. Major archaeological finds of Gallo-Roman wine-related objects strengthen the theory that wine was cultivated in Champagne fifty years after the birth of Christ.

Theatre of war

Champagne's history is coloured by many a bloody battle. No other region in France has been subjected to so much war, plunder and vandalism as Champagne. The Franks, the Goths, the Burgunders and the Vandals had their moments, but the worst by far must be Attila the Hun. In the year 451, the Katalaunian fields in Champagne were the scene of one of mankind's bloodiest clashes in which some 200,000 died. That battle forced Attila to retreat from western Europe, but Champagne's role as a theatre of war was not over. During the middle ages, the town of Épernay was burnt and plundered no fewer than 25 times, and the area was in the middle of major battles throughout World Wars I and II.

Wine from hills and valleys

The region's central position in France and Europe has also brought with it great advantages. The region's close proximity to Paris has played its part in helping to build its reputation. Louis I was the first to be crowned king of France in Reims, in the year 814 AD, which led to that city becoming the country's cultural centre.

As early as the 9th century, a difference was admitted between Vins de la Montagne (wine from the hills) and Vins de la Rivière (wine from the shore). The best villages were judged to be Bouzy and Verzenay up in the hills and Aÿ down in the Marne valley. Gradually, the name Vin de Champagne came to be marketed in its own right.

After Louis XIV's statement about champagne being "the only conceivable drink", champagne enjoyed a tremendously high status, as anyone who could followed the sun-king's advice. Champagne at this time was a pale red wine, and descriptions from the 16th century seem to confirm the picture of a wine with rosé-like tones.

In all probability, the acid content was too high in relation to the concentration of the wine, and with our taste today we would surely have considered it too sour. The aromas were often compared with that of peaches, a taste found today in rosé des Riceys (see page 112), an unique still rosé wine from Aube. We can also be quite sure that the vintage played an even more important role in the quality than it does today. Champagne's cold climate made the harvests something of a lottery, with profits arising only in warm years. (Burgundy's great Pinot wines are still too pale and unconcentrated every third year or so).

After the fermentation the bottles are put upside down, "sur pointes". This picture is taken at Krug in Reims.

Old family traditions

Aÿ, with its southerly slopes, had the best reputation of all Champagne villages, and Louis XII himself owned vineyards here in Champagne's greatest stronghold. Aÿ is also where we find the trail of the oldest surviving champagne house. As far back as 1555 the Gosset family began to make still wines, but they were far from being the first to sell champagne. That honour goes to Ruinart, which began sales in 1729.

However, it was not in Aÿ that the greatest individual producer names could be found during the 16th and 17th centuries. In 1543 the nobleman Pierre Brulart founded his wine company in the Grand cru village Sillery, athough the base for his best wines often came from the sunny slopes of Verzenay, just below the place where the famous windmill Moulin de Verzenay still stands today.

Immediately after Dom Pérignon succeeded in pressing white wine from black grapes, the Marquis de Sillery followed his example. The company succeeded therefore in remaining at the forefront of the region up until the French revolution, when the last Marquis, together with many other noblemen, went to the guillotine. Unfortunately the magnificent castle that Pierre Brulart built in the middle of the 16th century was also destroyed.

The village of Sillery has today a somewhat undeserved Grand crustatus, because it is often blended together with the far superior village of Verzenay.

Dom Pérignon

Dom Pierre Pérignon (1638-1715) is probably the most famous person in the whole history of wine. I can't count the number of times at wine tastings that I've been asked the question - did he invent champagne? Just as many times I've answered - no! The myth has to a great extent been built up by Moët & Chandon, who bought the rights to the name from Mercier at the beginning of the 20th century.

Moët & Chandon took over the monastery in Hautvillers where Dom Pérignon worked and made it into a popular museum. In 1936 they launched the world's first "cuvée de prestige", which appropriately enough bore the monk's name. Success was assured. The entire area has profited from the myth of champagne as the work of a single man, but the truth is quite different: the development from a still wine to a sparkling wine was a long drawn-out process, not a sudden discovery.

Wines from cold climates have bubbled since the first day they were made, whether the makers wanted it that way or not. All late-harvested wines had the problem of completing the fermentation process when the winter chill set in. The yeast that was used to turn the sugar into alcohol stopped doing its job, which meant that the fermentation continued after the wine had been bottled. When temperatures rose again in the spring, carbon dioxide was formed, creating bubbles - a great "failure"!

In 1531 however, the southern French monks at the St Hilaire monastery deliberately created sparkling wine with the so-called rurale method (see page 116). That wine still exists today and is called *Blanquette de Limoux*.

Rue Dom Pérignon is found at Hautvillers, the home village of the monk.

The Hautvillers monastery was built in the 5th century. One thousend years before Dom Pérignon made his first wines.

Experiments with sparkling wine

Another 150 years were to pass before the deliberate production of sparkling wines was to start in Champagne. Dom Pérignon was one of the first, but far from the only one, to experiment with bubbling wine. First and foremost though, he was a great winemaker with a unique reputation even during his own lifetime.

At first even Dom Pérignon viewed his wine's stubborn tendency to sparkle as a problem, but paradoxically enough, his efforts to achieve perfection only led to a greater risk for carbon dioxide in the wine.

Dom Pérignon left nothing to chance in his ambition to reach the peak of possible quality. This conscientiousness began out in the vineyard itself. He realised at an early stage the advantages of a low yield and so pruned the vines harshly, caring for them throughout the year. For the most part he used grapes from old vines, which gave higher concentration and better quality.

Dom Pérignon also revolutionised attitudes toward the harvest. Previously in Champagne the harvest had deliberately been carried out in the bright sunshine of the warmest autumn days, to extract as much colour from the grapes as possible. Dom Pérignon decided however that the harvest should be carried out on those days when there was mist or dew on the ground, in much cooler conditions. This would make the wine both fresher and more elegant, and would also allow more grapes to be picked, as they fell easier from the stems. The grapes were then carried very carefully in huge baskets that held hundreds of kilograms, so-called "mannequins".

Just as today's major champagne houses, Dom Pérignon had his wine presses located as close to the vineyard as possible. He realised that the earlier the grapes were pressed, the lighter and finer the wine would be. He asked himself not just when the grapes should be pressed but also how the procedure should take place. The traditional horizontal champagne press was invented by Dom Pérignon, and even today it has yet to be bettered in terms of speed and care. Of course, this quality-minded monk noticed quickly that the first pressing of the grapes gave the most delicate juice.

Dom Pérignon was probably the first to separate the wines from the three different pressings - the universally prevailing concept in Champagne to this day. After the first alcoholic fermentation the wine was drawn from one barrel to another twice, after which the wine was cleared with fish skin.

With his original thinking and experimentation, Dom Pérignon became the first to succeed in creating white wine from black grapes. He was also the first to get the white wines from Chardonnay to stay white. Previously they had gone brown after just a few months. All this led to Dom Pérignon producing clearer and finer wines than anyone in the area had ever managed.

Perhaps the famous monk's greatest contribution to the champagne of our day is the cuvée, i.e. the blending of various types of grape. Right up until merely a few years ago, his blending theory had such a grip on the winemaking industry that anyone suggesting that monocru champagnes were as good as blended wines would have been laughed out of the business.

Dom Pérignon's grapes came mostly from villages in the vicinity of Hautvillers. He could, with almost frightening certainty, sense from which vineyard the different grapes had come. He was also the first master of the difficult art of pairing together grapes from the right villages with each other. Then, as now, the aim was to balance powerful wines with acidic, almost unripe base wines in order to attain perfect harmony in the champagne.

Comte Audoin de Dampierre in Chenay still uses the traditional method with strings for his "prestige cuvée".

Corks and stronger bottles

As Dom Pérignon harvested under cool conditions, the acidity of the wine was increased, and the tendency to sparkle became stronger than ever. In order to keep spontaneously sparkling wines from exploding, he searched for stronger bottles and better methods of keeping the wine inside the bottle. At this point he began to use English glass — "verre anglais".

Several glass factories that used the new, stronger type of glass were established in the Argonne forest, the same forest that supplied the oak wood for the barrels. However, there were no cork trees in the forest, so Dom Pérignon turned to Spain in his search to discover if cork was the answer to his troubles. (In order to prevent the monk from suffering from hubris in his grave I should point out that, although it was he who first used corks in champagne bottles, there were several "rivals" well ahead of him in the use of corks elsewhere in France).

As more and more wines became sparkling, Dom Pérignon and others began to sell them, but at first sparkling champagne met a mixed reaction. The modern winemakers of those days now had the choice of trying to avoid the bubbles or encouraging them, and Dom Pérignon became the leading figure of the groups that chose the latter alternative. He probably made his first sparkling wines around the year 1690, but it took another hundred years to spread the new wine across the whole of France.

Finally, we should note that even if the monk from Hautvillers really did achieve a great deal, he was by no means alone in his discoveries. Another monk, Dom Oudard, worked in a very similar way in his monastery in Pierry, but as his monastery was less well-known, and the Chardonnay grapes he had to work with were regarded as inferior to the noble Pinot grape, he was always at a disadvantage. In different circumstances, perhaps Dom Oudard would now be known as "the father of champagne".

After Dom Pérignon

It was not until 1728 that the law forbidding the transport of bottled wine was lifted, finally making it possible to start a champagne house. Ruinart was first, in 1729, followed in quick succession by; Chanoine in 1730, Forneaux (now called Taittinger) in 1734, Moët in 1743, Vander-Veken (today Abelé) in 1757, Clicquot in 1772, Heidsieck in 1785 and Jacquesson in 1798.

From the middle of the 1730s the bubbling drink had taken a firm grip on the nightlife in Paris, which was awash with champagne. Every possible party or celebration had to be accompanied by the sound of corks popping.

Up until the beginning of the 19th century, all champagnes had sediment in the bottom of the bottle. The famous widow Clicquot came up with the brilliant idea of storing the bottles upside-down in wooden stalls (pupitres), so that the sediment accumulated next to the cork. Then, with a fast and precise movement, the sediment could be whipped out of the bottle and the wine recorked. This process is still in use and is called degorgement or disgorging.

In the beginning of the 19th century a French chemist by the name of M. François invented a tool called "le densimetre". With this tool one could measure the amount of sugar remaining after the fermentation process, which was important as it was necessary to know exactly how much yeast and sugar were needed for the second fermentation — in the bottle. This process was crucial in order to avoid exploding bottles, but was also a way of producing delicate small bubbles in the champagne. Although the instrument was cheap and simple to use, it was a long time before this measuring system made a real breakthrough.

Well preserved original labels from the beginning of the 19th century at the house of Jacquesson in Dizy.

Napoleon visiting his friend Jean-Rémy Moët during the summer of 1807.

Napoleon — more than just cognac.

As not even the most bloodthirsty revolutionaries had anything against the luxury product champagne, and the revolution was never the killing blow for the drink that it could have been. Napoleon entertained a great love for wine in general and champagne in particular. The companies that are thought to have been his favourite houses are manifold. Jacquesson, which received a medal from the emperor for the beauty and wealth of their cellars, should be seen as favourite number two, after Moët & Chandon. Napoleon became good friends with Jean-Rémy Moët, who was also the mayor of Épernay, and their mutual admiration knew no bounds. Jean-Rémy built two houses for Napoleon on the Avenue de Champagne, and after Jean-Rémy's efforts during the Russo-Prussian occupation of Épernay in 1814, Napoleon dubbed him a "chevalier of the legion of honour".

Were it not for these connections with Napoleon, Moët & Chandon would definitely not have become what it is today. Some claim that Napoleon would always take a detour through the Champagne region before a big battle to refill his supply of the strength-giving drink. Only once did he fail to perform his habit — on the way to the Battle of Waterloo!

Champagne goes east...

Napoleon was only one in a long line of famous rulers who came to love champagne. During the occupation of 1814, enormous quantities of Reims and Épernays champagne were drunk by the invaders. However, it's an ill wind that blows no good. The Russians acquired a taste for the sparkling drink and rumours of its greatness soon spread through their homeland. Monsieur Bohne, the agent for widow Clicquot, reported home that the wine was described as nectar and that pink champagne was the most popular variety in Russia.

Along with all the champagne agents of that time, Clicquot and Roederer's agents were quick to drum up interest in theatres of war directly after a battle. In this way Louis Roederer is thought to have inspired an interest in his products in Russia, not least in the palace of the Tsar. It was the Russian sovereign who ordered a specially-designed champagne in a transparent bottle of real crystal. The "Cristal" that Alexander II drank was much sweeter than the prestige champagne of the same name that Roederer has had so much success with today.

Sugar content in champagne

Extra Brut	0-6	gram/litre
Brut	0-15	gram/litre
Sec	17-35	gram/litre
Demi-Sec	33-50	gram/litre
Doux	50 <	gram/litre

...and west

Bollinger and Krug, formed in 1843, turned instead to the English market, with great success. In the middle of the 19th century some forty percent of all champagne was exported to the English Isles. Those companies which concentrated on attracting the English thus quickly gained a reputation as producers of the best champagne. The English liked their champagne much older and more mature, preferring it drier than the French. The French usually drank champagne with dessert, in contrast to the English, who wanted the bubbling drink as an aperitif. Bollinger, Clicquot, Pommery and Ayala released a "very dry 1865", and in the legendary year of 1874 Pommery launched what was probably the first wholly-dry champagne, marked "extra dry, reserved for England".

In those days we Swedes had an extremely sweet taste, something we still suffer from to this day. During my travels in the region, I am often told that producers don't want to sell their champagne to Sweden as we don't like dry champagnes. In the middle of the 19th century champagne with thirty grams of sugar per litre was exported to Sweden and Norway. The Russians wanted twenty grams, the Germans seventeen, the French fifteen and before 1874 the English had a mere twelve grams of sugar in their champagne. So one can safely say we have the English to thank for the fact that we can drink dry champagne today.

German knowledge

The technical advances made in the latter part of the 19th century enabled champagne sales to expand dramatically. However, we should remember that it was only a small number of champagne houses that made up the sales. At that time you had to be big to exploit the new technology to the full. Many of the most successful houses were founded by German immigrants such as Bollinger, Heidsieck, Krug and Mumm. Their knowledge of languages gave them an advantage over their French-speaking competitors on the export market.

Charles Heidsieck — "Champagne Charlie" — and Mumm then took a steady grip on the vital American market. Mumm succeeded in persuading the Americans to divide wine up into two categories: ordinary wine and champagne. A distinction that many people still make to this day.

Phylloxera and uproar

Just as the champagne industry was blossoming as never before, terrible, dark clouds rose over the horizon. The wine louse, an aphid called Phylloxera.

The tiny yellow Phylloxera was to present a greater threat to wine production than any of the human marauders that had spread terror through the Champagne region. The louse is so small that it can only be seen through a microscope, but even so, it is capable of devastating an entire district of vineyards. When the louse sucks the sap from the vine roots it leaves a poisonous saliva that infects the wound and prevents it from healing. The wine louse was discovered for the first time by an American entomologist in 1854 on wild vines in Mississippi. It had been around a long time before that of course, but as the American wild vines were resistant to Phylloxera, nobody was disturbed by the discovery.

It wasn't until 1863, when the louse crossed the Atlantic for the first time, that problems began to arise. From a boat in Marseille's harbour the louse spread to a vineyard in Provençe, near Nimes, and from there across Europe. As the European vines were not resistant to the bite of the louse, the destruction was enormous. Almost all the important winemaking areas were struck; Bordeaux and Portugal in 1869 (not Colares), Beaujolais and the Rhône valley in 1870, California in 1873, Australia in 1874, Burgundy in 1878, South Africa and Algeria in 1887 and Italy in 1888.

In the vineyard at the time of the Phylloxera scourge.

The only top-class wine districts that were spared were those to the north; Rhein, Mosel and Champagne. The hope was that the louse would not survive in a colder climate, but all hopes were dashed in 1890 when the pest was discovered on the outskirts of the western Marne valley. Möet & Chandon bought the vineyard and burned all the vines in an attempt to halt the march of the louse. However, two years later more vines were attacked — and just as quickly burned. When in 1894 the lice attacked several places simultaneously, no-one had the strength to apply the "scorched earth" policy one more time. Instead, several insecticides were tried. Some were effective, but were almost as poisonous to humans as to the lice. Even so, Champagne had a good deal of luck, as the lice moved more slowly in the cold climate than in other areas of France.

The final solution came from the United States and Canada, where thick domestic vines were resistant to the creature's bite. The problem was that the quality of these vines was far too low for them to adorn the slopes of Montrachet or Aÿ. In the end someone had the idea of grafting European cuttings onto American vines, in that way creating a resistant plant that produced grapes with a European taste. Nearly every example of "Vitis vinifera" vines worldwide was pulled up and replanted.

Today most would agree that the potential quality of the vines was greater before the global attack of the wine louse. Some also claim that the greater yield that comes from the grafted vines is an important factor in the shorter lifespan of the plants.

Anyone who has tasted *Bollinger Vieilles Vignes Françaises* from ungrafted vines, or *Romanée Conti* from a pre-Phylloxera vintage, will wish that the louse had never taken the trouble to cross the Atlantic.

Right next to the house of Bollinger in Aÿ you find this unique vineyard. The brick-walls didn't let the wine louse in. The ungrafted plants still provides Pinot Noir to one of the most magnificent wines in the world; Vieilles Vignes Françaises.

The Champagne Riots

At the beginning of this century, several events took place that were to have great importance for the way the wine-making area of Champagne Viticole looks today. The climax came with the so-called Champagne Riots of 1911.

As the Aube district lies both geographically and geologically closer to Chablis than it does to the rest of Champagne, the area's right to use the title "Champagne" for its wines was — with reason — brought into question. The soil consists mainly of Kimmeridge clay and not, as is the case around the Marne river, of Belimnite chalk. The quality of the wines from there will never be comparable to the great champagne. A group headed by the Aube growers claimed it was obvious that Aube should be part of Champagne Viticole, as the town of Troyes had previously been the capital of the entire Champagne province. The other side pointed to the difference in quality and argued that the province of Champagne and the wine with the same name should not be mixed.

At this time the 20,000 hectares were planted chiefly with Arbanne and Petit Meslier grapes, along with the Beaujolais grape Gamay. The yield was high and very few of the Aube producers cared overmuch about quality. Simply put, the Aube grapes were of such low quality that no champagne house would ever dream of using them in their cuvées. The Aube growers turned to both Champagne and Burgundy, but neither wanted to include Aube in their wine district.

The government acts

The rivalry between the two camps became so great in the end that the government decided to step in. On December 17th, 1908, the government decided which grapes could be used in champagne and which areas had the right to call their wines "champagne". There were two departments:

— The Marne department: all the municipalities by Reims and Épernay, including 35 municipalities around Vitry-le-François.

— The Aisne department: 82 municipalities around Château-Thierry and Soissons.

The Aube district was completely ignored! Understandably, the growers in the area were furious. Matters hadn't been helped by the fact that the area had been hit by crop failure for several years in a row. Despite the tough rules, many of the Marne valley producers used grapes from Midi, which enraged the Aube growers even more.

The Riots break out

Champagne had been transformed into a powder keg which could explode at any moment. In February 1911 the legislation was toughened even more, with threats of punishment for any producers using grapes from Aube or the rest of France in their champagne. The storm-in-a-champagne glass broke. All the Aube wine producers assembled in Troyes and there were loud, angry mass demonstrations.

The senate realised what was about to happen and temporarily withdrew the legislation, but it was too late. At two in the morning on April 11th, 1911, angry Aube residents broke down the cellar doors of a winemaker in Cumières

and one in Damery. By dawn the 5,000-strong growers' army had reached Aÿ, where any producers who were suspected of using grapes from Midi had their cellars, barrels and bottles destroyed. The streets flowed with wine. The authorities were asleep and the first forces from Épernay could only stand by helplessly and watch.

When the cellars were emptied the rioters moved towards the homes of the Aÿ producers and continued their mayhem. Bollinger was one of the few houses to escape the mob's actions. Madame Lilly Bollinger apparently heard later how the rioters had shown their respect for the house by lowering their revolutionary banners as they marched past. The area was declared a war zone by the government and 40,000 peacekeeping troops were brought in.

Reclassification

The government's new decision divided the sparkling wines into four types;

— Champagne (as earlier),
— Champagne Deuxième Zone (Aube, Seine-et-Marne),
— Vin Mousseaux (sparkling wine from the rest of France),
— Vin Gazéifié (artificially-produced sparkling wine).

In practice, the new law made it possible for the Aube growers to produce champagne, a right they could hardly have appropriated without this show of force. In 1927 the law was changed once again: the Deuxième Zone was dissolved and Aube was incorporated with the Champagne region.

Perhaps I will provoke a new Champagne Riot if I propose a return to the Deuxième Zone for the Aube grapes, but I believe that their quality can never equal that of the grapes from the heart of Champagne.

1911 Ayala was totaly destroyed by the growers of Aube.

BELLE EPOQUE

Building the Eiffeltower, 1888.

Cheerfully ignorant of the Champagne Riots and the Phylloxera louse, the wealthy world drank champagne as never before during the era that came to be known as the "Belle Epoque". The French had plenty of money and loved to be seen out and about with a glass of champagne in their hand. The fact was that many were so rich that the young, impetuous finance minister even considered introducing a new tax — income tax.

The "Belle Epoque" really started at the World Exhibition in Paris in 1889. France was becoming industrialised and times were changing. Gustave Eiffel had just built the period's greatest monument, the Eiffel Tower, which with its 300-metre height was a symbol of the new, positive view of the future. There were four restaurants in the tower, all of them swimming in champagne. Eugène Mercier built the largest wine barrel in world history, the contents of which could fill around 200,000 bottles. The barrel was pulled by 24 white oxen during a three-week journey to Paris, during which houses were demolished and roads rebuilt to enable the barrel to reach the exhibition in time.

Champagne on film

Eugène Mercier also showed the world's first advertising film at the exhibition. Not surprisingly, the film was about the Mercier champagne house. Copious amounts of the drink were consumed during the exhibition, and rumours of the wine's special joybringing qualities spread throughout the world.

Maxim's was the top meeting-place for the Parisians, where caviar, lobster and oysters were washed down with what was then a rather sweet drink. Social intercourse became hugely important for the French. One simply had to be seen out with the beautiful people, and if one had money one should wave it around as visibly as possible.

At the turn of the century the French had doubled their consumption compared to the middle of the 19th century, and it's easy to get the impression that everybody was drinking champagne at the time. Of course, almost everybody had drunk champagne at some point in their lives, but few could afford treating the sparkling drink as their everyday wine.

Free, fast and forward-looking

The lifestyle, art, fashion and architecture of the "Belle Epoque" was precocious, positive, bubbly and vulgar in an uncomplicated, life-assertive way. It was a liberated period when song and dance became provocative and the round forms of the female body were emphasised in art. Everything should have curves; furniture, vases, lamps and clothes all had inflated curves. The "Belle Epoque" was a fun time to be alive — at least, it was if you had money.

Museum and prestige champagne

The Perrier-Jouët champagne house has a particular love for the happy days before the first World War, and today there stands a museum with furniture from the period and pieces of Art Nouveau opposite their wine house in Épernay.

One of the most successful prestige champagnes is also sold under the title "Belle Epoque". The bottle, adorned with its distinctive anemones, was originally painted by the artist Émile Gallé around the turn of the century. He quickly became his time's greatest glass artist, alongside Daum and Tiffany. Nobody could guess that the flowery bottle would become a symbol for the entire period.

Émile Gallé (1846-1904) used an extremely delicate technique in which several layers of transparent glass were blown onto the bottles. They were then painted using an even more advanced method. The picture shows the original

Eugène Mercier built the largest wine barrel in world history, the contents of which could fill around 200,000 bottles.

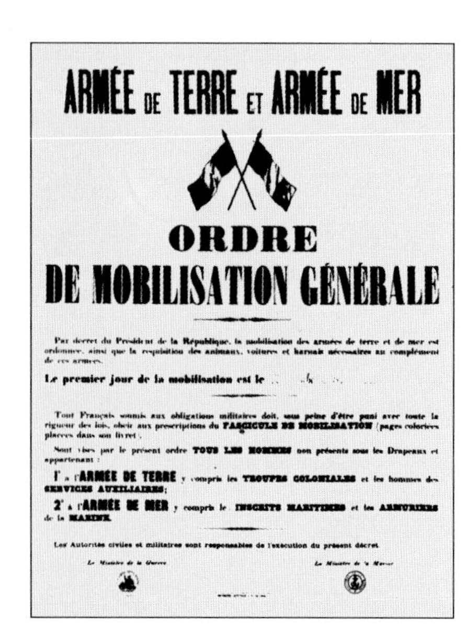

World War I

The outbreak of the first World War in 1914 was the start of a series of hard years for the population of Champagne.

Épernay and Château-Thierry had been evacuated the day before German troops entered France by way of the Marne valley on September 7th, 1914. The Germans had only a few kilometres left before they reached the strategically-important river Seine, and thus Paris.

Reims was occupied for ten days before the French managed to stem the tide at one of the most heroic battles in the country's history, "The first Battle of the Marne". Luckily, the Germans never reached the Seine. The clashes took place among the vines, and as usual the district's wines were a great asset for the French: many Germans were taken prisoner after over-indulging in champagne.

The front line ran straight through Champagne and the war became static. Sometimes weeks would go by before a new offensive was attempted. This crazy positional war continued for almost four years, up to July 18th 1918, when an allied attack gave the French a small taste of the sweetness of victory.

Harvest against the odds

The attacks kept coming and in the beginning of October all Champagne had been recaptured. Despite the trench warfare, certain brave souls succeeded in creeping out into the vineyards to reap a tiny but superb harvest in both 1914 and 1915. Sadly, twenty child pickers were killed during the 1914 harvest.

Maurice Pol-Roger was the mayor of Épernay during the war, and even though the Germans threatened to burn down the town and execute him, he stayed ramrod-straight throughout. His own *1914 Pol Roger* then became his favourite champagne, which he always carried with him for special occasions. Once, in 1944, he was so disappointed that the wine was so hard and immature that he asked his cellarmaster to disgorge a large number of bottles in advance, so that he would always have access to a mature champagne.

In May 1994 I had the great honour of sharing a bottle of the early-disgorged champagne from 1914 with the current owner of the firm, Christian Pol-Roger. Never before have I so clearly experienced the feeling that I was "drinking history". The wonderful quality of the champagne, with its coffee aroma and sweet richness, hardly made matters worse.

The Reims Cathedral attacked

Around the same time as Pol Roger's child pickers brought in the harvest of 1914, Reims experienced one of its darkest days. The Germans began to bomb the holiest of holies: the city's enormous gothic cathedral. In order to put a stop to the onslaught, the church was filled with 150 German prisoners, who were put through a great deal of suffering.

During the first raid a beggar was killed outside the doors of the cathedral. Afterwards, the "smile from Reims", the most famous of the many thousands of individual sculptures on the church's facade, fell to the ground. Among the prisoners panic broke out when two of their comrades were killed in the next attack. Thinot the Abbot climbed up inside the northern tower and raised a Red Cross flag, but nothing helped. The cathedral's huge roof, supported by great oak beams, caught fire and the heat was unendurable.

Sections of the beautiful rosette window exploded and people fled in panic, but the German prisoners remained inside. When the Germans realised that their countrymen were in the church building, they held their fire, but the flames from the roof spread to hundreds of surrounding houses. The cathedral survived, albeit badly damaged. Outraged, the French called on the Pope to condemn the attack, but his statement was milder than they had hoped, as the Germans had persuaded the Vatican that the French were using the cathedral for military purposes. The Kaiser considered the Pope's weak condemnation as a tacit acceptance of the attack, and on April 24th 1917 the cathedral was bombed again. A donation from the Rockefeller family made restoration possible, and incredibly it remains standing to this day, despite the severe damage the attacks caused.

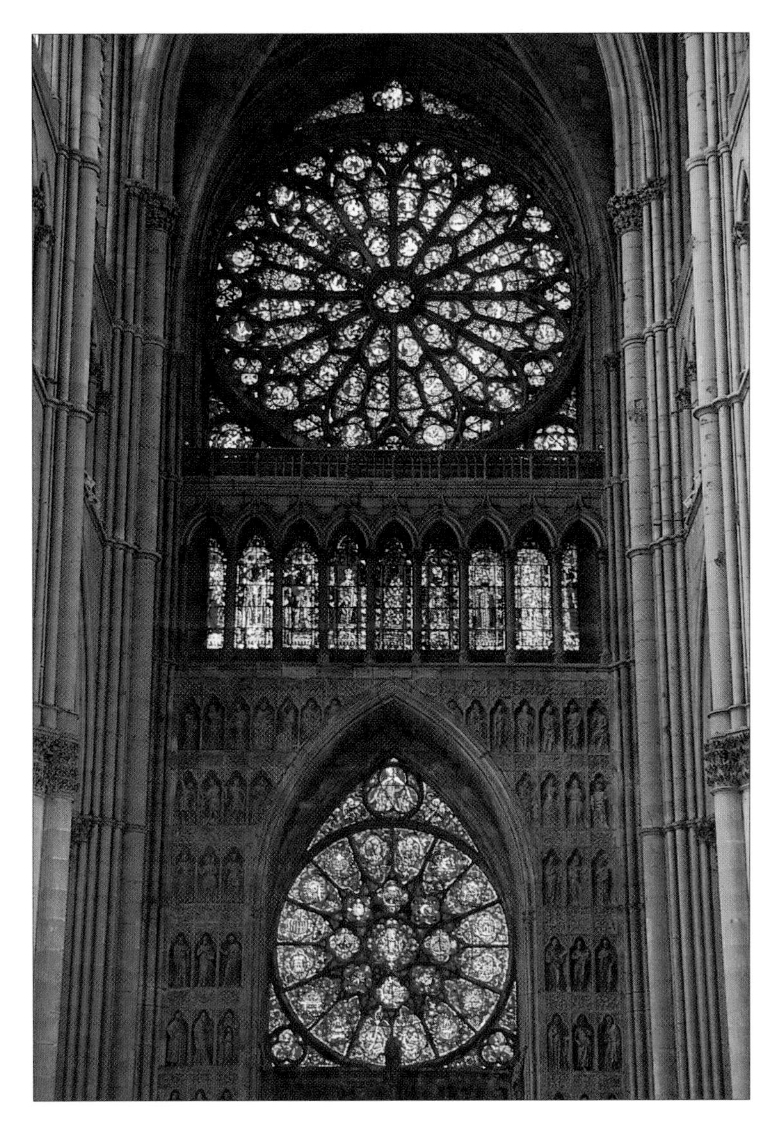

The famous rose window of Reims cathedral.

Between the wars

After the first World War Reims gathered all its strength in order to rebuild the city as fast as possible. The export market was tricky: the Germans were bankrupt after the war and the family of the Russian Tsar, which had been the biggest individual customer, had lost power in the country's revolution. The Americans were entering the age of prohibition and we Scandinavians followed them with our ration books for liquor. To top it all, it wasn't until 1926 that Champagne's tough climate succeeded in fostering a fine vintage once again.

Just when the Champagne area had recovered from Phylloxera and the war in the middle of the 1920s, the first signs of a global depression arose. In 1927, domestic sales of champagne in France were halved. In 1929 the infamous crash of the Wall Street stock exchange in New York plunged the entire western world into full-scale depression. The worst year of all, 1934, still managed to produce a superb vintage and remains so today, if a well-kept bottle can be found.

Champagne as a still wine!?

Many famous houses gave their wines simple labels in order to avoid the loss of prestige that came with selling first-class champagne at bargain-basement prices. The champagne producers used all the tricks to survive, and it wasn't unusual that firms sold their wines directly, and cheaply, to Paris as still wines. The still wines from Champagne soon became very popular.

It's terrible to think of 1928's wonderful wine virtually being given away as still wine, but unfortunately a large part of the harvest met this fate.

Many growers felt unhappy about selling potential top-class champagne as still wine, but as they didn't have the technical capability to produce sparkling wine themselves they formed many of the cooperatives that exist today. That the major champagne houses survived at all is thanks largely to the size of the domestic market.

During the second World War the head of Möet & Chandon, Robert-Jean de Voguë, put forward the revolutionary proposal that the price of grapes should be radically increased in order to ensure the survival of the growers and guarantee top quality grapes. De Voguë's idea wasn't received kindly by the other houses, but since then they have admitted that de Voguë saved the champagne industry with his drastic suggestion. He was also the leading figure when the Comité Interprofessionel du Vin de Champagne (C.I.V.C.) was formed with the Germans in 1941.

Champagne.

Nr.	Årg.			1/1	1/2
		PIERRE ARNAUD.			
191.		Extra Quality, Sec (halvtorr)		12:50	7:50
		J. BOLLINGER, AY-CHAMPAGNE.			
192.		Dry Extra (halvtorr)	Magnum 31:– (1/4 5:–)	15:50	8:75
193.		Carte Blanche (söt)		14:50	8:25
		LUCIEN CLICQUOT, REIMS.			
194.		Carte d'Or, Sec (halvtorr)		10:–	6:25
195.		Carte d'Or, Demi-sec (halvsöt)		9:50	6:25
		VVE CLICQUOT-PONSARDIN, REIMS.			
196.	1928	Brut (mycket torr)		23:–	
197.		Goût Américain, sec (halvtorr)	Magnum 37:–	18:50	10:25
198.		England, demi-sec (halvsöt)		16:50	9:50
		VVE GEORGE GOULET & Cie., REIMS.			
199.		Extra Américain (halvtorr)		14:50	8:25
200.		Extra Demi-sec (halvsöt)		14:50	8:25
		HEIDSIECK & Cie., REIMS.			
201.		Monopole Red Top (Goût Américain) (halvtorr)		14:–	8:–
		CHAMPAGNE ERNEST IRROY, REIMS.			
202.		Goût Américain (halvtorr)		16:–	9:25
		KRUG & Cie., REIMS.			
203.		Brut Réserve (torr)		19:50	10:75
204.		Goût Américain (halvtorr)		17:–	9:50
		MOET & CHANDON, EPERNAY.			
205.	1926	Brut Impérial (torr)	Magnum 32:–	16:–	9:–
206.		White Star (halvtorr)		13:–	7:75
		CHAMPAGNE MONTEBELLO, MAREUIL.			
207.	1928	Cuvée Extra Brut (torr)		19:–	
208.		Cordon Blanc (halvtorr)		15:–	8:50
		G. H. MUMM & Cie., REIMS.			
209.		Cordon Rouge (torr)		15:50	9:–

Bellmansro

20

Nr.	Årg.			1/1	1/2
210.		Goût Américain (halvtorr)	Magnum 26:–	13:–	7:75
211.		Cordon Vert (halvsöt)		13:–	7:75
212.		Grand Crémant (söt)		12:–	7:25
		POMMERY & GRENO, REIMS.			
213.	1928	Nature (mycket torr)	Magnum 44:–	23:–	
214.	1928	,, Rosé (mycket torr)		24:–	
215.		Drapeau Sec (halvtorr)		15:–	8:75
		COMTE DE REDDY, AY-CHAMPAGNE.			
216.	1926	Extra Quality, Carte Perle, demi-sec (halvsöt)		13:–	7:50
		LOUIS ROEDERER, REIMS.			
217.	1926	Brut (torr)		19:–	10:75
218.		Grand Vin Sec (halvtorr)		15:50	8:75
219.		Carte Blanche (söt)		13:–	7:75
		POL ROGER & Cie., EPERNAY.			
220.	1926	Brut, Cuvée de Réserve (torr)		23:–	12:50
221.		Brut Réserve (torr)		17:50	9:75
222.		Grand Vin Sec América (halvtorr)		17:50	9:75
		MOUSSERANDE BOURGOGNE.			
223.		White Cap, Special Dry (halvtorr), F. Chauvenet		9:–	5:50
224.		Bourgogne Mousseux Rouge (röd, söt), J. Calvet & Cie.		9:–	5:50
225.		Val d'Or (halvsöt), Jules Regnier & Cie.		9:–	5:50
226.		Perle de Bourgogne (halvsöt), J. Calvet & Cie.		8:50	5:–
		MOUSSERANDE ITALIENSKT VIN.			
228.		Gancia Asti Spumante, Fratelli Gancia & Cia (söt)		9:–	
		MOUSSERANDE TYSKA VINER.			
229.		Henkell Trocken (halvtorr), Henkell & Co.		12:–	7:25
230.		Sparkling Hock, Deinhard & Co. (halvsöt)		11:50	6:75
		MOUSSERANDE SVENSKA FRUKTVINER.			
231.		Borgskum (halvtorr), A. B. Th. Winborg & Co.		5:–	3:–
232.		Borgskum (söt), ,, ,, ,, ,,		4:–	2:50

"Skratta mina barn och vänner"

21

Winelist from 1934 in Stockholm.

World War II

Reims during the occupation.

When the German tanks rolled into France in 1940, the winemakers were far better prepared than they had been for the First World War. Hitler had been around on the international scene for a while and that was enough to inspire people to build false walls and hide large stores of champagne bottles from the Germans.

The Germans drank enormous quantities of champagne in Reims and Épernay, but after the surrender Hitler put a stop to the on-the-spot drinking. He wanted production to continue unaffected, so that Germany would be supplied with first-class champagne. One winemaker from the Rhein valley, Herr Klaebisch, became "Champagne's Führer", which was appreciated by the local growers.

Sales to private individuals were prohibited and around 350,000 bottles a week were to be sent to German troops on all fronts. Unfortunately for the Germans, the bottles were often sent the wrong way, and the quality of the champagne was as poor as the producers could make it. As no new planting took place during the war, the old vines also produced poor harvests.

Robert-Jean de Voguë was called into Klaebisch's room one day in the autumn of 1942 to be told that the Gestapo had condemned him to death. Happily, the execution order was never carried out, but he spent the rest of the war in various concentration camps.

The champagne producers were forced to be very cautious in their resistance to the Germans, as Himmler planned to blow up all the champagne cellars in order to give the German sekt industry an advantage after the war. However, General Patton's army moved in on August 28th, 1944, and as soon as the Germans had left Champagne all the cellars' false walls were torn down. An unexpectedly large quantity of champagne had been saved for the world in this way.

A war cemetery in Sept-Saulx.

War cemeteries

The two World Wars have left clear and frightening tracks after them in all the war cemeteries that exist in the area. If one has time to stop awhile between all the meals and wine visits in Champagne, one can wander around among the never-ending crosses marking the fallen and ponder on the madness of war. War has no winners, only losers, and here lie many of them.

One can also see how the different nations honour their dead. The French use wooden crosses, with the names engraved directly on the cross. The Italian wooden crosses have the victims' names engraved on plaques of rust-free metal. The British graves are marked with rectangular stones, while the Americans have raised marble crosses.

Perhaps the most beautiful is an American cemetery in Bois de Belleau outside Château-Thierry in Aisne, where General Pershing led a brave but inexperienced force to their deaths. Their sacrifice were not in vain, however. Thanks to their efforts, the enemy was stopped from crossing the Marne at a vitally important stage of the first World War.

Of the less ornate cemeteries, Marne chapel's in Dormans is the most remarkable, with the skeletons of some 1,500 unknown Frenchmen.

The presence of wars past is also made apparent by way of a number of monuments on the outskirts of the growing area. The enormous monument in Mondement in memory of The Battle of the Marne is placed there, as the Germans never reached further south than this point.

One monument that is hard to find is the one outside Mourmelan-le-Grand. In the middle of nowhere there is a white Russian church with two cupolas, and a Russian cemetery in the same style. Perhaps not what one would expect to find in this part of France.

After the War

Many were pessimistic about the future of champagne after the war was over. The champagne houses had financial problems and not much champagne left over, partly because of the march of the Germans through Europe. Almost the entire continent was flirting with socialism and royal families were falling like ninepins. The only people who could afford champagne in large quantities were the newly-rich Americans.

Things didn't look good at all, but the doubters were shown to be wrong. Thanks to the fantastic vintages of 1943, 45, 47, 49, 52, 53, and 55 the sales of champagne doubled within twelve years. During the next ten years they doubled again, until they were up to 64 million bottles per year. In 1976, 153 million bottles were sold, and in 1985, 195 million. Obviously, something dramatic had happened.

The most important explanation was that the industrialised nations quickly restored their economies after the war. Like most other luxury products, champagne was "democratised" and became a drink for almost everyone.

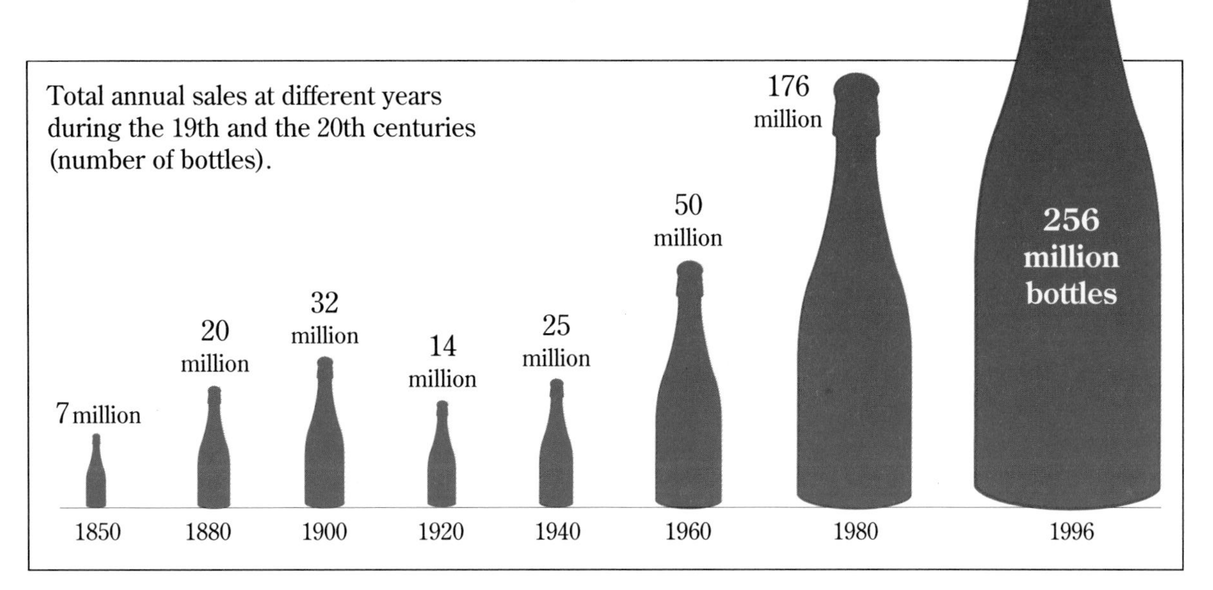

Champagne today

Today the media have contributed hugely to the spreading of the delights of champagne. The producers of the area should also be grateful for the enormous publicity that Moët & Chandon have given the region in every conceivable context. They have really succeeded in presenting champagne as a necessity when something is to be celebrated or made extra luxurious. The image that the James Bond films have given *Dom Pérignon* and *Bollinger R.D.* beats all the attempts of the producers to market their product to a wider audience. If you want to impress someone with your choice of wine at a restaurant, then a bottle of *Dom Pérignon* is the obvious choice.

Even if it's unusual for us Swedes to drink champagne unless we're at a party for New Year's Eve or someone's fiftieth birthday, I can assure you that a good many people in England and on the continent brighten up their days with the occasional bottle of champagne. Luxurious? Extravagant? Sure, but not particularly expensive if you compare it with the price of a few beers at a restaurant. Why not allow yourself the pleasure of this value-for-money luxury product, if you can appreciate the delights of the wine? Champagne is also a perfect drink to offer your guests. Pretty much everyone feels honoured if they're offered something special, and you don't need to explain that the champagne didn't cost much more than a bottle of ordinary wine.

Champagne in politics and sport

Although champagne really has become a democratised drink, consumption is still dominated by the upper class. All the world's royalty seem to be controlled by champagne. When the big names in western politics meet they often achieve successful agreements over a few glasses of cuvée de prestige, and the conflicts solved by politicians drunk on champagne are legion. Winston Churchill, who drank a bottle of Pol Roger a day, is a shining example. His son-in-law Christopher Soames was also a great admirer of Pol Roger's champagnes. When he was sent to Rhodesia to supervise the country's formal independence, he was asked when there would be peace in Rhodesia. He answered, "Rhodesia will have peace within exactly thirty days, as I have only thirty bottles of Pol Roger left".

After the death of Winston Churchill the Pol Rogers labels were decorated with a black boarder.

Since the war, champagne has also often managed to slip its way into the world of sport, and many are the victories that have been celebrated with champagne. Certain sporting events overflow with the fizzy drink: at Wimbledon, for example, champagne and strawberries is a must. The big houses nowadays sponsor lots of sporting events, such as the Americas Cup in sailing and the golf and Grand Prix circuits.

Fun and festivities

Wedding champagne is a classic in most countries, but otherwise Christmas is often the top champagne season. In many countries, including my own, New Year's Eve is the day when we drink champagne — or something we like to call champagne.

In many countries a vacation is also a time for champagne. When the Americans travel to Florida or the Bahamas, they gulp down colossal quantities of "bubbly", and in England people are out having champagne breakfasts in the open air as soon as summer has arrived.

As you see, there are plenty of excuses to open a bottle of champagne. The common denominator for those occasions when the cork pops is happiness. The idea of champagne as a symbol of festivities and fun is something the French have succeeded in marketing to us so well that the connection now seems obvious.

Production and techniques after the war

Let us take a look at what has happened within Champagne's borders since the second World War. Unfortunately for quality's sake, the harvest yield became greater, the vine-yards spread and as techniques improved, production increased. In the beginning of the 1960's most champagne houses had gone over to stainless steel vats from the cost-lier oak barrels. Remuage and degorgement became automated. More and more houses began to use a higher proportion of Chardonnay grapes in their cuvées, a trend that continues today. Whether it was the taste of the cuvées or the customers' taste that changed first rather depends on your point of view. But the growers suddenly had the technical capability of making champagne from their grapes themselves. In 1950 only 2.4 million bottles were sold directly from the growers. In 1980, 60 million bottles of growers' champagne were sold.

This development is both good and bad. The well-established houses don't always have access to the best grapes, which lowers their quality, but on the other hand new, interesting growers pop up all the time, making pure monocru champagnes of high class at extremely low prices.

The variations in taste are growing and today's consumer is no longer dependent on 18 champagne houses, as was the case before the war. The importance of the cooperatives has grown tremendously. Today several of the wine-producing villages have formed cooperatives which involve a large percentage of the village's population.

Big gets bigger

As for the champagne houses, the large have become even larger, as the houses buy one another up and continually form new business alliances. Moët-Hennessy is today part of a larger concern called LVMH, and even Veuve Clicquot and Pommery are parts of the group that controls almost 50% of the entire export market. Another important merged operation is the Seagram group, which includes Mumm, Heidsieck & Monopole and Perrier-Jouët. Even though most of the champagne houses are independent when it comes to their work with the wines, certain top producers are owned by outsiders. For example, Krug was before owned by Rémy-Martin, which has now incorporated both Piper-Heidsieck and Charles Heidsieck into its stable. As to the latter two, it should be noted that the house styles have begun to resemble one another since Daniel Thibault became "Chef de Caves" for both companies.

Of those that are still completely independent, most prominent is the big success story of the post-war years, the Laurent-Perrier house, led by Bernard de Nonancourt. Taittinger, Louis Roederer, Pol Roger and Bollinger are still wholly or partially family-owned firms, having been able to stay that way largely because of their easily-managed size. Louis Roederer was up until a couple of years ago the world's most profitable wine company, thanks mainly to the large number of vineyards they own.

Another important factor is the amazing success they had with their cuvée de prestige *Cristal*. Today that wine makes up a large part of the firm's total production and each bottle costs a small fortune.

Despite the great upswing experienced by the area after the war, the road hasn't been without its potholes. As late as in the beginning of the nineties champagne was hit by a recession and sales fell. The prices fell and the wine was stored in the cellars for longer than before, which means that we the consumers in the middle of the decade have gained most from the situation. We can also congratulate ourselves on the boon of a superb series of vintages up to 1990, but after that the weather gods turned their back, so be sure and stock up in the cellar!

Champagne's future

All over the world, more and more champagne is being drunk. However, fifty years ago the region accounted for thirty percent of the world's total consumption of sparkling wine, against a mere ten percent today. Two of the world's largest current producers of sparkling wines are Spain's Freixenet and Codorníu.

Should the champagne industry's leading figures be worried about this development? Hardly, as the market for sparkling wines is expanding and there ought to be room for both the simpler varieties and real champagne. The main competition quality-wise has come from the USA, where the champagne houses themselves, with their own know-how, have started the most successful companies.

This healthy competition woke many sleepy producers during the seventies. C.I.V.C. realised the danger at an early stage and has made a huge contribution to the raising of quality levels in Champagne in recent times. The latest legislation, which banned the third pressing (see page 61), has meant that today even the simplest champagnes have an elegance and purity which none of the world's other sparkling wines can match. Ten years ago, very few wine journalists heaped praise on the growers' champagne, but today the best of these is taken extremely seriously. Those champagne houses that don't take the competition from the best growers in the Grand cru villages seriously are in for a nasty surprise.

In the next century many of the winemakers will probably return to fermenting in oak barrels, as it is easier to catch the attention of wine writers with quality than with quantity. Champagne's development lies largely in the hands of the consumer. If we show that we want quality champagnes with individual characteristics, then the producers will be happy to supply them.

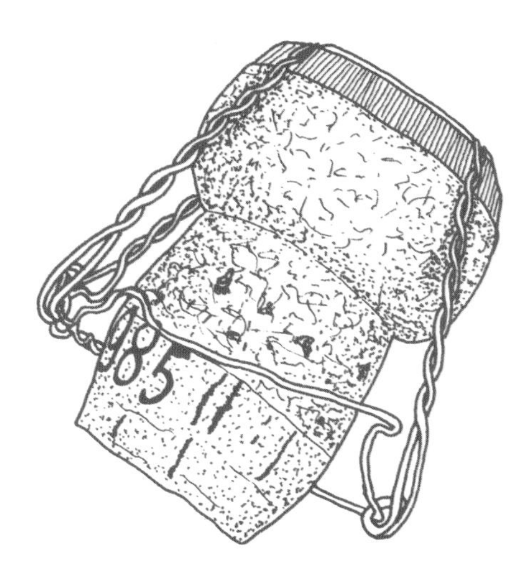

The new millennium

It can hardly have escaped anyone's notice that we are about to experience the most talked-about New Year's Eve in history. Our expectations for this evening have reached such heights that most of us will probably end up disappointed no matter what we do. They say that the world's computer systems will all collapse, and what's worse - there may not be enough champagne to go around!

Just how much truth there is in these tales is the subject of much debate. Some people say the great champagne houses have spread rumours of empty cellars in order to boost prices and increase sales. Other, highly credible, observers say that people will toast the new millennium with a bubbly of even greater quality than usual. According to this argument, someone who is usually content with a sparkling wine will want to buy real champagne for the occasion, and those who generally drink non-vintage champagne will instead choose a vintage, and so on. If this is true, then the champagne houses' reserves will certainly be considerably drained.

After 1990 came four poor vintages that are of little interest to the connoisseur. It's hardly a comfort to know that the harvests of 95 and 96 were of exceptionally high class, as these wines won't go on sale before the year 2000.

If you really must drink a vintage champagne on that magical stroke of twelve, then you should waste no time in acquiring some of the wonderful vintages that are already beginning to run out. Champagne has never been as inexpensive as it is at the moment, so the time is right to buy the three fantastic vintages of 1988, 1989 and 1990. If you are very lucky you may be able to get hold of a mature vintage from the sixties or seventies. Going for older champagnes may be a little risky.

Naturally the champagne houses would prefer people to buy their specially-designed jubilee bottles. Almost every producer is offering a champagne with a "2000" label at prices that are far too high. Those most talked about are the *1993 Dom Pérignon* and *1990 Cristal* in a majestic methusalem format. According to the bible, Methuselah lived for 996 years. Roederer have produced 2000 bottles of their "Cuvée 2000" at a price of 2,000 dollars apiece. The champagne is kept with its sediment until the summer of 1999 and will surely be extremely good, but the slow pace of a wine's development in such large bottles means the flavour will be very young.

Finally, I'd like to remind you that the stroke of midnight on New Year's Eve is seldom the perfect time to enjoy a great wine, but who cares? It's not every day you can celebrate the birth of a new millennium.

Champagne – king of the sparkling wines!

The view from Sacré-Cœur on July 14th, 1989. Paris in a glass.

All sorts of fruit and vegetables are at their most exquisite if they are grown on their northern boundaries in the northern hemisphere, and vice versa in the southern hemisphere. In our cool climate potatoes, apples, strawberries etc. struggle hard for their existence, but during the long process of ripening, complicated chemical combinations are developed in fruits and vegetables which give an especially elegant, fresh and balanced taste.

This phenomenon applies to grapes as well, of course. All the countless types of grape from which man makes wine demand their own particular growing conditions in the form of soil and climate. Some types of grape are happiest in the heat, while others can bear fruit as far north as Champagne or Mosel. Champagne is the northernmost AOC district (see page 45) to possess a climate which only a small number of grape varieties can put up with.

When making a sparkling wine, it is necessary for the ripe grapes to have such a large abundance of acidity which would be unsuitable in a still wine. The Chardonnay grapes harvested in Champagne would be regarded as unripe in Burgundy and vice versa. What one is striving after is a balance between acidity and sugar, but this balance varies depending on what type of wine one wants to produce. In a climate only marginally warmer than Champagne's, the wines would become clumsy and unbalanced compared to the original.

High and low temperatures

Champagne is occasionally hit by a heat wave, just like any other area. The years of 47, 59, 76 and 89 gave grapes with a potential alcohol content a couple of percentage points above normal. The acidity level was too low, and instead the wines had to rely on their large content of extracts and high alcohol level to keep themselves alive. It is due to the unique chalk soil of the area that the champagnes from these years don't remind us of crémant de Bourgogne.

The low annual average temperature in the region of 10.53°C forces the roots of the vines to dig down deep in the search for nourishment and water. At this depth the vines soak up a great deal of minerals from the earth, which give champagne its unique style. An interesting observation is that the average temperature outdoors is identical with that in the champagne cellars dug by the Romans. Wine actually thrives best at the same temperature as that in which the vine grew.

As artificial irrigation is forbidden in Champagne, the right amount of rainfall at the right time is crucial for the region. The average rainfall of 662mm per year puts the region somewhere between the drier Burgundy and the wetter Bordeaux districts, but Champagne does have a bountiful supply of water in the excellent network of rivers and canals within its boundaries. The Marne river, the most important water-carrier in the area, also functions as a solar reflector for the river's southern slopes. The river also helps to maintain a fairly constant temperature all year round, acting as a cooling agent in the summer and warming the vineyards up a little during the winter.

Winter in the vineyard.

Mareuil-sur-Aÿ's classic silhuett reflected in the Marne river. In the background Clos des Goisses is seen.

Soil linked with quality

It is quite clear that many areas around the world meet the description of the climatic conditions needed for top-quality wine production. However, it's more complicated than that. As I have pointed out earlier, the geology of the region is unique and definitely the most important factor in that which distinguishes champagne from other sparkling wines. It is perhaps easier to understand the importance of the soil if one examines the colossal differences in quality within Champagne. Aube to the south, with its Kimmeridge clay instead of Belimnite chalk, will never reach the giddy heights of which the Grand cru villages are capable. We don't even need to go as far as Aube to understand how vital the differences in soil are. Several villages that lie side-by-side with the same climate produce grapes with quite different qualities.

Although a wide belt of chalk stretches from Dover's white cliffs many kilometres eastwards into Europe, no other place in the world has such a high concentration of surface Belimnite and Micraster chalk as Champagne.

It is most common to find Belimnite chalk on the slopes and Micraster on the lower ground. It is easy to confuse limestone with chalk. All chalk is limestone, but only one type of limestone is chalk. The particular chalk soil gives the vines in Champagne their unique ability to produce ripe grapes with an unusually high acidity level. The disadvantage of the high chalk content is that it can limit access to iron and magnesium, which the vines need in order to avoid chloros.

As if it wasn't enough with the soil's perfect qualities, the area is also blessed with a suitable topography. The long, reclining hills — Les Falaises de Champagne —

make up yet another unique feature that aids the creation of sparkling wine of the very highest class.

In order to fully exploit the bounties of the soil, it is also necessary to continually renew and nourish the topsoil layer.

The topsoil is only a few centimetres deep, and is made up of sand, marl, clay, lignite and chalk gravel. It gradually loses its goodness and in heavy rain can also slide in great chunks down from the slopes.

"Black gold"

Under the forest-covered parts of Montagne de Reims lies Champagne's black gold — Cendre noires. A black, damp earth, rich in nourishment, especially sulphur and iron. The winegrowers have renewed the topsoil in the vineyards with this for hundreds of years, so much so that today they consist wholly of transported soil.

Certain environmentally-conscious people in the area are understandably beginning to be concerned about how long the black gold will last. Probably a few hundred years yet, but it is impossible to speedily replenish that which nature has taken millions of years to create. It's still quite normal to fertilise the ground with "boues de ville" — waste from Paris. The environmentally-dangerous mixture is always blue because of the blue plastic rubbish bags.

Cendre noires.

Conserve this heritage!

What the area needs are people who know how to care for nature's gifts. It is well-known all over the world that Pinot Noir and Chardonnay are the best grapes for sparkling wines. Their structure and classy aromas have no serious competitors. The grapes have been cultivated for a long time in Champagne, which means that clones have been carefully chosen to suit the region.

Pinot Noir is also a variety of grape that has a particular tendency to form mutations. Through the centuries unique local vines have been developed which have contributed to the richness of variety in terms of taste and quality. As in the other major wine districts, different sorts of yeasts have come to thrive in various areas, and they have then made their mark on the various villages' grapes.

As Champagne has all these unique assets for the creation of the best sparkling wine, the people too have always possessed a drive to improve the quality of the wine. Every winemaker in the world is faced with the quandary: quality or quantity? If the possibility of making a truly great wine is there, then the choice of quality seems the more likely. The development of the champagne methods in this particular region has not come about by chance, but any winemaker in the world can copy the method. The problem is that the process is expensive and the return in terms of quality is relatively small outside the Champagne district. Nor does everyone possess the inheritance of knowledge that tradition has passed down from generation to generation — a necessity if one is to set about creating what is without doubt the best sparkling wine in the world.

The wine world's most controlled district

No other wine district is so heavily regulated and protected as Champagne. It is not by chance that Champagne became France's first appellation. As early as in 1824 the farmers in the area managed to use legal means to forbid the use of the name Champagne on wines from chiefly Saumur and Touraine. They ruled that champagne wine is geographically defined, and not, as many people believe today, a type of wine.

Before 1900 there were groups of growers who got together to protect the name of champagne and to fight the misuse of the title. Between 1907 and 1911 the borders of the cultivation area were established, and in 1919 the "cru" system was created, whereby the prices of the grapes were graded according to their village of origin. During the thirties the forerunner to the C.I.V.C. (see below), the Comité de Châlons, was formed.

When the Appellation d'Origine Contrôllée (AOC) was formed in 1935, Champagne was already heavily regulated. The wines from here are today the only ones in the whole of France that don't require the letters AOC on their labels: the name of Champagne is sufficient as a stamp of quality.

In 1941 the Germans, amongst others, thought that the wine operation in the area needed a better organisation. That's why they made a large contribution to the creation of the Comité Interprofessionel du Vin de Champagne, or C.I.V.C. The organisation wasn't established in one go, but was rather the culmination of a long sequence of attempts to co-ordinate the interests of the wine growers and the champagne houses.

Today the C.I.V.C. is a huge organisation, which pulls in some fifty million francs a year through taxes on the wine producers. Around thirty percent goes to administration and other costs, while most of the money is used to finance equipment, research, PR etc.

The C.I.V.C. is an important and well-functioning body, where people enjoy their work, offer generous hospitality and have a strong passion for the wine. Nor is it any secret that everyone within the C.I.V.C. has a personal taste in wine, although their job is to represent all the producers in the area.

Clos du Mesnil in the heart of Le Mesnil.

House or grower?

It's said that some people within the C.I.V.C. used to represent the general misconception that a great champagne must always come from a blend from several villages, a theory which has been spread and maintained by the big houses for centuries.

I have also heard growers complain that they are not allowed to put the name of the vineyard on the label, even if the champagne is a monocru. They say that it is only the established houses who have dispensation for clos-wines. Examples of this are Krug's Clos du Mesnil, Bollinger's Vieilles Vignes Françaises, Cattier's Clos du Moulin and Leclerc-Briant's Les Authentiques series.

Pierre Peters in Le Mesnil make their prestige cuvée from grapes from one particular place — Les Chétillons — from 65-year-old vines, like Diebolt's exceptional blanc de blancs from Les Pietons in Cramant. Both of these growers would dearly like to have their cru named on the label!

Democratic organisation

Otherwise C.I.V.C.'s organisation is built up in a very democratic manner. It is controlled by a representative from the government, assisted by the growers' president and the president of the "Union des Maissons de Champagne" (the champagne houses). It is administered by a consultative committee made up of six growers' representatives and as many from the houses. All this to ensure that the small wine-producing growers have as much influence as the major houses.

C.I.V.C.'s main tasks

1. To seek a balanced market for both growers and champagne houses.

2. To work to maintain and develop the technical standards of wine production, through research and assistance to the winemakers, analysis and consultation. The organisation shall aim for quality at all stages of production through legislation and controls. For example, top quality vine plants are rewarded and the yield is carefully regulated. A tasting committee stop the worst wines, and there are tough penalties for those who break the rigorous rules of wine production. C.I.V.C. should also offer education for anyone within the business.

3. To work for a positive social climate between the parties involved in the business.

4. To strive for commercial expansion.

5. To work towards a better financial balance between the years. The problem is, as with so many agricultural products, that one is dependent on the quality and quantity of the harvest from year to year. The supply and demand for champagne must therefore be adjusted, using large stores of reserve and unsold wines in years when the harvest is poor.

6. One of the most important functions is PR. There is a special unit whose task is the marketing of the wines and the region.

7. Another important job for the C.I.V.C. is to defend the name of Champagne. There are of course many companies all over the world that want to exploit the attractive power the name brings with it. Today they are working actively to ban the name on wines from Canada, Colombia, New Zealand and Venezuela. In 1978 an agreement was reached with Spain that the Spanish sparkling wines should be called cava, and in 1973 the name "champagne" was struck from all Japanese wines. Some manage to get around such laws by calling their wines something similar. In the beginning of the eighties simple sparkling wine was sold in Brussels' nightclubs with Épernay becoming "Esternay-monopole a Aÿ" or "Eprenay". That particular bluff was squashed by the Belgians themselves. The other type of "counterfeiting" is to exploit the air of luxury that the name represents. German mineral water, English cider, Italian bubble bath and even Yves Saint Laurent's perfume "Champagne" are examples of this. The perfume was stopped by the C.I.V.C. but was still on sale in Sweden in 1996. However, sometimes one does wonder if it isn't the Champagne region that is the real winner from all the fuss surrounding these "fakes".

A striking resemblance, isn't it? The bottle in the middle is a Spanish cava with the champagne-sounding name of Paulponery. It is flanked by Dom Pérignon and Dom Pérignon Rosé.

How to read a label

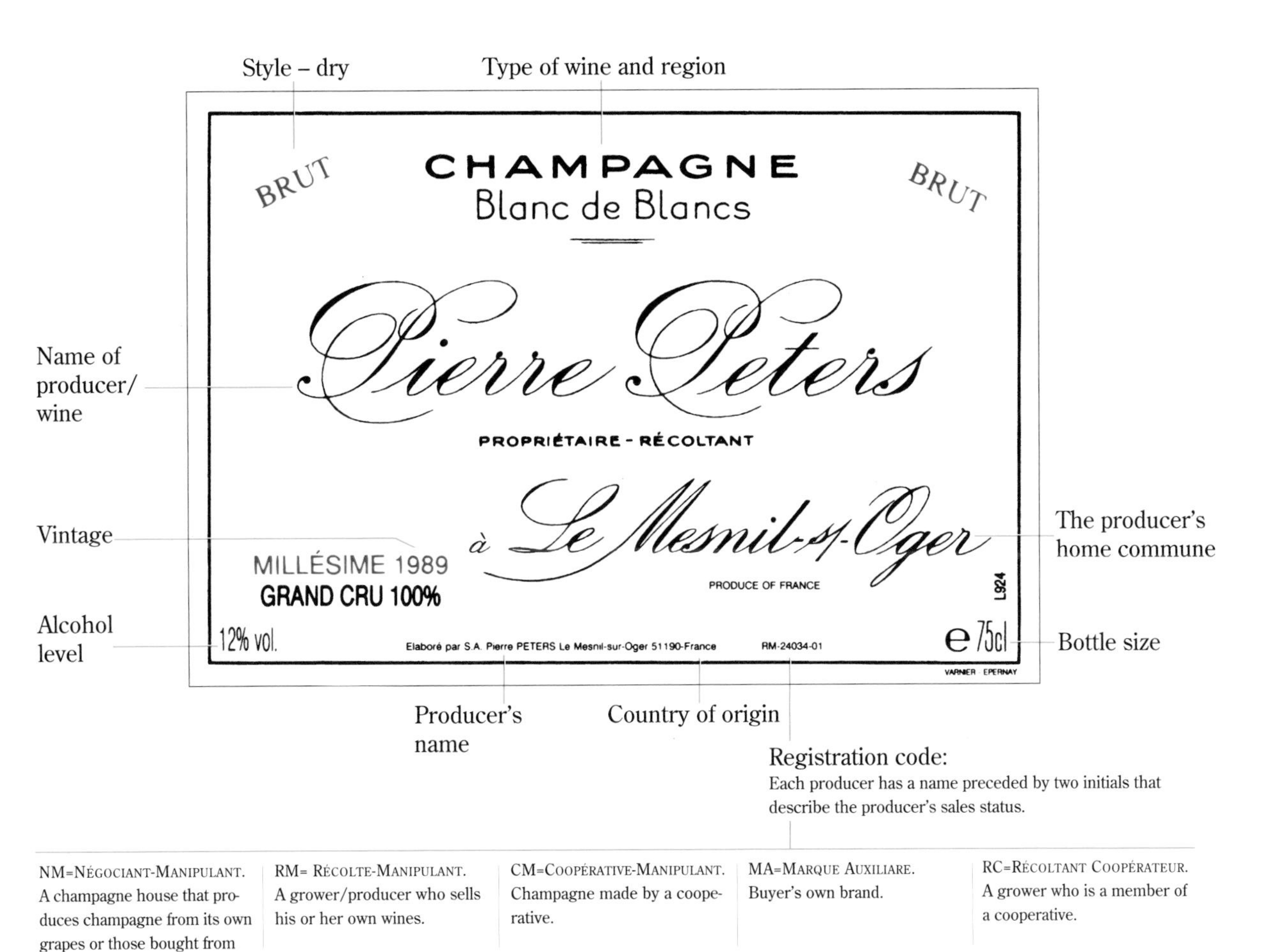

Champagne grapes and vines

The grapes

Only three varieties of grapes may be used in champagne: Pinot Noir, Pinot Meunier and Chardonnay. 35% of the winegrowing area cultivates Pinot Meunier, another 38% Pinot Noir and 27% Chardonnay. In the Grand cru villages one notices that it is the expensive Chardonnay grape that is most common. In Aube Pinot Noir is the variety grown most, while Pinot Meunier has a tight grip on Aisne and Seine-et-Marne. Even though most champagnes are made of a blend of varieties, the character of the various grapes should shine through. Naturally, good blanc de blancs and blanc de noirs should express the characters of the grapes from various areas.

Pinot Noir.

Pinot Noir

Pinot Noir is the wine grower's nightmare and at the same time the wine drinker's paradise: the grape is hard to cultivate but can make fantastic wine.

Pinot Noir, with its compact bunches, is extremely sensitive to rot, and disease was a major problem before the plants were checked for viruses. The grape is not only hard to grow but also sensitive: all contact with the skin must be avoided to ensure a white champagne. The grape juice is always darker than that from Chardonnay.

As opposed to Cabernet Sauvignon, which is grown successfully all over the world, Pinot Noir of the highest class is found only in Burgundy and Champagne. In Burgundy the grape gives the world's finest red wines an unmatched, multi-faceted aroma and a sweet, silky, fruity taste. In Burgundy too, however, they have problems with pale, watery, characterless wines. Only a tiny number of first-class wines come from a tiny number of producers.

Even though Pinot Noir in champagne can never attain the same strength or depth as in a red Burgundy, at least one can find similar aromas. In Champagne Pinot Noir is used chiefly to give backbone and structure to the companies' blends.

Alone, Pinot Noir seldom shows the same elegance as Chardonnay, but provides greater weight and better depth. In its youth, Pinot Noir reveals a strong fruity aroma and a soft if somewhat unbalanced flavour, only to develop as a ripe grape the quality of extending and softening the wine's aftertaste. It does take time for the Pinot Noir champagnes to develop their exciting vegetable and animal scents.

Even though *Bollinger Vieilles Vignes Françaises* is the best example of Pinot Noir in champagne, wonderful blanc de noirs are also made by the growers in Aÿ and Verzenay.

Pinot Noir has a great capacity to form mutations, which is why several hundred different clones of Pinot Noir can be found in Champagne. The grape is so genetically unstable chiefly because it is one of the very oldest kinds of grape. A lot of work in the district has been put into finding clones less sensitive to frost, which is a major problem for the growers, and today each village has a clone suited to their particular climate conditions and soil. Pinot Noir is so successful in Champagne because the region's soil is so high in calcium and because the grape's aromas become more harmonised and finely-tuned in a cool climate. A long ripening period free from disturbances is the key to success with the wine world's most exciting grape.

Pinot Meunier

Pinot Meunier.

Pinot Meunier is the grape that few talk about but which the majority use, and it totally dominates the regions of Aisne and Seine-et-Marne. Pinot Meunier first saw the light of day in the 16th century and is a close relative of Pinot Noir, but Pinot Meunier is easily distinguished from its relative by its downy leaves, which look as if they were covered in flour. This explains the grape's name: Meunier = miller.

Pinot Meunier is a very hardy grape and the only variety that ripens in really cold years. It is also less sensitive to spring frost, which explains why the grape is cultivated so much in the frost-hit Marne valley. Pinot Meunier also gives 10-15% higher yield than Pinot Noir, which is another reason for the grape's popularity.

Those producers who use a lot of Pinot Meunier often heap praise on the grape's fruity qualities. Wines made from Pinot Meunier mature quickly and reveal a tone of toasted or new-baked bread, candy and a simple fruitiness, along with a certain earthiness. Wines with a high percentage of Pinot Meunier, on the other hand, seldom age well. In certain older vintage wines from the major houses one notices how the Chardonnay and Pinot Noir parts are still lively, while the Pinot Meunier part has collapsed and destroyed the cuvée's overall impression. Pure blanc de noirs from Pinot Meunier are unusual and are rarely good for no more than ten years.

The two great exceptions that prove the rule about the maturing potential of Pinot Meunier is Krug and José Michel. Krugs legendary vintage from 1953 contain 30% Pinot Meunier and well-matured bottles retain their youth. The *1921 José Michel* is made only from Pinot Meunier and is one of the most impressive champagnes I have ever drunk. However, it should be remembered that the Pinot

Meunier Krug use has been integrated with the other grapes during the long maturing in the bottle, before degorgement. Krug's and Michel's grapes are also harvested from old vines in the special villages of Leuvrigny and Moussy. None of them uses malolactic fermentation, which is probably the main reason why their Pinot Meunier has enough acidity for it to mature over a longer period. Of course the small, 205-litre oak barrels play their part in the long lifespan of these champagnes.

At Louis Roederer they say that they would love to use Pinot Meunier if they had Krug's skill in handling the grape, but admit freely that so far they've failed to match their competitor.

The grape has its most important function in relatively cheap champagnes put aside for early consumption. Unlike its noble relative Pinot Noir, Pinot Meunier can give an easily-drunk, soft champagne after just three years.

Chardonnay grapes in Côte des Blancs.

Chardonnay

The world's finest white wine grape! Many are the producers the world over who dream of copying the great Chardonnay wines from Burgundy, Chablis and Champagne. In Australia and the USA producers like Leeuwin, Mount Eden, Mayacamas and Chalone make copies that come quite close to the originals, but which will never reach the standards of the top French wines. Chablis Grand cru from Raveneau and Dauvissat or first-class Burgundy from Ramonet, Coche-Dury, Lafon or Guy Roulot combine the grape's aromatic qualities with an elegance from the soil that can only be matched by champagne from Avize, Cramant and Le Mesnil.

The origins of the Chardonnay grape are not fully known, but it is obviously no relative of any other important grape in use today. Sometimes it is called "Pinot Chardonnay", which has added to the miscomprehension that Chardonnay is related to Pinot Noir and Pinot Blanc. All Vitis vinifera (all today's wine grapes) come from wild wines with green Muscat as their common ancestor. Chardonnay was probably one of the first new varieties of grape that developed from the Muscat grape, coming into Europe from the Middle East.

Today Chardonnay is a fashionable grape which is cultivated more and more in France. The greatest increase has in fact taken place in Champagne, where the growers see it as the crown jewel of grapes.

Often the grape's character is mingled with the character of oak, because many producers love to go to extremes in the use of new oak in their Chardonnay wines. The "new world" is the worst sinner when it comes to "over-oaked" Chardonnay, and sometimes the wine tastes more of planks and pencils than fruit. Chardonnay is otherwise the green grape that handles oak barrels best, and is in general a robust and pliant grape. The grape's own character is quite muted, but allows itself to be formed to perfection in various climates or soils. The grape's aroma is broad, buttery and elegant, and the fruit can go from apple in a cold climate to slightly melonish tones in a climate that is too warm.

The Chardonnay vines waste energy in producing leaves instead of using it to ripen the grapes. In Champagne they combat this with hard pruning and by planting the vines extremely close to each other. 7,500 plants per hectare is nothing unusual in Côte des Blancs. Despite its high quality, Chardonnay gives a high yield. The grape is very easy to cultivate and really has only one disadvantage: it is very sensitive to frost as it — like Pinot Noir — buds earlier than most other grape varieties.

In Champagne, Chardonnay gives wines an initial light body, high acidity and a refined bouquet. When young the scent is weak and flowery with clear elements of white flowers and Granny Smith apples. The flavour can be sharp and metallic, with weak citrus fruits and a high mineral content. Those who have been disappointed by a young blanc de blanc's discreet revelation should taste a mature Chardonnay champagne. From its harsh youth the wine is transformed to incomparable lushness and richness. The citrus aromas become more mature and are complemented by exotic fruits such as passion fruit, pineapple and mango. The nose becomes something with a lovely toasty feeling, with a touch of coffee thrown in. As the acidity is so high, Chardonnay wines have a very long lifespan, as anyone who has tasted old vintages of *Salon* will know what I mean.

Other grape varieties

Previously it was permissible to use three other grape varieties in champagne: Arbanne, Petit Meslier and Pinot Blanc. Happily, this is no longer the case. Today you will have to go a long way to find the odd vine that has been left growing, and those that are left will soon be replaced.

Arbanne

During the 19th century Arbanne was an important grape variety in Aube. Its characteristic flowery bouquet could dominate an entire cuvée, even though the actual content was small in percentage terms. The grape's sensitivity to mildew has meant it has disappeared from Champagne faster than Petit Meslier (see below). Arbanne is probably related to Chardonnay Blanc Musqué, which still grows at a plant school in Mâconnais.

Petit Meslier

The most important of the unusual grape varieties is Petit Meslier, still grown in Aube but now in fast retreat. Petit Meslier is very sensitive to viruses and grey rot. Besides, the buds come early and spring frost is a great threat to the harvest in Aube. The grape rarely manages to ripen in Champagne's central district and will only ripen in warm years in the southern parts of Aube. The classic grape varieties that grow in Aube give wines with a high alcohol content in warm years, and earlier the acidic and light Petit Meslier was used to lighten them up. On its own, the white grape is said to give unripe, sour wines with a fruity smell reminiscent of Pinot Meunier. Soon we will have the chance to taste this grape as Jacquesson will release a blanc de blancs made purely from Petit Meslier.

Pinot Blanc

Pinot Blanc is originally a descendant of Pinot Gris and a mutation of Pinot Noir. In Champagne and other areas in France the grape has been mistaken for Chardonnay. By studying the leaf, the difference between the grapes is easily distinguished. Pinot Blanc has flat leaves while Chardonnay's are concave and naked where the stalk meets the leaf. The Pinot Blanc that has crept into some of Champagne's vineyards is often there without the knowledge of the grower. The grape is clearly inferior to Chardonnay and gives neutral, high-alcohol wines that don't last long. That it is cultivated so frequently in Alsace and certain parts of Germany is mainly due to the high yield.

Gamay

This Aube grape was forbidden by law as far back as 1927, but with delayed effect so that the growers would have time to replant with the noble grape varieties. It was first in 1952 that it became illegal to add the lightly raspberry-tasting Beaujolais grape to Champagne's wines. Why the grape is still being grown is a mystery, as special permission is needed, and this is only granted if the grower is over the age of 95 and the vines were planted before 1948!

Gamay grapes.

An 80 year old vine.

The annual lifecycle of the vine

Vines follow an exact lifecycle, no matter what the grape. They rest throughout the winter, collecting strength for the spring. The twigs are bare during this period and have no sap, which has sunk down into the roots. Only when the ground temperature has risen to 9°C does any activity begin. This usually takes place towards the end of February/beginning of March, and after that the active phase of the plant takes between 160 and 200 days, usually divided up into eleven stages.

Thanks to the unique micro-climate, Salon's vines are always first to open their leaves in the village Le Mesnil.

1. **Sap secretion** — Les Pleurs. Sap is secreted from pruning wounds.

2. **Budding** — Le Débourrement. The rising sap forces the buds to open slowly. By the end of March the buds have opened completely.

3. **Leaves are formed** — La Feuillaison. In the beginning of April the first leaves show.

4. **Appearance of the embryo of grape bunches** - La Montre ou Sortie du Raisin. The more embryos that are formed, the greater the harvest - usually.

5. **The blossoming** — La Floraison. The blossoming at the end of May is a wonderful time to experience Champagne. In the evenings the scent of the vineyards, with their exotic passion-fruity aroma, is lovely. Unfortunately the blossoming doesn't last for more than three weeks.

6. **Pollenation** — La Fécondation. In order for the pollenation to start, the temperature in the vineyard must be at

least 20° C and a gentle wind is needed to spread the pollen. In order for the pollenation to succeed it should be over in a few days, as a long drawn-out pollenation period can mean no grapes are formed at all.

7. **Grapes are formed** — La Nouaison. Directly after the pollenation, during the summer months, the vine's energy is devoted to forming the grapes. At first the grapes are always green, small, hard, sour and amost entirely sugarless.

8. **The grapes ripen** — La Veraison. In August the grapes begin to ripen. They become softer and the Pinot grapes begin to develop their blue-black colour. The chlorophyll disappears, the acidity drops and the sugar content increases.

9. **The branches harden** — Aoûtement. At harvest time the branches and twigs harden in order to better survive the coming winter. A thin layer of bark covers the branches that had earlier sweated and breathed.

10. **The leaves change colour** - Le Dessèchement des Feuilles. When the chlorophyll disappears from the leaves in the autumn, they change colour to yellow or red, making the vineyards amazingly beautiful.

11. **The leaves fall** — La Chute des Feuilles. In the beginning of November the leaves dry up and fall easily in the late autumn winds. The sap now sinks down to collect its strength for the folowing year's efforts, and the vine settles down for its winter sleep.

Champagne during autumn.

The Champagne method - from the vine to the glass

What the Champagne method really means is that after the usual alcohol fermentation the wine undergoes a second fermentation in the bottle. Every stage in the process is carefully calculated and relatively complicated. But let us begin at the beginning.

"Aspersion" is the name of the method whereby the buds are protected from frost by water sprayed from a sprinkler system over the vines. The buds are encapsulated in the protective ice envelope and escape any frost damage.

The work in the vineyard

The vine farmer's work in the vineyard goes on all year round. At certain pre-ordained times he must prune, fertilise and spray his crop, and the struggle against viruses, parasites and rot is a never-ending one. The climate can also cause problems, especially the spring frost which can be a scourge to the blossoms.

A ground rule for all wine production is that the poorer the harvest yield, the better the grapes. The yield is usually measured in hectolitres per hectare. Depending on the extent of the harvest, a maximum yield is set every year in Champagne. During the exceptional harvest of 1982 the area reached the extremely high figure of 86 hectolitres per hectare, but most quality growers try to keep their yield figure under 50 hectolitres per hectare.

Another important ground rule is that the older the vines, the better the quality. Both these rules put the winemaker in a difficult position: they want to sell as much wine as possible, but as quantity and quality don't mix, they are forced to choose.

The average age of a vine in Champagne is around fifteen years. A vine that has reached the fine old age of thirty, when quality is at its peak, is generally replaced with a new plant by most producers today. It is of course extremely expensive to allow old, low-yield vines with expanding root systems to take up space in the vineyard, but there are enthusiasts who today harvest grapes from sixty to eighty year-old vines. Diebolt, Moncuit, Pierre Peters and Larmandier-Bernier separate the grapes from their oldest Chardonnay vines to go into a special

Old Chardonnay vines in Côte des Blancs bound in the Chablis style.

luxury champagne. Surprisingly enough, this variety costs no more than the champagne houses' ordinary vintage champagnes and has to be seen as a bargain.

The vines are at their most productive between 10 and 25 years of age. As the production of the grapes takes a lot of energy, the individual grapes have a less concentrated taste. Grapes from really old vines always contain more extract and a smaller amount of water than grapes from younger plants.

The positioning of the vines in the vineyard is critical to the results. Before the vine louse swept across Europe, Champagne's ungrafted vines were planted "en foule", which meant that the vines stood higgeldy-piggeldy at about six plants per square metre. The yield per unit space was higher than today, but as each individual vine produced far fewer grapes, the quality was maintained.

Bollinger still use this method for their ungrafted vines at Aÿ and Bouzy, which for some unexplained reason were never attacked by the lice. That they were spared the effects of the plague is a minor mystery.

Besides "en foule" there are four tying systems accepted in Champagne: Chablis, Cordon, Guyot and Vallée de la Marne.

The Chablis system comes, as the name suggests, from Chablis. Up to four branches are allowed on each vine — the fewer the branches, the more concentrated the fruit. Anselme Selosse in Avize always uses two branches, but if you take a look at the major houses' crops nearby you will only see vines with four branches. Almost all the Chardonnay vines in Champagne are tied according to the Chablis method.

The Cordon system is the most important form of tying for the Pinot Noir vines, where only one main branch is allowed.

The Guyot method is not allowed for Grand cru and Premier cru villages, but is often used in Aube for all three varieties of grape.

The Vallée de la Marne method is only used for the low-classed Pinot Meunier vines, and almost the whole of Aisne has vines that are tied in this manner.

After pruning the discarded branches are immediately burnt in metal wagons. The lovely smell of smoke that then covers the area is like that of Earl Grey tea.

The harvest

The harvest is the highlight of the year in any wine district. Everywhere the harvest festival is a colourful occasion that appears a touch exotic to us northerners. Even though the old guard think it was better in the good old days, harvest time can be pretty wild in Champagne nowadays. Champagne is the only district that does not allow mechanical harvesting, i.e. every grape is hand-picked and put in "les mannequins" (the grape baskets).

The C.I.V.C. decides when the harvest will begin in its annual proclamation "Ouverture des vendages", and two dates are given, one for Pinot grapes and one for Chardonnay. Earlier, nature had been the one to decide the harvest date — exactly one hundred days after the blossoming was over. Today that date often falls on the same day that the modern C.I.V.C. has ordained!

Of course, the date of the harvest varies from year to year, but it usually starts in the middle of September, and thousands of people come from all over France to help pick the grapes. The operation always starts at dawn, to prevent grapes from fermenting spontaneously, and the pickers are equipped with "Les Epinettes", a tool somewhere between a pair of scissors and secateurs.

The traditional baskets - "les mannequins" - are still used, although nowadays they have often been replaced by plastic crates.

Grey root

Just as in Bourgogne, Pinot Noir grapes in Champagne are sensitive to grey rot — Pourriture Gris — which should not be confused with noble rot — Botrytis Cinerea — which amongst other things gives the intensely sweet wines of the Sauternes. The grey rot, which gives a mouldy smell, is seldom a problem in Champagne.

As all the grapes are hand-picked, affected grapes can be thrown away at once. If for any reason a grape with grey rot makes its way into the champagne presses the taste is hardly noticeable as only the skin of the grape is affected. In Champagne any skin contact is avoided during the production of all white wines.

Sugar content and acidity decide

The grapes have to have achieved a high enough sugar content to produce 10-11% alcohol, while at the same time retaining enough acidity to balance the wine. The Germans measure "oechsle" and juice weight, while in Champagne they content themselves with checking the internal size of the acidity and sugar content.

The old monk Dom Pérignon studied and felt the grapes when they were ready to be picked. He also saw the advantage of harvesting in cool conditions and speedily transporting the grapes to the presses, and his principles are followed to this day. The entire harvest operation is strictly divided up and organised so that all the full baskets come up onto the lorries as quickly as possible and are taken directly to the presshouse.

The pressing

Hard work at a traditional Coquart press.

It is very important that all the grapes are whole and in the best condition when they reach the presshouse, which for this reason is always located as close to the vineyard as possible. Many of the smaller growers have their grapes pressed at the huge cooperative complexes. The major champagne houses always use their own presshouse in order to keep an eye on every stage of the process.

At harvest time the press houses are crawling with inspectors from the C.I.V.C. who check that the right amount of juice is extracted from each pressing. In 1992 the legally-set volumes for each pressing were altered, and the new law means that 2,550 litres should be extracted from 4,000 kilos of grapes.

First pressing (Cuvée)

The name is unfortunately the same as the one the French use for blend, which can be a little confusing. The first pressing gives the purest and most delicate juice direct from the grape's pulp, without any contact with the skin or the pips. A few producers, such as Jacquesson and Vilmart, go even further in the struggle for quality. They have discovered that only some of the cuvée is of the highest class, and they call that juice "Coeur de cuvée".

Second pressing (Premier taille)

Very few houses admit that they use anything other than the first pressing, but actually very few can afford the luxury of using only the cuvée. Wines made from the second pressing are slightly harsher and rougher. Using "premier taille" from both the black Pinot grapes can also give the colour of the champagne a reddish undertone.

Third pressing (deuxieme taille)

The third pressing used to make up an important ingredient of "supermarket champagnes" which brought shame on the region. New laws forbid the third pressing in order to put a stop to these inadequate champagnes.

Rebêche

Quite simply, Rebêche is what is left after the previous pressings. Pressing the almost completely dry skins gives an extremely high tannin content and is suitable only for distilling.

The champagne presses

When the grapes come in from the vineyards the pressing gets under way as quickly as possible.

At the traditional house of Krug the wine is racked from one cask to another through gravitational pull. The sediment thus stays in the bottom of the first cask.

New kinds of press are experimented with all the time in the region, but the conclusion usually is that Dom Pérignon's traditional vertical press — the Coquart — is still the best. The Coquart press is always made of wood and can be either round or square in shape, and with the aid of a large wooden plate the grapes are pressed quickly and carefully.

The other common type is the modern horizontal press, which is either pneumatic or hydraulic. It was received with great excitement and enthusiasm when it first arrived, but interest has waned somewhat since.

Oxidation

It is vital throughout the winemaking process that the juice is shielded from too much oxidation. Some winemakers do claim however that wine can be "vaccinated" against later oxidation by exposing the juice to oxygen at an early stage. The entire development of wine is a process of oxidation, so it would be wrong to say that it is wholly harmful, but the crucial point is how much the oxygen is allowed to affect the wine, and how fast the oxidation is allowed to occur. A wine made using oak barrels is exposed to a higher degree of oxidation than one that has been hermetically sealed in a stainless steel vat.

The chemical effect of excess oxidation is that the oxidation enzymes attack the wine's phenol constituents and colours the liquid brown, giving the wine a bitter, sherry-like taste. In order to protect the freshly-pressed juice, one must add around eight grams of sulphur dioxide per hectolitre. The sulphur also helps to kill wild yeasts which could otherwise trigger off an uncontrolled fermentation. However, it is highly unusual to be able to detect sulphur in the taste or the aroma: the dose is quite simply too small for that.

Débourbage

In order to remove unwanted particles and solid constituents the juice must go through a process called débourbage, which can be either natural or artificial. The artificial process is made up of centrifugation, filtration and precipitation through bentonite clay. Most of the winemakers in Champagne use the natural process though, where sediment is collected by cooling the juice down to a level just over the freezing point. A wine must go through many processes before it is ready, and the débourbage is the first stage towards that brilliant champagne.

Two firms with differing methods of fermentation.

Fermentation

When the grape juice has been taken to the fermenting vats it immediately starts to ferment, thanks to the yeasts that originally sat on the grape's skin. Selected yeast cultures are added, and they are either natural or grown, depending on what kind of champagne one wants to make. One of the secrets behind Moët & Chandon's "house style" is the yeast culture they use for all their cuvées, which gives a bread-like scent with hints of mushroom sauce.

Each individual Champagne village can hold hundreds of strains of wild yeast. The yeasts that are cultured in the laboratories all come originally from wild yeast.

Yeast needs nourishment in order to build up the strength needed to change the sugar in the grapes to alcohol and carbon dioxide, and it is found in the grape juice itself. In this are all the proteins, minerals and vitamins the yeast needs. A ripe Champagne grape contains around twenty percent sugar, which is quite enough for the yeast to begin the change to alcohol and carbon dioxide. Actually it is not the yeast cell that is responsible for the fermenting process, but rather a score of enzymes which the yeast cell carries. Each enzyme has its own particular task to perform during the complicated business of fermentation.

At the normal first fermentation — the alcoholic fermentation — the carbon dioxide built up is not used. At this stage the only thought is to raise the level of ethyl alcohol and change the grape juice into wine.

Vats of oak or steel?

Since the beginning of the sixties the champagne makers fermenting vats have mostly been made of stainless steel. Vats made of enamel, glass and fibre glass are also used to a small extent, but a small, quality-conscious elite, led by

Bollinger and Krug, ferment in oak barrels of various sizes. The classic size in Champagne is 205 litre barrels, so-called "pieces".

Many of the growers that use oak casks in Côte des Blancs today buy their barrels from Chablis: 225 litre "barriques". Jacquesson's prestige champagne Signature is fermented in 75 hectolitre "foudres", while a few producers own massive 600 litre "demi-muids".

The major champagne houses claim that the use of giant stainless steel vats has brought with it increased quality. Personally I take great delight in champagne that has been made in oak barrels. Without doubt the wine is given an extra dimension by the contact with the wood. The aromas become far richer and the depth is greater. However, that isn't to say that first-class champagne cannot be made in stainless steel vats. *Taittinger Comtes de Champagne*, *Roederer Cristal*, *Pol Roger Winston Churchill* and *Salon* are all shining examples of steel vat-fermented champagnes with wonderfully pure fruit and magnificent elegance. The oak-fermented wines from Krug, Bollinger and Jacques Selosse are, however, supreme when it comes to depth and complexity.

As champagne is such a finely-balanced and delicate wine, one has to be extremely careful that the oak aromas do not dominate the fruit of the wine. Using only new oak barrels, as is done in Rioja and Australia, is out of the question. An oak cask in Champagne is usually so old that the tannin and vanillin have disappeared through years of use. It wasn't until as late as in 1993 that an oenologist was able to prove clinically that Krug's champagnes did actually contain elements that came from the oak. Previously chemists had claimed that the oak character that is quite easy to detect in Krug's wines came merely from the breathing that the wine went through in the aged oak casks.

The content of both tannin and vanillin is higher in oak-fermented champagne than in that fermented in stainless steel vats. Another important difference is that the oak-fermented champagnes contain more glycerol, which makes the wine fatter and oilier. As the oak allows a small amount of air through to the wine the oxidation takes place a touch faster, giving a higher ester and aldehyde content.

Certain critics often judge oak-fermented champagnes from Bollinger and Krug to be defective at blind tastings, as they find a hint of sherry-like aroma and believe this is due to too much oxidation. I prefer to say that the tone is a faint and completely natural element in the classic oxidative character that a great oak-fermented champagne should have. Otherwise it can be hard to distinguish oak character from old Chardonnay in champagne — equally so in chablis wines. Both get a toasty, nutty and smoky basic tone, which sometimes hints at bread and coffee. Autolytic character, i.e. that aroma that champagnes develop when they've lain a long time in contact with sediment before being disgorged, can also easily be confused with oak character.

The quality-conscious champagne houses that use oak casks today never admit that they use a small number of new oak casks to give the wine a personal spice. Without naming any names however, I can honestly say that I myself have seen new oak casks filled with wine inside some famous champagne houses.

Anselme Selosse and Vilmart, on the other hand, make no secret of their experiments in this direction. Selosse claims that using 5-10% new barrels is only for the good of his bourgogne-like champagnes. He was also the first to release a champagne made entirely with new casks. His pure *87 Origine* does need decanting before it is drunk though.

Using oak barrels is of course very risky compared with stainless steel fermenting, as the wines that are made in the old handicraft manner with small barrels can show a disturbing degree of bottle variation. Occasionally they can be made in below-standard hygienic conditions, which results in a defective wine. For the big, mass-producing houses the stainless steel vat is certainly a blessing, making it hard to fail with a wine. The quality of the grapes and the ability of the cellar master to blend them are the elements in the process that determine how the final product will taste.

The cooper's craft is a dying one, but one or two firms still employ their own specialist.

Time and temperature

Two crucial factors in the fermentation are time and temperature. Usually fermentation takes ten days and takes place at a temperature of 18-20° C, but some winemakers ferment their wines at a lower temperature, enabling them to better retain the wine's fruit. Billecart-Salmon have become pioneers in the field of cold fermentation. Once again however, the most radical winemaker is Anselme Selosse, who ferments his wines for a couple of months.

Every cask is carefully checked before being refilled. Every year Krug and Bollinger discard barrels that don't meet their exacting demands.

The fermentation process is the phase that changes the grapes' ordinary juice into the unbeatable multi-faceted drink we know as wine. Wine made from grapes is the only drink that can contain the aroma of all the other kinds of fruit, collected together in one glass! Of course it can be interesting to go to a beer tasting session or a whisky tasting, but the unending combinations of taste that wine can achieve bear no comparison with any other drink in the world. The aromatic components of a great wine can reach the hundreds and include acids, alcohols, aldehydes, esters and cetones. If someone finds hints of apple or peaches in a champagne, then that person is likely to be completely right. Precisely those fifty components that create the apple's aroma can be part of a wine's complex constitution. Some smells are made up of far fewer components, such as almond (benzoaldehyde, acetain), hazelnut (diacetyl), honey (fenyl acetic acid) and banana (sioamylbuttyrate, butylamyllbuttyrate).

Personally I think it feels more appetising to describe a wine as having a hazelnut aroma than containing diascetylin.

Malolactic fermentation

The advantages and disadvantages of malolactic fermentation can really start a discussion between different winemakers. Whether they use it or not, they are all certain that their method is the correct one. This controversial biological process is based upon changing hard malic acid to gentler lactic acid.

The malolactic fermentation is speeded up if the fermenting vat is heated, and it is prevented if sulphur is added to the wine at a low temperature. The advantage with wines that have gone through malolactic fermentation is that they become gentler and easier to appreciate when young. Wines that have not gone through malolactic fermentation on the other hand are sharp and hard when young, but retain a lifegiving high level of acidity for much longer.

Several of the best and long-lived champagnes, such as *Krug*, *Salon* and *Selosse*, can taste tough in their infancy, but as they have not gone through malolactic fermentation their lives are greatly extended. However, when companies such as Piper-Heidsieck and Lanson avoid malolactic fermentation for their thin non-vintage champagnes, the point is lost. It should be said though that both Piper-Heidsieck and Lanson make vintage champagnes that begin their lives as pupae, but which with time develop into colourful, many-winged butterflies.

Much remains to be understood regarding malolactic fermentation. Some oenologists claim that the fermentation always occurs, the only question is - when? What is clear is that the process reduces a wine's acid content: ten grams of malic acid becomes 6.7 gram of lactic acid and the rest disappears as carbon dioxide.

You'll find more about the individual producers' attitudes towards malolactic fermentation in the producers' section.

Blending (assemblage)

When the wine has finished fermenting during the winter, it is usually racked twice. Racking means that the wine is separated from sediment that has sunk to the bottom by transferring it to a new vat. Certain producers who are terrified of the wine gaining too much character filter the wine once again, but happily enough more and more understand that they shouldn't do this as it removes important aromatic constituents.

In March/April one of the most difficult stages in the creation of champagne begins — the blending. This is when the cellar master — "Chef de Caves" — can stamp his and the house's own identity upon the wine. The fermented wines are completely still and usually lie in separate vats, divided up according to village. The richer the palette the cellar master has to choose from, the more he can influence the wine. Krug is a little different, with its unique 4,000 small oak barrels, so if they are disappointed with a particular cask they need only refuse that particular wine.

The cellar master at Moët & Chandon, Richard Geoffroy, can also play with an incredible mosaic of still wines, as his 800 giant tanks contain wines from 150 villages. A much lower basic quality than Krug's, but even so!

The small growers have an easier time of it. They usually put their better wines to one side for the cuvée de prestige, but rarely have a problem knowing which wines should be blended with which. Often they only have access to grapes from one or two crus. As usual Anselme Selosse goes a step further when he separates each location within the Grand cru village Avize into different barrels.

Anselme Selosse tasting from one of his oak casks.

It demands a great deal of experience and knowledge to create a non-vintage champagne with a special house style year after year because the raw materials vary so much with each vintage. The cellar master also has access to a huge store of reserve wines from previous years which he uses to balance the taste.

Krug keep their reserve wines in steel tanks as at this stage of the winemaking process the idea is to keep oxidation to a minimum. Louis Roederer go the other way, fermenting their wines in stainless steel vats but storing reserve wines in large oak barrels. Bollinger use the most refined method of all: their reserve wines are kept under low pressure in magnums.

The cellar master's magic

When the cellar master creates the cuvée he has a range of questions to consider:

— Will the wine develop harmoniously, so that the Pinot and Chardonnay won't be at different stages of development?

— Should he aim to follow the house style or the character of this particular vintage?

— How will the wine be appreciated when it has become sparkling?

— The big question is, which wines are best suited together? It isn't so simple as to merely blend the best sites. An unbalanced, sharp wine can provide the nerve that a heavy blend lacks, and a neutral, insignificant wine can function as a bridge between the lightest and fullest wines in a cuvée.

Certain crus don't work well together, even though they may produce great wines on their own. The job of the cellar master is very reminiscent of that of a chef, who must know exactly how much of each ingredient he shall use.

Ever since Dom Pérignon began to blend grapes from different villages, the idea of blending has been almost something holy in Champagne. I am one of those who believes that unblended, mono-cru champagnes can be of equally high class, but of course a skilful cellar master can work wonders with relatively simple grapes.

The Krug brothers gave me the oportunity to taste a "mini-Grande Cuvée". I can assure you that it was impressive!

The second fermentation (prise de mousse)

Thousands of bottles stored "sur lattes" in Boizel's cellar in Épernay.

When the cellar master has decided how the still wines should be combined, they are blended in giant tanks before bottling. It is at this stage that champagne's seal of nobility is formed — the snow-white mousse. The first fermentation builds carbon dioxide that disappears into the air, but the carbonic gas formed in the second fermentation stays in the bottle.

As the blended still wine has finished fermenting, more sugar and yeast must be added. The sugar and yeast are dissolved in wine, in a mixture called "liqueur de tirage". The dosage is strictly regulated according to how fizzy the champagne is to be. Usually 22 grams of sugar are added per litre of wine, raising the alcohol content of the wine by up to 1.2%.

When the solution has been added, the wine is bottled and sealed temporarily with a crown-cap instead of a proper cork. The inside of the crown-cap is covered with plastic in order to protect the wine from possible rust. The bottles are then carried down to the 10-12°C cellars and laid horizontally — "sur lattes" — stacked, one on top of the other, in enormous piles. The sight that meets you in the cellars of the larger companies is an impressive one: kilometre-long rows of bottles stretching as far as the eye can see.

Guarded storage

According to law the non-vintage champagne must lie untouched in this state for at least 15 months. A vintage champagne cannot be separated from its sediment until at least three years after bottling. Most of the quality producers will let their wines stay untouched for a couple of years more than the stipulated minimum.

The lower the temperature is in the cellar, the smaller and finer will be the bubbles formed by the fermentation. The fermentation itself is over after two weeks, and during that time the bottles are shaken several times by hand, an operation called "poignetage". These days it is unusual for bottles to explode during "prise de mousse", but before it became known exactly how much sugar and yeast was needed many a famous producer lost half his annual output that way.

During the fermentation a sediment is formed, called "depot" or "lie", which is made up of dead yeast cells and some unwanted chemical particles. The sediment enriches the wine with its own aroma, so-called autolytic character (see dictionary), and is a very important constituent of a complete champagne.

After the "sur lattes" stage, the bottles are placed with their necks downwards in large wooden racks called "pupitres". At first the bottles stand at a 45° angle, and the holes in which they are placed are constructed so that the angle can be gradually adjusted to 90°. A "remueur" twists the bottles an eighth of a revolution with a quick snap, thus slowly removing the sediment from the sides of the bottle. "Remuage", as the French call it, is today often done by large machines, called "gyropallettes". Undeniably this saves time, but it strips some of the glamour from the traditional handiwork of the wine producers.

From the quality point of view I can see only one disadvantage with "gyropallettes", and that is that not all the bottles are put through the same amount of movement. A "gyropallette" means that the bottles in the middle move less than those out on the edge of the apparatus.

After "remuage" the bottles are upside down, ready to lose their sediment. However, many producers prefer to mature the wine further "sur pointes" (on its toes), in order to be able to open a well-kept, fresh older bottle to order. Moët & Chandon are revolutionising the view of "remuage" with their "les billes": yeast capsules with thin skins made from an alginate that comes from marine algaes. The thin skin lets the liquid through but keeps sediment trapped inside the capsule. Remuage takes place in a few seconds, and the bottle is ready to be disgorged.

"Gyropallette"

Disgorging

The final important step in the champagne process is called disgorging ("degorgement"). These days the top of the bottleneck is frozen in freezing brine at a temperature of -28° C. The sediment becomes half-frozen and is shot out of the bottle by machine with a sharp mechanical movement.

Some winemakers still carry out this process by hand — "á la volée". With a swift, precise movement the sediment is shot out of the bottle, which at the same time is turned upright. The operation calls for years of training before one is sure of attaining yeast-free wine without spilling half of the contents. Salon in le Mesnil disgorge all their champagnes "á la volée" in order to control the scent of the wine.

The wine which is lost at this point is replaced with new wine, plus some sugar. How much sugar depends on what type of champagne one wants to produce.

This sugar solution is called "liqueur d'expédition" or "dosage". Some use older wine in their "dosage" to get a

Disgorging by hand and by machine.

more mature taste, but usually a few drops of the same wine are added. Up until the 1960's it was common to spice up the "liqueur d'expédition" with a little cognac. As this is forbidden, I have promised the winemakers not to reveal which of them still use cognac, but between us I can say that they number more than one! There are also many who have their own special "dosage". One small grower in Aÿ told me that he even uses honey in his blend!

On with the cork!

After the wine has been given its final "dosage", the bottle is supplied with the cork — so important when it comes to maturing the wine. At the start of this century all champagne corks were made in one piece, but today's high cork prices mean that they are now made up of several discs. The top part is agglamerated cork, and underneath are two or three discs of real cork. The part that is in contact with the wine is always of the highest quality. The length and quality of the cork are perhaps the most important factors in making it possible to mature the champagne over several decades. All the older champagnes that have been given high marks in the producers' section of this book have well-maintained corks. Looking at the difference in lengths of the corks in bottles from 1938 and 1979 makes you think: the older one is almost twice as long and made of one whole piece of cork!

When the cork is in, the bottle is shaken to mix the dosage with the wine, and the cork is then held in place by a wire muzzle.

Surprisingly a champagne cork is actually cylinder-shaped and quite straight before being inserted into the bottle. After a while in the bottle it becomes mushroom-shaped, then is squashed down as the years go by.

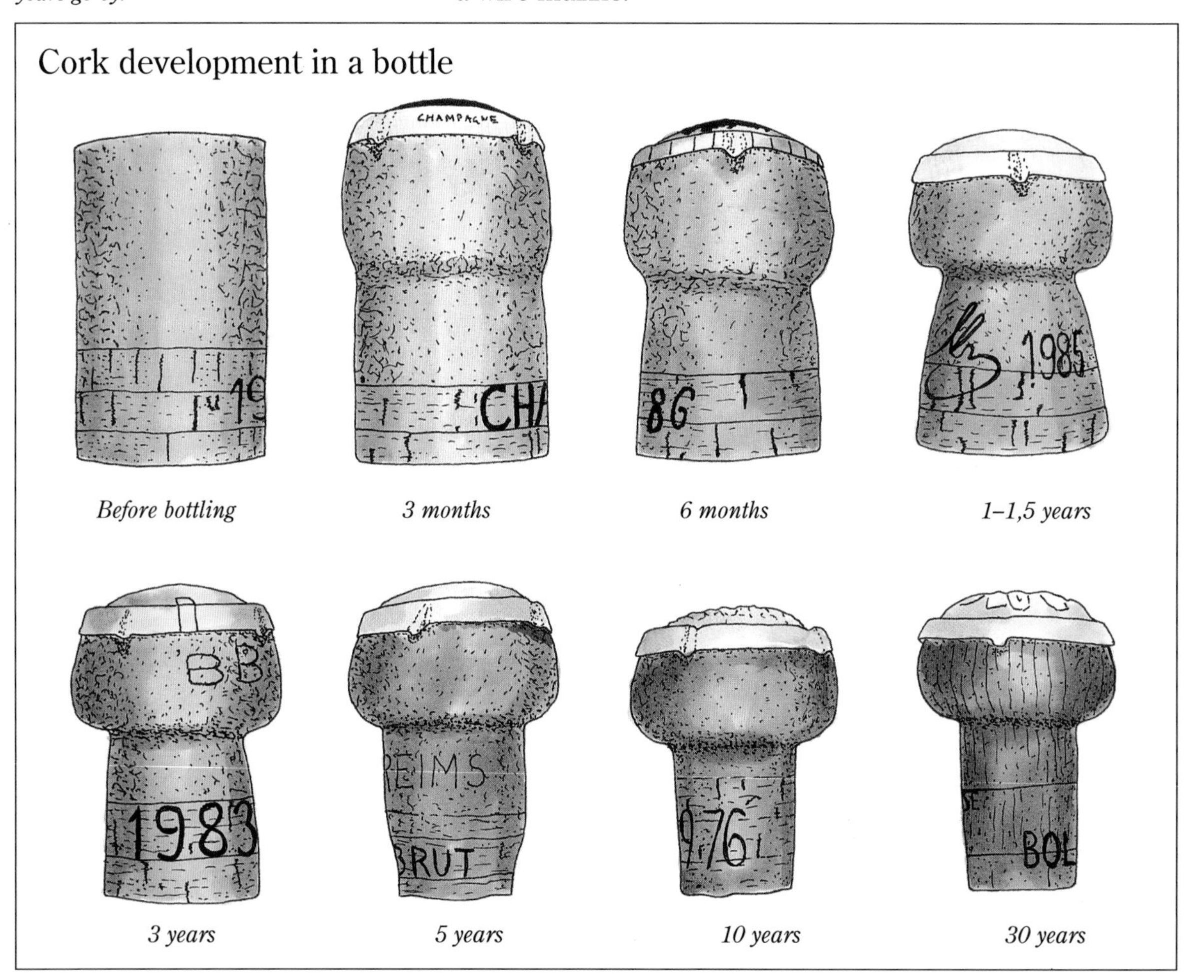

Beautiful labels

With the cork in place it is time for the labelling, whether manual or by machine. Unfortunately, champagne labels are given far too little attention by most people. Is there a wine district in the world whose labels can compare in beauty to those that decorate the bottles from Champagne? No, probably not, but then perhaps the champagne houses today spend far too much time launching new bottle shapes, labels and packaging in all conceivable materials instead of concentrating on the contents of the bottles. But you must agree that a beautiful label can make the bottle more attractive!

After the labelling, the bottles are stored for a short time at the producer's before the champagne is sent to the far corners of the globe. The long and laborious process that began in the vineyard many years ago has now reached its conclusion. Now all that is left is to open the bottle. And enjoy!

Buy, store and taste

Buying champagne

When we Swedes are out in the big wide world we get off to a good start. Stockholm's Arlanda airport Taxfree shop is perhaps the most well-stocked airport store in Europe when it comes to champagne. The price level is very low nowadays. At the end of the eighties champagne cost twice as much as it did in France, but today the difference is marginal. Charles du Gaulle, Heathrow and Schiphol are other airports that offer a great range of champagne. In the States the price level is rather high but bargains can be found in New York and San Francisco's wine and licquor stores.

Otherwise, quite the best method is to buy your wines directly from the producer, guaranteeing you wine in its best possible condition. Besides, you also get a chance to taste the wine before you buy. As opposed to the German winemakers, the champagne growers are not put off by having to open a bottle to sell one. The fact that you are willing to buy their champagnes seems enough to satisfy them.

In Reims and Épernay there are lots of luxurious champagne boutiques which charge outrageous prices. Only Madame Salvatore on the big square in Épernay maintains the same prices as the producers themselves.

Old champagne can almost only be bought in England. This is because the English have a traditional love for the great, sweet, mature style called Gout Anglais, and many are the lords and noblemen who have filled their cellars with champagne from the beginning of the century. Wander around in London and reconnoitre various wine shops, and you are bound to find more old champagne in a few hours than is on sale in the rest of the world. Older champagne is also relatively cheap on auction at Sothebys and Christies, but as the quality of older vintages varies so much depending on how the bottles have been kept, you are taking a great risk by buying anything before you've tasted it.

Choosing champagne

There are certainly many who ask why champagne has to be so expensive. The chief reasons are the rigorous quality threshold regulations and the costly method of making the drink. The cost of the bottle, the cork, the grapes, the production and storage make it impossible to sell champagne for less than fifty French francs (ffr).

Most matters concerning wine are naturally a question of taste and preference, but considering what *Château Petrus* or *Romanée Conti* cost these days, 600 ffr for *vintage Krug* has to be seen as a bargain. At most champagne houses the vintage wines are the best buys. For a few more francs we can buy the 1990 from Moët & Chandon and the 1989 from Bollinger, both of which are several classes better than their non-vintage champagne. The cuvée de prestige is usually even more refined and concentrated, but the question is whether the price is motivated by the difference in quality.

I believe one should avoid the very cheapest champagnes. They often have an unclean, earthy taste and don't give value for money. They usually contain a high percentage of wine from the second pressing and originate from Aisne or Aube, and the dominant grape in the wines is customarily Pinot Meunier. Most of the supermarket champagnes in Europe fit this description.

No, the real bargain in the champagne jungle is the high-class Grand cru growers' blanc de blancs.

In Burgundy the growers' wines are more expensive than the wine companies. In Champagne the situation is quite the opposite, as the rich companies solidly back the theory that good champagne should be made up of a blend of three sorts of grape. However, now that the growers are receiving more and more attention, they are sure to learn the lessons of how to ask for more. That's why we the price-conscious consumers should hurry now if we want to buy these masterworks at bargain prices. Some growers, such as Selosse and Vilmart, have already achieved such cult status that their wines are fetching sky-high prices in Paris and New York.

How about a nebuchadnezzar?

Bottle sizes

Nebuchadnezzar	(20 bottles)	15 litres
Balthazar	(16 bottles)	12 litres
Salamanazar	(12 bottles)	9 litres
Methusalem	(8 bottles)	6 litres
Rehoboam	(6 bottles)	4,5 litres
Jeroboam	(4 bottles)	3 litres
Magnum	(2 bottles)	1,5 litres
Bottle		75 cl
Half bottle		37,5 cl
Quarter bottle		18,7 cl

Whichever champagne you choose, you should check that the wine is in good condition. Never buy a champagne bottle that is kept standing in the shop, as the cork can dry out and ruin the wine. Hold the bottle up to the light to see if the champagne is clear or if there is sediment. If the champagne is older, then you should also smell the cork, and if you detect the unmistakable smell of madeira then there is a great risk that the cork has let in a harmful amount of air. The level of the wine also has tales to tell about the condition of the champagne: if it is clear that the wine level has sunk then that is a warning sign that something is wrong.

These small tips can help you to reject the worst examples, but there is one problem that cannot be detected even when the wine is poured: the ever-more widespread defective cork.

Intensive research is being conducted into corked wines, but so far no complete explanation has been found.

If you buy your wine in Champagne during the warm vacation weeks, don't keep the wine for long in a baking-hot car. The temperature there can easily reach some 50°C in the sun, so if possible leave the bottle in your hotel room until you journey home. If you can, keep the bottle in its packaging so as not to expose it to strong light. And of course, keep the bottle in a horizontal position all the way home.

Storage

The storage conditions the champagne producers maintain in their cold, dark, damp cellars are hard for us private wine lovers to reproduce. However, those of us living up here in Scandinavia have an advantage thanks to our cool climate. Many are sure to have access to an ordinary food cellar under the house or somewhere on their property. Even if the temperature varies somewhat between winter and summer, the cellar usually maintains a sufficiently constant temperature. The constancy of the temperature is more important than how cold it is, assuming that it never rises above 16-18° C. If you are thinking of storing your wines a really long time, then the perfect temperature is 10-12° C. If you live in an apartment, then you could always store wine in your refrigerator for a short time. This isn't recommended for longer periods, as strong smells from the food can make their way into the bottle and destroy the wine completely. There is also a risk that the cork will dry out if you keep the bottle in the refrigerator for too long.

If you can't afford to buy the hellishly expensive specially-designed wine refrigerators, you could always buy a second-hand example and keep your wines there. Champagne stored in this way keeps its freshness and elegance much longer than if it is kept at room temperature. A good friend of mine always "speed-matures" his champagnes in the pantry. If you want a softer, rounder taste in your champagne and know that the bottle won't lie longer than one year, then you can safely follow my friend's example.

Storage is, unfortunately, no exact science. Far too many times I've drunk tired and lifeless wines that have been stored in exemplary fashion, and on just as many occasions I've drunk wonderful wines that have been awfully abused in storage.

Wine is a living product and every bottle lives its own life, which makes the whole thing more fascinating.

Happily for those of us who live in the city, more and more wine clubs with their own premises have been started up, and members can rent their own racks. If you are so lucky as to have access to your own proper wine cellar, then you will improve your storage by organising your bottles according to district, type of wine and vintage. To keep a good overview of the contents of your cellar, make thorough notes in a cellar book or on your computer.

When maturing champagne, remember that magnums develop slowest and half-bottles fastest. This is because the relationship between air and wine in a magnum is quite simply ideal for fine, slow development. Too much air in relation to the amount of wine speeds up the whole process.

If you have the right furniture or other articles, such as wooden wine cases, in your private wine cellar, then with a little imagination and inventiveness you can create the appropriate atmosphere.

At the Cave Bouquet wine club in Stockholm's Old Town they pour out leftover drops of wine into the cellar's absorbent floor. This is done so that even visitors' olfactory senses are captured by the ambience.

Treasures of the deep

It was at dawn, on a clear day in the beginning of November, 1916, when a small Swedish motor vessel of only twenty metres was met by the German U-boat U 22. After a check of the ship's papers the submarine's captain ordered the Jönköping to be sunk with two explosive charges, and the ship's crew were taken on board the U-boat.

According to the papers the ship was carrying 29 tons of iron goods in the form of 54 crates of nuts and 200 boxes of hooks that were on their way to a Russian railway factory. The submarine captain decided these were contraband. He also decided it was unthinkable that the Tsar's army should get their hands on such quantities of champagne as were also found on board.

The 5,000 bottles of champagne were in fact a relatively small part of the overall cargo. There were also 40 tons of cognac in 67 oak casks and a large amount of unspecified wines on their way to Finland's Bank. The Finns made no protest as prohibition was in force there at the time.

Two Swedes named Peter Lindberg and Claes Bergvall had long shared a dream of finding this bountiful treasure chest. There were many pessimists who said it was impossible to locate such a small vessel in the deep waters outside the Finnish archipelago. Far fewer were the number who believed the cargo would still be drinkable if it was still on board.

After years of preparation the wreck was found in the summer of 1997 at a depth of 64 metres, and the cargo seemed relatively unharmed. The first cork was popped on the spot and the happy divers knew at once that the champagne was exceptional.

It's still unsure how many bottles are left, as the Germans must surely have filled up their own supplies. Who wouldn't have?

The first 500 bottles that were recovered were *1907 Heidsieck & Co. Gout Americain*, but it's hardly unthinkable that some of the cargo was non-vintage champagne. I myself have drunk this rarity on a number of occasions and am always struck by its youthfulness.

For some strange reason the water around the wreck must have been salt-free, and the temperature two instead of four degrees. These factors, combined with the calm darkness down there in the depths, served to preserve this fresh champagne.

This wonderful treasure discovered by Peter and Claes is of course worth a great deal of money, but there are still many questions to be answered. The issue of ownership is a tricky legal puzzle, as is the sale of the champagne.

Should the entire cargo be recovered at once? How should the rusted wire frames be replaced?

How will the wine age when the corks dry out?

Unfortunately it's probably impossible to allow the sea to continue its stewardship of the bottles, which would be the best option for the wine. I dream of a scenario in which you can always get your 1907 recently-salvaged instead of recently-disgorged. I'm allowed to dream, aren't I?

Probably rather an ordinary wine that under exceptional and perfect storage conditions has become fantastically personal and interesting. The two-degrees-warm, yet black water has apparently had a preserving effect on the semi-sweet champagne that was bound for the Russian army's officers. The colour is incredibly light, the mousse is perfect and the aromas fruity and youthful: A great historic pleasure to loosen one of the well-kept corks and admire this nectar.

90 year-old champagne, 1907 Heidsieck & Co. Gout Americain, that has lain on the bottom of the sea since 1916!

When to drink champagne

Champagne may be drunk on all kinds of occasions. The most important thing is of course that whoever is drinking it should get the most out of the wine. Whether you want to celebrate something, or just enjoy the wine for its own sake, you should always start by giving the wine a few moments' serious consideration.

If the circumstances allow, you ought to use the correct sort of glass and avoid disturbing smells like cooking, smoke, flowers or perfumes. If the champagne is to be drunk in more informal surroundings, then it's much better to take one of the cheaper bottles out from the cellar.

Personally I always drink my least desirable champagnes while shivering outside in the cold on New Year's Eve. The best bottles I save for serious tastings which often develop into well-composed dinners with champagne the guest of honour.

Drinking champagne outdoors during the summer months is perhaps the most pleasurable occasion of them all. Forget the fact that it is hard to correctly judge the wine's many qualities, as the wind, sun and scents of nature blend in with the wine's bouquet. It is a fact that champagne that comes into contact with the sun tastes different. I have never heard a wine expert comment on the subject, but supported by my closest friends I claim that the sun's rays bring forth a special aroma from all champagnes. I can best describe the smell as heavy, oily and with a hint of petroleum. This means that even Chardonnay champagne will be reminiscent of mature Pinot Noir, which is one reason why blind tasting outdoors demands extra years of experience.

Wine growers claim with all seriousness that even the moon's rays can change the nose of the wine. This so-called "gout de lune" is, however, something I've yet to experience.

Many times, together with my fiancée or a good friend, I've sat in the sunset with a wonderful view in front of me, sipping some favourite champagne. The euphoric feeling one gets when nature's theatre enhances champagne's wonderful taste is something every true romantic should experience.

Champagne's best age

An important question to address is at which age champagne should best be drunk. Once again, it's a question of personal preference. Do you prefer your champagne young and sharp, or do you appreciate an aged champagne's golden colour and honeyed bouquet? All the beginners' tastings that I have led in recent years have taught me that every style has its adherents. However, the average Scandinavian taste must be somewhere between "Gout Anglais" and the French love of sheer youth.

Disgorging makes it harder to predict a champagne's development compared to other wines. As long as the wine is in contact with its yeast sediment then the ageing process goes very slowly. The carbonic acid works as a conserver and very little oxygen comes into contact with the wine during the original bottling. However, during dis-

Average peak for vintage champagnes:

The age of the wine when disgorged	Time after dégorgement
3 – 4 years	1 – 5 years
5 – 8 years	3 – 30 years (far longer in some cases)
10–15 years	1 – 5 years
15–20 years	6 months – 2.5 years
30 years	0 – 6 months
40 years	0 – 2 months
50 years	0 – 1 week
60 years	straight away

gorging the wine is exposed to a lot of air, which kicks off the normal oxidation process. The tricky thing is that, the more the wine is developed at the time of disgorging, the faster the oxidation will proceed. Old recently-disgorged champagnes from the beginning of the century can thus be extremely vital and young in character, but just a few days after being disgorged they have become flat and oxidised. A normally-disgorged bottle on the other hand is much further developed than the recently-disgorged during the first day, and will then cope with the passage of time far better. This is the reason why the recently-disgorged *Bollinger R.D.* is best enjoyed within a couple of years of disgorging.

A champagne that is disgorged at an age of one to four years will never have time to take in enough nourishment from the yeast sediment, which means that it has no bright future prospects, despite the early degorgement. The ideal age for disgorging, if you want to mature your champagne, is generally between five and eight years.

Here in the margin is a table that shows when an average vintage champagne reaches its peak after being disgorged.

To complicate matters further, disgorging can shock some old wines. However, later on they can come into a beautiful second phase, probably after you've already drunk up the remaining bottles in the belief that they were on the road to ruin.

A bottle of *1914 Pol Roger*, disgorged in 1944, was quite wonderful fifty years later. The reason was probably that, despite its great age at disgorging the wine was hard and immature. It is not time that is the deciding factor, but rather how far developed the champagne was when it was disgorged.

The classical one-handed grip, perfectly demonstrated by a waiter at Trianon.

Opening and serving a bottle of champagne

There are of course a number of ways to open a bottle of champagne. If it's at a party, people want to hear the happy sound of a popping champagne cork. If you don't want to spill any of the expensive drops however, here are a few pieces of advice.

- Make sure the bottle is at the right temperature (8-10°C). A colder champagne is almost tasteless and a warmer one soon loses its freshness and mousse, even if the aromas are stronger and richer. Personally, I think that champagne tastes best between twelve and thirteen degrees, but be aware that it soon warms up in room temperature. This means it's far better to serve the wine too cold than too warm, so that the guests themselves can wait for the ideal drinking temperature and carefully make the acquaintance of the first, somewhat diffident wine.

If you're not drinking at express speed, you should continually fill up with a few drops of well-chilled champagne. Freshening up an already-developed, gentle, aroma-rich champagne with a little lively and active mousse gives the very best taste experience.

- Dry off the bottle with a towel and present the champagne for the people who are to drink it.
- Take away the foil around the neck of the bottle. Unscrew the wire frame carefully, while at the same time keeping your thumb on the cork.
- When the wire is off, take a firm grip on the bottom of the bottle with one hand, hold the cork in the other with your thumb on the top and fingers around the mouth of the bottle. Hold the bottle at an angle of 45 degrees, twist the bottle, not the cork, and maintain pressure on the cork with your thumb. When the cork comes loose this will enable you to avoid spilling any wine.
- If it is hard to loosen the cork, you may use tongs to grip between the head of the cork and the bottle's mouth.

The risk of the cork breaking is greater if you twist the cork than if you twist the bottle.

- Never point an unopened bottle at anybody. The majority of eye injuries in France are caused by champagne corks!

- Dry off the mouth of the bottle with a clean towel or with the bottom of the cork.

- Pour a little wine into the glass and let the froth die down. It's now much easier to pour the right amount without losing the mousse. Just like beer, champagne creates less froth if poured on drink that's already there. The carbonic acid stays in the liquid.

- Fill the glass to two-thirds full.

- Put the bottle back in the ice bucket/refrigerator, with or without a champagne stopper depending on the age and quality of the wine.

When you serve, it looks classy if you hold the bottle with one hand. The classical grip is with the thumb in the inward curve of the bottom of the bottle, and the fingers around the edge of the bottle as supports. If you do want to serve with one hand, this grip is the only way to do it when pouring from a magnum.

Twist the bottle a little as you stop pouring. This releases the last drops, which otherwise can easily end up on the tablecloth.

Jospehine Nordlind, sommelier at the Villa Pauli in Djursholm, Stockholm. A wonderful place to drink champagne!

A few small things to consider:

- If you use a towel in the same way as a wine waiter (or sommelier) at a restaurant, don't cover up the label.
- Never cool the glass with ice before pouring. It can affect the taste and leave moisture on the glass.
- Never use a champagne wisp. In thirty seconds it will destroy many years' hard work.
- Never leave the champagne bottle upside down in the ice bucket, as this is regarded as an insult to the producer.
- If you haven't been able to chill the wine in time, the fastest way is to use ice and cold running water. Some forbid the use of the freezer, but ten minutes in the freezer hasn't had any negative effect on the champagnes I've drunk, as long as the wine's temperature hasn't gone below six degrees C.

The importance of the glass

The greatest aid to the wine taster, apart from his or her own knowledge, is the wine glass. The importance of the glass cannot be overstated. The extra pennies one digs out of one's wallet to be able to drink a higher quality of champagne are wasted, if one doesn't have access to proper glasses.

In Champagne people have traditionally used the champagne flute. The flute shape, which dates back from Roman times, is far from an ideal glass. In the 16th century some of the most beautiful flute-shaped glases were made in the Italian town of Murano. They are still made today, with stylish decorations made of precious metals, but it was only during the 18th century that the Italian glasses began to be used in Champagne.

Before disgorging was developed, the sediment stayed in the bottle, and with the help of the shape of the glass it could be collected in the bottom.

The other typical form of champagne glass is called a coupe. This form was created originally in 1663 by Venetian glass blowers working in England. The famous champagne coupe is said to have been based on the shape of Marie Antoinette's breast! After enormous success in England the coupe crossed the Atlantic, where it became even more established. When American movies had their first golden era the glass was renamed the "Hollywood cup", and unfortunately one sees that the coupe is still used in American movies.

The design of the glass is quite wrong for champagne. Both the scent and the bubbles disappear through the wide opening from the ocean of surface that is in contact with the air. At least the flute retains the bubbles, although it spreads the bouquet out of reach of the taster's nose.

Narrow straight glasses are very common nowadays. They may concentrate the aromas to the minimal opening, but as the area of exposure is so small, very little of the champagne's aroma is released. It also makes it almost impossible for anyone to get their nose into the glass!

My own glass (in the middle) humbly called "Perfect", flanked by two regular tasting glasses.

The best glasses for tasting champagne are the ones best suited to all other sorts of wine — wine tasting glasses! Even if they don't look as charming as the flute, they capture the vitally-important aroma in all its majesty. There is however, one insoluble problem. No wine tasting glass can hold the mousse as long as a narrow glass. You must decide for yourself how important you rate the mousse compared to the aroma.

After many years' research into the form of the glass, an independent international organisation called ISO has produced a perfectly-formed standard design called the ISO glass.

Lots of glass manufacturers have launched their own wine tasting glass, based on this model — tulip or onion-shaped glasses with a straight leg. A common quality of all good wine tasting glasses is that the volatile vapours from the wine should be concentrated at an opening big enough to allow the nose into the glass. The bouquet should be held in the glass, and the wine should come into contact with the right amount of oxygen. One should be able to hold the foot of the glass quite easily, so as not to obscure the appearance of the wine or warm it up.

Whichever type of tasting glass you select for champagne, I believe it's best to use the same glass one uses for all other types of wine. By this means you can be sure of a constant frame of reference for all types of wine tasting.

I myself have chosen Orrefors' wine tasting glass. It is quite ideal, as long as one has the possibility of topping up the wine now and again to maintain the mousse. One interesting fact to note is how similar the Orrefors glass is to those used by the cellar masters in Champagne when they blend their cuvées. Coloured, decorated and frosted glasses should be avoided at all costs as they distort the appearance of the wine. Perhaps the best champagne glass of all is the very expensive "Les Impitoyable". However, one problem with it is that the bouquet gets so strong in the glass that the glass itself creates new aromas not found in other champagne glasses.

The way one treats the glass is almost as important as the shape. Never wash the glass up with washing-up liquid as that can affect both the aroma and the mousse. Rinsing agent polishes the inside of the glass so much that the carbonic acid has nothing to fasten on to, which means no bubbles. Instead, always rinse the glasses out by hand and dry them off with a clean, odour-free linen towel. Nor should champagne be served in glasses that come unrinsed from the cupboard, a home for dust in even the cleanest of kitchens. Take care that your fingers are clean when you rinse the glasses, and sniff each empty glass to make sure that it is completely clean. This is especially important if, as host, you are also cooking the meal. If, for example, you have just boned the salmon, then it would be wise to let someone else take care of rinsing the glasses.

Champagne tasting

If you want to learn a little more about champagne and quickly get a grasp on what this wine has to offer, then taking up wine tasting on a serious level is probably the best way. The qualifications needed for wine tasting in general apply just as much when it comes to champagne.

To begin with, the taster must be in good physical condition — catch a cold and you shouldn't be tasting. Your palate and tongue must be unaffected by smoke, spicy food, toothpaste, sweetmeats, medicine, alcohol or anything else that influences the taste buds.

There should not be any strong smells nearby: perfumes, flowers, cooking odours and smoke are the most common distractions. The room should have as normal a temperature as possible, usually somewhere around 20-22° C. Good lighting is needed if the wine's colour shall be judged correctly, and a white tablecloth can also be a help in this regard.

As any serious attempt to judge a wine demands intense concentration, the first phase of the tasting at least should be conducted in silence. Even experienced tasters are easily influenced by spontaneous comments about the wine from others present. It is absolutely acceptable to improve one's own judgement of a wine by taking up qualities that others have noted, but never before you have made your own judgement.

It is very rewarding to write down your own tasting notes and catalogue the wines according to your own taste. Firstly, this improves your concentration during the tasting itself, as you are forced to formulate your impressions for yourself. Secondly your notes will be of great help in remembering your reactions to each wine.

Champagne tasting at Bruno Paillard.

The three steps of wine tasting

Wine tasting can be divided up into three steps: appearance, nose and flavour.

Appearance

The wine's appearance can provide clues as to what sort of champagne you hold in your glass. If the champagne is muddy or unclear, with a dull surface and colour, then there is a great risk that the wine is off. Probably some microbiological disease is involved. Sediment which sinks to the bottom of the glass can be quite normal, if the champagne is very old. All great champagnes have a shining clarity and intensity in their colour, regardless of its depth or nuance. (The colour tones are judged chiefly by the grape blend and maturity.)

A high percentage of Pinot grapes and great age give the darkest colours, and thus a young blanc de blancs is the lightest wine to be found in Champagne.

As there are two parameters to take into account, it can be extremely difficult to decide just from the appearance what sort of champagne it is. An old Chardonnay is just about as dark as a middle-aged cuvée or a young blanc de noirs. Luckily it is possible to distinguish the nuances of the grapes' colours to a certain degree. Chardonnay often gives a greenish-lemon shade, while Pinot grapes can give reddish tones, like copper or bronze. Mature champagnes are almost always golden with an amber lustre before the oxidation has its way and turns the wine dark brown.

The importance of the appearance of the mousse in the glass is greatly exaggerated. It is true that Chardonnay grapes usually give smaller bubbles, and that older champagnes have a weaker mousse than their younger counterparts, but the various differences between glasses are just as clear.

Most champagnes made today have a fine mousse and it is only in the mouth that one can begin to judge the quality. A fine mousse always consists of small, fast and continuous bubbles. Top-quality mousse should melt like ice-cream in the mouth and gently burst against the palate, like a firework display of sparkling, enjoyable impulses on the tongue. The worst mousse is like foaming toothpaste and removes some of the taste experience instead of adding to it.

In general women have a better sense of smell than men.

The ring of bubbles that is formed around the glass after the foam has died down is called the "cordon". Even a champagne with a very fine mousse can be accused of having big bubbles, but that is usually because it contains air bubbles from the pouring process. They are removed effectively by knocking the foot of the glass firmly against the table a couple of times.

The wine's viscosity is another aspect judged at a tasting. When the glass is spun around, some of the wine runs very slowly down the sides of the glass, forming so-called legs. "Legs" or "tears" as they are also called, can be formed by glycerol, sugar or alcohol. The more of these constituents contained in the wine, the longer and clearer the legs.

Nose

Most of the clues to the quality of a wine are kept in the nose. Unfortunately, according to some scientists our sense of smell is not what it used to be and modern man too often goes through life without training his nose. What is clear is that it is possible to improve your sense of smell through training. Perfumerers and wine tasters can not only distinguish several shades of scent, they can also detect them at very low levels of concentration.

As a relic of those days when our sense of smell was better, a woman's sensitivity to odours increases during pregnancy, and the sense is generally at its height among teenage women.

When the freshly-poured glass has stood a little while on the table the prickly carbonic acid has died down and it is time for the "first nose". Without spinning the glass, poke your nose into it slightly and gently sniff the aromas of the untouched wine. The "second nose" is far stronger as it is preceded by a spin of the glass so that the wine has revolved a few times. This is done so that the wine comes into contact with oxygen and to remove unwanted gases, but chiefly to free the aromas in the wine. When you inhale the vapours it is important not to breathe in too powerfully or for too long.

It's good to alternate different wines during the tasting, as the brain has a tendency to get used to aromas. This explains why people that live close to evil-smelling factories don't move house. The nerve-circuits of their sense of smell are deadened after a while, and they no longer smell the fumes.

What does it smell of?

The fifty million or so nerve cells we have in our noses can register thousands of smells, but to simplify matters we usually divide them up into eight main categories. All aromas can be placed in one of these categories, but I have made a personal choice of the aromas that occur in champagne.

Animal aromas: wild, beef, fish, shellfish, oyster, sea, cheese, cream.
Balsam aromas: anything smoked, burnt, roasted and toasted; bread, hay, almond, nuts, coffee. Wood, leather, marzipan, cola, toffee, cakes.
Chemical aromas: spirits, acetone, vinegar, mercaptan, sulphur, yeast, oxidation, sherry, madeira, washing powder, glue.
Spicy aromas: all spices, but usually vanilla, pepper, cinnamon, mint, ginger.
Flower aromas: all flowers but usually apple blossom, honeysuckle, hawthorn, acacia, lily of the valley, jasmine, roses, violet and honey.
Fruit aromas: all fruits but usually lemon, apple, apricot, peach, strawberry, raspberry, wild strawberry, cherry, gooseberry, lime, grapefruit, banana, mango, kiwi, passion fruit, grape, mandarin, orange, figs, dates.
Vegetable and mineral aromas: chalk, limestone, mineral, flint, stone, herbs, autumn leaves, fungi, earth, tea, boiled vegetables, green peppers, broccoli, cauliflower, beetroot, green beans.

Another way to divide up aromas is:
– **Primary aromas:** Aromas that come direct from the grape.
– **Secondary aromas:** Those created by the fermentation.
– **Tertiary aromas:** Aromas arising from the vinification process and storage.

Upon sniffing champagne one should be met by a tremendous multi-faceted aroma, the elegance and delicacy of which can only be matched by the finest, sweet, German Riesling wines. The aromas should be rich with flowers and fruits, and the autolytic character should be revealed by aromas reminiscent of bread or bakery. The characteristic smell should also have a hint of chalk and mineral. If there is also a wealth of toasty aromas, along with cream and honey, then I for one am in heaven.

It's important to give the wine time in the glass so that one doesn't miss the crucial glass development. If there is an overabundance of sherry-like aromas, it is because there is too great an amount of aldehydes, indicating that the champagne has seen better days. On the other hand, if the wine smells very weak, it's probably because the champagne is too young.

Taste

As the tongue's taste buds can only register sweet, sour, salt and bitterness, the sense of smell is also the most important instrument of what we call taste. It is easy to understand how much we "taste through the nose" when we consider how our taste disappears during a cold.

In the same way as when one spins the glass to free the dominant aromas, so one lets the wine swirl around in the mouth, while one tries to breathe in air through the mouth. This takes some of the wine's constituents to the scent cells through the rear passages of the nose. It is also important to let the wine go properly around the whole mouth before swallowing or spitting out.

It you taste wine often, or have a large selection of wines in front of you, the wines should be spat out in order to retain your senses' sharpness.

New research has shown that the tongue feels more than sweetness on the tip, bitterness at the back, and salt and sour on the sides. There are instead lots of taste sensors spread across the entire tongue, even though they are concentrated at the areas I've just named. The tongue is also sensitive to touch, temperature, movement and consistence, so the quality of the mousse is best judged by the tongue.

When judging a wine's flavour, consideration should be given not only to the aromas, but also to the structure. Many wine tasters get stuck on a wine's lovely aromas and don't notice that it is unstructured. There are those who totally ignore the wine's true flavour, as long as it is well-formed and balanced. Fortunately the wine's good aromatic qualities often go hand in hand with a fine structure.

Henrik Arve and Guillaume Bruneau during a concentrated champagne tasting at the C.I.V.C.

An enjoyable wine should be formed according to the same principles that exist in all kinds of art. A painting by Chagall is full of contrasts and its parts are composed in harmony. Colour, form, light and content express feelings of harmony and tension. A symphony by Mozart is a wholeness. If we can discern the various instruments and follow the changes in the dynamic, tempo and rhythm of the piece and at the same time enjoy the accord of the elements, then we raise our enjoyment to another level.

A great champagne should be made up and enjoyed in the same way. In order to fully appreciate the whole, we must first analyse the separate elements. The interplay between concentration, extensions and expansions is just as important for wine as it is for music.

Wine should also have a backbone to build around, something that can balance opposites like weight/lightness, hardness/softness, sweetness/sourness etc.

Judging taste means making an analysis of the inner relationships of these opposites. One should also feel whether the wine has a good "attack" in the first taste, before judging the quality of the crucial aftertaste. A long aftertaste is always a sign of a great wine. The aromatic power of the aftertaste can stay with you for several minutes sometimes, if the wine is of the very highest class. However, it should be pointed out that it isn't always the taste of the wine that clings on to the palate: sometimes certain acids hang around without supplying any new aromas.

Extra marks go to a wine that doesn't only have a good "length", but which also presents a whole new tone in the aftertaste.

Practice makes perfect

It takes a long time to become a good taster. Personally I am convinced that a good general physical condition is a great help. Smoking weakens the senses of both smell and taste. It is also a good idea to think about training one's sense of smell in all sorts of situations, as we are surrounded by all kinds of odours and aromas that we are seldom conscious of. By, for example, systematically smelling flowers and learning their names you can improve your "aroma vocabulary" and extend your frames of reference.

There are no short cuts however to mastering the difficult art of wine tasting. A good sense of smell, a good memory, an ability to verbalise your impressions, imagination and a burning interest are all qualities demanded of a good taster.

The first four criteria are met by a great many women, but the burning interest that borders on the fanatic does seem, unfortunately, to be a male domain. The world is full of promising female wine tasters, but the drive to be best doesn't seem to be as strong as with the men. Most wine tasters in the world are men, as are most chefs in top restaurants, even though 90% of the world's food is surely made by women.

This is a subject worth its own book, so I won't go into it any further here, but I would be overjoyed if more women showed an interest in wine tasting. They have a great deal to give to an activity far too dominated by men.

Besides the prerequisites for a good taster I've already mentioned, the task requires an enormous amount of knowledge and experience. As all forms of art require education, the wine taster's taste will change the more he or she learns about wine.

Aromas that the beginner found distasteful can in later years become the taster's favourite.

Whether it's a question of wine, food, music, film, literature or art, the individual consumer will get the most out of it if it contains a base of recognisable components. Familiarity with the entire product is easily tiring, but if nothing is recognisable then the confrontation can be a shock. That's why it is important to have familiar ground to stand on when exciting new features in a wine excite one's interest.

If it's a blind tasting, then as soon as the champagne's appearance, aroma and taste have been examined try to piece together the various impressions so that a guess can be made. One should ask oneself questions like; how old is the wine? when was it disgorged? is it dominated by Pinot grapes or Chardonnay? was it made by a major or minor producer? has the wine gone through malolactic fermentation or matured in an oak barrel? And perhaps most important of all: how high is the champagne's quality level?

After a few years' training and a number of tasted champagnes, one can come quite close to the correct answer with a guess, which gives an extra kick and redoubled determination to learn more of the secrets of the noble wine.

A different kind of tasting

It is always fun to have some sort of theme for a tasting. The ordinary forms of tasting are vertical and horizontal tasting. At a vertical tasting, the same wine from various vintages is tasted, while a horizontal tasting means that several different wines from the same year are tasted.

I often think that wine tasters are too bound up in the traditional forms of wine tasting. Why not experiment a little and use your imagination?

One of the most amusing and productive variations is the "bring your bottle and come over" tasting: a very unpretentious occasion, where each taster brings a bottle from their own cellar and gives it to the host. The wines are then served blind. An advantage of this style is that you avoid prejudices about the wines, and that each participant decides for him or herself how much the tasting will cost. The wines can also be tasted half-blind, i.e. one knows in advance which wines will be tasted, but not in which order they come. If one knows what one is tasting it is called an "open" tasting.

One cold January in 1995 I organised a very special tasting where thirteen people met to enjoy nineteen champagnes from various vintages. One could say it was a vertical tasting vintage-wise, but from different champagne producers. The range of wines was as wide as possible, with pure Pinot Noir champagnes, cuvées and blanc de blancs.

In order to fool the tasters the wines were served in a random order. Some of the young wines certainly lost something by being placed next to certain mature wines, while others gained from their position. The wines were served in threes, accompanied by a suitable dish. I don't believe one can judge wines quite so categorically at a tasting like this, but the greatest advantage with this form of tasting is the unique possibility for each taster to get to know vintages, grapes and origins. Unfortunately several of the older wines were maderised, but it is quite natural that some of these old fellows can't cope with the passage of time. Sometimes we just have to blame bad luck and bottle variation. That, for example, the powerhouse of Bollinger couldn't produce a champagne that ages well in 1959 is something I know to be impossible.

The tasting group consisted of professionals within the wine business and experienced champagne amateurs. Taste is up to the individual, but all the tasters found favourites among the oldest and youngest vintages. Take a look at the results listed here and you'll note the range of tastes.

Even though it is unusual to have access to nineteen different vintages, this is a fun and very positive form of tasting which I recommend wholeheartedly. Perhaps four or five vintages and shrimps instead of Russian caviar would be enough to make the evening a memorable one.

Champagne	Origin
1) 1982 Bonnaire	(Cramant)
2) 1976 Michel Gonet	(Avize)
3) 1966 Moët & Chandon	
4) 1986 Selosse	(Avize)
5) 1989 Pierre Peters	(Le Mesnil)
6) 1973 Clicquot	
7) 1979 Louis Roederer	
8) 1961 Baron Donat	
9) 1988 Bonnaire	(Cramant)
10) 1987 Selosse	(Avize)
11) 1981 Pierre Laurain	(Aÿ)
12) 1953 Clicquot (not in perfect condition)	
13) 1959 Bollinger (not in perfect condition)	
14) 1983 Mailly	
15) 1990 Larmandier-Bernier	(Vertus)
16) 1985 Jacquesson Signature (slightly corked)	
17) 1975 H. Billiot (in poor condition)	(Ambonnay)
18) 1955 Canard-Duchêne (in poor condition)	
19) 1937 Charles Heidsieck (in poor condition)	

MOET
1966
J.SELOSSE
Charles Heidsieck
REIMS
BOLLINGER
Extra Quality
BRUT
REIMS

Champagne – the different types

Every champagne producer tries to build a broad portfolio of products in different styles and price brackets. The commonest assortment usually consists of a non-vintage champagne, a rosé champagne, a vintage champagne and a cuvée de prestige, but many firms also sell blanc de blancs, blanc de noirs, non-dosé, sweet champagne, crémant, late-disgorged champagnes, still wines and various liquors. The products on offer depend on the company's resources, position, vineyards and house style. Some producers maintain a constant level of quality throughout their assortment, while others can make a wonderful cuvée de prestige even though their non-vintage champagne tastes like a cheap sparkling wine.

In this chapter after every section I have made a brief list of recommended wines within the various categories. No consideration of price or vintage is taken. For more detailed descriptions see the Producers' chapter.

Non-vintage champagne

The law says that non-vintage champagne may not be sold earlier than 15 months after production and that it should contain ten percent alcohol. Non-vintage champagne is almost always the company's simplest. It should reflect the house style and be easy to drink. During a series of bad

vintages the quality is hit hardest among the growers' non-vintage champagnes, while the major producers with their large reserves can maintain a relatively constant level. On the other hand, few producers failed to make an unusually good non-vintage cuvée after the trilogy of great years 1988, 1989 and 1990.

A champagne producer usually uses both the first and second pressings in his non-vintage champagnes and has a higher dosage than in his vintage wines. The percentage of Pinot Meunier is usually higher in non-vintage champagnes, partly because the quality is poorer and partly because they mature faster and the non-vintage champagne is often sold for early consumption. However, almost all non-vintage champagnes gain from a few years in storage after being disgorged. Bottle age gives the wine soft, pleasant aromas of bread and honey and smooths away the rougher, harsher acidity from the champagne's youth. Those firms that can afford to age their non-vintage champagnes for four or five years, instead of two or three, will always be a touch classier. For most producers, non-vintage champagne is their most important wine as it makes up an average of 80% of production.

That is why some producers concentrate on raising the quality of their simplest wine by vinifying some of the wine in oak barrels or using a higher percentage of older reserve wines and only the cuvée. Krug's *Grande Cuvée* is undeniably the company's simplest wine and non-vintage to boot, and thus ought to be classed as a non-vintage champagne. But with its high price and a quality level that often beats *Dom Pérignon* and *Cristal*, it's hard not to agree with the firm's own judgement of the wine as a non-vintage "cuvée de prestige".

Best wines: Leclerc-Briant "Les Authentiques", Bollinger, Paul Bara, Gatinois, Jacquesson Perfection, Clouet.

Sweet champagnes

Very few demi-sec, sec or doux champagnes are made these days, happily enough. Besides, nearly all the producers use only their worst base wines for the sweeter sorts. The grape juice comes almost without exception from the "taille" and the Pinot Meunier content is high. The sugar camouflages the wine's qualities and removes the more subtle aromas. I must however admit that my first enthusiastic meetings with the sparkling drink often consisted of the sweet variety. It didn't take more than a couple of months though before my palate preferred the classic dry champagnes, and today I have trouble forcing down a glass of demi-sec or sec. As an introduction wine, these varieties can perform a useful function. The sweet champagnes we've had in Sweden are in any case among the more vapid examples of the style.

Best wines: Veuve Clicquot, Louis Roederer, Delamotte, Deutz, Pol Roger.

Vintage champagnes

The first vintage champagnes were probably made in the middle of the 18th century. According to the C.I.V.C's rules, all the grape juice must come from one single year, which should then be noted on the label. The alcohol content must be at least 11% and the wine may not be sold less than three years after being bottled. What is more the producer may not sell more than 80% of the harvest as vintage champagne. This guarantees that reserve wines are available for the next harvest and forces up the quality of the vintage champagne. Some minor firms sell vintage champagnes from weak years like 1974, 1978, 1980, 1987, 1991 and 1992. The idea is that only the best years should produce vintage champagnes. Bollinger underline this by calling their vintage champagnes *Grande Année*. Before the cuvée de prestiges were launched, the vintage champagnes were the cream of each producer's output. Even today, they are often the best buys, with a quality far beyond that of the non-vintage champagnes and at a much cheaper price than the prestige variety. Almost all the reputable champagne producers sell their vintage wines after around five years, perfect for a long storage.

If you find a vintage champagne you admire at a reasonable price, then by all means buy up a good supply so that you can follow the wonderful development of the wine from year to year. Most vintage champagnes are made from a blend of first-class Pinot grapes and Chardonnay. Up until the eighties most consisted of 60-70% Pinot Noir, while today the trend is to make lighter and more elegant wines, so a Chardonnay content of 60% is nothing unusual. It seems that Chardonnay began to dominate vintage champagne in the shift from 1988 to 1989. Krug and Bollinger are still majestic wines based on their large Pinot content and become impressively honeyed with age. In fact it is rare to see these two brands bettered in any vintage.

Best wines: Bollinger, Krug, Perrier-Jouët, Roederer, Pol Roger.

Le Mesnil.

Blanc de blancs

Up until 1980 a blanc de blancs could contain Chardonnay, Arbanne, Petit Meslier and Pinot Blanc, but nowadays all blanc de blancs champagnes are made only from the noble Chardonnay grape. In other districts the blanc de blancs may contain any kind of white grape. (Blanc de blancs means "white wine from white grapes").

There are blanc de blancs in all of Champagne's regions: Aube, Sézanne, Montagne de Reims and the Marne valley. But the fabulously elegant champagnes that are produced in Côte des Blancs lack an equal in the world of wine. No other wine can develop such charming, elegant aromas as a blanc de blancs from Avize, Cramant or Le Mesnil.

Many critics often find these wines to be a little too light and acidic, but few wines gain so much in complexity with age as these beauties. A young blanc de blancs is always extremely light, with a greenish hue. The nose may be closed and gently flowery, and the taste contains a slight tone of citrus or apply fruit with a penetratingly sharp acidity. The aftertaste too can feel short and immature, but even in youth one can sense the wine's purity and mineral elegance. On breathing one detects buttery and toasty aromas that will show tremendous development with age.

In their middle years the best Chardonnay champagnes have an excess of mature exotic fruits: mango, peaches and apricots dominate the now-mature lemon aromas. The feeling in the mouth is creamy and fresh at the same time. When the wine is fully mature the colour will be golden and the nose wonderfully full, a symphony of roasted coffee, bread and nuts. To me, the walnut aroma in an aged champagne from Bonnaire, Pierre Peters or Salon is an olfactory Olympus.

A few producers refuse to make a blanc de blancs as they want to use their best Chardonnay grapes in their prestige cuvées. Perrier-Jouët is an example of this. Otherwise the trend says that one should offer a blanc de blancs as part of a complete range. Blanc de blancs has been made throughout champagne's history, but the first commercial blanc de blancs to be launched was the *1911 Salon*, which became a great success at Maxim's in Paris. *Salon* is still one of the best champagnes, with a classically restrained and acidic style and a wonderful walnut aroma.

Taittinger Comtes de Champagne should be seen as the best of the exotic, gentle, slightly sweeter style. Krug's *Clos du Mesnil* leads the third style, which is less restrained than *Salon* but more serious than the charmer *Comtes de Champagne*.

Apart from these three there are many growers in Côte des Blancs' Grand cru villages who are knocking on the door, and a few that have already reached the top, like Selosse and Diebolt.

Many of the major houses make very fine blanc de blancs, but neither Pol Roger, Deutz, Billecart-Salmon, Roederer nor Ruinart can point to such a combination of purity and complexity as the best growers.

Best wines:
Non-vintage blanc de blancs: Selosse, Turgy, Charlemagne, A. Robert, Legras, Sugot-Feneuil, B. Schmitte, Paillard.

Vintage blanc de blancs: Bonnaire, Diebolt, Selosse, Charlemagne, Pierre Peters, Sugot-Feneuil, Legras, Roederer, Deutz.

Prestige blanc de blancs: Krug Clos du Mesnil, Salon, Taittinger Comtes de Champagne, Dom Ruinart.

Blanc de noirs

This type of champagne is nowhere near as common as blanc de blancs, even though more black grapes are cultivated than white in the area. A blanc de noirs can be made of either Pinot Meunier or Pinot Noir, or even both together. It's extremely rare for a producer to produce something under the title blanc de noirs even if the wine doesn't contain Chardonnay. Unfortunately far too few growers in the Pinot villages make their best wine in this manner any more. Instead they blend first-class Pinot Noir with Chardonnay from their own village, as they have heard for years how clumsy and unbalanced their Pinot champagnes are. A blanc de noirs cannot, of course, compete with a blanc de blancs when it comes to finesse and elegance, but as great wines they play an important role. Few blanc de noirs are aperitif champagnes, however — they cry out for food by their side. Blanc de noirs from Aÿ are unmatched concerning velvet-soft fruit and burgundy-like grape character. Producers like Fliniaux and Pierre Laurain come close to the unsurpassed power and richness found in Bollinger's *Vieilles Vignes Françaises*. The aromas can vary between the animal and vegetable tones, but they are always backed up by a heavy, dark fruit. With age come tones of smoke, honey, honeysuckle, toffee and mushroom creeping into the wine, and leather, fish and ripe cheeses are other descriptions used to portray great blanc de noirs. The Grand cru villages Verzy, Verzenay, Bouzy, Ambonnay and Mailly are also capable of producing first-class Pinot champagne. Bernard Hatté's example from Verzenay clearly shows the hardness and toughness that many blanc de noirs can have in their youth. Many are led to believe in a short life for Pinot champagne because of the low level of acidity they contain compared with blanc de blancs, but under the candy-like, simple fruit there lies a number of undeveloped extracts which need a longer time than a blanc de blancs to soften.

The Pinot wine then lasts about as long at its top as an average blanc de blancs. However, it's not the easiest thing in the world to appreciate an old blanc de noirs, when the gamey and vegetable aromas can almost be too much of a good thing.

Best wines: Bollinger Vieilles Vignes Françaises, Fliniaux, P. Laurain, P. Bara.

Cuvée de prestige

The prestige cuvées are always the company's most expensive wines and they should always be an essence of the very best the producer can achieve. A typical cuvée de prestige is made purely of Grand cru grapes from the best slopes. One uses the oldest vines, goes for a lower yield and vinifies the wine in a more pretentious way. Some use oak barrels and most only make cuvée de prestige during very good years. Some disgorge the bottle à la volée or use real corks during the fermentation in the cellar. The maturing time is much longer than for the vintage wine, and the presentation is as luxurious as possible: wooden boxes or decorated packages with specially-designed bottles the form of which often borrows from the 18th century bottles used by the monk Dom Pérignon and his contemporaries.

Moët & Chandon's *1921 Dom Pérignon* was the first cuvée de prestige, launched in 1936. Roederer's *Cristal* may have been sold earlier to the Russian tsar, but it didn't arrive on the market until the fifties, with a first vintage of 1945. The first vintage of *Taittinger Comtes de Champagne* was 1952.

In 1961 Bollinger decided to begin sales of its late-disgorged wines from the fifties under the title R.D. *1959 Dom Ruinart* was the second cuvée de prestige to be made entirely from Chardonnay grapes. The same year saw *Pol Roger Blanc de Chardonnay* launched for the first time, and on Duke Ellington's seventieth birthday Perrier-Jouët came out with *1964 Belle Epoque* with its beautiful white Anemones designed by Emile Gallé. Today that is the cuvée de prestige that is making the most ground. The latest in the successful row of prestige cuvées from the major houses is Pol Roger's *Winston Churchill*. The first vintage 1975 was only made in magnums.

There are no set rules for the manufacture of cuvée de prestiges. Some producers make non-vintage prestige cuvées such as Krug's *Grande Cuvée*, Laurent-Perrier's *Grand Siècle*, Perrier-Jouët's *Blason de France*, Alfred Gratien's *Cuvée Paradis* and Cattier's *Clos du Moulin*.

There are many producers that make wonderful prestige cuvées, but if we take away vintage-Krug, *Bollinger Vieilles Vignes* and those wines that I have presented in the section on blanc de blancs, then the champagnes below are the finest.

Best non-vintage cuvée de prestiges: Krug Grande Cuvée, Grand Siècle, Clos du Moulin, Origine.

Prestige cuvées: Cristal, Belle Epoque, Clos des Goisses, La Grande Dame, Signature, Dom Pérignon, P.R., Winston Churchill, Josephine.

Late-disgorged champagnes

The winemakers in Champagne have always saved old vintages that they have stored "sur point" up until they are disgorged. On special festive occasions they have disgorged their old wines and enjoyed them on the spot, without recorking or dosage. When Bollinger 1961 decided to sell their '52, '53 and '55 and simultaneously decided to disgorge them as late as possible, they enable consumers to be part of a privileged few, a group previously made up entirely of winemakers.

As I have written previously, the long contact with the yeast sediment gives a special bready taste called autolytic character. I have also explained the advantages and disadvantages with late disgorging (see page 82). What is obvious is that Bollinger have given us a new dimension with their R.D. wines. Today there are a number of producers that occasionally sell some old vintages that they disgorge late, but those brands that are sold continually in this category are few and far between.

R.D. stands for "Recently Disgorged" and is a patented trademark. the other producers have been forced to call their late-disgorged wines something else.

L.P Millesime Rare is a surprisingly cheap late-disgorged champagne. Bruno Paillard has a series of late-disgorged vintages that are valued highly by many. Many people believe — falsely — that *Krug Collection* is a late-disgorged version of the vintage wine, but the only difference is that the Collection bottles have lain untouched and normally-disgorged in Krug's cellars until the day of sale, and in this way the customer is guaranteed a bottle in perfect condition. The only late-disgorged commercially-available champagne that can be compared with *Bollinger R.D.* is *Jacquesson D.T.* (Degorgé Tardif). It has a great bready autolytic character and is reminiscent of Bollinger's full-bodied R.D. champagne, even though the grape is Chardonnay from Avize. Jacquesson also sell their *D.T.* at an even greater age than Bollinger. July 1997 saw *1985 Bollinger R.D.* and *1975 Jacquesson D.T.* on sale.

Best wines: Bollinger R.D., Jacquesson D.T.

Undosed champagnes

Ever since the English demanded drier champagne at the end of the 19th century, there have been examples of completely unsweetened champagnes. Laurent-Perrier has been a leading house in this category since they gave out their *1893 Grand Vin Sans Sucre,* and today they produce the best-selling completely-dry champagne, *L.P. Ultra Brut.* Piper-Heidsieck have a dosage-free champagne called *Brut Sauvage* and Besserat de Bellefon's contribution to the field is called *Brut Intégral.* Most young champagnes without dosage become too sour and sharp — by no means the kind of champagne one takes along to a friend who's trying the drink for the first time. At a ripe old age champagne no longer needs a dosage, as the maturity itself forms sweet, soft aromas. Therefore it's remarkable that those champagne houses that specialise in making powder keg-dry champagne don't store their wines even longer in order to balance them.

Jacquesson D.T., which I mentioned in the "Late-disgorged champagnes" section, is thanks to its age by far the best non dosé champagne available in the shops. As to the more conventional non-vintage, unsweetened wines, the "wine demon" Jacques Selosse's *Extra Brut* is quite outstanding. Here are various names for unsweetened champagnes that can occur: Extra Brut, Sans Sucre, Ultra Brut, Brut Sauvage, Sans Liqueur.

Best wines: Selosse Extra Brut.

Gently-sparkling champagnes

Champagne has recently lost the rights to the name crémant, which meant gently-sparkling champagne. Crémant de Alsace, crémant de Bourgogne and crémant de Loire have all managed to keep their names on the wines that contain a normal mousse. It's not surprising that the makers of champagne are upset that they can no longer use a term invented in Champagne.

Some producers still make a gentle sparkling champagne with a pressure of just 3.6 atmospheres. The wines don't last quite as long as their more powerfully sparkling counterparts, but the soft, creamy mousse can feel extremely delicate and melt like butter in the mouth. In the Chardonnay village of Cramant there was once a tradition of gently sparkling wines called crémant de Cramant. Mumm still make a wine like that but now call it *Mumm de Cramant.* Chauvet are alone in producing a crémant rosé, which is a great success. On the vintage side, Alfred Gratien is the greatest, even though one rarely thinks of their vintage as being gently sparkling.

Best wines: Alfred Gratien Millésime.

Rosé champagne

Rosé, or pink champagne became popular in the beginning of the 19th century, and it was the English and the Russians who expresses a special love for this romantic drink. Clicquot, who made their first pink champagne in 1777, should be seen as the pioneer house in rosé champagne, but the wine was not taken seriously by winemakers themselves for another century. Pink champagne gained the reputation of being a women's drink, which men would only drink at weddings if at all. Even today, pink champagne is the classical drink at weddings.

Up until the 1970's only a few producers made rosé champagne, and even fewer produced a vintage version. It is very unusual for the English auction houses to offer rosé champagnes from years before 1970.

Prestige rosés are above all a phenomenon of the eighties. As the Pinot grape's juice is colourless, the colour comes from the grape skin. In the rest of France rosé wines have to get their colouring from the release of pigment by the skin (maceration), which can occur at different phases of vinification. The colour may never be created by adding red wine to the white, except in one region: Champagne! Usually 8-20% still red wine from Bouzy or some other red wine village is used, together with Liqueur de Tirage. Even though the method is severely criticised, many of the best rosé champagnes are made with this technique, and it is practically impossible to tell the difference between blended rosés and macerated wines at a blind tasting. Perhaps one can detect a touch more raspberry and strawberry scent in a rosé champagne made with skin contact, as these aromas mostly come from the skin of the Pinot Noir grapes. Those producers that don't blend in red wine but use the so-called saignée method also claim that their method gives a more storable wine. Something that tastings have never managed to convince me to accept.

Rosé champagnes are made today in a colour scale from the palest rosé to the darkest red. They often have a blue-red hue when young, only to become almost orange between the ages of twelve and fifteen and amber some time after passing twenty, when they remind one strongly of an old "white" champagne about twice the age. Rosé champagne is often more costly to produce, so the price is often a little higher than non-vintage champagnes. For the most part the quality of the rosé is somewhat lower.

Growers' champagne from the best Pinot villages can often reach its peak as a rosé. As one is after the Pinot skin's strawberry and raspberry aromas, one should use as much Pinot Noir as possible in a rosé. Access to the Chambolle-Musigny-scented Pinot grapes from Aÿ can produce wonderfully juicy and enjoyable rosé champagnes. Growers such as Pierre Laurain and Fliniaux beat many prestige rosés with their concentration and grape aroma.

Once again I take Bernard Hatté's wine from Verzenay as a shining example of first-class Pinot in another style than the leather-aroma, caressing Aÿ Pinot. His rosé has a better spiciness and fruit tones of apple and plum, along with the red berries. A tiny number of prestige rosés are of even better class than these growers' rosés. The problem is just that they cost four times as much. *Krug Rosé* and *Jacquesson Signature Rosé* are heavyweights with extra finesse from their oak barrels. *Cuvée William Deutz Rosé* is very reminiscent of *Pierre Laurain Rosé* but with an aristocratic distinction that the growers cannot match.

My other two favourite rosé champagnes are not favourites because they are typical rosés, but because they are great champagnes. It would be impossible to point them out as rosés at a true blind tasting. Both *Cristal Rosé* and *Belle Epoque Rosé* are sensual masterworks with "white" noses of nuts, flowers and honey. *Dom Pérignon Rosé* and *Taittinger Comtes de Champagne Rosé* don't quite reach the same class, but are undeniably fine champagnes that develop wonderfully with the years. However, both would benefit from slightly lower dosage. The *1985 Dom Pérignon Rosé* however is a masterpiece.

Best wines: Pierre Laurain, Billecart-Salmon, Bernard Hatté, Fliniaux, Krug, Paul Bara, Clouet.

Vintage rosé: Cristal, Belle Epoque, Cuvée William Deutz, Signature, Taittinger Comtes de Champagne, Dom Pérignon, Roederer, La Grande Dame, Billecart Cuvée Elisabeth.

Old champagne

Champagne's incredible longevity is one of the factors that set it apart from the wine of other districts. When one visits the great houses as a tourist, one learns that champagne is a fresh product that can't abide being stored after disgorging. If one gets to know winemakers a little better, one soon finds out that they take out their champagne from the forties and fifties whenever there's a celebration on.

Most drink their old wines recently-disgorged without dosage, but a large number love champagne aged in the English way, i.e. several years after disgorging. The richness that a normally-disgorged old champagne can reveal is without compare. The bouquet is developed and rich in fruit because of the large quantities of esters and aldehydes formed by the contact with the minimal amount of oxygen between the cork and the wine.

On the other hand, there is a certain risk in buying a really old champagne, but if the cork is tight and the wine has been stored well, one may be in for a taste experience far beyond the ordinary. Perfectly-aged champagnes have a honeyed, exotic bouquet with features of coffee and chocolate. The taste is rich with a sensation of increased sweetness. Of course, the sugar content hasn't increased at all, but the esters and aldehydes create aromas of diverse sweetmeats. The complexity increases and the champagne is reminiscent of older white burgundies. Champagne from the best years of the sixties is wonderful today. If you want to try champagne that is even older, you can count on two or three bottles out of ten being maderised and lacking any mousse. However, I have drunk some fantastic champagnes from the forties and fifties with mousse invisible to the eye but quite noticeable on the palate. If there is a reservoir of carbon dioxide left in the wine, then the possibility of a culinary treat is very good indeed.

A recently-disgorged 1959 from the cellar of Camille Savès.

BLANC DE BLANCS

7 years old

15 years old

28 years old

BLENDED

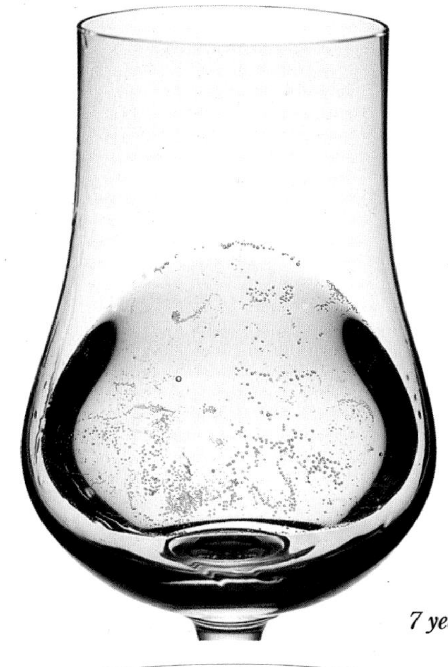

7 years old

15 years old

42 years old

BLANC DE NOIRS

ROSÉ

7 years old

7 years old

12 years old

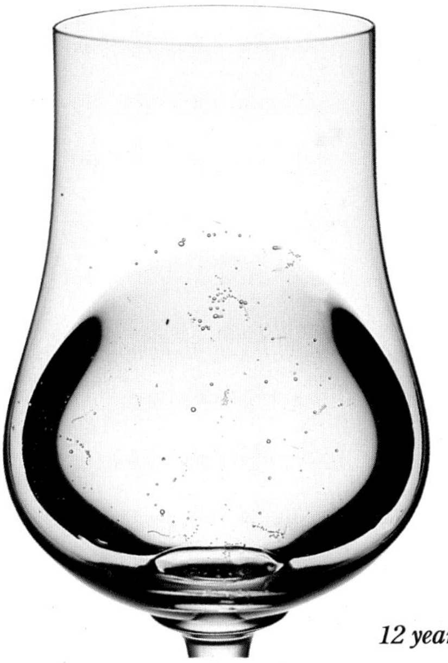

12 years old

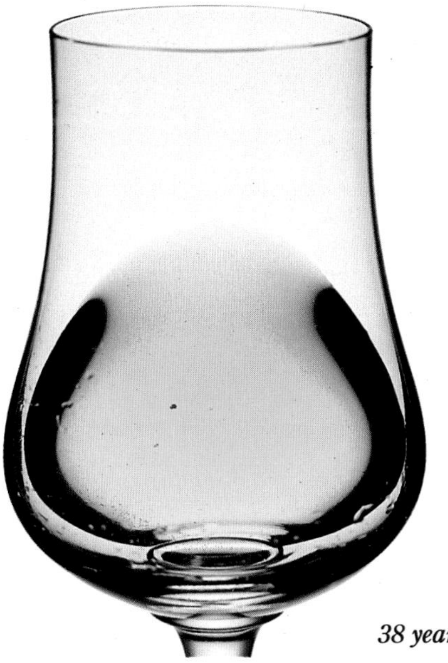

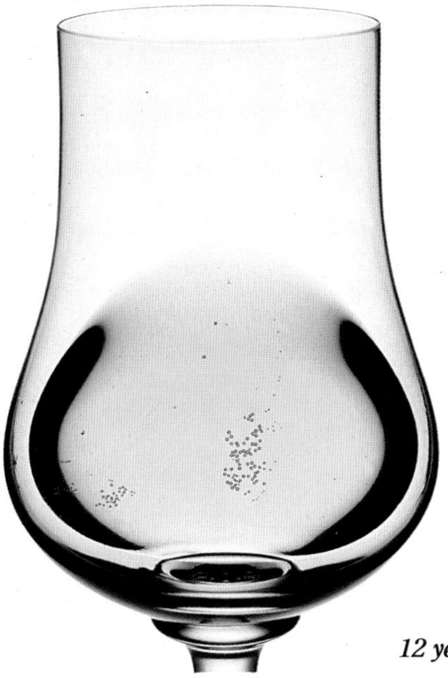

38 years old

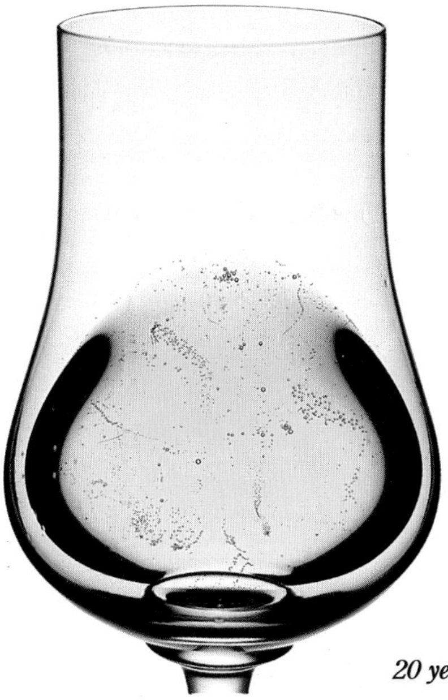

20 years old

AŸ · ROUGE
Coteaux Champenois
GATINOIS
1990

Still wines and spirits

Coteaux Champenois

Even though still wines were made in Champagne before the sparkling variety, the present appellation Coteaux Champenois didn't come into being until 1974. In 1927 the still wines from the area were called "Vin Originaire de la Champagne viticole", which in 1953 was changed to "Vin Nature de la Champagne".

Three types of wine are made under this appellation: rosé, red and white wine. The rare rosé wine is pale, thin and acidic, the white slightly better and the red really good. The problem with making still wines in Champagne is the cold climate, which means the grapes contain too little sugar and too much acidity. For this reason they are even more dependent than Burgundy on warm years to produce ripe Pinot Noir and Chardonnay. 1947, 1959, 1976, 1989 and 1990 are the best vintages since the second World War. As a rule the champagne houses produce rather uninteresting still wines, and the growers that have access to small plots of top-quality soil in Avize (for the white) and Bouzy, Aÿ, Ambonnay, Cumières and Mareuil-sur-Aÿ (for the red), make without doubt the most stimulating wines under the appellation.

Red wine

During very warm years the best growers in Grand cru villages produce red wine that is reminiscent of good, but not great, burgundy. The aromas can be top-class, but the structure can seldom be compared with a Premier cru wine from Burgundy. Raspberry, strawberry and exotic spices dominate the typical aroma of the grape, and the taste is light, acidic and elegant.

I recently drank a *1989 Bouzy Rouge* from Georges Vesselle with a lightly-spiced chicken fillet, and it was a culinary marriage made in heaven! All the tasters around the table were convinced that I had served a classy burgundy, which shows just how well the best wines from the appellation hold their own. Bollinger make one of the best reds in the area: *La Côte aux Enfants*, from a southern slope in Aÿ. Like many growers, they use small, new oak casks and only sell wines from exceptionally good years. Perhaps the best of them all are the recent vintages of *Gatinois Aÿ Rouge.*

Otherwise, Bouzy is best known for its red wines. Personally I think that, on average, Bouzy Rouge is of lesser quality than both Cumières and Ambonnay, but that the two best producers in Bouzy, Georges Vesselle and Paul Bara, are part of the elite. The king of red wine in Cumières is René Geoffroy and he was particularly successful in 1990. In Ambonnay, Secondé-Prevoteau have for several generations supplied Roederer with grapes for *Cristal*, and at the same time made an exemplary Ambonnay Rouge.

Best wines: Paul Bara (Bouzy), Secondé-Prevoteau (Ambonnay), G. Vesselle Cuvée Véronique-Sylvie (Bouzy), Bollinger La Côte aux Enfants (Aÿ), Gatinois Rouge (Aÿ), Coutier Rouge (Ambonnay), René Geoffroy (Cumières).

White wine

Even though these wines are the base for the fantastic Chardonnay champagnes, this type of wine is nothing to celebrate. Laurent Perrier's bestseller is a typical example of how thin and sour these wines often are. The nose reminds one of the striking side of a matchbox, and if any fruit is present at all, then unripe lemon is most likely. One reason why so few still white wines are of top class is that the best wines naturally go to the bubbly drink. Vin clair from the Avize wines of Selosse or Jacquesson are not unlike a young *Corton-Charlemagne* or Grand Cru Chablis. The best white wine commercially available in Champagne is Moët & Chandon's *Saran*, which is made from grapes that would otherwise have gone into *Dom Pérignon*. The taste is actually like a slightly diluted and relaxed "D.P.".

Best wine: Saran.

Rosé wine

The rosé Coteaux wines that I have tasted can be counted on the fingers of one hand. Few are produced and I have never heard a positive word spoken about any of them. Those I tried were simple, dried-out, sour and sharp.

Rosé des Riceys

Although Rosé des Riceys are a still rosé wine, they are not part of the Coteaux Champenois appellation, but an appellation all of their own. The sun king Louis XIV made this wine famous, something which has kept the tradition alive. In the little village of Les Riceys in Aube the producers really make an effort to make a first-class rosé wine. Along with the Rhône valley's Tavel, these wines are thought to be the best in the world, which may say more about rosé wines in general than the wines from Les Riceys. Having said that, Aube's pride ages well for a rosé wine, the relatively dark colour becomes orange and the strawberry and peaches aromas seem more like chocolate and mint. The depth of the flavour can be very interesting and the impression on the palate is always a gentle one. Alexandre Bonnet makes both the most expensive and the best wines in the village.

Best wines: Devaux, A. Bonnet, Morel.

Ratafia

Ratafia is a strong wine made from unfermented grape juice from the region's three types of grape, given extra strength by adding 90% spirit. The French drink their ratafia either as an apertif or as a digestive after food. It is a light brown, strong, raisin-scented drink, and the grapes must go through exactly the same quality checks as those that are used for champagne. As the grape juice is sweet by itself, no added sugar is needed, but most ratafia producers add a small quantity anyway. The alcohol content is around 20%, but the drink hardly feels as strong as that.

Very few use first-pressing grapes for their ratafia, but many of the best ratafia producers use Pinot Noir, which gives a softer, more grape-like taste than Chardonnay. After the addition of grape spirit — a process called mutage — the ratafia is stored in a barrel or vat for more than a year. Those stored in barrels get a sherry-like, oxidative taste which suits the aims of the drink. I have tasted too few to give an opinion on the quality of the various producers, but the great majority are made by the district's biggest distillery, Goyard in Aÿ. Jacques Selosse made a wonderful *1976 Ratafia* for his personal use only!

Marc de Champagne

As Cognac is a district in its own right and not a type of wine, the term is not used in Champagne. The wine that is made according to the same principles as cognac is locally called marc de Champagne. Marc is made from completely pressed-out grape leftovers that are fermented and distilled to an alcohol content of over 40%. Fine Marc, on the other hand, is made of wine that would have been used in the champagne production (but which didn't meet the quality requirements) and leftovers from the clearing and débourbage. The idea is that everything is used and made drinkable, but is it? Apart from some older marc from Burgundy and old cognac I personally dislike all forms of spirits, so I'm not the right man to judge the pride and joy of the region. The nicest marc de Champagnes I have sipped come from Comte Audoin de Dampierre and Pierre Peters.

Sparkling wines

No other place on earth shares Champagne's unique environmental conditions for the production of sparkling wine. This fact means that the number of ambitous sparkling wine producers around the world are far fewer than for the still variety. The best sparkling wines outside Champagne are made with the same sorts of grapes and vinification procedures as those used in the French region. The small number of wines that have gone through the champagne method and that have been stored with the yeast sediment as long as a cuvée de prestige can in the very best cases match the quality of a poor supermarket champagne. These sparkling prestige wines are very expensive to produce, often fermented in small oak barrels or gleaned from yields kept deliberately low. Therefore it's not so strange that the prices shoot up to levels close to those of the champagne houses' vintage wines. Actually, the market for these serious sparkling wines should be minimal as they can never be value for money.

Those areas that have the right sort of soil rarely have the appropriate climate, and vice versa. Franciacorta in Italy has soil that is extremely rich in minerals, but the climate is too warm for the cultivation of grapes with enough acidity. New Zealand's climate is similar to that of Champagne, but there the soil is far from ideal. The fact that the best sparkling wines are produced in California's subtropical climate is chiefly due to the "know-how" of the champagne houses being exported over there.

Every producer of sparkling wine around the world has the dilemma of whether to try to create a wine similar to champagne, or whether to use local grapes that give a more personal taste. The Germans' best sekt wines are all made from Riesling grapes. They are nothing like champagne but can be very good sparkling wines for all that, with aromas typical of the grape and an elegant freshness.

Not only the champagne method...

Up until quite recently it was all right to use the champagne method if the label included the term "Méthode Champenoise". Foolishly, that term has now been abolished. Apart from the champagne method, there are plenty of other ways to make sparkling wine, none of them gives such long-lasting delicate bubbles or anywhere near as much of that vital autolytic character that the champagne method delivers. The other methods are:

Cuvée Close or the Charmat method

Eugène Charmat invented this method in 1907 and lent it his name. It means that yeast and sugar are added to the still wine for a second fermentation in a pressure-free stainless-steel tank. Then the sparkling wine is pumped under pressure through a filter into the bottle, together with a dosage. As the entire process is over in a couple of weeks it's easy to understand why it's so popular. The result is superior to the carbonated method, but a long way short of champagne's supremacy. However, the Charmat is today the commonest means of putting bubbles into wine.

The Rurale method

A predecessor to champagne. The monks at the St Hilaire monastery were making sparkling *Blanquette de Limoux* as early as 1531 with this method. At that time the wines began to ferment a second time in the barrel after the winter as they lay in contact with the sediment. Nowadays the wines are bottled before the fermentation is completed so that a relatively weak mousse is created. In actual fact the wine does not go through a second fermentation in the bottle, as the process is merely a continuation of the first fermentation. Even today, *Blanquette de Limoux* is the only wine made according to this principle, and as the wine is not filtered or disgorged it can never be completely clear.

The Transfer method

Yeast and a sugar solution are added to the bottled wine, causing a second fermentation. However, instead of putting the wine through remuage and disgorging it is transferred to a tank where the sediment sinks to the bottom. The clear wine is filtered prior to being bottled under pressure. This method, a cross between the Rurale and more straightforward Charmat methods, is used chiefly in the United States.

The Dioise method

This is a development of the Rurale method and is only used to make the Rhône valley sparkling Muscat wine Clairette de Die. The wine ferments for four months before it is filtered.

The Gaillacoise method

This method is used only in Gaillac in south-west France, and is yet another variation of the Rurale technique. The fermentation is really only a continuation of the first fermentation, and no extra sugar or yeast is added.

The carbonated method

This is the simplest and cheapest way of all of getting bubbles into the wine. The carbon dioxide is injected into a large wine-filled tank and bottling is pressurised. The big, fizzy bubbles which this method creates are fine for mineral water and sodas, but absolutely unsuitable for wine.

France

Loire

Many producers use their very worst grapes to make sparkling wine. Their reasoning goes like this: if you've got a wine nobody wants to drink, then a little carbon dioxide will do the trick. Even in Loire, where the excellent crémant de Loire is produced from Chenin Blanc, many of the best producers only make sparkling wine in the years that are too poor for good still wine.

Gaston Huet of Vouvray, a maker of some of the finest sweet wines in the world, does claim that the poor years are the only times the grapes contain enough acidity to make them suitable for sparkling wine. In any case, it would be interesting to see how good the sparkling wines would be if made from southern-slope grapes in a good year. In *1979 Huet* made hardly any still wines, so all the grapes that usually end up in his wonderful moelleux wine were used for sparkling wine. The company's wine is one of the best sparkling drink from the Chenin Blanc grape. Sparkling wines from the Vouvray and Saumur districts are very popular, and for a small outlay one can buy a light and fresh wine with a little of the elegance of champagne. However, far too often the grape gives a rubbery undertone that becomes more and more penetrating in older wines.

Marc Bredif's sparkling wines should be regarded as the closest thing to champagne in the area, with a reasonable autolytic character and a fine mineral tone. The best sparkling wine from Loire — *Tresor* — is however not made purely from Chenin Blanc, but is also 30% Chardonnay grape. The oak barrel-fermented wine is made by Bouvet-Ladubay and is so good that it could be mistaken for a basic champagne.

Taittinger, who have business interests in Bouvet-Ladubay, are by no means the only champagne house to show interest in crémant de Loire. The Saumur firm Gratien & Meyer is owned by Seydoux, who also own the Alfred Gratien champagne house in Épernay, but the wines they produce in the Loire valley are not even pale imitations of Gratien's champagne. A total of around 25 million crémant de Loire are produced annually and the region is certainly one of the best behind champagne.

Burgundy

The only district in France that consistently makes better sparkling wines than Loire — apart from Champagne — is Burgundy. What they lose there in soil conditions and climate they make up for in the grapes. Of course, both Aligoté and Pinot Blanc are used occasionally, but most of the crémant de Bourgogne produced each year contains only Pinot Noir and Chardonnay. The foremost producers of them all are probably Simonnet-Febvre in Chablis, who with their crémant de Bourgogne Blanc challenge the poorer growers in Aube. As Chablis rests on the same kimmeridge clay as Aube, and isn't so far away, it's hardly surprising that there are similarities. Unfortunately most crémant de Bourgogne is made by cooperatives that concentrate more on quantity than quality.

André Delorme is one of the biggest producers of sparkling wine in Burgundy, Mâconnais have their challenger in Henri Mugnier from Charnay, and another producer that makes fine champagne-like wines is Cave de Bailly, based south of Auxerre, outside Chablis. Usually though, the overall tone is lowered by a strong earthiness in most crémant de Bourgogne.

Alsace

The third area that is allowed to use the term "Crémant" is Alsace, and in 1976 the region won its own appellation "Crémant d'Alsace". Although almost all the wines under the appellation are made according to the champagne method, the quality is clearly inferior to both Burgundy's and Loire's crémant wines. Most of the sparkling wines from Alsace are made from the characterless grape Pinot Blanc. More and more Chardonnay vines are being planted for production of crémant d'Alsace, so it is possible that we have an exciting and bubbling future to look forward to in this French/German wine district. Otherwise, a very exciting wine made in the area today is crémant d'Alsace Rosé, made from Pinot Noir grapes. Just as in Burgundy, most sparkling wines here are made by cooperatives.

Elsewhere in France

The Alpine districts Jura and Savoie produce surprisingly good sparkling wines from local grapes. Rousette, Molette, Jacquére, Clairette and Chenin Blanc are the grapes that go to make up the fresh champagne-method wine called Seyssel Mousseaux. In south-west France, where the first sparkling wines were made in the 16th century, Blanquette de Limouex is still being produced by the cooperative in Limouex. It is a pleasant, fresh wine very similar to Seyssel Mousseaux. The 650-member cooperative chiefly uses the local Mauzac grape, along with small quantities of Chenin Blanc and Chardonnay. Blanquette de Limouex's neighbouring district Gaillac also uses Mauzac for its sparkling wines, without achieving quite as good a result.
Perhaps the most un-French sparkling wine made in the country is Clairette de Die, made from Mauzac grapes. The Rhône valley's contribution to the world of sparkling wines is by no means dissimilar to the simple elderflower-flavoured spumante wine from Asti in Italy. Buffardel Fréres and Achard-Vincent are the top producers in the area.

Recommended producers: Bouvet-Ladubay (Loire), Simonnet-Febvre (Chablis), Huet (Loire), Henri Mugnier (Mâconnais).

The rest of the world

Italy

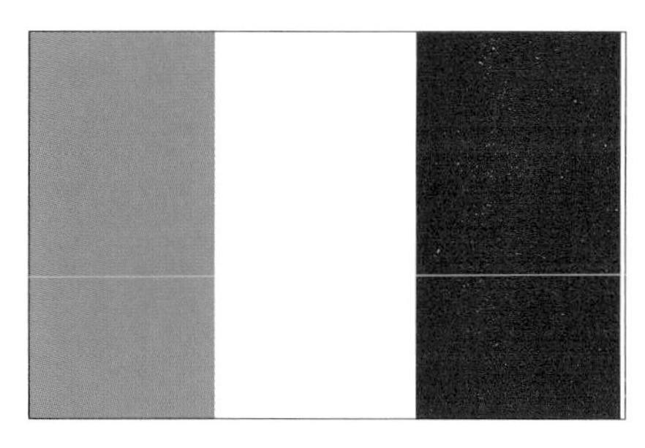

Italy produces about as much sparkling wine per year as Champagne, but very few of the country's winemakers put their sparkling wine at the top of their range. Spumante, as the Italians call their bubbly, is quite simply a party drink that doesn't deserve the same effort as the more serious red wines. The great majority of Italy's sparkling wines are made with the Charmat method. Asti spumante from Piemonte, perhaps the country's most famous sparkling wine, is often sweet, with a scent of elderflower. The Muscat grape very often gives a taste of raisin seeds.
The wines from Trentino-Alto-Adidge in northernmost Italy are far more interesting. The Trentino producer Ferrari is one of the most fascinating sources of sparkling wine outside Champagne. Their *Ferrari Brut* is not quite up to champagne quality, and neither the vintage wine nor the prestige version *Giulio Ferrari Riserva* distinguish themselves much from the standard wine.
Italy's best sparkling wine — *Franciacorta* — is made in Lombardy, around the beautiful Iseo lake. from here, Cá del Bosco produce well-structured, bready and mineral-rich sparkling wines that are among the five best outside Champagne. The winemaker learned his craft at Moët & Chandon and uses oak barrels for his reserve wines. Apart from Pinot Noir and Chardonnay, the neutral Pinot Blanc grape is often used, and compared to Ferrari the firm's vintage wine is in another league from the non-vintage wines.

Piemonte's Muscat grapes are used for the popular sparkling wine, Asti spumante.

Recommended producers: Cá del Bosco and Ferrari.

Spain

Spain is really far too warm to make sparkling wine, but despite this the Spanish cava wines are popular in large parts of the world. Is it because of the attractive bottles or the low prices?

The giant Freixenet company's *Cordon Negro* has, for example, been a great success thanks to the lovely black bottle, but sadly the wine is by no means as pleasant.

I see the Spanish winemakers as being extremely serious about what they do, but unfortunately they face an unbeatable foe — the climate! Modern vinification techniques may mean that the grape juice can be kept fresher and fruitier than before, but the Spanish sparkling wines still have an unpleasant earthiness in both smell and taste, combined with a robust, indelicate, oily fruit.

The Spanish wines that have gone through the champagne method are called cava, and one thing they have in common is that maturity offers no improvement. The mature tones that a cava develops with age are extremely earthy and smoky, and the truth is that the wine's natural development creates an aroma that brings to mind a cork defect! For several years I thought that the corks from there were of particularly poor quality, but after having tasted a great many cavas of various ages I have realised that the cork-like taste is unavoidable in older wines.

In Catalonia, which totally dominates the cava industry, the commonest grape is called Parellada, although Mácabeo and Xarel-Lo are also used. Many firms are experimenting with Chardonnay, which will avoid the earthiness but in the warm climate will give pure tutti-frutti aromas at best.

One of the world's biggest producers of sparkling wine, Codorníu, make a simple but nice *Anna de Codorníu* from a blend of local grapes and Chardonnay. However, the country's two commercial giants, Codorníu and Freixenet, must admit defeat to Segura Viudas. This is the only producer in the country that has succeeded in making biscuity, tasteful wines with features of lemon. An autolytic character is unmistakably present in all their wines, but at its best in *Reserva Heredad Brut*.

Recommended producers: Segura Viudas.

Germany

The Germans have at last dealt with the problem of foreign grapes in their sparkling wines. Today almost all German sekt is actually made from grapes cultivated in Germany. Awful blends like *Henkell Trocken* have given the German sekt an undeservedly poor reputation. Of course, most of the country's sparkling wines taste like pear cider, but those quality producers that make their sekt purely from Riesling grapes have a wine that may not show much resemblance to champagne, but which is very enjoyable anyway.

Ten to fifteen year-old sekt wines from the Rheingau company Fürst von Metternich develop aromas all their own: petroleum with a touch of toffee and honeysuckle. The wines retain their freshness throughout their development thanks to the high acidity level in the Riesling grapes. *Deinhard Lila*, so popular, usually reveals too much elderflower, but in good years Deinhard makes a wonderful but incredibly expensive sparkling wine from the famous Bernkasteler Doctor vineyards. Even though the wine is nothing like champagne, *Bernkasteler Doctor Sekt* is the best sparkling wine I have tasted outside Champagne.

Doctorsberg in Bernkastel.

Recommended producers: Deinhard, Fürst von Metternich.

Austria and eastern Europe

The Austrians should follow the German example and use Riesling in their sparkling wines. Today they are made mostly from Welschriesling and Grüner Veltliner, but neither of these grapes have the acidity level required for sparkling wine.

Schlumberger is the biggest and best sekt house in Austria, and is one of the few producers to use the classic champagne method for their wines.

Before the Russian revolution, vast quantities of real champagne were drunk in Russia, and the tsar's interest in sweet champagne inspired many Russian wine districts to begin producing a sparkling wine called Shampanskoye. Then, as now, a lot of sweet, flat and mediocre wine was produced that Russians enjoy immensely. The Crimean peninsula has some of Russia's finest vineyards and *Abrau Durso* is judged by most observers to be the country's best sparkling wine (and one of the few to be made the champagne way). Georgia is the other important wine province, but it too produces basic, sickly sweet wines.

About as much sparkling wine is made in the former Soviet Union as is produced in Champagne, but the quality is hardly comparable. Even the pear-flavoured *Zlata Radgonska Penina* from Slovenia and *Backarska Vodika* have made more of an impression on me than any Russian sparkling wine has managed.

USA

About half of USA's states are home to a producer of sparkling wine, with Tedeschi Vineyard on Hawaii perhaps the most exotic example. After California, New York is the state that makes the most sparkling wine. Moët & Chandon were heavily criticised when they established the Domaine Chandon company in Napa Valley. The United States is, after all, the country that had abused the name of champagne more than any other: every other sparkling wine from California had previously exhibited the famous title in large letters on the label. Besides, many Frenchmen were frightened of the competition America would bring in the long term.

Today, most Californian producers strive to imitate champagne, and without doubt it is the Americans who have come closest to copying the real thing. Moët & Chandon's special variety of yeast is in common use and the vinification method is almost identical to Champagne's.
In order to come as close to the original as possible, the grapes are picked virtually unripe so that the acidity level will be sufficiently high. The harvest usually takes place in the coolest hours of the night. The Chardonnay grapes that grow in California can easily become heavy and clumsy, which makes the coldest parts of the state the most suitable for making sparkling wines. Anderson Valley and Potter Valley seem to enjoy the best conditions, and in Anderson valley the Roederer Estate make the most champagne-like wines in the world. They are not just like the French wine, they actually resemble very closely *Louis Roederer Brut Premier*. Only a slightly exaggerated chocolate tone that arises when the glass warms up reveals the wine's place of origin. Roederer and Moët are by no means the only champagne houses that have made the journey to California: Maison Deutz in Santa Barbara, Domaine Mumm in Napa Valley and Piper-Sonoma in Sonoma are the best-known, but many more are moving in. Other European wine companies have also followed in the French footsteps: the Chianti firm Antinori are working together with Bollinger, and both the Spanish giants Codorníu and Freixenet own land way out west.

Apart form the Roederer Estate, two native companies make first-class sparkling wine.

- Claude Thibault at Iron Horse is rightfully proud of his dry wines. Both the blanc de noirs and blanc de blancs are pure and elegant.
- The other wholly-American competitor to the Roederer Estate is Schramsberg in Napa Valley. Their wines are more controversial than the other top wines as they are much heavier and fuller. They are usually called "USA's Krug" and make partial use of oak fermentation and a long maturing period before disgorging. As with most American producers, they use brandy in their dosage. *Schramsberg Cuvée de Pinot* is a great sparkling wine in those years when the acidity is high enough, but I for one haven't yet discovered any similarities with Krug.

Recommended producers: Roederer Estate, Iron Horse, Schramsberg.

Australia and New Zealand

In the northern parts of New Zealand's southern island and the eastern parts of the north island, the climate is almost ideal for the production of sparkling wines. The grapes that are cultivated here have a naturally high level of acidity and a delicate character. As New Zealand is such a young wine-making country, many potentially brilliant winemakers are still at an experimental stage. Wonderful burgundy-like Chardonnay wines are made at the Morton Estate, which is probably the most promising property for sparkling wines too. The best results have been achieved by producers using a lot of Chardonnay in their cuvées.

Compared to New Zealand, Australia has come a lot further in its wine production. Just as in the United States, several champagne houses have shown interest in Australia. Bollinger's cooperation with the legendary winemaker Brian Croser at Petaluma is the most successful venture so far. Today Petaluma produces, together with Seaview, the best sparkling wines in the southern hemisphere.

The first sparkling wine that was made in Australia was *Seppelt's Great Western show champagne*. It is usually called "Australia's Bollinger R.D." as it lies in contact with its sediment for at least ten years. It is a remarkable wine made from Ondenc grapes: the fruit resembles Gewürztraminer and doesn't suit the autolytic character of Seppelt's prestige wine.

Recommended producers: Seaview, Petaluma.

Other countries

A respectable amount of sparkling wine is made in a number of unexpected countries around the world.
In Canada the cool climate is quite suitable for sparkling wines, but so far no thrilling dry wines have emerged. The great masters of sweet wines Château des Charmes and Inniskillin are however, making great strides with their sparkling experiments.

Moët & Chandon are very active in South America, and wines under the title of "M.Chandon" are made in both Brazil and Argentina. One wonders how many are disappointed when they drink "M.Chandon" in the belief that it is a genuine champagne?

The top winemaker in Spain, Miguel Torres, has just launched a reasonable sparkling wine from Chile, while Concha Y Torro are the leading domestic producers there.

The most interesting wine from "the rest of the world" is definitely *Omar Khayham* (previously *Marquise de Pompadour*), which is made in India. With the help of champagne house Piper-Heidsieck, the Indians have produced a fresh and well-balanced sparkling wine from Ugni Blanc, Pinot Blanc and Chardonnay. The warm climate in the Maharashtra district outside Bombay is a difficult opponent which is combated with high-technology and French know-how. The grapes are picked at night to avoid the boiling hot sun.

Sparkling wine is even being made up in the north, although most are made from low-quality grapes bought in from lands to the south. Some are fruit wines made from apples or elderflower. Even in Sweden low-quality sparkling wine is made, using imported grapes. Åkesson from Brösarp have a strong grip on the market in my country.

Among the other countries where sparkling wine is made are England, Luxembourg, Hungary, Romania, Portugal, Switzerland, Israel, Mexico, Colombia, Venezuela, Japan and South Africa.

Champagne and food

In France they usually drink champagne with dessert, while the rest of the world treats it as an aperitif. Champagne is of course the perfect aperitif, with its appetising acidity and fast-working, refreshing effect, but with the right food one can take the drinking experience to even higher levels. As we all know, the French are world champions in the kitchen, and their greatness comes from a combination of tradition, knowledge and access to good fresh ingredients. Each province has its own local dishes that enjoy a global reputation, but in French terms Champagne is no classic culinary province. The best restaurants there tend to serve dishes from other parts of France, but despite that the local kitchen is rich and varied. The nearby rivers hold an abundance of freshwater fish, and as the Ardennes forests north of Reims are still one of Europe's richest wildlife areas, red and fallow deer and game birds form the base of many local dishes.

Lamb and pork dishes are also more common than beef.

They love soups and salads of all kinds in Champagne, with potato, swede and other vegetables the dominating ingredients. Fish are prepared in many imaginative ways, but always, always with wine involved.

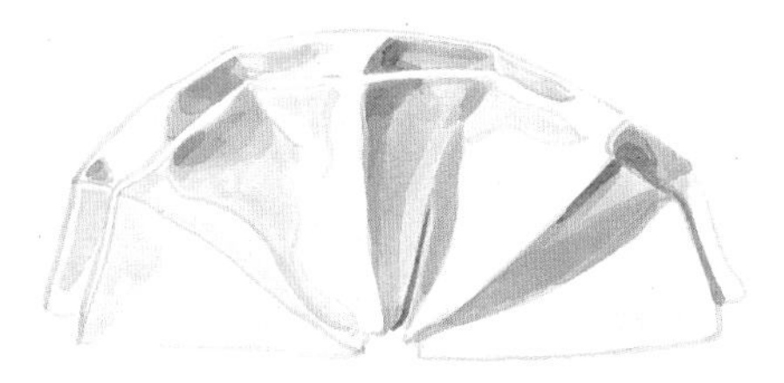

Champagne's greatest contribution to the world-famous French kitchen can be found among the cheeses. It is a real pleasure to travel around the outskirts of Champagne and buy cheese straight from the farmers. The characterless factory-made cheeses should be avoided if you're after that certain extra something. The most famous cheeses are the bries, such as the delicate Brie de Meaux with its creamy taste. If you ever have the opportunity to choose from a well-filled cheese tray in Champagne, be sure to try Arrigny, Boursault, Caprice des Dieux, Chaumont, Explorateur or Maroilles.

Champagne is also well-known for its pastries — especially the different fruit cakes. For those with a sweet tooth I can recommend a trip to the bountiful, extravagant chocolate shops and pâtisseries in Reims. Do be careful not to serve up the chocolate truffles with the champagne, something which many Frenchmen do, unfortunately. If, against all good sense one decides to drink champagne with dessert, then one should at least choose a sweet champagne. Sugar is dry champagne's enemy No.1. Dry champagne has an unerringly sour taste together with desserts, and the only sweet course that I believe goes with champagne at all is strawberries (on their own). Even then, I must admit that I prefer a German Riesling Spätlese with my delicate summer berries.

Successful combinations

Champagne is a perfect partner for the culinary delicacies of the sea.

When it comes to combining food and wine, the old rule always applies. The heavier and stronger the dish, the heavier and more full-bodied the wine should be, and vice versa. A fish course should be served with white wine, and red meat with red. Nowadays it is fashionable to stray from these principles in a spirit of experimentation, but every analysis shows that certain substances react negatively together. One example is the sea salt in shellfish, which separates when it meets the tannin in red wine. White wines with meat are a better bet, but they rarely cope well with the powerful tastes often dominating the sauce or spices.

However one chooses to compose one's meal, it is important to consider the balance between food and drink. This can be achieved by having a wine that adds something the food lacks, or by choosing a wine with aromas that match those of the dish in question. For example, a game course can quite happily be accompanied by a red wine with animal tones, or a nutty caviar dish by a champagne with a similar hint of nuts. Restauranteurs all over the world are looking for new, successful combinations where balance is the most important goal, whether attained through complimentary or matching aromas in the food and wine.

Many people believe that champagne can be drunk with all sorts of food, without being especially good with anything. It may be true that champagne fits an unusual number of dishes, but the wine can be heavenly when combined with the right course. The bubbles and acidity cuts like a knife through cream or butter-based sauces, purées, egg and other fat, mild dishes. Vegetable dishes, fish and shellfish are lifted by the elegant champagne, while the drink can also clean the mouth from other, more powerful tastes. However, one should avoid more acidic foods: champagne together with citrus fruits or vinaigrette sauces produces a sour sensation.

Champagne together with red meat is something I customarily avoid, preferring a good red wine, but the *1986 Clos des Goisses* I drank with beef during a visit to Philipponnat in November 1994 was a fabulous feast.

A shame that so many of these delicacies are so expensive!

Treasures of the sea

Naturally it is possible to combine champagne with relatively basic and inexpensive dishes, but I think one should be ready to spend a little more on something a little special when one opens a bottle of the bubbly. Oysters and champagne is of course a classic, as is champagne and Russian caviar. In such cases it is important to choose a young, dry and light Chardonnay-based champagne that can cope with the taste of brine.

Oysters develop a milder flavour if they are baked in the oven with a little creamy sauce or some mild cheese. As to the Russian caviar, try and avoid the salty Sevruga and plump instead for the milder Beluga or the nutty and slightly rarer Oscietra. By all means serve the caviar over a Russian Blini with Smetana or Créme fraiche (and leave out the lemon slice!).

All forms of shellfish go well with champagne, although the question is whether lobster and champagne is the very best pairing. Salmon and flatfish with white wine sauce paired with a middle-aged cuvée champagne is another successful gastronomic marriage. Even lightly-smoked fish can go well together with a champagne that boasts its own roasted aromas, such as a mature blanc de blancs.

Truffles, asparagus and Japanese food.

Truffles taste wonderful together with a Pinot-based champagne with its own animal and vegetable tones. Asparagus is generally seen as being a "difficult" companion to wine, but champagne is a shining exception. Asparagus in hollandaise sauce accompanied by a delicate cuvée champagne is like drinking in the spring!

The discreet flavours of the Japanese kitchen are perfect for the sparkling drink, and Champagne's master chef Gérard Boyer is a pioneer who uses curry and ginger superbly in his food combinations. However, watch out for Asian dishes that contain a lot of soy or strong spices.

Poultry

A blanc de noirs is extremely well-suited to poultry. These Pinot champagnes are also the only ones, together with perhaps rosé champagnes, that cope well with mild, hard and goats' cheeses.

I personally believe that the perfect combination is old champagne and duck liver. The sweet, toffee-like aromas in a fully-matured champagne are a far more refined choice to liver than sauternes or the clumsy Gewurztraminer wines from Alsace. The acidity in the champagne prevents the fatty liver from become too powerful an experience. A duck liver terrine is even better than the fried variant, as the burnt aromas from the frying surface can easily dominate. Both duck and goose liver are incredibly expensive in most countries, but there are cheaper alternatives, such as goose paté or duck mousse which contains some liver. Most of the really old champagnes that you can read about in the producers' section are ones I have tasted in all their lonely majesty, before a good portion of duck liver has kept the wine company.

If you want to have a special theme for a champagne supé, there is a particularly delightful idea — the rosé dinner. Serve rosé champagne throughout to a first course of lobster and main course of pink salmon. Finish with strawberries or raspberry soufflé. Make sure all the candles, serviettes, tablecloth etc. are pink, and decorate the table with some pink roses. A more romantic meal would be hard to imagine. A simpler alternative is a champagne picnic in the countryside, with a fresh chicken salad or toast and caviar.

Jacky Michel at the "Hôtel d'Angleterre" in Châlons-sur-Marne doesn't believe in the old adage "Too many cooks spoil the broth".

Restaurant food

Several champagne houses experiment with various food combinations. Bollinger and Krug are perhaps more than any other the champagnes of the large meal. Their weight and depth can match any number of exciting dishes. Rémi Krug cooperates closely with some of the world's top chefs and together with them composes special Krug dinners. Appropriately enough, *Krug Rosé* is almost always alongside the obligatory cheese tray, but I do question the oldest vintages of *Krug Collection* being drunk to accompany dessert.

Food from Swedish restaurants

I have asked some of the leading personalities in the food and wine business in my home town of Stockholm to choose a dish and the appropriate champagne from their restaurant's menu.

De fyras krog

Järntorgsgatan 5, 111 29 Stockholm, 08-24 14 14

Poached halibut, melted butter and horse radish

Boil the water, a few decilitres of white wine, the juice of half a lemon and some white pepper grains. Let the fillet of halibut (4-5cm wide) simmer for around five minutes or until it shows some resistance to the touch. Melt the butter over a low temperature and remove the scum that is formed. Blanch some spring onions or leek that have been finely chopped. Form a bed of onion on which to lay the fish. Pour over the melted butter and cover with grated horse radish. Serve with new potatoes. Voilà....enjoy! Simple and delicious. Notice particularly the way the nutty aroma of the butter unites with the champagne from Krug.

Johan Blanche (Former President of the Swedish Sommeliers' Association).

Franska matsalen, Grand Hôtel

S Blasieholmshamnen 8, 111 48 Stockholm, 08-679 35 84

Fried Swedish wood pigeon with ginger and beans

6 pigeons	1 tablespoon of soy
3dl beef stock	1 tablespoon of sherry vinegar
3dl white wine	150g butter
2dl sweet sherry	100g various dried beans
2 onions	200g broad beans
1 carrot	1 sweetcorn cob
1 fresh ginger	1 whole garlic

6 portions. This is what you do.
Fry the pigeons until brown and cook them for around ten minutes in the oven until bloody. Peel an onion and dice the carrot, then fry in the butter until it colours, then sprinkle over some sugar and pour on the sherry. Let it cook dry. Pour over the wine and boil together a while. Finally pour on the beef stock and let it boil until the taste is good. Strain and flavour with grated ginger, soy, vinegar, salt and pepper.

Soak the dried beans for a few hours and then boil them until soft in chicken boullion. Boil the corns from the cob in salt water until soft. Soften the cloves of garlic in butter. Blanch the broad beans and remove the shells. Blend all the ingredients into the sauce and heat.

With this we serve a *1986 Dom Ruinart Rosé*, the power of which makes it an excellent champagne partner for the pigeon.

Roland Persson Anders Nordqvist.

Leijontornet

Lilla Nygatan 5, 111 28 Stockholm, 08-14 23 55

Parcel of Salmon and St. Jacques mussels

4 sheets of rice paper
4 large mussels
200g fresh salmon
8 large spinach leaves

Dressing:
1dl rape seed
1/2 teaspoon grated fresh ginger
A few drops of sesame oil
1 teaspoon coriander, shredded
1 pinch of finely chopped fresh pepper
1/2 pinch of ground black pepper
1 teaspoon salt
Juice from one lime
2 tablespoons of water

Olle Lindberg.

Wet the rice paper. Slice the mussels into three parts. Slice the salmon into pieces of equal size. Mix the dressing and marinate the pieces for an hour or so. Parboil the spinach and dry well. Lay out two leaves on the rice paper. Apply alternate layers of salmon and mussels. Brush egg white over the edges and fold into small knots.

Brush with butter and bake the knots in the oven for 4-5 minutes at 200°C. Pour the dressing onto the plate, lay out the knots and add a few drops of soy onto the dressing. To this we serve a *Deutz Blanc de Blancs.*

Videgård

Regeringsgatan 111, 111 39 Stockholm, 08-411 61 53

Mussel variation

Recipe for 4 people

8 large Pilgrim scallops
1kg vongoule scallops
2 large baked potatoes
1dl black beans
1dl red beans
1dl Black Eye Beans

Ingredients for red bean sauce

1 tablespoon red bean pasta
2cl sesame oil
2cl sugar
2 tablespoons of water
1/2cl vinegar
1/2cl MSG (Korean salt)

Ingredients for picked lettuce

4 endive leaves
4 frisée leaves
4 lollo leaves
4 rossi leaves
2 tablespoons peanut oil

Ingredients for lime and mustard dressing

1dl olive oil
1/2 tablespoon French mustard
1 tablespoon lime juice
1 tablespoon finely chopped herbs; chives, parsley, tarragon, thyme and a little sage

Ingredients for tomato fondue

10 tomatoes
1/2 clove of garlic
1 pinch of fresh thyme
1 bay leaf
2 shallots
2 tablespoons olive oil

Erik Videgård.

Begin by dividing up the tomatoes and squeezing out the seeds. Cut into smaller pieces, blend in the herbs and boil dry. Boil the vongoule scallops and open them. Steam the scallops for one minute and let them cool. Boil the beans in chicken stock, cooking each kind of bean separately. Mix the ingredients for the red bean sauce, then do the same for the lime and mustard dressing. Shred the lettuce and mix with the peanut oil. Thinly slice the potatoes and fry so that the slices become round.
Lay the shredded lettuce in the potato basket, slice the scallops thinly and mix with the lime and mustard dressing. Lay this over the lettuce. Mix the beans with the tomato fondue. Lay on the plate with the vongoule scallops over the bean mix. Pour lines of red bean sauce over the vongoule scallops.
We serve *1990 Pierre Peters* with this dish.

NF
NF

A Champagne journey

It doesn't take long to reach Champagne from Paris, and one can travel the 150 kilometres by road or rail. If you are driving around France on vacation, Champagne makes a perfect short trip or a slight detour on the road toward the sun-soaked south. Wherever you're coming from, the landscape outside the wine growing area is rather flat and monotonous, and it's first when you reach the wine villages or the towns of Champagne that you discover the beauty of the region. And Champagne is beautiful! The open landscape, with small villages lying squeezed in between the rolling hills, gives you a feeling of freedom and release from the stresses and strains of modern living.

Everyone loves champagne!

The people of Champagne have a relaxed charm and inner warmth that's far from superficial. Their temperament and disposition is actually very similar to the Scandinavian character. The locals have good organisational sense, but the tempo of their lives is a far cry from the big city life of nearby Paris.

The directors of the major champagne houses are of course globetrotters with well-filled diaries and they are always being invited to countries all over the world to attend dinners and balls as ambassadors for Champagne in general and their house in particular. Many of these directors live a life of considerable luxury: some have their own planes while others collect expensive cars. However, the majority work closely with their staff and show great respect for their professional capabilities.

The small growers don't live in such high society, of course, but they do share a commitment to the wine. As they are present during all the stages of vinification they often know more about their product than do the "big house" bosses.

Staying the night

The standard of hotels in the area is high, with prices relatively low. If it's nightlife you're after, the best place to stay is Reims, as Épernay is deathly silent after midnight. If you prefer to sample the unique atmosphere of the area then the possibilities of staying at some "auberge" out among the vineyards are many. They are often to be found on the wine road "Route Touristique du Champagne".

The wine road

Cycling around among the historic wine villages is a joy. Stop for a picnic on the top of some hill of vines or visit some of the thousands of producers in the area for a look around their cellars and a taste of their wines.

Get to know a champagne grower well and you've got a friend for life. Champagne is a fascinating place if you want to try and discover unknown producers. While in Burgundy

and Rhône the best growers have long since been surveyed and established, here there is still a great deal left to explore.

Sitting on a hill and enjoying a chilled champagne from the area while one looks out over the ground, the wine sprang from is a fantastic experience. Many times I've tasted a champagne from a vineyard and at the same time examined the wine's birthplace. There is no better way to fix in your mind the importance of the actual place where the grapes grew for the wine's eventual quality. Such enjoyable experiments make one wonder how one could ever misplace the wine at a blind tasting. Back home however, and the unthinkable is likely to happen.

Pause for food

After drinking an aperitif among the vines, it doesn't feel out of place to enjoy a delightful French meal at one of the many culinary manors in the area. Gérard Boyer's restaurant "Les Crayères" in Reims is one of the best in the world. The food and the wine list are of course quite exceptional, and the surroundings in the Parque Pommery are also impressive. The beautiful garden was created by the famous landscape architect Redon, and the building itself is a real stately home in prime condition. Add the stylish furnishings and the perfect service and you'll understand that Boyer offers a culinary experience that shouldn't be missed.

If the wallet starts to complain, there is a great variety of very fine restaurants in a somewhat lower price range. In Vinay, just south of Épernay, is "La Briquetterie".

Nowhere else in the world are champagne and food combined as well as by Gérard Boyer at the three-star restaurant "Les Crayères" in Reims.

This is a wonderful restaurant with the best duck liver I've ever eaten. The charming place is a one-star restaurant in Guide Michelin. In my opinion it certainly deserves two stars.

"Royal Champagne" is one of the area's many star-studded restaurants. This manor lies high up in Champillon, with a fantastic panoramic view, and the house speciality is a superb fresh asparagus served with truffles. Here, as at Boyer's, one can stay in the same building as the restaurant. "Royal Champagne" is owned by Moët & Chandon, which explains why the *Dom Pérignon Rosé* is quite cheap.

Another pearl can be found in Sept-Saulx: "Cheval Blanc", with a relaxed rustic atmosphere and well-cooked food.

There is only one truly top-class restaurant in the centre of Épernay - "Les Berceaux" - but there are several personal and charming restaurant/bars such as "Chez Pierrot" and "Au Petit Comptoir".

In Reims, apart from Boyer's restaurant, one can find "Le Florence", "Le Chardonnay" and above all "Le Vigneron". This restaurant is run by Hervé Liégent, a moustachioed gentleman with a great passion for old champagne. "Le Vigneron's" champagne list is probably the leading one of its kind in the world, with several producers represented from

Besides his impressive wine list, Hervé Liégent also has an amazing collection of old champagne posters and wine curiosos.

pretty much every vintage since the end of the 19th century. Order an oldie from "the brown pages" of the wine list and you'll be allowed to follow Hervé across the street and down into his remarkable cellar. The prices are never set: you pay according to which champagne monsieur recommends that particular day. Previously the prices were also lowered the more times you visit the cellar on the same evening. The last two years have seen prices double and even worse, the prices have been removed from the wine list! This move has lead quite a few raised eyebrows on the presentation of the bill. This is where champagne makers themselves had come to drink old vintages of their own wines. When everyone else was out of a vintage, it was always worth a try to pay a visit to Hervé at "Le Vigneron". I hope the glorious ancien régime at "Le Vigneron" is soon restored.

In Côte des Blancs a perfect idea is stopping by at "Le Mesnil" in the village of the same name. The prices are low and the well-cooked food is relatively simple, but the greatest feature of the place is the atmosphere. Many growers drop in for lunch and drink some of their colleagues' champagne from the Grand cru village. If you enjoy blanc de blancs, then this is the spot for you.

Other interesting restaurants in the area are "Le Foch" and "Le Univers" in Reims, "Le Grand Cerf" in Montchenot, "Aux Armes de Champagne" in L'Epine and "Hôtel d'Angleterre" in Châlons-sur-Marne.

Château Louvois.

Sightseeing

If you want to do more than just eat and drink in Champagne, then you'll find there's a great range of things to see. The area is full of historically interesting places and buildings. If you are interested in French castles, then you should visit those in Boursault, Louvois, Mareuil and of course the very biggest, Château de Montmort. The most beautiful of all is clearly worth seeing: the Château de Brugny, and the wall of graves that surrounds it.

Those with a historical bent should also make time for the citadel in Langres and the fort at Rocroi. Both offer English-speaking guides who will relate in full the tale of Champagne's precarious situation during both world wars. The monastery at Hautvillers where Dom Pérignon worked is of course the most famous and popular of all the region's monasteries, boasting a fine museum and the grave of the old monk himself.

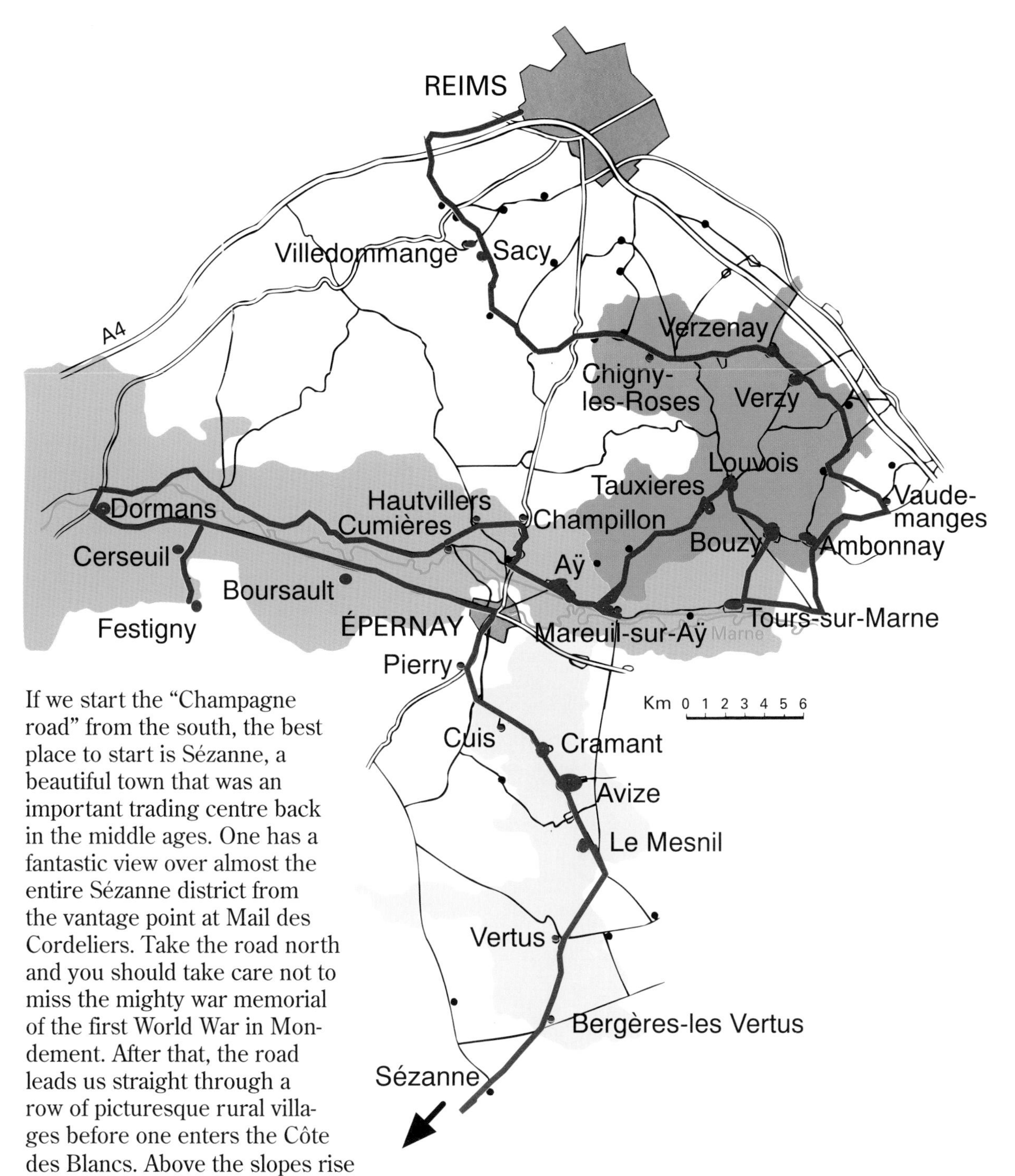

If we start the "Champagne road" from the south, the best place to start is Sézanne, a beautiful town that was an important trading centre back in the middle ages. One has a fantastic view over almost the entire Sézanne district from the vantage point at Mail des Cordeliers. Take the road north and you should take care not to miss the mighty war memorial of the first World War in Mondement. After that, the road leads us straight through a row of picturesque rural villages before one enters the Côte des Blancs. Above the slopes rise the famous Champagne hills in all their glory. Bergères-les-Vertus is the southerly outpost with its 237-metre high peak Mont Aimé, a vital strategic point for many a warlord. Tsar Alexander is perhaps the best-known.

Through Vertus the journey now takes us north towards the seat of class and finesse, Le Mesnil. There is something magical about that name. The village is filled with famous winemakers and vineyards, so there is nothing else that need bother the visitor during a stay at this particular spot.

In Avize one is greeted by a gorgeous church and the region's university for budding winemakers. Just as in Le Mesnil and the next village Cramant, here it's hard to think of anything other than champagne, but one should take a moment to be awed and bewitched by the lovely countryside. Travelling from the south, on the right side of the road is Butte de Saran, on which one can see Moët & Chandon's Château de Saran. In front of the Château are

This 33-metre high statue of Pope Urbain II stands in Châtillon-sur-Marne. Just like the Statue of Liberty in New York there are steps inside the arm that aren't to be recommended to those suffering from claustrophobia.

Parts of the thick forest in Montagne de Reims are classed as a national park. One of the great Sunday pastimes for local families is to wander along the many paths through the forest.

the vineyards from where the grapes are taken to be used in the firm's prestige champagne *Dom Pérignon*. All the Grand cru villages in Côte des Blancs are buzzing with exciting producers who will gladly sell a bottle or two for a reasonable sum (see the producers' section).

Leaving Côte des Blancs via Cuis one begins to approach Épernay, but first there should be time to visit the 12th century church at Chavot. In Pierry there is the chance of looking around Taittinger's property "la Marquetterie", which includes the vineyards that supplied the monk Jean Oudart in the beginning of the 18th century.

The Marne valley

In Épernay you will find the peerless Avenue de Champagne, the home address for many famous champagne houses. The C.I.V.C. is also based in Épernay, but otherwise the town is quite unremarkable. It lies in the middle of Champagne, and from here one can travel northwards towards Montagne de Reims or further west into the Marne valley. On the south side of the river lies Boursault, with its castle and the charming, leafy villages Festigny, Cerseuil and Troissy, which are all worth a visit.

The road continues its journey on the north bank of the river in Dormans and passes through a row of Pinot Meunier-dominated villages where the countryside is beautiful but the wines less so. Once in Damery and Cumières and one is back in first-class grape country, and by the road in Cumières one can see Leclerc-Briant's three clos locations — Les Crayères, Chèvres Pierreuses and Clos des Champions.

After Cumières we reach the cradle of Champagne, Hautvillers, with its medieval monastery. The landscape is hilly and famous villages jostle for position. After Dizy and Champillon one comes to the small champagne town Aÿ with its rich wine history and its silky-smooth Pinot champagnes. Pierre Laurain has an interesting wine museum adjoining the "Vieux Pressoir" restaurant in the town centre.

In Mareuil-sur-Aÿ one passes the Abel Lepitre, Billecart-Salmon and Philipponnat champagne houses (worth a visit!) before one sees the steep southerly slopes at Clos des Goisses just by the road. This is where the grapes grow that make up some of the area's most majestic champagnes of the same name (see the producers' section).

Montagne de Reims

Our journey progresses through Mutigny, Tauxières, Louvois and Bouzy before we come back to the Marne canal at Tours-sur-Marne, the home of Laurent-Perrier and Chauvet. Down by the water there is a delightful "auberge" called " La Touraine champenoise".

Ambonnay is the next Grand cru village, with its fascinating network of streets that radiate from the hub of the community, Place de la Fontaine. Vaudemange is the easternmost point on our tour before we come to the northern side of Montagne de Reims. Verzy contains one of the most remarkable sights in Champagne: Faux de Verzy, the haunted wood, a perfect environment for the witches and elves of fairy tales. The short trees, with their twisted, octopus-like branches and knotted trunks present an almost unnatural and spooky sight. No-one knows why the trees have become so deformed, but one theory is that it is due to a mineral imbalance in the soil. Another explanation is that the beech trees have formed mutations caused by a virus infection.

The age of the trees is another subject of discussion, but most scientists claim that they are around 2,000 years old. It doesn't take more than a couple of minutes to turn off the "champagne road" from Verzy to this miracle of nature. The forest is full of paths that lead to the beeches or to the viewpoint from Mount Sinai. Do remember not to leave anything of value in the car, as the unguarded car parks are easy pickings for thieves.

Both Verzy and Verzenay give the impression of being aristocratic, lying as they do high up on the steep hills, with the Reims plain below them. After a few twisting curves on the road to Verzenay one comes face to face with the famous windmill "Moulin de Verzenay" on Mount Boeuf, the only mill left in the whole of Champagne. It was built in 1823 and used as an observation post in the first World War, then by the French Resistance in World War II and finally the American troops at the end of the war. Heidsieck & Monopole later bought the mill and used it as a restaurant. As a landmark and a symbol of Champagne the mill still has an important role to play.

The next village on the journey westwards is the Grand cru village of Mailly, dominated by the cooperative of the same name. A place where it's easy to creep in to an unplanned tasting.

Chigny-les-Roses is almost as lovely as it sounds, and in fact the village is unusually well-blessed with flowers for Champagne. Otherwise it's normal for houses to have their gardens in the inner courtyard, and only a few hanging baskets adorn the small number of windows facing the street.

At Montchenot one can leave the "Route Touristique du Champagne" and take the N51 straight to Reims. If you continue on the "Champagne road" you will travel a very beautiful stretch of road through Petit Montagne, even though the champagne that is made here seldom reaches the heights. Don't miss the divinely beautiful churches in Sacy and Villedommange. The road goes through an enchanting wood before it passes the motorway and enters Gueux, with its famous race track and excellent golf course.

Faux de Verzy.

Moulin de Verzenay.

The sights of Reims

The final destination of the journey is the city of Reims, with its 200,000 inhabitants. Unlike Épernay, Reims is a place of many possibilities. The city centre has recently been rebuilt and modernised in a not-too-successful manner. What happened to all the greenery? The Place d'Erlon is still there in all its glory, but is now surrounded by artless hotels and car parks. However, the city is still a wealth of architectural masterpieces. The city's history began when the Gaulish tribe of Remi aided Caesar in one of his wars, and Reims became the capital of the Belgica secunda province. The town became a bishopric in the 3rd century and an arch bishopric in the 5th century.

The nation that is France began its history when Clovis was crowned by Saint Rémy in the year 496 in Reims, and up until 1825 Reims was the city where the rulers of France were crowned. Reims was an old Roman town called Durocortorum in the beginning, and there are still several ruins and building work left over from the Roman times. The Porte Mars is perhaps the most impressive of the individual buildings.

The cathedral

Reims is also a town rich in churches. The oldest church in the city, the St Remi basilica from the 12th century that has its own museum, is something extra special. Anyone who has the time should also visit the Cryptoportique and its well-kept Gallo-Roman colonnades.

Learned experts the world over argue about which is the world's most magnificent Gothic cathedral. For me, no other cathedral on earth exudes the same utter harmony as the one at Reims. The size and power, combined with the many thousands of statues, give the same type of balanced, deep impression as an old and vibrant vintage champagne from Krug. My good friend Frank Ward often uses the expression "a Cathedral of a Wine". I believe he must be referring to the cathedral at Reims.

No-one could be unmoved by this building, which with its slenderness, sculptural decoration and glass paintings reaches for the skies. The cathedral is quite simply one of the greatest creations of the High Gothic era.

A cathedral was built here as early as the 9th century, but it burnt down in 1210. The fire also destroyed large parts of the town, but one year later to the day archbishop Aubry de Humbert laid the first stone of the present cathedral, which took almost a hundred years to complete. The original plans were for a giant spire where the transepts were to meet and six smaller spires on the towers of the facade, but they had to be scrapped after a fire among the roof trusses in the 15th century.

The church was almost completely destroyed in the first World War. After years of restoration work the building was damaged once again, in the second world conflict. Many of the statues that were destroyed have been replaced and the originals can be seen in the archbishop's palace, Musée du Tau, beside the cathedral.

The interior of the cathedral is awesome: a nave, 38 metres high by 115 metres long, is separated from the side transepts by pillars, and furthest in is a large chancel and five chapels. The pillars at the front are closer together and in this way heighten the perception of depth.

Even though several of the church's famous windows were destroyed during world war one, there are, happily, still a few left from the 13th century. The best of all is the west side's huge rose window which is best seen when the sun is low. In the centre is the death of Mary and around

Chagall's glass windows on the cathedral's east side.

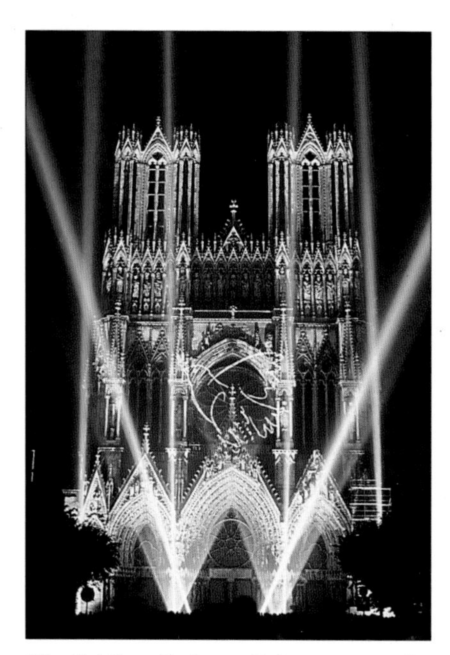

The lighting display at Reims - a remarkable show under a summer night sky.

The famous chalk cellars of Reims.

her the twelve apostles, angels and furthest out the prophets and kings that welcome her to heaven. Perhaps the most famous of the "new" windows are those done by Marc Chagall, which show Jesus' death and resurrection and other biblical scenes.

The exterior, and in particular the west side, is extremely impressive. It is adorned by several sculptures, one of which is the angel with the famous "smile of Reims" — "Le sourire de Reims". Of course I cannot go into all the details here, but anyone interested in the High Gothic style, much of which originated in the sculptors' huts in Reims, can find some excellent literature in the tourist bureau by the cathedral.

One final sight to recommend appears every Friday and Saturday evening in the summer, when the cathedral is the scene of a fantastic display of light and sound. Even for those who don't understand a word of French, it's an unforgettable experience. Afterwards the light display continues on the giant west side, describing the history of the cathedral.

The Gallo-Roman cellars

Champagne's most popular tourist attractions are probably the Gallo-Roman cellars, i.e. the chalk cellars excavated by the Romans. Les Crayères offer unique storage conditions for the wines and a perfect situation for the formation of bubbles, "Prise de mousse". The cellars are dark, damp and free from sound, vibrations and draughts, and the temperature is always close to the ideal of 10° C.

The Roman chalk quarries were originally dug by slaves so that the giant blocks could be used when Reims was built. The quarries were dug in the shape of a pyramid and the blocks were lifted out using primitive cranes. Even today there are houses in Reims that were built with stone blocks from Roman times.

In the beginning of the 18th century, Claude Ruinart took over some of the old quarries, which then began to be used to store wine. Since then the underground network has been extended so much that below the surface Reims looks like a Swiss cheese. There are cellars two hundred kilometres long, while under Épernay they are as long as one hundred kilometres. The combined storage capacity for both towns has been calculated at three hundred million bottles.

The champagne cellars were used as bomb shelters throughout both world wars. Some people enjoyed it so much that they stayed underground for several months, doing practically everything they usually did above ground. Trade was maintained and concerts and plays were performed while bombs laid waste to the town. Without doubt the deepest and most beautiful cellars lie under Reims. The cellars belonging to the firms Pommery, Ruinart, Henriot and Taittinger are my personal favourites, with their great halls that taper off up to a small opening in the ground, allowing in a magical beam of sunlight.

With their underground train Piper-Heidsieck may have gone a little too far in their exploitation of the historic cellars, but this train ride was my personal maiden voyage into the delights of Champagne. After a visit to Piper-Heidsieck in July, 1986, I began to read all I could find about the area, and a lifelong passion was born.

Hundreds of thousands of people visit the Moët & Chandon and Mercier cellars in Épernay each year, and they too use trains for the guided tour. For the first-time visitor these cellars are a must, but the best way is of course to contact the company's agents in your home country, and they will gladly help to arrange a suitable itinerary. Bollinger and Pol Roger are two companies that accept visitors in a very humble manner, despite their fame. Only Krug and Salon are all but impossible for those outside the wine trade to visit.

Visitors enjoy a train ride through Mercier's cellars.

Go your own way

I've shown one road through Champagne, a road that has given me many fine experiences and great memories. Naturally there is much, much more to discover in this exciting area, and indeed the best places are always those you discover yourself. I wish you a pleasant journey with many wonderful moments. Only time, resources and you yourself can decide when your journey is over.

Champagne's classification system

The cru system

As the growers in Champagne have, for the most part, sold their grapes to the major houses, the classification system in Champagne is based on grape prices. The system is called "Echelle des Crus" and ranks all the wine villages at between 80% and 100% on a cru scale. Today the free market reigns, but in previous years the C.I.V.C., together with the growers and the champagne houses, fixed the annual price for a kilo of grapes. Thus grapes from a 100% village would cost the houses full price, which would then be reduced according to the percentage the village is ranked on the scale.

When the cru system was first introduced in 1919, the scale went from 50% to 100%, and in recent years there have been many calls for a return to the wider scale. The critics claim that there is not enough variation in price between, for example, basic Pinot Meunier grapes from the Marne Valley and Grand cru Chardonnay.

Another problem with the scale is that it only notes which village the grapes come from, and not where within the village they were cultivated.

Several cru villages were re-classified in 1985, with five new villages receiving Grand cru status alongside the original twelve. A lot of villages improved their status, and none lost status. There are still villages that are extremely overrated and others that deserve promotion. There are also certain areas in some Premier cru villages that achieve Grand cru quality. Personally, I believe that Burgundy's cru scale is fairer, with every cultivation area judged on its own merits.

Grand cru

In Burgundy it is taken for granted that the best and most expensive wines come from the Grand cru vineyards. However, what isn't generally known is that Champagne has a similar system with Grand cru and Premier cru. I maintain that there is just as great a difference between a champagne from Aÿ and Verzenay as there is between a *Chambertin* and a *Musigny*. More and more champagne makers lay stress on having access to wine from the Grand cru areas.

The reason the Grand cru system isn't better known is that the major houses have always promoted cuvées from a mosaic of villages, with lowly-ranked areas included. The small firms and growers who have had access to first-class grapes have not had the same PR machinery behind them as the giants of Moët, Mumm, Clicquot, Pommery, Lanson and others. On the other hand these companies haven't been shy about the fact that they use only Grand cru grapes in their prestige cuvées.

The best growers from the Grand cru villages now make textbook champagnes with a wonderful character of the place where the grapes once grew. The price of the Grand cru champagnes from these growers isn't in the same league as those of Grand cru wines from Burgundy. In fact, they're a bargain.

Certain vineyards give grapes of a completely different intensity from others. My favourites are Aÿ and Verzenay for Pinot Noir, and Avize, Cramant and Le Mesnil for Chardonnay. These villages have a special luminosity about their product, whether they are part of some classic cuvée de prestige from a famous house or coping by themselves in a monocru champagne direct from the growers.

The quality of the raw material is obviously very important in the creation of a first-class champagne. Fortunately more and more consumers are awakening to the benefits of Grand cru champagne, which has led to the growers also beginning to market the concept.

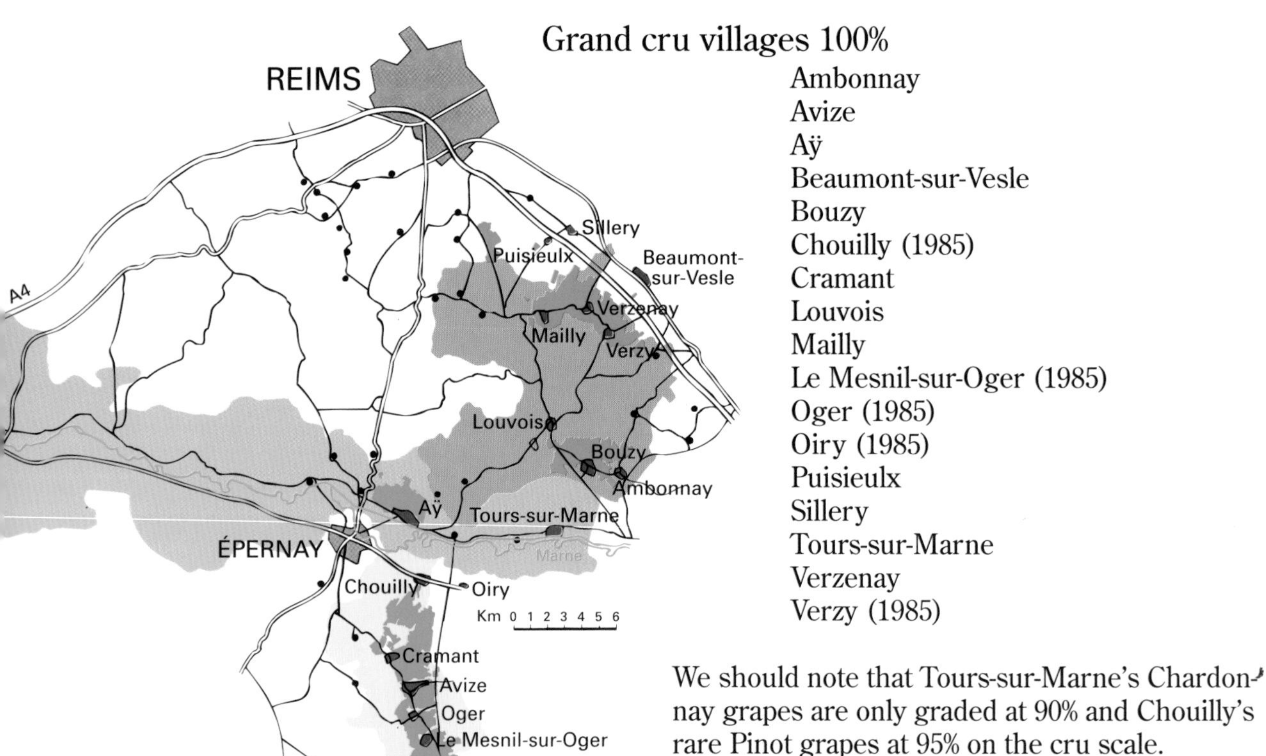

Grand cru villages 100%

Ambonnay
Avize
Aÿ
Beaumont-sur-Vesle
Bouzy
Chouilly (1985)
Cramant
Louvois
Mailly
Le Mesnil-sur-Oger (1985)
Oger (1985)
Oiry (1985)
Puisieulx
Sillery
Tours-sur-Marne
Verzenay
Verzy (1985)

We should note that Tours-sur-Marne's Chardonnay grapes are only graded at 90% and Chouilly's rare Pinot grapes at 95% on the cru scale.

Premier cru

Premier cru villages are those ranked between 90 and 99% on the cru scale. Counting the Premier cru grapes produced by Chouilly and Tours-sur-Marne there are forty Premier cru villages, but the true figure is 38. Some Premier cru villages actually outdo certain Grand cru villages, so it is good to know the growing conditions and reputation of the various villages. Even if the ranking is fair, there can be areas within the village that provide Grand-quality grapes. The Mareuil-sur-Aÿ location Clos des Goisses has some of the district's finest grapes and should definitely have Grand cru status.

Other Premier cru villages of high quality are Cuis, Dizy, Grauves, Trépail, Vertus, Chigny-les-Roses, Rilly-la-Montagne, Avenay, Champillon and Cumières.

Premier cru villages 90-99%

99%
Mareuil-sur-Aÿ
Tauxières

95%
Bergères-les-Vertus (white grapes only)
Billy-le-Grand
Bissueil
Chouilly (black grapes only)
Cuis
(white grapes only)
Dizy
Grauves
(white grapes only)
Trépail
Vaudemanges
Vertus
Villeneuve-Renneville
Villers-Marmery
Voipreux

94%
Chigny-les-Roses
Ludes
Montbré
Rilly-la-Montagne
Taissy
Trois-Puits

93%
Avenay
Champillon
Cumières
Hautvillers
Mutigny

90%
Bergères-les-Vertus
(black grapes only)
Bezannes
Chamery
Coligny (white grapes only)
Cuis (black grapes only)
Écueil
Étréchy (white grapes only)
Grauves (black grapes only)
Jouy-les-Reims
Les Mesneux
Pargny-les-Reims
Pierry
Sacy
Tours-sur-Marne
(white grapes only)
Villedommange
Villers-Allerand
Villers-aux-Noeuds

Unclassified villages 80-89%

Only a small part of Champagne's cultivated land goes to make up the Grand and Premier cru villages.

Most of the champagne produced today contains grapes ranked only between 80 and 89% on the cru scale, usually called unclassified. All the villages in the outer regions of Champagne, like Aube, Sézanne and Aisne, come into this category. Few of the low-classed villages have any real personality of their own, but there are exceptions, such as Bethon, Damery, Urville, Leuvrigny, Mancy, Montgenost and Les Riceys.

The main task of the unclassified wines is to act as a "taste-broadener" in Champagne's cuvées. The relatively neutral wines can balance the top wines with greatly differing characters and create a harmonious whole. The non-vintage cuvées of the major houses are often made of hundreds of unclassified wines.

89%
Coulommes-la-Montagne
Damery
Moussy
Sermiers
Venteuil
Vrigny

88%
Chavot-Courcourt
Épernay
Mancy
Monthelon
Reims

87%
Allemant (84% Pinot)
Barbonne-Fayel (85% Pinot)
Bethon (84% Pinot)
Broyes (85% Pinot)
Celle-sous-Chantemerle
(85% Pinot)
Chantemerle (85% Pinot)
Courmas
Fontaine-Denis (84% Pinot)
Montgenost (84% Pinot)
Nogent l'Abbesse
Saint-Thierry
Saudoy (85% Pinot)
Sézanne (85% Pinot)
Thil
Trigny (85% Pinot)
Vindey
Villenauxe-la-Grande
(85% Pinot)
Villers-Franqueux

86%
Binson-Orquigny
Bouilly
Branscourt
Brouillet
Brugny-Vaudancourt
Courthiézy
Crugny

Cuisles
Faverolles
Hourges
Lagery
Lhéry
Montigny-sur-Vesle
Reuil
Sainte-Euphraise
Saint-Martin d'Ablois
Savigny-sur-Ardres
Serzy et Prin
Soulières
Tramery
Treslon
Unchair
Vandeuil
Vandiéres
Vauciennes
Verneuil
Villers-sous-Châtillon
Vinay
Vincelles

85%
Barzy-sur-Marne
Bassu
Bassuet
Baye
Beaunay
Celles-sur-Ource
Cernay-les-Reims
Coizard-Joches
Congy
Cormoyeux
Courjeonnet
Étoges
Fèrebrianges
Fleury-la-Rivière
Germigny
Givry-les-Loisy
Gueux
Janvry
Loisy-en-Brie
Mondement
Ormes
Oyes
Passy-Sur-Marne
Prouilly
Romery
Saint-Lumier
Talus-saint-Prix
Trélou-sur-Marne
Vert-Toulon
Villevenard
Vitry-en-Perthois

84%
Baslieux-sous-Châtillon
Belval-sous-Châtillon
Berru
Boursault
Broussy-le-Grand
Cerseuil
Châlons-sur-Vesle
Champvoisy
Chenay
Cuchery
Festigny
Hermonville
Jonchry-sur-Vesle
Jonquery
Leuvrigny
Mardeuil
Mareuil-le-Port
Marfaux
Merfy
Mesnil-le-Hutier
Montigny-sur-Vesle
Morangis
Moslins
Nesle-le-Repons
Neuville-aux-Larris
Oeuilly
Olizy-Violaine
Passy-Griny
Pévy
Port-á-Binson
Pontfaverger-Moronvilliers
Pouillon
Pourcy
Prouilly
Sainte-Gemme
Selles
Villers-Franqueux

83%
Bligny
Breuil
Brimont
Cauroy-les-Hermonville
Celles-les-Condé
Chambrécy
Champlat-Boujacourt
Chapelle-Monthodon
Chaumuzy
Chavenay
Châtillon-sur-Marne
Cormicy
Connigis
Courcelles-Sapicourt
Courthiézy
Crézancy
Dormans
Igny-Conblizy
Poilly
Reuilly-Sauvigny
Rosnay
Saint-Agnan
Sarcy
Soilly
Try
Vassieux
Vassy

82%
Arcis-le-Ponsart
Aubilly
Bergères-sous-Montmirail
Bouleuse
Cortagnon
Courville
Méry-Prémecy
Nanteuil-la-forêt
Orbais l'Abbaye
Romigny
Saint-Gilles
Ville-en-Tardenois

81%
Châlons-sur-Vesle

80%
All the remaining villages in the Marne and the Aube department. The most important villages in terms of quality are:

Avirey-Lingey
Balnot-sur-Laignes
Bar-sur-Seine
Bligny
Buxeuil
Charly-sur-Marne
Château-Thierry
Columbé-le-Sec
Fontette
Gyé-sur-Seine
Les Riceys
Urville
Ville-sur-Arce

Vintages

The quality of different vintages varies much more in northerly wine districts than in those in warmer climes. The problem has been solved in Champagne by blending different vintages with one another in order to balance the wine. Vintage champagnes are made in the years when the grapes ripen to perfection, and these wines should reflect the style of the producers and the year in which the grapes were harvested.

There is no formula for the perfect year. The style of the vintage depends upon a series of complicated factors of which temperature, solar energy and rainfall are very important. The way these components are divided up during the year is decisive. The different personalities of the vintages are a wine taster's great joy. Some are happiest with the powerful vintages like 1947, 59, 76 and 89, while others prefer years which gave more elegant and delicate champagnes, such as 1966, 69, 71, 79, 85 and 88. Whichever is your favourite, the different vintages have a richness of variation which makes tasting so much more fascinating.

It is tricky to give the vintages a grade according to their general quality, as some are extremely generous in their younger years while others take an eternity to develop. Keep in mind that the table of vintages that follows is extremely general in nature. Those vintages that have high marks have wines that live long and have a high maximum level. Several of the vintages that have low marks can be extremely good to drink now as they have already reached their peak. Check the assessments of the various wines in the Producers section.

19th century

1874 is thought to be the best champagne vintage of the 19th century. Other great years were 1858, 1880, 1884, 1892, 1898 and 1899.

1900

Large harvest of high quality. Often compared to the somewhat more storable vintage of 1899.

1904

A rich harvest of famous vintage wines in an elegant style of great longevity.

1906

Normal harvest and average quality. The wines have lasted longer than at first thought.

Vintage chart

Vintage	Grade
1900	4
1904	4
1906	4
1907	2
1911	4
1914	5
1915	4
1919	4
1921	5
1923	3
1926	3
1928	5
1929	4
1932	2
1933	3
1934	4
1937	5
1938	4
1942	2
1943	4
1945	4
1947	5
1948	3
1949	5
1951	2
1952	4
1953	4
1955	5
1959	5
1961	4
1962	3
1964	5
1966	5
1969	4
1970	3
1971	4
1973	4
1974	1
1975	4
1976	4
1978	2
1979	5
1980	2
1981	4
1982	4
1983	3
1985	5
1986	3
1987	2
1988	5
1989	4
1990	5
1991	2
1992	2
1993	3
1994	(2-3)
1995	(4-5)
1996	(5)
1997	(3-4)
1998	(3-4)

1907
A potentially fine vintage that became lighter then expected due to rain at harvest time. Few houses released a vintage and Heidsieck & Co. is the only one I have come across.

1911
A classic vintage with many wines that are still lively. Pol Roger is magnificent.

1914
A large vintage harvested under difficult conditions at the cost of many lives. The hardness of the wines when young took a while to pass, but since then they have lasted a very long time.

1915
A well-liked vintage which does not have quite the life span of 1914.

1921
One of the greatest white wine vintages this century throughout Europe. In champagne it may have been beaten by 1928, but the quality was excellent with bottles even more lively today. *1921 Dom Pérignon* was the first cuvée de prestige.

1923
Unknown vintage with very small harvest. At first the wines were elegant and acidic. Probably some champagnes from the top houses retain a glimmer of life if there are any bottles left.

1926
A vintage that is almost forgotten today, after falling in the shadow of 1928. A bottle of *1926 Krug*, drunk in 1994, did lack mousse but was reminiscent of a noble *Château d'Yquem* from the twenties with its sweet, toffee-like aromas.

1928
The vintage of the century! Krug from this year is judged by many experts to be the most perfect champagne ever made. 70 year-old champagne may be risky, but if you get the chance for a '28 then buy it!

1929
A very good vintage which has been forgotten beside 28 and is not always as long-lived.

1933
Of little interest today, but a good vintage in its youth.

1934
Elegant, long-lived wines which can even be good today.

1937
Very big, rich wines which are said to be a great experience in the nineties. I have only tasted some fresh examples, *1937 Krug* hits the bullseye.

1938
A large harvest made acidic wines which were first thought to be good, but not exceptional. Imagine my surprise when *1938 Krug* turned out to be the best champagne I have drunk so far, despite being over half a century old.

1943
A fine vintage that gave wines of great finesse. There are few good examples left today however.

1945
The best vintage of the second World War but not up to the levels of the 47 and the 49. 1945 also saw the debut of *Roederer Cristal*.

1947
All Bordeaux lovers will have heard of *47 Cheval Blanc*. Not quite so heroic wines were made in Champagne, but the 47s are known for their extra-richness and masculine strength. Despite low acidity levels a long-lived vintage.

1948
A year forgotten between 47 and 49, but successful in Côte des Blancs.

1949
The wines were almost as mighty as in 47, but with better acidity. Long life span.

1952
Very long-lived and balanced wines, but sadly their relative youth is the best feature of the vintage. Certain 52s are incredibly youthful although not particularly impressive champagnes. *Taittinger Comtes de Champagne* made its entry this year.

1953
Quite the opposite of the 52 wines, the 53s are easily maderised and not fresh. Those bottles still lively do however give sensual and pleasurable wine experiences. *1953 Diebolt* is one of the best champagnes I have ever tasted.

1955
A fantastic year which can still reach the heights. Acidic, fine wines with a lovely toasty bouquet and perfect balance.

1959
A large harvest of champagnes which ended up with almost 13% alcohol because of the extremely hot summer. The wines have shown themselves to be eminently storable, despite low acidity. The energy and concentration are amazing whether the wine is dominated by Pinot or Chardonnay. A wonderful champagne year of its style! Many prestige cuvées made their debuts this year, such as *Dom Ruinart* and *Pol Roger Blanc de Chardonnay.*

1961
As the Bourdeaux 61s have become so famous Champagne's 61s cost more than a 59, 64 or 66, even though the quality is usually lower. *1961 Krug* is monumental and some famous tasters regard *1961 Dom Pérignon* as the best champagne they have tasted.

1962
This is often an underrated vintage in many champagne circles, but the year has given great, rich and soft champagnes, although they may lack in stringency.

1964
This wonderful vintage is often compared to 1966. Today, with few exceptions, the 64s have a scent of mint chocolate, bergamot oil and new-baked bread and a full-bodied, sweet and concentrated taste that is at the very peak of its life cycle. If you want to taste old champagne but don't want to take a risk, then a '64 may be one of the safest choices. The flower-gilded cuvée de prestige *Belle Epoque* was introduced this year.

1966
Frost and hail combined to limit the harvest and lifted what was expected to be an ordinary vintage up to heavenly heights. The great cuvées are full of life, with all manner of exotic fruit aromas and an elegant structure. The rare blanc de blancs are exceptionally elegant and the great name of Pinot has made powerful, vegetable-suggestive champagnes. Just try a *Bollinger 66,* which reminds one of a great *La Tâche* in its aromas.

1969
After a number of problems during the year a tiny harvest was collected, with acidic grapes which gave sharp, basic wines at first. Today the best have attained true greatness and unmatched elegance. *Bollinger Vieilles Vignes Françaises* and *Jacquesson Blanc de Blancs* are great favourites.

1970
Potentially a very fine vintage, but overproduction reduced the quality somewhat. A medium quality vintage for champagne with *Bollinger R.D.* as an exotic honeysuckle-scented favourite, after the creamy and concentrated *Vieilles Vignes Françaises.*

1971

This year had a series of problems in store for the vineyards, but produced a small harvest on September 18th. The wines from this vintage are uneven. They are usually light and elegant but lack sufficient life-preserving acidity. As usual, *Krug* is the clear winner.

1973

Another hot year that meant a late harvest at the end of September. The wines were seen as a short-term lot, but the best have lasted tremendously well. Just as with the 71s, there are some tired cases, but the 73s are always rounder and richer with particularly good blanc de blancs.

1974

A cold, rainy year which produced a wet harvest on September 28th. The wines are mediocre and diluted, with only Vertus and Aube producing grapes worthy of the name. *Roederer Cristal* is regarded as the best from this thin vintage.

1975

The experts are at odds over this vintage. Some say this is the storage vintage to beat the best, while others claim that a '75 should be drunk as young as possible if they are to retain their charming fruitiness. I think the 75s lack charm but are good for storing and well-balanced. Pinot Noir was generally more successful than Chardonnay, the proof of which lies in, amongst others, the lovely *La Grande Dame* and *Bollinger R.D.* from 1975.

1976

A giant harvest of sun-ripened grapes gave slightly fleshy and extra-rich champagnes reminiscent of 47 or 59, but not quite up to their standard. Fairly often there's a detectable earthy or smoky hint to the taste coming through the fatty, oily structure. *Cristal* and *Salon* are my favourites, having avoided clumsiness in such a hot year.

1978

In my recent travels I have heard more and more growers speak well of 78s. The champagnes seem to have developed unexpectedly well. I myself have little experience of this vintage.

1979

A wonderful, classic vintage with incredibly elegant wines backed up by a large portion of concentration. Few factors in the weather reveal this as a top-quality vintage. Most 79s are wonderful to drink now with their fragrant, toasty and nutty tones. Only the future will tell if they are to become even better. *1979 Krug* was for many years the most multi-faceted champagne I had drunk.

1980

The sugar content of the grapes could only muster an alcohol level of 8%, which led to over-chaptalised wines (see Dictionary). The few producers who harvested from the southerly slopes early in November did however find grapes of quite high quality. *Comte Dampierre Blanc de Blancs*, *Dom Pérignon* and *Bonnaire* are some of the best champagnes from 1980.

1981

As Champagne had experienced small harvest for several years, there were hardly any reserve wines left. Hopes were high for a major harvest, but it didn't happen. The 81s are delicate, elegant champagnes with an exceptional feminine balance in the Pinot Noir, but sometimes a rather light-bodied Chardonnay. Sadly a great deal of potentially fine vintage wine was used in non-vintage champagne. Look for champagnes with a large proportion of Aÿ Pinot from this year. *Bollinger Vieilles Vignes Françaises* and *Krug* are landmarks.

1982

At last, a year of huge production (295 million bottles). The vineyards of Côte des Blancs were so overloaded with grapes that the vines were bowed by the weight. The over-production meant that far too many 82s have not lasted as well as expected. 1982 was above all a Chardonnay vintage. If you find some of the Grand cru growers' 82s then you are in for an exotic experience. At a tasting of 82s in 1993, with all the big names present, many of the blanc de blancs emerged on top. *Krug* and *Bollinger Vieilles Vignes Françaises* were the only exceptions. *Krug Clos du Mesnil* won just ahead of *Jacques Selosse* and *1982 Krug*.

1983
The previous year's record of 295 million was immediately beaten by the 1983 harvest: 300 million bottles were filled. The last time two years had succeeded with both quantity and quality had been 1857 and 1858! The wines do have more acidity than in 82, but most have matured at worrying speed the last two or three years and are unlikely to last especially long, with some exceptions.

1985
One of my true favourites. The winter brought temperatures of -25° C to Champagne, destroying a tenth of the vines. An indian summer in September/October rescued a small harvest which later proved to be of outstanding quality. Both the Pinot and Chardonnay have exceptional balance.

1986
A hard winter was followed by late budding. It rained during the early part of the harvest, but those with nerves of steel enough to wait out the heat harvested rich, ripe grapes. An average vintage with one "superstar" – *1986 Jacques Selosse* – with a lot of acidity.

1987
Anyone who made a vintage champagne did so for financial reasons. The wines are thin and raw.

1988
The trilogy that began with 1988 is without compare in the history of champagne. Choosing one's favourite from these three years is more a question of style than quality. The '88 is the most classic, which in its more refined, balanced way reminds one of 85 and 79. The Pinot Noir was especially high-class this year.

1989
The '89 was the richest and best-developed vintage right from the start. The weather was similar to that during 47, 59 and 76. This meant sweet, extra-rich wines with a high alcohol content and low acidity. I can imagine that 89 is the vintage that holds most delights for the general public.

1990
Champagne from 1990 is more reserved than that of 89, but richer than 88. 88 may be the more classic of the two, but 1990 is something special. I am too young to have experienced a '28 in its heyday, but I believe they must have had the same compact, impressive structure and closed but magnificent aroma. The wines are so rich you can chew them. It will be tremendously exciting to follow the famous trilogy in their journey through time.

1991
Pinot grapes of high quality were harvested, but they were used in non-vintage champagnes, hardly for any vintage wines.

1992
A poor year with wines of low acidity and alcohol levels. No vintage quality here either.

1993
Harsh, rainy weather at harvest-time killed all chances of a good yield. The winemakers were getting impatient: three years without a vintage champagne! The '93 has turned out better than originally expected.

1994
In Sweden we remember 1994 for a lovely hot summer and success for the nation's football team in the World Cup. In Champagne everything looked promising up until the harvest, which was once again partially rained away. However, barrel tastings from Jacques Selosse, Krug and others show that some good wines were made in the area this year.

1995
A superbly balanced vintage which will develop faster then the superior 96 vintage.

1996
Probably one of the best vintages ever made, extremely high alcohol and acidity.

The Producers

In most French wine districts the growers make wine from their own grapes. Since the days of Dom Pérignon the philosophy of blending has reigned supreme in Champagne, and has led to the formation of major champagne houses with the capacity to make champagne from grapes grown in a number of villages.

Today the development has changed, and cooperatives and growers make up an increasing proportion of the annual production. It has become more and more vital for champagne houses to own their own vineyards, or to sign long-term contracts with growers to maintain their supply of grapes. The champagne house that is entirely self-sufficient in grape production just does not exist.

If you are unsure about which type of producer has made the champagne you intend to drink, then look for the initials on the label. They are often found low down on the left-hand side, followed by a producer number. N.M. (Négociant-Manipulant) means a champagne house, R.M. (Récoltant-Manipulant) a grower and C.M. (Coopérative-Manipulant) means it was made by a cooperative.

The champagne houses

The difference between a champagne house and a grower is that the champagne house has the right to make champagne from grapes bought from throughout the region.

The champagne houses have always had a strong position in the area. Today there are 265 champagne houses of varying size. The ten largest houses answer for around half of total sales, and in 1964 the "Syndicat des Grandes Marques de Champagne" was formed to defend their position. Membership of this body doesn't mean so much today, as many of these firms produce mediocre champagnes and several of the top names are absent.

The original members were Ayala, Billecart-Salmon, Bollinger, Clicquot, Delbeck, Deutz, Heidsieck & Co. Monopole, Charles Heidsieck, Irroy, Krug, Lanson, Massé, Moët & Chandon, Montebello, Mumm, Perrier-Jouët, Joseph Perrier, Piper-Heidsieck, Pol Roger, Pommery, Prieur, Roederer, Ruinart, Salon and Taittinger.

The growers

As I hinted earlier, the growers are becoming a major power in the area, as today's new technology gives them the possibility of producing better wines than before. Some own land in areas where the grapes lack the quality to be vinified separately, while others grow world-class grapes. There are now 5,152 growers who make their own champagne from their own grapes.

The cooperatives

The number of cooperatives in Champagne has grown dramatically the past few years. There are today 44 cooperatives where the growers in the village have joined forces for help with the vinification of their grapes. They had previously sold all their grapes to the big champagne houses, but today they have the possibility of becoming a Récoltant-Manipulant or joining their neighbours in a cooperative.

The cooperatives are divided up into four categories.

1. Pressing-house cooperatives that press grapes for others.
2. Cooperatives that press grapes and make still wines.
3. Sur lattes cooperatives that press grapes, vinify still wines and make the wines sparkling before they are sold under someone else's label.
4. Selling cooperatives that make champagne and sell it under their own name. Their labels are always marked with the initials C.M. (Coopérative-Manipulant).

Today there are several high-technology cooperatives that make pure and original champagnes, but few of them have achieved the same level of quality as the best individual growers. The resources are there but few of the cooperatives dare to concentrate on a cuvée de prestige made from a strict enough selection of grapes or with exclusive vinification techniques. This is often because opinions differ within the cooperative about who grows the best grapes.

The well-established cooperative in Mailly is an admirable example, producing better champagne than the individual growers in the village. The cooperatives from Avize and Le Mesnil are hardly the pick of their own villages, but with the excellent raw materials to which they have access they make pleasant champagnes in all price ranges.

It is chiefly in the Pinot Meunier-dominated villages that the cooperatives have made a marked difference to the quality. Beaumont des Crayères in Mardeuil or H. Blin in Vincelles have really lifted the reputation of their villages. The fact that more and more growers are joining cooperatives makes it easier for those of us who want to know how the individual villages' wines do taste. The number of growers one must keep track of becomes more easily manageable. Something that does complicate the picture more though is that many cooperative members also sell champagne under their own grower's label R.C. (Récoltant-Coopérateur).

The buyer's own brand

M.A. (Marque d'Acheteur) means that a major buyer, such as a hotel chain or a store, uses its own name on the label even though the wine is made by a cooperative or a champagne house. It is common in England for department stores to have "their own champagne", but in order to prevent consumers from being cheated the producer number and the letter M.A. must be shown on the label. Some champagne houses have specialised in making "buyers own brand", while others are far too proud and careful of their good name to let their wine be sold under another's label. If you are lucky then there may be some extraordinary winemaker hidden behind the label. Several of the top French restaurants have, for example, Legras from Chouilly as their house champagne under the restaurant's own name. However, behind department store chain's house champagne there often hides a winemaker of lesser quality, as the store is keen to sell its champagne as cheaply as possible. As a specially-labelled champagne costs a lot to produce it means that customers must buy in volume for the whole thing to succeed economically, so it is not a enterprise for every local bar or pub.

Producers Section

Introduction

In this section of the book I have attempted to chart as carefully as possible the most important Champagne villages and their producers. The villages are divided according to the cru system, and they are placed in alphabetical order within each category — Champagne towns, Grand cru, Premier cru and other villages of interest. The producers, on the other hand, are ranked according to quality in each village or town.

The placement of the producers caused me many headaches as some of them have a very uneven range, while others make a fantastic non-vintage champagne without the resources to make a vintage wine. How, for instance, should one rank Moët & Chandon, who made *Dom Pérignon*, one of the world's finest champagnes up until the middle of the seventies, but who today make a basic non-vintage champagne, a decent vintage rosé, a good vintage champagne and a very good *Dom Pérignon*? The answer must be that one must take the way the producers are divided up with a pinch of salt.

Far more exact and much more interesting is my judging of the individual wines, subjective though it may be. It is based on serious tastings between 1987 and 1999 and is one of the most comprehensive evaluations of champagne that has ever been made.

The vintage wines receive two marks: one for the quality when last tasted, and one for the quality when the wine is at its best. The non-vintage wines are judged only for quality at the time of sale. Certain non-vintage wines do however improve with storage. It is usual that one also says when the wine will be at its best, but as the maturity of champagne is so much a question of personal taste I have resisted making any such judgements.

If there is a very large gap between the mark given from the latest tasting and the potential points, then I should assume that the wine needs more time in the cellar than if the opposite is the case. Then it is a question of your own experiments to find which state of maturity suits you best.

I have chosen to work with a 100-point scale as I think it's best to use as wide a scale as possible. A wine that is not pleasurable to drink shouldn't get any points at all in my opinion, so my scale starts at 0. However, I should add that all champagnes — apart from the defective ones — hold such a high standard that they are all quite fun to drink. 50 points is an average mark for a non-vintage champagne, but the average for this category is somewhat higher as I have concentrated on the most name worthy of the 5,461 producers. Had I had the chance to try all of them, I am convinced the mark would be closer to 50. The full 100-point score is reserved for the perfect champagne, which I hope I have yet to drink.

My system is not divided up into different points for various qualities, but is rather an overall judgement of the wine as a whole. At the end of the producers section there is a list of the best wines from each vintage, from each decade and a Top 100 which covers everything.

Let me point out once again that this is a subjective evaluation and that champagne is a living product which can vary greatly between bottles. The points system is valuable however, as it helps you to understand what sort of quality a wine has. Perhaps my descriptions of the champagne's personality and style will say even more.

Hopefully this will be a help as you make your choice out in the "champagne jungle". It's also important to remember that the points system cannot do justice to the pleasure of drinking a simple champagne with a view across the vineyards or in fascinating company. I have tried to close my mind from such situations when I make my judgements here.

Symbol key

PIERRY = the name of the village.

% = The village's rank according to Champagne's 100% scale.

[grape symbol] = The grape proportions which tell how much of the village's land is planted with each variety.

Vollereaux = The name of the producer.

[telephone symbol] = The producer's telephone number.

Production: = The number of bottles produced per year.

1989 Vollereaux = The wine's name in red italics.

65 = The first points refer to the mark at the latest tasting.

(Aug 95) = The time I last tasted the wine.

78 = The second points refer to the wine's potential maximum mark. Vintage champagnes only.

▼ = The wine is past its best and will deteriorate.

(50% PN, 10% PM, 40% CH) = The approximate blending of the various grapes, which constitute the wine. Varies greatly from year to year in non-vintage wines.

PN = Pinot Noir, PM = Pinot Meunier, CH = Chardonnay.

Other producers = Producers in the village whose wines I have never tasted or lack enough information on. There is certainly an occasional "oversight" who makes wonderful champagne! Look around yourself, especially in the Grand cru villages!

The Champagne Towns

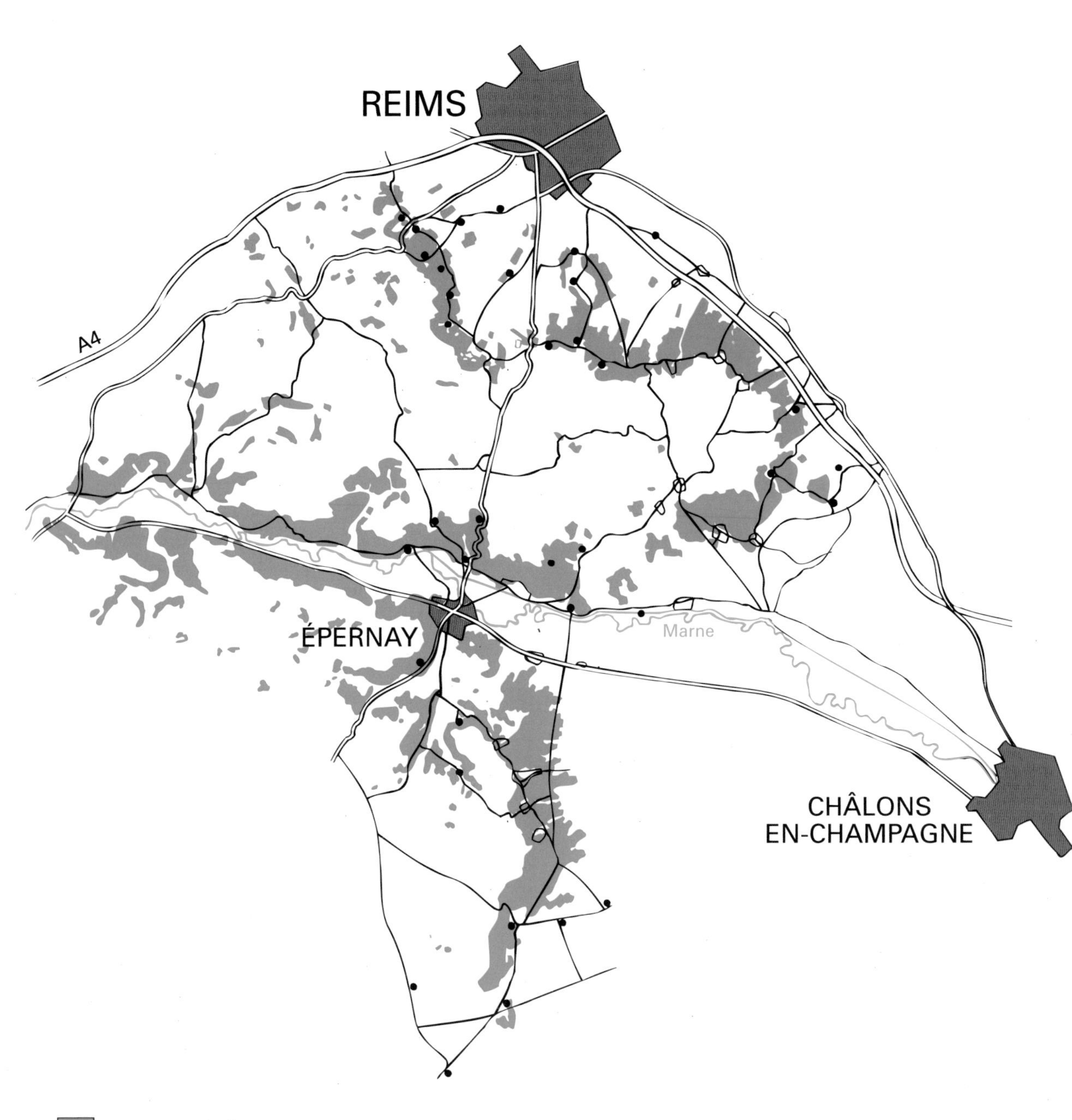

CHÂLONS-EN-CHAMPAGNE

Châlons-sur-Marne was once upon a time an important champagne town. Today only two champagne houses are left in the town and the closest vineyard is far away. Châlons has a tremendously rich history and is full of relics from Roman times. During the middle ages Châlons became the capital of the Champagne region. Nowadays a great deal goes on apart from sparkling wine production, and the town has a well-developed food industry. The price of champagnes can in fact be lower here than in the tourist-filled Epernay and Reims. The restaurants are definitely cheaper and of a very high class. A vist to the Hôtel d'Angleterre is a must!

Joseph Perrier

69 av. de Paris, 51016 Châlons ☎ 03 26 68 29 51

Production: 600,000 bottles.

The only champagne house of any consequence in Châlons today. And it is perhaps due to its geographical location that Joseph Perrier is often forgotten when the finest champagnes are discussed. Ever since the firm was started in 1825 it has maintained a low profile but is well-known among wine experts.

The methods of vinification are modern, apart from the use of 600 litre oak barrels for the reserve wines. J-C Fourmon, however, denies the use of cognac in the dosage, which is occasionally alleged in wine books. The company's style is based on the excellent Pinot locations they have in their 20 hectares in Cumières, Damery and Hautvillers. The wines are always fruity and soft, with a great deal of elegance. Owned by L.-P.

Joseph Perrier Brut 73
(35% PN, 30% PM, 35% CH)
Earlier one of my favourites among non-vintage champagnes. A sorry disappointment a few years ago, when the great mature citrus aroma has become gooseberry and elderflower. Today back on the right track.

Joseph Perrier Rosé 68
(38% PN, 37% PM, 25% CH)
Lovable romantic low-price champagne, quite irresistable. Drink it outdoors in order to fully appreciate the flowery aroma of the wine.

1989 Cuvée Royale 84 (Jul 97) 88
(45% PN, 5% PM, 50% CH)
The house has succeeded in creating a champagne which perfectly reflects both the vintage and house style. The wine is laid-back and charming, with a delightful tone of toffee.

1985 Cuvée Royale 87 (Dec 98) 89
(50% PN, 50% CH)
A generous and well-interlaced wine with a chewy taste similar to meat paté and a heavy, almost overripe fruity nose.

1982 Cuvée Royale 84 (Aug 97) 86
(50% PN, 50% CH)
A soft and easy to drink champagne, with lots of fruit aromas.

1979 Cuvée Royale 93 (Jan 99) 94
(50% PN, 10% PM, 40% CH)
Fantastically youthful, with a beautiful honey flower nose and a sensual citrus flavour. I bought a case of this classic wine and certain bottles had already developed a toffee-flavoured maturity.

1976 Cuvée Royale 91 (Jan 99) 91
(50% PN, 50% CH)
This wine always give a clear reflection of the vintage. Anyone who values the 76's highly won't be disappointed by the extra fatness and butterscotch aroma in this champagne. The '79 is more a classic.

1975 Cuvée Royale 92 (Jan 99) 92
(47% PN, 8% PM, 45% CH)
I can't think of a better way to learn the character of different vintages than holding a vertical tasting of Joseph Perrier. The '75 is classically structured but a little less friendly than the other vintages of the seventies.

1973 Cuvée Royale 89 (Mar 96) 89
(50% PN, 50% CH)
This is powerful and definite tasting, Finishes in a lovely taste of warm bread.

1985 Josephine 91 (Jan 99) 93
(50% PN, 50% CH)
Josephine is one of the new prestige cuvées. It's inspired by the ***Belle Epoque*** with its flower-adorned bottle, and the contents are just as romantic and sensual as the original. ***Josephine*** has joined the ranks of classic prestige cuvées. The '85 is much like the '82, although slightly less developed. The nose is full of sweet honey tones and Earl Greyish aromas, and the flavour can be compared with a juicy peach.

1982 Josephine 94 (Jan 99) 94
(55% PN, 45% CH)
Closed in the glass, strangely enough, considering that the aromas are so sweet and ripe. Ten minutes later an explosion of coconut, bergamot oil, mint and coffee. A sweet, long and almost erotic flavour.

Cent Cinquantenaire 90
(50% PN, 50% CH)
It took a long time before I found a bottle of this threatened species in England. The house style is instantly recognisable, and the step up from the vintage wine is hardly noticeable. Just as with ***Grand Siècle***, this cuvée de prestige is made from grapes from three vintages.

Albert le Brun

93 av. de Paris, 51016 Châlons ☎ 03 26 68 18 68

Production: 300,000 bottles.

This house is one of two left in what was once an important champagne town. The Le Brun family have held the reins ever since the start in 1860 in Avize. The cellars they own today are the ones that Napoleon rewarded Jacquesson for.

Cuvée Reservée Brut 52
(65% PN, 35% CH)
A non-vintage champagne made from Hautvillers, Vertus, Avize, Bethon and Troissy. A rustic wine with a bone-dry aftertaste and a rough, bread-like nose.

A. le Brun B. d. B. 81
(100% CH)
Without doubt the company's best wine. A pure Avize champagne with a scent of ripe apples. Perhaps the resemblance to apple cider is too great.

1983 Cuvée Reservée 69 (Jul 90) 74
(41% PN, 59% CH)
Strong nose of licorice and almond cake. Bushy and restless on the palate.

1986 Vieille France 72 (Jul 90) 77
(54% PN, 46% CH)
Very similar to the preceding wine, with an added taste of apples in the finish.

1983 Vieille France 73 (Jul 90) 80
(54% PN, 46% CH)
Very weak but rather elegant nose. Rather more restrained than the '86, but shorter in growth.

1986 Vieille France Rosé 70 (Jul 90) 73
(80% PN, 20% CH)
Dark and heavy thoughout its figure. Powerful smokiness in both taste and nose, with a slighly clumsy licorice finish. This champagne demands meat!

Societe Champenoise d'exploitation vinicole

51016 Châlons ☎ 03 26 68 18 68

Chenevaux Premier 53
A light colour with some copper tones. The champagne is a little rough, with elements of red apples and bread, and a touch of bitterness in the finish.

ÉPERNAY

There is hardly a person alive in Épernay who isn't connected to the champagne industry in some way. There are 25 champagne houses in the town, with Moët, Pol Roger, Perrier-Jouët and Mercier the most famous. Several are located on the grand street Avenue de Champagne which opens by the giant Moët & Chandon by the town's obelisk. The fact is that Épernay also has vineyards just outside the town rated 88% on the cru scale. These 222 hectares are owned by the houses and 26 grower/producers.

% 88% 25% PN, 24% PM, 51% CH

Pol Roger

1 rue Henri Lelarge, 51206 Épernay ☎ 03 26 59 58 00

Production: 1.4 million bottles.

No-one else means more to their house than Christian Pol-Roger. The manner in which he welcomes wine lovers in Champagne is beyond compare. Christian both looks and acts like some English aristocrat, with a dry humour that wouldn't shame Sir Alec Guiness. His joyful lifestyle is as charming and effervescent as his champagne. He loves his house, his home town and his champagne and lets his friends share his delight.

Together with Christian de Billy he runs Winston Churchill's favourite house in the same spirit as his ancestors. Christian de Billy, the son of an air force officer and his wife, born Antoinette Pol-Roger, is an affable greying man of about sixty. He is perfectly suited to the rule of guardian of the temple. The house was founded in 1849 by Pol Roger, who was succeeded by his sons Maurice and Georges. At the turn of the century the Roger family changed its name to Pol-Roger.

Maurice was the mayor of Épernay during the week-long occupation of the town by the Germans in September, 1914. Despite the German threats to shoot him and burn the town, he remained ramrod-straight and later hailed as a hero of his town. He was voted honorary mayor for life.

England has always been the main export market for Pol Roger, and when Winston Churchill died the wine's label was black-edged in his memory. When the period of mourning was deemed to be over, the *1975 Cuvée Sir Winston Churchill* was launched, in magnums only. The wine is made in a style they believe Winston would have appreciated. His favourite vintages were 1928, 34 and 47.

Today the firm owns 85 hectares of vineyards, most of them close to Épernay: Mardeuil, Chouilly, Pierry, Moussy, Chavot, Cuis, Cramant and Grauves. They meet 45% of the firm's needs, and the rest is taken from Pinot villages to give the wine backbone. Pol Roger's vinification is quite normal, which leads me to the conclusion that the secret lies in the quality of the grapes and above all the skill of James Coffinet in assembling the cuvées. The wines are medium-bodied with a lovely fruity balance and perfect dosage. The mousse is exemplary, with smaller bubbles than usual because of a cellar temperature half a degree below the average.

I love the entire range of the firm's product, although I am still slightly critical of the idea of three prestige cuvées. If they had only made one on top of the vintage wine, then the quality of the two would probably be even higher. Who is king of Épernay — Pol Roger or Perrier-Jouët? It depends on who's in form on the day!

Pol Roger Brut 80
(33% PN, 33% PM, 34% CH)
Some of the best bottles of non-vintage champagne I have tasted have been well-stored Pol Roger. The ability to age with grace despite its Pinot Meunier content is the wine's best asset. In recent years some sharp and thin examples of this wine have disappointed me, but now we are back on track again.

Pol Roger Extra Dry 80
(33% PN, 33% PM, 34% CH)
Reserved for England. This champagne has a nice bottle age, and an effervescent charm.

Pol Roger Demi-Sec 55
(33% PN, 33% PM, 34% CH)
This is one of the best in this uninteresting category. The light-hearted house style handles the sugar quite well.

1988 Pol Roger Rosé 84 (Aug 98) 89
(60% PN, 40% CH)
Very pure and delicate with better structure than the '86, but without its sensual style.

1986 Pol Roger Rosé 80 (Jul 94) 89
(65% PN, 35% CH)
After I had said this wine tasted like Billecart-Salmon, Christian Pol-Roger revealed it was James Coffinet's first champagne for Pol Roger. He had earlier worked for Billecart. Fine pale colour, ultra-elegantly pure and fruity. Weak hints of nut and raspberry.

1985 Pol Roger Rosé 60 (Mar 93) ?
(65% PN, 35% CH)
Orange colour, remarkable lavender nose. Unusual and spicy. However, the taste is better, with restrained acidity and a correct structure. Needs retasting.

1982 Pol Roger Rosé 86 (Dec 98) 86
(65% PN, 35% CH)
By no means an obvious rosé if you don't consider the colour. The nose is heavy and complex, with hints of diesel fumes, thorn bushes and smoke. Aromas of woodlands are present in the full-bodied but vigorous taste.

1979 Pol Roger Rosé 89 (Jul 96) 89
(75% PN, 25% CH)
A salmon-pink rosé, with an abundance of ripe fruits and toasty aromas. Exellent acidity.

1990 Pol Roger 86 (Feb 99) 91
(60% PN, 40% CH)
So typical Pol Roger style. Sophisticated and utterly charming. Fruity, creamy and lingering.

1989 Pol Roger 85 (Apr 97) 90
(60% PN, 40% CH)
More generous than the '88, with a mighty nose of mature Pinot Noir and a bold, rich and juicy flavour of mature Chardonnay. The house style isn't lost however, despite the rich vintage.

1988 Pol Roger 85 (Jul 98) 90
(60% PN, 40% CH)
Pol Roger's vintage champagne ages well. It wouldn't surpise me if the '88 transformed dramatically after the year 2000. Today this is a tight, restrained champagne with purity and a stunning dryness.

1986 Pol Roger 85 (Feb 95) 89
(60% PN, 40% CH)
Much more generous than the '88 even when launched, and very enjoyable today. The spectrum of aromas includes jasmine, orchids, sweets and lemon. The taste is juicy and well-balanced, refreshing and lush.

1985 Pol Roger 85 (Dec 93) 90
(60% PN, 40% CH)
Classic vintage champagne with a convincingly tight structure. Pure fruit dominates the biscuity aromas. Complex medium-bodied taste with a long acidic aftertaste of green apples.

1983 Pol Roger 86 (Oct 98) 86
(60% PN, 40% CH)
The '83 should been viewed as a failure for Pol Roger, especially when you consider that no prestige cuvées were made this year. So the best grapes are in this rather insignificant wine. Totaly matured in 1998.

1982 Pol Roger 88 (Jul 98) 89
(60% PN, 40% CH)
The entire wine is typical of the vintage. Broad nose of bread and rich fruit. Medium-bodied and soft with vanilla aftertaste. The wine has developed a touch too rapidly these past few years for it to be a real long-term hope.

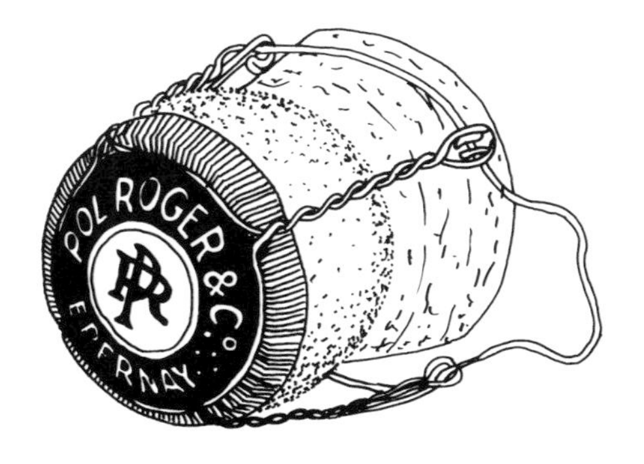

1979 Pol Roger 88 (Jan 99) 88
(60% PN, 40% CH)
Tasted when freshly disgorged and without dosage in Pol Roger's cellar. Needs dosage and a few more years in the bottle! Not a generous wine, with a slightly thin structure, but clear aromas. The same wine normally disgorged and without dosage is quite flat but superb in magnums.

1976 Pol Roger 91 (May 98) 91
(60% PN, 40% CH)
The '76 is much fatter and more developed than the '75. The wine is extremely generous, with strong aromas of chocolate and coffee. The maturity is impressive and the sweetness rich. Hardly a great vintage but a good champagne.

1975 Pol Roger 94 (Oct 98) 94
(60% PN, 40% CH)
The '75 is a buttery, seductive and loveable champagne. The fruit is very rich and the nut aromas are almost woody. Rich, soft and balanced.

1973 Pol Roger 91 (Jul 97) 91
(60% PN, 40% CH)
Lusty and homogenous with its rich chocolate-like mature style.

1971 Pol Roger 87 (Mar 97) 87
(60% PN, 40% CH)
Pol Roger presents quite a powerful '71, with a big, muscular body and chocolate aromas. Low acidity and on the way to losing its grip on what holds the building-blocks together.

1966 Pol Roger 94 (Nov 98) 94
(65% PN, 35% CH)
Tasted both freshly-disgorged and normally-disgorged. Like all of Pol Roger's wines they gain from maturing in the bottle. That's when the new-baked bread is revealed and the citrus fruits progress to a peach-like complexity. Very long, full taste of chocolate and marzipan, and one of the most prolonged aftertastes I've experienced.

1961 Pol Roger 94 (Apr 95) 94
(65% PN, 35% CH)
Great bottle variation, but always wonderfully creamy, soft and peach-flavoured despite the dark, aged colour. Much more charming than many tough 61's. Old champagne, when it succeeds in combining the tones of old wood with apricot and peach aromas, is one of the most enjoyable things in the world. Certain bottles of *Pol Roger 61* have reached even higher on the points scale.

1955 Pol Roger 95 (Dec 98) 95
(60% PN, 40% CH)
A wonderfully well-kept champagne with toasty and nutty aromas. The fruit is intense and exotic. The aftertaste is a little short.

1952 Pol Roger 93 (Nov 98) 93
(70% PN, 30% CH)
Tom Stevenson's favourite champagne! Incredibly light and well-maintained. Almost like a champagne from the eighties. Delicate young sweet nose of cream, sweets and white flowers. The taste is bursting and light with elegant notes of bread and creamy Chardonnay fruit.

1949 Pol Roger 96 (Feb 99) 96
(60% PN, 40% CH)
Quite wonderfully fresh and elegant, somewhat lighter than expected but with a Krug-like depth and elegance. It reminded me of a '66. The nose is dominated by candy floss, peach and exotic fruit.

1947 Pol Roger 96 (May 97) 96
(70% PN, 30% CH)
Winston Churchill's favourite champagne and "a Churchill of a wine" according to Christian Pol-Roger. This magnum '47 was planned as the highlight of a Pol Roger dinner in Stockholm in 1993. Imagine my disappointment when the 500 dollar magnum had transformed into madeira and was poured away at once. Of course Christian let me taste a recently-disgorged bottle from his cellar which was almost too young but wonderfully complex and balanced.

1945 Pol Roger 94 (Jan 99) 94
(70% PN, 30% CH)
The wine is just as splendid as it should be from this year of peace. A colossal cognac-like bouquet with hints of walnut and plum. The taste is superbly vital, like an lady who has aged with grace. Pol Roger in good form.

1928 Pol Roger
(70% PN, 30% CH)
Only one badly stored and maderised bottle tasted. Unjudged. Should still be magnificent.

1914 Pol Roger 97 (Oct 98) 97
(80% PN, 20% CH)
It's hard not to be influenced by the occasion when one is drinking a ***1914 Pol Roger*** together with the owner in Winston Churchill's favourite room in the house. To then hear Christian tell the fascinating story about this wine was almost too much. The greatest wine experience of my life! Remove the story and occasion from your thoughts and the wine is still no disappointment. The bottles do apparently vary greatly, but the one I had the honour of tasting was perfect. The colour was deep and shining like a golden pagoda. Weak but consistent mousse. Remarkably large, complex nose with loads of sweetmeats, honey, rum, chocolate, coffee and syrup. The taste was chewy and tremendously sweet, almost like an old sauternes.

1988 Blanc de Chardonnay 82 (Jul 97) 88
(100% CH)
This label is so consistent throughout the years. The '88 is charming and distinguished, with a light citrus tone and soft aftertaste.

1986 Blanc de Chardonnay 80 (Apr 95) 87
(100% CH)
Pol Roger has, as we know, many fine Chardonnay vineyards. The style of their ***Blanc de Chardonnay*** is always broad, polished and refined, but it lacks the depth and concentration of the true greats. The '86 is slightly creamy with a young, fresh and flowery bouquet. Somewhat lighter than the vintage champagne of the same year.

1985 Blanc de Chardonnay 84 (Feb 95) 89
(100% CH)
Classical and typical for the house, with a lovely youthfulness. The fruit is bursting with vitality and under the surface lie weak tones of freshly-ground coffee beans.

1982 Blanc de Chardonnay 92 (Nov 98) 92
(100% CH)
A great favourite among journalists that has never fully convinced me. The mineral tones are stony, almost earthy, disturbing the rich, buttery and orange-like Chardonnay taste.

1979 Blanc de Chardonnay 87 (Dec 89) 91
(100% CH)
It took ten years for the skeleton to get some meat on the bones. Only then did a volatile bouquet of lemon, hawthorn and toasted bread and a well-balanced buttery softness emerge. Perfect aperitif wine.

1959 Blanc de Chardonnay 95 (Apr 98) 95
(100% CH)
The debut year for Pol Roger's Chardonnay champagne. At the age of 36, still a light colour and a lively mousse. Aromas of tobacco, chocolate and lime. The house style and character of the grape become more recognisable in the taste, Creamy, acidic and well-balanced, with a very long, strong and somewhat sharp finish rich in tannin.

1988 P.R. 92 (Jan 99) 95
(50% PN, 50% CH)
Here Pol Roger has hit the nail on the head. The '88 is quite wonderful today, with its sensual bouquet and crystal-clear, balanced flavour. If you have the patience then put a few bottles in your cellar and eventually you'll experience something even more magical. The best ***P.R.*** I've tasted.

1986 P.R. 88 (May 95) 91
(50% PN, 50% CH)
For me the ***P.R.*** is just as great a champagne as the ***Cuvée Sir Winston Churchill***. The '86 is as light as that vintage usually is, with lots of citrus and mineral aromas. The taste is flowery and light with a long, elegant Chardonnay aftertaste.

1985 P.R. 90 (Jan 94) 92
(50% PN, 50% CH)
The '85 is a robust, massive wine, more toasty and nutty than the ***Winston Churchill*** but slightly less concentrated. Tasting them together is always a great experience.

1982 P.R. 90 (Apr 93) 92
(50% PN, 50% CH)
The '82 resembles ***Dom Pérignon*** in many ways. A little lighter than usual and with a more toasty and exotic fruity style. The aftertaste contains many citrus aromas and hints of mango and peach.

1979 P.R. 92 (Feb 90) 93
(50% PN, 50% CH)
It's incredible that the Pinot content isn't greater. The wine reveals a heavy, almost Bollinger-like, robust character with strong chocolate and powerful, oily aftertaste. The '79 lacks some elegance but is a very impressive wine.

1986 Cuvée Sir Winston Churchill 89 (Jun 98) 92
(secret)
Christian Pol-Roger refuses to reveal the grape content after making a promise to the Churchill family. However, I think my guess of 65-70% Pinot Noir and the rest

Chardonnay is close to the truth. The wine is made mainly from the firm's own Grand cru vineyards. This is the wine from Pol Roger that needs the longest storage. The '86 is hard and young, but has a great richness of extracts and a high concentration.

1985 Cuvée Sir Winston Churchill 93 (May 97) 96
(secret)
The favourite champagne among Swedish journalists. It combines magnificent richness of taste and concentration with a public fruity style. Both the nose and taste create a silky-smooth impression and a layer of toasty aromas spice the rich fruit. A great wine.

1982 Cuvée Sir Winston Churchill 92 (Jan 99) 92
(secret)
Like the ordinary '82, very typical for its year. That means that the wine is also a touch impersonal. This year the ***Winston Churchill*** was definitely lighter than *P.R.* Superb toasty aromas in magnums.

1979 Cuvée Sir Winston Churchill 83 (Jan 88) 90
(secret)
Tasted only once, early in my career. My impression was that the '79 was very elegant and well-balanced, full of promising fruit but lacking that extra dimension that you expect from a cuvée de prestige. Needs retasting.

1975 Cuvée Sir Winston Churchill 95 (Apr 97) 97
(Secret)
The first vintage of this cuvée was made in magnums only. Christian Pol-Roger was kind enough to allow me to taste a recently-disgorged magnum of this classic. The nose wasn't fully developed, but the flavour was phenomenal. What depth! What length! An almost perfect champagne with dense fruit and toasty aromas.

Perrier-Jouët

26 av. de Champagne,
51201 Épernay 03 26 53 38 00
Production: 3 million bottles.

This house was founded in 1811 by Pierre-Nicolas-Marie Perrier-Jouët. Under the leadership of his son Charles the company became famous with its nickname P-J. In 1959 Mumm bought a majority shareholding in the company and the house became part of the Canadian Seagram group. Michael Budin, who led the firm up until the late eighties, was a great admirer of Art noveau and opended a Belle Epoque museum in 1990, twenty years after launching the cuvée de prestige of the same name.

Belle Epoque has become a great success everywhere, and the Americans in particular have fallen for the flower-bedecked bottle. The house owns 108 hectares in seven villages and the other 65% of the grapes are bought in from 40 villages. The most important village is Cramant, where the firm owns 29 hectares of the very best slopes. Compared to other houses the heritage has been kept well.

The vines are very old and produce fantastic grapes that can dominate an entire cuvée even if small in proportion to the total content, and the delicate house style is dependent on these Chardonnay grapes. Perrier-Jouët compete with neighbouring house Pol Roger for the number one spot in Épernay. Both make fruity medium-bodied champagnes in a broad and sophisticated style, but Pol Roger's wines are somewhat drier and Perrier-Jouët's more personal. The vintage wine is a classic and both the *Belle Epoque* wines are a great source of joy for the romantic wine lover.

Perrier-Jouët Brut 69
(33% PN, 45% PM, 22% CH)
Far greater Chardonnay aroma than the grape content reveals. Always a fruity, well-balanced non-vintage champagne of the lighter style. The citrus aromas becomes nutty with age.

1976 Perrier-Jouët Rosé 90 (Jun 97) 92
(70% PN, 30% CH)
The wine was so pale that my friends doubted it was a pink we were drinking. The nose was typical for a rosé from the seventies, with a basic tone of rose-hip, strawberries and a slight, sour tone that separates them from their white opposite numbers. A well-structured, balanced '76 that will develop.

1990 Perrier-Jouët 87 (Feb 98) 93
(40% PN, 33% PM, 27% CH)
Lovely as usual with a developed fruity and toasty nose. Naturally a biscuit aroma and all the sweet richness we've come to expect.

1988 Perrier-Jouët 82 (Dec 94) 90
(40% PN, 33% PM, 27% CH)
It took a few years for me to discover just how good the ordinary vintage wine from Perrier-Jouët really is. Now I never miss a vintage as the wine is always well-made and full of Chardonnay elegance. The '88 is still young, but one catches a hint of freshly-baked bread, the ready-to-burst Chardonnay and the silky-smooth fruity taste.

1985 Perrier-Jouët 93 (Nov 98) 94
(40% PN, 30% PM, 30% CH)
Hugely well developed, flowery nose with hints of spun sugar, sweets, popcorn, coffee beans, chocolate biscuits and raspberry vinegar. After this broadside of scent impressions it's lovely to sip the unified taste, where peach and toffee set the tone. A veritable bullseye! Extremly toasty in magnums.

1982 Perrier-Jouët 90 (Nov 92) 92
(60% PN, 40% CH)
Even better than the ***Belle Epoque*** of the same vintage. A fabulous toasty and buttery bouquet. A balanced, creamy taste with medium body.

1978 Perrier-Jouët
(60% PN, 40% CH)
Only a badly stored bottle tasted. Unjudged.

1976 Perrier-Jouët 90 (Jul 91) 90
(60% PN, 40% CH)
Fully mature and slightly overloaded with heavy fruit and vanilla aromas. Fabulously rich, but a little too powerful and sweet.

1975 Perrier-Jouët 90 (Sep 96) 90
(60% PN, 40% CH)
Rather waxy nose, but good dry, crisp taste. Fairly powerful yet elegant.

1964 Perrier-Jouët 95 (Jul 93) 95
(60% PN, 40% CH)
Old champagne with its aromas at their most lovely. Unusually developed, could even be ten years older. "After Eight" and toffee dominate both taste and nose. A medium-bodied taste carried by a weak mousse and reasonable acidity, very long. Drink soon.

1961 Perrier-Jouët 94 (Dec 98) 94
(60% PN, 40% CH)
Wonderfully toasty and buttery with all the flowers of the garden wrapped in an oily structure. The '61 has many years left on the scene.

1959 Perrier-Jouët 93 (Oct 97) 93
(60% PN, 40% CH)
Almost still, but light in colour and very creamy in style.

1953 Perrier-Jouët 93 (Apr 94) 93
(60% PN, 40% CH)
Incredibly one can detect the firm's style clearly in this aged wine. A certain oxidation and weak mousse. But a great wine that has probably been even greater. Rich, toffee-like and gracefully scented in the middle of the nineties. Very complex. A few years left.

1947 Perrier-Jouët
(60% PN, 40% CH)
A perfect looking magnum was totally maderised in October 97. Unjudged.

1943 Perrier-Jouët 93 (Oct 97) 93
(50% PN, 50% CH)
A majestic and powerful champagne typical of the vintage.

1928 Perrier-Jouët 92 (Jan 99) 92
(60% PN, 40% CH)
My first wine from the vintage to end all vintages. The champagne was just as majestic as I had hoped, but only for a couple of minutes. After that the wine is maderised very rapidly even though the heroic structure remains. The colour was quite golden, and the mousse was detectable in the mouth. The great nose hinted of cream and beachcombed wood. The aftertaste was amazingly long and rich, with veal and port wine my immediate association.

Blason de France 83
(36% PN, 34% PM, 30% CH)
Much cheaper than *Belle Epoque* and perhaps better value for money. Rich, mature character in a slightly fuller style than the firm's other prestige cuvées.

Blason de France Rosé 86
(47% PN, 27% PM, 26% CH)
Young and delicate aroma of green apples. An inferior wine to *Belle Epoque Rosé*, but even here there are hints of orange. This rosé ages very well.

1973 Blason de France 93 (Oct 96) 93
(60% PN, 40% CH)
The wine is very similar to the *Belle Epoque* from the same year, if somewhat less intense. The balance between the contrasts is taken from the higher school and this delicate wine demands your full attention if it is to give the best effect.

1966 Blason de France 95 (Jul 95) 95
(60% PN,40% CH)
Fabulously well-balanced and fresh champagne with enormous attack and rich citrus fruit. A hint of chanterelle mushrooms in the nose.

1989 Belle Epoque 93 (Jan 99) 95
(30% PN, 22% PM, 48% CH)
A magical wine whose super-elegant toasty form is so reminiscent of a fine *Montrachet*. The nose explodes in the glass with tones of flowers, fruit and roasted coffee. The flavour is exotic and classical simultaneously, with an amazingly enjoyable toffee finish.

1988 Belle Epoque 90 (Dec 98) 94
(30% PN, 22% PM, 48% CH)
The first times I tasted *Belle Epoque* I thought the bottle was more beautiful than the contents. In recent years I've been converted. The wines always have a brilliant flowery elegance which they keep for many years. Added to the elegance is a nutty and roasted coffee aroma of true greatness. The '88 has all these qualities encapsulated in a youthful shell.

1985 Belle Epoque 93 (Jan 99) 95
(50% PN, 50% CH)
A more elegant cuvée champagne does not exist! The wine is full of young, subtle nuances. If you know how beautifully the '73 (for example) developed you will understand how these aromas are magnified with the years. Today one is met by a scent like a bouquet of flowers in the spring, and a rich but restrained fruit aroma backed up by vanilla, coffee and saffron.

1983 Belle Epoque 90 (Jan 99) 92
(50% PN, 50% CH)
The nose is full of aromas that wrestle with each other without ever really reaching out. It is as if someone has placed a lid over the wine: if it is lifted off the wine will bloom in a lovely manner. The taste is light and Chardonnay-influenced with a clear vanilla aroma.

1982 Belle Epoque 82 (Sep 91) 86
(50% PN/PM, 50% CH)
The ordinary vintage wine and the rosé are better than the *Belle Epoque* of this year. Probably so much effort went into delicacy that the wine turned out a little thin. The aromas are fine but weak, and the acidity is relatively low.

1979 Belle Epoque 94 (Jan 98) 94
(50% PN/PM, 50% CH)
The '79 has a nose like an entire coffee-roasting house. The taste is more creamy, like coffee-flavoured ice cream. Relatively light but wonderfully long and full of aromas.

1976 Belle Epoque 91 (Mar 97) 91
(50% PN/PM, 50% CH)
Not quite the elegance we're used to. The vintage has left its fat fingerprints here. Very nice, naturally.

1975 Belle Epoque 91 (Jan 96) 91
(50% PN/PM, 50% CH)
Slightly disappointing considering the vintage, it is in any case a delightfully elegant champagne with lively acidity, mousse and a rich fruit with exotic overtones.

1973 Belle Epoque 95 (Nov 94) 95
(50% PN/PM, 50% CH)
Light orange with exceptional mousse. Fantastically delicate, complex nose where the flower, fruit and honey aromas fight for ascendancy. An equilibristic elegant taste. Light to medium-bodied, with hints of peach, apricot, spun sugar and vanilla cookies in the aromas. Typical — and outstanding — house style.

1988 Belle Epoque Rosé 90 (Feb 98) 94
(47% PN, 23% PM, 30% CH)
The nose has tones of petroleum like a great Riesling, but also a classical biscuit tone and dense fruit. Wonderful balance and elegance, but wait a while into the next century before loosening the cork.

1986 Belle Epoque Rosé 89 (May 94) 93
(47% PN, 23% PM, 30% CH)
Belle Epoque Rosé is one of the greatest pink champagnes. The wine has a personal style and the '86 is no exception. Lovely orange colour. Broad, deep nose of mature, musty Pinot Noir with uplifting tones of fruit and sweets. Meaty classic strawberry fruit with hints of orange and coffee. Superb elegance.

1982 Belle Epoque Rosé 93 (Jun 98) 95
(50% PN, 20% PM, 30% CH)
Mature orange colour, fine tiny prolonged bubbles. Incredibly complex elegant nose of fresh-ground coffee, roast chestnuts, tangerine and cocoa. Cristal-like and barrel-like in character. Wonderfully rich creamy orangey taste spiced with the same aromas as the nose. Delightful buttery Chardonnay finish.

1979 Belle Epoque Rosé 94 (Dec 95) 94
(50% PN, 20% PM, 30% CH)
Just as delicate and seductive as it looks. Divine elegance, a light, buttery toffee tone and a classically smooth, mature Pinot finish.

Trianon.

Moët & Chandon

20 av. de Champagne, 51333 Épernay ☎ 03 26 51 20 00
Production: 24 million bottles.

The Moët family originally comes from Holland, but has been active in Champagne since the 15th century. The champagne house was founded in 1743 by Claude Moët, but rose to fame under the leadership of Jean-Rémy in the beginning of the 19th century. Napoleon, who studied at the military academy in Brienne, became good friends with Jean-Rémy, who soon became the mayor of Épernay. It was the start of a fabulous story of success!

In order that Napoleon should have a worthy place to stay on his many visits to Champagne, the Le Trianon palace was built opposite Moët & Chandon on the Avenue de Champagne. Just before Napoleon was arrested and sent to Elba, he visited Moët to present Jean-Rémy with the Legion of Honour. Despite his defeat at Waterloo, Moët's champagne increased in popularity.

In 1832 the name was changed to Moët & Chandon and the company was successful throughout the industrialised world. Millions of bottles were being sold at the beginning of this century, and since then production has steadily increased, apart from a brief hiatus early in the nineties. Robert-Jean de Vogué was another strong man who ran the company in the thirties, and was also the man behind the C.I.V.C.

Moët & Chandon was the first champagne house introduced onto the Paris stock market in 1962, and since then the quality of their famous wines has fallen a bit. The non-vintage chamapgne is conventional, the vintage is very good but hardly as long-lived as previously. ***Dom Pérignon*** is still a very elegant champagne, but financial interests have the upper hand and the millions of bottles produced today are far too many for the wine to retain sufficiently high concentration. The company's strength lies in the large number of crus they have access to in assembling their cuvées. If the wines were stored a little longer and the yield in their Grand cru vineyards reduced, then perhaps Moët would win back those wine lovers who once had adored Moët & Chandon. Recent vintages show Moët & Chandon recovering their former glories.

Moët & Chandon Brut Imperial 65
(50% PN, 40% PM, 10% CH)
The most successful champagne in the world. A bottle of Moët is opened every other second somewhere in the world. The quality is uneven even if the basic style is consistent. The grapes are basic and storage time is only two and a half years. The mousse is fine, the nose always has hints of bready Pinot Meunier, creamed mushroom and orange. The taste can vary between elderflower in its youth to complex exotic fruits in some well-kept magnums. The dosage is often to high.

Moët & Chandon Brut Premier Cru 78
(33% PN, 33% PM, 34% CH)
Wonderful house style and charming aromas of white flowers. Easy to drink, but will probably age quite well.

Moët & Chandon Demi-Sec 30
(40% PN, 40% PM, 20% CH)
Drinkable if it is stored for four or five years after being disgorged, but if not bottle-matured it is often merely sickly sweet and oily. Strawberries are a big help in getting this down the throat.

1992 Moët & Chandon Rosé 76 (May 98) 80
(52% PN, 10% PM, 38% CH)
92's never reach greatness, and nor does this rosé. There is a range of aromas, including apricot, roses and passion fruit. A rather full but short flavour.

1990 Moët & Chandon Rosé 87 (Aug 98) 90
(47% PN, 22% PM, 31% CH)
A success that combines the house style with the stringency of the vintage in an excellent manner. Pure, clear fruit and good balance.

1988 Moët & Chandon Rosé 75 (Dec 96) 80
(60% PN, 15% PM, 25 % CH)
Deep colour, developed cheesy style with sweets and raspberry. Deep, ripe and abrupt Pinot taste.

1986 Moët & Chandon Rosé 78 (Mar 97) 79
(47% PN, 22% PM, 31% CH)
Rounded, bready and easily drunk, with a pleasant, unpretentious fruit and a rather short aftertaste.

1985 Moët & Chandon Rosé 76 (Feb 94) 81
(55% PN, 10% PM, 35% CH)
The colour was tremendously developed and orange, but the nose and taste showed more restraint. Unusually delicate rosé from the firm with mineral character.

1981 Moët & Chandon Rosé 65 (Jun 90) 70
(60% PN, 15% PM, 25% CH)
Pale colour, sweet toffee nose, rough charmless taste.

1978 Moët & Chandon Rosé 80 (Nov 95) 82
(60% PN, 15% PM, 25% CH)
Unexpectedly fresh with a nose dominated by vegetables. A very fruity flavour that lacks terroir character.

1992 Moët & Chandon 78 (May 98) 82
(45% PN, 15% PM, 40% CH)
The nose is all right, but the flavour is much too thin and short. Although Moët & Chandon should receive some praise for such a low dosage in this weak year.

1990 Moët & Chandon 88 (Jun 98) 90
(50% PN, 20% PM, 30% CH)
Moët's vintage wines are always of a relatively high class, without costing much more than the non-vintage wine. The '90 is more restrained and stricter than usual. The taste is both buttery and creamy with a weak toasty tone and lemonish complexity.

1988 Moët & Chandon 87 (Jul 96) 88
(50% PN, 20% PM, 30% CH)
Moët in a nutshell. Mature, charming nose of yeast, creamed mushroom, orange and toasted bread. Soft, weakly toasty taste with a sweet, medium-long aftertaste. Good value for money.

1986 Moët & Chandon 78 (May 92) 80
(50% PN, 20% PM, 30% CH)
A lightweight when it was launched. With a couple of years in its favour it matured extremely quickly. Strong nose of smoke, mushrooms and banana. Good soft flavour of exotic fruit and mostly passion fruit.

1985 Moët & Chandon 87 (Sep 98) 89
(50% PN, 20% PM, 30% CH)
Much more storable and stricter than the charmer of 86. The nose is weak but Chardonnay-influenced. In the mouth a very concentrated taste that stays on the palate. Less exotic than usual.

1983 Moët & Chandon 83 (Jan 91) 89
(50% PN, 20% PM, 30% CH)
A successful vintage for Moët, with the wine having a lovely nose of liver paté and creamed mushrooms. The taste is very vigorous and vibrates with fruit.

1982 Moët & Chandon 81 (Apr 94) 85
(50% PN, 20% PM, 30% CH)
If someone was to ask me to describe Moët's house style, I'd open a bottle of this champagne. A form that shouts out Moët!

1981 Moët & Chandon 85 (Nov 95) 85
(50% PN, 20% PM, 30% CH)
Very pleasant clean and creamy nose. A distinctive taste with nice weight.

1980 Moët & Chandon 70 (Dec 90) ▼
(50% PN, 20% PM, 30% CH)
For me this is a nostalgic wine, as it was the first champagne I bought. Sadly it has shown itself to be a difficult vintage, and the smoky tones of the nose have taken over completely since the beginning of the nineties.

1978 Moët & Chandon 86 (Jun 98) 86
(50% PN, 20% PM, 30% CH)
During a trip with the SAS Wine Club I bought a couple of recently-disgorged bottles of this vintage. The wine is undoubtedly fresh and fruity but lacks any great complexity and has a herbal finish of unripe grapes. The toasty nose is much better.

1976 Moët & Chandon 84 (Jan 97) 84
(50% PN, 20% PM, 30% CH)
Fleshy and heavy. Not my type of champagne. The bread aromas are good but slightly over-dimensioned.

1975 Moët & Chandon 93 (Jun 98) 94
(50% PN, 20% PM, 30% CH)
This year there was very little to choose between *Dom Pérignon* and the vintage wine. Here we have a classical tight structure with plenty of ballast, a sparkling mousse and fresh acidity. The nose is seductive after a while in the glass, oozing tones of coffee, peach and jasmine.

1973 Moët & Chandon 90 (Sep 98) 90
(50% PN, 20% PM, 30% CH)
Lively and creamy-mushroom nose, typical of the Moët house with soft acidity and mature, unified taste.

1971 Moët & Chandon 83 (Dec 96) ▼
(50% PN, 20% PM, 30% CH)
The only bottle I tasted was in worse condition than a *Silver Jubilée* from the same year. However, I was struck by the similarity in structure and the delicious mango aroma that was slightly spoiled by oxidation.

1970 Moët & Chandon 86 (Jun 98) 86
(50% PN, 20% PM, 30% CH)
Beautiful straw colour, medium large nose of berries, mango and basil. Tastes like a rich burgundy with fat, smoky Chardonnay. Very long indeed, but a bit to sweet.

1969 Moët & Chandon 86 (Aug 98) ▼
(50% PN, 20% PM, 30% CH)
Fine reddish colour and alert mousse. The Pinot Meunier part has completely collapsed! This means the wine is no longer a harmonious whole, even though the Chardonnay part is still full of vigour.

1966 Moët & Chandon 92 (Jan 97) 92
(45% PN, 20% PM, 35% CH)
This wine held its own at "a different kind of tasting". By no means a great wine, but well-kept and at its peak now. Very fine mousse despite the deep colour. Unified, mature toasty champagne nose and very ingratiating taste of nectarines. Medium long.

1964 Moët & Chandon 91 (Mar 97) 91
(50% PN, 10% PM, 40% CH)
This is almost a parody with its exaggerated tones of roasted coffee. But it is a lovely champagne with a well-composed tight taste and long toasty aftertaste.

1962 Moët & Chandon 93 (Oct 98) 93
(40% PN, 5% PM, 55% CH)
The last year of the oak barrel for the vintage wines. One notices immediately a completely different concentration and complexity in the wine. An almost artificial pear soda colour and extremely lively mousse. Large exotic nose of sweat, cheeses, sea, smoke and leather. Tastes like a ***Meursault*** with a long aftertaste of oak and nuts.

1961 Moët & Chandon 93 (Jun 97) 93
(40% PN, 5% PM, 55% CH)
Classic stuff!

1959 Moët & Chandon 94 (Dec 98) 94
(50% PN, 20% PM, 30% CH)
Volume and strength dominate this fantastic wine. I've only tasted it from a magnum, but I hardly think you'll be disappointed if you find a bottle of normal size.

1947 Moët & Chandon 94 (Aug 97) 94
(45% PN, 20% PM, 35% CH)
The mousse is hardly visible but there's a spry yellow colour and a pure chocolate nose. Magnificently full-bodied, while the wine's viscosity is bourne up by fresh acidity and a long, buttery flavour.

1945 Moët & Chandon 85 (Oct-97) ▼
(45% PN, 20% PM, 35% CH)
Wonderful for a couple of seconds, very speedy maderisation in the glass.

1921 Moët & Chandon
(45% PN, 20% PM, 35% CH)
Only three more or less maderised half-bottles tasted. Should still be magnificent in regular bottles. Unjudged.

1919 Moët & Chandon
This half-bottle may have been maderised and hardly representative but under the skin there was wonderful acidity and a buttery concentration which surely must dominate the few full-size bottles left. Unjudged.

1990 Dom Pérignon 90 (Jan 99) 95
(42% PN, 58% CH)
Very youthful and elegant with typical *Dom Pérignon* finesse. It will be a pleasure to follow the internal development of the '88 and '90. A great debut for Richard Geoffroy!

1988 Dom Pérignon 90 (May 98) 93
(55% PN, 45% CH)
Dom Pérignon is the most famous champagne in the world, and the '88 will probably become the greatest "Dom" since 1973. It's tones are as clear as the purest diamond. The nose is extremely fine. I associate it with toast, coffee beans and fresh orange-like fruit. The taste is also brilliant with clear, sharp uplifting aromas of fruit and nuts.

1985 Dom Pérignon 92 (May 97) 93
(40% PN, 60% CH)
I was more impressed with this wine when it was launched than I am today. The lovely coffee tones are there already but the exhaust-fume tone and mushroom aroma are less advantageous. The flavour is delicate and fruitly elegant with a sophisticated smoothness and long aftertaste that reminds me of toffee and oranges.

1983 Dom Pérignon 88 (May 97) 90
(50% PN, 50% CH)
A typical *Dom Pérignon* style! The wine has a style similar to many others, but once you have the wine in your glass there is no doubt as to the origin. The '83 has more orchid, creamed mushroom and diesel fumes than the '85, but fewer toasty tones. The champagne is easy to drink and juicy, rather like chewing a sweet peach.

1982 Dom Pérignon 92 (Apr 98) 93
(40% PN, 60% CH)
Tasted a score of times since May 1988, this wine is easy to identify at blind tastings. It was developed relatively slowly and has an even quality from bottle to bottle. The complex nose has a perfect balance between the Pinot and the Chardonnay. Exhaust fumes, creamed mushroom, orchids and orange are some of the most obvious aromas in this medium-bodied champagne.

1980 Dom Pérignon 90 (Mar 98) 90
(50% PN, 50% CH)
One of the best from 1980. Light, but very well-developed in its toasty style. Sea and shellfish, along with mint chocolate, are present in the wide spectrum of aromas. Fresh and crisp but somewhat too hollow to be seen as a great *Dom Pérignon*.

1978 Dom Pérignon 89 (Apr 98) 89
(50% PN, 50% CH)
Fruitier than the '80 but without its restrained elegance. An aroma of creamed mushroom and bread-like taste with well-rounded edges.

1976 Dom Pérignon 92 (Apr 95) 92
(50% PN, 50% CH)
Not one of the greats. This wine has a fully-developed golden colour, toasty bouquet and nutty taste with a smidgin of earthiness in the finish. Wide bottle variation already.

1975 Dom Pérignon 93 (May 97) 94
(50% PN, 50% CH)
A pure *Dom Pérignon* with everything in its rightful place. Perhaps this wine lacks charm compared to some other vintages, and I go against the grain in prefering the '73.

1973 Dom Pérignon 96 (Jul 98) 96
(50% PN, 50% CH)
The last of the great "Doms"? The '73 is a remarkable wine with a lovely walnut bouquet interweaved with coffee and nougat aromas. The aftertaste is oily and spotted with walnut aromas. Not quite as concentrated as the "Doms" of the sixties, but just as enjoyable aromatically and elegant.

1971 Dom Pérignon 94 (May 98) 94
(50% PN, 50% CH)
All the older vintages of *Dom Pérignon* develop a clear tone of roasted coffee beans. The '71 is full of such aromas. The taste is slightly thinner than the '73 and without its walnut tones, but the aftertaste is actually longer.

1970 Dom Pérignon 91 (May 97) 91
(50% PN, 50% CH)
A strong nose with toasty elements. The flavour is fruity and good but the wine hardly lives up to its label.

1969 Dom Pérignon 95 (May 98) 95
(50% PN, 50% CH)
The last vintage in oak barrels. Lighter than all the old vintages of *Dom Pérignon* I have tasted, with a sensual acacia honey nose and the usual hint of coffee. It dances in the mouth. Almost blanc de blancs in style. Long, pure aftertaste.

1966 Dom Pérignon 96 (May 98) 96
(50% PN, 50% CH)
A completely wonderful wine which almost brought a good friend of mine to tears. It is full of life and vigour. Similarities to *Krug 66* are many. The nose is fluent and appetising with lots of fruit aromas from apricot and peach to mango. Weak tones of chocolate, nuts, oak and coffee are there too, of course. In the mouth one can perceive the finest marmelade and small uplifting bubbles. Majestic aftertaste.

1964 Dom Pérignon 98 (Apr 98) 98
(50% PN, 50% CH)
Believe it or not, but the '64 may even be a touch sharper than the '66. The winner of a tasting with twelve of the best vintages from *Dom Pérignon*, *Krug* and *Bollinger*. This wine combined the large nutty tones of age with young acidity and fresh attack. The wine has everything, where the butterscotch taste is separated from the fruit and nut aromas. This taste remains all the way and makes up the entire, exceptionally long, aftertaste.

1962 Dom Pérignon 94 (Apr 98) 94
(50% PN, 50% CH)
One of the best 62's, although only marginally better than Moët's ordinary vintage champagne. Actually less concentrated and with a shorter aftertaste. On the plus side, a silky-smooth fruit that is always outstanding in *Dom Pérignon*.

1961 Dom Pérignon 95 (Sep 90) 95
(50% PN, 50% CH)
The only champagne given six stars by Michael Broadbent in his book on vintage wines, where the maximum is five stars! A little too impersonal for me to be equally smitten. It does however have a majestic spice-like nose with a lovely depth and cocao dominated tones. Very full-bodied and barrellish long aftertaste with several nuances, with coffee the most obvious, as usual. Needs retasting. Richard Geoffroy holds this as the best *Dom Pérignon* made after the war.

1959 Dom Pérignon 94 (Oct 98) 94
(50% PN, 50% CH)
Completely overshadowed by the *59 Cristal* at a major tasting recently. Extremely viscous with a lively mousse. A strong, nutty nose and a long almond flavour.

1955 Dom Pérignon 95 (Dec 96) 95
(50% PN, 50% CH)
Even more full-bodied and richer than any other *Dom Pérignon* vintage. Some of the finesses have been lost in this compact, unified wine. The wine's fruitiness is overshadowed by the dark, deep cellar aromas, the smokiness and the almond taste.

1952 Dom Pérignon 95 (Nov 98) 95
(50% PN, 50% CH)
A deep golden colour with a healthy mousse. A very idiosyncratic *Dom Pérignon* without the usual fruit and roast bonanza. Instead the wine is dominated by truffles, leather, meat and tar.

1943 Dom Pérignon 94 (Mar 96) 94
Apparently the same wine as the *Coronation Cuvée*. Here it held up better in the glass though. A wonderful flavour and a lovely, luxurious feel in the mouth.

1985 Dom Pérignon Rosé 94 (May 98) 96
(50% PN, 50% CH)
A marvellous wine with a nose marked by the extraordinary Aÿ Pinot. Moët & Chandon have succeeded in the art of making a wine with a powerful Pinot nose and at the same time a buttery, elegant Chardonnay texture. One of the best rosés I've tasted.

1982 Dom Pérignon Rosé 91 (Oct 97) 93
(40% PN, 60% CH)
D.P.R. is always amazingly expensive and seldom worth the money. The '82 has an orange colour, an elegant fruity nose and a powerful taste of orange sweets, leaving quite a definite impression on the palate.

1980 Dom Pérignon Rosé 90 (Oct 97) 92
(65% PN, 35% CH)
Very reminiscent of the '82, with a lovely orange bouquet and a classic taste.

1978 Dom Pérignon Rosé 86 (Sep 88) 89
(60% PN, 40% CH)
Dark red colour, cheesy nose, concentrated, fruity long taste. Sweeter and more full-bodied than the white "Dom". Certainly more winey, but less elegant. Spend your money elsewhere.

1975 Dom Pérignon Rosé 93 (Mar 95) 93
(60% PN, 40% CH)
Extremely dark red colour, mousse almost foaming. The nose is unexpectedly fruity and young, with a broad spectrum of orange, strawberry, plum, black and red-currant tones. At first the taste was young and full of strawberry. It was only in the accelerating fat aftertaste that the wine's greatness shone through.

1983 Anniversary Cuvée 83 (Oct 93) 89
(secret)
A special blend from Moët's vineyards, according to Moët themselves. For me it is confusingly similar to the ordinary '83 in a later-disgorged guise.

Moët & Chandon Silver Jubilée 1977 92 (Jan 97) 92
This jubilee bottle is actually a pure '71 with a nose of newly-washed sheets that have dried in the wind. The dominant element in both the nose and the full balanced flavour is mango.

Moët American Independence 84 (Oct 97) 84
Champagne made for the bicentennial 1776-1976.
To sweet for my taste, but charming and fresh, with aromas of almonds and ripe apples.

1943 Moët & Chandon Coronation Cuvée
94 (Sep 96) ▼
This special cuvée was made in honour of Queen Elisabeth's coronation in 1952, and gave myself and my companions a truly historic experience. The colour was deep and the nose oxidised quickly in the glass, but the fresh, majestic flavour was wonderful.

Alfred Gratien

30 rue Maurice Cerveaux,
51200 Épernay
03 26 54 38 20

Production: 150,000 bottles.

Founded in 1864 in Épernay, this is one of the most traditional champagne houses. All wines are fermented in small oak barrels and the reserve wines are stored in large oak vats. The malolactic fermentation is also avoided. The chief reason why Gratien doesn't make wines as great as Bollinger or Krug is that the grapes purchased from outside are not of the same class. Pinot Meunier also makes up a surprisingly large proportion of the grape content. The wines that are made by Jean-Pierre Jaeger are very good. Champagnes for the cellar.

A. Gratien Brut 75
(10% PN, 45% PM, 45% CH)
One of my favourite non-vintages a few years ago. Today the nose is often sharp and acidic. However, still an above-average champagne.

A. Gratien Rosé 67
(20% PN, 20% PM, 60% CH)
Young, sharp malic acidity tone down the other qualities of the wine. One of few oak-fermented rosés. Needs to be stored in order to smooth the sharp edges and lengthen the aftertaste.

1989 A. Gratien 89 (Nov 98) 91
(10% PN, 30% PM, 60% CH)
Much more open and opulent than the '88. Already honeyed and rich, With an acidic long aftertaste.

1988 A. Gratien 90 (Nov 98) 94
(16% PN, 26% PM, 58% CH)
Closed on the nose at first, after some breathing glorious nut chocolate aromas emerge. Dry, clean, acidic and extremely long lingering taste.

1985 A. Gratien 85 (Oct 97) 88
(24% PM, 76% CH)
Lovely flowery bouquet and minty aromas. A strange wine when it was released, but today it is very elegant.

1983 A. Gratien 91 (Nov 98) 93
(33% PN, 6% PM, 61% CH)
Many similarities with Bollinger's wonderful '83. Classically nutty and woody nose. Powerful, balanced taste with good attack.

1982 A. Gratien 86 (Nov 98) 91
(40% PN, 20% PM, 40% CH)
The toasty aromas border on burnt rubber and are slightly exaggerated. The taste is undeveloped, but very promising.

1979 A. Gratien 91 (Nov 98) 91
(22% PN, 22% PM, 56% CH)
Quite mature with a lovely combination of exotic fruit and toasty aromas. Actually already on the slippery slope downhill, with acidity beginning to soften and the fruit losing strength. Some bottles are still very fresh.

1976 A. Gratien 87 (Sep 92) 87
(14% PN, 15% PM, 71% CH)
Rather one-dimensional, like many 76's. Weak nose, but with heavy, meaty tones. Hard finish of an initially creamy-smooth taste.

1969 A Gratien 93 (Mar 94) 93
(22% PN, 39% PM, 39% CH)
One of my greatest wine experiences at the end of the eighties, but when I drank it in March 1994 my impressions were of a lower key. The nose is mature and biscuity, the taste fresh and elegant. The aftertaste gives this wine its high class, lasting for several minutes.

1969 A. Gratien B. d. B. 93 (Oct 97) 93
(100% CH)
Very fresh and acidic, but at the same time old aromas of almonds and mushrooms. A bit thin in the aftertaste.

1966 A. Gratien
(30% PN, 30% PM, 40% CH)
Brownish colour, weak mousse, tokay and madeira in nose and taste, but still drinkable. Unjudged.

1964 A. Gratien 94 (May 92) 94
(100% CH)
Not the conventional '64, but a special cuvée that is offered freshly-disgorged on grand occasions at Gratien. Aromas typical of the vintage: coffee, mint, biscuits, vanilla, dwarf banana, honeysuckle and cream. Almost the perfect nose. The taste is a little too steely and light.

1955 A. Gratien 98 (Oct 97) 98
(100% CH)
Only Mesnil and Cramant. An absolutely fantastic champagne with extraordinary mousse and green/yellow colour. Excellent flowery bouquet with hits of lime, wet stones and brioche. Perfect balance and as close to perfection you can get.

1953 A. Gratien 82 (Jul 90) 82
(100% CH)
Aged amber colour of good clarity. Lovely nose of dried fruits, mocha and banana. Full-bodied taste with hints of old wood and unfortunately a large dose of madeira in the aftertaste. Better kept bottles should still be good.

Cuvée Paradis 85
(16% PN, 26% PM, 58% CH)
Gratien's new cuvée de prestige is a pure '90. Still a closed nose, but on airing it reveals vanilla, honeysuckle and violet. The taste is light and elegant, not at all typical for the house, but delicate.

Cuvée Paradis Rosé 80
(20% PN, 20% PM, 60% CH)
Another pure '90 with slightly minty, discreet and elegant nose, unexpectedly weak, delicate taste with no direct rosé character. Rather like the white variety.

Leclerc-Briant

67 rue Chaude-Ruelle, 51204 Épernay ☎ 03 26 54 45 33
Production: 250,000 bottles.

Lucien Leclerc made his first bottles of champagne in 1872 and since 1978 the grandson Pascal Leclerc-Briant stood at the tiller for 30 hectares of classic property. Vineyards in six villages of which Cumières produces a large part of the grapes. It is in Cumières that Leclerc-Briant make three fantastic Clos wines in a series called "Les Authentiques". Better examples of the importance of the soil are hard to find, and the laughably low prices don't hurt either.

All three *Les Crayères — Chèvres Pierreuses* and *Clos des Champions* — are some of the best non-vintage wines Champagne has to offer. Pascal Leclerc, one of the region's most innovative winemakers, grows his crop biodynamically and is a pioneer when it comes to teaching visitors about Champagne's unique conditions. I thought long and hard before placing Leclerc-Briant after Moët & Chandon in Épernay. Seen historically, Leclerc-Briant doesn't have a chance against Moët's incredible series of old vintages, but if we consider what the firm offers today then a house that produces three non-vintage champagnes just under the 90-point line is to be reckoned with. The choice wasn't easy.

Leclerc-Briant Extra Brut 69
(70% PN, 30% PM)
Even though the non-vintage wine isn't in the same league as the Les Authentiques series, it maintains high class with its delicate, fragile and lime-tasting style.

Leclerc-Briant Brut Resérve 74
(70% PN, 30% CH)
Greater freshness and pureness in the fruit than the previous wine. Low dosage and a mature aftertaste of licorice.

Leclerc-Briant B. d. B. 79
(100% CH)
Only tasted briefly, but my impression was positive. Lime, coffee and juicy fruit.

Clos des Champions 85
(70% PN, 30% CH)
This is one of three Clos wines in the fantastic Les Authentiques series. The wines are sold together at a ridiculously low price. The wines are not vintage, although those I have tasted were pure 1990. All three are harvested from old vines, with an average age of thirty. Clos des Champions is a walled-in area with an extremely warm micro-climate. This wine is the richest of the three, with a sensual nose and full of white flowers and exotic fruit. A good initial attack and citrus tones. Long, fat aftertaste of mature Pinot.

Chèvres Pierreuses 86
(55% PN, 5% PM, 40% CH)
The tiny five percent Pinot Meunier comes from some of the oldest vines I've seen in Champagne — around 100 years old! This is my favourite of the three. The nose is a masterwork, where goat's cheese, minerals and yellow roses compete for the upper hand. It has a perfect balance in the mouth with its appetising acidity, lime and lemon tones and long taste of honey.

Les Crayères 84
(90% PN, 10% PM)
Here we see the importance of the soil. This area is named after the mineral-rich chalk earth. The fact is the wine has nearly the same aromas as a blanc de blancs from Côte des Blancs even though it's a blanc de noirs! This is the lightest of the three, the nose is cold, fresh and flowery with a large portion of lime aroma. The taste continues on the same discreet theme. The aperitif of the trilogy.

1989 Rubis de Noirs Rosé 80 (Jul 97) 83
(100% PN)
Juicy, focused, sophisticated and tasty, but lacking any meaningful potential. Buttery finish.

1988 Divine 84 (May 95) 89
(50% PN, 50% CH)
Perhaps not as close to the gods as the name suggests, but very rich and enjoyable with a lovely Pinot structure and substantial fruity nose, where plum and sticks of rock are present. The colour is deep and indicates a greater content of Pinot than is actually the case.

Heidsieck & Monopole

17 av. de Champagne,
51200 Épernay ☎ 03 26 59 50 50
Production: 1.5 million bottles.

This is a label which became part of the Canadian Seagram group in 1972, but later the house was taken over by the Vranken group in October 1996. The honourable Reims house owns 112 hectares of first-class Pinot country in Verzenay, Bouzy, Verzy and Ambonnay, amongst others. They also owned the mill in Verzenay and the vineyards that accompany it. The firm, which was first called Heidsieck & Co, was founded in 1834 and took its present name in 1923. It was first when I had the chance to taste some of the sixties vintages that I understood how good Heidsieck & Monopole had once been. Those wines that are sold today are sadly of much lower class.

Heidsieck & Monopole Brut 56
(45% PN, 25% PM, 30% CH)
Despite a large proportion of high class Pinot grapes, this is a constantly one-dimensional and charmless, if concentrated, champagne.

Heidsieck & Monopole Demi-Sec 40
(45% PN, 25% PM, 30% CH)
Heavy and powerful with an oily structure.

1982 Heidsieck & Monopole 70 (Dec 91) 79
(67% PN, 33% CH)
A lustreless colour without clarity, together with an exaggerated foaming mousse hardly invites confidence in the wine's other qualities. The nose is yeasty and heavy and the flavour continues along the same lines.

1979 Heidsieck & Monopole 82 (Oct 96) 82
(67% PN, 33% CH)
Despite its toasty aromas this was a weak, watery vintage at a time when the firm had entered a rut. When will they come out of it?

1975 Heidsieck & Monopole 90 (Feb 96) 90
(67% PN, 33% CH)
More harmonious and mature than *Diamant Bleu* from the same year. The wine is fresher than the '73 but displays much the same aromatic spectrum.

1973 Heidsieck & Monopole 88 (Jan 96) 88
(67% PN, 33% CH)
Chocolate, nut and honey are the first things I associate with the flavour and nose of this smooth, mature wine. That perfect stringency may be missing, but the aromatic spectrum is extremely enjoyable.

1969 Heidsieck & Monopole 94 (Jul 95) 94
(67% PN, 33% CH)
An old, mature champagne in its element. Filled with enjoyable toffe and mint chocolate aromas and a sensual, melting, long aftertaste of honey.

1966 Heidsieck & Monopole 95 (Apr 95) 95
(67% PN, 33% CH)
A brilliantly pale orange colour and sparkling mousse. The champagne makes a slightly more lively and fruity impression than the '64, with tones of mango, orange and chocolate in the flavour. The delightful nose is dominated by orchids, roasted coffee beans and butter melting in the frying pan.

1964 Heidsieck & Monopole 95 (Apr 95) 95
(50% PN, 30% PM, 20% CH)
The same deep orange colour. The mousse is a bit tired, but there's a more masculine power in the vinous flavour. The nose is also older than the '66, with a Krug-like mint chocolate tone that I have a weakness for.

1959 Heidsieck & Monopole
(75% PN, 25% CH)
I've only tasted a poorly stored bottle. Considering the potential of both firm and vintage this should be a great wine. Unjudged.

1955 Heidsieck & Monopole 95 (Apr 97) 95
(67% PN, 33% CH)
When the wine was poured I detected some impurity in the nose, but this was soon aired out and along came the old majestic wine with a carpet of fine white mousse. Great depth and dark aromas that are as thrilling as a Hitchcock movie.

1921 Heidsieck & Co. 96 (Dec 96) 96
(75% PN, 25% CH)
Richer than the 1919, with a dense aftertaste of dry cocoa. As so often, the wine is borne up by a wonderful Pinot aroma.

1919 Heidsieck & Co. 94 (May 96) 94
(70% PN, 30% CH)
A vintage that had been totally unknown to me, but this magnum was an unforgettable experience. A powerful mousse, medium-deep colour and wonderfully assembled bouquet of dried roses, orange, coffee, mint chocolate and wood. The flavour was light and fresh, and dominated by apricot, peach and dark chocolate.

1907 Heidsieck & Co. Gout Americain 91 (Sep 97) 91
(70% PN, 30% CH)
90 year-old champagne that has lain on the bottom of the sea since 1916!

Probably rather an ordinary wine that under exceptional and perfect storage conditions has become fantastically personal and interesting. The two-degrees-warm, yet black water has apparently had a preserving effect on the semi-sweet champagne that was bound for the Russian army's officers. The colour is incredibly light, the mousse is perfect and the aromas fruity and youthful. The nose is dominated by apple and bananas, but there is also a deeper side with tones of tar and petroleum. The flavour's sweetness is no problem, but instead gives the pure flavour of Scandinavian autumn fruit extra length. The wine is rather light, which is to be expected with this vintage, but what an historic pleasure it is to loosen one of the well-kept corks and admire this nectar.

1982 Diamant Rosé 83 (Apr 90) 89
(50% PN, 50% CH)
Only 15,000 bottles were made of this prestige rosé. It had an intensely beautiful salmon colour and a sophisticated, slightly restrained, nose. With time in the glass this rare and expensive champagne produced aromas of toffee, nuts and strawberry.

1985 Diamant Bleu 79 (Jul 95) 86
(50% PN, 50% CH)
It takes a few minutes in the glass before the tones of dill and beef stew are blown away and replaced by a mineral-rich Chardonnay aroma. Medium-bodied and pleasant, but certainly a disappointment.

1982 Diamant Bleu 83 (May 90) 87
(50% PN, 50% CH)
A pretty fruit and more bread aromas than the '79, but I have to admit that the *Diamant Bleu*, with its stony finish, is far from being one of my favourite champagnes.

1979 Diamant Bleu 83 (May 90) 86
(50% PN, 50% CH)
You can really chew on the stony mineral flavour. Both the nose and the flavour have an ungenerous fruit and allow the minerals to take over. Verzenay dominates the impression emphatically.

1976 Diamant Bleu 94 (Oct 95) 94
(50% PN, 50% CH)
One of the best '76's and better than the '75. The wine is aristocratic, with a sophisticated, buttery tone from the vintage which adds a touch of charm to what is otherwise a rather barren wine.

1975 Diamant Bleu 87 (May 97) 93
(50% PN, 50% CH)
The first year of the new bottle. I was surprised when this 22 year-old revealed a youthful, rebellious, almost pubertal streak. The acidic flavour isn't fully balanced yet. The aftertaste has a strong Verzenay character.

1964 Diamant Bleu 97 (Jun 97) 97
(50% PN, 50% CH)
This wine, the subject of many a myth and rumour, is a legend that lives up to expectations. I've heard that it's best in magnums, but considering the freshness it displayed from an ordinary bottle, I wonder. *Diamant Bleu* is lighter and more elegant than the vintage wine, but they have in common a mint chocolate aroma and an improbable mineral finesse.

Other wines: Rosé.

De Venoge

30 av. de Champagne,
51200 Épernay ☎ 03 26 55 34 34

Production: 1.5 million bottles.

Along with all the Germans who founded champagne houses there is one Swiss man, Marc-Henri de Venoge. He started work in Mareuil-sur-Aÿ in 1837, but soon moved to Épernay. Throughout the 20th century the house has belonged to the most important producers in Champagne. Half of the firm's produce is exported to the German-speaking countries and to Great Britain. 90% of the grapes are bought in and vinified in modern steel vats. The firm's style is created by huge blends, like many other large houses. The non-vintage champagne is the house's best buy together with the lovely *Des Princes*.

De Venoge Brut Cordon Bleu 75
(35% PN, 40% PM, 25% CH)
This wine goes from clarity to clarity. The reserve wines must be of very high quality. classical, strong, bready nose and rich, fruity taste of Pinot.

De Venoge Demi-Sec 50
(40% PN, 35% PM, 25% CH)
Pure and well made dessert champagne for those with a sweet taste. Ages very well.

De Venoge Princes Rosé 68
(72% PN, 10% PM, 18% CH)
De Venoge Rosé has a colour unlike any other. It is actually more yellow than red. Even the taste is distinctly personal, and the closest description I can come up with is dried toffee. Weak mousse and slightly sour aftertaste mean lower marks.

De Venoge B. d. B. 60
(100% CH)
A wine from 1982, according to Hervé at the "Le Vigneron" restaurant. Despite the light colour, the nose is acrid and aged. Juicy curiouso that has seen better days.

De Venoge Blanc de Noirs 78
(80% PN, 20% PM)
Many years since last tasted, but my memory of the champagne is of an overwhelming fruitiness and a soft, fine taste.

1990 De Venoge Blanc de Noirs 82 (Jan 97) 88
(80% PN, 20% PM)
Sophisticated and smooth big house style. Full-bodied and polished in balanced fashion. Quite unlike any B. d. N. from a grower. None of the typical Pinot character, despite the grape content.

1990 De Venoge B. d. B. 80 (Feb 97) 85
(100% CH)
Smoky and tough, with tones of tar and forest. The fruit flavour is generous though, with hints of apricot.

1989 De Venoge 82 (Jan 97) 86
(51% PN, 34% PM, 15% CH)
A deep, beautiful colour with a snow-white mousse. A broad, mature Pinot nose with clear tones of chocolate and toffee. A balanced buttery flavour with big, rich fruit.

1988 De Venoge 82 (Jan 99) 84
(51% PN, 34% PM, 15% CH)
Not as fat as the '89, but otherwise the same spectrum of tastes and the same house style. Chocolate, chocolate, chocolate.

1986 De Venoge 82 (Jan 99) 84
(51% PN, 34% PM, 15% CH)
Developed and toasty nose with elements of chocolate. Something of a one-track, mature flavour with low acidity and respectable fruit. A decent drink, no more.

1982 De Venoge 87 (Jan 97) 87
(51% PN, 34% PM, 15% CH)
Highly developed nose, packed with coffee aromas. Sadly the aftertaste is a bit short, but otherwise a very nutty and pleasant champagne at a modest price.

1979 De Venoge 90 (Dec 95) 90
(51% PN, 34% PM, 15% CH)
Toasty, nutty and bready are the usual judgements on the 79's. They are admirably apt here. Now fully mature.

1990 Des Princes 87 (Jan 99) 92
(100% CH)
Brilliant, shining bright with ultra-fine bubbles. Also a faint, subtle nose that reveals the truth: this is a multicru. A smooth mousse and flavour, which is similar to the *Deutz B. d. B.* from the same vintage.

1989 Des Princes 90 (Jan 99) 92
(100% CH)
An extremely refined champagne with a glimmering green hue. A glorious nose of lime, lily of the valley, mint and toasted bread. Multi-faceted, crystal clear flavour with aristocratic elegance and fat structure.

1985 Des Princes 90 (Jan 99) 92
(100% CH)
At first a perplexing champagne almost without aroma and a cold, sharp and nondescript taste, but an incredible length. Today concentrated and fat.

1982 Des Princes 92 (Jan 99) 92
(100% CH)
Very much its own nose of pine trees, turpentine and hawthorn. However, there is a familiar hint of lemon and toasted bread. Delicate and light with a long, nutty finish.

1979 Des Princes 93 (Jan 99) 93
(100% CH)
Parts of the nose are classically toasty, but there is also a very personal hint of ginger and hawthorn. Creamy, nutty, delicately mature taste. Ages in grace.

1971 Des Princes
(100% CH)
Kept in an upright position and too warm. Maderised and of course not judged.

Madame Rouques-Boizel.

Boizel

14 rue de Bernon, 51200 Épernay ☎ 03 26 55 21 51
Production: 3 million bottles.

Boizel still has eleven bottles from 1834, the year when the firm was founded in Épernay. This treasure-store is unique in Champagne, with several undisgorged wines from the 19th century. The cellars lie under the Avenue de Champagne by the house where Christian Pol-Roger lives. Boizel has always been better-known abroad than home in France. Evelyne Roques-Boizel is president of the company today, but all her decisions are made together with her very likeable husband.

Chanoine and Bruno Paillard are now shareholders in the noble champagne house. Boizel buy grapes from fifty different villages, which are then blended by Pascal Vautier, the oenologist on the nineteen-man staff. Boizel are best known for their low prices, but I think the quality deserves better. Both the *Blanc de Blancs* and the cuvée de prestige *Joyau de France* are of very high class in their respective categories.

Boizel Brut 63
(55% PN, 15% PM, 30% CH)
A very soft and rounded champagne with powerful flavour. Suitable for simpler meat dishes.

Boizel Rosé 72
(50% PN, 40% PM, 10% CH)
A light and delicate rosé, despite the large proportion of black grapes. Quite a "white" taste, with good acidity and mineral character.

Boizel B. d. B. 85
(100% CH)
The grapes come from one single year and originate from Cuis, Cramant, Vertus, Chouilly and Le Mesnil. A beautiful champagne with a lovely mousse and ochre-yellow colour. A romantic nose of summer flowers and vanilla. Broad, likeable, buttery style.

1988 Boizel 73 (Apr 95) 81
(60% PN, 10% PM, 30% CH)
Slightly vigorous, extrovert champagne with spiced aromas and rich, slightly licorice-like taste. Development hard to judge!

1976 Boizel 85 (Feb 96) 85
(60% PN, 10% PM, 30% CH)
Rich, chocolate flavour and nutty bouquet.

1988 Joyau de France 88 (Jan 99) 92
(65% PN, 35% CH)
A pure Grand cru champagne of high class. Incredibly tight and promising with a Belle Epoque-like spectrum of aromas where coffee, lime and minerals set the tone. The taste is hard, but concentrated.

Mansard-Baillet

14 rue Chaude-Ruelle,
51200 Épernay ☎ 03 26 54 18 55
Production: 2 million bottles.

M. Mansard is a relaxed man who runs one of Champagne's fastest-growing houses. He owns 17 hectares in Marne, covering a third of his needs. Today he uses some 25 villages in his blends and creates well-balanced wines in a typical Épernay style. Malolactic fermentation is used in all wines except for *Tradition.*

Mansard-Baillet Brut 69
(25% PN, 25% PM, 50% CH)
Has an uplifting citrus tone that *Du Triomphe* lacks, even though the wine is lighter and less concentrated.

Du Triomphe 64
(15% PN, 15% PM, 70% CH)
I can imagine myself drinking this champagne sitting in a café on the Champs-Elysées looking up at the Arc de Triumph. Its easily-drunk fruity style certainly suits the wider public. The nose is simple with hints of elderflower. The large proportion of Chardonnay is apparent in the mouth with its lovely creaminess.

Mansard-Baillet Rosé 80
(65% PN, 35% PM)
A very impressive champagne with blood-red colour and burgundy-like taste. The taste is brilliantly complex with a wonderfully rich Pinot-fruity nose. The nose reveals the presence of Pinot Meunier. Eggnog and strawberries are mixed with animal tones.

Cuvée des Sacres 88
(40% PN, 60% CH)
A cuvée de prestige in a limited edition and only in magnums. The blend is made from the vintages of 85, 86 and 87. A lovely champagne with *Dom Pérignon* overtones. Less toasty, but the same gorgeous, delicate fruit and sophisticated style.

1988 Cuvée des Sacres 82 (May 95) 88
(30% PN, 70% CH)
The grapes come from Mareuil, Cumières, Chouilly, Vertus and Le Mesnil. Surprisingly it is the Pinot character that makes itself known here. Dark, tight and oily. Very well-fed and extremely rich with aromas from dark berries. Not as elegant as the non-vintage *Cuvée des Sacres*.

1989 Tradition de Mansard 85 (May 95) 90
(10% PN, 90% CH)
The grapes originate from Mareuil, Chouilly, Oger, Mesnil, Avize and Cramant. A lovely rich Chardonnay fruit. Superbly mature already.

De Cazanove

1 rue des Cotelles, 51200 Épernay ☎ 03 26 59 57 40
Production: 3 million bottles.

The house of C.G. de Cazanove was founded in Avize in 1811. However, the firm had to wait until the end of the 1970's before it achieved its breakthrough. The company produces very easily-drunk champagnes for the public at low prices, except for the *Cuvée Stradivarius*. The non-vintage champagne *Brut Azur* was one of the top five at a large tasting of forty non-vintage champagnes in Sweden in 1994.

De Cazanove Brut Classique 60
(65% PN/PM, 35% CH)
Not the same roundness and rich, creamy bottle maturity as *Brut Azur*. This wine lives more on its uplifting freshness and crispy Granny Smith taste.

De Cazanove Brut Azur 78
(50% PN/PM, 50% CH)
Beautifully massive maturity! One of the best value non-vintage champagnes on the market. Round peach and vanilla aromas in both nose and taste.

De Cazanove Rosé 68
(5% PN, 95% CH)
A featherlight rosé painted with delicate brushstrokes. Light and plenty of minerals, but the finish feels a little diluted.

1989 De Cazanove 76 (Feb 97) 79
(60% PN, 40% CH)
The nose is full of toasty aromas and sweet exotic fruit, but the flavour is somewhat less impressive.

1990 Stradivarius 84 (Jul 97) 88
(30% PN, 70% CH)
The wine smells and tastes like a smooth, polished B. d. B. It has lime, grapefruit and apples in abundance.

1989 Stradivarius 80 (Mar 97) 86
(33% PN, 67% CH)
A luxurious nose of sweet grapes, a medium-bodied, bold taste which would have been happier with a lower dosage.

1985 Stradivarius 80 (May 95) 84
(30% PN, 70% CH)
After having been impressed time after time by *Brut Azur* I had great expectations of this luxury champagne. I found a very fine mineral tone and a discreet toasty tone in the nose. However, the taste was too unconcentrated and simplistically lemony to elevate it among the greats.

De Castellane

57 rue de Verdun, 51204 Épernay ☎ 03 26 51 19 19
Production: 3.2 million bottles.

The noble Vicomte de Castellane founded his house in 1895. Today it is best known for its remarkable water tower below the Avenue de Champagne. They also have a wine museum and a butterfly house with species from all over the world.

Previously the champagne had fermented in all manner of containers, including giant oak barrels. The style became a personal one, but never particularly pure. Since Laurent-Perrier took over in 1985 the vinification and the wines have been modernised, leading to greater purity but less personality in the champagnes. The firm's wines are not only sold under the title De Castellane, but also as Maxim and Ettore Bugatti.

De Castellane Brut Croix Rouge 60
(40% PN, 30% PM, 30% CH)
This was previously a very personal wine with a nose of Earl Grey tea. Today we're dealing with a more neutral interpretation of the champagne art. Pure, light and slightly sweet.

De Castellane Tradition 64
(40% PN, 25% PM, 35% CH)
Somewhat fresher than their other non-vintage brut.

De Castellane Maxim's 64
(40% PN, 25% PM, 35% CH)
Same wine under another label.

De Castellane Chardonnay Brut 72
(100% CH)
Soft, balanced, with citrus aromas. A bit short in the aftertaste.

De Castellane Rosé 50
(60% PN, 40% CH)
Dark pink colour. Strong nose of banana gum and raspberry soda. Soft, sweet soda-like champagne.

1986 Cuvée Chardonnay Royal 76 (Nov 94) 76
(100% CH)
Lovely yellow colour, slightly overripe rounded nose with sophisticated citrus fruitiness and polished, ready-to-drink taste. Do not store.

1986 Cuvée Florens De Castellane 77 (Jan 95) 77
(10% PN, 90% CH)
Very similar to the *1986 Royal*. The difference in price is by no means justified. Mature.

1980 De Castellane B. d. B. 80 (Oct 97) 80
(100% CH)
A rather faint nose with a fragrant flavour.

1989 De Castellane 80 (Aug 97) 82
(53% PN, 7% PM, 40% CH)
Well made commercial blend, very soft and fruity. Quite mature.

1983 De Castellane 79 (Jun 97) 79
(50% PN, 25% PM, 25% CH)
Mature but flat, featureless vintage champagne.

1969 De Castellane
(50% PN, 25% PM, 25% CH)
One of the few 69's that have completely collapsed. Unjudged.

1964 De Castellane 91 (Jul 91) 91
(50% PN, 25% PM, 25% CH)
Alert and in top condition. Relatively faint nose but with a delightful hint of peppermint and new-baked vanilla buns. The aromas are the same in the taste, where the wine reveals a certain lack of concentration and length, despite its elegant vitality.

1962 De Castellane 82 (Oct 96) 84
(50% PN, 25% PM, 25% CH)
Tasted on three occasions from magnums. As young as an eighties wine every time. The aromas are faint and flowery and the wine is a touch too light and unconcentrated.

1988 Cuvée Commodore 84 (Jan 95) 89
(70% PN, 30% CH)
This is where the firm shows a new face that apeals to me far more than the other wines. A Dom Pérignon-like nose with a wide spectrum of bread and cocao aromas. Concentrated chocolate-filled taste with good body. Very enjoyable now, but will develop even more.

1975 Cuveé Commodore 91 (Feb 96) 91
(75% PN, 25% CH)
Magnificent champagne, with a lovely nutty bouquet and a full awesome taste.

Other wines: Commodore Rosé.

Charbaut

17 av. de Champagne,
51205 Épernay ☎ 03 26 54 37 55

Production: 1.2 million bottles.

André Charbaut founded his house as late as 1948. When he died in 1986 the firm was taken over by the commercially-minded sons Guy and René. In 1995 Charbaut became part of the Vranken-Lafitte's empire and in future the wines will be made by oenologist Thierry Gomerieux, who is responsible for all the concern's wines. Charbaut had a very good reputation during the sixties and seventies, but in the eighties only the cuvée de prestige *Certificate* received regular praise.

Charbaut Brut 58
(60% PN, 20% PM, 20% CH)
Here the house succeeds in its ambition of making an uncomplicated, easily-drunk party drink, but that's all it is.

Charbaut B. d. B. 69
(100% CH)
A beautiful champagne without much fuss and with pleasant primary fruits like apple and pear.

1985 Charbaut 70 (Nov 92) 78
(50% PN, 50% CH)
Irritating foamy mousse lowers the marks. Slightly rough nose but not without elegance in the taste.

1985 Charbaut Certificate 89 (Apr 98) 89
(100% CH)
Today a completly mature and rustic blanc de blancs with walnutty depth and complexity.

1982 Charbaut Certificate 86 (Jan 93) 90
(100% CH)
A critically-praised cuvée de prestige that is really good. It has a smoky complexity together with the soft, exotic fruit and vanilla taste.

1979 Charbaut Certificate 82 (May 91) 83
(100% CH)
I often prefer the '79 to the '82, but despite a delightful toasted tone in the nose the '79 doesn't quite hit the heights. The wine is quite simply too unconcentrated to be great.

Other wines: Rosé, Vintage Rosé, Certificate Rosé.

Mercier

75 av. de Champagne,
51200 Épernay ☎ 03 26 51 22 00

Production: 6 million bottles.

Eugéne Mercier is one of the most important people in the history of champagne. In 1858 he began his work in Épernay, digging 18 kilometres of cellar that he showed off to many celebrities. They even say a car rally sped off from here!

Eugéne Mercier was a very PR-conscious champagne entrepreneur. He had the world's biggest oak barrel built which was pulled by 24 white oxen to the World Exhibition in Paris in 1889. He also made an advertising film about champagne for the Exhibition that received a lot of attention.

In 1970 Mercier merged with Moët & Chandon. Even today Mercier is very careful about its marketing. A tourist train goes through the cellars, carrying an enormous number of visitors each year.

Mercier is definitely a great house to visit for any beginner. They buy basic grapes and use wine from the second pressing in their cuvées. Moët & Chandon concentrate more on exports, while Mercier maintain an interest almost exclusively in the domestic market.

Mercier Brut 59
(40% PN, 40% PM, 20% CH)
Unfortunately an uneven champagne that tastes different on different markets. The best bottles have a broad, warm nose of chocolate and new-baked bread, while others can be so green and immature that one wonders if it really is champagne in one's glass.

Mercier Demi-Sec 40
(55% PN, 45% PM)
No Chardonnay is included in this rather serious demi-sec. If you can stand the sweetness, this is a decent champagne.

Mercier Rosé 55
(60% PN, 40% PM)
Only rarely tasted. The impression was of a wine that was much more pale than the colour advertised. A neutral and slightly diluted rosé despite the Pinot grapes.

1990 Mercier 81 (Aug 97) 86
(32% PN, 28% PM, 40% CH)
This vintage is a sure thing whatever the name of the producer. Here Mercier have made a very enjoyable and easy-going champagne.

1982 Mercier 79 (May 93) 84
(50% PN, 50% CH)
Here the cooperation with Moët & Chandon is very noticeable. The same nose of orange and creamed mushroom, with a somewhat less clear, slightly rough taste.

1966 Mercier 92 (Aug 95) 92
(45% PN, 20% PM, 35% CH)
Lovely round and chocolaty '66 with good length.

1962 Mercier 92 (Nov 93) 92
(55% PN, 20% PM, 25% CH)
Just like Moët, Mercier have made a very good '62. Rather young colour, rich mousse and a large smoky nose with chocolate and hints of earth. Good weight, hard attack and a mature sweet aftertaste.

1955 Mercier
Totally maderised and undrinkable. Unjudged.

1942 Mercier
Only a maderised half bottle tasted. Unjudged.

1966 Mercier B. d. B. 92 (Aug 95) 92
(100% CH)
A brilliant champagne with a slender structure and delicate, ultra-refined fruit aromas. Also a touch of roasted coffee beans.

Other wines: Bulle d'Or.

Collective Testulat

23 rue Léger Bertin, 51200 Épernay 03 26 54 10 65

Testulat Brut 70
A pleasant acquaintance a couple of years ago. Very fine mousse and delicate aromas throughout. Digestive biscuits and mandarines among the tones. I would guess that the proportion of Pinot Noir is considerable in this champagne.

Besserat de Bellefon

19 av. de Champagne, 51200 Épernay 03 26 78 50 50
Production: 2.2 million bottles.

Founded in Aÿ in 1843. Bought by Pernod-Ricard in 1971. Today housed at Marne et Champagne. Marie-Laurence Mora is responsible for keeping the quality at Besserat on an acceptable level. Vincent Malherbe is the man behind the cuvées, and the grapes come from 30 communities. The wines are vinified in ultra-modern style and filtered so hard that the aging potential is minimal. The firm has a good reputation in France for their fruity crémant wines, but they should be drunk when young. Other brands: de Monterat, de Vauzelle.

Grande Tradition 75
(35% PN, 25% PM, 40% CH)
Sensationally good non-vintage champagne with a marked toasty Chardonnay nose.

Cuvée des Moines 67
(45% PN, 35% PM, 20% CH)
Not at all as classy a nose as the ***Tradition***, but the taste has a pleasant, picquant fruitiness that resembles the lime overtones of a Riesling.

Cuvée des Moines Rosé 67
(60% PN, 20% PM, 20% CH)
A critically-praised rosé in youthful style. Flowery nose and feather-light flavour.

1989 Besserat de Bellefon 80 (Aug 97) 82
(25% PN, 14% PM, 61% CH)
Discreet flowery and young on the nose. Correct, but rather charmless in the mouth.

1985 Besserat de Bellefon 74 (Nov 94) 79
(45% PM, 55% CH)
Similar to ***Tradition***, but not so much toast to the nose. The taste is, however, a little more concentrated.

Grande Cuvée B. d. B. 67
(40% PN, 60% CH)
It's very seldom that the cuvée de prestige isn't a firm's best champagne, but with Besserat de Bellefon I prefer the vintage wine. The nose is a little strange with tones of egg and paper, but the taste is light and thin with pure citrus tones.

1975 Brut Intégral 88 (Dec 95) 88
(50% PN, 50% CH)
Dry, long but lacks finesse.

Bauget-Jouette

60 rue Chaude-Ruelle, 51200 Épernay 03 26 54 44 05
Production: 200,000 bottles.

A rarity. A grower's champagne from Épernay. The work began in 1822 with grapes from 15 hectares in Mancy, Monthelon, Grauves, Damery, Venteuil and Hautvillers. Their wines have received a great deal of attention in the international press in recent years. Traditional methods are used. The firm's style is made up of uncomplicated bready champagnes for the broader public and the cuvée de prestige doesn't cost more than the major houses' non-vintage champagnes.

Bauget-Jouette Carte Blanche 54
(10% PN, 50% PM, 40% CH)
A nice but simple Meunier champagne where new-baked bread and apples bombard the senses.

Bauget-Jouette Rosé 62
(80% PN, 20% CH)
Massive breadiness in the nose and a soft, easily-drunk, charming cherry taste. Aftertaste a little too sweet.

1990 Bauget-Jouette 78 (Jul 95) 81
(30% PN, 70% CH)
A '90 that has developed a touch too early, with buttery and creamy nose and taste.

1990 Bauget-Jouette B. d. B. 78 (Jul 95) 84
(100% CH)
Somewhat more restrained and elegant than the blended '90. Short aftertaste.

Cuvée Jouette 81
(30% PN, 70% CH)
Delicate, mineral rich nose and a precious, stony taste with hints of digestive biscuit. Can develop!

Mignon & Pierrel

24 rue Henri Dunant, 51200 Épernay ☎ 03 26 51 93 39

A small champagnehouse in Épernay that is represented in my home country.

1988 Mignon & Pierrel Grande Cuvée 78 (Mar 95) 84
A medium-size nose that is very delicate, with creamy Chardonnay tones in both nose and taste.

Beaumet

3 rue Malakoff, 51200 Épernay ☎ 03 26 59 50 10

Production: 1.5 million bottles.

Beaumet was founded in 1878 in Pierry. Today the company is owned by Jacques Trouillard and is situated together with Oudinot and Jeanmaire in the beautiful "Parc Malakoff". Beaumet holds over 80 hectares spread across Champagne, and about half the grapes are bought in.

Couronne d'Or 50
(40% PN, 30% PM, 30% CH)
A big seller in Sweden for many years. A particularly varied champagne. A certain breadiness can sometimes give a decent champagne character.

Couronne d'Argent 25
(40% PN, 30% PM, 30% CH)
I loved this sickly-sweet champagne in my youth. It may still be pure, but the sugar hides all else.

Marquis d'Auvigne 50
(40% PN, 30% PM, 30% CH)
Low-price wine. Not generous, but pure.

Beaumet Rosé 50
(70% PN, 30% PM)
There may be a leathery Pinot aroma, but it is too much like a child's fruit drink and unbalanced, with an artifical like apricot colour.

1989 Beaumet Grand Cru 77 (Oct 98) 79
(60% PN, 40% CH)
Pure, pleasant but a little artificial. Full of apple and citrus fruits but a flavour that lacks personality.

1982 Cuvée Malakoff 85 (Jun 98) 88
(100% CH)
Large impressive buttery blanc de blancs with a lovely mature style.

1982 Cuvée Malakoff Rosé 80 (Jun 95) 81
(100% PN)
A well-kept but insignificant, fruity '82 without complexity.

Oudinot

12 rue Godard-Roger, 51200 Épernay ☎ 03 26 59 50 10

Production: 1.5 million bottles.

The company was founded at the turn of the century by a grower from Avize. Today the house style is still based on high-class Chardonnay grapes. In 1981 Oudinot and Jeanmaire became part of the Trouillard group. The non-vintage champagne is aged for three years before being sold and exports are somewhat greater than sales in France. I can't comment on the firm's house style, but those reports I have had bear witness to well-made and slightly neutral champagnes.

Oudinot B. d. B. 68
(100% CH)
A pure and light blanc de blancs with faint citrus aromas and a rather short aftertaste.

Oudinot Blanc de Noirs 78
(100% PN)
Polished, buttery and good, but the flavour disappears swiftly.

Other wines: Brut, Rosé, Vintage, Cuvée Particulière, Cuvée du Centenaire.

Jeanmaire

12 rue Godard-Roger, 51200 Épernay ☎ 03 26 59 50 10

Production: 2 million bottles.

Today Jeanmaire is owned by Trouillard and shares facilities with Oudinot. The house was founded in 1933 by André Jeanmaire. The Trouillard concern began to concentrate on *Jeanmaire* and *Beaumet* in 1982, after both had become popular low-price champagnes in Sweden. Jeanmaire buy in half their grapes and use some 37 crus in their cuvées. Chouilly and Avize are the villages where the firm owns its largest vineyards.

Jeanmaire Brut 48
(40% PN, 30% PM, 30% CH)
Just a touch better than the sparkling alternatives from elsewhere in France. Avoid *Jeanmaire* in half-bottles especially! There is not even a hint of autolytic character which can be found in the full size bottles.

Jeanmaire B. d. B. 50
(100% CH)
A simple low-price blanc de blancs with strong nose of yellow apples and short taste somewhat sour from the second pressing. Soon lost in the glass.

Jeanmaire Rosé 45
(70% PN, 30% PM)
Made using skin contact, which gives a rather deep red colour. The bouquet is attractive with its red fruits, but the taste is a little immature and short.

1989 Jeanmaire 75 (Oct 98) 76
(60% PN, 40% CH)
A neutral and rather nondescript champagne with good purity and decent length.

1988 Jeanmaire 68 (May 95) 77
(60% PN, 40% CH)
Made from Grand cru grapes. Round and likable. Pleasant apple finish.

1982 Elysée Rosé 75 (Jul 98) 80
(100% PN)
A Grand cru rosé aged in the company's darkest cellar for at least seven years. Despite that I was not impressed by this champagne. Very light colour and delicate, small bubbles. The taste is dominated by mineral tones. Medium length.

1990 Elysée 80 (Oct 97) 86
(100% CH)
Fresh nose of lemon peel, young on the palate, with aromas of crisp bread and mineral. Almost aggressive in the aftertaste.

1985 Elysée 81 (Mar 95) 85
(100% CH)
Charming Chardonnay overtones are found in this prestige bubbly. A creamy nose with vanilla and butterscotch. The same soft style meets the taste buds and leads to a slender finish.

1976 Elysée 90 (May 95) 90
(100% CH)
The grapes come from Avize, Chouilly and Cramant. Sensationally good and well-kept. Deeply shimmering green, indecent nose of goat's cheese, truffels, forest and port wine. The champagne is oily and concentrated, with a typical autolytic Chardonnay aroma not unlike *Jacquesson D.T.*

Other wines: Vintage Rosé, Blanc de Noirs.

Contet

23 rue Jean Moulin, 51200 Épernay ☎ 03 26 51 06 33

Today the firm is owned by Martel and shares the same address.

Contet Brut 70
Slightly bloated but powerful non-vintage champagne with a mature, yeasty bouquet and soft, muscular Pinot taste. The non-vintage champagne's Arnie Schwarzenegger.

Demoiselle

42 av. de Champagne,
51200 Épernay ☎ 03 26 53 33 20

Production: 2.5 million bottles.

Paul-François Vranken, an ambitious businessman from Belgium, owns one of Champagne's most powerful groups. In 1976 he formed Vranken-Lafitte and today owns Demoiselle, Charles Lafitte, Barancourt and Charbaut. Both Demoiselle and Charles Lafitte use a great deal of grapes from Aube and Sézanne. The company's headquarters in Épernay look more like an advertising agency than a champagne house, and without a doubt the firm goes more for quantity than quality. Thanks to the extremely skilful oenologist Thierry Gomerieux, who creates all the cuvées, both Demoiselle and Charles Lafitte are not bad champagnes at all, and Barancourt and Charbaut can be very good on occasion. However, one big drawback is the firm's ridiculous attempt to get their non-vintage champagne to look like a cuvée de prestige.

Demoiselle Brut "Tête de Cuvée" 68
(15% PN, 85% CH)
Tantalisingly sweet perfumed nose: this tastes like a simple blanc de blancs with very little resistance to the swallow.

Demoiselle Grande Cuvée 69
(30% PN, 70% CH)
A touch more flowery than ***Tête de Cuvée***, otherwise quite similar in style.

Demoiselle Rosé 40
(15% PN, 85% CH)
Here the butteriness feels a little artificial and vulgar.

Other wines: Vintage.

Charles Ellner

6 rue Côte-Legris, 51207 Épernay ☎ 03 26 55 60 25

This firm specialises in the "buyer's own brand" under various labels. They own 52 hectares.

Philippe d'Albertcourt Brut 65
Broad, bready, developed nose of richness and charm. Oily, one-dimensional mature taste.

Marquis d'Estrand 60
Rather fresh and fruity champagne with elements of citrus fruits and minerals.

Charles Ellner Rosé 64
I have to admit that Charles Ellner was completely unknown to me before this rosé came to Sweden. It proved to be an honest, rustic rosé champagne well worth its price. Probably suitable alongside fish dishes with its meaty, full style.

Sacotte

13 rue de la Verriere, Magenta,
51200 Épernay ☎ 03 26 55 31 90

Founded in 1887 by Léon Sacotte, the father-in-law of Gaston Burtin, who ran the company until he started his own, highly successful, champagne house (Marne & Champagne). Sacotte make simple low-price champagne which is popular in England.

Sacotte Carte Rubis Brut 39
(30% PN, 40% PM, 30% CH)
Rather a pale and tame champagne in every aspect.

Sacotte B. d. B. 49
(100% CH)
Slightly fruitier, good acidity, but with no character to speak of.

Marne & Champagne

22 rue Maurice Cerveaux,
51200 Épernay ☎ 03 26 78 50 50

Production: 11 million bottles.

Moët & Chandon is often - and somewhat unfairly - given the label "coca cola champagne". This description fits Marne & Champagne far better. The firm was formed in 1933 by Gaston Burtin, a man who was far more interested in business than he ever was in champagne. Today the company is the second largest in Champagne, despite the fact that they shy away from all forms of advertising. Instead, Paul Messin has chosen to buy the cheapest available grapes in order to produce as much as possible as cheaply as possible. The company now leads the market in "buyers' own brands". I've come across any number of champagnes with the buyer's label that have been produced by Marne & Champagne. Although I was impressed by the low price at first, I'm always extremely disappointed by the quality. The different labels are very confusing, with Gautier, Eugéne Clicquot, Pol Gessner and Giesler all conveyor-belt champagnes from the Marnes & Champagne science-fiction style industrial complex.

The firm's giant steel tanks have a capacity of 200,000 hectolitres of wine! The only champagne from the house for which I have any appreciation is Alfred Rothschild. However, the company does have a role to play - it uses grapes and juice no-one else wants and makes neutral but uncommonly cheap champagnes.

Pol Gessner Brut 29
(40% PN, 40% PM, 20% CH)
A puerile champagne which lacks autolytic character and has been filtered too hard.

Gautier Rosé 32
(45% PN, 35% PM, 20% CH)
Large, wavy nose of red fruits but a wholly unripe and diluted taste.

Eugéne Clicquot Brut 35
(40% PN, 40% PM, 20% CH)
The quality is extremely variable. At times mature with chocolate but old and tired, at other times immature and green.

A. Rothschild Brut 61
(35% PN, 25% PM, 40% CH)
Quite a different depth from the firm's other wines. The champagne character is unmissable, and in blind tastings this champagne is often confused with those from the bigger names Clicquot and Moët.

A. Rothschild B. d. B. 68
(100% CH)
Smooth and attractive pineapple flavour which probably comes from Sézanne. A perfect wine for beginners!

1989 A. Rothschild Rosé 60 (May 97) 68
(15% PN, 40% PM, 35% CH)
A deep, blue/red colour, fine mousse and strong bouquet of crispbread, paper and red fruit. A simple but correct flavour which becomes less enjoyable the more you drink.

1989 A. Rothschild 73 (Jul 96) 76
(10% PN, 25% PM, 65% CH)
There's a certain degree of richness and good fruit here, but the overall impression is of a somewhat one-dimensional and messy wine. I'm one of those people who wants to hear all the instruments in an orchestra.

1986 A. Rothschild 79 (Apr 94) 80
(35% PN, 10% PM, 55% CH)
Mildness, maturity, marzipan - three m's that describe this wine very well.

1976 A. Rothschild 88 (Nov 95) 88
(50% PN, 50% CH)
Luscious and spicy, with layers of caramel flavours.

1988 Grand Trianon 85 (Mar 97) 86
(40% PN, 60% CH)
Fantastically close to ***1988 Moët & Chandon***. Perhaps a touch lighter but an almost identical nose of fresh bread and chocolate orange. Enjoyable for a wide audience.

G. H. Martel & Cie

4 rue Paul Bert, Magenta,
51201 Épernay ☎ 03 26 51 06 33

Founded in 1869 by a grower from Avenay. When the firm's owner died in 1979 the house was taken over by Rapeneau.

Martel Carte d'Or 67
A pleasant surprise with fine champagne character and pure acidity. Martel's cuvée style reminds me of several big brands.

Other wines: Vintage, Crémant, Blanc de Blancs, Rosé, Cuvée Henry Leopold.

A. Desmoulins

44 av. Foch, 51201 Épernay ☎ 03 26 54 24 24
Production: 95,000 bottles.

Founded in 1908 by Albert Desmoulins and still a family business. Almost all wines are sold via mail order.

Other wines: Prestige, Réserve.

Desmoulins Rosé 62
(26% PN, 7% PM, 67% CH)
Beautifully orange-coloured, a discreet nose with elements of pineapple and grapefruit. The flavour has a raw, recently-disgorged approach.

1988 Desmoulins 76 (May 97) 81
(100% CH)
Unexpectedly vinous and powerful for a B. d. B. The fruity nose is quite bushy and the flavour is focused but one-dimensional.

Trouillard

2 av. Foch, 51208 Épernay ☎ 03 26 55 37 55

Production: 250,000 bottles.

A house which is better known for its change in ownership than its champagne. The Trouillard group is well-known. The firm is currently run by Bertrand Trouillard.

Trouillard Cuvée Diamant 55
(60% PN, 40% CH)
A somewhat impersonal champagne that is very fresh and has a weak toffee tone in the finish.

Trouillard B. d. B. 70
(100% CH)
A good, even mousse, elegant on the nose, crisp and fruity on the palate, but rather short.

1988 Trouillard Cuvée Fondateur 80 (Apr 96) 85
(100% CH)
A good, pure B. d. B. at a very reasonable price. Even a certain finesse about it.

Other wines: Sélection, Vintage, Rosé.

Gonet Sulcova

13 rue Henri Martin, 51200 Épernay ☎ 03 26 54 37 63

Production: 120,000 bottles.

This grower works in what is perhaps Épernay's most run-down building. 80% of the 15 hectares they own are full of Chardonnay. The man in charge is Vincent Gonet, probably yet another family member in Côte des Blancs.

Gonet Sulcova B. d. B. 59
(100% CH)
Here we're dealing with quite a polite B. d. B. with sweet tutti-frutti aromas and pleasing elements of lemon and lime. Sweet finish.

Other wines: Brut, Club des Viticulteurs.

Coop. Esterlin

25 av. de Champagne,
51200 Épernay ☎ 03 26 59 71 52

Production: 1.2 million bottles.

Mancy's cooperative was formed in 1948 and today has 145 members harvesting 140 hectares. Now in Épernay.

Esterlin Brut 52
(20% PN, 50% PM, 30% CH)
A correct but impersonal and somewhat one-dimensional non-vintage champagne.

Esterlin Rosé 53
(25% PN, 55% PM, 20% CH)
Very similar to the firm's non-vintage variety. Despite a rather dark red colour, it tastes quite "white".

Esterlin B. d. B. 50
(100% CH)
An extremely soft and easily-drunk champagne with a hint of eggnog in the aftertaste.

Other wines: Vintage.

De Castelnau

18 rue de Reims, 51200 Épernay ☎ 03 26 51 63 09

Production: 80,000 bottles.

Champagne de Castelnau was first produced in 1916, in honour of General de Castelnau, one of the leaders involved in the Battle of Marne. After a long period in the wings, Sylvain Batteux moved the champagne house centre stage and now has a portfolio of three low-price wines. All the grapes are bought in.

Castelnau Brut 51
(33% PN, 33% PM, 34% CH)
A new acquaintance in which I can't seem to find much of a personality. Correct but dull.

Castelnau Extra Quality 50
(33% PN, 34% PM, 33% CH)
A well-made and pure champagne in a popular style. It's so normal and ordinary that I can't find any words to describe it.

Other wines: Rosé, Chardonnay.

Jules Pierlot

15 rue Henri Martin, 51200 Épernay 03 26 54 45 52

Production: 125,000 bottles.

In 1889, just as the world exhibition got off the ground in Paris, Jules Pierlot started his house. The family still owns the company, which makes champagne under three names: Jules Pierlot, Veuve Chauvet and the most prestigeous, Lido de Paris, which is made up of 70% first-class Chardonnay. Untasted.

Rapeneau

4 rue Paul Bert, 51201 Épernay 03 26 51 06 33

Production: 1.8 million bottles.

Founded in 1901 by E. Rapeneau, and today linked with Martel. Despite the relatively high production level, I've never come across these champagnes (see Contet).

Wines: Brut, Grande Réserve, Blanc de Blancs, Vintage.

Janisson Baradon

65 rue Chaude Ruelle, 51203 Épernay 03 26 54 45 85

Production: 55,000 bottles.

This Épernay property was founded in 1922, and the owner these days is Richard Janisson. Wines not tasted.

Wines: Sélection, Brut.

Delabarre

7 rue Irène Juliot Curie,
51200 Épernay 03 26 54 78 57

Production: 200,000 bottles.

The firm is now in its fourth generation of ownership, with Jacky Brochet and Elisabeth Collignon in charge. Wines not tasted.

Wines: Rosé, Vintage, Brut, Prestige Pierre Balmain.

Achille Princier

9 rue Jean Chandon Moët,
51200 Épernay 03 26 54 04 06

Production: 115,000 bottles.

This house was recently founded by J-C. Hébert, who has been a champagne broker for the last 35 years. Wines not tasted.

Wines: Tradition, Passion, Rosé, Grand Art, B. d. B.

Other producers in Épernay:

René Arrois	03 26 59 90 12
Christian Coquillette	03 26 54 38 09
Jacquinot	03 26 54 36 81
Jacquot	03 26 54 10 17
Michel Picault	03 26 54 12 61
M. Ragouillaux-Mangin	03 26 54 13 14

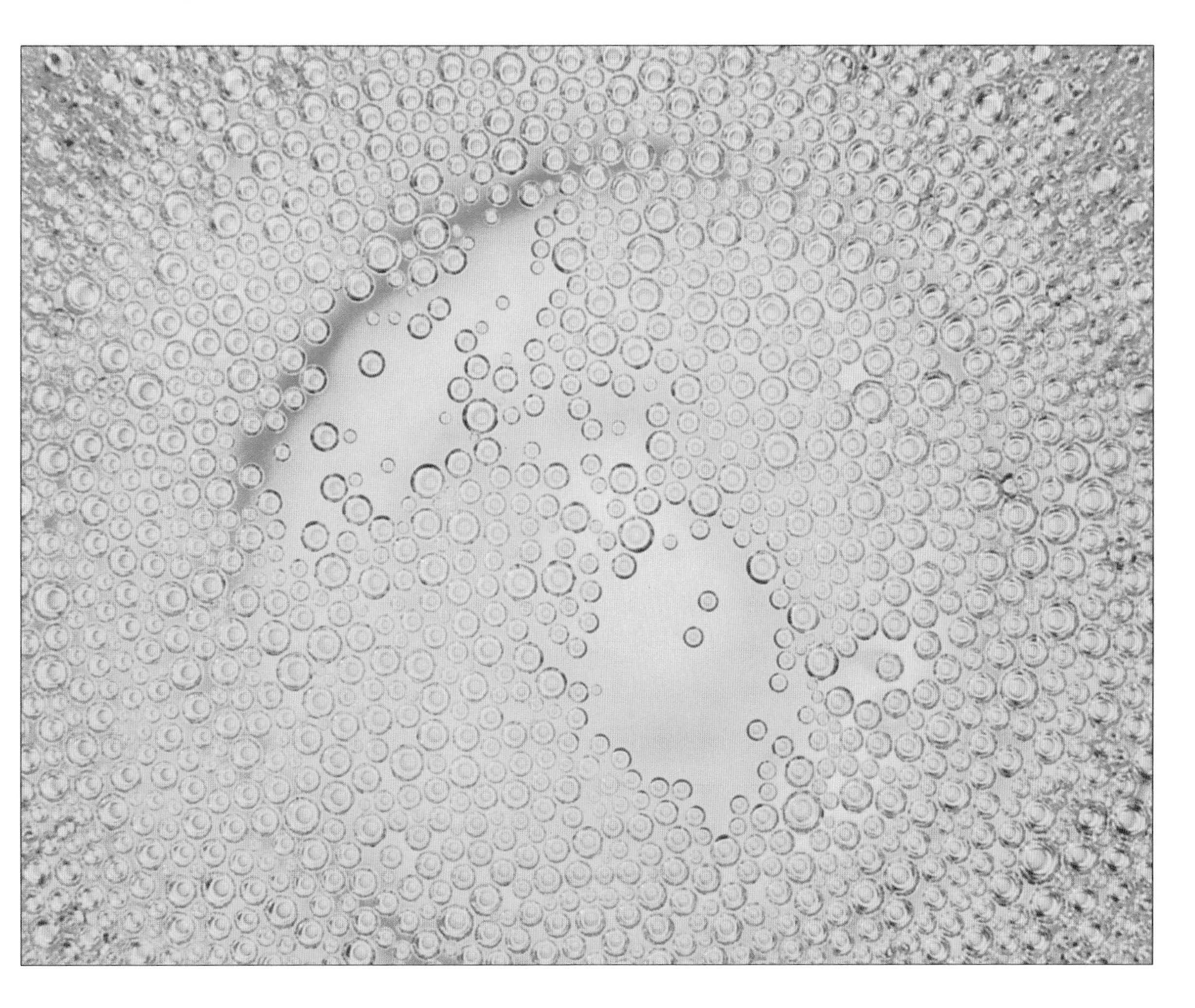

The smile from Reims, the most famous of the cathedral's thousands of statues, is found above the main entrance.

REIMS

Although Reims does possess vineyards that stretch over 49 hectares, that's hardly the reason it has become famous as Champagne's stronghold. Fifteen of the most well-known champagne houses are here, most of them blessed with Gallo-Roman chalk cellars for the storage of millions of bottles. The town has a wonderfully rich history and is now a major draw for tourists with a lots of activities on offer. Everywhere the visitor is reminded of the sparkling wine's presence. It's always easy to pop into a bar and order a champagne coupe from some locally-based house. Reims competes with Épernay for the crown of the capital of Champagne, but with houses like Krug, Roederer, Taittinger, Clicquot, Heidsiecks, Mumm, Lanson and Pommery here, Reims is my choice for the title every time.

% 88%   31% PN, 38% PM, 31% CH

Krug

5 rue Coquebert, 51100 Reims   03 26 84 44 20

Production: 500,000 bottles.

For me, Krug is more than a champagne. It is a word that stands for artistry, tradition, craftsmanship and moments of pure pleasure. The Krug family has used the same methods since the house was founded in 1843 by Johann-Joseph Krug from Mainz. It is hardly likely that the Krug philosophy will be abandoned in the foreseeable future since it has brought so much success.

Put simply, that philosophy means that all the wines are fermented cru by cru in well-aged 205-litre barrels from the Argonne. The wines are never filtered: Just two rackings by gravity, from cask to cask. Nor do they go through a malolactic fermentation, which is one of the reasons for Krug's fantastic aging potential. None of the wines is disgorged before it is six years old and the reserve wines are stored in stainless steel tanks from the Swedish Alfa Laval company. The firm's simplest wine, *Grande Cuvée*, is made from fifty or so wines from various vintages. Naturally the raw materials are also of the very highest class. Twenty hectares in Aÿ, Le Mesnil and Avize are owned by the house, but above all it is the network of prestigious contracts with some of the region's best growers that answers for the quality, as the growers consider it an honour to supply Krug with grapes.

Johann-Joseph Krug, the founder, learnt his champagne craft at Jacquesson, and when he regarded himself as qualified after nine years there, he set of to Reims to start his own house. After Joseph's death his son Paul took over and built the powerful Krug dynasty, followed as he was by Joseph Krug II in 1910 and Joseph's nephew Jean Seydoux in 1924. It was he, together with Paul Krug II, who created the famous cuvées, and it was only in 1962 that today's winemaker, Henri Krug, took over.

Today Henri leads the company, together with his more business-minded brother Rémi. They work undisturbed and independently, despite the fact that the firm is part bŷ LVMH. All Krug's wines are small masterworks, and although *Grande Cuvée* may be lighter and fresher than its predecessor *Private Cuvée*, after a few extra years in the cellar it outshines the competitors' vintage champagnes. *Clos du Mesnil* is a newcomer which simultaneously combines the best blanc de blancs and distinguishes the wine with the house's own distinct style. Vintage Krug competes with today's *Clos du Mesnil*, but if we go backward in time, it is without doubt the best champagne. If the opportunity arises, never miss the chance to drink a Krug!

Krug Grande Cuvée 93
(50% PN, 15% PM, 35% CH)
Strangely enough, this exceptional wine is one of the champagnes I've drunk on the greatest number of occasions - more than seventy times, in fact. Almost every time some new tone is revealed, and as it is blended from ten different vintages and 47 different wines from 25 villages, the variation is understandable. However, I've only missed out on identifying it at a blind tasting once, which shows that the basic style is unique. The extremely tough acidity, combined with the heavy, rich Krug aromas, is the clearest clue. Always check how straight the cork is in order to decipher when the wine was disgorged. The acidity can feel a touch too hard when young, and as a middle-aged or aged wine the *Grande Cuvée* is a magically complex nose and taste which is dominated by honey and nuts. The aftertaste is always long and majestic, and the best bottles deserve even more points than I have given here.

Krug Rosé 92
(55% PN, 20% PM, 25% CH)
Krug Rosé is a relatively new product from the Krug brothers. Their aim was to make a wine with a proper house style where the pink colour was the only clue that it was a rosé. The colour is actually an extremely light salmon-pink, and the nose is definitely Krug! Their unmistakable symphony of full, complex aromas is backed up by a whiff of raspberry. The taste is tremendously austere and acidic, but less generous than a *Grande Cuvée* and definitely a wine to store.

1989 Krug 95 (Jan 99) 97
(47% PN, 24% PM, 29% CH)
A vintage Krug is the standard by which all other vintage champagnes are measured. Incredible balance and elegance. Wonderful today but magic after the year 2000.

1985 Krug 94 (May 98) 96
(48% PN, 22% PM, 30% CH)
The '85 was first sold in early 1994. These majestic wines demand a long time stored in the bottle, but the '85 is surprisingly accessible at once, with its wonderfully roguish nose of smoke, cream, honey, nuts, peaches and vanilla. The oak character is not particularly obvious, but instead this wine relies on a velvety fruit. A very long aftertaste of vanilla.

1982 Krug 96 (Aug 96) 98
(54% PN, 16% PM, 30% CH)
Krug 82 will soon join the ranks of the legendary wines. It has all the building bricks needed to build a mighty castle. The fruit is enormous, the acidity, the concentration, the house's barrel tones: all are present and correct. The '82 is the most full-bodied wine to come from the property since 1976, but has a far greater elegance than that vintage. The nose's spectrum embraces nuts, coffee, butter, sun-dried sheets, sweet wrappers, orchids, vanilla, balsam poplars and orange. Most of these aromas are found once again in the explosive taste.

1981 Krug 95 (Feb 98) 95
(31% PN, 19% PM, 50% CH)
This wine probably lacks the qualities needed to become legendary and achieve longevity, but at the age of eleven it was a sensual wine experience. A *1985 Le Montrachet* from Drouhin felt clumsy compared to this elegant bottle of Krug. The fruit is rich, elusive and exciting, and the bouquet is multi-faceted, with tones of apple cake and custard, coffee, honey and white chocolate.

1979 Krug 97 (Oct 98) 97
(36% PN, 28% PM, 36% CH)
Although this wine will probably live long, it will never be better than it was in 1990. Then there was a life and a glass development which was an unmatchable pleasure to follow. First a closed but top-class nose which opened up after ten minutes into a Montrachet-like depth of the loveliest of aromas. It has a classically well-balanced structure with a long, nutty aftertaste which is close to perfection. Later bottles have shown an even greater richness of taste, but some of the elegance has been lost.

1976 Krug 94 (Feb 98) 94
(42% PN, 26% PM, 32% CH)
Loads of Krug aromas and voluptuousness, gigantic body and warm fruit. Even so, this is the vintage that has constantly failed to impress me. The vanilla aroma is a little exaggerated and the elegance is greater in *Cristal* and *Salon*, to take two examples, this year.

1976 Krug Collection 90 (Dec 96) 92
(42% PN, 26% PM, 32% CH)
Robust and limited for a Krug. The wine is hardly worth its Collection title.

1975 Krug 94 (May 98) 95
(50% PN, 20% PM, 30% CH)
This marvelous champagne is truly classic and will last very long. Deep nutty flavour and great length.
A good, but not great Krug.

1973 Krug 95 (Aug 96) 95
(51% PN, 16% PM, 33% CH)
A wonderfully accessible champagne which fills the room with its euphoric bouquet of honey, peach and apricot. The taste is concentrated and developed, with an expansive fruit and silky-smooth structure. The '73 is made in the same style as the '79 and '66. A classic Krug!

1973 Krug Collection 95 (Oct 96) 95
(51% PN, 16% PM, 33% CH)
A bit younger than the vintage, otherwise identical.

1971 Krug 96 (Mar 93) 96
(47% PN, 14% PM, 39% CH)
This is what Krug is all about! Mature and exotic, the nose of the '71 is unbeatable. The taste lacks the right concentration and length to take the score up to 100 points, but the nose is perfect, as is the aromatic breadth in the taste. The innumerable aromas are honeysuckle, honey, cakes, strawberry jam, boiled vegetables, popcorn - the list is as long as you care to make it. Unusually, the taste hints more at Chardonnay than Pinot Noir.

1971 Krug Collection 94 (Feb 97) 96
(47% PN, 14% PM, 39% CH)
Seems to be lighter than the vintage. Of course it's not. Keep this champagne a few more years in your own cellar.

1969 Krug Collection 93 (Sep 95) 95
(50% PN, 13% PM, 37% CH)
"Collection" merely means that the champagne has been stored in Krug's cellars much longer than is usual. Disgorged after six or seven years, the '69 is smoky and tough and is reminiscent of the austere *1969 Bollinger R.D.*

1966 Krug 98 (Mar 96) 98
(48% PN, 21% PM, 31% CH)
One of the most elegant vintages from Krug that I'm aware of. Lots of unmistakable Krug aromas in the bouquet, with a richer fruit and floweriness than usual. The taste is like a gentle brush of deep, mature, exotic fruits. Very fresh acidity, unbeatable long elegant taste with all the most enjoyable tones that can be found in a champagne. The '66 is a lot like the '79.

1964 Krug 95 (Sep 95) 95
(53% PN, 20% PM, 27% CH)
Yet another legendary vintage which many select as the best ever to come from the property. However, despite its greatness, I contend that this is no more than a normal Krug. At the age of thirty it's still very youthful and acidic. The oak tones have a delightful nerve and are supported by the aroma of a bakery in the morning. The mid-palate is more impressive than the aftertaste, which is dominated by ripe apple and vanilla.

1962 Krug 94 (Mar 94) 94
(36% PN, 28% PM, 36% CH)
An even richer wine than those of 64 and 66, although lacking their elegance, the '62 probably reached its peak in the early eighties. The nose is so strong that you feel it in the room when the wine is poured. It holds the scents of the travelling fair: popcorn, candy floss and vanilla ice cream. In the mouth the champagne expresses an oily weight and an incredible explosion of riches. Lots of Krug tastes, but slightly heavy in the rump compared with other vintages.

1962 Krug Collection 94 (Dec 96) 94
(36% PN, 28% PM, 36% CH)
Indentical to the straight vintage wine.

1961 Krug 98 (Jan 99) 98
(53% PN, 12% PM, 35% CH)
One of history's most heroic champagnes! When those of us in our thirties see our waistlines expanding, this '61 will have just finished building up its body. Even though I prefer the '38's aromatic merits, the '61 is the grandest monument to the craft. The colour is still light, with touches of bronze and copper. The nose has a side with all the roasted aromas from the cask, and another with fascinating tones from the sea and the forest. The superb taste is also on the dark, masculine side, with truffles, duck liver, mushroom, earth cellar, wood and fish. The fruit is by no means ingratiating, but the depth and breath of the wine are amazing. The aftertaste is actually the longest I've ever experienced!

1959 Krug 97 (May 98) 97
(50% PN, 15% PM, 35% CH)
Krug have deliberately made a more acidic and drier wine than usual as the character of this vintage is so heavy and rich in itself. This is undeniably one of the giants of the history of wine. A gigantic nose of freshly baked bread, apple pie and vanilla. The taste has elements of that wonderful mint chocolate tone that vintage Krugs gain with age. Extremely fat, oily, majestic burgundy-like structure. Fantastic!

1955 Krug 95 (Jun 97) 97
(50% PN, 20% PM, 30% CH)
A legend that still has a way to go before peaking! The acidity is amazing and the mousse almost aggressive. I'm still waiting for the mint chocolate tone that will pop up in ten years or so, but otherwise the wine is quite complete.

1953 Krug 96 (Sep 95) 96
(35% PN, 30% PM, 35% CH)
One wonders how Pinot Meunier can survive for so long. Incredibly fresh and acidic on the palate, with a colossal, meaty richness. Superb!

1952 Krug Collection 92 (Feb 97) 92
(43% PN, 19% PM, 38% CH)
Despite the fact that the wine was in prime condition, it was a great disappointment and one of the wines I've tasted that gave least value for money. The '52 is slender and fine, with a faint nose of burnt butter and oak. The flavour is very acidic and vigorous but lacks both charm and depth.

1947 Krug 94 (Sep 94) 94
(43% PN, 15% PM, 42% CH)
A legendary wine which was, however, not as good as expected. The wine was in perfect condition with a light colour and highly active mousse and the nose was closed but opened in the glass, which is highly impressive for a 47 year-old wine. A typical Krug nose of nutty complexity with ageing tones of tar and wood. An extreme attack and length, a dry, austere taste slightly lacking in fruit but with lovely tones of cocoa and wood.

1945 Krug 90 (Oct 97) 90
(42% PN, 16% PM, 42% CH)
A legendary wine, which was a huge disappointment for me. Good structurè and nice acidity. Charmless though.

1938 Krug 99 (Mar 94) 99
(57% PN, 16% PM, 27% CH)
A year which is almost completely forgotten, but which produced the best champagne I ever drank. It was a shock of the positive kind when the cork flew off at great speed, and seeing the bubbling drink with its clear middle-aged colour. The nose cannot be described with words, but it was very like the *1945 Mouton Rothschild,* with its tremendously rich tone of mint chocolate. There were also layers of fruit and minerals, and the wine was chewy and huge, with a divinely minty, bready and nectarine basic taste. The finish was majestic, with a clear tone of truffles and aged wood, alongside the mint chocolate. Is the '28 even better?

1937 Krug 95 (Jan 99) 95
(49% PN, 19% PM, 32% CH)
A deep golden colour, active mousse and a thought-provoking bouquet. Unified taste of peach and chocolate.

1928 Krug
(70% PN, 8% PM, 22% CH)
The most famous of all champagnes. Only tasted from a half-bottle. Incredible power, but maderised. Unfortunately unjudged. Call me if you find a magnum!

1926 Krug 95 (Nov 94) 95
(55% PN, 20% PM, 25% CH)
Orange-brown, with only a thin line of bubbles. A developed mint chocolate aroma in less sophisticated style than the '38, but with a greater dessert character. chocolate, rum and honey in the nose. The taste is a revelation of sweet Yquem-like style with layers of toffee, caramel and dried fruit. Probably even better 20-30 years ago.

1989 Krug Clos du Mesnil 95 (Oct 97) 98
(100% CH)
Is there a better wine in the world than *Krug Clos du Mesnil*? I doubt it.

1985 Krug Clos du Mesnil 96 (Sep 97) 99
(100% CH)
The height of elegance! The '85 reminds me of the '79, but I wonder if this wine doesn't reach even greater peaks. What balance and indescribable finesse! Sadly it's rare these days that I become so awestruck by a wine that I go through an almost religious experience. This wonderful lime-fruity champagne with its polished butteriness and sparkling clarity succeeded in inducing that feeling three days in a row during a tour with Henri Krug in November, 1995.

1983 Krug Clos du Mesnil 93 (Mar 96) 96
(100% CH)
The 1.87 hectare vineyard Clos du Mesnil, in the heart of the village, is a location that sums up all that Le Mesnil's champagne stands for. In Krug's hands this is the essence of Chardonnay. The '83 has a little way to go before it is fully mature: the colour has a clear green gleam, the nose is young, finely balanced and flowery, with lily of the valley, fresia and white lilies clearly definable. There is also a complex creamy side filled with toasty aromas, young fruit and damp wool. The taste is long and dry, with massive elegance and feminine frivolity.

1982 Krug Clos du Mesnil 95 (Mar 96) 97
(100% CH)
A wine with more Krug style than Mesnil. The colour is reminiscent of an oak-fermented great white burgundy and the nose is that way inclined too. It has an oriental spicy aroma, but toffee, honey, coffee, lime, cream, sun-ripened oranges are all there too. Wrapped in a Corton-Charlemagne-like, fat, nutty, enormous taste. Very high acidity, which is however hiden under layers of sweet fruit.

1981 Krug Clos du Mesnil 93 (Apr 97) 94
(100% CH)
In 1981, 12,793 bottles were made of a discreet and developable *Clos du Mesnil.* Today this wine is wonderfully elegant with a long zesty finish.

1979 Krug Clos du Mesnil 98 (Apr 98) 99
(100% CH)
A perfect blanc de blancs and a "decent" first try by the Krug family. The nose lives more on finesse than richness. Juicy Cox Orange apples, cointreau and acacia honey raise high expectations for the taste, and they are met with flying colours. There is a wonderfully exotic richness which reminds me of *Taittinger Comtes de Champagne,* but with an aftertaste even richer in glycerol honey sweetness.

Krug Private Cuvée 94
(55% PN, 20% PM, 25% CH)
I drank a magnum from the fifties in September 1995, and was astonished over how youthful and fresh the champagne was. The nose is restrained, but the taste is very deep and has a classic Pinot character.

Louis Roederer

21 bd Lundy, 51100 Reims ☎ 03 26 40 42 11
Production: 2.5 million bottles.

Roederer didn't get their present name until 1833, but were in existence as far back as 1776 under the name of Dubois Père & Fils. Louis Roederer was a hardworking man who succeeded in selling his champagne on several important export markets. Roederer's real ace was, as with Clicquot, the Russian market. Tsar Alexander II wanted a more impressive label to show his guests and in 1876 he made a special order for the first transparent *Cristal* bottles, which at that time were actually made of real crystal. The wine was stuningly sweet and gave Roederer certain problems of disposal after the Russian revolution, when the firm was lumped with unpaid invoices and stores full of sweet champagne that no-one else wanted. The company recovered in the thirties, when Camille Olry-Roederer took the helm. The money earned from sales was invested in some exceptional vineyards in Aÿ, Hautvillers, Cumières, Louvois, Verzy, Verzenay, Vertus, Avize, Chouilly and Le Mesnil.

Today the firm is the most financially successful in the region, thanks largely to these vineyards, which supply Roederer with some 75% of its grapes. The house is now run by Jean-Claude Rouzaud, who works according to the same principles as held in the past decades. All the wines ferment separately, cru by cru, in small steel vats while the reserve wines are stored in large oak barrels. This is said to give the company its special "vanilla touch". I'm not alone in wondering if certain wines for the prestige variety *Cristal* aren't stored in these barrels, as it is precisely in *Cristal* that one can sometimes discover a nutty, oily and vanilla tasting barrelish character. Apart from that, up to 20% of the oak aged reserve wine is used in the non-vintage champagne *Brut Premier*. Roederer has no set receipe regarding the malolactic fermentation - the personal qualities of the wine differ from case to case. It should be noted that the prestigeous house uses "taille" which are centrifuged before blending. Roederer is without doubt a brilliant champagne house with an exceptional portfolio of wines.

The non-vintage champagne is appreciated by many, the rosé and blanc de blancs offer an aristocratic elegance typical of the house, and the vintage wine is always among the best. *Cristal* is today the most sought-after cuvée de prestige and has perhaps the most appetising appearance of any wine in the world.

Louis Roederer Brut Premier 79
(62% PN, 8% PM, 30% CH)
A non-vintage champagne which is constantly praised, with a high proportion of reserve wines stored in large oak barrels. Four years in the bottle before being disgorged, first pressing only, etc. Everything points to a superb champagne, but I don't think this applish wine belongs among the elite. On the other hand, the aging potential is very good.

Louis Roederer Extra Dry 50
(62% PN, 8% PM, 30% CH)
With 16 grams of sugar this is reasonably dry and drinkable.

Louis Roederer Grand Vin Sec 49
(62% PN, 8% PM, 30 % CH)
Light and elegant with good acidity, with the sugar just a slight distraction.

Louis Roederer Carte Blanche 48
(62% PN, 8% PM, 30% CH)
Always one of the best sweet champagnes. Richer and more mature than *Grand Vin Sec*, which is good because the ripe, chocolate Pinot aroma is the only one that has the strength to carry such gruesome amounts of sugar.

1991 Louis Roederer Rosé 84 (Oct 97) 88
(75% PN, 25% CH)
It's surprising that a quality house should produce a '91. The wine hardly reaches normal standard, but is very good considering its vintage. Pale colour.

1989 Louis Roederer Rosé 86 (Apr 96) 89
(70% PN, 30% CH)
Flowery, light and full of rich red fruit. Unfortunately it's too sweet.

1988 Louis Roederer Rosé 86 (Nov 96) 90
(70% PN, 30% CH)
Roederer's rosé has a very good reputation. I myself was surprised to discover when I wrote this book that I had only tried a few vintages of this fine wine. The '88 is a crystal clear, stylish champagne with pure, vigorous Pinot aromas of plum and raspberry.

1976 Louis Roederer Rosé 91 (Sep 96) 93
(70% PN, 30% CH)
Fat and concentrated, with a strong rooty Pinot nose. Concentrated, elegant, fruity taste.

1966 Louis Roederer Rosé 94 (Jul 95) 94
(70% PN, 30% CH)
This wine is proof that rosé champagnes can be aged. Only the colour reveals the wine's identity. The nose is divine, with a broad spectrum of sweet aromas typical for this vintage. The taste is very tight and elegant, with tones of nut, toffee and honey.

1952 Louis Roederer Rosé 96 (Jul 96) 96
(70% PN, 30% CH)
An incredible champagne with amazing fruit, elegance and breeding. The vitality is awesome, as is the length of the magical aftertaste of butter and wild raspberry.

1990 Louis Roederer B. d. B. 91 (Jul 98) 95
Superbly sophisticated wine with a juicy and easy-to-drink overall feel. The flavour is loving and romantic, with tones of vanilla cakes and sweet lemon.

1989 Louis Roederer B. d. B. 85 (Jul 97) 93
(100% CH)
Really it's just a question of style as to which Roederer '89 you prefer. All of them share a sophisticated house style. Personally, I have a weakness for this outstandingly fresh B. d. B., which in common with *Cristal*, has more malic acid than usual.

1983 Louis Roederer B. d. B. 90 (Apr 92) 92
(100% CH)
Roederer's blanc de blancs are very rare. The '83 is a wonderful wine with great similarities to the *Cristal* of the same vintage. The nose is powerful and elegant with nuts, pastries and sweet, juicy fruit. The wine has a softness and maturity which is so typical in high-class grapes. Long, classic aftertaste.

1955 Louis Roederer B. d. B. 96 (Jun 97) 96
(100% CH)
Tasted alongside the ordinary '55, this has a deeper colour and weaker mousse. If possible, the nose is even more delightful, filled with toffee aromas. The flavour is magically smooth and fruity. A minor masterwork.

1990 Louis Roederer 86 (Oct 97) 92
(66% PN, 34% CH)
Wonderful balance and refinement. Creamy and classic, with a high degree of acidity.

1989 Louis Roederer 84 (Feb 97) 90
(66% PN, 34% CH)
So classical and enjoyable at the same time. Both the nose and the flavour have clear elements of fudge and dark chocolate. The wine is made in a balanced and medium-bodied style with masses of authority and charm.

1988 Louis Roederer 85 (Feb 97) 90
(66% PN, 34% CH)
Promising, but far too young to drink now. Applish, dry and long. Store for at least ten years.

1986 Louis Roederer 85 (Mar 97) 87
(66% PN, 34% CH)
Light and pretty with a citrus-fresh breeze and tones of toffee. Somewhat unconcentrated.

1985 Louis Roederer 85 (Jan 92) 91
(66% PN, 34% CH)
A wonderful wine which conceals depths of beauty under the subdued surface. Pure, slightly buttery, classical build and perfect balance. Drink after the year 2000.

1983 Louis Roederer 80 (Jul 89) 89
(66% PN, 34% CH)
Only tasted in its youth. Then it was very fresh and Granny Smith influenced. Clear, pure, medium-bodied with good acidity. Promising!

1982 Louis Roederer 83 (Sep 89) 90
(66% PN, 34% CH)
Pure house style with polished, ultra-sophisticated character and uplifting freshness.

1981 Louis Roederer 84 (Dec 94) 84
(66% PN, 34% CH)
The 1981 is usually dominated by an elegant fruit aroma, but here Roederer have instead produced a creamy and fat champagne with plenty of toffee in the nose. Short aftertaste.

1979 Louis Roederer 93 (Oct 98) 93
(66% PN, 34% CH)
This wine is perhaps the best example I know of which shows that champagne ages best in magnums. In the magnum, this '79 has an exotic nose of orchids and honeysuckle, along with several jars of roasted coffee. The taste is a sensual experience with a richness reminiscent of nut-filled chocolate. Long and classical. In the normal sized bottles the dosage feels too much and the fruits of the wine are almost undeveloped and subdued. Hard one to judge.

1978 Louis Roederer 88 (Aug 96) 88
(66% PN, 34% CH)
A rare vintage with great depth and caramel flavour. Honeyed nose.

1976 Louis Roederer 93 (Jul 98) 93
(66% PN, 34% CH)
Roederer are apparently the firm to go for this year. This '76 achieves a rare richness and sophisticated fruit sweetness. Very much like the *Cristal* from the same vintage, but slightly richer chocolate aromas and less buttery Chardonnay taste. Long and united.

1975 Louis Roederer 91 (Jul 91) 93
(66% PN, 34% CH)
The nose isn't as nice as the '76, but the acidity and the attack boast of a longer life. The nose played on a vegetable theme, accompanied by a weak but clear gorgonzola tone. The Pinot Noir is more apparent here than in the '76, despite the fact that the grape proportions are identical.

1973 Louis Roederer 85 (Nov 96) 85
(66% PN, 34% CH)
Not a great vintage for Roederer. Very matured, almost old without sparkle.

1971 Louis Roederer 87 (Apr 96) ▼
(66% PN, 34% CH)
It's probably been a few years since this wine hit its peak, but it still gives a good deal of pleasure with its oily richness and developed nut and leather aromas.

1971 Louis Roederer Crémant 89 (Jun 88) 89
(100% CH)
A weaker mousse than usual. Buttery and slim in a wonderful way. In 1988 the acidity was a little low, and the wine may well be on the way out.

1961 Louis Roederer 88 (Jan 95) 
(66% PN, 34% CH)
It's rare to see a champagne with such an effervescent mousse combined with a brown amber colour. The broad nose is very similar to an old tokay with tones of prune, overripe apple and damp wood. A heavy Pinot taste, with sweet, toffee-like aromas. Not completely clean however, and the aftertaste is a touch maderised.

1955 Louis Roederer 96 (Jun 97) 96
(66% PN, 34% CH)
A perfect mousse, Roederer's unmistakable toffee nose and a nervous, acidic undertone in this wonderfully balanced honeyed wine.

1949 Louis Roederer 96 (Oct 97) 96
(66% PN, 34% CH)
As always with this vintage, a wonderfully fresh and flowery champagne. Reminds me of the *'66 Cristal* with its elegant style.

1945 Louis Roederer 96 (Oct 97) 96
(66% PN, 34% CH)
Greater volume and strength than the '45, but without its seductive refinement.

1928 Louis Roederer 97 (Dec 96) 97
(70% PN, 30% CH)
I finally got the chance to see how great the 28's could be. Roederer's perfect champagne has a colossal, irrepressible power combined with a toffee flavour so typical of the house.

1990 Cristal 91 (Feb 99) 96
(55% PN, 45% CH)
A classic *Cristal* which is more open and a bit fatter than the '89. Otherwise it has the same delightful aromatic spectrum, with Roederer's typical toffee tone and rich but subtle fruit.

1989 Cristal 91 (Jan 99) 96
(55% PN, 45% CH)
Many of my friends are disappointed with this wine, but even though I agree that the delicate nose is young and restricted, I am delirious with pleasure over the super-concentrated flavour. Everything is there, with dominant elements of candy, apple and hazelnut. By all means decant this expensive wine if you're thinking of opening it before the year 2000.

1988 Cristal 93 (May 98) 95
(50% PN, 50% CH)
Roederer Cristal has a place among the elite of the cuvées de prestige. It combines Bollinger's and Krug's heavy, nutty Pinot-based style with ***Taittinger Comtes de Champagnes'*** enjoyable exotic fruitiness and butterscotch taste. The '88 is young and classical, with rich fruit and the beginnings of nuttiness, plus great depth.

1986 Cristal 87 (Feb 95) 87
(50% PN, 50% CH)
To be honest, this is a very weak ***Cristal***. It reached full maturity at the early age of eight and will last just a couple more years. Buttery, sweet and easy to drink, but without freshness or concentration.

1985 Cristal 91 (Dec 94) 94
(60% PN, 40% CH)
Right now this wine is in a sleeping phase, when the nose is slightly less lush than in its childhood. The *85 Cristal* is otherwise just as delightful as it sounds. An aristocratic champagne with a superbly long aftertaste of butterscotch.

1983 Cristal 93 (Dec 98) 93
(60% PN, 40% CH)
Far more developed than the '85, with a broad, impressive, nutty and buttery nose. A deep, mature taste of sweet fruit, nougat and butterscotch. Unnecessarily high dosage.

1982 Cristal 95 (Mar 98) 95
(55% PN, 45% CH)
One of this vintage's real top wines. Luxuriously scented and creamily rich. Slightly high dosage, but devastatingly good with its overflow of vanilla, almonds, honey, white chocolate and citrus aromas. Drink it soon!

1981 Cristal 93 (Dec 92) 94
(60% PN, 40% CH)
Cristal has few superiors in this vintage. A classic, with pure buttery Chardonnay and wonderfully mature chocolate Pinot. Incredibly nutty bouquet.

1979 Cristal 94 (Apr 98) 95
(60% PN, 40% CH)
Still very young in style, a very refined and toasty nose. The taste is superb, with an amazingly rich, exotic fruitiness.

1978 Cristal 93 (Jan 96) 93
(60% PN, 40% CH)
Perhaps a little thinner than usual, but it contains the entire range of aromas. The lovely nose includes elements of lilies, apricot and nut chocolate.

1977 Cristal 93 (Jan 99) 93
(60% PN, 40% CH)
Definitely the best wine of the vintage. Charming and refreshing, but with a somewhat short aftertaste. Very elegant.

1976 Cristal 95 (Mar 91) 96
(60% PN, 40% CH)
One of the most perfect *Cristals* I've ever experienced. It sums up everything the firm stands for in such a magically concentrated and buttery drink. The fruit is astoundingly rich and the freshness is outstanding - this wine is wonderful and easily understood.

1975 Cristal 93 (May 95) 93
(60% PN, 40% CH)
The '75 is impressive and intense, but it's a touch rough and has an exaggerated smoky character which stops it being a truly great *Cristal*. If asked to taste this blind, I'd probably say it was a '76 with its full, low-acidic, mature taste. The Pinot grapes are dominant here.

1974 Cristal 91 (Jan 99) 91
(60% PN, 40% CH)
Roederer never fails to make great wines even in the worst vintages. Creamy, nutty and delicious.

1973 Cristal 89 (Mar 91) ▼
(60% PN, 40% CH)
Owing to overproduction in the early seventies, the '73 is a little unconcentrated. The structure is relaxed and the unusually thin taste is dominated by an almond aroma.

1969 Cristal 97 (Apr 98) 97
(60% PN, 40% CH)
This is in fact more developed than the '66, which this wine otherwise so resembles. The colour, mousse and the explosive nose are perfect. The flavour is tremendously rich and fruity, with a luxurious fat finish.

1967 Cristal 93 (Mar 97) 93
(60% PN, 40% CH)
Incredibly good with all the classic *Cristal* aromas, and the only weak point is an aftertaste that is too short and flat. Definitely the best wine of the vintage.

1966 Cristal 98 (Mar 97) 98
(60% PN, 40% CH)
It's hard to conceive of a wine being more enjoyable than this one. The fruit is incredibly dense and the style is unimpeachable. A classic champagne which has everything and more. A little lighter and more elegant than the awesome '59.

1964 Cristal 98 (Oct 98) 98
(60% PN, 40% CH)
There's something magical about *Cristal*. Every vintage from the sixties is wonderful and stylish. I wonder if the '64 isn't the best of them all. Here we find all the usual points: the sweet toffee tone, the creaminess and the amazing balanced fruit. The seductive flow is supported this time by a La Tâche-like Pinot depth which is unmatched anywhere.

1959 Cristal 99 (Jan 96) 99
(60% PN, 40% CH)
Majestic and irresistible. As usual *Cristal* manages to charm both the expert and the novice with its beautiful, exotic sweetness and creamy toffee flavour. This wine doesn't show us anything new or unexpected, but quite simply offers more of all the good things one finds in these wines. Call me if you find a wine that gives you more pleasure!

1953 Cristal 94 (Dec 96) 94
(60% PN, 40% CH)
A monumental wine that has been even better. If Roederer have any bottles left in their cellar then they're probably as close to perfection as you can get. The only example I've tasted had a faint madeira tone but still reached 94 points.

1949 Cristal 98 (Mar 97) 98
(60% PN, 40% CH)
Wonderfully good! Both one of my own favourite champagnes and favourite vintages. Naturally the result is bound to be brilliant if you, like me, manage to find a well-kept bottle.

1988 Cristal Rosé 95 (Jul 98) 98
(70% PN, 30% CH)
Potentially the best rosé I've tasted. There's finesse and crystal clear elegance which just makes me happy. This rosé reminds me of the white '89, with its perfect balance, sparkling freshness and irresistable aromatic purity.

1985 Cristal Rosé 94 (Dec 96) 96
(70% PN, 30% CH)
What a wine! The price may well be considered ludicrous, but the elegance is inimitable, and after a few years in the cellar the honey and toffee tones will break out in full bloom. Undeniably one of the very best rosé champagnes available.

1983 Cristal Rosé 90 (Jan 97) 94
(70% PN, 30% CH)
A light and young creation with a classic *Cristal* flavour. However, I should note that the rosé of this vintage is both drier and more acidic than its white cousin. The long aftertaste is superb, with sackfuls of Granny Smith aromas.

1981 Cristal Rosé 93 (Aug 91) 94
(70% PN, 30% CH)
Cristal Rosé is one of the champagne world's pearls. The '81 has a very light colour and behaves more as if it was a white champagne than a rosé. Only a very faint strawberry tone distinguishes it from its white sibling. An entrancing bouquet of honey, hazelnuts and milk chocolate. Fantastically balanced and well-oiled, with an aftertaste of white Toblerone.

Taittinger

9 pl. St. Nicaise, 51100 Reims ☎ 03 26 85 45 35
Production: 4 million bottles.

The house of Forneaux, as Taittinger's predecessor was called, was one of the first champagne houses when it was founded in 1734. The firm's first financial upturn came when it was bought by the Taittinger family in 1932. Pierre Taittinger bought a palace called La Marquetterie and built up an impressive arsenal of vineyards. Today's owner, Claude Taittinger, took over in 1960, and the company now has 256 hectares in 26 villages, which supply some 45% of its grape needs. Experiments with small numbers of new oak barrels have begun with the prestige wine *Comtes de Champagne*, but otherwise all the wines are fermented in large steel tanks and put through malolactic fermentation. The firm is well-known for its efforts to support major projects outside the local region. For example, the company owns two hotel chains, two wine firms in the Loire valley and one in California. The artistically-formed Collection bottles have become a huge success in terms of sales despite the exorbitant prices.

The non-vintage champagne is a touch uneven but it often reflects the flowery, soft house style well. The vintage wine is a real charmer which sadly lacks storage potential. The real star is the *Comtes de Champagne*, a classic blanc de blancs which is one of the best in the region, with its soft, exotic and creamy style. I imagine that the *Comtes de Champagne* is the champagne which is appreciated by the broadest public. It contains no difficult aromas, but instead a flood of charmingly sweet and soft tastes in an elegant and luxurious style. In any case, it contains an aromatic spectrum that is exciting enough for the most fastidious expert to fall head over heels for its beauty.

Taittinger Brut 70
(42% PN, 20% PM, 38% CH)
Very uneven. Often too sweet and scented, sometimes with such a creamy Chardonnay character that it can be mistaken for a vintage champagne. Recently very good.

Taittinger Prestige Rosé 54
(70% PN, 30% PM)
Sweet, ingratiating and public style that doesn't appeal to me. Ages very well-though.

1991 Taittinger 81 (Oct 97) 83
(60% PN, 40% CH)
Soft and charming. Aromas of vanilla and butterscotch.

1990 Taittinger 84 (May 97) 90
(60% PN, 40% CH)
A faintly cheesy nose which is quickly blown away until it becomes a subdued but fruity and chocolate-laced bouquet. First and foremost it's the full flavour which impresses me. The '90 is packed with fruit and bold, biscuity layers. A perfect dosage and balance.

1988 Taittinger 83 (Apr 94) 83
(45% PN/PM, 55% CH)
Taittinger's vintage champagnes are made for early consumption and so rarely reach the heights of their most famous competitors. The '88 is good, sure, but does it have any more to give? Bushy, ingratiating, generous, sweet and a hint of saffron in the nose.

1985 Taittinger 87 (Sep 98) 88
(50% PN/PM, 50% CH)
Early developed and ingratiating, like most of the vintages of this wine. The delicate mousse forms beautiful pearl necklaces in the glass. The nose is broad and exotic, with vanilla and saffron leading the field. The taste is sensual with its fruit sweetness and long, chewy fullness.

1983 Taittinger 80 (Aug 89) 86
(60% PN/PM, 40% CH)
Identical to the ***Taittinger Collection*** but much cheaper. Broad, Pinot-dominated nose, full, impersonal and with scope for development.

1982 Taittinger 83 (Sep 94) 87
(60% PN/PM, 40% CH)
This wine has caused me to doubt that ***Collection*** and ***Millésime*** are the same wine. ***82 Collection*** has always impressed me, while this wine has had similar aromas without the magnificent build of ***Collection***.

1980 Taittinger 81 (Jul 91) ▼
(60% PN/PM, 40% CH)
Bready, mushroom aromas without fruit in the bouquet. However, the taste is fine, with sweet, plum-like fruit. The wine is rich and pleasant, but loosely hung.

1979 Taittinger 86 (Dec 96) 86
(60% PN, 40% CH)
Like an ice lolly, agreeable immediately with an exotic fruit flavour.

1970 Taittinger
(60% PN/PM, 40% CH)
All the worst aspects of old champagne. Flat and flabby with a lot of maderisation. Unjudged.

1959 Taittinger 94 (Apr 96) 94
(60% PN, 40% CH)
I believe this type of vintage is necessary for Taittinger's vintage wines to show that they can be stored. A typically stubborn '59 with incredible power and a long, strong flavour of nuts and smoke.

1988 Comtes de Champagne 91 (Oct 98) 94
(100% CH)
As with so many 88's, almost hard in its stringency when it was introduced. Today there is a nutty weight and veils of mint aromas that are waiting to burst out in full bloom very soon.

1986 Comtes de Champagne 88 (May 98) 90
(100% CH)
Comtes de Champagne is one of my favourite champagnes. Creamier and more easily-drunk champagnes just don't exist! The '86 is made in that style, but it's not counted as one of the great vintages. It is creamy with a long finish of almond and honey. Dosage a touch high.

1985 Comtes de Champagne 95 (Feb 98) 97
(100% CH)
A brilliant deep yellow revelation with an astoundingly beautiful mousse. The '85 is a light and refined wine with an incredible range of nuances in its rather broad nose. Red apples, cocoa, syrup and butter are obvious participants. Classical blanc de blancs structure with an uplifting citrus taste. Dry initially, but with an exemplary sweet, tropical aftertaste.

1983 Comtes de Champagne 94 (Feb 98) 94
(100% CH)
I misjudged the '83 in its youth. It went on to mature rapidly in 1993 and 1994, and suddenly its bouquet and taste were huge. A tidal wave of sweet tones meets the palate, imbedded in an oily, silk-smooth structure. A long aftertaste of almond and vanilla.

1982 Comtes de Champagne 94 (Feb 98) 94
(100% CH)
Comtes on top form! Overwhelming, rich, romantic and euphoric champagne. Bubbling mousse with that unique pearl necklace formation. The generous buttery nose includes masses of exotic ripe fruit, red apples, cocoa and a nutty complexity. The sweetness is tangible in the juicy taste. Creamy, fat, full-bodied, buttery and wonderfully long. The wine melts in the mouth like ice cream and runs down the throat like nectar.

1981 Comtes de Champagne 90 (Feb 98) 91
(100% CH)
Light and slightly closed at first. The pearl necklaces the mousse formed are among the most beautiful I have seen in a champagne glass. The nose is feminine and unusually discreet. Flowery, with tones of newly-washed sheets that have been hung to dry outdoors. The acidity is pure although the dimensions are smaller than usual. All the exotic fruits are there, but to a lesser degree than usual.

1979 Comtes de Champagne 95 (Feb 98) 95
(100% CH)
A relatively light vintage for the company. Unmistakeable style, with refreshing creamy citrus and butterscotch tones. Wonderful perfume of white flowers and a crystal-clear nutty taste. It has had a sensational development in recent years.

1976 Comtes de Champagne 96 (Feb 98) 96
(100% CH)
This '76 was one of the champagnes that made me obsessed with the area and its wines. Never before had I tasted something as exotic, fruity and enjoyable. It still holds up well, even though the character has changed somewhat. The butter has now been replaced by a broad nose and the taste of sweet lemons. That may be found in many mature champagnes, but never as clearly as in the ***Comtes de Champagne 76***.

1975 Comtes de Champagne 90 (Aug 89) 94
(100% CH)
An unusually restrained example of this cuvée de prestige. With a creamy nose and slightly exposed, long and mineral rich taste. A clear scent of cocoa in the empty glass. Should be perfect for the millennium.

1973 Comtes de Champagne 93 (Feb 98) 93
(100% CH)
This '73 should in all likelihood begin to withdraw from its peak now. In the late eighties it was fully mature, with a dark colour and an almost overripe sauternes nose. Colossally powerful, like a dessert. Who could fail to be impressed by this bounteous champagne?

1971 Comtes de Champagne 95 (Feb 98) 95
(100% CH)
Quite simply a fabulous champagne. Rich exotic taste which lingers for several minutes.

1970 Comtes de Champagne 84 (May 89) ▼
(100% CH)
Definitely a very good champagne that was at its peak between the ages of ten and fifteen. However, the acidity wasn't high enough to keep the wine alive for a longer period. When *Comtes de Champagne* gets too old it develops its very own oxidation tones. The sweetness becomes huge and the structure is very fat.
A manzanilla-like tone disturbs the whole.

1966 Comtes de Champagne 93 (Oct 98) 93
(100% CH)
Some bottles are on its way downhill. Deep colour and a manzanilla-like bouquet. Fresh and nutty on the palate.

1964 Comtes de Champagne 97 (Sep 90) 97
(100% CH)
"Comtes" at its best. with its lively deep yellow appearance. Full-bodied, fat, oily and creamy. Packed with aromas from dried fruits, magnificently rich and smooth with the same softness and sweetness in the long aftertaste.

1993 Comtes de Champagne Rosé 85 (Feb 98) 92
(100% PN)
I really wonder why this famous and expensive champagne is sold as a baby. The colour is salmon pink and the taste is soft and creamy as usually. The dominating aromas are cherries and apple peel. Put it away in the darkest corner of the cellar.

1991 Comtes de Champagne Rosé 87 (Feb 98) 89
(100% PN)
I haven't seen a pink Comtes 1988, 89 or 90, and then suddenly along come '91 and '93. I don't get it! The champagne itself is fine and typical of this house, with a soft and long vanilla aftertaste.

1985 Comtes de Champagne Rosé 81 (Nov 93) 90
(100% PN)
As opposed to the white version of *Comtes de Champagne*, the rosé contains only Pinot grapes. Bouzy is usually the dominant village, and so it is in the '85. Broad, full-bodied and robust rosé with good raspberry-like fruitiness. The colour is always deep. Put down for ten years.

1981 Comtes de Champagne Rosé 82 (Aug 89) 90
(100% PN)
The Taittinger rosés always take a long time to mature. The '81 had only begun its mature period at the age of nine. Huge, well structured and tight.

1976 Comtes de Champagne Rosé 93 (Mar 96) 93
(100% PN)
Fat and sweet with wonderful concentration. Hardly a classic but a wonderful explosion of fruit aromas.

1973 Comtes de Champagne Rosé 94 (Jul 94) 94
(100% PN)
When my fiancée tasted this champagne blind in a Sardinian sunset, she was convinced it was a white, aged champagne. The colour was actually a lot like an amber coloured bubbly from the fifties. The mousse was weak, but fine. The nose was exemplary, with exciting elements of cranberry, gooseberry, mushrooms and honey. The best thing about the wine, however, was the taste. Today the '73 is purest nectar. The sweet ripe fruit taste contains tones of apricot, peach, mango, passion fruit and an entrancing aftertaste of acacia honey.

1970 Comtes de Champagne Rosé 91 (Jun 97) 93
(100% PN)
The nose may not be generous, but this is compensated for by a delightful, concentrated nectar-like flavour. The fruit tones resemble blood orange, grapefruit and mango.

1990 Taittinger Collection
84 (May 97) 90
(60% PN, 40% CH)
Wonderfully buttery. A charmer with good prospects for the future.

1986 Taittinger Collection
83 (Nov 94) 86
(60% PN, 40% CH)
Highly expensive, artistically designed bottle with a gaudy plastic case, the '86 is a mature sweet wine that is typical of this house, without much chance of development.

1985 Taittinger Collection
88 (Mar 98) 90
(60% PN, 40% CH)
Tasted alongside the ordinary '85, this *Collection* felt even more complex, due perhaps to its greater autolytic charcacter.

1983 Taittinger Collection
80 (Aug 89) 86
(60% PN, 40% CH)
Designed by Da Silva and identical to the 1983 Vintage. Full-bodied, well-made but slightly dull champagne.

1982 Taittinger Collection 92 (Oct 93) 93
(60% PN, 40% CH)
The bottle is formed by the artist André Masson, and the wine is made in a Cristal-like style. High class aristocratic champagne with overflowing fruit. The concentrated taste is perfectly balanced and has a lovely finish which brings to mind English butterscotch.

1981 Taittinger Collection 83 (Sep 88) 85
(60% PN, 40% CH)
Arman's surreal golden string instrument against a black background is my favourite among the Collection bottles even if the contents aren't so much to get excited about. It's finely tuned and refined, sure, but lacks the expected concentration.

1959 Taittinger Rosé 84 (Jul 97) ▼
I have to admit that the existence of this wine was a complete surprise to me. Probably made almost entirely from Pinot Noir. Still a very powerful wine with a deep colour. Unfortunately much of the fruit had been lost and the oxidation was very obvious.

Veuve Clicquot

12 rue du Temple, 51100 Reims ☎ 03 26 89 54 40
Production: 10 million bottles.

The house was founded in 1772 by Philippe Clicquot, then his son François married Nicole-Barbe Ponsardin, who took over the company at the age of 27 when she found herself a widow. By her side was Comte Edouard Werlé and the firm's "Chef de Caves", Antoine Müller. Together with Müller she developed "remuage" using "pupitres". One Heinrich Bohne then helped to take the Russian market by storm. Throughout the 19th century and right up to the 1970's, Clicquot was reckoned as one of the top three or four champagne companies, a position that was lost when the decision was made to increase sales by several hundred percent. At first the company merged with Canard-Duchêne, but today it is a part of the powerful Louis Vuitton-Moët-Hennesy group. The 284 hectares owned by Clicquot in 22 villages is enough for around three of the ten million bottles produced each year.

The most important crus for *La Grande Dame* and the vintage wine are Ambonnay, Bouzy, Avize, Cramant, Le Mesnil, Oger and Verzenay. Since 1962 modern vinification techniques and stainless steel tanks are used. If you find old well-kept vintages they'll be very like Bollinger and Krug. Despite the factory scale, the house has managed to keep its Pinot-based classic style, where dough, bread and pepper are clear elements. Jacques Peters, who is brother to François Peters in Le Mesnil and an equally gifted winemaker, should get the credit for Clicquot's quality today. The vintage wine often gives best value for money. A classic house!

Veuve Clicquot Brut 80
(56% PN, 16% PM, 28% CH)
Despite increased production François Peters' brother Jacques succeeds in making a classically rich and dry non-vintage champagne of top quality. Clicquot's style is impressive, with a yeasty bouquet and rich fruits, along with elements of pepper.

Veuve Clicquot Sec 55
(56% PN, 16% PM, 28% CH)
The "Yellow Widow". If you really have to drink unnecessarily sweet champagne, then Clicquot is a good choice. Clicquot and Roederer use the correct base wines with a good portion of maturity which carries the sugar with head held high. Yeasty, bready nose with a full-bodied taste. If only it wasn't so sweet!

Veuve Clicquot Demi-Sec 55
(56% PN, 16% PM, 28% CH)
Precisely as with Roederer, Clicquot has even more bottle maturity in its sweetest wine before sale. A trouser-opener, as the Germans say. Honey, strawberry and toffee, but sickly sweet after a while. A good way to introduce someone to champagne.

1989 Veuve Clicquot Rich Réserve 68 (Feb 98) 78
(68% PN, 32% CH)
A famous Swedish wine writer recommends this together with herrings! For me this is very good for dessert.

1988 Veuve Clicquot Rich Réserve 60 (May 97) 75
(68% PN, 32% CH)
Sweet vintage champagne! Full-bodied and bready, with autolytic character. Smooth, rich flavour. A well-made wine but hardly the thing for those of us who love our champagne dry. I rather have the concentrated 1990.

1988 Veuve Clicquot Rosé 82 (May 97) 86
(73% PN, 27% CH)
A typical rosé from Clicquot with good balance and a faint element of strawberry. Otherwise the nose is broad and bready and the flavour is smooth and delicate with a sweet touch.

1985 Veuve Clicquot Rosé 86 (Oct 98) 88
(73% PN, 27% CH)
The colour is medium-deep, with elements of copper and bronze. The nose is unique, with earthy aromas that remind one of hyacinths and pelargonia. The flavour is balanced and continues on the same theme, combined with a peppery aftertaste. More creamy with age.

1983 Veuve Clicquot Rosé 68 (Sep 92) ▼
(73% PN, 27% CH)
It was wonderfully mature in 1990, but had fallen away a great deal two years later as the fruit has dried out and been replaced by a little rough flavour. Needs retasting.

1979 Veuve Clicquot Rosé 80 (Sep 88) 83
(73% PN, 27% CH)
If the wine's fruit is sufficient the '79 will last long. Toasty, nutty with barrel-like aromas and full Pinot flavour.

1978 Veuve Clicquot Rosé 84 (Jul 88) 84
(73% PN, 27% CH)
Sensual, successful '78. Biscuits and perfumed tones blended with mature cheeses and strawberry aroma. Soft, creamy and somewhat one-dimensional, medium long flavour.

1976 Veuve Clicquot Rosé 68 (Dec 87) ?
(73% PN, 27% CH)
A clumsy and square '76 with tough spicy aromas and a lack of fruit. Maybe an ugly duckling.

1932 Veuve Clicquot Rosé
(75% PN, 25% CH)
Sadly the cork was too loose, and the wine was oxidised. Several competent tasters appreciated this champagne, but I regarded it as defective. Unjudged.

1989 Veuve Clicquot 86 (May 98) 88
(67% PN, 33% CH)
The '89 is a touch fruitier than usual, with clear elements of mature Chardonnay, even if the classical breadiness is there in the background.

1988 Veuve Clicquot 86 (Oct 97) 90
(67% PN, 33% CH)
The Clicquot vintage wine is always a good bet with its bready, yeasty and peppery nose, and rich autolytic flavour. The '88 is no exception.

1985 Veuve Clicquot 85 (Jan 95) 90
(67% PN, 33% CH)
More typical of the house and classical than *La Grande Dame* of the same year. Broad, mature, peppery and bready Clicquot nose. The full-bodied flavour is in tune too.

1983 Veuve Clicquot 77 (Mar 92) 85
(62% PN, 5% PM, 33% CH)
Bready and bushy Clicquot nose with a peppery flavour and undeveloped aftertaste.

1982 Veuve Clicquot 90 (Jan 99) 92
(62% PN, 5% PM, 33% CH))
As *La Grande Dame* wasn't made this year, this is the firm's best wine from 1982. The champagne has a good well-built body and promising young fruit. Lovely in magnum.

1980 Veuve Clicquot 83 (Feb 88) 87
(67% PN, 33% CH)
One of the first champagnes I ever bought. Extremely restrained and mineral-rich to be an '80. Pure fruit and long, stony aftertaste.

1979 Veuve Clicquot 93 (Aug 98) 93
(67% PN, 33% CH)
Extremely well-kept and youthful, with aromas of chocolate, nut, cellar and fresh bread. A fine attack and a pure, fruity flavour with length.

1978 Veuve Clicquot 80 (Jan 88) 82
(62% PN, 5% PM, 33% CH)
Mature and smoky champagne that demands food. One-dimensional and robust.

1976 Veuve Clicquot 89 (May 88) 92
(67% PN/PM, 33% CH)
If the rosé of 1976 was clumsy, the white '76 was far more successful. Warm, open generous nose of new-baked bread and classically mature Clicquot flavour.

1975 Veuve Clicquot Wedding Cuvée 94 (Dec 94) 94
(67% PN, 33% CH)
Oh Clicquot, what a year 1975 was for you! Wonderfully well-kept, vibrant wine with generous toasty and nutty tones which are similar to Bollinger in style. Superbly mature brioche flavour and fresh fruit.

1973 Veuve Clicquot 90 (Dec 94) 90
(67% PN/PM, 33% CH)
The flesh is looser than in the '75, but with just as much chocolaty richness. An old-fashioned dark and woody aftertaste feels very piquant.

1969 Veuve Clicquot 92 (Sep 96) 92
(67% PN/PM, 33% CH)
Meaty nose, dry long nutty flavour and nice acidity.

1966 Veuve Clicquot 94 (Aug 95) 94
(67% PN/PM, 33% CH)
Not as massive as the '64, but with an aristocratic stature and freshness that is of the highest class. A textbook Clicquot.

1964 Veuve Clicquot 94 (Aug 95) 94
(67% PN/PM, 33% CH)
Heavy and vinous with the vintage's typical mint chocolate aroma, along with a fat, long aftertaste with layers of vanilla. One of the vintage's most full-bodied champagnes.

1961 Veuve Clicquot 97 (Aug 97) 97
(67% PN/PM, 33% CH)
The colour indicates great age but the mousse is exemplary, as is the nutty and complex flavour. One of the greatest Clicquot vintages I've ever tasted.

1959 Veuve Clicquot 95 (Jan 99) 95
(67% PN/PM, 33% CH)
Not quite as monumental as the '61, but meaty, broad and well-structured. The fruit and the acidity are more obvious than in most other '59's. The nose is nutty, with elements of mushroom and bread. The everlasting flavour is focused and fruity.

1955 Veuve Clicquot 98 (Jan 99) 98
(67% PN/PM, 33% CH)
This champagne is perfection with its lovely nose of roasted coffeebeans and unbeatable freshness.

1953 Veuve Clicquot 93 (Dec 94) ▼
(67% PN/PM, 33% CH)
Maderised on three occasions, so *53 Clicquot* is defintely not a sure thing. The two well-kept examples I have drunk were wonderful. The wine had a richness and concentration you seldom find in today's champagne. The mousse is often very weak, but the oily wine has a burgundy-like bouquet and a honeyed flavour.

1949 Veuve Clicquot 95 (Mar 96) 95
(67% PN/PM, 33% CH)
Quite wonderfully fresh and elegant, with great fruitiness and toasty aromas. Great length.

1947 Veuve Clicquot 90 (Jan 94) ▼
(67% PN/PM, 33% CH)
Sadly, a touch aged to be quite "whole", but a gigantic wine of monumental dimensions. A nose like a great cognac and fiery, aged, massive chewy and long flavour, with a sherry-like touch.

1945 Veuve Clicquot 96 (Mar 96) 96
(67% PN/PM, 33% CH)
One of the top 45's. A young, many-layered nose with a feminine form. Extravagantly long, fresh and deep flavour.

1943 Veuve Clicquot
(67% PN/PM 33% CH)
In appearance, deep old gold, but a maderised nose and a flat taste. Unjudged.

1942 Veuve Clicquot
(67% PN/PM, 33% CH)
Now loose and tired. Unjudged.

1937 Veuve Clicquot 94 (Feb 96) 94
(67% PN/PM, 33% CH)
A very deep colour and a weak but appreciable mousse. Incredibly concentrated, fat, fruity flavour with a long, impressive aftertaste of honey.

1928 Veuve Clicquot 95 (Aug 95) 95
(67% PN/PM, 33% CH)
A hardly visible mousse but a surprisingly light appearance. A bouquet full of finesses like butterscotch and roses. A magnificent flavour of damp wood and bitter chocolate. Holds well in the glass.

1923 Veuve Clicquot
(67% PN/PM, 33% CH)
Unfortunately I've only tasted it maderised. Unjudged.

1919 Veuve Clicquot 95 (Jun 97) 95
(67% PN/PM, 33% CH)
What a superb, lively vintage! The nose is more developed than the flavour. It reveals dark chocolate, plum and orange,while the mouth enjoys two layers of flavour, one incredibly fresh and acidic, and the other extremely buttery and rounded. A hugely long citrus-influenced aftertaste.

1989 La Grande Dame 90 (Feb 99) 92
(60% PN, 40% CH)
Developed, chocolaty and full of honey. A touch richer than the '88, but not as good as the exotic 1990.

1988 La Grande Dame 90 (Feb 98) 93
(62% PN, 38% CH)
The new bottle has brought with it a change in style. The champagne is now more toasty and feels lighter, less majestic, but with a honeyed aftertaste.

1985 La Grande Dame 90 (May 98) 92
(66% PN, 34% CH)
This was the year when Clicquot changed bottles. Those sold in the new bottle are reminiscent of *Dom Pérignon*, while the older, more curvacious bottle contains a wine more typical of the house, with deep chocolate tones. I doubt that the disgorging is the only reason for this.

1983 La Grande Dame 90 (Feb 98) 91
(67% PN, 33% CH)
Heavy, powerful and old-fashioned, but with an earthy side-tone that has crept into the chocolaty, rich whole. The latest bottles i have tasted were surprisingly sublime and fresh.

1979 La Grande Dame 95 (Jan 98) 95
(67% PN, 33% CH)
This rich Pinot-dominated champagne is a classic. At the age of eight, applish and fresh, elegant and long. At ten it had developed Bollinger-like richness and weight. Flowing with chocolate, honey, nuts, cheese, champagne cellar and huge fruit of mature red apples. Very consistent through the years. A real diamond.

1975 La Grande Dame 95 (Aug 90) 95
(67% PN, 33% CH)
The wine of the vintage! Dark, but brilliant and full of vigour. What dimensions! The nose is of an entire bakery full of pastries: dark and milk chocolate and nougat are all easily-definable tones. Bigger, softer, fruitier and longer than the famous *1975 Bollinger R.D.*

1988 La Grande Dame Rosé 92 (Jul 98) 94
(62% PN, 38% CH)
What an outstanding debut! It's surprising that this rosé house has waited so long before launching a prestige wine. The house style is instantly recognisable, with its full-bodied chocolaty Pinot character, but there's a rarely seen fruity element that lifts this multi-faceted wine up among the elite of prestige cuvées.

Charles Heidsieck

4 bd Henri Vasnier, 51100 Reims ☎ 03 26 84 43 50
Production: 3 million bottles.

Even though Charles Heidsieck is both the best and most famous of the three Heidsieck houses, it was the last of them to enter the scene. It took 66 years after Florens-Louis Heidsieck laid the foundations for the Heidsieck clan before Charles-Camille Heidsieck founded the house in 1851. Six years later, Charles-Camille embarked on his first journey to America. He was soon dubbed "Champagne Charlie" by the yanks and became so famous that his name was a feature of burlesque song lyrics all over the States. Charles-Heidsieck was owned for a while by Henriot, but was sold in 1985 to the Rémy-Cointreau group. Daniel Thibault is "Chef de Caves" both here and at Piper-Heidsieck, and before the hero Thibault came along, the house owned no vineyards of its own. Today the firm owns 30 hectares in Ambonnay, Bouzy and Oger. The non-vintage champagne *Brut Reséve* is among the best on the market today and the vintage wine is always a pleasure to follow. The decision to stop the *Champagne Charlie* line and replace the cuvée de prestige with a *Blanc de Millénaires* has been praised by many, but personally I reserve my judgement, as the company built up its strong image through its mature Pinot-influenced style.

Charles Heidsieck Brut 67
(40% PN, 40% PM, 20% CH)
The forerunner to the successful *Brut Réserve*. Much more restrained wine with a fulsome Pinot character and slightly hard finish. Ages extremely well.

Charles Heidsieck Brut Réserve 79
(40% PN, 35% PM, 25% CH)
From a hundred or so villages and 40% reserve wines Daniel Thibault makes one of the very best non-vintage champagnes produced by a large house. With a couple of years extra storage in the bottle it develops a high-class nose of toasted bread and a long complex fruitiness with a smooth aftertaste of toffee.

1985 Charles Heidsieck Rosé 83 (Oct 96) 83
(70% PN, 30% CH)
Huge overripe rosé with a loose bready style. A generous, soft, round and pleasurable flavour which gives a far sweeter impression than the '83.

1983 Charles Heidsieck Rosé 66 (Jun 92) 76
(65% PN, 15% PM, 20% CH)
Applish, fresh, almost hard but long aftertaste.

1982 Charles Heidsieck Rosé 70 (Jun 90) 78
(70% PN, 5% PM, 25% CH)
Extremely fruity, more generous than the '83, but with a shorter aftertaste.

1976 Charles Heidsieck Rosé 85 (Nov 95) 85
(75% PN, 25% CH)
A richly flavoured wine, long and clean on the finish. Mellow nose.

1989 Charles Heidsieck 83 (Aug 96) 88
(70% PN, 30% CH)
Lots of coffee and toasted bread in the nose, as usual. A rich, pleasurable orange fruit and a long, generous aftertaste.

1985 Charles Heidsieck 87 (Feb 98) 87
(70% PN, 30% CH)
Open and generous Heidsieck, with a more typical "big house" style. Broad, toasty and orange fruity. Slightly overdeveloped already and a touch sweet.

1982 Charles Heidsieck 85 (May 97) 86
(60% PN, 40% CH)
Drier than the '85 with a bursting, chewy fruit and bread aroma typical of the house.

1981 Charles Heidsieck 83 (Sep 98) 83
(55% PN/PM, 45% CH)
Nice bouquet of orange-chocolate and coffee. The taste is rather one-dimensional.

1975 Charles Heidsieck 89 (May 91) 90
(75% PN/PM, 25% CH)
Straw-yellow colour, brioche nose and a rich well-structured flavour with elements of peach. Also somewhat one-dimensional.

1970 Charles Heidsieck 80 (Sep 87) 88
(55% PN, 45% CH)
It would be interesting to try this champagne again. That is to say, it was very underdeveloped at the age of 17. Closed nose and long acidic flavour.

1969 Charles Heidsieck 94 (Nov 94) 94
(75% PN, 25% CH)
What a magical nose! So sweet and charming, with all the flowers and fruits of the garden. The flavour is also magnificent, although not quite so outstanding. Unfortunately the dosage is a little high and there's a somewhat short aftertaste.

1966 Charles Heidsieck 94 (May 92) 94
(75% PN, 25% CH)
For those who don't know what dry cocoa smells like, I can recommend a sniff of this champagne. Golden, fresh colour with a virile mousse. The full-bodied, dry taste is a little withdrawn at first, but with some time in the glass a lovely length develops, with aromas of coconut, mandarin and orange.

1964 Charles Heidsieck 94 (Dec 96) 94
(75% PN, 25% CH)
Not as elegant as the '66, but big, bold, nutty and full of mouth-filling flavours.

1959 Charles Heidsieck
(75% PN, 25% CH)
Unfortunately one of the few 59's that has already passed its peak. In the middle of the nineties it was totally maderised. Unjudged.

1955 Charles Heidsieck 84 (Feb 95) ▼
(75% PN, 25% CH)
A weak pop! Mousse that is hardly visible, broad chocolate nose with weakly oxidised elements of overripe apple. Good, rich and united flavour. On the way out, but still a pleasure to drink.

1953 Charles Heidsieck 90 (May 92) 90
(75% PN, 25% CH)
Plenty of life and mousse, but a surprisingly weak nose. The divine flavour of old marine wood inspires forgiveness.

1949 Charles Heidsieck 94 (Oct 97) 94
(75% PN, 25% CH)
Extremely light and youthful. Fantastic freshness in the long aftertaste.

1937 Charles Heidsieck
(75% PN, 25% CH)
Totally defective at a tasting in 1994. Black and cloudy, like water mixed with the contents of an ashtray. Unjudged.

1985 Blanc de Millénaires 86 (Aug 98) 89
(100% CH)
Although very good, I must admit to a certain disappointment with this citrus-fruity, toasty wine. I long for ***Champagne Charlie***!

1983 Blanc de Millénaires 87 (Nov 94) 90
(100% CH)
Heidsieck's new cuvée de prestige is a constant winner at blind tastings all over the world. I'm less impressed by the deep yellow drink with its fine but rather miserly classical nose and buttery Chardonnay flavour. Clean and attractive, like a well-produced record of American west coast rock.

1983 Charles Heidsieck B. d. B. 90 (Mar 97) 90
(100% CH)
A sensational champagne with an overwhelming toasty nose. My colleagues were two decades out when they guessed wrong at a blind tasting in Cannes in 1996. The flavour was lighter and younger, without the many nuances that would take it up among the greats.

1982 Charles Heidsieck B. d. B. 88 (Apr 96) 90
(100% CH)
Bold and rich with a toasty nose and fine flavour of ripe grapes.

1981 Charles Heidsieck B. d. B. 80 (Jul 89) 87
(100% CH)
Straw-coloured, bursting with life, a characteristic hawthorn nose typical of the vintage and slightly rough flavour.

1976 Charles Heidsieck B. d. B. 85 (Oct 92) 85
(100% CH)
Sulphur colour and a lively mousse. Mature, heavy and oily. The Chardonnay fills the senses, although citrus tones do the groundwork.

1971 Charles Heidsieck B. d. B. 59 (Nov 90) ▼
(100% CH)
A fragile wine that hasn't had the strength to withstand the ravages of time. Light and thin with clear hints of maderisation as early as 1990.

1969 Charles Heidsieck B. d. B. 94 (Jun 97) 94
(100% CH)
Superbly multi-faceted and a teasing, flowery nose quite without any toasty undertones. A flavour that is a nectar that melts in the mouth, with lively citrus tones wrapped up in a smooth chocolate veil.

1961 Charles Heidsieck B. d. B. 91 (Apr 96) ▼
(100% CH)
A way past its peak with aromas of overripe apples and raisins. Even so, a muscular B. d. B. with a pure finish and magnificent butteriness.

1981 Champagne Charlie 90 (Aug 91) 91
(50% PN, 50% CH)
The name Champagne Charlie didn't go down so well in the English-speaking world, so Charles Heidsieck decided to discontinue this lovely champagne. Juicy, exotic and well-balanced with a good grip and long aftertaste of mango.

1979 Champagne Charlie 93 (Jan 99) 94
(50% PN, 5% PM, 45% CH)
The '79 is made in the same juicy exotic style, but based on an even better backbone of Pinot grapes. Delightfully enjoyable. My mouth waters when I think back to that delicious mango flavour.

1973 La Royale 90 (May 96) 92
(75% PN, 25% CH)
Powerful and exceptionally potent for a vintage which sees most wines now beginning to near their end. The nose is classical and bready and the flavour acidic and tough, with an afterthought of cocoa.

1966 La Royale 96 (Jun 97) 96
(75% PN, 25% CH)
This must be one of the best champagnes Charles Heidsieck has ever made. The nose is filled with breakfast aromas, like toast, coffee, butter and some exotic fruit marmelade. The flavour is very elegant and invigorating, with a strong tone of peach.

Bruno Paillard

Av. de Champagne, 51100 Reims 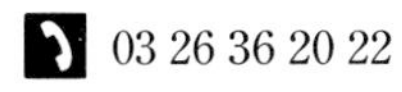 03 26 36 20 22
Production: 300,000 bottles.

Bruno Paillard is one of Champagne's most influential figures. His impressive height and stylish appearance, combined with great knowledge and a large dose of humility have given him places on the boards of various organisations in Champagne. He started his house in 1981 after having worked for many years as a broker in the business. In order to get going he bought stores of wine from champagne houses threatened with bankruptcy, or from growers. He is the first to admit that he didn't create the cuvées in the early years of Bruno Paillard champagne. The '83 is his first real effort, and it marks a leap in quality.

Bruno Paillard is determined to become one of the top champagne producers. He has 120 permanent contracts with wine growers in 32 villages. He uses 15% oak in all his champagnes, except the rosés. He is also careful to have a large store of old reserve wines in barrels for six months. Only the cuvée is used in Paillard's champagne - a measure he finances by using the second pressing wines for his other labels. The Pinot grapes mostly come from Bouzy, Mailly and Verzenay, and the Chardonnay from Mesnil, Vertus, Cuis and Sézanne. Paillard, who also has a fondness for Jaguars and art, has followed in Mouton-Rothschilds' footsteps and allows various artists to decorate his vintage labels each year.

Paillard is also one of the few who releases the disgorging date on all of his wines. In August 1994, Paillard and Chanoine had the majority of shares in Boizel. De Venoge and Philipponnat are now also included in the group.

Paillard Brut Première Cuvée 75
(45% PN, 22% PM, 33% CH)
Weak reddish copper tone. Hard, slightly restained nose with elements of newly-baked bread and yeast. A young flavour of both red and green apples. Storage potential. Certain similarities with *Roederer Brut Premier.*

Paillard Chardonnay Réserve Privée 86
(100% CH)
The bottles I have tasted been based on the harvest of 1989. Almost transparent colour with a greenish tone, an incredibly sophisticated, flowery nose of acacia, yellow roses and fresia. The flower theme returns in the light flavour and is enriched with vanilla and lime aromas. Reminds me of Deutz and Pol Roger.

Paillard Rosé 71
(85% PN, 15% CH)
Once again a broad wine with all the advantages of a blend. Multi-faceted, bready and berry-filled nose with a sweet flavour and long aftertone of wild raspberry. Perhaps the dosage is too high.

1985 Paillard 91 (Apr 95) 93
(45% PN, 55% CH)
A wonderful wine with a deep golden colour and Krug-like aromas. Nuts, honey, marzipan and the hard crust of wholemeal bread can all easily be distinguished in the broad and tight nose. Oily, deep and very rich flavour of all the products of the bakery.

1983 Paillard B. d. B. 87 (Sep 94) 89
(100% CH)
A richer and more full-bodied wine than the non-vintage blanc de blancs, with a less refined bouquet. Slightly smoky nose and a strong citrus aroma in the long taste.

1979 Paillard 81 (Jul 91) 84
(40% PN, 60% CH)
A thin '79 of purity and some elegance, but without concentration.

1976 Paillard 84 (Jul 90) 87
(40% PN, 60% CH)
Surprisingly light wine considering the vintage. Light colour, elegant nose of bakeries and honey. Stylish flavour that lacks length.

1973 Paillard 86 (Apr 96) 86
(50% PN, 50% CH)
Broad, aged and toasty nose with elements of chocolate and dried fruit. The flavour is quite full with certain signs of age.

1969 Paillard 87 (Jul 94) 
(60% PN, 40% CH)
A champagne in the English style, huge autolytic character and certain oxidative flavour. Buttery, broad and compact.

Ruinart

4 rue des Crayères, 51100 Reims  03 26 77 51 51

Production: 1.7 million bottles.

Dom Thierry Ruinart, a priest from Reims who was a good friend of Dom Pérignon, passed on enough knowledge to his nephew Nicolas Ruinart to enable him to form the first champagne house in 1729. Thus it's quite logical that Ruinart should belong to the Moët-Hennessy group.

The firm soon became successful on widely different export markets and was a popular place to visit due to its deep, exceptionally beautiful chalk cellars, which are now classified as a historical monument. Deep down in these cellars the best wine waiters of the world compete in the Trophée Ruinart. The company president Roland de Calonne holds over 15 hectares in Sillery and Brimont, which stands for 25% of the grape supply. The other 75% is bought in from 200 villages. Ruinart's wines often have a strong toasty character, combined with fine purity and good richness of minerals. The prestige wine *Dom Ruinart* is of very high class.

Ruinart Brut 68
(48% PN, 5% PM, 47% CH)
The high proportion of Chardonnay makes *Ruinart* a storable non-vintage champagne which becomes delightfully toasty after a few years. However, when it comes to direct consumption, it's hardly exciting, with its weak bread tone and hint of citrus aromas in a somewhat sharp taste.

Ruinart Rosé 48
(36% PN, 23% PM, 41% CH)
Less pure than its white colleague, slightly sour in the finish and an earthy tone in the nose.

1990 Ruinart 81 (Jul 97) 87
(59% PN, 41% CH)
As so often, a fine toasty tone in the nose but here it's backed up by a clear, deep Pinot aroma. The flavour is quite full with a Moët & Chandon-like basic tone. The reliability of this vintage is confirmed once again.

1988 Ruinart 70 (Oct 93) 81
(50% PN, 50% CH)
Like the *88 Moët* with its developed mushroom paste and citrus style. Mighty Pinot-inspired nose, but the taste isn't so good, unclear and earthy as it is.

1985 Ruinart 73 (Apr 93) 84
(50% PN, 50% CH)
Steely hard style all the way through, possibly some good development possibilities.

1982 Ruinart 74 (Apr 93) 83
(50% PN, 50% CH)
Once again steely, applish and hard.

1981 Ruinart 82 (Nov 95) 82
(50% PN, 50% CH)
A quite powerful '81, full of depth and flavour. Bready and toasty nose.

1947 Ruinart 87 (Mar 97) 87
(70% PN, 30% CH)
Lively and light with a faint nose of tar and crème brûle. Lots of fruit at first, but it is quickly replaced by darker aromas of wood, tar and cigars. Dry finish.

1986 Dom Ruinart Rosé 90 (Sep 98) 90
(20% PN, 80% CH)
The colour has an orange hue, the nose is full of pleasing mature aromas and an undefinable berry essence. Today the taste is very round and mouthfilling. Some tasters think this champagne tastes like a red burgundy and others speak of Bordeaux.

1985 Dom Ruinart Rosé 80 (Nov 93) 84
(10% PN, 90% CH)
Fine salmon colour, aggressive mousse, vinous style with tones of tobacco and leather. Powerful tobacco flavour but a touch short for it to be completely satisfying. It is hard to judge this champagnes future.

1982 Dom Ruinart Rosé 75 (May 98) 78
(20% PN, 80% CH)
Just like the white '82, a huge disappointment. The nose was finely balanced, as was the initial flavour, but the aftertaste is sour and short.

1979 Dom Ruinart Rosé 80 (Feb 90) 83
(20% PN, 80% CH)
Deep orange colour. Strong nose of boullion and bread. Full but short flavour. An untypical '79.

1978 Dom Ruinart Rosé 93 (Sep 97) 93
(20% PN, 80% CH)
A superbly good and personal '78 with a wonderfully toasty bouquet and a fresh, long, exotic flavour.

1976 Dom Ruinart Rosé 93 (Jan 99) 93
(20% PN, 80% CH)
Splendid! The nose is like a mature, top-class red burgundy. The strong bouquet is followed by a sweet ice-cream-like round and mild raspberry flavour. Mature.

1988 Dom Ruinart 93 (Jan 99) 95
(100% CH)
Surprisingly developed and generous already, with a massive tropical wealth of mangoes and oranges. Also a strong attack and sophisticated, multi-faceted, long aftertaste to follow into the 21st century. An unbeatable *Dom Ruinart*!

1986 Dom Ruinart 84 (Sep 98) 89
(100% CH)
Weak currant tones backed up by roasted chestnuts and a discreet element of acacia honey. The flavour is still very young and aggressive but the attack is promising. An unusually storable '86 that shouldn't be consumed before the year 2000.

1985 Dom Ruinart 80 (Nov 92) 86
(100% CH)
Here we have the remarkable tone of blackcurrants easily discernible in the nose. Several professional wine tasters thought this was a Sauvignon Blanc at a large SAS tasting in 1992. However, I recognised the style from earlier *Dom Ruinarts*. Even though the blackcurrant character was a bit too dominant, this is a tasty wine.

1983 Dom Ruinart 90 (Jan 94) 92
(100% CH)
Gorgeous green/yellow colour and a prolonged, fast mousse. Broad, smoky, enormously toasty nose that is exquisite, although slightly over-dimensioned. The mature currant-like fruit is noticed first in the soft aftertaste.

1982 Dom Ruinart 80 (Jun 91) 86
(100% CH)
Much-praised wine which so far has yet to offer itself at all. Closed nose and a pure, unripe, mineral-rich flavour.

1979 Dom Ruinart 93 (Mar 93) 93
(100% CH)
This lovely vintage seldom leaves one disappointed. Ruinart's '79 is very personal, with its classic toasty basic tone. The fruit is made up of aromas very much like fresh beef tomatoes and redcurrants. The acidity is wonderful and the length magnificent.

1978 Dom Ruinart 90 (Feb 90) 90
(100% CH)
A great, overpowered wine with a unique nose of overripe oranges and yeast. Massive round flavour of ripe fruit, low acidity.

1976 Dom Ruinart 90 (Dec 96) 90
(100% CH)
Extremely green colour, a touch miserly on the nose but a concentrated, exotic fruit flavour with a soft, fine aftertone.

1975 Dom Ruinart 70 (Aug 89) 70
(100% CH)
What happened to Ruinart in 1975? Hollow and at best a mineral-rich wine. Stingy and smelling of fish. Needs retasting.

1973 Dom Ruinart 94 (Sep 96) 94
(100% CH)
This is great stuff! A bold bouquet of toasted bread and overripe lemons. A full, intense flavour with the same aromas.

1969 Dom Ruinart 90 (Jun 93) 91
(100% CH)
Ochre yellow nuances in a basic lime green colour. Extremely active and youthful. A decadent cold nose of sea, oyster shell and rubber. On the palate the impressions are more classical and tasting of lime. Full, fat and long.

1961 Dom Ruinart 93 (Aug 95) 93
(100% CH)
Still very fresh, with lovely active acidity. The nose suggests leather, vanilla and clean sheets. The flavour is slightly short but very refreshing and sophisticated, with a certain lemon freshness.

Henriot

3 pl. des Droits del Homme,
51100 Reims ☎ 03 26 89 53 00

Production: 1 million bottles.

Joseph Henriot is one of Champagne's most powerful men. After having been the boss of Veuve Clicquot for many years he returned home to Henriot in 1994. The Henriot family were growers in Champagne as far back as in 1640 and they started their own champagne house in 1808. The firm's strength has always been the top class vineyards they've owned in Côte des Blancs. Today they have 100 hectares in Le Mesnil, Chouilly, Oger, Beaumont, Avize, Épernay, Vertus, Villeneuve, Verzenay, Verzy, Trépail, Aÿ, Avenay, Mutigny and Mareuil-sur-Aÿ. This is sufficient for 75% of production, which is an outstanding figure for a champagne house. The total proportion of Chardonnay is over 40% and dominates the house style with its pure, fresh citrus fruit.

The Henriots have always had strong links with Charles Heidsieck and until quite recently shared their office and wine production plant. They share cellars, on the other hand, with Clicquot. The company's largest export market is Switzerland, where Henriot's dry, slightly discreet champagnes are extremely successful.

Henriot Souverain Brut 70
(60% PN, 40% CH)
It's great to avoid Pinot Meunier in a large firm's non-vintage champagne. The large proportion of Chardonnay is apparent first in the delicate, light flavour. The house style is striking.

Henriot B. d. B. 79
(100% CH)
The wine resembles the non-vintage champagne in many ways, but the nose is a touch more mature and open, with elements of apple jam. Good but expensive.

1988 Henriot Rosé 81 (Feb 97) 87
(52% PN, 48% CH)
A pure and well-made rosé with good red and blackcurrant tones and excellent mineral riches.

1989 Henriot 82 (Feb 97) 86
(55% PN, 45% CH)
Henriot have made a very light and elegant '89 with a subdued, flowery bouquet. The taste of minerals and citrus is appetising.

1988 Henriot 80 (Feb 97) 86
(55% PN, 45% CH)
A restrained and elegant champagne with signs of maturity in the nose and a pure, agreeable flavour.

1975 Henriot 80 (Aug 90) 83
(67% PN, 33% CH)
A surprisingly well-kept and youthful champagne, with a pure but characterless fruit. One of the thinnest 75's I've tasted.

1973 Henriot 81 (Aug 96) 81
(67% PN, 33% CH)
Surprisingly loose and clumsy. The house style seems to have disappeared. Instead we have a wine that is generous and full of chocolate, with an impure earthy secondary tone.

1971 Henriot 85 (May 96) 85
(67% PN, 33% CH)
The concentration fails to impress, and otherwise the wine is light and brittle with a fine acidity and intact mineral tones. A little too open and naked to make an impression with me.

1985 Les Enchanteleurs 85 (Jan 99) 88
(45% PN, 55% CH)
The firm's new cuvée de prestige is identical to *Cuvée Baccarat*. Their efforts to make a light and discreet champagne are fully rewarded in this wine. Rather light with a flowery elegance.

1983 Cuvée Baccarat 81 (May 94) 85
(45% PN, 55% CH)
Both the '83 and the '85 lack concentration. The wines are light, bordering on the brittle. The colour is light with hues of green. A weak, smoky mature tone is noticed in the flowery nose. The flavour is also flowery rather than fruity. A frail vanilla tone appears in the discreet aftertaste.

1982 Cuvée Baccarat 89 (Feb 97) 90
(45% PN, 55% CH)
A somewhat broader and meatier nose than usual, but otherwise the same laid-back, balanced big house style that we've come to expect. A classical champagne character all the way, but a touch impersonal.

1981 Cuvée Baccarat 88 (Sep 91) 90
(45% PN, 55% CH)
The '81 is a textbook example of an elegant cuvée champagne. It is smooth, generous and easy to appreciate, with its bouquet of mature Chardonnay and exemplary soft mousse. The flavour is woven together with veils of exotic fruit.

1979 Cuvée Baccarat 90 (Aug 96) 90
(40% PN, 60% CH)
Elegant and charming champagne. The lovely balanced taste is full of vanilla.

1981 Baron Philippe de Rothschild 83 (Jan 89) 87
(50% PN, 50% CH)
The equal proportions of Pinot and Chardonnay give the wine balance. ***Baron Philippe*** is always a heavier and more full-bodied champagne than *Baccarat*.

1979 Baron Philippe de Rothschild 83 (Jan 90) 88
(50% PN, 50% CH)
The Baron's own champagne from 1979 is similar to the '81 for the most part. The fruit may be a touch richer in this wine.

1973 Baron Philippe de Rothschild 93 (Apr 96) 93
(50% PN, 50% CH)
A fully-mature thoroughbred with class, charm and authority. The nose is complex and paradoxically youthful and mature. There are tones of yoghurt, orange and cheese and the flavour is exuberant, with a crispy finish and pure tone of orange chocolate.

1983 Cuvée Baccarat Rosé 84 (Feb 97) 87
Slender-limbed and sophisticated bread aroma and a hint of spring flowers in the nose. The rather full-bodied, restrained flavour has fine mineral tones.

Pommery

5 pl. du Général Gouraud,
51100 Reims
03 26 61 62 63

Production: 7 million bottles.

In 1856 Pommery & Greno was founded after having been known as Dubois-Gosset for the previous twenty years. The firm established a sales channel to the English as early as in the 19th century and were pioneers with their dry champagne - quite without a dosage. The Marquise de Polignac was one of the first owners and the man in charge of blending the cuvées, Prine Allain de Polignac, can trace his ancestry all the way back to her. In 1990 Pommery was one of those firms who ended up as part of the Moët-Hennessy group, but they do all they can to retain their house style. Pommery is one of the firms that own the most land in the Grand cru villages, but what is less well known is that their locations within the area are not always the best. Besides Pommery's own grapes, 60% of the supplies come from all over Champagne, and are vinified in modern style. Pommery is undoubtedly a great name in historical terms, but it was long since they made really great champagnes. The house style is made up of dry, restrained, ageworthy champagnes with an ascetic fruit and unmissable steeliness. The cuvée de prestige *Louise Pommery* doesn't fit that description, but instead is far too soft and polished to compete with the top wines of its competitors. The last four to five years have shown a clear improvement in quality.

Pommery Brut Royal 72
(40% PN, 30% PM, 30% CH)
At times I'm struck by the richness of Pommery's non-vintage wines, and at other times it's harder and meaner than most. The style is always an uncompromising dryness. Better after storage. An improvement in quality. Now it often has a biscuity, rich taste.

Pommery Extra Brut 60
(35% PN, 35% PM, 30% CH)
Wine mostly made for the German market. Ash dry, hollow champagne, quite without maturity and generosity.

Pommery Rosé 55
(60% PN, 40% CH)
Pale colour, mineral rich and simple nose of wild strawberry. Sweeter than expected, short aftertaste and a hint of licorice.

1990 Pommery 83 (May 97) 90
(50% PN, 50% CH)
This label has been given the Grand cru name for the first time. This is really a great year for Pommery. Steely, classical, closed but with a nose ripe for development, backed by undertones of butter and apple.

1989 Pommery 84 (Jun 98) 89
(50% PN, 50% CH)
Steely, metallic and hollow when young. As opposed to the '88 there is however a hint of toasty Chardonnay tones. Today completely changed for the better.

1988 Pommery 60 (Aug 94) 75
(50% PN, 50% CH)
Light, pure, with an incredibly acidic apple cider style. Neutral and aggressive. This ungenerous champagne makes me wonder how the firm became so popular. The style is not easily accessible.

1987 Pommery 60 (Aug 92) 70
(50% PN, 50% CH)
Only financial reasons can have motivated Pommery's decision to sell an '87. They shouldn't have.

1985 Pommery 78 (May 92) 86
(50% PN, 50% CH)
More buttery and softer than other Pommery vintages. Open caramel nose with elements of seaside rock and flowers.

1983 Pommery 80 (May 91) 87
(50% PN, 50% CH)
Surprisingly good and rich with Clicquot-like Pinot fruit and pepperiness. Bready flavour with good acidity.

1982 Pommery 80 (Dec 98) 84
(50% PN, 50% CH)
Fresh and applish, but with Pommery's metallic hardness. Some lemon licorice and burnt rubber had crept in around the age of ten.

1980 Pommery 75 (Mar 88) 80
(50% PN, 50% CH)
Tasted at the beginning of my interest in champagne. Faint metallic nose. Rich, bready, slightly loose flavour which lacks fruit.

1976 Pommery 84 (Dec 95) 84
(50% PN, 50% CH)
Faint and restrained, albeit masculine, nose. Powerful, smoky flavour with low acidity. Overall a little clumsy.

1969 Pommery 93 (Jun 97) 93
(50% PN, 50% CH)
A superb flowery and attractive wine with a broader nose than is usually the case with Pommery. In the mouth one finds toffee and smoky elements and an elegant crispy Chardonnay finish.

1964 Pommery 80 (Mar 93) ▼
(50% PN, 50% CH)
I've tasted this wine twice, both times from magnums. One bottle was completely maderised, the other had a toasty bouquet and great richness, but even there the aftertaste was filled with sherry aromas.

1961 Pommery 91 (Dec 93) 91
(50% PN, 50% CH)
Once again a restrained nose. Dark bouquet of tar, tobacco, molasses, forest and turpentine. A full-bodied flavour of wood, earth and chocolate, long and very well-built. A wine for macho men.

1955 Pommery 84 (Dec 91) ▼
(50% PN, 50% CH)
The bottle I tasted had a perfect level and gave a confidence-building hissing sound. The colour was also promising, but the champagne had too small a nose and the flavour was too much like tokay for its too reach brilliance. Not as good as the '53.

1953 Pommery 93 (Feb 94) 93
(50% PN, 50% CH)
The '53 has a dark amber colour, but the mousse seems indestructible. The nose is weak, with tones of molases, syrup and burnt sugar. The flavour is wonderfully rich, with a lovely peach-like aroma and sweet, aged aftertaste.

1952 Pommery 95 (Feb 97) 95
(50% PN, 50% CH)
Lots of 52's are youthful and fresh, but very few are as delicate as Pommery's. The colour is light and the microscopic bubbles stream around the glass like tiny pearls. The nose resembles a great white burgundy from the seventies and the tight, restrained flavour with its elements of cream candy is to all intents and purposes perfect.

1949 Pommery 95 (Oct 93) 95
(50% PN, 50% CH)
Only tasted once, from a magnum. No apparent mousse, only a slightly broad nose but plenty of purity where elements of toffee, cream, cocoa, cola and coffee can be distinguished. The flavour was one of the richest I've experienced. Exceptionally fruity with plums, mango, pastries and an extremely sweet aftertaste of milk chocolate. I can hardly imagine how many points it would have amassed if the mousse had been intact.

1947 Pommery 92 (Apr 93) 92
(50% PN, 50% CH)
Just as with other older vintages of Pommery, the flavour was more impressive than the nose. The cork was pulled with a corkscrew and the "pop" was weak. Deep amber colour and almost invisible mousse. The nose contained gingerbread, dates and dark chocolate. The flavour was nowhere near the lovely fruity sweetness of the '49, but had a massive wall of alcoholic power and character of raisins. No madeira tone.

1945 Pommery
(50% PN, 50% CH)
As with so many 45's, Pommery has been on the way downhill for some time. Unjudged.

1943 Pommery
(50% PN, 50% CH)
Slightly fresher than the '42, but to old. Unjudged.

1942 Pommery
(50% PN, 50% CH)
Maderised and therefore unjudged.

1929 Pommery 96 (Oct 98) 96
(50% PN, 50% CH)
Superb stuff! Classic and majestic.

1928 Pommery 88 (Sep 97) ▼
(50% PN, 50% CH)
What tremendous power and structure! Sadly a little too much sherry in the nose, but vigorous acidity and a long chocolaty aftertaste show that the wine's not on its death bed quite yet. Well-kept bottles may well be worth their high price.

1988 Louise Pommery 86 (Jan 99) 91
(40% PN, 60% CH)
The first vintage carrying the beautiful white label. The wine too is lovely, and tasteful to boot. The nose is already mature, with elements of cheese, cream candy, and licorice. The flavour, on the other hand, is much less developed, with dry freshness and aromas from Avize Chardonnay.

1987 Louise Pommery 82 (Feb 97) 85
(40% PN, 60% CH)
A pleasing nose of pastries and chocolate. Somewhat too hollow and thin fruity flavour for a cuvée de prestige.

1985 Louise Pommery 86 (May 95) 90
(40% PN, 60% CH)
The firm's cuvée de prestige is always made in a softer and more refined style than the vintage wine. The '85 has an exceptionally soft and luxuriant mousse, The nose is typical of *Louis Pommery*, with a cheesy, mature element combined with vanilla, fresh baked bread and orange. A tremendously melting and easily-drunk champagne. Stylish, but a touch too carefully arranged.

1982 Louise Pommery 85 (May 92) 88
(40% PN, 60% CH)
Attractive both to look at and to drink, but without that little extra. Medium-bodied and very soft and charming house style.

1981 Louise Pommery 83 (Dec 93) 84
(40% PN, 60% CH)
Most 81's in Champagne live on an exquisite flowery elegance. *Louis Pommery*, on the other hand, trusts its mature Aÿ Pinot, with plenty of cheese and charming chocolate aromas. The wine is medium-bodied and has a relatively short aftertaste.

1980 Louise Pommery 82 (Mar 94) 84
(40% PN, 60% CH)
Very discreet when young. Far broader and larger as the years go by. The colour is till very light, and the nose is expansive, like an '82 with polished and toasted bread tones. The toasted aromas return in the flavour, which is fat and finished.

1989 Louise Pommery Rosé 80 (Mar 97) 87
(57% PN, 43% CH)
Chalky, cold and hard, but with an underlying strength and a dry, elegant, fresh flavour with a hint of strawberry.

1982 Louise Pommery Rosé 84 (Sep 91) 87
(40% PN, 60% CH)
Very expensive and praised to the skies by many. A good rosé champagne with bready nose, delicate fruit, but too short an aftertaste.

1943 Pommery Rosé
A wine that has collapsed and is suitable only for madeira sauce. Unjudged.

Abelé

50 rue de Sillery, 51100 Reims ☎ 03 26 87 79 80

Production: 400,000 bottles.

Degorgé à la glace (see dictionary) was invented in Abelé's cellars. When Téodore Vander-Veken founded the firm in 1757 he laid the foundations for the third champagne house in history. Abelé stayed within the family until 1828, when Auguste de Brimont took over and began an experimental cooperation with Antoine Müller, Clicquot's innovative "Chef de Caves". After a short-lived move to Ludes, the champagne house is now back in Reims. José Ferrer Sala of the Spanish Freixenet was so delighted by Abelé's wines at a tasting that he bought the company in 1985. Abelé's wines are marked by a purity and lightness that closely resembles Henriot.

Abelé Brut 75
(33% PN, 33% PM, 34% CH)
Young and pure non-vintage champagne which surprises with its Chardonnay aromas of hawthorn and grapefruit.

Abelé Rosé 68
(45% PN, 25% PM, 30% CH)
Not at all as much Chardonnay fruit as the non-vintage champagne, but the same light fruity and mineral-rich aftertaste.

1985 Abelé 70 (Mar 94) 82
(60% PN, 40% CH)
The nose is less developed than in the delightful *Abelé Brut*. Steely acidity and a slightly thicker body point to the '85 developing well. Today however, I prefer the non-vintage.

1966 Abelé 93 (Dec 95) 93
Brilliantly flowery nose and elegant, sensual flavour - as so often in this perfect vintage.

1988 Soirées Parisiennes 84 (May 98) 87
(35% PN, 25% PM, 40% CH)
Very elegant and young, with nice acidity and a steely finish.

1986 Sourire de Reims 83 (May 95) 86
(25% PN, 75% CH)
An enormously expensive bottle decorated with a golden plastic angel. The champagne almost feels like a blanc de blancs in the nose, with flowery and animalist tones. The flavour is well-balanced, with a fine, mineral-rich champagne character.

1976 Abelé Imperial Club 85 (Oct 95) 85
(40% PN, 60% CH)
Dry and long, but lacks any interesting fruit aromas.

Lanson

12 bd Lundy, 51100 Reims ☎ 03 26 78 50 50

Production: 6.7 million bottles.

Lanson was founded in 1760 by François Delamotte as one of the first champagne houses. François' son Nicolas-Louis, who was a knight in the Maltese Order, took over in 1798 and decided to use the Maltese Cross as the company's symbol. The name Lanson didn't appear before 1837, and it wasn't until twenty years later that the firm moved to the present address in Reims.

Unfortunately, after a brief period in the Louis Vuitton group, Lanson ended up as part of Marne & Champagne in 1991. The house doesn't own its own vineyards, but instead buys grapes from 60 different villages. A controversial thing about Lanson, and Piper-Heidsieck for that matter, is that they stubbornly avoid malolactic fermentation without possessing a rich and good enough basic wine to get away with it. Both the non-vintage champagnes are sour and by no means easy to drink. The vintage champagne stings the teeth and stomach during its first years on the market, but does actually develop well as it gets older. Old vintages of Lanson are good buys and value for money. If you have the patience, put the latest vintage down in the cellar for ten years or so and then enjoy the bready and still fresh champagne.

Lanson Black Label 50
(50% PN, 15% PM, 35% CH)
Lanson Black Label is one of the most famous champagnes despite its unreasonable hardness. Just like Piper-Heidsieck, Lanson avoid malolactic fermentation, which means sharp, prickly wines when the body and extract is missing. Watch out for airlines' quarter-bottles with a screwcork! You have to look hard to find a worse representative for the region.

Lanson Demi-Sec 20
(50% PN, 15% PM, 35% CH)
At the first sniff thoughts go to ripe apples, but as the wine warms up, and when it is tasted, one wishes one were a beginner. They are the only people who could appreciate this champagne.

Lanson Rosé 37
(53% PN, 15% PM, 32% CH)
Light, sour and characterless, with an earthy sub-tone.

1990 Lanson 80 (Jan 99) 87
(50% PN, 50% CH)
Drinking this wine now is like getting up at dawn on a Sunday. It's too early. There are hard acids that burn in the stomach, but don't be surprised if great complexity and fine, toasty aromas turn up and take over in a few years.

1989 Lanson 72 (Jun 95) 78
(56% PN, 44% CH)
Few know that this is in fact a Grand cru champagne. The grapes come from Verzenay, Aÿ, Bouzy, Oger, Chouilly and Cramant. With acidity at 5.5 grams it's far softer than the '85, which has 7 grams of malic acid. Rounded and pleasant, but it loses it all worryingly quickly in the glass.

1988 Lanson 70 (Jun 95) 78
(51% PN, 49% CH)
Surprisingly soft and candy-influenced champagne without much openness in the nose and a somewhat impure finish.

1985 Lanson 84 (Feb 97) 88
(50% PN, 50% CH)
At first a very sharp and hard to drink, where the apple tang is intrusive. The nose is stylish and fresh however, with an appealing breadiness. An embryo that has developed into roundness and maturity.

1983 Lanson 75 (Feb 89) 81
(50% PN, 50% CH)
Unexpectedly developed bready nose, but that ungenerous house style reappears in the taste and the apple tang is intrusive again.

1981 Lanson 88 (Jun 97) 88
(54% PN, 46% CH)
1981 is a lovely vintage for Lanson. Few have succeeded in making such classical champagnes with a good grip and faint roasted aromas.

1980 Lanson 90 (Feb 99) 80
(50% PN, 50% CH)
Fresh and creamy nose. Hard, sour and somewhat short flavour.

1979 Lanson 90 (Feb 99) 92
(50% PN, 50% CH)
The '79 has all the advantages of the vintage. A particularly elegant wine with a round Pinot nose and well-built structure. The apple tang is well integrated with this wine. Long and thin as a supermodel.

1976 Lanson 91 (Dec 98) 91
(46% PN, 54% CH)
Relatively mature colour, incredibly toasty, almost burnt character. Impressive with its dill and brioche. Slightly heavy in the rump, with a structure resembling the '59, without that year's purity. Very young in magnum.

1975 Lanson 92 (May 97) 92
(55% PN, 45% CH)
Aside from the horrible bottle design this champagne creates a lovely overall impression. Mature, full of chocolate and a fresh, long flavour.

1971 Lanson 90 (Nov 95) 90
(50% PN, 50% CH)
Pure and honeyed. Light to medium-bodied with a charming apple character which reminds me of Cox's Orange apples.

1959 Lanson 94 (Nov 94) 94
(50% PN, 50% CH)
Without a doubt the greatest Lanson I have tasted. The wine is almost heroic in its dimensions, and amazingly vital in its colour and mousse. The nose opens slowly to reveal all the colours of the peacock's tail. The champagne is very masculine, with nuances of cedar and havanna cigars. The wine is astoundingly heavy and full-bodied, with the same aromas as the nose. The finish is a textbook example of the vintage, very dry and tough, fiery and rich in tannin.

1945 Lanson
(50% PN, 50% CH)
Despite their reputation, very few 45's have shown the stamina needed to stay the pace over half a century. Lanson is no exception. Totally maderised. Unjudged.

1988 Noble Cuvée 85 (Jun 98) 88
(40% PN, 60% CH)
A pure Grand cru champagne from Avize, Cramant, Chouilly, Verzenay and Ambonnay. Restrained and concentrated with an aromatic spectrum which augurs well for the future.

1985 Noble Cuvée 83 (Mar 95) 88
(40% PN, 60% CH)
I have only drunk one glass of this wine. It seemed to be much more restrained than the '80, but with more of a mineral accent and less generous fruit.

1981 Noble Cuvée 83 (Jun 96) 89
(40% PN, 60% CH)
Flowery and fine like so many '81's, with candy tones and juicy acidity, and the promise of a long life.

1980 Noble Cuvée 86 (Jul 89) 87
(20% PN, 80% CH)
The colour was a deep yellow and the nose was filled by mature Chardonnay, but with a perceptible element of eggnog. Richly peach-like, soft and medium-long taste.

1989 Lanson B. d. B. 83 (Jul 98) 88
(100% CH)
The firm's new cuvée de prestige is made from equal portions of Chouilly, Cramant and Avize grapes. A textbook appearance and an attractive nose of biscuits and lemon. The flavour is complex and elegant today.

1983 Lanson B. d. B. 85 (Feb 95) 89
(100% CH)
12.7% alcohol is extremely unusual! The wine also has an extraordinary power for a blanc de blancs. The nose is marked by petroleum and overripe lemons, with a weak toasty element. In the mouth the company's apple tang comes in handy in an otherwise rather mature wine. Somewhat one-dimensional grapefruit taste.

1981 Cuvée 225 92 (May 96) 93
(45% PN, 55% CH)
A brilliant Lanson! Everything's gone right here. The wine has a classical champagne character, full of minerals, toasted bread and delicious citrus-influenced fruit. The harmonies in the flavour are also outstanding.

Piper-Heidsieck

51 bd Henry-Vasnier,
51100 Reims 03 26 84 43 00
Production: 5 million bottles.

All three Heidsieck houses originate from the same company, Heidsieck & Co, which was formed in 1785 by Florens-Louis Heidsieck. The Piper-Heidsieck branch was founded in 1834 by Christian Heidsieck. The house remained within the family right up to 1989, when it became part of Rémy-Cointreau. Daniel Thibault, who makes the cuvées at Charles Heidsieck, is also the man responsible at Piper-Heidsieck, but he is careful to maintain the two houses' separate identities. Piper own 21 hectares and buys in most of its grapes from 60 villages. Today the wines are going through the malolactic fermentation, but Piper used to prevent it which led to knife-sharp wines without extract. All the firm's champagnes gain a great deal from being cellared, which is unfortunately something Piper neglects to inform consumers about. Florens-Louis and the vintages from the sixties are stunning. Their extremely well-designed cellar tours are constructed in the very best Hollywood style, something which should suit their American customers admirably. As I've remarked before, it was a train ride around Piper's cellars that confirmed my fascination for champagne.

Piper-Heidsieck Brut 60
(55% PN, 30% PM, 15% CH)
Previously i wondered why they didn't use malolactic fermentation in such a thin wine? The acidity is thrust upon the drinker when the extract isn't there. It should be noted, however, that Piper has improved enormously since Thibault became "Chef de Caves" a couple of years ago. Today the wine is fruity and sound.

Piper-Heidsieck Demi-Sec 26
(55% PN, 30% PM, 15% CH)
Sour and sweet at the same time. Need I say more?

Piper-Heidsieck Rosé 50
(45% PN, 40% PM, 15% CH)
Heavy and clumsy as a basic red wine. The still wine doesn't seem to be wholly integrated with the champagne. Sweet and fruity aftertaste.

1982 Piper-Heidsieck Rosé 78 (Oct 95) 84
(75% PN, 25% CH)
Still undeveloped and hard to judge. To be honest I haven't found enough extract to persuade me to believe in an ugly-duckling story here.

1975 Piper-Heidsieck Rosé 84 (Feb 96) 84
(50% PN, 50% CH)
As with all older vintages from Piper, this wine retains a youthful freshness. This '75 is, however, too weak in the nose and limited in flavour to send me jumping through hoops.

1989 Piper-Heidsieck 75 (Feb 97) 87
(70% PN, 30% CH)
Too early to drink yet. There are hard acids that burn in the stomach, but don't be surprised if great complexity and fine, toasty aromas turn up and take over in the next century.

1985 Piper-Heidsieck 80 (May 98) 85
(55% PN, 15% PM, 30% CH)
This wine demands a customer with a good sense of smell! It's all there, but very very weak. The flavour is light, soft, agreeable and ultra-modern. If you look well enough you'll find hints of orange, chocolate, lime and licorice.

1982 Piper-Heidsieck 78 (May 91) 81
(55% PN, 15% PM, 30% CH)
Unusually sweet and soft. Nice enough to drink but lacking any major development possibilities.

1976 Piper-Heidsieck 84 (Oct 98) 90
(60% PN, 10% PM, 30% CH)
This rich year suits Piper's brittle. Developed, chocolatety in regular bottles. Vigorous and balanced, with very young apperance.

1975 Piper-Heidsieck 84 (Feb 96) 84
(60% PN, 10% PM, 30% CH)
A faint nose with hints of breadiness. The flavour is fresh and light, with a short, pure aftertaste of minerals.

1964 Piper-Heidsieck 95 (Oct 98) 95
(65% PN, 35% CH)
Surprisingly my first bottles of Piper´s '64 was completely maderised. Monsieur Liégent at the "Le Vigneron" restaurant used that champagne in his sauces. Other bottles are fantastic!

1961 Piper-Heidsieck 91 (Mar 96) 91
(65% PN, 35% CH)
A really mineral, almost salty nose. Finishes in a lovely taste of bread.

1955 Piper-Heidsieck 96 (May 94) 96
(65% PN, 35% CH)
A magical, sensational champagne. I opened it as an extra bottle one evening when we'd met to enjoy the legendary *1947 Krug*. This wine was even better! Light and with a mousse that didn't look a day over ten years old. A superb nose of roasted coffee, bread, wood, nuts, honeysuckle, lily of the valley and wet wool. Vigorous and fat flavour where lime and peaches have the upper hand. Remarkable balance!

1928 Piper-Heidsieck 90 (Oct 97) 90
(65% PN, 35% CH)
Almost without sparkle, but still an impressing champagne. Deep old taste of tar, dried fruit and leather. Only one half-bottle tasted.

1988 Brut Sauvage 73 (Jan 97) 84
(70% PN, 30% CH)
A weak nose that is typical of the house, with discreet fruit and a cold, clear flavour with biting acidity and shy fruit.

1985 Brut Sauvage 75 (Jan 97) 82
(70% PN, 30% CH)
The champagne was heavy and bready in the nose. The flavour on the other hand is somewhat raw and sharp. A hint of rubber tones lowers the overall impression in what is otherwise a very full-bodied champagne.

1982 Brut Sauvage 77 (Jun 94) 84
(70% PN, 30% CH)
Quite without dosage. What I call a "big house style", with broad and blended tones, polished and pure. Tangerine, orange and minerals dominate the acidic flavour.

1979 Brut Sauvage 73 (Jun 88) 80
(70% PN, 30% CH)
To be honest this would have been better with a dosage! Stingy and ascetic.

1988 Piper Rare 78 (May 97) 86
(35% PN, 65% CH)
Very discreet on the nose, lovely acidity and length.

1985 Piper Rare 73 (Mar 95) 85
(35% PN, 65% CH)
Sour, full of minerals and relatively thin, but with good development possibilities.

1979 Piper Rare 73 (Mar 94) 85
(35% PN, 65% CH)
A lightweight with a surprisingly small suit. You have to search hard for the mineral tones that are there, somewhere.

1976 Piper Rare 84 (Oct 88) 89
(35% PN, 65% CH)
A masterwork of elegance in this powerful year. A nose of sea and flowers, and a crispy, multi-faceted flavour with minimal bubbles that burst against the palate like pellets of caviar. Unfortunately the wine is too light and fragile to make me fall head over heels.

1975 Cuvée Florens-Louis 83 (Aug 88) 87
(20% PN, 80% CH)
This cuvée de prestige disappeared from the market a long time ago, to be replaced by *Piper Rare*. To me the wine tasted a lot like its successor, light and elegant without any great depth.

1973 Cuvée Florens-Louis 91 (Feb 96) 91
(20% PN, 80% CH)
Somewhat richer than the '71, but with less outspoken elegance and length. I suppose that most would prefer the '73 above the '71 as it's been painted with a broader brush and clearer strokes. Personally I prefer the teasing refinement of the '71.

1971 Cuvée Florens-Louis 93 (Jul 95) 93
(20% PN, 80% CH)
Tasted blind at the "Le Vigneron" restaurant, I had no problems naming the year and the producer. The wine is light but very elegant, due to the lack of malolactic fermentation.

George Goulet

1 av. de Paris, 51100 Reims ☎ 03 26 66 44 88

Production: 1.3 million bottles (100,000 sold as Goulet).

A firm with a complicated history. François André Goulet started the business in 1834, and in 1960 the house was taken over by Abel Lepitre, who let the well-respected name fade away. Today most of the operation has moved to Vaudemanges, where Luc Chaudron is determined to push Goulet's name up into the top circles once again. Goulet was a supplier to the Swedish Royal Family for many years. Only 10% of production is sold under the Goulet name, with most marketed under the "buyer's own label", or as Chaudron & Fils. The company makes some lovely soft Pinot-based champagnes of great quality.

G. Goulet Brut 76
(66% PN, 34% CH)
Well-stored and pure non-vintage champagne which is always a pleasure to drink. Soft and full-bodied with an agreeable mature flavour of Pinot Noir.

G. Goulet Rosé 75
(70% PN, 30% CH)
The house style is clear here, with its soft Pinot fruit and generous character. A pleasing aftertaste of blackberry.

1988 G. Goulet 80 (Nov 94) 86
(66% PN, 34% CH)
In the nose I found mostly Chardonnay tones like flowers and cream. The flavour on the other hand is dominated by the characteristic house aroma of soft Pinot Noir. Long, almond aftertaste.

1973 G. Goulet 89 (Oct 96) 89
(60% PN, 40% CH)
Full, big, fruity and mature on the palate. Chocolaty nose.

1985 Veuve G. Goulet 80 (Nov 94) 89
(50% PN, 50% CH)
Young, undeveloped champagne which holds much of interest within it. Fine bakery tones in the nose and good attack in the mouth, but the aftertaste needs a few more years in order to develop a satisfactory length.

1982 G. Goulet B. d. B. 78 (Dec 96) 78
(100% CH)
Light, faint nose. Lacking flesh and with a slightly metallic flavour.

1973 G. Goulet B. d. B. 79 (Sep 97) 79
(100% CH)
Very youthful and well-kept, but lacking charm. Light colour, lively mousse and a mineraly, dried-out, short flavour. A disappointment.

Thiénot

14 rue des Moissons, 51100 Reims ☎ 03 26 47 41 25

Production: 600,000 bottles.

Thiénot is a relatively new house that was formed as late as 1980. Most of the grapes are bought in from reasonably good areas. The founder, Alain Thiénot, is still at the helm. M. Thienot is very hospitable and charming, but in that respect he's overshadowed by his lovely wife.

Thiénot Brut 60
(50% PN, 25% PM, 25% CH)
This wine seems to be a lot younger and less ripe a couple of years ago. The last few times I've drunk the champagne it's had a pleasant biscuity maturity and a deeper colour.

1985 A. Thiénot Grande Cuvée 85 (May 96) 88
(60% PN, 10% PM, 30% CH)
The first vintage that A. Thienot was satisfied with, and understandably so. The '85 is very sophisticated and worthy of its prestige label. The wine has brilliant balance between mature Pinot aromas and refreshing top-class Chardonnay in a medium-bodied style.

Other wines: Vintage, Vintage Rosé.

Mumm

29 rue du Champ de Mars,
51100 Reims 03 26 49 59 69

Production: 8 million bottles.

Mumm is one of the very biggest champagne houses. They have a particularly steady grip on the American market, which really loves *Cordon Rouge*.

In 1827 the house was founded by two Germans, Peter-Arnold de Mumm and M.Giesler. The Mumm family was by then established in the Rhine valley but wanted to try the sparkling French wine. World War One was particularly troublesome for Mumm, due to the German origins of the owners. Between the wars René Lalou became the man with the drive to restore the Mumm name, and after World War Two the firm expanded enormously by pushing the export market hard. Since 1969 the company has been owned by the Canadian concern Seagram. Today Mumm owns 327 hectares with an average rank of a high 95%, but three quarters of the grapes are bought in from far simpler vineyards. The non-vintage champagne has Aube's unmistakable sticky style and is one of the worst dry champagnes around.

Mumm Cordon Rouge 31
(50% PN, 25% PM, 25% CH)
A decent champagne a few years ago, but today hopelessly loose, sticky and unstylish. Pull your socks up!

Mumm Cordon Vert 20
(55% PN, 35% PM, 10% CH)
An even sweeter case which I would definitely not recommend.

Mumm de Cramant 69
(100% CH)
Previously *Crémant de Cramant*. Known as the 'right' sort of wine for those who have a feeling for class. In which case I don't belong in that category. Waterish colour, weak flowery nose, slightly fragile and short flavour.

1982 Mumm Rosé 49 (Jul 88) 68
(70% PN, 30% CH)
After having been really disappointed by this wine I have decided to avoid buying any more vintages. It may be that other vintages are much better, but the '82 had an almost non-existent applish nose and a hard, sharp flavour of tart apple. Needs retasting.

1959 Mumm Rosé 96 (May 97) 96
(72% PN, 28% CH)
What a sensational wine! The concentration is outstanding. The champagne is almost treacly and fat, with a nectar-sweet assembly of exotic fruit. The nose is hardly exceptional but extremely satisfying with dense fruit and smoky complexity.

1988 Mumm 80 (Jul 96) 87
(70% PN, 30% CH)
A broad, developed, biscuity, Moët & Chandon-like, high-class nose. The flavour is more ordinary, with a rich fruity sweetness and fair balance.

1982 Mumm 83 (Jul 93) 84
(62% PN, 38% CH)
Abrupt and musky nose, rich, full-bodied, food champagne. Probably already at its peak.

1979 Mumm 92 (Mar 93) 92
(75% PN, 25% CH)
A lovely, mature and well-structured wine, with a full body and tones of chocolate and nut aromas. A long aftertaste of calf gravy. Actually a better wine than the *79 René Lalou*.

1976 Mumm 90 (Nov 96) 90
(75% PN, 25% CH)
Anybody looking for elegance and appetising freshness in their champagne shouldn't bother with this. Here we have an old-fashioned food champagne with a robust character and steady backbone strong enough to carry a heavy meat dish.

1975 Mumm 91 (Jan 96) 91
(75% PN, 25% CH)
A very good vintage for Mumm, as the large Pinot content has been given room to move and all the building blocks have fallen into place. This wine has a long life ahead of it, but is unlikely to get better than it is now.

1971 Mumm 70 (May 87) 73
(70% PN, 30% CH)
Meaty and clumsy champagne which isn't especially typical of either the producer or the vintage. Probably passé by now.

1966 Mumm 92 (Aug 95) 92
(70% PN, 30% CH)
The room was filled with the strong bouquet when the wine was poured out. The champagne is very well-kept and outstandingly fine on the nose, but with a somewhat short, sweet aftertaste.

1964 Mumm 93 (Aug 95) 93
(70% PN, 30% CH)
Absolutely pure and balanced, like so many 64's. A stylish nose of vanilla and hazelnuts. In the mouth the wine is compact and genuine, with tones of cream and roasted coffee beans.

1961 Mumm 92 (Oct 97) 92
(70% PN, 30% CH)
Strong stylish wine, with lots of power and a dry classic finish.

1959 Mumm 83 (Aug 95) ▼
(70% PN, 30% CH)
The '59 has in all likelihood seen its best days. Of course, it may still be enjoyable with its fat, oily toffee flavour and chocolate-filled nose, but the vitality is about to die and the wine is lost quickly in the glass.

1955 Mumm 94 (Apr 95) 94
(70% PN, 30% CH)
Oh my, this was good! Alive and vital at the age of 40. The nose has a magnificent spectrum of coffee and honey, there's a medium-bodied fruity flavour and a beautiful long aftertaste of candy and popcorn.

1953 Mumm 80 (May 93) ▼
(70% PN, 30% CH)
A curious wine with an exemplary appearance, the nose of a dry, high-class sherry and a long but extremely dry flavour for such an old champagne.

1949 Mumm 94 (Oct 97) 94
(70% PN, 30% CH)
A voluptuous wine with a wonderful nose of vanilla and butterscotch. Good to look at and easy to drink.

1947 Mumm 89 (Jul 92) 89
(70% PN, 30% CH)
Mumm made rather an ill-fitting wine in this great year. Some sherry aromas have crept in, but the one-dimensional, meaty structure keeps the wine from drowning for a few more years.

1985 Grand Cordon 83 (Feb 93) 83
(50% PN, 50% CH)
The firm's latest cuvée de prestige has an exceptional softness and decent concentration, but the aromas are far too like the sweet, vapid flavour in the company's basic non-vintage champagne. The first time I tasted this wine blind my spontaneous comment was - a very refined version of *Mumm Cordon Rouge.*

1985 René Lalou 88 (Oct 98) 90
(50% PN, 50% CH)
Mild aromas that resemble herbal tea meet the olfactory senses. The flavour is more concentrated and intertwined with a medium body.

1982 René Lalou 85 (Dec 91) 89
(50% PN, 50% CH)
This champagne is recognisable by its rich, juicy fruit and melon-like aftertaste.

1979 René Lalou 90 (Dec 98) 92
(50% PN, 50% CH)
Tremendously enjoyable in the beginning of the nineties, the wine lacked the necessary concentration it needed to develop further. A weak toasty bouquet with elements of peach and violet. The peaches returned in the soft, fruity medium-long flavour. Still very young.

1976 René Lalou 88 (Jul 96) 88
(50% PN, 50% CH)
Like the '75 this is relatively light and comes equipped with a perfect mousse. The nose is faint and closed. The wine's best sides are only shown in the mouth, where it achieves a perfect balance in the long flavour of crème brûle and vanilla.

1975 René Lalou 86 (Jul 96) 86
(50% PN, 50% CH)
Deepish colour, broad, open but youthful bouquet of exotic fruit. After a while in the glass the nose becomes clumsy and typical of this house. The flavour is full and young, with a hard, dry finish.

1982 Mumm de Mumm 85 (Jan 97) 86
(50% PN, 50% CH)
Rounded and rich champagne that lacks a little acidity and freshness. A pleasant aftertaste of butterscotch.

Palmer

67 rue Jacquart, 51100 Reims ☎ 03 26 07 35 07
Production: 300,000 bottles under its own label, a total of 2 million in all.

Palmer is an unusual creature - a cooperative in Reims. The original idea of a cooperative came up among some growers in Avize who needed some Pinot grapes from Verzenay in order to create a competitive cuvée. This happened in 1947, but when the firm became too big in 1959 Palmer moved into Teofile Roederer's old cellars in Reims. Jean-Claude Colson and his right-hand man Roland Priem lead a modern and effective team who have access to grapes from forty crus. Colson's philosophy is to combine traditional methods with the latest advances made by science. The firm is very proud of its 8,000 kilo press from which they only use cuvées for Palmer. The wines are well aged after four years in the cellar and carefully tested in the company's modern laboratory. Palmer has an unusually large amount of older vintages for sale, which are disgorged to order. The wines are a little too impersonal and clinical for my taste. Perhaps they would have more character if they weren't put through cold stabilisation and double filtering.

Palmer Brut 68
(45% PN, 5% PM, 50% CH)
It feels refreshing to avoid the Pinot Meunier character in the nose in a non-vintage champagne from a major company. The nose is good and nutty with a correct Pinot taste, which sadly finishes too quickly.

Palmer Rosé Rubis 60
(53% PN, 3% PM, 44% CH)
A very fruity rosé with raspberry and licorice tones in both nose and flavour.

1985 Palmer B. d. B. 49 (May 95) 55
(100% CH)
Palmer has no set receipe for its vintage wines. In 1985 they decided that Chardonnay was of such high quality that a blanc de blancs was motivated. I was very disappointed with this pale champagne, where the mousse grew just as it should not do in the mouth.

1982 Palmer 84 (Jan 98) 86
(60% PN, 40% CH)
A well-built wine with chocolate-laced maturity and rounded, balanced flavour.

Amazone de Palmer 87
(50% PN, 50% CH)
A Grand cru champagne from 1985 and 1986, with deep colour and lovely toasty aroma of wholemeal bread and coffee beans. The flavour is dominated by mature Avize-Chardonnay with an added weight from some first-class Pinot Noir.

Irroy

44 bd Lundy, 51100 Reims ☎ 03 26 88 37 27

Production: 500,000 bottles.

Taittinger's second house was founded in 1820. Originally one of the top names, but today almost invisible.

1943 Irroy 94 (Aug 97) 94
(70% PN, 30% CH)
One of the few champagnes from this house that I've tasted. ***43 Irroy*** is judged by many to be the best champagne from this vintage! It is still majestic with its irrepressible energy, lively mousse and fiery finish. The wine is marked by oak aromas and heavy Pinot Noir. The nose is Krug-like, with aromas of honey and nuts, and the full flavour is dominated by cocoa aromas.

1928 Irroy 95 (Jan 99) 95
(70% PN, 30% CH)
If the storage has been good this '28 is a remarkable and aristocratic champagne. The strength is huge and the taste is like nectar. Some bottles are not in perfect condition though.

Other wines: Brut, Cuvée Marie Antoinette.

Jacquart

5 rue Gosset, 51100 Reims ☎ 03 26 07 88 40

Production: 7 million bottles.

Today this is one of the largest champagne producers, despite the fact that the cooperative is only 35 years old. When Robert Quantinet originaly collected together a group of growers they produced 100,000 bottles. Today that figure is up to seven million every year, and the cooperative controls over 1,000 hectares from 64 villages in Marne. Just like Reims' other large cooperative, Palmer, they use the new 8,000 kilo presses at their ultra-modern plant. The wines have a surprisingly good name among critics.

Jacquart Brut Sélection 58
(35% PN, 15% PM, 50% CH)
Not my choice, if I had to choose, but amazingly rich in its bready, slightly over-explicit style.

Jacquart Tradition 64
(33% PN, 33% PM, 34% CH)
A bit more elegant and fruitier than ***Sélection***. Clean and well made.

Jacquart Rosé 55
(45% PN, 15% PM, 40% CH)
Closed mineral-like nose and weak, almost diluted flavour which does return in a surprisingly long finish.

1990 Jacquart 78 (Feb 97) 82
(50% PN, 50% CH)
A rounded wine made for early consumption, already including aromas of peach, apricot and chocolate.

1990 Ritz 78 (Feb 97) 82
(50% PN, 50% CH)
This seems to be exactly the same wine as the ***90 Jacquart***. The fruit is generous, with concentration that brings chocolate pudding to mind.

1988 Cuvée Nominée 84 (Oct 97) 86
(40% PN, 60% CH)
Cheese and chocolate on the somewhat unclean nose. Much better on the palate. Soft taste filled with exotic fruit.

1986 Cuvée Nominée 83 (May 97) 83
(60% PN, 40% CH)
Fully developed at the age of ten. Enjoyable, round and full of honeyed fruit with some exotic overtones. The wine is oxidative and gives a Pinot-dominated impression.

1985 Cuvée Nominée 78 (Nov 94) 85
(40% PN, 60% CH)
When many firms make their cuvée de prestige, they strain so hard to make a soft and refined wine that they tend to remove some of the wine's character. ***Cuvée Nominée*** is just such a cuvée de prestige. Very sophisticated style with a smooth mousse and weak, delicate peach aromas and discreet breadiness in the nose.

1992 Jacquart B. d. B. 83 (Oct 97) 84
(100% CH)
Charming and mature, but without any potential.

1992 Cuvée Mosaique 80 (Oct 97) 83
(100% CH)
Excellent mousse, ripe buttery nose. The texture is creamy and the champagne is very charming.

1990 Cuvée Mosaique 86 (Oct 97) 89
(50% PN, 10% PM, 40% CH)
All these champagnes share an exotic rich juicy chewable taste. Ripe and gutsy.

1986 Mosaique Rosé 78 (Apr 97) 80
(45% PN, 15% PM, 40% CH)
As with so many 86's, this wine felt a little loose. There are elements of cheese and other mature tones, the flavour has popular appeal but lacks complexity and length.

1985 Cuvée Nominée Rosé 87 (Sep 98) 87
(50% PN, 50% CH)
A beautiful and delightful champagne with charming aromas and a creamy structure.

Ferdinand Bonnet

12 allée du Vignoble, 51055 Reims ☎ 03 26 84 44 15

Production: 1 million bottles.

Stephane Lefebvre runs this recently-started house with its roots in Oger. The original firm's ten high-class hectares are retained, but 90% of the grapes are bought in. Remy-Cointreau took over management in 1988 (See F. Bonnet in the Grand cru village Oger).

F. Bonnet Héritage Brut 67
(32% PN, 50% PM, 18% CH)
This is a prizewinning non-vintage champagne which is made to appeal to a broad public. The similarities with Charles Heidsieck are striking. The nose is faintly toasty and biscuity, with a fine apple aroma, and the flavour shadows the nose skilfully.

F. Bonnet Princesse Brut 67
(32% PN, 50% PM, 18% CH)
I'm more and more convinced that Bonnet's champagnes are set to attract a large following. This wine is less toasty than the *Héritage*, but has sufficient richness and a jammy fruit.

F. Bonnet Brut Prestige 66
(70% PN, 30% CH)
Tight and focused, with exciting aromas of nestles and spinach. I was left searching for a little elegance.

Médot

30 rue Werlé, 51100 Reims ☎ 03 26 47 46 15
Production: 250,000 bottles.

A small house in Reims which was founded in 1897 by Jules Pascal. The firm has stayed within the family and is now run by Philippe Guidon, and it is best known for producing one of the area's few Clos champagnes, *Clos des Chaulins*.

1989 Médot 68 (Aug 95) 69
(50% PN, 50% CH)
A water-coloured champagne with meagre nuances. Best appreciated when young when it's at its freshest.

Clos des Chaulins 79
(100% PN)
Pinot grapes from a southerly slope in Pargny-les-Reims. Tones of licorice, candy and blackberry dominate this rare clos wine. The mousse is perfectly soft and the wine is suitable for storage in the cellar.

Other wines: Brut, Blanc de Blancs.

Delbeck

39 rue du Général Sarrail,
51100 Reims ☎ 03 26 77 58 00
Production: 350,000 bottles.

An historic house which was formed in 1832 and which rapidly gained a tremendous reputation after founder Frédéric Delbeck married the widow Ponsardin's niece. For several years Delbeck champagne was the royal champagne at the French court. In the sixties the company was broken up, only to be resurrected in 1993, and the wines were made at Bruno Paillard on the outskirts of Reims. The company is almost self-sufficient, buying only around 30% of its grapes, which gives it great control over the work in the vineyards. In 1995 Pierre Martin took the helm.

Delbeck Brut Héritage 52
(80% PN, 20% CH)
Dry and well-made, but a little too reserved and shy.

Delbeck Rosé 61
(90% PN, 10% CH)
Just as pale as the colour suggests. A wine that doesn't dare give of itself, despite the wealth that lies under the surface.

1988 Delbeck 83 (Aug 97) 88
(70% PN, 30% CH)
Restrained, meaty and dry. Today rather fishy on the nose. Good future.

1985 Delbeck 70 (Oct 93) 75
(70% PN, 30% CH)
There is great personality and intensity to be found in Delbeck's '85. The question is only if one should be wholly satisfied with a champagne that smells of elder and burnt rubber.

1945 Delbeck 94 (Jun 97) 94
A strong nose that you feel in the room when the wine is poured. Superb taste of duck liver, truffles and chocolate.

1943 Delbeck
Maderised and therefore unjudged.

Chanoine

Av. de Champagne, 51100 Reims ☎ 03 26 36 61 60
Production: 500,000 bottles.

Philippe Baijot is one of the district's tallest and humblest gentlemen. He had a long career behind him before he decided to start up his own house. He works closely with Bruno Paillard and has just built a giant facility with temperature-controlled cellars on the slope south of Reims. Chanoine will certainly gain more attention as the wines are good and very inexpensive.

Chanoine Brut 57
Not as dry as I'd like, but its charming fruit has a broad appeal. The wine reminds me of *Moët & Chandon Brut Imperial* at a much lower price.

Chanoine Brut Rosé 69
The richest and most accessible of Chanoine's wines in its category. Soft, meaty tones and a hint of cheeses are to be found in both the nose and the rather full taste.

1988 Chanoine 80 (Apr 96) 85
I must have misjudged this wine when I wrote the Swedish version of this book. The last time I tasted this champagne it may still have had an excess of almond aromas, but the fruit felt a great deal richer than at the first tasting.

1973 Chanoine 92 (Apr 96) 92
Good-looking, enjoyable mature champagne with plenty of chocolate tones and exotic fruit.

Massé

48 rue de Courlancy, 51100 Reims ☎ 03 26 47 61 31
Production: 700,000 bottles.

Founded in 1853 in Rilly-la-Montagne. A label you often find in Denmark, actually. A low-price champagne which is in practise Lanson's second wine, although the company is one of the exclusive members of the "Syndicat des Grandes Marques".

Massé Brut 45
(45% PN, 20% PM, 35% CH)
A basic wine with clear similarities to *Lanson Black Label*. Sharp acidity which isn't supported by the wine's fruit.

Cuvée Henry Massé 53
(40% PN, 20% PM, 40% CH)
Slightly rounder and with less aggressive acidity. Here too there is a lack of body and grip which prevents it lasting the distance.

Baron Edouard 53
(45% PN, 35% PM, 20% CH)
Lighter and more pure than the other wines from this house, but with no great complexity.

Montaudon

6 rue Ponsardin, 51100 Reims ☎ 03 26 47 53 30
Production: 1.2 million bottles.

For over one hundred years the Montaudon family has succeeded in keeping the firm in its own hands, and today it is run by Luc Montaudon. The firm's own vineyards lie in Aube and they are very happy with the grapes there, even though most of the grapes are bought in from Marne. The wines are uncomplicated and fruity with a spicy tone that has many supporters. Personally, I remain unimpressed.

Montaudon Brut "M" 51
(50% PN, 25% PM, 25% CH)
Reddish colour. Lots of Pinot Meunier in the nose, with bread, ripe apples and a simple caramel tone. Simple, flowery and short flavour.

Montaudon Sec 30
(50% PN, 25% PM, 25% CH)
The nose is actually very nice with a Clicquot character. The wishy-washy sweetness camouflages all hint of quality.

Montaudon B. d. B. 38
(100% CH)
One of the worst blanc de blancs I've ever tasted. Very basic aromas of candy and far too sweet.

1989 Montaudon 67 (May 96) 78
(60% PN, 40% CH)
A relatively developed Pinot nose of ripe grapes. Rounded and well-built champagne with a correct dosage.

1988 Montaudon 52 (Nov 93) 60
(60% PN, 40% CH)
Here the firm may have made a basic wine, but this time there is at least a bready champagne character and a small portion of Chardonnay fruit.

1979 Montaudon 79 (Jul 95) 79
(60% PN, 40% CH)
Fresh, lively mousse, brilliant colour and perfect maturity. However, still a basic champagne with some clumsy cheese tones.

1990 Montaudon Rosé 55 (May 96) 68
(65% PN, 35% CH)
Purer than previous vintages, but plenty of Aube Pinot in the nose and there's a total lack of mineral elegance in a rich and fruity flavour.

1988 Montaudon Rosé 32 (Nov 93) ?
(65% PN, 35% CH)
A dark red colour of Aube Pinot. Impure nose where boiled eggs and lemon muffins fight it out. The flavour is full and artificial.

Marie-Stuart

8 pl. de la République, 51100 Reims ☎ 03 26 47 92 26
Production: 1.7 million bottles.

The Scottish queen Marie Stuart, who was very popular in Reims during the 16th century, gave her name to this house in 1919. Today the company is a very commercial operation which has gone in hard for "buyer's own brand" wines and has specialised in world record bottle sizes. Both the largest and smallest champagne bottles in the world come from this house, which has no vineyards of its own.

Marie-Stuart Brut Tradition 40
(50% PN, 25% PM, 25% CH)
Rough, unripe flavours without any champagne character. Probably a large proportion of grapes from the second pressing.

Marie-Stuart Rosé 39
(60% PN, 20% PM, 20% CH)
This champagne too is rough, unpolished and lacking in fruitiness.

1988 Marie-Stuart 70 (Aug 95) 70
(10% PN, 90% CH)
A clear nose of crispbread and beer poured out on coals in a sauna. Unified tough taste with a round toffee finish.

Cuvée de la Reine 76
(10% PN, 90% CH)
Marie-Stuart's cuvée de prestige is smoky and potent with a pure, elegant Chardonnay flavour.

Chaudron

1 av. de Paris, 51100 Reims ☎ 03 26 66 44 88
Production: 180,000 bottles.

The firm was founded by Paul Dauchet in 1820 and current owner Lionel Chaudron controls 25 hectares. Wines not tasted.

Wines: Brut, Rosé, Sélection, Extra Brut.

Other producers in Reims:

Balahu de Noiron	03 26 54 45 53
Rémy Paillard	03 26 40 07 06
Paul Bur	03 26 07 34 10

Grand cru villages

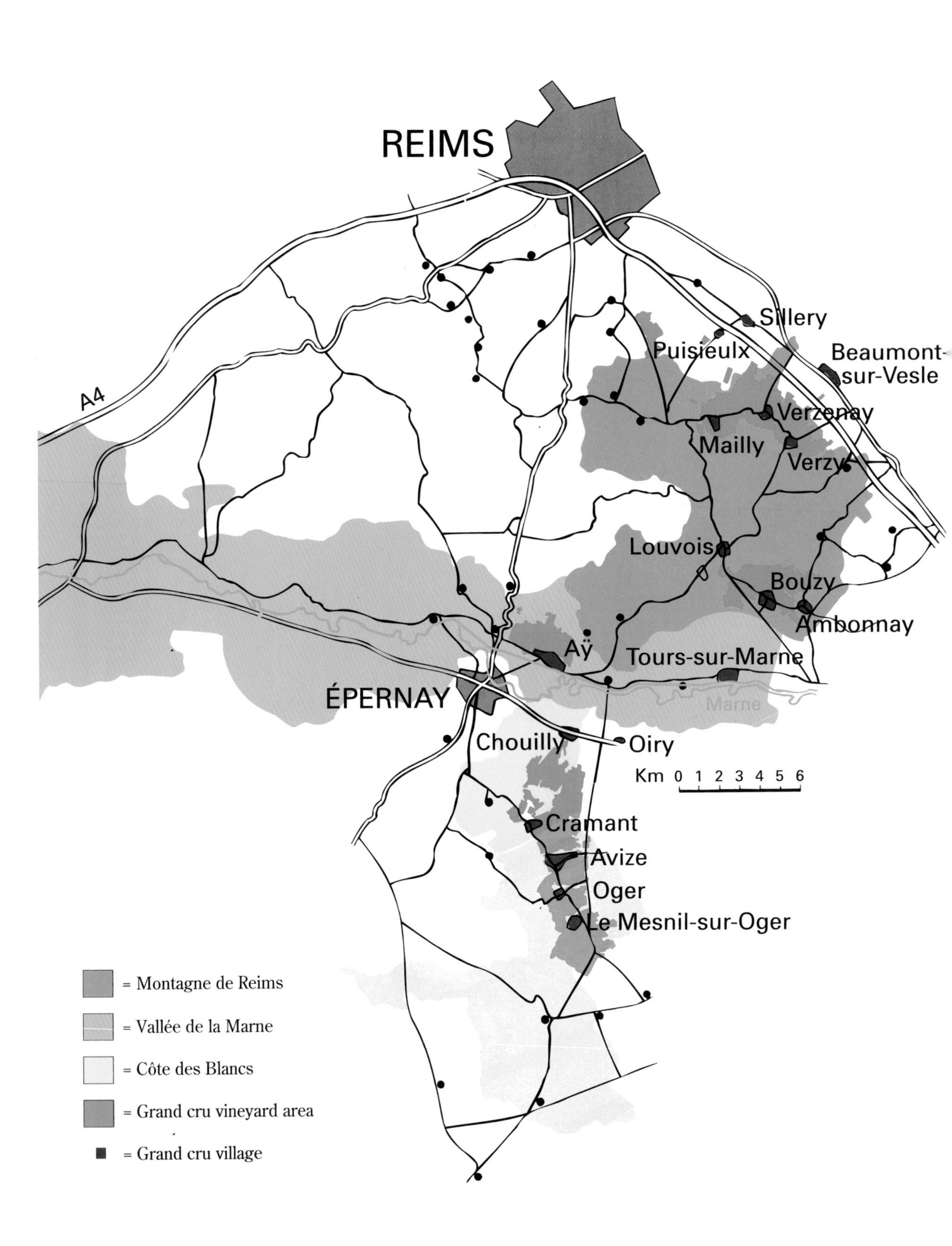

AMBONNAY

Ambonnay is one of the largest Grand cru villages, with its 378 hectares of vineyards. Today it is full of growers who are part of the cooperative, but who also sell small quantities of their own champagnes. Some of the better sites in the village are owned by R. Coutier, H. Billiot, Soutiran-Pelletier and the major houses Moët, Clicquot, Mumm and Taittinger. It is above all in the cuvées where Ambonnay shows its greatness. Their soft, oily but slightly neutral taste can function as a bridge between, for example, the musty, aromatic Aÿ-Pinot and the knife sharp, ultra elegant Avize-Chardonnay. taken on its own, Ambonnay seldom reaches the same dizzying heights as the pure blanc de noirs from Aÿ and Verzenay. As with Sillery and Bouzy, Ambonnay's wines gain a great deal from their contact with oak barrels, but sadly there is only one grower in the village who uses oak. Anyone who doubts that an oak barrel can give increased complexity to Pinot wines should taste a still Ambonnay wine from Krug.

Geographically and geologically, Ambonnay is an extension of Bouzy's vineyards to the east. The best slopes in the village have a southwesterly exposure and lie north-west of the picturesque village, with its narrow streets. Just as with Bouzy's vineyards, the quality can vary wildly within the village, and the finest grapes are harvested at a height of around 150-180 metres above sea level. Unfortunately for champagne lovers, far too many of these grapes are used to make still red wine, called Ambonnay rouge.

% 100% 80% PN, 20% CH

René-Henri Coutier

7 rue Henri III, 51150 Ambonnay 03 26 57 02 55

Production: 25,000 bottles.

This classic firm was founded in 1880. Coutier own seven hectares in the village but sell 80% to the cooperative. Malolactic fermentation is used on half of the still wine. The father of the present owner was the man who first planted Chardonnay in Ambonnay, back in 1946. Coutier is now the uncrowned king of Ambonnay.

R. H. Coutier Brut 73
(70% PN, 30% CH)
Young, compact, fresh fruit with a lovely structure, but the aromas are a touch basic.

R. H. Coutier Rosé 78
(50% PN, 50% CH)
Extremely delicate and pure grape aromas. After a few more years in the bottle this rosé takes on aromas of seaweed and oyster shell. Personally I prefer the wine when young.

R. H. Coutier B. d. B. de Ambonnay 77
(100% CH)
Wonderfully rich young pear aromas. Juicy, soft taste with elements of pear and pineapple. Very full-bodied and with scope for development in April 95, when the base wine came from the 1990 harvest.

1990 R. H. Coutier 85 (Feb 98) 91
(75% PN, 25% CH)
A wine that is personal and hard to judge. It has fresh acidity and youthful fruit, with clear elements of melon, kiwi and Alexander pear.

1988 R. H. Coutier 90 (Aug 95) 94
(75% PN, 25% CH)
Colossally elegant and sophisticated. The wine's aromas resemble Roederer's *Cristal* from the same year. Nuts and butterscotch back up the pure fruit.

1978 R. H. Coutier 88 (May 98) 90
(75% PN, 25% CH)
A harmonious champagne with a complete, elegant nose of nuts, marzipan and brioche. Unfortunately somewhat short.

1964 R. H. Coutier 95 (Jul 95) 95
(100% PN)
Wonderfully golden and lively. A magnificent wine with a dark nose of cigars, brioche, syrup, chanterelle mushrooms, plums, truffles and rotten wood. The flavour is exceptionally tight and concentrated, with an accelerating aftertaste like a great Bordeaux wine in its tones of cigars and leather.

Henri Billiot

Pl. de la Fontaine, 51150 Ambonnay 03 26 57 00 14

Production: 45,000 bottles.

The minimal amount of bottles that annually leave Billiot's cellars are bought almost exclusively by committed fans in Britain. His wines are so rare that I had never come across one before I managed to arrange a visit to the property in 1994. It was with mounting excitement that I opened the gate to the vineyard itself. How was this cult figure among winemakers going to look? Had the pressures of fame gone to his head, as they had with so many of Burgundy's minor demonic growers? No. It was with great relief that I found that he, like Selosse, Peters and Diebolt, had kept his feet firmly on the ground. M. Billiot is a very unassuming and humble person, who was dressed in his worn jeans and knitted sweater throughout our visit. When you've just come from one of the major houses with their slim, Armani-clad, business-minded directors, it's wonderful to meet a real vine farmer in the true sense of the phrase.

The British believe that he ferments his wines in oak barrels. Can this misunderstanding originate from the fact that Billiot prefers to speak German with his guests? They also believe that his two hectare-large vineyards contains only Pinot Noir. He is very proud of his Chardonnay plants and uses most of their fruit in his cuvée de prestige, *Cuvée Laetitia*, which is named after his daughter. Billiot's greatness depends chiefly upon his hard work out in the vineyard. Old vines and low yield are the recipe. Despite the high quality, Billiot's champagnes are hardly for beginners, as the malolactic fermentation has not been used. The concentration and richness that lies under the surface can be hard to appreciate in the wine's youth. All of his wines demand at least a further five years in the bottle to mature properly.

H. Billiot Tradition 70
(70% PN, 30% CH)
Always a blend of three vintages, with four years fermentation and some second pressing. A deep copper colour, a somewhat foamy mousse and a muffled fruity nose. It's in the mouth that this wine shows its inherent strength and almost chewable fullness. Fat but young fruit.

H. Billiot Cuvée de Réserve 79
(90% PN, 10% CH)
Only the first pressing is used for this champagne, which is stored for five years in the grower's cellars. Once again, copper-coloured and a closed nose. Under the surface one detects top class creamy Pinot Noir. The taste is uneasy and unbalanced, but the depth of the masculine fruit is particularly impressive. Unfortunately this champagne, though suitable for storage, has a mousse that is rather too rough and frothy.

H. Billiot Cuvée de Réserve Rosé 78
(100% PN)
Dark red with elements of violet. The mousse is a little unsubtle and the nose is closed, but one is struck yet again by the enormous concentration and richness to be found in this grower's champagnes.

Cuvée Laetitia 85
(40% PN, 60% CH)
According to the winemaker, there are a number of secrets in this cuvée. It is a blend of nine different vintages, but involvement of oak barrels is something he strongly denies. The colour is a deep green/yellow and the nose is buttery and mature. The flavour is fruity and sweet in a positive way, unified and with a long aftertaste of honey. 1982 is the dominant vintage in my mouth. Sure, this is a jolly good champagne, but I would rather have seen a cuvée de prestige nade entirely out of Pinot grapes.

1975 H. Billiot
(100% PN)
A vintage the grower is extremely proud of. I tried it three months after dégorgement here at home (see "A different tasting"). The appearance was vital and promising, but what had happened to the nose? One of the queerest defects I've ever come across. It smelled just like a defrosted refrigerator. My guess is that something went wrong during the disgorging process. Unjudged.

1959 H. Billiot 90 (Apr 95) 92
(100% PN)
Once again recently-disgorged and youthful, but filled with power and aromas typical of the grape. Heroically built without finesse.

Egly-Ouriet

15 rue de Trépail, 51150 Ambonnay ☎ 03 26 57 00 70
Production: 60,000 bottles.

One of Robert Parker's favourite champagnes. The company started out in 1930 and today Michel Egly owns six hectares in Ambonnay, 0.5 in Bouzy and 0.5 in Verzenay. The vines are over thirty years old on average, and for the prestige wine they're fifty.

Egly-Ouiret Tradition 79
(70% PN, 30% CH)
A copy of Bollinger's non-vintage champagne. Chocolate, hazelnut and ripe apples, a broad, masculine full style and power.

Egly-Ouiret Rosé 70
(80% PN, 20% CH)
The same base, with the addition of a little Ambonnay rouge. The nose is weaker with a tone of red and blackcurrants. The balance is inferior to that of the white version.

Egly-Ouriet Blanc de Noirs 83
(100% PN)
Grapes from Pinot vines cultivated in 1946 give the wine an extra weight and concentration. The fruit is rich and dense, and the potential for cellar storage is huge.

1989 Egly-Ouriet 83 (May 96) 88
(60% PN, 40% CH)
This champagne is already highly developed and bold, and the meaty and sweet Pinot aromas link together in perfect harmony. Several tasters guessed an older vintage from Bollinger, which I couldn't understand as the wine had none of the nutty and smoked aromas found there.

Paul Dethune

2 rue du Moulin, 51150 Ambonnay ☎ 03 26 57 01 88
Production: 30,000 bottles.

This Ambonnay domain is among the most beautiful and well looked-after in the whole of Champagne. Every flower in the garden is "well pruned". The freshly-polished facade of the house is half-covered by a gorgeous ivy which stylishly follows the colour changes of the seasons. Inside, in the tasting room, everything is just as perfectly handled. It's a pleasure to sit in front of the firepalce with the shy Madame Dethune who makes the wines now. That the excellent care which goes into the property comes from a woman is perhaps no surprise, although when it comes to the wines I'm less overwhelmed. Dethune is the only producer in Ambonnay to ferment and store their wines in oak barrels, but I managed to detect oak tones only in the cuvée de prestige. The wines are often dry and restrained and lack that dimension which the cask should have given them.

Paul Dethune Brut 53
(100% PN)
Very ungenerous nose and a surprisingly light, neutral flavour.

Paul Dethune Rosé 50
(100% PN)
The same wine, with a splash of Ambonnay rouge added. The red wine fails to raise the basic wine though, and the overall impression is young and neutral.

1990 Paul Dethune 85 (Oct 97) 90
(50% PN, 50% CH)
Lovely nose of vanilla, butterscotch and hazelnut. Marvelous ripe, oily texture and a honeyed aftertaste.

Princesse Dethune 79 (Dec 90) 87
(100% PN)
Only after twenty minutes in the glass does a hint of oak appear, in the guise of a weak nutty tone. The wine has astounding lightness and elegance, and those who guess at a blanc de blancs in a blind tasting need feel no shame. Worth storing into the next century.

Secondé Prévoteau

This house has really frustrated me over the years. For many years I tried to arrange a visit to the property, but the names of the owners have changed, as has the address. Those champagnes I have managed to locate have been very good. André Secondé's family has always sold grapes to Louis Roederer, and the Russian Tsar's rosé champagne was coloured by still red wine from Secondé's great slopes in Ambonnay. The firm's Ambonnay rouge is one of the best in the region. The company owns 12 hectares in Ambonnay, Bouzy and Louvois, but for the moment it lies fallow.

Princesses de France 70
(88% PN, 12% CH)
An astonishingly elegant champagne with exceptionally fine mousse for Pinot Noir. The nose is soft but weak, and the taste is mild and balanced.

Princesses de France Rosé 76
(88% PN, 12% CH)
A lovely burgundy-like rosé with impressive Pinot fruit and elements of leather.

Other wines: Blanc de Blancs, Fleuron de France.

H. Petitjean

12 rue St Vincent, 51150 Ambonnay ☎ 03 26 57 08 79

Production: 100,000 bottles.

Petitjean was founded in 1846 but was of negligible importance until Henri Petitjean took over. In 1959 it was the turn of Michel Petitjean to take the helm, and the firm is still owned by the family today. Only 5% of the grapes come from the house's own vineyards in Ambonnay, and the remainder is bought in from seven high-ranking villages. In 1993 the firm launched something as tasteless as three different Pavarotti champagnes that were accompanied by CD's. I have nothing against the concept of champagne and opera in itself, but as a commercial idea the union is rather more doubtful. Fortunately the champagne is far from tasteless.

1985 Bal Maschera, Fernando Pavarotti 82 (Jan 94) 87
(60% PN, 40% CH)
Golden colour, aristocratic toasty nose and a creamy long taste that reverberates at least as long as Pavarotti's high C.

Soutiran-Pelletier

12 rue St Vincent,
51150 Ambonnay ☎ 03 26 57 07 87

Production: 105,000 bottles.

Also known as Vueve Victorine Mongardien. Today Alain Soutiran makes the wines while his daughter Valérie runs the tiny house with steely determination. It is one of those companies that would rather lie on the Côte des Blancs. They praise the Chardonnay grapes without having any great ability to grow them. If you want to get to know Soutiran's wines, go to their shop in the middle of the village, called "La Palette de Baccus".

Soutiran-Pelletier Rosé 48
(100% PN)
A rough, earthy Pinot aroma without elegance, according to my latest notes from October 1994.

Angéline Godel Brut 61
(50% PN, 10% PM, 40% CH)
Somewhat charmless and hard, but with sharp nails and plenty of potential. Very low dosage.

1989 Cuvée Victorine 70 (Jan 95) 76
(50% PN, 50% CH)
This is a wine that is hard to understand. A beginner would probably be scared off immediately by the animalist and slightly "dirty" nose. Personally I felt both dread and delight. The flavour is powerful and long, but far from charming.

1985 Cuvée Victorine 76 (Sep 94) 78
(50% PN, 50% CH)
I was alone among ten tasters to be fascinated by this vegetable-scented champagne. Boullion and stables were other judgements that tripped off the tongue. Once again though, good power and authority.

Claude Beaufort

16 bd des Bermonts,
51150 Ambonnay ☎ 03 26 57 01 32

Today Claude is the Mayor of Ambonnay and his daughter is married to the village's top grower, R. H. Coutier.

Claude Beaufort Cuvée Réserve 65
(15% PN, 85% CH)
Much heavier than the high proportion of Chardonnay would suggest.

Claude Beaufort B. d. B. 65
(100% CH)
One of the meatiest B. d. B.'s I've tasted. The finesse is absent but the pineapple and lemon are tell-tale signs of the grapes' origin.

Claude Beaufort Rosé 63
(50% PN, 50% CH)
Cherry aromas have been added to the house style, but I'm not sure the combination is so successful. The blend of pineapple and cherry doesn't feel completely harmonious.

André Beaufort

1 rue de Vaudemanges,
51150 Ambonnay ☎ 03 26 57 01 50

Production: 25,000 bottles.

André Beaufort founded his company in Ambonnay in 1933. Today Jacques Beaufort owns seven hectares planted with 65% PN. This grower is among the select group that sell older vintages.

André Beaufort Brut 47
(66% PN, 34% CH)
Aromas of glue and banana. The colour is red/yellow. Full-bodied and lacking elegance.

1985 André Beaufort Demi-Sec
(66% PN, 34% CH)
Nose like a beerenauslese from Rheinfalz. A funny sparkling wine where the special aromas of vegetables and meat comes back in the aftertaste. To peculiar to be judged.

1990 André Beaufort 78 (Oct 97) 85
(66% PN, 34% CH)
Strong nose of dill and meat stew. Quite heavy and cumbersome without food. Idiosyncratic.

1989 André Beaufort 78 (Oct 97) 80
(66% PN, 34% CH)
Beetroot, meat stew and blueberries on the nose. Very round and full-bodied taste of blueberries, like in a Australian Shiraz.

1987 André Beaufort 82 (Oct 97) 82
(66% PN, 34% CH)
Totally different from the others. Creamy aroma of melted butter, peach, banana and chewing gum. Soft exotic fruit and Chardonnay aroma on the palate.

1986 André Beaufort 82 (Oct 97) 82
(66% PN, 34% CH)
Fully developed nose of honey and spun sugar. To sweet for my taste, but with a rich exotic fruit. Aftertaste of licourice.

Coop. Vinicole d'Ambonnay

Bd des Bermonts, 51150 Ambonnay ☎ 03 26 57 01 46
Production: 400,000 bottles.

Most of the growers in the village are members of the cooperative that sells its champagnes under the names Saint-Reol and Elégance. Today the cooperative is run by Marcel Billiot, the brother of Henri.

Saint-Reol Brut 49
(80% PN, 20% CH)
Vegetable and gamey tones too strong for my taste. One-dimensional.

1988 Ouiret-Patur 82 (Oct 97) 86
(50% PN, 50% CH)
Focused and very well structured champagne. Fine pinhead bubbles, a rich, fruity nose.

Other wines: Elégance, Rosé, Blanc de blancs, Prestige d'Argent.

AVIZE

The eastern slopes of Avize are completely covered with Chardonnay vines. The grapes that come from these steep slopes give finer and more delicate wines, but in a blend the more robust wines from the relatively flat ground below the village play their part. In general Avize means slightly more powerful wines than the more well-scented Cramant or Le Mesnil. Nor is the village as full of top growers as the latter two. Apart from the wine demon Anselme Selosse, the best wines in the village are made by the major houses. *Jacquesson D.T.* is a pure Avize champagne which demonstrates the village's powerful style in a highly concentrated form. The nose is never as nutty or toasty as those from the neighbours, but instead reminds you of chocolate, leather and truffles as it ages. The famous prestige cuvées from the major houses often contain a large proportion of Chardonnay from Avize. The harvest area is as much as 455 hectares, giving more than one million bottles per year.

% 100% 100% CH

Jacques Selosse

22 rue Ernest Vallé, 51190 Avize ☎ 03 26 57 53 56

Production: 40,000 bottles.

I've mentioned the name of Anselme Selosse on several occasions earlier in this book, partly because he's my favourite grower, and partly beacuse he's the most original winemaker in all of Champagne. The charismatic Anselme is influenced by his time studying at Lycée Viticole in Beaune, where he studied together with several famous winemakers from Burgundy. Anselme was determined to attempt to make a great champagne using Burgundy methods. His father Jacques already owned some of the best strips of land in Côte des Blancs, full of old vines, so Anselme did have some excellent basic materials to work with.

Today Anselme owns four hectares in Avize, one in Oger, one in Cramant and one in Aÿ. The location in Aÿ is right next to Bollinger's Côte aux Enfants, from where Anselme plans to make an oak fermented blanc de noirs (the vin clair from 1994 are superb). All of Selosse's 35 Chardonnay locations are vinified separately in small Burgundy barrels bought in from Domaine Leflaive in Puligny-Montrachet. Anselme, the perfectionist, does almost everything himself. The old vines - average age 38 years old - are pruned to the maximum in order to minimise the harvest. The grapes are harvested later than most and are individually picked. After the pressing the juice is tapped into 225-litre barrels, where it stays for a year. Once a week Anselme lifts up the sediment with a steel rod in order to further enrich the wine, in a traditional Burgundy process called "bâtonnage". Selosse categorically rejects malolactic fermentation, which gives his rich wines a bite that is unbeatable. The wines are then stored up to eight years in the bottle before being disgorged. Just as with Krug, all Selosse's well-kept wines need at least six months' bottle age after being disgorged in order for them to be accessible. The dosage is always very low, and only fruit sugar is used to maintain the wine's natural balance.

Selosse's wines have given champagne a new dimension with their unique vinous Chardonnay style. The forty year-old from Avize has swiftly become Champagne's cult grower number one, after having been chosen as France's top winemaker in all categories by the magazine Gault Millau in 1994. Despite this fame, his wines cost nothing compared with *Petrus, Romanée-Conti* or *Krug Clos du Mesnil.*

J Selosse Tradition 81
(100% CH)
Selosse's youngest champagne needs a few months after being disgorged for it to develop those Selosse aromas that are so hard to describe. Undoubtedly a great champagne which with time will both taste and smell of Brazil nuts.

J Selosse Vieux Réserve 83
(100% CH)
Old reserve wines from relatively unsuccessful vintages, according to Anselme. Mature, oxidative soft style with a broad spectrum of tastes, from exotic fruit to mature cheeses.

J Selosse Extra Brut 84
(100% CH)
My own house champagne! Disgorged after five years in the cellar and without any dosage, this wine demands one more year in the bottle to round off that sharp malic acidity. Loads of peaches, mango and nutty barrel tones. No-one knows how good this wine can become, but between 10 and 15 years after disgorging should be a perfect period of storage.

J Selosse Origine 93
(100% CH)
A new invention from the genius of Avize. Very young indeed, but already a wonderful wine with Krug-like depth and viscosity. It's made from reserve wines from 87-90 but still the wine needs decanting.

J Selosse Rosé 84
(10% PN, 90% CH)
Powerful and full in Selosse's unmistakeable style. The champagne has high acidity and wonderful length.

1989 J Selosse 90 (Aug 98) 93
(100% CH)
A very great wine which is still a touch closed, but that extra richness and acidity will keep it alive long into the 21st century.

1989 Selosse "N" 92 (Sep 98) 96
(100% CH)
Since 1988 Anselme separates out a tiny portion of his wine from his two best locations in Avize, which are planted with very old vines. In deference to the extreme concentration of the wine, Anselme uses 85% new oak barrels! Despite all that, the wine feels balanced. Naturally this burgundy copy requires long storage, but it is already highly impressive with its rich velvet-smooth fruit and majestic aftertaste.

1988 J Selosse 89 (Sep 98) 95
(100% CH)
More acidity than the '89 and with a less developed style. Pure and rich in minerals, this wine lies in wait for a few years before its toasty aromas and oily fruit come to astound us.

1987 J Selosse Origine 88 (Jul 97) 90
(100% CH)
The first champagne to be wholly vinified in new oak barrels. An experiment that was more successful than expected. After decanting, the oak was integrated and the wine became much like a white burgundy. Broad aroma of peaches and butterscotch.

1986 J Selosse 95 (Jun 98) 97
(100% CH)
The wine that gave Anselme the title of "Winemaker of the Year in France 1994". A majestic wine with outstanding personality. The nose is like a smorgasbord - it contains everything and is unlike anything else: sesame oil, oriental spices, and a particularly acidic fruity tone. The flavour is amazing, with a tropical wealth and supported by the freshest attack I've ever felt in a champagne. The fact is that Selosse succeeded in making a wine with 35% higher acidity than the '85 (11grams!). Need I add that the aftertaste is phenomenally long?

1985 J Selosse 89 (May 95) 91
(100% CH)
Selosse is one of the few producers to have made a better champagne in 1986 than the previous year. This has caused the '85 to be neglected , but the nose is buttery and spicy, with Selosse's unmissable exotic wealth and nut aromas. Slightly square and full-bodied taste with good length.

1983 J Selosse 86 (Oct 92) 87
(100% CH)
Plenty of the "Avize apple" and ripe pears in the nose. Woody, full flavour with a rather rough finish where bananas and cinnamon leave their fingerprints. Not a great Selosse.

1982 J Selosse 94 (Mar 93) 95
(100% CH)
One of the greatest 82's. A very rich blanc de blancs which closely resembles *Comtes de Champagne* from the same vintage. The nose is like a fruit firework display with butter and vanilla as added extras. The same exotic fruitiness meets the palate, and the aftertaste is bettered only by Krug this year.

1981 J Selosse 87 (Dec 95) 87
(100% CH)
Well developed, hazelnuts, almonds and vanilla are evident flavours.

1979 J Selosse 94 (May 94) 95
(100% CH)
Basically somewhat lighter than the '82, but with deeper mature tones in the nose. Brioche and duck liver are hinted at, together with the creamy fruit. Long, delicate aftertaste of hazelnut.

1976 J Selosse 70 (May 92) ▼
(100% CH)
Anselme's first attempt was a failure. A rough blanc de blancs with a nose of green peppers, lettuce and tar. Powerful and warm taste with good length but some strange aromas.

1975 J Selosse 93 (Apr 95) 93
(100% CH)
The last year when the good Jacques was the winemaker. I've never encountered such a scent of truffles in a wine before. Rich autolytic flavour which resembles the *1975 Jacquesson D.T.*, which also comes from Avize.

Franck Bonville

9 rue Pasteur, 51190 Avize ☎ 03 26 57 52 30
Production: 130,000 bottles.

The firm was founded in 1947, and today Franck Bonville makes very rich, nutty champagnes in the English style. His '83 was mistaken for a *Krug Grande Cuvée* in a big blind tasting in Stockholm in 1992. Personally I think that Bonville is the only grower in Avize who comes close to Selosse.

F Bonville Sélection 79
(100% CH)
Imagine, if only more producers could make non-vintage champagnes like this! Quite uncomplicated, but a classic, mature and nutty champagne.

1985 F Bonville 68 (Dec 93) ?
(100% CH)
Undeniably a bastard! The structure, mousse and colour are blameless, but the aromas must have originated from wild yeast which has gone off on a tangent. Capris, perfume and dill-flavoured meat lay a blanket over the citrus aromas.

1983 F Bonville 90 (Aug 92) 90
(100% CH)
The oak character takes one's thoughts to Bollinger or Krug. Smoky, broad champagne with a lovely depth and classical oxidative style. Drink within a couple of years.

De Sousa

12 pl. Léon-Bourgeoise, 51190 Avize ☎ 03 26 57 53 29
Production: 50,000 bottles.

The firm was founded in 1986 and Erick De Sousa owns five hectares in Avize, Cramant and Oger, where the average age of the vines is over thirty years. Despite its short time on the champagne scene, the company has already established a good name for itself.

De Sousa Tradition 61
(25% PN, 25% PM, 50% CH)
Well-made but young and neutral with aromas of digestive biscuits and almonds.

De Sousa B. d. B. 73
(100% CH)
Deep nose typical of this village, with elements of sun-melted butter, nuts and spices. Powerful flavour with good length.

1990 De Sousa 84 (May 98) 91
(100% CH)
Young, closed nose, but an open, oily, rich flavour of butter and strawberry.

1988 De Sousa 80 (Jul 95) 86
(100% CH)
More developed but somewhat smaller dimensions than the '90.

Agrapart

57 av. Jean-Jaurès, 51190 Avize ☎ 03 26 57 51 38
Production: 65,000 bottles.

Agrapart owns ten hectares in Avize and produces storable wines vinified in oak barrels of varying sizes. The wines are a bit rustic, but rich in extracts.

Agrapart Brut 70
(100% CH)
1/3 has fermented in oak barrels, which is readily apparent. The nose is a little rough and barrelish, the flavour is rich and impressive with good weight.

Agrapart Réserve 73
(100% CH)
The same wine as *Agrapart Brut*, but with an extra year in contact with the yeast. The same aromas with even more weight.

Cuvée de Demoiselles Rosé 73
(7% PN, 93% CH)
I don't usually like rosé champagnes based on Chardonnay, but here Agrapart have created an interesting wine with great elegance and a seductive nose of lilac, roses and hyacinth.

1988 Agrapart 80 (Mar 97) 87
(100% CH)
The '88 has a fine nose of products from the bakery and a vinous, powerful flavour with great potential for the future.

1985 Agrapart 77 (Feb 93) 87
(100% CH)
A huge, masculine wine loaded with unripe extracts with give a slightly bitter aftertaste. Almost a Pinot structure, which makes it suitable to drink with food.

Gérard Dubois

67 rue Ernest Vallé, 51190 Avize ☎ 03 26 57 58 60
Production: 30,000 bottles.

Paul Dubois started the business in 1930 in Avize. Today's owner Gérard has access to six hectares.

Other wines: Brut, B. d. B., Spéciale.

Gérard Dubois Réserve 73
(100% CH)
Crisp, dry, with slightly green tinge. very good firm taste.

1985 Gérard Dubois 88 (Aug 97) 89
(100% CH)
Full, rich blanc de blancs, with mature aromas and good structure.

1981 Gérard Dubois 88 (Aug 97) 88
(100% CH)
Mature, clean and creamy. A nice nutty, dry aftertaste.

Michel Gonet

196 av. Jean-Jaurès, 51190 Avize ☎ 03 26 57 50 56
Production: 300,000 bottles.

One of Champagne's biggest growers in terms of volume, and one of the most colourful personalities in the region. Michel Gonet, who is a keen huntsman, controls forty hectares in Avize, Le Mesnil, Vindey, Montgeueux, Oger and Fravaux. 80% of the ground is planted with Chardonnay, and three-quarters of production is exported to English-speaking countries, where his dubiously-named champagne ***Marquis de Sade*** is a big hit. Michel Gonet makes plenty of commercial and basic wines, but his vintage champagne has a very good reputation.

Marquis de Sade 65
(100% CH)
The grapes come from Sézanne and Côte des Blancs. Lots of Cox Orange apple in the bouquet, the flavour is rather rough but there's a rich aftertaste of cinnamon.

Michel Gonet Brut 59
(50% PN, 50% CH)
This is a surprisingly compact wine, with a silky structure and slightly insipid aromas of violet tablets.

Michel Gonet Rosé 45
(100% PN)
A rather messy champagne with a flavour of apricot marmelade.

1992 Michel Gonet Rosé 59 (Sep 97) 61
(100% PN)
The grapes all come from Fravaux, and the nose initially reminds one of a crémant de Bourgogne. Later an interesting spectrum opens up, with tones of blackboard chalk, dust, pineapple and cherry. Rather a basic flavour.

1988 Marquise de Sade 73 (Jul 96) 83
(100% CH)
A concentrated and rich champagne with good vinosity but without the charm or elegance that one has the right to demand from Avize.

1982 Michel Gonet 84 (Apr 96) 85
(100% CH)
Rich and fruity, with a luscious finish.

1976 Michel Gonet 92 (Feb 95) 92
(100% CH)
The '76 is a great wine full of manly power, richness and spice. One of the vintage's stars, with its oily fruit and remarkable smokiness.

Union Champagne

7 rue Pasteur, 51190 Avize ☎ 03 26 57 94 22
Production: 1 million bottles.

The Avize cooperative is perhaps the best in Champagne. The grapes comes from eleven subsidiary cooperatives which use only Premier and Grand cru grapes. More than half of the production is sold as still wines to the larger houses. The cooperative's wines are ingredients in, for example, ***Taittinger Comtes de Champagne***, ***Grand Siècle*** and ***Dom Pérignon***. Their own wines are sold under several names: ***St Gall***, ***Pierre Vaudon*** and ***Orpale***.

Bernard Cugnart 68
(100% CH)
The Avize cooperative have made a champagne with a youthful, apple flavour that should be stored for a while yet.

Pierre Vaudon Brut 55
(70% PN, 30% CH)
A pure and lively champagne with just the right dosage and a correct structure.

St Gall B. d. B. 72
(100% CH)
The champagne is bursting with life and Granny Smith aromas - a crispy champagne with a divine character.

1985 Orpale 88 (Jan 95) 90
(100% CH)
One of the best cooperative champagnes I've ever drunk. The wine is creamy-soft and is rich in minerals and elegance. Oranges and tangerines are clearly-detected aromas.

Assailly-Leclaire

6 rue de Lombardie, 51190 Avize ☎ 03 26 57 51 20
Production: 25,000 bottles.

Assailly-Leclaire B. d. B. 69
(100% CH)
An almost transparent lightweight, with a weak flowery nose and a tender, delicate apple taste.

Callot & Fils

31 av. Jean-Jaurès, 51190 Avize ☎ 03 26 57 51 57

Opposite Michel Gonet on the Avize high street, you will find Callot. My fleeting acquaintance with this grower's champagne took place on Jersey in 1992.

Pierre Callot Grande Réserve 74
(100% CH)
Despite a relatively recently-disgorged bottle, the colour was a deep gold. Slightly impure nose of woolly mittens and honey. The taste hinted at Avize's power, but the edges were too smooth.

Warris et Chenayer

1 rue Pasteur, 51190 Avize ☎ 03 26 57 50 88
Production: 80,000 bottles.

The firm was founded in 1898 and is one of the village's most respected growers. Alain Warris runs this property.

Warris et Chenayer B. d. B. 68
(100% CH)
A medium-bodied blanc de blancs full of vigour and lemon-fresh acidity.

Other wines: Super Imperator, Rosé, Vintage, Cuvée Etrusque.

Bricout

29 Rempart du Midi, 51190 Avize ☎ 03 26 53 30 00
Production: 4 million bottles.

In 1820 the young German Charles Koch came to Avize and started his operations. His three sons began working with Arthur Bricout, a former winemaker for De Venoge in Épernay. The company never grew to be as big as was hoped, and it was only in 1966, when Andreas Kupferberg renovated the firm's premises, that Bricout established itself as a famous house. Today it's the largest company in Avize. Almost all the grapes are bought in and the vinification methods are extremely modern. In 1998 Bricout was sold to Delbeck.

Bricout Cuvée Réserve 38
(35% PN, 25% PM, 40% CH)
Impure and sharp as a model pupil's pencil. Metallic.

Bricout Cuvée Prestige 61
(45% PN, 55% CH)
The firm's finest non-vintage champagne with four years of aging. The Chardonnay is easily noticeable in the citrus fruit flavour. An unimpeachable non-vintage champagne.

Bricout Rosé 60
(20% PN, 80% CH)
Crisp, with an uplifting floweriness and a fine mousse. Unfortunately the flavour is without character.

1986 Bricout 70 (May 96) 73
(60% PN, 40% CH)
Some lovely toasty and buttery aromas that fail to conceal a lack of concentration and length.

1985 Arthur Bricout 82 (Dec 93) 87
(40% PN, 60% CH)
In the space of just a few years, Bricout's cuvée de prestige have had three different names. ***Cuvée Elegance, Charles Koch*** and now ***Arthur Bricout***. Obviously, they're not satisfied with the sales of their cuvée de prestige. The '85 has a toasty nose that almost forces itself upon you, and which many of my colleagues perceive as burnt rubber. I connect the nose with toasted bread that has fastened in the toaster for too long. This wine is undeniably good, but perhaps one expects a greater wealth of nuances in a cuvée de prestige.

Waris-Larmandier

608 remparts du Nord, 51190 Avize ☎ 03 26 57 79 05
Production: 8,000 bottles.

Vincent Waris started the company in 1984, and his minimal production comes from three hectares in Avize, Cramant and Chouilly.

Waris-Larmandier B. d. B. 73
(100% CH)
Despite the minimal production this is an elegant and pure champagne with wonderfully clear acidity and a subtle flowery bouquet.

Michel Fallet

56 rue Pasteur, 51190 Avize ☎ 03 26 57 51 97
Production: 30,000 bottles.

One of the chefs at Boyer recommended this producer, who I had known nothing about. At first I thought it was strange that I had missed Fallet, but when it became apparent that the gate lacked a sign I began to understand why. The wines are only sold direct to customers who knock on the door.

The elderly widow Fallet runs what is now a rather run-down property. However, there is plenty of potential with 75 year-old vines in excellent locations.

Michel Fallet Brut 45
(100% CH)
Sweet and clumsy as a demi-sec. A cautionary example of the destructive power of sugar.

Michel Fallet Extra Brut 65
(100% CH)
Sweet aromas of honey, banana and pear. A very rich champagne with an oily structure and striking roundness which gives a sweet overall impression.

Coop. des Anciens de la Viticulture d'Avize

Lycée Viticole, 51190 Avize ☎ 03 26 57 79 79
Production: 130,000 bottles.

Monsieur Anglade started the cooperative in 1952, together with the students at the oenology school in Avize. The champagne that is sold today is made by the students and is sold under three names: Sanger, Louise Puisard and Vaubécourt. Sanger is the cooperative's top brand, and only the cuvée is used. The grapes come from 35 villages and the wines are always technically correct.

Sanger B. d. B. 68
(100% CH)
A pure and light sour apple champagne with no frills.

Sanger Rosé 61
(10% PN, 90% PM)
The tiny percentage of Pinot Noir is hardly noticed. Instead a very basic, candy-flavoured fruitiness dominates.

Other wines: Sanger Brut, Vaubécourt, Louise Puisard, Vintage.

Veuve Lanaud

3 pl. Léon-Bourgeois, 51190 Avize ☎ 03 26 57 99 19

Production: 160,000 bottles.

This little champagne house was founded seventy years ago by Henry Léopold Tabourin. The firm's largest export market is Belgium. The wines are sold under three labels: Veuve Lanaud, Ed Gauthier and Charles Montherland.

Veuve Lanaud B. d. B. 66
(100% CH)
A really thin, crispy champagne where the charm takes second place to purity.

Simon-Selosse

20 rue d'Oger, 51190 Avize ☎ 03 26 57 52 40

Production: 20,000 bottles.

Together with Jacques Selosse's sister, Philippe Simon runs this property opposite the wine school in Avize. They own three hectares in Avize, Cramant and Oger.

Simon-Selosse B. d. B. 60
(100% CH)
Quite mature and extremely full-bodied champagne. All the wines from this property oxidise quickly in the glass.

Simon-Selosse Extra Brut 60
(100% CH)
Drier, but otherwise as above.

1990 Simon-Selosse Cuvée Prestige 70 (Apr 95) 73
(100% CH)
At first the wine felt tight and harmonised, but in the glass it fell apart like a house of cards. When poured the champagne was ungenerous but gave fleeting glimpses of a buttery theme.

AŸ

Aÿ was the big name in the area long before wines became sparkling, and many were the kings and popes who counted Vin d'Aÿ as their favourite wine. Today the town, population around 4,000, hosts 19 more or less famous champagne houses and around fifty grower/producers. The vineyards slope down steeply to the village by the Marne river, and the best locations are just over the town, sheltered from the wind and with maximum exposure to the sun. Several of these locations provide the base ingredient for Bollinger, Krug, Fliniaux and Laurain champagnes. The Chardonnay master Anselme Selosse has bought the lot next to Bollinger's Côte aux Enfants, from where he hopes to create an oak barrel-fermented blanc de noirs. Pinot Noir from Aÿ has an unbeatable combination of purity of aromas, richness of flavours and a silk-smooth structure.

% 100% 86% PN 4% PM, 10% CH

Bollinger

16 rue Jules Lobet, 51160 Aÿ ☎ 03 26 53 33 66

Production: 1.3 million bottles.

Joseph Bollinger was the German from Würtemberg who founded this ancient house in 1829. The French called him simply "Jacques". The firm's large estates in the best Pinot villages were bought by his sons Georges and Joseph, and in 1918 it was time for the next Jacques to take over the property. He became the mayor of Aÿ, but died during the German occupation at the age of 47. The most colourful person in the history of the house is his widow, Lily Bollinger, who kept an eye on the vines by cycling through the vineyards regularly. Her rigorous demands for quality still run through the house to this day. Now Bollinger is run by Ghislain de Montgolfier and Michel Villedey, who control over 144 hectares, providing 70% of the grape supply.

Besides the house's exceptional vineyards, they also use very expensive vinification methods. All the vintage wines are fermented in small, aged oak barrels and are never filtered. Nor is any malolactic fermentation, which would probably take place very late in the process, at all encouraged.

The reserve wines are stored at low pressure in magnums. Unfortunately the handcrafted champagnes created by Bollinger vary from bottle to bottle. Nowadays it's not at all unusual to come across charmless Bollinger bottles which lack fruit. However, when everything works, they have few superiors. Bollinger make the heaviest and most full-bodied champagnes of any house, and their wines always have a smoky and hazelnutty complexity which is very hard to beat. The vintage wines are among the very best, but the question is if the curious *Vieilles Vignes Françaises*, made with grapes from non-grafted vines, doesn't reach even greater heights.

Bollinger Spécial Cuvée 80
(60% PN, 15% PM, 25% CH)
Previously one of my great favourities among non-vintage champagnes, but since the beginning of the nineties the wine is only four years old and vinified in steel vats. Even so, it's fascinating to see how much 12% old reserve wines, vinified in oak barrels and stored in magnums, do to lift the product. The oakish, smoky and deep Bollinger style develops after a couple of years in the bottle, but the wine is not quite what it used to be.

1988 Bollinger Rosé 87 (Oct 98) 91
(74% PN, 26% CH)
Very good house style, light orange colour. A "Bolly" nose and a round feel of ripe grapes.

1985 Bollinger Rosé 73 (Jul 93) 78
(68% PN, 32% CH)
Rosé champagnes have never really been taken seriously by Bollinger themselves, which shows. A relatively uninspired wine with a bready nose and full fruity taste, with elements of bitter almonds. Needs retasting.

1982 Bollinger Rosé 68 (Jun 88) 75
(70% PN, 30% CH)
What happened to the Bollinger character? The red wine wipes out the wine's positive aspects. Fruity and neutral.

1976 Bollinger Rosé 90 (Jul 96) 90
(60% PN, 40% CH)
Fat, rich and fruity with a creamy, mature finish.

1973 Bollinger Rosé 84 (Sep 96) 84
(75% PN, 25% CH)
Oaky and leaden-footed rosé champagne without elegance. However, a good, full-bodied champagne with food.

1989 Bollinger 87 (Aug 98) 90
(61% PN, 39% CH)
A somewhat unbalanced and overpowerful champagne that lacks a little acidity. Very mature, broad and bold, but hardly one of the great Bollingers.

1988 Bollinger 90 (Oct 98) 93
(75% PN, 25% CH)
I always get a tingling sensation in my stomach when I hear that a new vintage Bollinger has come onto the market. The '88 is classical and promising, but so far drinking it is still like eating the turkey long before Christmas.

1985 Bollinger 92 (Jun 97) 95
(65% PN, 35% CH)
This is what Bollinger is all about. The colour is deep and the concentrated, glycerol-rich champagne forms clear "legs" along the edge of the glass. The nose combines weight with complexity. Biscuits, hazelnuts, chocolate and toasted bread, together with a faint element of oyster shell. The life-bearing malic acidity is restrained and fine and lift this powerful chewy wine up among the greats.

1985 Bollinger R. D. 92 (Oct 98) 94
(65% PN, 35% CH)
Surprisingly little true *R.D.* character yet, with a delicate flowery bouquet which hints at more Chardonnay than is actually the case. A fresh, fruity flavour rich in nuances, with a stifled, underlying power which reveals its origin in the end.

1983 Bollinger 92 (Oct 98) 92
(70% PN, 30% CH)
Even more enjoyable than the great '85. For me the '83 is the most Krug-like of all of Bollinger's wines, as it has more nougat and honey tones than usual. It also has a somewhat richer fruit.

1982 Bollinger 93 (Oct 98) 93
(70% PN, 30% CH)
Certain bottles are already showing signs of age, while others resemble the successful *R.D.* version. Whether or not this is due to the date of disgorging I don't know. At its best it's round and rich with a good aftertaste.

1982 Bollinger R.D. 92 (Jan 99) 92
(70% PN, 30% CH)
R.D. (Recently Disgorged) is the same as the vintage wine, but stored a few more years in contact with the yeast. The '82 has a more vigorous fruit than the normally-disgorged wine. In this vintage the rich autolytic character and muscular build come in very handy.

1979 Bollinger 90 (Dec 93) 90
(70% PN, 30% CH)
Elegant and nutty with a much weaker body, but better fruit than the *R.D.* from the same vintage.

1979 Bollinger R.D.
(70% PN, 30% CH)
A little over the 90 point line at the launch, but now on its way downhill. Bottles sold in Sweden showed a troublesome degree of bottle variation. Whether or not this was due to the house, or to careless handling during transport, is something I couldn't comment upon. The wine is meaty and smoky, but lacks fruit. Some magnums are amazingly fresh. Unjudged.

1976 Bollinger 87 (Oct 98) 87
(50% PN, 50% CH)
Completely mature at the tender age of twelve. Buttery and rich, but the flesh is a little loose and baggy.

1976 Bollinger R.D. 90 (Oct 98) 90
(50% PN, 50% CH)
A touch lighter than expected, considering the house and the vintage. The hazelnut aromas and smoke tones are weaker than usual. The '76 relies instead upon a fat fruitiness. Unusually short aftertaste.

1975 Bollinger 94 (Jun 98) 94
(70% PN, 30% CH)
Just as big, bold, nutty and full of chocolate that one might expect after having tasted *R.D.* on twenty or so occasions.

1975 Bollinger R.D. 94 (May 98) 95
(70% PN, 30% CH)
For several years the best champagne I'd drunk. The critics are unanimous - this is a great vintage for Bollinger. Some bottles with the *Année Rare* label have been too young and closed. The wine is best appreciated two or three years after being disgorged, when its classical hazelnut tones and rich flavour of truffles, cheese and chocolate appear more clearly in the relatively hard and acidic wine. The aftertaste is majestic, with layers of nut and leather aromas.

1975 Bollinger R.D. Année Rare 92 (Mar 94) 95
(70% PN, 30% CH)
The same basic vintage champagne kept for even longer sur pointes. This one was too young !

1973 Bollinger 92 (May 96) 92
(75% PN, 25% CH)
Considering the full development of the *73 R.D.*, I was afraid that this wine would have seen its best days. Actually they're very similar to one another, and only a tone of hay and toffee separates them.

1973 Bollinger R.D. 92 (Mar 93) 92
(75% PN, 25% CH)
Broad tannin-rich champagne with musky and gamey nose. Bollinger's characteristic "sauna tone" from the oak barrels take centre stage. A mature, slightly abrupt power-pack with charm.

1973 Bollinger R.D. Année Rare 92 (Mar 94) 92
(75% PN, 25% CH)
Same impressions as the *R.D.*

1970 Bollinger 93 (Feb 97) 93
(70% PN, 30% CH)
The flavour is full of berries and surrounded by a veil of oak character. Its bouquet is delightful and stimulating, with strong elements of my favourite flower, the honeysuckle.

1970 Bollinger R.D. 94 (Jan 90) 94
(70% PN, 30% CH)
The wine of the vintage. The flavour is somewhat less concentrated than both the '73 and '75, but the nose is among the most exquisite I have experienced. Never before has honeysuckle dominated a wine so clearly. The house's typical hazelnut aroma is also part of the family here. A wine to lose yourself in.

1970 Bollinger R.D. Année Rare 94 (Mar 94) 94
(70% PN, 30% CH)
Same impressions as the *R.D.*

1969 Bollinger 95 (Sep 98) 95
(70% PN, 30% CH)
A classic Bollinger vintage.

1969 Bollinger R.D. 95 (Oct 93) 95
(70% PN, 30% CH)
A beautiful golden colour and a sensual spectrum in the nose, where flower and fruit aromas are more prominent than usual. Paradoxically fresh and mature at the same time. There is a faint vegetable element in the refined flavour of exotic fruits and popcorn.

1966 Bollinger 98 (Oct 98) 98
(75% PN, 25% CH)
Momentous, almost statesman-like vintage. At that time there were grapes from the non-grafted vines from Aÿ and Bouzy in the wine, something which is actually quite noticeable. The wine expresses Aÿ pinot at its very best. Orange colour, animalish, vegetables and toasty aromas hit you in the glass. The nose actually resembles a mature *La Tâche* from D.R.C. The attack is enormous, despite the wine's meaty structure and rich fruit. The aftertaste accelerates in the mouth and it takes a long, long while before one is left with just the popcorn aroma lingering on the palate.

1966 Bollinger R.D. 94 (Sep 98) ▼
(75% PN, 25% CH)
Not so recently-disgorged any more. Wonderful, but flagging a little.

1964 Bollinger 96 (Oct 98) 96
(75% PN, 25% CH)
The '64 is a touch less generous in the fruit and a bit tougher in its acidity than the '66, but the wine is just as great, full of truffles, coffee and chocolate aromas. After a stringent first taste, the aftertaste gets going in the mouth and leaves a honeyed tone that lasts for several minutes.

1964 Bollinger R. D. 94 (Mar 97) 97
(75% PN, 25% CH)
Tasted when recently-disgorged in a magnum. It was still a young champagne with enormous inner power, but of course the date of dégorgement was decisive.

1961 Bollinger 90 (Sep 90) 90
(75% PN, 25% CH)
Very light, young colour. Few nuances, but there's good stringency and earth cellar aromas, along with a powder-dry barrel character. Slightly lacking in fruit.

1961 Bollinger R.D. 84 (Nov 93) ▼
(75% PN, 25% CH)
Red wine notes that remind you of a heavy Barolo. A weak mousse and somewhat dried-out fruit. Meaty and vinous. Disgorged in 1972, so examples disgorged more recently may be considerably better.

1959 Bollinger 97 (Oct 97) 97
(75% PN, 25% CH)
A majestic and powerful champagne full of life.

1955 Bollinger
(75% PN, 25% CH)
This ought to be one of Bollinger's finest champagnes. Unfortunately I've only encountered a poorly-stored bottle of low quality. I will taste it again soon. Unjudged.

1953 Bollinger 94 (Aug 94) 94
(75% PN, 25% CH)
Not a bubbly champagne exactly, but definitely a great wine. The '53 is an amber-coloured drink with faint reservoirs of carbon dioxide. The nose is dominated by oak and dried roses, with a very unique, red wine-like bouquet. This is a very well-built and muscular champagne with huge dimensions. The dry cognac-like aftertaste lasted for an entire three minutes!

1952 Bollinger 80 (Dec 96) 
(75% PN, 25% CH)
Despite a high level and total lack of sediment, the two bottles I tasted had long since passed their peak. Surprisingly strong oxidation for this vintage.

1947 Bollinger 80 (Apr 96) 
(75% PN, 25% CH)
I tasted only a half bottle. No mousse to speak of and a clear maderised tone that is disturbing. Otherwise a remarkably well-structured wine that would certainly have reached the 95 point mark in a magnum.

1945 Bollinger 96 (Dec 96) 96
(75% PN, 25% CH)
It's not often that 45's are as brilliant as this. Bollinger have made a refined wine with teasing aromas and a romantic bouquet. It's easy to swallow this caress of a wine, with its smooth fruit and lively freshness.

1989 Vieilles Vignes Françaises 96 (Jan 99) 98
(100% PN)
Champagne's greatest rarity is made from grapes from ungrafted pre-phylloxera vines in Aÿ and Bouzy. No other champagne can present such richness as this. As usual, almost perfect. So far the wine is Yquem-like, with its enormously sweet, concentrated, exotic fruit. Only when aired does there appear a magnificent secondary aroma of cep mushrooms.

1988 Vieilles Vignes Françaises 94 (Jan 99) 97
(100% PN)
When first introduced onto the market it was unusually raw and abrupt. At the time I missed the creamy complexity that previous vintages had shown in their infancy. One year later it was all there; the creaminess, the power and the tons of fruit. A giant!

1986 Vieilles Vignes Françaises 92 (Dec 95) 95
(100% PN)
The '86 may not be one of the great vintages, but here too there is an unbending power which lifts it over its competitors. The colour is always dark, with elements of mahogany, and the nose is astoundingly broad, with layers of fruit and vegetable aromas. The wine is compact, with a strict finish. Drink during the coming century.

1985 Vieilles Vignes Françaises 96 (Oct 98) 99
(100% PN)
One of the rare champagnes in this book that have received 99 points. It's always equally difficult to describe in words the very best wines, so let me say instead that this champagne is close to perfection, with its deep golden colour, outstandingly mature, multi-faceted bouquet and shocking attack. The acidity is wrapped up in an incomprehensibly rich and elegant fruit. A masterwork!

1982 Vieilles Vignes Françaises 93 (Aug 93) 97
(100% PN)
A brilliant colour, like red gold. Undeveloped compact nose which is full of minerals, cold and deep, full of exciting aromas. The yoghurt that you sometimes find in red burgundies is a very clear element here. Cream, olives, iron, tar, figs and orange are other clearly-discernible nuances. At first the flavour is as harsh as a red *Hermitage*, but goes on to develop a toasty, wonderful complexity. Don't touch it for ten years!

1981 Vieilles Vignes Françaises 94 (Nov 93) 96
(100% PN)
A wonder of delicacy. That a blanc de noirs can be so elegant and multi-faceted astonished an entire tasting group in November 1993. The nose is only of medium scope, but has a lovely romantic, flowery style. Along-side the flowers there is a broad spectrum of all the treasures of the bakery, white chocolate, marzipan, lilies and lime.

1975 Vieilles Vignes Françaises 96 (Sep 96) 97
(100% PN)
Still quite young, With a strong nose, cosiderable length and a gorgeous Pinot flavour. Perfection.

1973 Vieilles Vignes Françaises 91 (Nov 93) 91
(100% PN)
This has to be the mightiest champagne I've ever drunk. The nose was amazingly broad, but the quesiton is if it wasn't too overwhelming. The champagne as a whole resembles a great red burgundy. Boiled vegetables, paprika, green beans, beetroot, fish, raw meat and gunpowder smoke. The gigantic flavour runs along the same lines, with extra tones of cauliflower, lavender, basil, tar and duck liver. The richest and most idiosyncratic champagne I've tasted, but hardly worth the exorbitant price.

1970 Vieilles Vignes Françaises 98 (Oct 98) 98
(100% PN)
After having read both Sutcliffe and Broadbent's judgements on this wine I was extremely surprised by its character. Along with my British colleagues I was impressed by the wine's concentration, but the aromas were very different from those I'd noted in other vintages of this pre-phylloxera wine. The aromas were fruity and creamy, like a Cramant B. d. B. The nose was tactful and the flavour fat and full of exotic mango aromas. The wine's concentration and length confirm that the label isn't on the wrong bottle.

1969 Vieilles Vignes Françaises 97 (Nov 93) 97
(100% PN)
A fantastic vintage and one of the greatest champagnes I've tasted. I managed to get a bottle from the last remaining case the producer had. This is also an unique wine in that it's the first vintage of *Vieilles Vignes Françaises*. A very dark golden reddish colour, perfect mouse and a magnificent bouquet. There are none of the 73's vegetable tones, but instead the wine is dominated by sweet licorice, dark chocolate, tobacco, apricot and peach. The texture is oily and fat, but the acid attack is impressive under the benign surface.

Deutz

16 rue Jeanson, 51160 Aÿ  03 26 55 15 11

Production: 1 million bottles.

Two Germans, William Deutz and Pierre Gelderman, founded this honourable firm in 1838 in the village of Aÿ. Deutz was hard hit by the champagne riots of 1911. Since the seventies the house has been run by André Lallier, who has invested heavily in other wine districts, including properties such as Delas in the Rhône valley, Maison Deutz in California and another sparkling wine from the Loire valley. In 1993 Louis Roederer bought a majority shareholding in the company. And today the skilful Fabrice Rosset runs the famous house.

75% of the grapes are bought in from Grand and Premier cru vineyards, although Deutz owns land in five villages, including some of the most beautiful locations in all champagne. The style is laid-back, elegant and sophisticated, with a medium body and crystal-clear fruit, along with a first-class mousse. All the wines are extremely good, but *Cuvée William Deutz Rosé* has that little extra something.

Deutz Brut Classic 78
(38% PN, 32% PM, 30% CH)
Good quality champagne, but sold too early. Lay it aside in the cellar for a couple of years and it will develop a fine, bready nose which plays down the exaggerated apple fruit.

Deutz Demi-Sec 52
(38% PN, 35% PM, 30% CH)
The dosage is 35 grams, but the house style is maintained.

1990 Deutz Demi-Sec 70 (Jul 97) 75
(40% PN, 30% PM, 30% CH)
Deutz is another to have latched on to the trend of sweet vintage champagnes. This wine is identical to the *90 Deutz*, swamped with a spoonful or two of sugar. Certainly fine with a crème brûle.

1990 Deutz Rosé 83 (Sep 97) 90
(100% PN)
14% red wine from Bouzy. A smooth nose of cream and butterscotch. Softly delicate, laid-back, rich and fruity flavour of good length.

1988 Deutz Rosé 82 (Mar 95) 87
(100% PN)
The firm has a well-deserved reputation for its rosé champagnes. The '88 has a lovely Pinot character and a fresh, bubbling liveliness.

1985 Deutz Rosé 87 (Sep 96) 90
(80% PN, 20% CH)
A pale orange colour and a delicate, multi-faceted nose containing elements of cream. The palate is lined with delicate, smooth sensations. Creamy, elegant and developed.

1981 Deutz Rosé 88 (Feb 97) 88
(100% PN)
Big, bold and elegant all at the same time, with a lightness that is typical of this vintage. The aromatic spectrum includes tones of orange, lemon and Aÿ Pinot.

1975 Deutz Rosé 89 (Aug 96) 89
(80% PN, 20% PM)
Meaty and mature with a smoky nose that reminds one of an old-fashioned butcher's shop. A sweet, mature fruit flavour that edges towards plums and sun-ripened tomatoes. Good with plenty of personality.

1990 Deutz 83 (Jul 97) 88
(40% PN, 30% PM, 30% CH)
Incredibly fruity and rich, with a relaxed charm so typical of this house. Good balance and harmony.

1988 Deutz 77 (Feb 95) 86
(45% PN, 20% PM, 35% CH)
A wine in the Deutz laid-back, polished style. Young and soft at the same time.

1985 Deutz 83 (Jul 91) 86
(40% PN, 25% PM, 35% CH)
This chocolaty champagne has developed early, with a broad, ripe fruit in the flavour. Only the length will be improved by a few years in the cellar.

1982 Deutz 79 (Aug 93) 83
(40% PN, 25% PM, 35% CH)
A relative disappointment, where tones of freshly-baked bread gave the most positive impressions.

1990 Deutz B. d. B. 80 (Feb 95) 88
(100% CH)
Deutz Blanc de Blancs reminds me of Pol Roger's Chardonnay wine. Both are ultra-sophisticated and aristocratic, but lack that character that a really great wine needs. The '90 is typical of its vintage, with a tight structure and a collected inner power.

1989 Deutz B. d. B. 91 (Jul 98) 94
(100% CH)
For once this feels like a grower's champagne of the highest class from Le Mesnil. The wine is clearly influenced by the village's terroir character, with smoky and mineral-rich undertones and a fat, concentrated, acidic flavour, which is an advantage in my eyes.

1988 Deutz B. d. B. 79 (Dec 93) 89
(100% CH)
Light green/yellow colour and fine, microscopic mousse. A textbook blanc de blancs with superb finesse and overflowing with young acidity. A delicate and faintly toasty tone complements the floweriness. Pure, dry and long.

1985 Deutz B. d. B. 88 (Oct 94) 92
(100% CH)
When I was confronted with this champagne in 1990, I was impressed by its wealth of finesse. Whether it is in a weaker phase or should have been enjoyed when very young, only time will tell.

1982 Deutz B. d. B. 86 (Mar 91) 89
(100% CH)
Delicate, easily-placed blanc de blancs with an underlying sweet rounded fruit. *Deutz Blanc de Blancs* is undeniably relatively insensitive for its vintage, but the house style makes its point, as always.

1979 Deutz B. d. B. 82 (May 90) ▼
(100% CH)
This wine is a little too thin and soft for it to be particularly good for storage. A green, mature Chardonnay colour and faint toasty nose with an element of vanilla. The flavour is dominated by pineapple and grapefruit tones.

1975 Deutz B. d. B. 92 (Jan 96) 92
(100% CH)
Lighter and weaker in the nose than expected. All is forgiven when the citrus-crispy flavour is as delicate and never-ending as it is here.

1988 Cuvée William Deutz 93 (Aug 98) 95
(50% PN, 10% PM, 40% CH)
A wonderfully balanced champagne that makes me sing the praises of blending. The slender Aÿ Pinot is lifted by a Chardonnay finish that is citrus-fresh and full of minerals.

1985 Cuvée William Deutz 90 (Apr 98) 92
(62% PN, 8% PM, 30% CH)
Brilliant appearance, classical champagne nose and flavour, but somewhat impersonal in its medium-bodied, polished style at first. Today full and rich.

1982 Cuvée William Deutz 86 (Aug 93) 90
(62% PN, 8% PM, 30% CH)
Well copper-coloured, clear and brightly shining with a stylish cordon. A delicate, mineral-rich nose with faint ripe tones. Medium-bodied, elegant flavour of young Pinot. A touch short.

1979 Cuvée William Deutz 86 (Jun 89) 90
(62% PN, 8% PM, 30% CH)
Wonderful rich vanilla aroma that dominates the wine. The fruit had more to give when I tasted the champagne, but otherwise it was rather undeveloped and ingratiating.

1975 Cuvée William Deutz 94 (Jun 98) 94
(60% PN, 10% PM, 30% CH)
More developed than most other 75's, but still showing superbly high quality. The wine is very similar to *Bollinger*, with its nutty richness and mushroom aromas. Aÿ Pinot also provides a concentrated, impressive aftertaste.

1973 Cuvée William Deutz 90 (Sep 96) ▼
(60% PN, 10% PM, 30% CH)
Definitely a high-flier with an early peak. When I tasted the champagne it was beginning to go downhill but still achieved an impressive ninety points. Balance, charm and chocolate aromas still delightful.

1971 Cuvée William Deutz
(62% PN, 8% PM, 30% CH)
Totally flat and lifeless. A chocolate nose with elements of earth, raisins and maderisation. Rather unconcentrated and short flavour without lustre. Unjudged.

1961 Cuvée William Deutz 94 (Oct 97) 94
(60% PN, 10% PM, 30% CH)
Old-fashioned, oaky and heavy. A food champagne that was perfectly suited to duck liver. Apparently the first vintages of this cuvée de prestige were made in a more full-bodied style than today's.

1976 Cuvée Georges Mathieu 90 (Jul 95) 90
(60% PN, 15% PM, 25% CH)
The wine avoids the fatness of the vintage and is instead stylish and pure. However, personality and length went missing here.

1985 Cuvée William Deutz Rosé 94 (Jul 97) 94
(100% PN)
This prestige rosé is without doubt the crown jewel of Deutz's assortment. Both the '82 and the '85 are magnificent romantic wines that almost make me cry with happiness. The '85 doesn't really have the same concentration as the '82, but it has more restrained acidity. The nose is lush, with a gorgeous tone of Aÿ Pinot. Leather, cheese and chocolate are aromas which gives the strawberry tone greater nuances, and the flavour is incredibly long.

1982 Cuvée William Deutz Rosé 96 (May 98) 96
(100% PN)
Absolutely one of the best rosé champagnes I've ever drunk. Only Grand cru grapes have been used, with Aÿ dominant. Deep red colour, tremendously broad nose of ripe berries, leather and nougat. The flavour is fat and concentrated and contains an explosion of sweet fruits. Extremely balanced.

Deutz Anniversaire 81
(70% PN, 10% PM, 20% CH)
The jubilee cuvée with wine from 1979, 81 and 82. Delicate and refined champagne with a taste of lemon licorice, but disappointing in terms of the very high price.

1975 Deutz Aÿ 95 (Jun 97) 97
(100% PN)
Too good to be sold! said Deutz's winemaker. The most striking thing is that this 100% Pinot Noir wine is so elegant. There is a superb multi-faceted and toasty nose with strong acidity and a light, buttery Chardonnay-like character. A masterwork that reflects Deutz more than Aÿ.

Gosset

69 rue Jules Blondeau, 51160 Aÿ ☎ 03 26 56 99 56
Production: 500,000 bottles.

Ruinart may be the oldest champagne-producing firm, but Gosset was a maker of still wines much earlier. As long ago as in 1584, Pierre Gosset sold his vin d'Aÿ as a négociant. Today the family owns 12 hectares in the villages of Aÿ, Bouzy, Mareuil and Rilly, all of which are full of Pinot Noir. This meets a fifth of the firm's needs, but the character of the villages is clearly noticeable in the vintage wines. Gosset is one of the real traditionalists in the area, with hand-produced labels and disgorging. They also use old oak barrels where the vintage wines are stored for a short time, giving only a hint of oak character. The wines are always full and rich, with a heavy element of Aÿ-Pinot.

Gosset Brut Excellence 77
(42% PN, 9% PM, 49% CH)
Less mighty and concentrated than the *Grande Réserve*, but more enjoyable in large amounts. The wine is rich in Pinot fruit and chocolate aromas. The dosage is unnecessarily high in both of Gosset's non-vintage champagnes.

Gosset Grande Réserve 77
(40% PN, 12% PM, 48% CH)
A fat and oily champagne with tons of ripe apples and a meaty Pinot taste. Only in the mineral-rich finish does one notice the Chardonnay grapes.

1990 Grand Millésime Rosé 81 (Feb 97) 87
(18% PN, 82% CH)
This light wine has an aroma of oak-fermented Chardonnay that hasn't gone through malolactic fermentation. The resemblance to *Selosse Rosé* is striking. It has a fine attack and plenty of personality and richness.

1988 Grand Millésime Rosé 83 (Nov 94) 88
(18% PN, 82% CH)
60% of the wine has been vinified in oak barrels, which hardly makes a difference. Here the elegant Chardonnay is the mark of distinction. So far the excellent nose of strawberry, cream and mineral is rather discreet. The flavour is more impressive with deep, thought-provoking and elegant nutty Chardonnay.

1985 Grand Millésime Rosé 93 (Jul 97) 94
(18% PN, 82% CH)
Sensational, outstanding, unique champagne with a ripe orange colour and amazingly multi-faceted nose. The dominant tones are mint chocolate and forest mushrooms. The flavour is creamy and tremendously buttery.

1982 Grand Millésime Rosé 81 (Aug 98) 81
(12% PN, 88% CH)
A much-discussed rosé made in the modern way. Today mature and rich without any elegance. A laid-back wine that certainly doesn't stick its neck out.

1989 Grand Millésime 81 (Oct 97) 86
(34% PN, 66% CH)
A broad, powerful wine which many will view as being mature. In my opinion the overwhelmingly sweet, oxidative fruit is a touch unbalanced right now. The wine reminds me of the mighty '83.

1985 Grand Millésime 90 (Feb 98) 94
(38% PN, 62% CH)
The best champagne from Gosset that I've tasted. A wine in perfect equilibrium, with an impeccable appearance and a refined spectrum in the nose of white flowers, nectar, passion fruit, mango and a faint barrel tone. The wine hasn't gone through the malolactic fermentation, which gives a frisky bite to the pure, flowery and fruity aromas.

1983 Grand Millésime 83 (Aug 97) 85
(60% PN, 40% CH)
Almost chewy and viscous, with a developed reddish colour. The nose is overwhelming, with tones of figs and windfall.

1983 Gosset Cuvée Suzanne 82 (Apr 96) 85
(60% PN, 40% CH)
Sadly too sweet, but enjoyably round. Undeniably rich and impressive.

1982 Grand Millésime Green Label 84 (May 91) 89
(55% PN, 7% PM, 38% CH)
A weak, nutty and stylish champagne for the aesthete. Lighter and more restrained than the "Red Label".

1982 Grand Millésime Red Label 89 (May 94) 89
(60% PN, 40% CH)
A mature Pinot style. The home ground of Aÿ has certainly left its mark in this round and overflowing, full-bodied, plum-like flavour.

1979 Gosset 83 (Jan 89) 87
(34% PN, 5% PM, 61% CH)
Weak, smoky and clear tones of champagne cellar in the nose. Unexpectedly light mineral-rich flavour which I would never have connected to a Gosset in a blind tasting.

1976 Gosset 93 (Oct 97) 93
(50% PN, 50% CH)
Amazingly fresh acidity intergrated with an oily texture and marvelous aromas of tea, apricot and honey.

1975 Gosset 88 (Mar 88) 92
(60% PN, 40% CH)
I imagine that the '75 is wonderful today. At the age of 13 it still had its youth left, but one could detect a hint of the chocolate aromas to come. Massive, rich, fat fruit with a long, dry and stringent aftertaste.

1971 Gosset 93 (Nov 96) 93
(60% PN, 40% CH)
The '71 has almost become a creature of myth. I didn't think it was all that wonderful. However, this is a muscular '71 with a smoky Pinot character á la Bollinger.

1959 Gosset 94 (Mar 96) 94
(60% PN, 40% CH)
The *59 Gosset* is as good as it sounds. Muscular and round all at once, with a delightful attacking hazelnut flavour and a smooth aftertaste of honey.

1952 Gosset 93 (Dec 95) 93
(30% PN, 70% CH)
A delightful wine with many delicate nuances of flowers and toasty tones. Youthful, with a long and lively toffee flavour.

1988 Gosset Célebris 88 (Mar 98) 93
(34% PN, 66% CH)
Lighter and more delicate than usual, with an appetising, flowery nose and an exquisite, crispy lime flavour.

Pierre Laurain

2 rue Roger Sondag, 51160 Aÿ ☎ 03 26 55 18 90
Production: 60,000 bottles.

After having sold Collery to Germain, Alain Collery continued under the name of Pierre Laurain. Today he has a wine museum and a popular restaurant in the middle of town, while he simultaneously take good care of his exceptional properties in Aÿ and Mareuil-sur-Aÿ. When Collery was sold, he kept a store of older vintages in order to have the possibility of selling fully mature wines to us Collery fans.

Pierre Laurain Brut 67
(previously Collery Brut)
(70% PN, 20% PM, 10% CH)
A robust champagne which needs several years of extra aging. When young it can feel unbalanced in a meaty way, but with a little time in the bottle it settles into a lovely harmony.

Collery Brut 67
(70% PN, 20% PM, 10% CH)
The same wine as ***Pierre Laurain Brut.***

Pierre Laurain Demi-Sec 52
(100% PN)
Unexpectedly dry and drinkable, with a rooty Pinot flavour.

Pierre Laurain Rosé 88
(previously Collery Rosé)
(100% PN)
One of the best rosé champagnes in existence. Aÿ Pinot gives the most burgundy-like aromas in all of Champagne, and no rosé champagne shows this more clearly. The colour is dark and clear, the nose screams out Pinot aromas with all their gamey tones, cheeses, spices and strawberry-like fruit aromas that one would expect. The flavour is compact, with a deep, juicy Pinot aroma and exquisite length.

Collery Rosé 88
(100% PN)
The same wine as ***Pierre Laurain Rosé.***

1989 Pierre Laurain 70 (Mar 93) 84
(20% PN, 80% CH)
A slightly strange wine which was hard to judge when young. A strong, rank bouquet of mushrooms and boiled vegetables. A sharp attack with highly concentrated vegetable power. Not a wine for beginners.

1985 Pierre Laurain 91 (Oct 97) 94
(previously Solange Collery)
(100% PN)
A pure Aÿ blanc de noirs, with a good deal of variation in the bottle. Some are full of vegetables, while others have a roasted nose and an astonishingly young flavour. The greatest wines are dominated by leather, mushroom, truffles and hazelnut.

1985 Solange Collery 91 (Jun 95) 94
(100% PN)
The same wine as ***1985 Pierre Laurain.***

1981 Pierre Laurain 92 (Aug 95) 92
(previously Collery Herbillon)
(90% PN, 10% CH)
A champagne made in the Bollinger style with smoky complexity, a full nutty aroma and vigorous fruit. Perfect with game.

1981 Collery Herbillon 92 (Aug 97) 92
(90% PN, 10% CH)
The same wine as ***1981 Pierre Laurain.***

1980 Collery Herbillon 90 (Apr 93) 90
(100% PN)
Not as restrained and massive as the '81, but with a seductive nose of honey and chocolate. The flavour is medium-bodied with a creamy finish.

1976 Collery Special Club 93 (Oct 95) 93
(100% PN)
Mouth-filling and awesome in its volume. Marvelous with young rabbit!

1973 Collery Herbillon 90 (Sep 88) 90
(90% PN, 10% CH)
Drunk when I was a beginner in this field, but it will be a while before I forget the incredible power or the interwound aftertaste of licorice.

Collery

4 rue Anatole France, 51160 Aÿ ☎ 03 26 54 01 20
Production: 30,000 bottles.

We must hope that Alain Collery intends to carry out his plan of buying back Collery from Germain. Collery was previously one of my favourite houses, but Alain sold the name in 1991 while keeping his vineyards in Aÿ and he now bottles wines under the label Pierre Laurain. (See Pierre Laurain)

Pierre Cheval.

Gatinois

7 rue Marcel Mailly, 51160 Aÿ ☎ 03 26 55 14 26
Production: 30,000 bottles.

The man who runs Gatinois today, Pierre Cheval, reserves his greatest pride for his red wine from Aÿ. Together with Bollinger, Gosset-Brabant and Gotourbe, he is alone in making an Aÿ rouge. The Gatinois family have been winemakers inn Aÿ since 1696 and own 29 pieces of land in Aÿ with a total area of seven hectares. Half of the harvest is sold annually to the neighbours Bollinger. Gatinois produces classical Aÿ champagne that takes many years to reach full maturity.

Gatinois Tradition Brut 73
(90% PN, 10% CH)
Dark copper colour, faint nose of leather and plums. Good, acidic, pure and one-dimensional flavour of red apples.

Gatinois Réserve 80
(90% PN, 10% CH)
A blend of three vintages. A very red colour, massively sweet nose of honey, banana and raisins. A broad, complex taste of mature Pinot grapes and strawberries.

Gatinois Rosé 80
(100% PN)
A delicate Aÿ rosé that contains a wide spectrum of flowery and spicy aromas and a long, elegant, balanced flavour.

1990 Gatinois 89 (Oct 97) 94
(90% PN, 10% CH)
A deep colour, honeyed nose and magnificent long sweet aftertaste.

1989 Gatinois 86 (Apr 96) 90
(100% PN)
Extremely deep colour, more orange than copper. A sweet honeyed nose that is typical of the vintage. The flavour is strong and full of character.

1983 Gatinois 81 (Apr 95) 85
(100% PN)
Pierre Cheval's favourite vintage. Light colour, faint nose of vegetable boullion and stewed meat. An oily, gamey flavour with good acidity, thanks to the malolactic fermentation being left out this year.

Roland Fliniaux

1 rue Léon Bourgeois, 511160 Aÿ ☎ 03 26 55 17 17

Production: 85,000 bottles.

Fliniaux is one of the champagne houses closest to my heart. A better Pinot Noir producer is hard to find. Regis Fliniaux, who has had a great deal of success in the German-speaking countries, now runs the company in the same uncompromising spirit as Roland had done. They own four hectares in Aÿ, which constitutes 25% of production needs. Most of the grapes that are bought in come from Aÿ. No oak barrels are used, but the richness in Fliniaux's wines are reminiscent of Bollinger. The champagne is nothing for acid fetischists, or those who are seeking elegance in their wines. Fliniaux's greatness is built on power and a wealth of flavours - just as it should be from this little town.

Fliniaux Cuvée de Réserve 75
(80% PN, 20% CH)
The firm's most basic wine is typical of the house, with a Pinot nose and round taste.

Fliniaux Carte Noir Brut 80
(80% PN, 20% CH)
The same foundation wine as its predecessor, but stored longer. A massive yet charming wine, with a broad meaty nose of leather and hazelnut. Rich, round fruit taste of raisins, plums and banana.

Fliniaux Rosé 88
(100% PN)
A textbook rosé which expresses a lot of the character of the soil, together with the grape's wonderful strawberry aroma. The dark colour puts many people off, but just close your eyes and let yourself be washed away by the incredibly rich grape character.

1988 Fliniaux Rosé 90 (Jul 93) 93
(100% PN)
Somewhat lighter in colour than the above. More restrained and younger, but with even more potential. The last glass was a symphony of the Pinot grape's various incarnations, where the aftertaste reverberated like a singer's voice in a cathedral.

1985 Fliniaux 90 (Jul 95) 90
(100% PN)
Massive gunpowder scent in this Aÿ champagne, with good attack and a superb length.

1983 Fliniaux Cuvée Prestige 85 (Feb 94) 89
(100% PN)
Fliniaux's wines resemble *La Grande Dame* with their generous, soft and chocolaty Pinot aromas. The '83 isn't as magnificent as the '79, but has better acidity and a teasing resistance, along with a tone of roasted chestnuts.

1982 Fliniaux 83 (May 95) 83
(100% PN)
Fat, round, mature and gutsy. Drink up!

1982/83 Fliniaux 82 (Jul 90) 85
(100% PN)
The rounder and softer vintage of 1982 dominates the wine with a vengeance. For once the structure is loose, even though the aroma of chocolate and banana is overwhelming.

1979 Fliniaux 92 (Jul 93) 92
(100% PN)
Once one of my favourites, which I regularly placed ahead of *79 Bollinger R.D.* at blind tastings. Some bottles are losing it, but most are at the peak of their abilities. If you're lucky you'll experience an outstandingly rich wine with an exotic nose of honeysuckle, honey, hazelnut, mushroom and chocolate candy. All these tones return on the palate in a luxurious soft package.

De Méric

17 rue Gambetta, 51160 Aÿ ☎ 03 26 55 20 72

Production: 150,000 bottles.

This family firm is one of my later discoveries. Christian and Patrick Besserat come from the family that owned Besserat de Bellefon, but in 1960 Christian left to start his own house in Aÿ. They still control 10 hectares in the village, with an unusually high percentage of Chardonnay. Those grapes that are bought in come from the Côte des Blancs. Only the cuvée is used, and only the best of the first pressing goes into the cuvée de prestige. De Méric is one of the few producers who admit that they use cognac in their dosage.

De Méric Brut 78
(70% PN, 30% CH)
I wish I could give this unstinting praise, but some bottles hardly make it over the 50 point level with their artificial rubber scent. On other occasions I've been so impressed by this gunpowderish champagne that I've found similarities with young vintage Bollingers.

De Méric B. d. B. 76
(100% CH)
A pure Côte des Blancs champagne with a mild, delicate nose and a slightly diluted, easily-drunk style.

De Méric Rosé 72
(89% PN, 11% CH)
More consistent than the non-vintage champagne, but the nose is more muffled. The aftertaste is magnificent, with its cheeky combination of citrus aromas and wild strawberry.

1988 De Méric 76 (Mar 95) 84
(70% PN, 30% CH)
A blend of Aÿ and Oger. Despite that, nothing out of the ordinary. The smoky house style is combined here with a hint of green apples.

Cathérine de Médicis 89
(50% PN, 50% CH)
The company's cuvée de prestige is made completely from the grapes of Aÿ. Always a blend of three vintages, with an average age of thirteen. A very mature and aromatic wine in the English manner. Slightly exaggerated oxidative character, but gorgeous banana and chocolate aromas. The flavour is also wonderful and full of sweet, mature tones, but the aftertaste is devalued by an ounce of sherry tones.

Ayala

2 bd du Nord, 51160 Aÿ ☎ 03 26 55 15 44

Production: 800,000 bottles.

When Edmond de Ayala, the son of a Colombian diplomat, married into Aÿ society in 1860, he started up a champagne house which quickly became one of the most popular around. The firm's best market was England, and it still owns the Château de Mareuil and the champagne house Montebello. Their own vineyards are in Mareuil-sur-Aÿ, but 80% are bought in from 95% grapes. The house was run by the former president of the C.I.V.C., the legendary J.-M. Ducellier, but in 1996 his son Alain took the helm. The house style has always been influenced by Pinot and the wines have a fine roundness.

Ayala Brut 65
(50% PN, 25% PM, 25% CH)
A rather uncomplicated but pleasant non-vintage champagne with good maturity and pure fruit.

Ayala Demi-Sec 50
(30% PN, 60% PM, 10% CH)
Resonably good despite the huge amount of Pinot Meunier and sugar.

Ayala Rosé 66
(100% PN)
A peach-coloured rosé with a lovely nose of Aÿ-Pinot and a surprisingly restrained fruity flavour.

1990 Ayala B. d. B. 76 (Jul 95) 79
(100% CH)
The wine resembles the precocious style of an '89. Hardly elegant, but enjoyable with its soft fruit.

1988 Ayala B. d. B. 67 (Mar 95) 71
(100% CH)
The same neutral impression as the '82. Ayala are better with Pinot!

1982 Ayala B. d. B. 66 (Jul 89) 70
(100% CH)
Despite the excellent vineyards in Côte des Blancs, this champagne is a little too light and characterless.

1979 Ayala B. d. B. 78 (Oct 95) 78
(100% CH)
A real disappointment with some peculiar aromas and a somewhat loose structure.

1990 Ayala 78 (Feb 97) 84
(70% PN, 30% CH)
Ayala have pulled off a decent piece of workmanship, but no more. This rich and relatively mature '90 has a sweet fruit that reminds one of the 1989 vintage.

1989 Ayala 81 (Jul 95) 86
(75% PN, 25% CH)
A fruity Pinot-dominated champagne bursting with life, with a smooth, long aftertaste.

1985 Ayala 81 (Dec 96) 85
(70% PN, 30% CH)
Great weight and meaty Pinot aromas flow through this well-built '85.

1982 Ayala 80 (Jul 91) 86
(75% PN, 25% CH)
Typically generous, fruity Ayala nose with a rich and uncomplicated flavour.

1979 Ayala 87 (Aug 96) 88
(75% PN, 25% CH)
An intense, fruity wine, with a pleasant butterscotch finish.

1975 Ayala 91 (Apr 96) 91
(75% PN, 25% CH)
Very lively and fiery, with clear Pinot aromas and a powerful aftertaste.

1973 Ayala 84 (Jun 97) ▼
(75% PN, 25% CH)
On its way to the grave, but still enjoyable though.

1964 Ayala 95 (Apr 95) 95
(75% PN, 25% CH)
A wonderful, classical '64! Deep golden colour and minimal bubbles which ever stop streaming upward out of the glass. A broad, mature nose with a wide spectrum of lovely aromas, such as toffee, mint chocolate, honey and dried fruit. A wonderfully sweet flow through the mouth with a romantic, ultra-long aftertaste of butterscotch.

1961 Ayala 92 (Jul 95) 92
(75% PN, 25% CH)
Rather light and lively 33 year-old. Slightly vegetable nose, with elements of licorice, tobacco, tar and leather. Rich, dry, masculine and long champagne with some severe acidity. One of the last years that Ayala used oak barrels.

1945 Ayala
(75% PN, 25% CH)
Maderised and therefore unjudged.

1928 Ayala
(75% PN, 25% CH)
Maderised and unjudged.

1988 Grande Cuvée 84 (Jul 95) 89
(30% PN, 70% CH)
An extremely delicate champagne with tones of white chocolate and jasmine. Light and stylish.

H. Goutorbe

9 bis rue Jeanson, 51160 Aÿ ☎ 03 26 55 21 70

Henri and his son René Goutorbe are known for their Aÿ rouge, but they also make some fine champagne. This is one of few firms that sell older vintages.

H. Goutorbe Brut 68
(65% PN, 5% PM, 30% CH)
Rounded honey aromas claim attention in an otherwise fruity nose with mineral elements. Good attack and a pure, dry flavour.

H. Goutorbe B. d. B. 68
(100% CH)
Buttery and round champagne with clear vanilla tones in a surprisingly short flavour. 100% Bisseuil!

H. Goutorbe Rosé 61
(100% PN)
A somewhat lighter colour than expected, with elements of yellow. The nose and flavour are fruity and harmoniously discreet, but with a slightly rough mousse.

H. Goutorbe Prestige 73
(65% PN, 5% PM, 30% CH)
The long time spent in the bottle gives a complex and strong autolytic wine.

1989 H. Goutorbe Special Club 84 (Apr 97) 88
(50% PN, 50% CH)
A pure Aÿ champagne with golden colour and a nose featuring roses, plums and cream. A fresh, rich flavour that needs a few more years for the aftertaste to lengthen.

1988 H. Goutorbe Special Club 85 (Jul 95) 89
(70% PN, 30% CH))
Incredibly rich, round and accessible, creamy and sweet.

1987 H. Goutorbe Special Club 80 (Apr 96) 82
(66% PN, 34% CH)
An elegant and focused '87 with a fine tone of brioche and vanilla. Somewhat hollow and green with a pleasant vanilla tone returning in the aftertaste.

1983 H. Goutorbe 90 (Sep 96) 90
(66% PN, 34% CH)
A sensual champagne with a lovely nose of honeysuckle, oyster shell and leather. The flavour may not be quite so sensational but is rich enough to take it up to the magic 90-point mark.

1982 H. Goutorbe 86 (Jun 96) 86
(66% PN, 34% CH)
A supreme nose of honeysuckle and a sweet, mature honeyed flavour with elements of plum.

1976 H. Goutorbe 86 (May 96) 86
(66% PN, 34% CH)
This oldie was still on sale in May, 1996. Rather recently disgorged and very well-kept, it's a good representative of the house style. There's power beneath the elegant surface, and the mineral tones are very clear.

Pascal Henin

22 rue Jules Lobel, 51160 Aÿ ☎ 03 26 54 61 50
Production: 8,000 bottles.

The tiny but well-run Aÿ house was founded in 1920. Pascal Henin owns vineyards in Chouilly and Aÿ that he blends in equal proportions in all his wines.

Pascal Henin Brut 70
(50% PN, 50% CH)
A fine, creamy Chardonnay aroma and a perfectly pure mineral tone. A strong backbone made up of sanguine Aÿ Pinot.

Pascal Henin Rosé 70
(50% PN, 50% CH)
Deep red with a mighty nose. Aÿ Pinot is in there, screaming for attention, along with additional aromas of winegums and raspberry.

1990 Pascal Henin 87 (Feb 97) 88
(50% PN, 50% CH)
Amazingly impressive beside ***Krug Grande Cuvée***. Shares weight and an aroma normally found in Bollinger, but sadly loses some freshness when aired.

Ivernel

6 rue Jules Lobet, 51160 Aÿ ☎ 03 26 55 21 10
Production: 100,000 bottles.

Since 1989 this historical house has been owned by Gosset, which in practice looks upon Ivernel as its second label. The Ivernel family has lived in Aÿ since the 15th century, but didn't start their champagne house until 1955. All the grapes are bought in from outside, and Ivernel have specialised in supplying France's top restaurants.

Ivernel Brut Réserve 72
(30% PN, 30% PM, 40% CH)
A lot like Gosset in terms of style, with rich honey aromas and an ingratiating sweet, fruity flavour.

Ivernel Rosé 51
(20% PN, 80% CH)
Lighter than the firm's other wines, but with a similar tone of honey and almond paste.

1989 Ivernel 76 (Aug 95) 80
(45% PN, 12% PM, 43% CH)
Round and powerful. Just as could be expected, considering the vintage and the producer. Hardly one for the cellar.

Guy Dauby

22 rue Jeanson, 51160 Aÿ ☎ 03 26 54 96 49
Production: 60,000 bottles.

Guy Dauby Brut 78
A grower worth investigating. I was very impressed by the typical Aÿ character in the non-vintage champagne the one and only time I tasted it.

Gosset-Brabant

23 bd du Maréchal-de-Lattre-de-Tassigny, 51160 Aÿ ☎ 03 26 55 17 42

Remarkably, many growers in Côte des Blancs praise this grower and neighbour of Bollinger. The family have grown vines in Aÿ since 1584, and Gosset-Brabant are one of the few who make Aÿ rouge.

Gosset-Brabant Tradition 71
(90% PN, 10% CH)
Broad and, at the same time, elegant nose from the soil. Leather and chocolate dominate both flavour and nose.

1989 Cuvée Gabriel 74 (Jul 95) 83
(70% PN, 30% CH)
The nose is creamy and full of sweet plums. A good initial taste, but the length is insufficient.

Other wines: Rosé, Cuvée Réserve.

Ed. Brun

14 rue Marcel Mailly, 51160 Aÿ ☎ 03 26 55 20 11
Production: 250,000 bottles.

The house was founded in 1898. Ed. Brun uses 5% oak barrels and the grapes come from 23 villages.

Ed. Brun Cuvée Spéciale 39
(60% PN, 38% PM, 2% CH)
An unripe champagne with elements of elderflower in both nose and flavour.

Ed. Brun Cuvée de Réserve 61
(95% PN, 5% CH)
Quite another complexity than the *Cuvée Speciale*. A mature, well-kept and cheesy champagne with good structure.

Ed. Brun B. d. B. 63
(100% CH)
A somewhat rough and unpolished B. d. B. which does, however, have its aromatic advantages.

1988 Ed. Brun 69 (Jan 97) 83
(60% PN, 40% CH)
Completely closed nose. Well-structured and rich champagne with a smoky undertone that could develop well.

1982 Ed. Brun 61 (Jul 88) 73
(70% PN, 30% CH)
A dreadfully thin '82. Pale colour, almost nonexistent nose and a one-dimensional, unripe apple taste.

1971 Ed. Brun 88 (Mar 88) ▼
(80% PN, 20% CH)
Not a great champagne, but an enjoyable wine that was best when freshly poured, before it collapsed in the glass. At first a seductive nose of honey and butterscotch. Soft honeyed flavour without much acidity or mousse.

Henri Giraud

71 bd Charles de Gaulle, 51160 Aÿ ☎ 03 26 55 18 55

I discovered this grower in a Finnish women's magazine. The Aÿ grower doesn't give any details about his wines, but will happily sell a few bottles to anyone who knocks on his door.

Henri Giraud Brut Réserve 79
(100% PN)
A dark, masculine wine with great depth and cellar tones. Forest mushrooms, leather and nuts rise to the surface in a beautifully aged flavour. A great champagne to food.

Henri Giraud Rosé 30
(100% PN)
How someone can make such a poor rosé when the non-vintage champagne is a minor masterpiece quite escapes me. Giraud's rosé is very unclear and plump. The nose is dominated by overripe cheeses and sweat. Dies quickly in the glass.

1991 Henri Giraud 69 (Apr 96) 73
(50% PN, 50% CH)
Unripe and unfocused, with vegetable aromas and a full flavour.

E. Driant

12 rue Marie-Coquebert, 51160 Aÿ

Founded in 1920 by Émile Driant. The firm owns only 20 hectares in Mareuil-sur-Aÿ, but buys grapes from Aÿ and Côte des Blancs.

E.Driant Brut 65
(60% PN, 40% CH)
Broad cheesy nose with elements of the "degenerated training shoe". The flavour, on the other hand, is fresh and pure with a good attack and a fat, long aftertaste.

Husson

2 rue Jules Lobet, 51160 Aÿ ☎ 03 26 55 43 05
Production: 80,000 bottles.

Husson Brut 50–60
(70% PN, 30% CH)
I tasted this champagne together with Madame Husson and a good friend who remarked that the wine had a smoky bouquet before he noticed the open fire burning in the heath. The nose was almost impossible to judge, and the flavour was ordinary at best.

Husson Rosé 65
(100% PN)
Plenty of strawberry aromas in both nose and flavour, but lacking in distinction.

René Brun

4 pl. de la Libération, 51160 Aÿ ☎ 03 26 55 21 24

Production: 200,000 bottles.

The Brun family have grown vines in Aÿ for at least five generations, and house status was achieved in 1941. The proportion of Chardonnay grapes is surprisingly high, thus removing some of the village character from the wines.

René Brun Brut 48
(60% PN, 40% CH)
A light and thin champagne with citrus tones in both flavour and nose.

René Brun Rosé 39
(60% PN, 40% CH)
A "dirty" nose of Danish cheese and sweat. Soft, pure and long flavour of summer berries.

1985 René Brun 70 (Jun 92) 76
(40% PN, 60% CH)
The same citrus aromas as the non-vintage champagne, although somewhat heavier and more complexity.

Other wines: Blanc de Blancs.

Juget-Brunet

5 rue Roulot, 51160 Aÿ ☎ 03 26 55 20 67

Juget-Brunet Brut 71
(80% PN, 20% CH)
A typically bold and full Aÿ champagne with a deep colour, broad mushroom nose and mighty leather-like flavour.

E. Hamm

16 rue Nicolas Philipponnat, 51160 Aÿ ☎ 03 26 55 44 19

Production: 250,000 bottles.

Émile Hamm started as a grower in Aÿ at the beginning of this century and received house status in 1930. The firm owns 3.5 hectares in Aÿ and buys in 90% of its grape supplies.

E. Hamm Brut 53
(35% PN, 35% PM, 30% CH)
A simple "straight-to-the-point" champagne. Dark hue and full of flavour in a rustic sort of way.

E. Hamm Réserve 1er Cru 68
(40% PN, 20% PM, 40% CH)
Aromas of crisp bread and apple. Nice acidity, but a somewhat sweet aftertaste.

1987 E. Hamm 71 (Mar 95) 75
(50% PN, 50% CH)
Why make a vintage wine this year? This '87 held no explanation. Abrupt fruity nose and a somewhat hollow, short taste.

Other wines: Rosé.

Raoul Collet

34 rue Jeanson, 51160 Aÿ ☎ 03 26 55 15 88

Production: 3 million bottles.

The best known of the two Aÿ cooperatives was founded in 1921 in Dizy. The firm's current name came about when the director Raoul Collet died in 1960.

R. Collet Carte Noir 53
(40% PN, 60% PM)
The champagne has a fine mousse and a nose of Christmas spices and caraway bread. The flavour is very different too. Could this be because of the particular grape content?

R. Collet Rosé 60
(100% PN/PM)
It's rare to see a real pink champagne, but this wine is definitely as pink as a piglet, with a powerful spicy nose that includes elements of redcurrants and ginger.

1988 Raoul Collet 80 (Oct 97) 84
(80% PN, 20% CH)
Here we are dealing with a pure Aÿ champagne. The most obvious aromas are leather, plums and licorice.

Serge Godmé

1 rue Roger, 51160 Aÿ ☎ 03 26 55 43 93

This Godmé shouldn't be confused with Bertrand Godmé in Verzenay.

Serge Godmé Brut 39
It was several years ago that I tasted this champagne, and as the grower's non-vintage champagnes vary considerably from year to year, the quality may have improved. In July 1990 the champagne cut a particularly characterless figure.

Montebello

2 bd du Nord, 51160 Aÿ ☎ 03 26 55 15 44

Production: 250,000 bottles.

The Montebello champagne house was founded in 1834 by the count of the same name in the magnificent Château de Mareuil. He was the son of one of Napoleon's best friends, Maréchal Lannes. The firm has long been owned by Ayala, and is nowhere near the class of its big brother. A couple of years ago they lost their membership of the Syndicat des Grandes Marques at last. I haven't tasted the company's champagnes, and in fact I've never even seen one of their bottles.

Vatel

5 rue de la Brèche, 51160 Aÿ ☎ 03 26 55 44 05

Production: 80,000 bottles.

The least-known of Aÿ's two cooperatives. The champagne is also sold as Champagne del la Brêche and Gérard. Wines not tasted.

BEAUMONT-SUR-VESLE

Beaumont-sur-Vesle's 28 hectares of arable land are flat and don't deserve Grand cru status. The wines from here are light and thin. The village lies beside the poorest part of Verzenay's large area of cultivated land and as with Sillery and Puisieuix it is helped by this situation. Today the land is mostly cultivated by growers who sell grapes to the major houses. The village has only three producers.

% 100% 95% PN, 5% CH

BOUZY

With its 380 hectares, Bouzy is one of the most famous villages in Champagne. That reputation comes to some degree from the village's still red wine Bouzy rouge, which can vary from watery beaujolais efforts to burgundy-like greatness from growers like Paul Bara and Georges Vesselle. This clear difference in quality within the village is also very apparent in those grapes that are used for the sparkling wines. The answer lies in the soil - geology and the slope of the ground. The cultivated area is divided up into three strips. The most northerly and highest strip produces top class Grand cru grapes that make wines with a juicy fruit and great depth. The middle strip gives the same peach-like aromas, but lacks the concentration produced by the vineyards that lie higher up. The vines from the flatter ground around the village itself make strangely perfumed, slightly insipid wines with a loose and lazy structure. Even though the cru is overrated, Bouzy's high class is shown by the the fact that the major champagne houses either own or buy grapes from the village's southern slopes for their prestige cuvées.

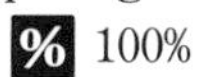 100%  88% PN, 1% PM, 11% CH

André Clouet

8 rue Gambetta, 51150 Bouzy 03 26 57 00 82

Production: 65,000 bottles.

The young Jean-François aims to match Bollinger's style and quality, and sometimes he succeeds. These wines are among my most recent discoveries and the rare vintage wine comes from old vines beside Bollinger's ungrafted plants in Bouzy.

Clouet Brut 72
(60% PN, 40% CH)
A younger and lighter wine than the big, bold *Silver Brut*. Easy to drink and full of ripe fruit aromas, with a really good length as well.

Clouet Grande Réserve 82
(100% PN)
The same wine as *Silver Brut*, but with a dosage.

Clouet Silver Brut 83
(100% PN)
A tremendously powerful champagne with an ugly/ pretty label. The mature reserve wines give weight and softness and round off the completely dry aftertaste. Bollinger-like.

Clouet Grand Cru Rosé 85
(100% PN)
Almost the colour of red wine, with a heavy nose of almonds, smoke, nuts and honey. Tight and chewy with amazing concentration. One of the most full-bodied rosé's I know of.

1990 Clouet 91 (Feb 99) 94
(50% PN, 50% CH)
A very interesting wine full of explosive apple peel aromas and restrained acidity. Focused, honeyed and chewy all at the same time. A superbly balanced and classy champagne.

1989 Clouet 89 (Aug 97) 90
(50% PN, 50% CH)
Very ripe and powerful champagne, with bready aromas and a meaty finish.

1986 Clouet 84 (Apr 96) 86
(50% PN, 50% CH)
Bushy, developed nose of mature fruit. Sadly it's a bit short.

1961 Clouet 92 (Apr 97) 94
(100% PN)
Jean-François, born in 1973, doesn't usually like older champagnes, but even he was forced to bow to this lively powerpack. Personally I'd prefer to wait for the maturity that comes from a few more years in the bottle.

Paul Bara

4 rue Yvonnet, 51150 Bouzy 03 26 57 00 50

Production: 90,000 bottles.

Paul Bara is a living legend in Champagne. He took over the firm as a teenager sixty years ago and remembers every vintage in perfect detail. He belongs to the sixth generation since the company was founded in 1833. Many major champagne houses have approached Bara over the years to try to buy the 30 exceptional locations he controls in the village. The average age of the vines is around 25 years, but those that produce the vintage wines are closer to 40. The butterfly-collecting legend is, together with Camille Savès and André Clouet, the most quality-obsessed grower in Bouzy. Only the first pressing is used, the wines are aged for at least four years in the cold cellar, and the yield is maintained at the lowest possible level. Despite the traditional methods, Bara's wines have a very elegant fruitiness which is unique in Bouzy. It is incomprehensible that he is best known for his red wine when his champagne is of world class.

Paul Bara Brut 80
(80% PN, 20% CH)
It's a lovely, life-enhancing experience to drink a glass of the rich, fruity Pinot champagne. Aromas of green apples dominate in its youth, but with time a rich chocolate flavour takes over.

Paul Bara Rosé 84
(90% PN, 10% CH)
A very masculine and well-built rosé champagne with burgundy-like form and a unified aroma. Suitable for aging.

1989 Paul Bara 86 (Apr 98) 92
(100% PN)
A dark yellow blanc de noirs with outstandingly tight honeyed nose and massive buttery candy flavour. Focused and concentrated without being clumsy. The wine has a special sweet complexity which only old vines and a warm year can give.

1989 Paul Bara Special Club 85 (Apr 98) 90
(70% PN, 30% CH)
What the wine wins in elegance it loses in concentration with the addition of Chardonnay. The nose is closed but has an extra dimension of jasmine. Very good attack but a shorter aftertaste than the vintage wines.

1978 Paul Bara Special Club 90 (May 96) 90
(100% PN)
Rich and mellow, with ripe plum flavours and good length.

1985 Comtesse Marie de France 85 (Apr 95) 91
(100% PN)
An incredibly elegant and delicate '85. A typical champagne nose with elements of toasted bread, chestnuts and lemon peel. The wine leaves a pared-down, crystal-clear impression on the palate, with its equilibristic, restrained aftertaste.

1983 Comtesse Marie de France 78 (Apr 93) 84
(100% PN)
An odd perfumed wine with an exaggerated nose of banana and blackcurrants. The flavour is of a much higher class with its pure, slightly one-dimensional hazelnut aroma.

1959 Paul Bara 96 (Apr 95) 96
(100% PN)
I asked Paul Bara which vintage he was most satisfied with during his lifetime. "Come here and I'll show you," he said, and he fetched a normally-disgorged half bottle of this peerless wine. The mousse was weak and the colour glowed amber. In the nose I was met by an undescribably wonderful wave of sensations, mint chocolate, rum, peaches, wood and honey. The flavour was even more impressive, if that's possible, with an Yquem-like structure and sweetness. The flavour was precipitous, uniting mint chocolate with rum liqueur. When Pinot Noir tastes like this, even the most confirmed Chardonnay lover can't fail to be converted.

Camille Savès

4 rue de Condé, 51150 Bouzy 03 26 57 00 33
Production: 60,000 bottles.

Definitely one of the highlights of Bouzy. The Savès - father and son - are among Champagne's most passionate winemakers. The wines are stored in the cellar for at least five years and the harvest yield is very low. The malolactic fermentation is avoided, the reserve wines are stored in oak barrels and only the cuvée is good enough for the Savès. Their vines have an average age of 25.

C. Savès Brut 77
(75% PN, 25% CH)
Rich but closed nose of honey and almonds. Impressively pure, full and a nice taste of marzipan and plum. Very long.

C. Savès Rosé 76
(75% PN, 25% CH)
A powerful and impressive rosé champagne with a nose of raw potato, plum and leather. Tight, soft and concentrated Pinot flavour with the firm's own almond aroma.

1988 C. Savès 89 (Sep 97) 92
(75% PN, 25% CH)
Surprisingly light colour and small bubbles for Pinot Noir. An expansive nose of hazelnut and cocoa, with a wave of marzipan and thick, dark fruit. The malic acidity support the rich flavour and lead on to a classic finish.

1959 C. Savès 94 (Apr 95) 94
(80% PN, 20% CH)
It was very exciting to taste two 59's from Bouzy on the same day. Paul Bara's example was a normally-disgorged half bottle, and Savès' a recently-disgorged full size bottle. The difference was apparent, despite a better mousse and freshness in Savès' wine, I prefered the amazingly concentrated nectar from Paul Bara. Both had an alcohol level of 13% and a deep golden colour. Savès' 59 had a nose of forest, fresh mushrooms, boiled vegetables and smoked meat. The flavour was broad, with big, sweet plums and a deep aftertaste of tar tablets. The wine resembles an old red burgundy.

Other wines: Brut Réserve.

E. Barnaut

2 rue Gambetta, 51150 Bouzy ☎ 03 26 57 01 54
Production: 60,000 bottles.

The property was founded in 1874 and covers 15 hectares in Bouzy. Philippe Secondé is always the last in the village to harvest his grapes and he handpicks the ripest. The wines are stored for at least five years before being sold.

E. Barnaut Extra Brut 80
(90% PN, 10% CH)
A multi-vintage made from older wines. Incredibly tight and focused. The colour is red-brown and the aromas almost meaty.

E. Barnaut Grande Réserve 71
(80% PN, 20% CH)
The nose and initial flavour are ordinary, but the length is astounding. A non-vintage worth keeping.

E. Barnaut Cuvée Douceur Sec 50
(66% PN, 34% CH)
With twenty grams of sugar, this is a surprisingly balanced wine. Perhaps the full-bodied Pinot Noir is needed to integrate the sugar content?

E. Barnaut Rosé 79
(100% PN)
Less powerful than the firm's other wines, but with an added fruity elegance.

1990 E. Barnaut 76 (May 97) 86
(50% PN, 50% CH)
Unexpectedly elegant nose of apple and almonds. The flavour is acidic and quite full, with interesting mineral tones. The origin is, as usual, much easier to trace after a moment's breathing.

Georges Vesselle

16 rue de Postes, 51150 Bouzy ☎ 03 26 57 00 15
Production: 145,000 bottles.

The best of the Vesselles. The good Georges had previously worked for Mumm and had time to become the Mayor of Bouzy. He owns 17.5 hectares in Bouzy and Ambonnay and makes some of the best red wines in the area. His champagnes are nothing to sniff at either.

Georges Vesselle Brut 80
(90% PN, 10% CH)
A ten year-old half bottle of this champagne is among the nicest non-vintage champagnes I've tasted. Chocolaty and rich as a dessert. Recently-disgorged full size bottles are naturally less generous and developed, but they contain a mighty fruit which is ready to burst into full bloom.

Georges Vesselle Rosé 45
(90% PN, 10% CH)
A great disappointment with its candy aromas and artificial fruit of wild strawberry. Needs retasting

1989 Georges Vesselle 84 (Apr 97) 88
(90% PN, 10% CH)
More developed and broader than the '88, but lacking its restrained mineral finesse. Honey and chocolate are already the dominant aromas.

1988 Georges Vesselle 81 (Feb 95) 89
(90% PN, 10% CH)
This is how a Pinot champagne should be built. Deep golden colour, tight, young, creamy nose with elements of olive and iron. Powerful, acidic and masculine flavour with good length.

1988 Georges Vesselle Brut Zero 82 (Jul 97) 89
(90% PN, 10% CH)
The same champagne without any dosage.

Cuvée Juline 77
(90% PN, 10% CH)
This cuvée de prestige is the most expensive in the village, but hardly the best. There is a basic Chenin Blanc like perfume and an uncomplicated, sweet fruit with an aftertaste of vanilla.

Bernard Tornay

2 rue Colbert, 51150 Bouzy ☎ 03 26 57 08 58

One of Bouzy's top growers. The entire wine plant is contained in his normal-sized villa on the outskirts of the village. His vineyards aren't located in Bouzy's best belt, but the yield is low and above all he keeps his wines in the cellar longer than anyone else. The style is made up of uncompromising food champagnes with smoky complexity and aromas of hazelnut.

Bernard Tornay Brut 72
(100% PN)
Broad, rich and gamey Pinot champagne.

1981 Bernard Tornay 80 (Sep 92) 82
(100% PN)
This vintage was sold in 1992 (eleven years old). The broad nose was majestic, while the flavour couldn't quite hold up its end. The spectrum of aromas included honey, almond, leather and plum.

Bernard Tornay Cuvée Belle Dames 88
(100% PN)
The cuvée de prestige is a blend of three vintages aged together with the yeast for at least eight years. Clumsy compared to a blanc de blancs, but wonderful together with breast of pheasant in morel sauce.

Pierre Paillard

2 rue du 20ème Siècle,
51150 Bouzy ☎ 03 26 57 08 04

Production: 60,000 bottles.

The firm was founded in 1946, and today this grand owner works with a large proportion of oak barrels to contain his Chardonnay. The average age of the vines is 23 years, and shoots up to 40 for the vintage wines.

Pierre Paillard Brut 70
(60% PN, 40% CH)
Four and a half years in the bottle. Always a low dosage. Full-bodied, with a character typical of the village. Good attack and stringency.

1989 Pierre Paillard 86 (Jun 97) 90
(40% PN, 60% CH)
A sensational champagne with its own style as all the Chardonnay comes from Bouzy and has been fermented in new oak barrels! A broad nose of lilies and pineapple. Around the acidic, dry flavour there is a lovely separate vanilla tone.

1985 Pierre Paillard 83 (Feb 98) 87
(50% PN, 50% CH)
A classic Bouzy champagne with a great almond nose and a powerful, dry masculine flavour.

1973 Pierre Paillard 86 (Apr 96) 87
(50% PN, 50% CH)
Tasted recently-disgorged without dosage. A nose of Swiss nuts, leather and licorice. High alcohol content and good freshness.

Paul Clouet

10 rue Jeanne d'Arc, 51150 Bouzy ☎ 03 26 57 00 82
Production: 45,000 bottles.

A property owned by Marie-Therese Bonnaire, who is married to the famous winemaker in Cramant! It is he who makes those classic Bouzy champagnes in his modern headquarters in Cramant. Definitely a name to remember. The Chardonnay comes from Chouilly.

Paul Clouet Rosé 60
(33% PN, 33% PM, 34% CH)
Now the same wine as ***Bonnaire Rosé***. No great shakes with its caramel tone and raspberry squash-like flavour.

1994 Paul Clouet 70 (Jun 97) 80
(80% PN, 20% CH)
A pure fruit in this young and undeveloped wine. A plum aroma and meaty structure with a somewhat short aftertaste.

1993 Paul Clouet 82 (Jun 97) 89
(80% PN, 20% CH)
Wow, what dense, mighty power! The wine is creamy and smooth with lots of plum and chocolate aromas.

1992 Paul Clouet 84 (Jun 97) 87
(80% PN, 20% CH)
Even in such a weak vintage Bonnaire succeeded in making a buttery, round, fat Bouzy champagne full of plums.

Brice

3 rue Yvonnet, 51150 Bouzy ☎ 03 26 52 06 60
Production: 65,000 bottles.

Jean-Paul Brice founded this company as recently as 1994, after previously having been one of the trio behind Barancourt. Michel Joly is "Chef de Caves" and has set terrroir champagnes as his top priority. Very good value for money.

Brice Tradition 50
(45% PN, 5% PM, 50% CH)
A wine that has grown in the last two years. At first it was pathetically sour and uneven but will probably improve as the reserve wines grow older.

Brice Cramant 73
(100% CH)
Crisp, delicate and upright, with young, pure fruit and a very fine mousse.

Brice Bouzy 80
(80% PN, 20% CH)
Surprisingly light, with a deliciously pure and fruity bouquet and a crystal clear flavour which reminds me of green apples.

Brice Aÿ 83
(90% PN, 10% CH)
The purity of the aromas is striking, even if I miss the maturity that gives Aÿ Pinot its characteristic weight. Definitely worth time in your cellar.

Brice Verzenay 83
(75% PN, 25% CH)
Very good cru character from this famous village. Rich creamy style and a lovely long aftertaste.

Alain Vesselle

8 rue de Louvois, 51150 Bouzy ☎ 03 26 57 00 88

Production: 130,000 bottles.

Alain went his own way in 1958 and works mainly with his Bouzy rouge. He owns 18 hectares in Bouzy.

Alain Vesselle Cuvée St Eloi 77
(50% PN, 50% CH)
Soft and slightly fluffy flavours with a shy but vegetable nose. Surprisingly good length.

Other wines: Brut, Rosé, Demi-sec.

Jean Vesselle

2 pl. J. B. Barnaut, 51150 Bouzy ☎ 03 26 57 01 55

Jean Vesselle is the family member who makes the least wine (70,000 bottles), and he also makes the youngest and unpredictable champagnes. The family is very hospitable and enthusiastic, but the problem seems to be a limited area to cultivate and vines that are too young.

Jean Vesselle Brut 75
(100% PN)
Only tasted when old in the bottle, as shown by the straight cork. Lovely chocolate flavour in which all the vegetable elements had been smoothed away.

Jean Vesselle Rosé 30
(100% PN)
"Lingonberry drink" noted four of eight tasters about the nose in May,1993. I agree, and would add a basic structure and artificial tones.

Jean Vesselle Partridge Eye 49
(100% PN)
Somewhere between a rosé and blanc de noirs, with the pink colour from the skin very pale. Pale describes the nose too, and the flavour is aggressive.

1985 Jean Vesselle 67 (Dec 92) 71
(100% PN)
Artificial banana flavour, pear and elderflower aren't exactly what you expect to find in a cuvée de prestige. Not recommended.

Barancourt

B.P. 3, 51150 Bouzy ☎ 03 26 53 33 40

Production: 800,000 bottles.

In 1966 a trio of winemakers from Bouzy joined together to form Barancourt. Twelve years later, Brice, Martin and Tritant bought a vineyard in Cramant in order to make cuvées from Grand cru grapes. For many years, Barancourt has been seen as a producer of good storable wines, but despite my passion for that style, I've never been convinced about this company's greatness. Certainly the wines do have a personal style, with their vegetable aromas, but they don't come close to greatness. In 1994 Barancourt was taken over by the Vranken group and today their grapes come from ten different villages, including a couple of places in Aube.

Barancourt Brut 67
(50% PN, 10% PM, 40% CH)
More charm and fruit than *Bouzy Brut*, good attack and structure.

Barancourt Bouzy Brut 56
(80% PN, 20% CH)
This champagne has never impressed me. It has a musky nose and a flavour laced with vegetables.

Barancourt Rosé 70
(40% PN, 60% CH)
Vegetables and raspberry doesn't sound like a successful combination, but here Barancourt have managed to unite those tones in an exciting manner in a full and lively champagne.

Barancourt Cramant B. d. B. 68
(100% CH)
"Like a Riesling" is the comment most often heard about this champagne. Otherwise a fresh, vigorous champagne without the village's usual creamy style.

Cuvée Fondateurs 80
(80% PN, 20% CH)
Bouzy only. Weak, musky nose lifted up by vegetable aromas, a fine mousse and a promising structure. Worth storing awhile.

1988 Cuvée Fondateurs 82 (May 95) 87
(80% PN, 20% CH)
The vegetable and animal tones return here, but are now backed up by much-needed creaminess and a crispy fruit that makes this the firm's very best wine.

1983 Cuvée Fondateurs 78 (Sep 93) 79
(50% PN, 50% CH)
Equal measures of Bouzy and Cramant. The style is one-dimensional, with a heavy and slightly bushy flavour of vegetables and smoke. The creamy Chardonnay from Cramant is readily noticeable in the flavour.

1985 Barancourt Bouzy Brut 79 (Apr 95) 75
(90% PN, 10% CH)
Nor does this vintage Bouzy make me swoon. The wine is actually rather light and flowery, but lacks any great finesse.

Herbert Beaufort

32 rue de Tours, 51150 Bouzy ☎ 03 26 57 01 34

Production: 140,000 bottles.

Beaufort owns 17 hectares in Bouzy and has a good reputation for its range of Bouzy reds. One Swedish club chose to invest in this producer's non-vintage champagne to drink as the clock strikes twelve to start the year 2000. Just how this normally-disgorged Bouzy will taste then will be interesting to find out.

H. Beaufort Carte Blanche 69
(70% PN, 30% CH)
This champagne gave a mature impression back in 1992. The nose was friendly, with sweet, oily fruit and candy. The flavour is also ingratiating and soft with a sweet and long aftertaste.

Le Monarque Bleu 69
(70% PN, 30% CH)
The same wine as *H. Beaufort Carte Blanche.*

H. Beaufort Carte d'Or 74
(100% PN)
A purer wine of stringence and potential. The nose has a toasty element which makes one think of Chardonnay.

H. Beaufort Rosé 60
(100% PN)
Many people are impressed with this skin-contact rosé, but I'm a bit bothered by the tutti-frutti aromas and the somewhat artificial, if well-built, structure.

1981 H. Beaufort 82 (Jul 90) 87
(100% PN)
The colour is brilliant and the nose is full of apple blossom and hawthorn. The flavour is long and impressive.

Hubert Dauvergne

33 rue de Tours, 51150 Bouzy 03 26 57 00 56

Production: 45,000 bottles.

Fernand Dauvergne started the business in 1860. 87% of the 6.5 hectares are planted with Pinot Noir.

Hubert Dauvergne Brut 69
(87% PN, 13% CH)
Chocolate, almonds and honey in the nose and a developed, well-filled flavour.

H. Dauvergne Elégance Rosé 76
(50% PN, 50% CH)
Raspberry and cherrys on the nose. Fresh, full and lively on the palate.

Other wines: Fine Fleur de Bouzy, Cuvée Saphir.

Maurice Vesselle

2 rue Yvonnet, 51150 Bouzy 03 26 57 00 81

Production: 40,000 bottles.

The business was started in 1955 and includes 8.3 hectares in Bouzy and Tours-sur-Marne. There are plenty of producers who make Bouzy rouge, but Didier Vesselle is one of the few to make a Bouzy blanc.

Maurice Vesselle Brut 68
(85% PN, 15% CH)
I missed acidity in both of Maurice's wines, but they are very rich and concentrated.

Maurice Vesselle Rosé 75
(100% PN)
I should think that this wine is superb when the base wine comes from acidic vintages. Here the freshness was missing, but the wine was very pompous and impressive.

Other wines: Vintage, Réserve.

Jean Lefevre

26 rue du Général de Gaulle,
51150 Bouzy 03 26 57 06 58

Jean Lefevre Brut 60
A champagne whose greatest asset is its soft flavour. The nose was wild and full of such unusual bedpartners as licorice, acetone and lemon.

Alfred Tritant

23 rue de Tours, 51150 Bouzy 03 26 57 01 16

Production: 30,000 bottles.

This producer started his business in 1930 in Bouzy and still uses traditional methods. He now owns 3.5 hectares in Bouzy.

A. Tritant Grand Cru Brut 68
(60% PN, 40% CH)
Very fruity nose of young Pinot Noir. Undeveloped dry flavour, with decent length.

1989 A. Tritant 82 (Sep 97) 85
(60% PN, 40% CH)
Bready, fishy and powerful. Ripe flavour of figs and mushrooms.

Bandock-Mangin

3 rue Victor Hugo, 51150 Bouzy 03 26 57 09 09

Production: 10,000 bottles.

Yannick Bandock founded the firm as late as in 1988. He owns 3.5 hectares in Ambonnay and Bouzy but sells most of his grapes to the cooperative in Bouzy. Wines not tasted.

Wines: Brut, Rosé, Vintage.

Louis Martin

3 rue Ambonnay, 51150 Bouzy 03 26 57 01 27

Louis Martin Brut 47
(80% PN, 20% CH)
An unsuccessful champagne from Bouzy with a perfumed nose and powerful, rough flavour which leaves a sour taste.

René Lallement

22 rue Gambetta, 51150 Bouzy 03 26 57 00 68

René started up in 1950, but his grandfather was producing champagne in Bouzy back in 1928. All the wines are stored for a minimum of three years in contact with the yeast. Wines not tasted.

Wines: Carte Blanche, Rosé, Vintage.

CHOUILLY

Note that Chouilly is one of those villages that have differing cru status for Pinot Noir and Chardonnay. In this case that doesn't matter so much, as the proportion of Pinot vines is only 2%.

The best locations in the village all lie next to Cramant and many growers have land in both villages. One area of particularly fine quality is a thin strip on Butte de Saran's south side, which gives grapes very like those in Cramant. Unfortunately, the quality within Chouilly itself varies greatly. A great deal of the village's 498 hectares is flat ground, which produces rather mediocre Chardonnay grapes. In my opinion Chouilly lies a touch under Avize, Cramant, Oger and Le Mesnil. Many wines from Chouilly have a clear almond tone, and the village's champagnes rarely exhibit a toasty or nutty character. In general they are a little rougher and more full-bodied than their more well-known neighbours. The village has 68 grower/producers and several champagne houses are pleased to have property here. Henriot, Pol Roger, Moët and Roederer all use a lot of Chouilly grapes and Legras produces exceptional champagnes from Chouilly alone.

% 100% CH, 95% PN   2% PN, 98% CH

R. & L. Legras

10 rue des Partelaines, 51530 Chouilly ☎ 03 26 54 50 79

Production: 250,000 bottles.

House status was achieved in 1973. This impeccably-run firm now owns 13 hectares in Chouilly's finest vineyards. Monsieur Barbier, who is a big man in more ways than one, runs his company with a successful mixture of modern and traditional vinification methods. Even though the wines go through malolactic fermentation, they retain a very high degree of lifegiving acidity for decades. Legras is the house champagne at many of France's three-star restaurants and must be counted among the top producers in all of Champagne.

Legras B. d. B. 81
(100% CH)
One of the very best non-vintage champagnes! The nose is an olfactory pleasure of the highest class. The stringency and purity are striking, as are the crisp aromas of Granny Smith apples. The flavour is fresh and clear as a mountain stream, and is dominated by citrus and minerals. The long aftertaste puts many a vintage champagne in the shade.

1989 Présidence 83 (May 93) 92
(100% CH)
The company style surfaces here in all its glory. Few match its restraint and elegance, both of which are supported by a sunripe wealth from the vintage.

1985 Présidence 86 (Apr 92) 93
(100% CH)
Much lighter than the '89, but with a greater wealth of nuances. Extremely light in colour, with glowing shades of green. A faint buttery nose with layers of flower aromas. Feminine, delicate and harmonious flavour with a faint element of hazelnuts which will only grow with time.

1979 Présidence 92 (Aug 96) 92
(100% CH)
Lovely toasty nose. Creamy and a bit crisp, with a pungent spiciness.

1990 Cuvée St Vincent 86 (Jul 98) 92
(100% CH)
A lovely young, vigorous, citrus nose, fresh and attractive with plenty of potential.

1988 Cuvée St Vincent 88 (Jul 98) 94
(100% CH)
Tremendously elegant and sophisticated with superb creaminess and smooth acidity. Feminine and graceful.

1983 Cuvée St Vincent 90 (Jun 98) 92
(100% CH)
In certain years the grapes from the very oldest vines in the village are seperated for this cuvée de prestige. The '83 has a mature green colour, a broad, complex nose and a honey-scented and long flavour.

1975 Cuvée St Vincent 92 (Jul 97) 92
(100% CH)
This wine really reminds me of *Salon*, with its classic bouquet of walnuts and steely taste.

1969 Cuvée St Vincent 95 (Jun 98) 95
(100% CH)
There's always something special with normally-disgorged champagne that are stored in the producer's cellar. During a visit to the firm in 1992, Monsieur Barbier chose this expensive, oak-fermented specimen from his cellar. The colour was a fierce gold, and the mousse was sparse but consistent. The nose was wonderful, with its Salon-like aroma of walnut. There was also an exotic element that verged on petroleum and sensual perfume. Another layer of aromas appeared to be smoky, oaky and tar. The freshness and length were seriously impressive.

1959 Cuvée St Vincent 96 (Jun 98) 96
(100% CH)
In his exultation over my correct analysis of his '69, Monsieur Barbier sent a runner off to fetch something even older. 1959 is a legendary vintage which was strongly influenced by a very warm summer. The elegance and freshness weren't so tangible as in the '69, but the power and weight were magnificent. Nor does top-class Chardonnay ever feel clumsy. Legras' example exhibited a remarkably broad, aromatic spectrum with clearly definable tones of chocolate, nuts, vanilla, coffee and honeysuckle.

Nicolas Feuillatte

B.P. 210, 51530 Chouilly ☎ 03 26 59 55 50

Production: 16 million bottles.
(2.8 million bottles as Feuillatte)

The French-American businessman Nicolas Feuillatte founded this firm together with the Centre Vinicole de la Champagne in Chouilly in 1971. Today he is constantly on the move, working as an ambassador for the cooperative's champagnes. 200 gigantic fermentation tanks of stainless steel tower over the ultra-modern wine plant, which has a production capacity of 16 million bottles. The grapes from the various cooperatives come from 130 crus and are all blended in the giant tanks. Every stage in the champagne-making process is automated, and the cellars contain some 33 million bottles. Those wines that are released under the name of Nicolas Feuillatte contain Premier and Grand cru grapes only.

Nicolas Feuillatte Réserve Particulière 53
(50% PN, 30% PM, 20% CH)
Reddish colour, weak, bready nose. Steely acidity and clear fruit.

Nicolas Feuillatte B. d. B. 50
(100% CH)
A pure but neutral, diluted and characterless blanc de blancs.

Nicolas Feuillatte Rosé 48
(60% PN, 30% PM, 10% CH)
A surprisingly light champagne considering the high proportion of black grapes. Very faint nose of cakes and wild strawberry, with a yeasty, light and dry flavour.

1992 Nicolas Feuillatte B .d. B. 75 (Oct 98) 79
(100% CH)
Nice ripe nose and a biscuity lingering taste. Aftertaste of green apples.

1990 Nicolas Feuillatte 84 (Jun 97) 86
(40% PN, 40% PM, 20% CH)
A lovely, fruity wine with plenty of immediate charm and toasty aromas. There's also an explosive, juicy flavour of peach. The Chardonnay grapes must be top class.

1988 Feuillatte Cuvée Spéciale 78 (Jun 97) 84
(40% PN, 20% PM, 40% CH)
Not much to celebrate. Stringency and potential but at the age of nine it felt a bit unbalanced.

1985 Nicolas Feuillatte 86 (Aug 97) 87
(50% PN, 25% PM, 25% CH)
Sensational biscuity nose and a rich long mature flavour of honey.

1982 Nicolas Feuillatte 80 (Dec 93) 84
(50% PN, 25% PM, 25% CH)
Light and lively. An exciting nose of hawthorn, red and blackcurrants and orange marmelade. Good, dry, mineral-rich and medium-bodied flavour with an aftertaste that is a touch too short.

1990 Palmes d'Or 84 (Mar 98) 90
(40% PN, 60% CH)
Green colour, faint flowery nose. Delicate, fine taste on the same theme, with an added tone of green plums in the luscious finish.

1985 Palmes d'Or 90 (Jul 97) 90
(40% PN, 60% CH)
A lovely champagne, classically built and bursting with vitality. Even so, I can't help thinking it's reached its peak.

1992 Nicolas Feuillatte Rosé 62 (Oct 97) 62
(60% PN, 30% PM, 10% CH)
Rather sweet and easy-going. Well-made but quite basic.

Lucien Vazart

2 rue d´Avize, 51530 Chouilly ☎ 03 26 55 61 15
Production: 50,000 bottles.

The village of Chouilly is packed with producers called Vazart or Legras. Lucien is one of the more well-known. As with R. & L. Legras, the almond aroma so typical of the village is avoided in favour of a purer, more classical Chardonnay style.

Lucien Vazart Private Cuvée 75
(100% CH)
Almost colourless and with fast, minimal bubbles. Perfectly pure, pale, young, steely nose with excellent character from the soil. The flavour exhibits a broad spectrum of faint, delicate nuances. A perfect aperitif champagne.

Hostomme

5 rue de l'Allée, 51530 Chouilly ☎ 03 26 55 40 79
Production: 140,000 bottles.

The Hostomme family has produced Grand cru champagne for three generations. They are the principal owner of Chouilly's rare Pinot Noir vines and even make a blanc de noirs with a lot of Chouilly Pinot.

Hostomme B. d. B. 66
(100% CH)
Light, flowery nose with a pure, brittle flavour of grapefruit.

Hostomme Grande Réserve 68
(100% CH)
Slightly deeper and more full-bodied than the above, with a hint of almond in the light flavour.

Hostomme Rosé 53
(50% PN, 50% CH)
A featureless wine with a neutral albeit pure nose.

Hostomme Blanc de Noirs 60
(80% PN, 20% PM)
This champagne is highly personal, with a broad and bushy nose of pear and apple shampoo. Round and rather soapy taste with elements of banana.

1989 Hostomme 70 (Jul 95) 80
(100% CH)
Unexpectedly light, with weak, creamy tones and a certain elegance.

Michel Genet

22 rue des Partelaines,
51530 Chouilly ☎ 03 26 55 40 51
Production: 40,000 bottles.

Right next to Legras there is a medium-sized villa where Michel Genet lives and makes champagne. He owns 6.5 hectares.

Michel Genet B. d. B. 65
(100% CH)
A one-dimensional blanc de blancs which is dominated by almond aromas in both nose and flavour. Dry, fine finish.

1990 Michel Genet 81 (Jan 97) 86
(100% CH)
Genet's wines are always perfectly pure but slightly thin and too tactful. In this vintage the weather helped him to fill the empty spaces with an exotic richness.

1986 Michel Genet 73 (Apr 93) 85
(100% CH)
A shining revelation. Faint but pleasant nose of hawthorn and citrus fruits. The flavour is powder dry, with exciting mineral tones. The aftertaste is a little short, however.

Other wines: Brut, J-B Fleuriot.

Banchet-Legras

8 rue du Pont, 51530 Chouilly ☎ 03 26 55 41 53

A small grower who I've never visited but often tasted in restaurants in Épernay. I've never come across a single champagne producer outside of Chouilly who has known of this firm's existence.

Banchet-Legras B. d. B. 70
(100% CH)
A robust and oxidative blanc de blancs, which gives an oily sensation in the mouth and a nose of ripe apples.

Vazart-Coquart

7 rue Dom Pérignon,
51530 Chouilly ☎ 03 26 55 40 04
Production: 100,000 bottles.

The Vazart-Coquart father and son are extremely proud over what they achieve, and the firm has many fans. The winemakers are innovative and ready to experiment with their own ideas. The family is often arranging exciting tastings with the same wines with varying bottle sizes, sugar content or date of disgorging. Vazart-Coquart use plenty of old reserve wines in their champagnes. They have also released a champagne called *Fois Gras* (goose liver) which contains wines from around ten old vintages and which should suit the fat delicatess admirably. Despite these laudable ideas I'm not so impressed by the company's champagnes. There is always an excess of clumsy almond aromas and a dosage that is often too high - something which they themselves agree, strangely enough. They appear to have disregarded their own ideals in favour of an anticipated demand from the public.

Vazart-Coquart Grand Bouquet 62
(100% CH)
Deep, mature colour from the large proportion of old reserve wines. The nose is friendly and bushy, dominated by oxidative almond aromas that return in the soft and overripe flavour. Much too sweet.

Vazart-Coquart Cuvée Fois Gras 74
(100% CH)
A corny name and an ugly label in a wine with high ideas about itself. Dark, banana-smelling, rich, oily and pleasant, but once again the dosage is too high. One bonus point for the long aftertaste of honey.

1989 Vazart-Coquart Grand Bouquet 75 (Dec 96) 77
(100% CH)
Honey and almonds are typical aromas for both the producer and the vintage.

1988 Vazart-Coquart 75 (Aug 93) 76
(100% CH)
This is the most restrained and elegant wine I've drunk from this property. The nose is intensely flowery, with a touch of butter and almond. The ground wine is fruity and lemon-fresh, but the dosage transforms the village's almond aroma into marzipan.

1982 Vazart-Coquart 76 (Jul 93) 76
(100% CH)
Amazingly like the '88, but in another stage of maturity. The nose is open and exotic, with exciting tones of acacia and orchids. The flavour is fat, almost mawkish, with rich mango fruit. The almond element has turned into meringue.

CRAMANT

Cramant is perhaps the most beautiful of all Côte des Blanc's villages. The landscape is hilly, with a wonderful view over Moët's glorious Château de Saran. The village itself lies surrounded by a sea of Chardonnay vines, exposed to the south and east. The locations that are directly to the south of the village towards Avize, and the slopes below Château de Saran in Chouilly, give some of Champagne's finest grapes. The wines have a bouquet which can only be matched by Le Mesnil, and a marvellous toffee cream flavour. Another of the cru's advantages is its consistency. Really poor champagnes from Le Mesnil are unfortunately not a rarity, but so far I've never drunk an unpleasant wine from Cramant. The wine from here matures more quickly than its neighbours, but maintains its peak for just as long. Besides Diebolt, Bonnaire, Sugot-Feneuil and others, the major houses own some of Cramant's best-regarded locations. Perrier-Jouët's vineyards are the best-kept, but Moët, Taittinger, Clicquot, Laurent-Perrier, Pol Roger, Oudinot, Mercier, Pommery and Mumm all own considerable areas of the village's cultivatable land.

% 100% 100% CH

Diebolt-Vallois

84 rue Neuve, 51530 Cramant 03 26 57 54 92
Production: 70,000 bottles.

Jacques Diebolt and his family are some of the nicest people I've met in Champagne, and the fact that they produce Chardonnay wines of world class doesn't hurt either. Several producers in the village make supremely enjoyable champagnes, but personally I think Diebolt gives the cru another dimension, especially with those wines that haven't gone through malolactic fermentation, and which were harvested from the 65 year-old vines in Les Pietons. There is a thought-provoking depth which reminds you of Le Mesnil, combined with Cramant's creamy structure. Unfortunately, the demand for Diebolt's wines is so great that they are forced to sell the champagne far too early. Diebolt was an unknown name before the firm was awarded Champagne Producer of the Year in 1992 by the magazine Gault Millau, but since then the connoisseurs of the world have fought over their bottles.

Diebolt B. d. B. 72
(100% CH)
Made from fine Grand cru grapes and probably extremely storable, but far too young and pear-tasting when it arrives on the market.

Diebolt Prestige 91
(100% CH)
A pure '90 harvested from one location - Les Pietons - from 65 year-old vines. Colossal concentration of amazingly sweet, saffron-scented fruit. Yellow plums are there to be found in both nose and flavour, this wine is partially vinified in oak barrels.

Diebolt Prestige Wedding Cuvée 88
(100% CH)
This wine was made for the Diebolt son's future wedding from the vintages of 1982, 83, 85 and 86. I hope he waits a while yet before tying the knot, so that the delightful but undeveloped wine has time to show off its best side. Here I'm tempted to alter my principles and give points for potential to a non-vintage wine. In that case this wine would be close to 95 points, but really it's only of interest to the Diebolt family themselves as the 100 bottles produced will never go on sale.

1990 Diebolt 88 (Jul 95) 94
(100% CH)
It's not far from Perrier-Jouët's best location in Cramant. This champagne is very similar to *Belle Epoque* with the characteristic vanilla and cake tones. The wine's fruits ways toward peach, tangerine and mango. The concentration is somewhat less than that of the prestige wine, but the aromas are utterly charming.

1989 Diebolt Prestige 93 (May 98) 95
(100% CH)
Harvested from the old vines and vinified without malolactic fermentation. An incredibly fine wine that resembles some of the best 85's from Le Mesnil. The fleeting nose has many facets and the tones of petroleum, roasted coffee, walnuts and pure minerals. A superb blanc de blancs with a marvellous attack.

1988 Diebolt 83 (May 94) 90
(100% CH)
Pure, fine nose of white flowers, cherries, Williams pears and almonds. Once again similar to Le Mesnil with its deep, authoritative style. Undeveloped, pure and vigorous flavour. We'll meet again sometime next century.

1985 Diebolt 92 (Feb 97) 93
(100% CH)
A Grand cru blanc de blancs from 1985 always provides a wonderful experience with its toasty aromas and clear brioche-like subtleties. Diebolt have made a classic '85.

1982 Diebolt 91 (Feb 97) 91
(100% CH)
The '82 is richer and bushier than the balanced '85. I enjoyed this freshly-disgorged bottle tremendously in the company of the Diebolt family.

1961 Diebolt 97 (May 98) 97
(100% CH)
I've been present several times when a producer has opened a new bottle of the same vintage because he wasn't satisfied with the first. Jacques, on the other hand, is the only one who's opened a new bottles in order to show how bad the wine can be! At its best the '61 has a fantastic, almost Pinot-like nose of truffles, autumn leaves, barrels and boiled vegetables, while the other he opened was more like mushroom soup. The structure was impressive in both, however.

1953 Diebolt 98 (May 98) 98
(100% CH)
One of the best champagnes I've ever tasted. Drunk when newly-disgorged and undosed in Diebolt's cellar. The wine is made in oak barrels without malolactic fermentation. The colour was a brilliant, beautiful golden yellow, and the bubbles continued to stream out of the glass two hours after the wine had been poured. The nose received maximum points! The entire wine was like a great symphony by Sibelius - full of melancholy, happiness, nature and romance. The freshness and the agile lightness, combined with the wine's length, were outstanding, but the nose's focused complexity was probably the most impressive feature of the champagne. Coffee, syrup, bergamot oil, brioche, walnuts, lime and passion fruit were the most clearly- defined aromas. When will we meet again?

Other wines: Tradition.

Bonnaire

120 rue d'Épernay B.P.5,
51530 Cramant ☎ 03 26 57 50 85

Production: 200,000 bottles.

The biggest individual producer in Cramant was originally called Bonnaire-Bouquemont, and for many years Bonnaire has provided us with some of the creamiest Chardonnay wines the world has ever seen. A few years ago Jean-Louis Bonnaire moved his office and reception down to the ultra-modern plant in the middle of the village's vine rows. He owns 13 hectares of Cramant's best locations, and the grapes from here are always used in the vintage wine or the *Special Club*. These wines in particular are among the area's real charmers, if they are given about ten years in the cellar. The malolactic fermentation is used and so the wines gain a buttery, mature character in their youth, but the acidity is always very high, lifting up the wines to an exotic wealth in their middle age and a splendid nutty fullness when mature. Bonnaire make textbook Cramant for the sensualist.

Bonnaire Carte Noire 60
(30% PN, 30% PM, 40% CH)
Fresh and healthy, but basic. Save your money for the *Blanc de Blancs.*

Bonnaire B. d. B. 77
(100% CH)
Lighter and less concentrated than the vintage wine, but wonderfully enjoyable and pure, with a tense taste of citrus fruits that will develop well in the cellar.

Bonnaire B. d. B. non Dosé 75
(100% CH)
The same impression, but an even greater need of time in the bottle.

Bonnaire Crémant de Cramant 79
(100% CH)
The weakly sparkling champagne is always disgorged somewhat later, which in this case makes Cramant's creamy structure and butterscotch aromas all the more clear.

Bonnaire Rosé 68
(10% PN, 90% CH)
It feels a bit wrong to sniff the nose of a creamy Chardonnay and experience Cramant's typical buttery flavour clad in a pink disguise.

Bonnaire Sélection 83
(100% CH)
A blend from 1984 and 1985 which in its light and ingratiating style is one of Monsieur Bonnaire's personal favourites.

1992 Bonnaire Blanc de Noirs Bouzy 83 (Apr 97) 87
(100% PN)
Love has taken Bonnaire to its opposite, Bouzy. This blanc de noirs will be very good in a few years, but naturally feels a little clumsy in comparison with the blanc de blancs.

1993 Bonnaire 80 (Jun 97) 89
(100% CH)
Restrained, pure, compact and classical. It wouldn't surprise me if it became even better than predicted in my points total.

1992 Bonnaire 79 (Apr 95) 86
(100% CH)
Not yet out on the market. The wine will of course be better after more time together with the yeast sediment.

1991 Bonnaire 83 (Apr 98) 89
(100% CH)
Acidic and tough today, and less round than the '92. Just released in 1998.

1990 Bonnaire Special Club 92 (Jan 99) 94
(100% CH)
As expected, Bonnaire have succeeded well with this classic vintage. We will have to wait a couple of years before the '90 is on the market, but those who wait for something good never wait in vain. Rich and chewable.

1989 Bonnaire 84 (Jun 97) 91
(100% CH)
A wine more typical of the vintage than the house. The nose is heavy and exotic with elements of saffron and petunia. The flavour is deep and spicy.

1989 Bonnaire Special Club 88 (May 98) 92
(100% CH)
Full of incredibly sweet, charming fruit. A fat flavour with a slightly loosely assembled structure.

1988 Bonnaire 86 (Jul 95) 91
(100% CH)
A textbook Bonnaire. Impossible to miss in a blind tasting. Light colour, ultra-fine mousse, buttery nose of toffee, white flowers and wild strawberries. Long, tight and creamy flavour.

1988 Bonnaire Special Club 89 (Oct 97) 93
(100% CH)
Harvested from some of the village's best locations. Always very similar to the vintage wine, but less developed after six or seven years. After that the *Special Club* unfailingly exhibits a somewhat greater concentration of similar aromas.

1987 Bonnaire 90 (Jul 97) 90
(100% CH)
Perhaps Bonnaire's greatest asset is that he has always succeeded in harvesting fully ripe grapes from his southerly slopes in Cramant. The '87, together with *Origine*, is the top wine of the vintage.

1986 Bonnaire 90 (Nov 96) 93
(100% CH)
A little less restrained than the 87. The wine is full of sun-ripened fruit and a whiff of toasty aromas. An incredible attack and yet, paradoxically, soft and buttery.

1985 Bonnaire 90 (May 97) 92
(100% CH)
1985 is a special vintage for Bonnaire. The wines contain less of the toffee aroma, but display a fascinating, baffling spectrum in the nose and have a more restrained form. An intellectual wine.

1985 Bonnaire Special Club 94 (Apr 97) 95
(100% CH)
I love this champagne in the young phase it's going through right now. There is a refinement lacking in the ultra-generous '82. Restrained, elegant and withdrawn, with a Montrachet-like tone of nut and a crystal clear mineral flavour.

1983 Bonnaire 93 (Nov 93) 93
(100% CH)
Bonnaire's '83 and '82 are among the most enjoyable and generous champagnes one can find. The grower's answer to the *Comtes de Champagne*. Astoundingly rich, exotic and creamy.

1983 Bonnaire Special Club 93 (Jun 97) 93
(100% CH)
Almost identical to the vintage 83.

1982 Bonnaire 94 (Jul 95) 94
(100% CH)
The '82 is, if possible, even greater, with its mango-dominated fruit and toasty nose. The winner of "A different tasting".

1982 Bonnaire Special Club 94 (Apr 97) 94
(100% CH)
Even softer and more concentrated, but less acidity.

1981 Bonnaire Special Club 95 (Feb 98) 95
(100% CH)
A sensation, which I fell head over heels for. Supremely elegant and a broad nose of toasted bread and Dom Pérignon-like explosive fruit. Extraordinary balance and a delicate flavour which reminds me of the '85. One of this vintage's very finest champagnes.

1980 Bonnaire Special Club 90 (Nov 93) 90
(100% CH)
A bastard child. Dark and smoky tones: it's incredible that oak barrels weren't used. Awesome power - this wine demands food.

1978 Bonnaire Special Club 92 (May 97) 92
(100% CH)
Always reliable and sound. Rich, lemony and luscious.

1975 Bonnaire 91 (May 95) 91
(100% CH)
Surprisingly, a discreet '75. Light colour and weak mousse. The nose is delightfully flowery and young. The whole wine shines with youth and freshness, but lacks richness.

1974 Bonnaire 89 (Jun 97) 89
(100% CH)
A wonderful nose of butter and Salon-like depth. Fat initially, then a little thin and dried out in the finish, with tones of tea leaves and fine sherry. Loses it in the glass.

1973 Bonnaire 94 (Apr 97) 94
(100% CH)
This is a Bonnaire in full maturity. The colour is dark, the nose incredibly broad with smoky, deep, Salon-like aromas. Massive nutty fullness and a rich body.

1971 Bonnaire 91 (Nov 93) 91
(100% CH)
More restrained than the '73, with delicious young acidity and a very long citrus flavour. The maturity is only hinted at in the faintly smoky nose.

Sugot-Feneuil

40 impasse de la Maire,
51530 Cramant 03 26 57 53 54

Production: 100,000 bottles.

This masterly grower in Cramant owns seven hectares in Bergères-les-Vertus, Chouilly, Oiry and above all Cramant. Only Chardonnay grapes are used in the vintage wine. Robert Sugot is the fourth generation of winemakers in the family, and Sugot-Feneuil's champagnes, so wonderfully typical of the village, are some of my absolute favourites. The *Special Club* is made from three excellent locations called Les Beurons, Biennes and Mont-Aigu, with 30 year-old vines.

Sugot-Feneuil B. d. B. 82
(100% CH)
Lovely non-vintage champagne that is full of lust for life, with a toffee aroma so typical of the village, and a hint of hazelnuts.

Sugot-Feneuil Carte Perle 75
(100% CH)
Gentle mousse and creamy flavours hinting at lemon yoghurt.

1988 Sugot-Feneuil Special Club 91 (Jul 98) 94
(100% CH)
Relatively closed nose but with the entire aromatic spectrum of Cramant and a creamy structure.

1986 Sugot-Feneuil Special Club 88 (Sep 97) 88
(100% CH)
A fast-matured wine which is a pleasure to enjoy today. Open nose of honey nectar and butterscotch, and a soft, creamy, focused flavour of peaches and fudge.

1985 Sugot-Feneuil Special Club 87 (Oct 92) 93
(100% CH)
A restrained classic with a multi-faceted flowery nose and a lightly toasty and balanced flavour with overtones of lemon.

1983 Sugot-Feneuil Special Club 87 (Jan 96) 88
(100% CH)
A bit shy and ungenerous with clear aromas, and a twist of lemon acidity on the finish.

1979 Sugot-Feneuil 94 (Apr 95) 95
(100% CH)
M. Sugot's favourite vintage, and it's easy to understand him. The wine has a young, greenish colour and a euphoric nose of chocolate, nuts, coffee, lily of the valley and white Toblerone. A nutty flavour with lovely depth for the aesthete and layers of fruit for the romantic.

1978 Sugot-Feneuil Special Club 87 (Jul 97) ▼
(100% CH)
Already going downhill. Still an enjoyable wine though.

Other wines: Rosé, Carte Perle.

Lilbert

223 rue du Moutier, 51530 Cramant ☎ 03 26 57 50 16
Production: 30,000 bottles.

Georges Lilbert is the man who makes the toughest wines in all of Cramant. His vineyards lie in Chouilly and Cramant, the yield is low and the wines are stored for at least five years before being sold. The fact is that the wines are so hard and acidic that I've seldom tasted a mature bottle. I think that his vintage wine should be about thirty years old in order to reach full maturity.

Lilbert B. d. B. 78
(100% CH)
Wonderfully fine, fruity bouquet dominated by apple and honey. Stringent, almost hard, developable flavour in which the soil leaves some clear fingerprints.

Lilbert Brut Perle 77
(100% CH)
Gently sparkling, fairly dry, clean, with good acidity.

1990 Lilbert 86 (Feb 97) 93
(100% CH)
Sweeter than the usual bone dry champagnes from Lilbert. The fruit is rich and typical of the village, with a little extra fatness.

1989 Lilbert 87 (Jul 97) 88
(100% CH)
Ripe, deep and rich, Great vinosity.

1985 Lilbert 87 (May 94) 93
(100% CH)
Broad and exquisite Cramant nose, where petroleum and nuts together build a symphony. The flavour is far more restrained, with plenty of potential.

1983 Lilbert 86 (Feb 97) 88
(100% CH)
Undeveloped and with a longer life than most 83's. Very fresh and flowery, with only a faint smoky undertone hinting at the wine's considerable age.

1982 Lilbert 89 (May 94) 93
(100% CH)
A heavy, smoky masculine nose that doesn't softsoap you. The palate is met by a sensational attack, where the hard, acidic mineral taste whispers of wonderful future possibilities.

1964 Lilbert 95 (Feb 97) 95
(100% CH)
It was a great honour to share this pearl with Monsieur Lilbert in his cellar. Despite a complete lack of dosage the wine gave off a very sweet scent and a velvet-smooth, concentrated, rich, exotic flavour. There were also tones of mushroom, truffles, tar and smoke, like those of certain 61's.

Larmandier

B.P. 4, 51530 Cramant ☎ 03 26 57 52 19
Production: 100,000 bottles.

The Larmandier family have been leading wine growers in Cramant for several generations. It was only in 1978 that they received house status, through Dominique Larmandier. Today the firm is closely linked with Gimonnet in Cuis. The house owns eight hectares in five crus in Côte des Blancs.

Larmandier B. d. B. 73
(100% CH)
Buttery and delicate style which ought to be appreciated by more than just connoisseurs.

1989 Larmandier Special Club 83 (Mar 96) 91
(100% CH)
A surprising nose of stew and cheese which I've only previously found in Le Mesnil. The wine is hardly charming but has a good structure.

1988 Larmandier Special Club 90 (Mar 96) 93
(100% CH)
Much richer and sweeter than the '89. The wine gives a juicy impression which is irresistible.

1982 Larmandier 79 (Jul 92) ▼
(100% CH)
Tasted beside the *1982 Gimonnet*. Far more developed and mature, a creamy champagne with rich fruit and a small side-tone of garlic cheese.

G. Morizet & Fils

19 rue du Moutier, 51530 Cramant ☎ 03 26 57 50 92

G. Morizet Grand Cru Brut 72
(100% CH)
It's hard not to be seduced by Cramant's fragrance and toffee flavour. Morizet's wine is a shining example of the cru character, although the suit may be a size too small.

Pertois-Lebrun

28 rue de la Libération,
51530 Cramant ☎ 03 26 57 54 25

Production: 80,000 bottles.

This Cramant grower owns six hectares in the village and also makes charming champagnes that are typical of the cru. The result would be even better with a lower dosage.

Pertois-Lebrun B. d. B. 71
(100% CH)
The creaminess is there, as is a weak tone of melon and honey. Unnecessarily high dosage.

1989 Pertois-Lebrun 78 (Nov 94) 85
(100% CH)
Here too the dosage is a little heavy-handed, which is a shame when the grapes themselves have such lovely sweet aromas.

Lancelot-Pienne

1 allé de la Foret, 51530 Cramant ☎ 03 26 57 55 74

Production: 100,000 bottles.

This firm was founded in 1870, and is one of two with the knight's name of Lancelot. The cuvée de prestige is called *Table Ronde*, refering to the knights of the round table.

Lancelot B. d. B. 69
(100% CH)
Ingratiating nose of butter and saffron. Rich, sweet flavour, once again with saffron tones.

Lancelot-Pienne Table Ronde 85
(40% PN, 60% CH)
This small grower has succeeded in imitating the big houses in his cuvée de prestige. If I tasted this blind I'd probably go for a Pol Roger. The wine is sophisticated with a fine toasty tone and broad style of a big house.

Other wines: Brut, Rosé.

Lancelot-Royer

540 rue Général de Gaulle,
51530 Cramant ☎ 03 26 57 51 41

Production: 30,000 bottles.

This generous producer holds property not only in Cramant, but also in Avize, Oger and Chouilly. The average age of the wines is 25 years and the reserve wines are stored in oak casks.

Lancelot-Royer B. d. B. 66
(100% CH)
Buttery Cramant style: young, smooth and uncomplicated fruit.

Lancelot-Royer Extra Dry Chevalier 70
(100% CH)
A powerful champagne with tones of pear and pineapple.

89/90 Lancelot-Royer 78 (Jul 97) 84
(100% CH)
Medium-bodied and honey scented with good roundness and exotic fruit.

1983 Lancelot-Royer 76 (Apr 96) 82
(100% CH)
The flavour is harmonious with a fine citrus tone, but the gamey style of the nose is demanding.

1982 Lancelot-Royer 82 (Apr 96) 84
(100% CH)
Unusually developed '82 with a unified flavour of cream and licorice.

1969 Lancelot-Royer 81 (Apr 96) ▼
(100% CH)
A wine on its last legs. English oxidative flavour with leather and licorice saltiness.

Courtois-Camus

270 rue du 8 mai 1945,
51530 Cramant ☎ 03 26 57 91 18
Production: 8,000 bottles.

The friendly owner, who possesses what are probably the largest hands in Champagne, met me in his villa during a spontaneous visit in April, 1996. Unfortunately he said vintage wines weren't worth considering as the family had such a modest output. They own only two hectares in Cramant, but they are spread out among 22 different locations. The company is well worth a visit, not least to feel the firmest handshake in the region.

Courtois-Camus Tradition 74
(100% CH)
A rounded, pleasing flavour with elements of cream and butter. The wine comes from two locations in Cramant.

Courtois-Camus Carte Rouge 70
(100% CH)
A higher dosage than the *Tradition*. Less sophisticated and somewhat shorter.

Wanner-Bouge

177 rue du 8 Mai 1945,
51530 Cramant ☎ 03 26 57 52 35

Production: 250,000 bottles.

The firm was founded in 1870. Jacques Wanner produces slightly thin but elegant champagnes from his seven hectares in Cramant, Oiry and Chouilly.

Wanner-Bouge Grande Réserve 58
(20% PN, 20% PM, 60% CH)
Light and pleasant, with a style influenced by Chardonnay.

Wanner-Bouge B. d. B. 68
(100% CH)
Impeccably pure. The aftertaste isn't on a par with the wine's other qualities, unfortunately.

1990 Wanner-Bouge 69 (Jul 95) 80
(100% CH)
Closed and surprisingly thin, but with aromas typical of the village.

Voirin-Jumel

555 rue Libération, 51530 Cramant ☎ 03 26 57 55 82

Voirin-Jumel B. d. B. 60
(100% CH)
Rather an uninteresting and somewhat unripe Cramant champagne with only a smidgin of the delightful cru character.

1990 Voirin-Jumel 75 (Feb 97) 80
(100% CH)
This is a very rich and chocolaty wine, with a fat structure and pompous expression. I do miss some of Cramant's purity.

1982 Voirin-Jumel 60 (Apr 96) 60
(100% CH)
Quite a dirty champagne with cheese aromas and tones of sweat. The creaminess doesn't cover all the sins here.

LOUVOIS

Unusually, Louvois' vineyards lie in a large glade in a wood. It's a remarkable sight to see rows of vines planted along the slopes below the edge of the forest. The village lies hidden and although Louvois is a Grand cru village, the wines aren't so well-renowned.

Most people I've talked to during my work with this book agree that this village shouldn't be ranked as a Grand cru. They are probably right, but the still wines from the village I've tasted have impressed me.

Geologically speaking, Louvois and Bouzy come from the same wrinkle in the earth's surface. Louvois is the westernmost point of Bois de Dames, and today 18 winemakers grow grapes in the village's 41 hectares. Of the large houses, Bollinger, Clicquot, Roederer and Laurent-Perrier own most of the land.

% 100% 90% PN, 10% CH

Yves Beautrait

4 rue de Cavaliers, 51150 Louvois 03 26 57 03 38
Production: 65,000 bottles.

This grower owns 16.5 hectares in Bouzy, Louvois, Tauxières and Tours-sur-Marne. Beautrait's cellars are clinically clean and the equipment is highly modern, considering that production is relatively minor.

Yves Beautrait Brut 76
(75% PN, 25% CH)
A real wine for keeping, packed with undeveloped extract, acidity and potential. The nose is closed and the flavour is dry and restrained.

1983 Yves Beautrait Special Club 76 (Jul 89) 80
(60% PN, 40% CH)
Made completely from Bouzy grapes. The nose isn't as complete as the non-vintage champagne, but in the mouth one is met by a concentrated, long, Pinot flavour.

Guy de Chassey

1 rue Vieille, 51150 Louvois 03 26 57 03 32
Production: 40,000 bottles.

In 1993, when Guy de Chassey passed away, his two daughters took over the firm. This grower is one of few who make expressly Louvois champagne.

Guy de Chassey Brut Grand Cru 76
(95% PN, 5% CH)
The wine creates a focused and united impression, as do so many monocru champagnes. A closed but deep nose of top-class Pinot. A full, long, spicy and harmonious flavour.

Guy de Chassey Brut de Brut 68
(65% PN, 35% CH)
The same wine without dosage.

Guy de Chassey Reservée 75
(35% PN, 65% CH)
Very good structure and nice acidity. A true Grand cru champagne.

1990 Guy de Chassey 80 (Jul 98) 86
(50% PN, 50% CH)
40 year old vines! Closed on the nose. Wonderful inner power.

Guy Méa

1 rue de l'Eglise, 51150 Louvois 03 26 57 03 42
Production: 65,000 bottles.

Guy Méa's champagne first saw the light of day in 1953. The wines are stored for three years in the cellar before they go on sale. The vineyards cover 8.5 hectares, divided among the villages of Ludes, Tauxières, Bouzy and Louvois.

Guy Méa Brut 71
(70% PN, 30% CH)
This well-built Grand cru champagne has quite a closed style, at least when recently-disgorged. It's the flavour that impresses, with its power and length.

Other wines: Rosé, Prestige.

MAILLY

Mailly is a worthy Grand cru village. However, I would like to point out that the conditions don't appear to be so advantageous on the surface. Large strips of vineyards are on flat ground, but instead of relying entirely on the sun's rays the plants are warmed by a local hot airstream which expedites the ripening of the grapes. The village's plantations face all the hands of the compass, apart from directly west. The microclimate and other conditions mean that there are excellent locations both on the northerly and southerly slopes. The very best location in the village lies right under the Mailly cooperative's base and is owned by its members. Some say that Mailly competes with Verzenay for first place in Montagne de Reims. My feeling is that Mailly lacks the little extra necessary for its wines to be labelled as great. However, the wines from here are extremely reliable. They are well-structured and develop at an early stage those chocolate aromas in the nose that are so typical of high-class Pinot Noir. The village also possesses a considerable number of Chardonnay plants that received Grand cru status in 1972.

% 100% 89% PN, 4% PM, 7% CH

Coop. Mailly Grand Cru

28 rue de la Libération, 51500 Mailly 03 26 49 41 10
Production: 450,000 bottles.

Some seventy members of this cooperative control as many hectares in a highly professional and successful manner. Mailly Grand Cru is definitely one of the best and most well-known cooperatives in the entire district, and their marketing strategy is well-organised and intence.

Mailly Brut Réserve 55
(80% PN, 20% CH)
A touch sweeter than the cooperative's other wines. The added sugar really is necessary because there's an unripe monster lurking under the surface.

Mailly Extra Brut 74
(75% PN, 25% CH)
A seafood champagne that is bone dry. Good attack and a hint of licorice in the nose. Worth keeping.

Mailly Blanc de Noirs 79
(100% PN)
In this Pinot champagne they have used grapes from the youngest vines to prevent the wine from being too heavy and obtrusive. The nose is young yet mighty: chocolate and licorice fill the mouth together with a surprisingly high acidity.

Mailly Rosé 73
(90% PN, 10% CH)
Thanks to the skin contact method, the colour stays light. The nose is good but with quite basic tones of raspberry. The flavour is charming and round.

1990 Mailly 80 (Oct 97) 87
(75% PN, 25% CH)
Superb freshness and vivacity. This "vin de garde" has got a good lingering aftertaste and a great structure.

1989 Mailly 86 (Oct 97) 89
(75% PN, 25% CH)
Surprisingly even better than the '90. Balanced, fresh and full of ripe fruit aromas. Nice nose of chocolate and coffee beans.

1988 Mailly 78 (Apr 95) 84
(75% PN, 25% CH)
I found dried fruit in this vintage champagne which tends to lift up the typical house aroma of licorice and chocolate.

1983 Cuvée 60e Anniversaire 87 (Sep 97) 87
(60% PN, 40% CH)
A lovely champagne with elements of roasted almonds and chestnuts. The mature flavour is full and well-balanced.

Cuvée de Échansons 89
(75% PN, 25% CH)
Always a blend of two vintages. Many wine journalists often complain that the wine is oxidative, but I got quite another impression. The colour shone and there was a fine mousse, the nose was creamily soft with elements of mushroom paste and leather. The aromas returned in the soft, enjoyable flavour.

LE MESNIL-SUR-OGER

For more than forty years, a mere percentage point separated Le Mesnil from Grand cru status, and it wasn't until 1985 that the promotion came, even though many saw the village as the best of them all. Those grapes which grow is a belt at a height of 160-220 metres provide the most elegant champagnes the world has tasted. The cru has a very special Chardonnay clone which give a penetrating bouquet even when the actual content in a cuvée is small. Mesnil's wines are often shy and acidic when young, only to explode in a burst of colour and sensational pleasures.

Walnuts and coffee combined with a roguish, exotic fruit are usually the main ingredients in the wholly mature champagnes from the village. Unfortunately there are plenty of basic Le Mesnil champagnes, which goes to show how much the microclimate within the village varies. The most famous locations are Chétillons, Musettes, Jutées, Cocugneux, Champ d'Alouettes and, above all, Clos du Mesnil, which was previously owned by Julien Tarin. This unique walled area in the centre of the village was bought in 1971 by Krug, who immediately began planting new vines. It wasn't until 1979 that the Krug brothers thought the wine was good enough to go on sale. In historical terms it is Salon, another monocru champagne, that has given the village a global reputation. The cultivated land area now covers 432 hectares, shared among some forty grower/producers and a few houses that have managed to buy the extravagantly expensive land in time. Krug, Clicquot, Salon, Moët and Henriot are among the happy few.

% 100% 100% CH

Salon

5 rue de la Brèche d´Oger,
51190 Le Mesnil 03 26 57 51 65
Production: 50,000 bottles.

Salon is the most desirable champagne among real connoisseurs. This magnificent wine is so rare that only a few people have had the chance to taste the quintessence of Le Mesnil. In 1867 a perfectionist by the name of Aimé Salon was born. He grew up in Champagne and dreamed of creating the perfect champagne at an early age. After a short period as a teacher he became a successful fur trader, which gave him the capital needed to buy two small vineyards covering a total of one hectare in Le Mesnil. He made his first champagne in 1911 and formed a champagne house in 1914.

As early as in 1920, Salon became the house wine at Maxim in Paris. *Salon* was the first commercial blanc de blancs and a monocru besides. It's quite remarkable that the fame and praise heaped upon the firm has continued through the years, as the big names see Salon's philosophy as a direct antithesis. In principle *Salon* is a grower's champagne, considering that the wine contains only one kind of grape from just one cru. *Salon* may well be the best "grower" of all, but the success shows that Selosse, Peters, Diebolt and Charlemagne are all on the right course after all. When even the masters of the blend - Krug - made a monocru champagne from Le Mesnil, it became harder for the major companies to sing the praises of blending in such dogmatic fashion.

After Aimé died in 1943, the firm stayed within the family up until 1963, when Besserat de Bellefon took over the show. In 1989 Salon was bought up by Laurent-Perrier, and today the firm is run by the infinitely charming and spiritual Didier Depond, who had worked for Laurent-Perrier.

Recently the oak barrels have been thrown out, but that hardly affects the flavour, as the Le Mesnil Chardonnay grapes take up the most nutty and toasty aromas you could think of without even having seen an oak cask. Salon's two areas in the village are always the ones where the leaves come out first, which shows that the microclimate there is exceptional.

The average age of the vines is around fifty, and the other 75% of the grapes needed are chosen each year from the best growers in the village. *Salon* demands longer storage than any other champagne. The wines do not go through malolactic fermentation and have a razor-sharp acidity in their youth, which carries the wine through the years to unparalleled heights. A mature *Salon* expresses a gigantically broad aromatic spectrum and has a burgundy-like vinosity. The stringency is maintained throughout the wine's life, and as *Salon* has almost no dosage the wine never becomes an exotic charmer like *Taittinger Comtes de Champagne*, but it is unmatched in terms of class and purity. *Salon* is only made in exceptionally good years, and in other years the grapes go to make up Delamotte. Since 1921 the following vintages have been produced: 1921, 25, 28, 34, 37, 43, 46, 47, 48, 49, 51, 52, 53, 55, 59, 61, 64, 66, 69, 71, 73, 76, 79, 82 and 83. Nor should you miss the coming vintages of 1985, 88 and 90.

1990 Salon 94 (Jan 99) 98
(100% CH)
At the age of five the '90 still felt like a vin clair! Perfectly pure and appley, with chablis-like aromas and a magnificent young fruit. An embryo that is difficult to judge.

1988 Salon 90 (Jan 99) 96
(100% CH)
The '88 isn't on the market yet, for which we should be grateful. This is without a doubt the least developed champagne of this vintage. The nose hints at nuts and chocolate but the flavour is mercilessly hard so far. A great wine in six to ten years' time.

1983 Salon 93 (Jan 99) 94
(100% CH)
The aromas were a touch clearer than in the '82. The nose was spicy and flowery with a sweet honeyed depth. The flavour was creamy with citrus aromas and a powerful aftertaste of walnuts and melted butter. Aging fast.

1982 Salon 94 (Feb 98) 96
(100% CH)
It took a few years before the '82 really found itself. Now it is wonderfully harmonious if a little uneven from bottle to bottle. A classic *Salon* with brilliant acidity and an exceptionally dry aftertaste of lanolin and butter.

1979 Salon 94 (Jul 97) 95
(100% CH)
Incredibly hard and closed for many years before it opened up a classically walnut-scented depth at the age of 14. The flavour is still restrained, dry and full of malic acid. The mineral-rich aftertaste is textbook stuff.

1976 Salon 95 (Jul 97) 95
(100% CH)
A quite wonderful toasty Mesnil bouquet with elements of coconut, coffee and autumn leaves. Outstandingly rich, almost fat and hardly one of the most elegant champagnes to have come from this house, but it competes with *Cristal* for the title of "Wine of the vintage".

1973 Salon 88 (Feb 94) ▼
(100% CH)
A perfect level, colour and mousse, but somewhat over-ripe and with a hint of maderisation. Rich fruit and nut aromas although still a disappointment.

1971 Salon 89 (Jun 94) ▼
(100% CH)
Great bottle variation. Certain bottles contain cider-like apple tones and are on their way out. Others are very fresh but slightly thin.

1969 Salon 97 (Jan 99) 97
(100% CH)
This book's photographer and illustrator, Pelle Bergentz, joined this project after having tasted this heavenly wine. The colour was light, clear and bright, and all the flowers of the garden were present in the almost narcotically seductive bouquet. The toasty tones were there already, albeit muffled. The flavour is a fresh and life-enhancing experience. An equilibric masterpiece of the very top drawer.

1964 Salon 97 (Nov 98) 97
(100% CH)
Not as sensual as the *1964 Comtes de Champagne*, but just as good in a more restrained and younger style. Light lime green colour and prolonged, minimal bubbles. A strict nose that needs airing for it to open up the inner depths of Salon's typical aromas. Exquisitely balanced with an intense attack and acidity. *Salon* in a nutshell!

1959 Salon 97 (May 93) 98
(100% CH)
As light as a champagne from the eighties. At first a very closed nose that wanted a quarter of an hour in the glass before it developed a momentous depth of autumn leaves, walnuts, chocolate, smoke and jasmine aromas. The flavour softened with time, but was extremely concentrated and hard. The power is beaten only by the *Bollinger Vieilles Vignes Françaises*. Not the most charming *Salon* vintage, but one of the best I've tasted. The thought-provoking depth, combined with the wine's dazzling youth, make *1959 Salon* one of my greatest experiences of wine. And it can develop even further!

1955 Salon 98 (Jan 97) 98
(100% CH)
Somewhere between the '53 and '47 in terms of style. Superbly classical, toasty and nutty with a strong feel of woodlands. Acidic, amazingly long flavour with tones of walnut and lemon.

1953 Salon 98 (Oct 95) 98
(100% CH)
This is an incredible and wonderful wine that has united youthful vigour and majestic maturity in an unsurpassable manner. The fresh nose is borne up by aromas that transport you straight into some deep, autumnal forest. The vinosity and mineral richness give the eternal flavour perfect balance.

1951 Salon 93 (Jan 99) 93
(100% CH)
A distinctly odd vintage. The freshness is almost laughable. The colour is once again like a champagne from the eighties and the nose is flowery with faint nutty tones. The flavour is sensational with all its acidity and youthfulness. Naturally it's not as rich in extracts as the classical vintages, but high in alcohol.

1947 Salon 98 (May 97) 98
(100% CH)
A legend which costs a fortune and is actually worth its price. The nose is remarkable, with tones of hay, toffee, walnut, cognac and burnt butter. However, clearest of all is a tone of crème brûle. The flavour is tremendously full and rich, with an accelerating, smoky aftertaste.

Pierre Peters

26 rue des Lombards,
51190 Le Mesnil ☎ 03 26 57 50 32

Production: 150,000 bottles.

The Peters family came originally from Luxembourg, before Pierre settled in Le Mesnil. The always smiling and tremendously skilful François Peters controls 17.5 hectares, 12 of which lie in the very best parts of Le Mesnil. For several years grapes from the old vines in Les Chétillons were included in the vintage wine, but nowadays they make a *Cuvée Spéciale* from grapes from this unique location. The enthusiasm over this wine all over the world is huge - before anyone has had a chance to taste a mature bottle. Mesnil's wines take a long time to mature, but champagne from Peters offers from the start an accessible fruitiness that resembles tangerine and a large portion of butterscotch and nut aromas. With age they become majestic and deep as a water well, full of coffee and walnut aromas and a fleeting, vibrant exotic fruitiness. Pierre Peters is a hidden treasure of Champagne, so far anyway, which makes the prices laughable considering the quality of the wines.

Pierre Peters Cuvée de Réserve 81
(100% CH)
Sadly the bottle variation is great. The quality is always high, but some mature examples rise above the rest with their toasty Mesnil character.

Pierre Peters Perle du Mesnil 80
(100% CH)
Weakly sparkling, citrus fresh and easily drunk, but without any great complexity.

1991 Pierre Peters 78 (Aug 97) 85
(100% CH)
The tangerine aromas are already there, but it lacks the structure needed to bring it up to the producer's normal standard.

1990 Pierre Peters 91 (Jul 98) 93
(100% CH)
The '90 is a little bit special, with a personal style in which the yoghurt-like red fruit nose is often confused with Pinot Noir. The structure is incredibly tight and focused. A great wine in the making.

1990 Pierre Peters Cuvée Spéciale 92 (Jan 99) 96
(100% CH)
A superbly concentrated Chardonnay wine which brings a smile to my lips as I take up the pen. The wine combines the 89's muscular tangerine aroma with the 88's stony stringency. Wonderful today, magical after 2010.

1989 Pierre Peters 86 (Jul 95) 91
(100% CH)
The '89, with grapes from Oger, Mesnil, Avize and Chouilly. During 1995 the champagne developed very quickly and is now large and bushy, filled with toasty tones. The flavour is somewhat loose, but it is creamy and packed with fruit.

1989 Pierre Peters Cuvée Spéciale 91 (Sep 98) 94
(100% CH)
This Vieilles Vignes champagne from seventy year-old vines in Les Chétillons has been part of the very elite since its very first vintage. The wine's rich tangerine flavour leads many to expect a short life. In actual fact this exotically rich and toasty champagne is full of life-sustaining acidity that lie in wait under the surface.

1988 Pierre Peters Cuvée Spéciale 91 (Oct 97) 95
(100% CH)
The '88 isn't quite so rich and fruity as the '89, but it has an even more classical form and a fresher, more multi-faceted flowery nose with elements of roasted coffee beans.

1986 Pierre Peters 83 (Nov 94) 84
(100% CH)
Juicy, mature and chocolate scented. Drink within a couple of years.

1985 Pierre Peters * 92 (Oct 97) 94
(100% CH)
Perfectly pure and beautiful, with vigorous young tones in both nose and flavour. Packed with mineral aromas and seductive tones. Dry and restrained and extremely potent.

1985 Pierre Peters Cuvée Spéciale 90 (Apr 95) 96
(100% CH)
The owner's own favourite wine. At the age of ten the acidity was still huge, and the flowery nose is extremely fine but somewhat closed. The flavour resembles a drier and more elegant version of the *1985 Roederer Cristal.*

1982 Pierre Peters 92 (Jun 97) 92
(100% CH)
Honeyed soft, buttery and easily drunk.

1979 Pierre Peters 94 (Apr 95) 95
(100% CH)
An outstanding wine that shows how beautifully the village's wines age. In a normal bottle the wine has a nutty nose and from the magnum one is struck by a perfect aroma of butter-fried chanterelle mushrooms. The flavour is identical in both bottle sizes. The elegant, acidic flavour is wrapped in an oily envelope and displays aromas of beeswax, tobacco, coffee and walnuts.

1978 Pierre Peters Special Club 91 (Apr 97) 91
(100% CH)
Incredibly elegant and refreshing champagne with stringent acidity and broad toasty aromas, plus a delicious citrus flavour. One of the pearls of this vintage.

1973 Pierre Peters 96 (Jun 93) 96
(100% CH)
Only *Dom Pérignon* can compete for the title of "Champagne of the vintage". Peters' '73 is golden nectar with a fabulous Montrachet-like bouquet. Petroleum, walnuts, melon, mango, autumn leaves and coffee fill the room when the wine is poured. The flavour is oily and smooth as honey.

1973 Pierre Peters Special Club 91 (May 96) 91
(100% CH)
The old club bottle's shape has proved to be unsuitable for long aging. Compared to the unreal '73 this version is far more developed, with certain signs of oxidation. Both the nose and flavour are delightfully rich, but any finesse is subdued.

Guy Charlemagne

4 rue de la Brèche d'Oger,
51190 Le Mesnil 03 26 57 52 98

Production: 130,000 bottles.

This elegant firm was founded in 1892. Guy Charlemagne and his son, Philippe, make some of the purest champagnes on the market, and the Le Mesnil character is, if possible, even more tangible than in wines from the neighbouring Salon. Besides eight hectares in Le Mesnil they own two in Oger, four in Sézanne and eight in Cuis. The average age of the vines is an impressive thirty, and in the vintage wines there are grapes from three locations: Vaucherot, Aillerand and Masonière. They have recently begun using small oak barrels for some 20% of the harvest.

Guy Charlemagne B. d. B. 83
(100% CH)
This champagne, which is aged for three years, is made from grapes from Oger and Le Mesnil. It's one of the most elegant non-vintage champagne I've ever had! The nose is incredibly pure and flowery, like a Chablis Grand cru from Louis Michel. The flavour is also romantically light and multi-faceted - the perfect aperitif on an early summer evening.

Guy Charlemagne Rosé 60
Quite uninteresting wine from this wonderful producer.

1992 Guy Charlemagne 78 (Sep 97) 85
(100% CH)
Youthfully light and flowery. It may be pure and balanced, but I miss the customary concentration.

1990 Guy Charlemagne 80 (Jun 97) 91
(100% CH)
Still tightly closed and restrained, but after 20 minutes in the glass one can discern the origin and high quality.

1990 Mesnillesime 90 (Feb 98) 95
(100% CH)
The 90's nose is slightly closed and personally I prefer the similar *Pierre Peters Cuvée Spéciale* from this year. However, the flavour is superb, packed with layers of intense Chardonnay experiences. A little *Salon* in the making.

1988 Mesnillesime 91 (Apr 95) 96
(100% CH)
One of the best 88's. Despite only 0.4% sugar content, we have here a astonishingly honeyed wine with the broad spectrum of aromas that only Le Mesnil grapes can give. The oak barrel provides yet another dimension in the fantastically concentrated flavour. The wine contains everything, and offers a whole lot of that already.

1982 Guy Charlemagne 89 (Apr 95) 91
(100% CH)
Once again, diamond-clear seductive tones of jasmine, yellow roses and lily of the valley. The flavour is full of toffee and is very reminiscent of Chardonnay from Cramant.

1979 Guy Charlemagne 93 (Apr 95) 94
(100% CH)
All the wines from this property are light, with a rare crystal clarity. The '79 is a delicate, feminine wine, full of innumerable aromas. Lime, white roses and toasted bread are the front-runners. A sensual lightweight.

Other wines: Cuvée Centenaire.

Launois Père & Fils

2 av. Eugene Guillaume,
51190 Le Mesnil 03 26 57 50 15
Production: 180,000 bottles.

The firm was founded in 1872 and owns 21 hectares, most of which lie in Le Mesnil. Bernard Launois has recently set up a fantastic wine museum on his property. Few winemakers in Champagne have such a well-stocked cellar full of old vintages as Bernard's. Even fewer are as generous and willing to share as this connoisseur of life.

Since 1970, grapes from Avize, Oger and Cramant are all part of Bernard's wonderful wines. Launois' finest wine, ***Special Club***, is a blend of equal parts of Le Mesnil (Les Chetillons) and Cramant (Les Justices).

Launois Brut 73
(100% CH)
A lovely, uncomplicated champagne with delicious, juicy Chardonnay fruit and elements of mango.

Launois Réserve B. d. B. 79
(100% CH)
A powerful blanc de blancs with plenty of attack and good length.

Launois Mesnil Sablé 79
(100% CH)
Delicate, pure and creamy. Definitely good for very long storage.

1990 Launois 90 (Jan 99) 94
(100% CH)
Plenty of toffee and saffron aromas, but also a steely, acidic finesse which is typical of this unbeatable village.

1990 Launois Special Club 91 (Jun 98) 95
(100% CH)
More affected by Mesnil than the '88. Amazingly tight and plenty of capacity for development.

1988 Launois 86 (Jul 97) 91
(100% CH)
A classic Mesnil champagne which is at its best in magnums. The wine already has a typical village perfume which is quite wonderful.

1988 Launois Special Club 93 (Apr 96) 95
(100% CH)
Bonnaire's favourite champagne, and I understand him! Cramant shines brightly in this wonderful solo piece.

1988 Launois Sablé 86 (Apr 96) 91
(100% CH)
Faintly sparkling, a broad meaty nose with tones of roasted chestnuts and citrus fruits. A delicate mousse and extremely pure young flavour.

1986 Launois Cuvée 2000 83 (Aug 97) 85
(100% CH)
The colour is close to green, the nose is thoroughly toasty and there's an acidic, one-dimensional taste.

1985 Launois 90 (May 98) 92
(100% CH)
A wine with a tightly focused style, closed and stringent, but with a long, acidic and developable aftertaste.

1985 Launois Special Club 80 (Apr 92) 93
(100% CH)
A closed package of minerals which literally feels like drinking chalk soil. The wine has not gone through malolactic fermentation and has very hard acidity. The fruit is stingy but very elegant and worth storing awhile. Don't drink before the year 2000.

1985 Launois Sablé 91 (Jul 97) 92
(100% CH)
This lovely, languidly-sparkling wine is like a piece of jewellery with beautiful, delicate features. Lime and whipped cream are what come to mind when you try to describe the aromas. Launois has done it again!

1982 Launois 88 (Jul 91) 91
(100% CH)
Extremely fine, small bubbles that give a gorgeous pearl necklace in the glass. Subtle nose of mineral and newly-baked bread. I have an obvious weakness for blanc de blancs of this calibre.

1981 Launois Special Club 94 (Jun 97) 95
(100% CH)
Several 81's are beginning to show previously unimagined qualities, with a flowery elegance common to them all. Launois' example is among the most beautiful, with its shining green/yellow colour, ultra-elegant nose and exotic fruit flavour.

1979 Launois 94 (Jul 97) 94
(100% CH)
Great freshness on the nose, bouquet of fresh hay that has just been cut. Wonderful taste of walnuts.

1975 Launois 89 (Apr 92) 89
(100% CH)
A brutal blanc de blancs that steams ahead with deep chocolate aromas and a corpulent body.

1971 Launois 92 (Apr 92) 94
(100% CH)
Tasted together with the '75, this vintage was lighter and its bouquet more refined. A typical example of how easily older blanc de blancs can be confused with oak character.

1966 Launois 96 (Jun 97) 97
(100% CH)
What a magical champagne! The wine has an elusive, refined nose that I've only previously encountered in *1985 Krug Clos de Mesnil*. The feminine elegance returns in the buttery, eternal flavour.

1947 Launois 97 (Apr 96) 97
(100% CH)
What a pearl! Not as elegant as the '66 but much richer, with a youthful nose of seaside rock, passion fruit and a magically concentrated nectarine flavour. A wine for everyone to love.

1932 Launois 92 (Apr 96) 92
(100% CH)
Leather, meat and truffles in the nose. When in the mouth, it's dominated by old butter and licorice aromas.

Michel Turgy

17 rue d'Orme, 51190 Le Mesnil ☎ 03 26 57 53 43

When you travel around the growers in Le Mesnil there is one name, besides Salon, that always turns up. Old vintages from Turgy are regarded by several growers to be the best wines ever made in the village. After Michel's recent death the sale of vintage wine was blocked, and this means that the non-vintage champagne also contains wine that would normally be classed as a vintage. The blend on sale in 1995, for example, was based on 1988's harvest and contained very old reserve wines! As Le Mesnil wines have such longevity Turgy, together with Guy Charlemagne and Selosse, offers the very best non-vintage champagne if we discount *Krug Grande Cuvée* from that category.

Michel Turgy Sélection 83
(100% CH)
I've drunk purer non-vintage champagnes, but hardly any more enjoyable. The honeyed nose is very broad. The flavour is filled with mint chocolate and has a complex aftertaste of old reserve wines.

Alain Robert

25 av. de la République,
51190 Le Mesnil ☎ 03 26 57 52 94

Production: 100,000 bottles.

Alain Robert is one of Champagne's most unique winemakers, with control of vineyards in five Chardonnay villages. The grapes are picked by hand, the Mesnil grapes ferment in oak barrels and the youngest non-vintage champagne is nine years old. In May of 1995, they sold 1978 and 1979 as vintage champagnes! All this is made possible by asking an awfully high price. A. Robert's prestige wine is in fact the second most expensive in Champagne after *Krug Collection*. Unfortunately I haven't tasted his vintage wines, but the rich non-vintage examples are very good, if a trifle rustic.

A. Robert Sélection 73
(100% CH)
The wine contains 60% Sézanne grapes and is vinified in steel tanks. This pure '86 is broad and bushy with a smoky, slightly sweet element. The flavour is full and heavy, with good acidity.

A. Robert Brut 82
(100% CH)
A pure '85 with a rich honeyed bouquet in a classic oxidative style. The power and maturity are superb, as is the long aftertaste of walnut and butter.

A. Robert Mesnil Sélection 80
(100% CH)
A pure '83. Broad, nutty, classical old-fashioned nose with buttery, rich, somewhat one-dimensional flavour.

A. Robert Vieux Dosé 90
(100% CH)
Made from thirty year-old vines from the harvests in 1980 and 1982. Completely vinified in oak barrels and for sale ten years after being disgorged! A lovely, golden champagne with green elements and a classical toasty, barrelly nose. The wine is mature but holds up terrifically well in the glass.

Other wines: Vintage.

Philippe Gonet

6 route de Vertus, 51190 Le Mesnil ☎ 03 26 57 53 47

Production: 90,000 bottles.

This Gonet is of course a relative of Michel Gonet in Avize. The family firm has been around now for six generations and has one of the most impressive collections of old vintages in all of Champagne. Of Gonet's 18 hectares, six lie in Oger and Le Mesnil.

P. Gonet B. d. B. 68
(100% CH)
Light colour and a fresh, fruity nose. A sparkling, sharp flavour with good potential.

1990 P. Gonet 82 (Feb 97) 88
(100% CH)
A rich wine typical of the vintage, with a clear aroma of saffron and a long aftertaste.

1988 P. Gonet 75 (Jul 95) 85
(100% CH)
Pure, elegant and bone dry.

1989 P. Gonet Special Club 80 (Jul 95) 88
(100% CH)
Made from 66 year-old vines in Les Hauts Jardins. So fat and chewy that it almost feels clumsy.

1988 P. Gonet Special Club 86 (Jul 95) 92
(100% CH)
Incredibly concentrated and rich champagne with tones of red fruit, almonds and beeswax. A deceptive impression of maturity.

F. Billion

4 rue des Lombards,
51190 Le Mesnil 03 26 57 51 24

Production: 80,000 bottles.

Robert Billion was previously responsible for wines at Salon, but still found time to make a small amount of champagne under his own name. Even today, Billion still sells grapes to Salon and has some similarities of style. The smokiness and nut aromas are very broad, but Billion lacks the elegance that the very best producers in Le Mesnil have in common. A. Robert and F. Billion lead the heavier oak barrel-fermented Mesnil school.

F. Billion Vinesime 73
(100% CH)
A well-muscled champagne in overalls. A broad, powerful nose of almonds, barrels and ripe yellow apples. Sweet and fat flavour that lacks the proper clarity.

F. Billion Brut 75
(100% CH)
Lots of honey and walnut aromas, but even fatter structure than the *Vinesime*.

1989 F. Billion 83 (Apr 97) 86
(100% CH)
Both the vintage and the producer usually produce fat wines, but this one retains its balance. If there's anyone who doubts that asparagus and champagne can work together, I can recommend this wine, which goes up a few gears when alongside the golden treasure of spring.

1988 F. Billion 80 (Dec 94) 84
(100% CH)
A wealth of tastes and very friendly. Packed with exotic Chardonnay fruit and buttery charm, but aging too quickly.

1985 F. Billion 90 (Sep 95) 90
(100% CH)
A rustic version of Salon's aromas. Dark yellow colour, oaky nose backed up by butter and honey. Vinous as a white burgundy. Impressively old-fashioned.

Bernard Schmitte

12 ruelle des Jutées,
51190 Le Mesnil 03 26 57 54 14

Unfortunately the good Bernard Schmitte doesn't sell any vintage champagne at the moment. His non-vintage blanc de blancs is however a pure '89 of high class. He is rated among the top growers in Le Mesnil.

B. Schmitte B. d. B. 81
(100% CH)
A richly seductive wine, with a strong honey and candy nose. The flavour is full of exotic fruits and almond aromas. The champagne possesses a concentration which can be explained by the old vines the grower harvests.

Pertois-Moriset

13 av. de la République,
51190 Le Mesnil 03 26 57 52 14

Production: 100,000 bottles.

Yet another grower in Le Mesnil to keep an eye on. Pertois-Moriset also owns vineyards in Pinot villages from which he makes three blanc de noirs.

Pertois-Moriset B. d. B. 80
(100% CH)
Rich, developed Chardonnay aromas in both nose and flavour. The wine relies on its richness more than any finesse, which is unusual for Le Mesnil.

1988 Pertois-Moriset Special Club 86 (May 95) 92
(100% CH)
A wonderfully rich wine with an almost perfumed flowery Mesnil nose. Tight and creamy structure with a taste of mango and vanilla.

Other wines: Blanc de Noirs, Sélection, Vintage, Brut, Rosé.

Leon Launois

3 ruelle de L'Arquebuse,
51190 Le Mesnil 03 26 57 50 28

Production: 100,000 bottles.

Jacky Launois and his wife created such a strange impression during my visit in April 1995 that it seems a miracle that they make such good champagne. Launois controls 18 hectares of first-class vineyards in Le Mesnil and claims in all seriousness that all wines in Le Mesnil taste the same!

Leon Launois B. d. B. 75
(100% CH)
A trifle thin, slender-limbed blanc de blancs with good prospects for the future.

1992 Leon Launois 70 (Feb 97) 73
(100% CH)
Thick and loose-skinned with pleasant aromas of red fruits. Ages quickly in the glass.

1989 Leon Launois Cuvée Prestige 82 (Apr 95) 90
(100% CH)
Slightly closed in the nose, but with pure Le Mesnil tones in the flavour. Dry and fine, and very promising.

Other wines: Rosé, Cuvée Perlée.

Robert Moncuit

2 pl. de la Gare, 51190 Le Mesnil 03 26 57 52 71

Far less well-known than Pierre Moncuit, but the champagnes that I tasted were distinctly promising.

Robert Moncuit B. d. B. 77
(100% CH)
A feminine champagne with elusive, multi-dimensional tones. Typical of the village.

1987 Robert Moncuit 80 (Feb 97) 84
(100% CH)
A full-bodied, rich champagne typical of the village, with tones of nutshell and pears. This wine resembles *F. Billion*.

1982 Robert Moncuit 80 (Feb 97) 83
(100% CH)
A weakly, liqueur-like element disrupts the young nose. The flavour is youthfully fresh and short.

André Jacquart

6 av. de la République,
51190 Le Mesnil 03 26 57 52 29

Production: 100,000 bottles.

André Jacquart is one of the growers who is moving up in the world and can soon be expected to demand sky-high prices. At their command they has seven hectares in Aube and the Marne valley, but it's their eleven hectares in Le Mesnil that are making them famous.

André Jacquart Brut 49
(30% PN, 30% PM, 40% CH)
Appreciated by many, but to my mind it's a sticky and candy-sweet champagne.

André Jacquart B. d. B. 72
(100% CH)
Quite rich with tones of saffron and red fruit. Uneven from year to year.

1989 André Jacquart 77 (Jul 95) 86
(100% CH)
Tough and unexpectedly light, with high acidity and a strong mineral tone.

1989 André Jacquart Special Club 80 (May 96) 89
(100% CH)
As usual, superior concentration and roundness in the *Special Club* when compared to the ordinary non-vintage champagne, with identical aromas.

1986 André Jacquart Special Club 81 (Jul 95) 83
(100% CH)
Mature and rounded with a creamy flavour.

1985 André Jacquart Le Mesnil 87 (Jun 93) 92
(100% CH)
This is where Jacquart displays their greatness with a classic blanc de blancs in a mature style. An almost exotic nose of mango and peach, and funnily enough the toasty elements only arrive in the flavour.

Robert Charlemagne

Av. Eugène Guillaume,
51190 Le Mesnil 03 26 57 51 02

Production: 35,000 bottles.

Guy Charlemagnes' cousin owns 4.3 hectares in the village, divided up into 36 locations.

R. Charlemagne B. d. B. 72
(100% CH)
A few years ago it was too sweet and tutti-frutti flavoured, but charming and pleasant. Today it's more serious.

1989 R. Charlemagne 85 (Aug 95) 91
(100% CH)
An extraordinarily sophisticated champagne where the lightness and finesse are intertwined in outstanding fashion. The wine's aromatic spectrum is dominated by nutty candy, seaside rock, tangerine and grapefruit. The family resemblance to the famous cousin is marked.

René Jardin

B.P. 8, 51190 Le Mesnil 03 26 57 50 26

Production: 130,000 bottles.

Louis Jardin founded the company in 1889, and today the pure Mesnil champagnes are made by M. Jardin.

Jardin B. d. B. 70
(100% CH)
Faintly smoky and rather fat blanc de blancs with a long aftertaste of pineapple.

Jardin Prestige 76
(100% CH)
The nose is toasty and contains a bunch of flowers. The flavour is restrained but develops aromas of bacon with time.

1990 Jardin 79 (Feb 97) 86
(100% CH)
A clear tone of saffron has crept into many of Le Mesnil's 90's, a trend that is illustrated nowhere better than in this champagne. The flavour is rich and a touch rustic.

1988 Jardin 76 (Aug 95) 84
(100% CH)
Once again burnt, smoked and aromatically carrying tones of bacon. Very long.

1985 Jardin 83 (Jul 95) 87
(100% CH)
Beautiful developed colour. A nose of meat stew that is also found in Pierre Moncuit's wines. The flavour is much better. Rich, buttery and long.

Claude Cazals

28 rue du Grand Mont,
51190 Le Mesnil 03 26 57 52 26

Production: 100,000 bottles.

One of Le Mesnil's better-known producers. He makes fast-maturing, toasty champagnes in a somewhat unconcentrated style.

C. Cazals B. d. B. 65
(100% CH)
Unexpectedly dark colour. Open, toasty and slightly fleshy nose with an appealingly rich and fruity flavour. The first glass always tastes better than the last.

C. Cazals Vive Extra Brut 70
(100% CH)
Powder dry, lively and sharp with pure apple aromas.

1990 C. Cazals 84 (Jan 97) 90
(100% CH)
An extremely focused and flowery B. d. B. Pure and typical of the village.

1988 C. Cazals 84 (Jan 97) 85
(100% CH)
Surprisingly toasty character. A little artificial and looser than the '90.

1985 C. Cazals 83 (Dec 92) 84
(100% CH)
Another developed wine with an immediate charm. Surprisingly complete for an '85.

Bardy Père & Fils

3 rue d'Oiry, 51190 Le Mesnil ☎ 03 26 57 57 59

Production: 60,000 bottles.

Unfortunately Monsieur Bardy no longer makes vintage wines from his six hectares full of 25 year-old vines.

Bardy B. d. B. 65
(100% CH)
Far too young, but filled with a potent gooseberry fruit.

Bardy Cuvée Réserve 75
(100% CH)
Five years old and with a heavy autolytic nose. The flavour is full but somewhat one-dimensional.

Delamotte

7 rue de la Brèche d'Oger,
51190 Le Mesnil ☎ 03 26 57 51 65

Production: 300,000 bottles.

This neighbour of Salon was founded as far back as 1760, and although closely linked with Lanson for a period it was taken over by the Nonancourt family in 1949. Since Laurent-Perrier bought Salon in 1989 Delamotte has functioned as Salon's second label. Delamotte owns five hectares in Le Mesnil and has access to Salon's vineyards during those years when *Salon* isn't produced. Didier Depond runs both firms with feeling and enthusiasm. Delamotte buys in 75% of its grapes, mostly from Premier cru villages.

Delamotte Brut 64
(30% PN, 20% PM, 50% CH)
Kind, almost feeble champagne where everything is weak although it's all there somewhere.

Delamotte B. d. B. 74
(100% CH)
A non-vintage wine that gains from years in the cellar. In its youth you can find rhubarb and pineapple, but as it matures the wine's creaminess and complexity grow.

Delamotte Rosé 65
(100% PN)
Not precisely what one expects from Delamotte. A pure Pinot Noir champagne with meaty style.

1990 Delamotte Demi-Sec 78 (Jul 97) 83
(100% CH)
Sensationally good sweetened champagne with a perfectly pure nose and elegant, citrus-fresh flavour. It's first in the aftertaste that the dosage reveals itself, which is exactly what is required.

1990 Delamotte 83 (Jan 99) 87
(100% CH)
A great vintage for Delamotte, giving them better concentration and greater depth than usual.

1985 Delamotte 79 (Feb 95) 83
(100% CH)
A fine nose of elegantly youthful Chardonnay. Once again pineapple and rhubarb in a kindly style.

1976 Delamotte 87 (Jun 97) 87
(25% PN, 75% CH)
A well-structured '76 which has reached its peak but can still be stored for a few years yet. The wine lost in comparison to the *Salon*, of course, but anyway it has a charming, toasty bouquet with elements of biscuits and bread.

1976 Delamotte B. d. B. 89 (Jun 97) 89
(100% CH)
This rich vintage suits what is normally a rather light wine very well. Here we find the muscles that Delamotte sometimes lacks.

Nicolas Louis Delamotte 75
(100% CH)
A pure '83 with clear tones of maturity and roasted elements. The flavour is light but the dosage is a touch high for me.

Dominique Pertois

13 av. de la République,
51190 Le Mesnil ☎ 03 26 57 52 14

Production: 100,000 bottles.

Dominique Pertois B. d. B. 67
(100% CH)
Pale and vaguely flowery, with a light, pure flavour which makes one long for Pinot Noir.

Other wines: Vintage.

Pierre Moncuit

11 rue Persault Maheu,
51190 Le Mesnil ☎ 03 26 57 52 65

Production: 125,000 bottles.

Nicole Moncuit runs this well thought-of domain, which owns twenty hectares in Le Mesnil, including a share of Les Chétillon's old vines. Moncuit is often mentioned in the same breath as greats like Selosse, Diebolt and Peters, which is something I have trouble understanding. Moncuit's wines are remarkable: when young they are more closed and sharp than most, only to suddenly develop some very odd tones of maturity. The nose becomes perfumed and the flavour gains a queer tone of lingonberry, which isn't what you expect from Le Mesnil. To be honest I think that Moncuit's hygienic conditions are doubtful. I've noticed the same strange lingonberry aroma in their cuverie and seen a few things there that don't belong in a fermentation tank. However, there is little doubt that the grapes are fantastic.

P. Moncuit B. d. B. 60
(100% CH)
The colour is a shimmering green and the mousse is perfect. This champagne has tremendous acidity and attack, but is almost wholly devoid of aromas.

1989 P. Moncuit 75 (May 94) 82
(100% CH)
Here the shimmering green wine has a closed nose. The flavour is rich and full-bodied, but the aftertaste is short.

1988 P. Moncuit 76 (May 94) 84
(100% CH)
Bitingly acidic and hard, but a promising structure and young, unripe fruitiness.

1988 P. Moncuit Vieilles Vignes 81 (May 94) ?
(100% CH)
For the first time Moncuit separate their oldest vines in Les Chétillons for use in the cuvée de prestige. The nose is closed for half an hour in the glass, but suddenly gooseberry, pear and lingonberry arrive. The structure in the mouth is fat and concentrated. This wine will probably become great, but don't bet too heavily on it.

1986 P. Moncuit 83 (Jan 95) 84
(100% CH)
Very enjoyable and creamy blanc de blancs of a classical style.

1982 P. Moncuit 30 (Sep 92) ?
(100% CH)
This is a wine I'd like to forget. Something went wrong here. The wine is loose and lingonberry-scented.

1981 P. Moncuit 87 (Mar 92) 88
(100% CH)
Definitely the most enjoyable champagne from this firm

I've tasted. An extremely multi-faceted, flowery nose spread with citrus fruits and mint. The flavour is light, delicate and uplifting.

1980 P. Moncuit 85 (May 94) 85
(100% CH)
A deep colour. A mature champagne that has not developed lingonberry aromas. Instead one notices the vintage's smoky style and the proper weight.

J-L Vergnon

1 Grande rue, 51190 Le Mesnil ☎ 03 26 57 53 86

Production: 40,000 bottles.

Jean-Louis Vergnon grows vines in five hectares in Côte des Blancs and was once a favourite of many growers in the district. That's a club I haven't joined. His wines are full of flavour but lack the village's elegance. No malolactic fermentation for the vintage wine, which comes from 40 year-old vines. Sadly the company is probably going downhill at the same rate as its owner.

J-L Vergnon B. d. B. 50
(100% CH)
A rough, almost gamey and vegetable nose. A good wealth of extracts and expansive fruit.

J-L Vergnon Extra Brut 73
(100% CH)
My friends were lyrical about this tasty, oxidative champagne. A little too rustic for my taste.

1988 J-L Vergnon 70 (Jun 96) 78
(100% CH)
At first a somewhat impure bouquet which happily disappears when aired. The wine is typical of the cru but is still something of a disappointment.

1987 J-L Vergnon 86 (Jan 96) 87
(100% CH)
Delightful, sensational wine, with a personal, perfumed nose and a classically pure, chalky flavour. The dominant fruit aroma is kiwi and melon.

1986 J-L Vergnon 76 (May 92) 76
(100% CH)
An almost Australian Chardonnay nose with mango, acacia, butter and bacon. Creamy and fat but a somewhat exaggerated meaty style.

1982 J-L Vergnon 70 (Jul 90) 77
(100% CH)
A prizewinning '82 of broad dimensions, but the back end's a bit too heavy for my taste.

Bliard-Moriset

2 rue Grand Mont, 51190 Le Mesnil ☎ 03 26 57 53 42

Production: 20,000 bottles.

This grower owns six hectares in Le Mesnil which are divided up into ten locations.

Bliard-Moriset Réserve 68
(100% CH)
Green/yellow colour and a slightly rough but correct style. A champagne that can be stored and which opens nicely in the glass.

Alain Moncuit-Bigex

5 av. Gare, 51190 Le Mesnil ☎ 03 26 57 95 65

Alain Moncuit-Bigex 70
(100% CH)
Hardly typical of the village, but concentrated and with popular appeal. Perhaps the dosage is a little high, but the wine harmonises well with asparagus and sauce hollandaise.

Jean Pernet

6 rue Breche d'Oger,
51190 Le Mesnil ☎ 03 26 57 54 24

Jean Pernet 66
(100% CH)
Extremely light and weak. Nor is it particularly elegant for a Mesnil champagne.

A. Lebis

11 rue Jean Baptiste Morizet,
51190 Le Mesnil ☎ 03 26 03 61 65

R. Lebis B. d. B. 50
(100% CH)
Oxidative, boring style. A poor example of Le Mesnil.

Michel Poyet

9 imp. Richebout, 51190 Le Mesnil ☎ 03 26 57 97 41

Michel Poyet B. b. B. 65
(100% CH)
Very light and pale, lacks concentration.

François Gonet

1 rue du Stade, 51190 Le Mesnil ☎ 03 26 57 53 71

Production: 30,000 bottles.

François is the brother of the more famous Philippe Gonet and owns eleven hectares in Le Mesnil, Cramant and Monteux. 50,000 bottles are sold sur-lattes annually, and those under his own label are among the village's more basic wines. The company is just as proud of its property in Loire, Domaine de Cathyanne.

F. Gonet Brut 53
(50% PN, 50% CH)
A very penetrating Pinot aroma in the nose and a slightly earthy subtone in the perfumed flavour.

F. Gonet Demi-Sec 33
(50% PN, 50% CH)
Tart, sour, boring and to sweet.

F. Gonet Rosé 48
Rooty Pinot flavour, soft and rather obvious.

F. Gonet Réserve 58
(50% PN, 50% CH)
Somewhat richer than the *Brut*. Good backbone of rooty Pinot Noir.

Other wines: Vintage, Special Club.

Coop. Le Mesnil

11 rue Charpentier Laurain,
51190 Le Mesnil ☎ 03 26 57 53 23

Production: 100,000 bottles.

This cooperative had all the opportunities to become something a little bit special, but careless grape handling and a yield that is far too high have led to inferior wines. Some growers in the village have their labels marked with the letters R.C. (Récolteur-Coopérateur). Such a champagne is made by the cooperative in the village under various labels.

Michel Poyet 67
(100% CH)
Tasted recently-disgorged during the festival of St Vincent in 1997, this wine from the Mesnil cooperative was pure but somewhat unconcentrated.

Christian Robinet 67
(100% CH)
A light and pure champagne with good balance and a flavour of burnt almonds. A little thin.

Deshautels 25
(100% CH)
Actually a pure '82. Unclean nose of flour and wet wool. The taste of dirty vinification!

1988 Jean-Pierre Launois 79 (May 95) 84
(100% CH)
The best champagne from the cooperative that I've tasted. Powerfully vinous nose and hard malic acidity.

1985 Deshautels 40 (Jun 95) 
(100% CH)
Impressive for a few minutes but then collapsed like a house of cards. Rough and unclean, but with plenty of power.

Michel Lorin

24 Grande rue, 51190 Le Mesnil 03 26 57 54 13

Michel Lorin B. d. B. 19
(100% CH)
You'll have to go a long way to find a worse Grand cru wine. The wine tasted as unclean as the grower's property looks. The nose is OK, but the flavour resembles calvados and the aftertaste is like old bacon.

OGER

Oger received its rightful Grand cru status in 1984, when that last, vital percentage point arrived. The village, which stands almost entirely upon Belimnite chalk, is often forgotten among its more famous neighbours. The difference between Oger and Le Mesnil-sur-Oger is mostly due to Oger's much younger vines, but the wines have a classic Chardonnay character. The best grapes come from the same long stretch of southeasterly slopes as Avize and Le Mesnil-sur-Oger. Clicquot is the biggest individual landowner, and today the vines cover an area of 350 hectares. The village surely hides a whole chest of treasures among its growers and is therefore well worth investigating at first hand.

% 100% 100% CH

Ed Bonville

3 rue du Gue, 51190 Oger 03 26 57 53 19

Production: 40,000 bottles.

The Bonville family have always used oak barrels in both Avize and Oger, and Ed Bonville's entire production is vinified in this fashion. The malolactic fermentation is avoided, giving even the non-vintage champagne good storage potential. Bonville own seven hectares in the village.

Ed Bonville B. d. B. 80
(100% CH)
100% oak + 100% Grand cru + 100% Chardonnay is an infallible receipe for a tasty champagne. Bonville's non-vintage blanc de blancs is one of the best of its genre. The nose is always broad with hazelnut tones from the barrel and the flavour is both rich and fresh.

F. Bonnet

1 rue de Mesnil, 51190 Oger 03 26 57 52 43

Up to 1988 it was an independent company. This well-run house is presently owned by the Rémy-Cointreau group, and has close connections with Charles Heidsieck. The house was founded in 1922 by Ferdinand Bonnet and owns ten hectares in Oger, Avize and Vertus. The house is well known in connoisseur circles and those champagnes I have tasted have left me wanting to taste more. See Ferdinand Bonnet Reims on page 214.

F. Bonnet Crémant 68
(10% PN, 90% CH)
What's the point of the Pinot content? The overall impression is of a light and flowery champagne with a powder dry aftertaste.

1983 F. Bonnet Sélection 85 (Jul 90) 90
(100% CH)
Surprisingly dark colour. An almost erotic nose, with smoky and spicy perfumed tones. The same aromas return in the mouth.

1982 F. Bonnet Sélection 83 (Jul 92) 88
(100% CH)
The wine doesn't have the same stringency and romantic tension as the '83, but it is a classic multicru blanc de blancs with juicy fruit and fine breadiness.

Jean Milan

4 rue Avize, 51190 Oger 03 26 57 50 09

Production: 80,000 bottles.

Henry Milan is not the name of a football team, but rather one of few clever, visionary growers in Oger. Just as with Ed Bonnville he uses a great many oak barrels - 100% in fact, for the cuvées de prestige. Jean Milan's champagnes are all good, but who wouldn't miss having a Van Basten up front?

Jean Milan B. d. B. 70
(100% CH)
Hard acidity and a classic Chardonnay aroma in both nose and flavour.

Cuvée Jean Charles Milan Sélection 82
(100% CH)
One of the firm's two prestige cuvées. Vinified exclusively in oak barrels, it has a restrained, tight, buttery nose with orange and honey. A well-balanced and concentrated blanc de blancs with good potential for the future.

1990 Terres de Noël 80 (May 98) 83
(100% CH)
From the firm's oldest vines comes this cuvée de prestige via more oak barrels. Lighter and fruitier style, less concentrated and with a tingling flavour of yellow apples.

Desautels-Roinard

1 rue de Mesnil, 51190 Oger 03 26 57 53 75

Desautels-Roinard Réserve 35
(100% CH)
This wine has a cava-like, earthy nose with elements of cardboard. The flavour is pure but uninteresting.

Desautels-Roinard Cuvée Prestige 60
(100% CH)
The Oger grower's prestige wine is made from older wines and undoubtedly feels mature. The colour is deep yellow and the nose is broad and honeyed. Plenty of flavour but it's a touch impure.

Henry de Vaugency

1 rue Avize, 51190 Oger ☎ 03 26 57 50 89

Henry de Vaugency Carte Noir 49
(100% CH)
A pale champagne with an earthy and yeasty nose. Apple flavour.

OIRY

This village may lie a long way from Côte des Blancs' main strip, but the vineyards belonging to the village are next to Cramant and Chouilly. I have myself stood together with a grower by this three-way junction and heard him bemoan the fact that his oldest vines and best grapes grew on the Oiry side, which made them less valuable. The quality of the grapes that grow on the lower slopes of Butte de Saran are actually of very high quality, but most of Oiry's 95 hectares of vineyards lie at the bottom of the slope. The chief reason for the grapes being of lower quality than those in Avize and Cramant is the lack of Belimnite chalk. Instead there is a wide strip of Micraster chalk in the soil. The village's finest locations are at a height of 150 metres over sea level and are owned by Pol Roger and Larmandier. Up to 1985 Oiry was merely a Premier cru village.

% 100% 100% CH

Lang-Biémont

Les Ormissets, 51530 Oiry ☎ 03 26 55 43 43

Production: 500,000 bottles.

A married couple began selling Lang-Biémont champagne in 1875, and today the very modern property is run by Lionel Chaudron. Lang-Biémont buy in grapes from a widespread area, but the basic ingredient is Chardonnay from Oiry.

Lang-Biemont Réserve 61
(10% PN, 90% CH)
A clear, shining colour, a nose of yellow plums and a sweet fruity flavour.

1986 Lang-Biémont B. d. B. 80 (Jan 95) 85
(100% CH)
A well-made wine with good depth and a high acidity which leads the grapefruit aromas on to a neat finish.

Other wines: Carte d'Or, Rosé, Exception, Cuvée III.

PUISIEULX

It's a mystery that this village could become a member of the Grand cru club. Puisieulx has long ridden on the back of Sillery's reputation, and Sillery in turn has gained fame from grapes grown in Verzenay. With its 18 hectares, Puisieulx (so hard to pronounce!) is by far the smallest Grand cru village. It lies east of Reims, on the slope north of Montagne de Reims, and the vines grow in an unusually gravel-rich soil that doesn't contain much chalk. Most of the cultivated area is owned by Moët and there are no producers among the 300 inhabitants of the village. Puisieulx is perhaps the best example of the unfairness of Champagne's cru system.

% 100% 60% PN, 9% PM, 31% CH

SILLERY

Earlier on in this book I wrote about the Marquis de Sillery who made famous wines way back in the 16th century. As all the Marquis' wines were sold under the name of Sillery the village held an undeservedly good reputation which should instead have gone to Verzenay. The vineyards of Sillery lie on the frost-sensitive flat ground north of Montagne de Reims and today cover an area of 94 hectares. The wine-growing conditions are definitely not the best, but many of the biggest firms own land in the village. you should be aware that many of the major firms' cuvée de prestige contain grapes from the less good Grand cru villages, which makes it possible for them to claim that the wine is made from Grand cru grapes only.

Considering the steadily increasing amounts that are made of certain famous superbubblies these days, one can with some justification suspect that the proportion of basic Grand cru wines has increased in recent years. Ruinart are proud that their *Dom Ruinart Blanc de Blancs* contain a large proportion of Chardonnay grapes from Sillery, but otherwise the village is best known for its Pinot Noir. Normally Sillery's wines are unconcentrated and characterless, but a taste of Lanson's Sillery wine stored in oak barrels at another champagne house has made me realise that there is first-class Pinot Noir in Sillery.

% 100% 48% PN, 8% PM, 44% CH

François Secondé

6 rue des Galipes, 51500 Sillery ☎ 03 26 49 16 67

Production: 30,000 bottles.

François Secondé is the uncrowned king of Sillery. From his four hectares he makes first-class wines with a wonderful cru character.

François Secondé Brut 66
(80% PN, 20% CH)
Definitely one for storing. When really young the nose is candy-like and full of basic fruit aromas that resemble banana and pear. The flavour is concentrated and long with a lingering tone of leather and wood.

François Secondé Demi-Sec 40
(80% PN, 20% CH)
A good basic wine has been injected with so much sugar that I personally have trouble appreciating the taste. The nose is pure and elegant though.

François Secondé Rosé 81
(80% PN, 20% CH)
What a pleasant surprise! Personal and classical simultaneously. A deep, thought-provoking nose with aromas of truffles, leather, blackberry and caramel. A smooth, creamy elegant flavour in which a tone of strawberry in the finish provides sensual satisfaction.

1992 François Secondé B. d. B. 80 (Mar 96) 83
(100% CH)
An exciting wine where the village character provides fullness and leather aromas and the grapes contribute with an exotic fruitiness.

François Secondé Intégral 79
(80% PN, 20% CH)
First a sauternes-like, fiery nose that turns into a collected whole, with elements of leather. The flavour too is tight and concentrated.

TOURS-SUR-MARNE

Tours-sur-Marne has a special place in my heart after my numerous visits to the charming hotel La Touraine Champenoise. The village is just the right size and holds much of the elements that make up Champagne's soul; the Marne river, vineyards, growers and two famous champagne houses. The atmosphere in the village is always relaxed and open, but the grapes from here aren't much to write home about. The best southerly slopes give a wine which resembles that from the outskirts of Bouzy. The aromas can be perfumed and fruity in a basic way, and while the structure is often correct it's not as well-built as one can demand of a Grand cru. It should be noted that the village's Chardonnay grapes don't have Grand cru status.

% 100% PN, 90% CH   60% PN, 40% CH

Laurent-Perrier

32 av. de Champagne,
51150 Tours-sur-Marne   03 26 58 91 22
Production: 7.5 million bottles.

L.P. is the biggest success story since the second World War. The family firm was on the verge of going under in the early fifties but now is among the largest and most respected companies in all of Champagne. The house was founded by Monsieur Laurent, a cooper from Chigny-les-Roses. His son married Mathilde Perrier, a stubbornly ambitious woman who really established the house. The first World War strained the house's chances of survival to the limit, as several of the appointed heirs were killed. Marie-Louise de Nonancourt bought the firm just as World War II broke out, and her son, whom she had prepared to run the company, was killed in that war. Her other son, Bernard, survived despite a leading role in the Resistance and later returned home to take over the business. This genius of a businessman, Bernard de Nonancourt, set out to capture new export markets. He began in West Africa and supplied his agents with fresh, recently-disgorged champagne that would cope with the tropical heat. Back home he specialised in coteaux champenois, an area in which the house is leader on the white wine side.

Today L.P. is part of a holding company which, besides the champagne houses Salon, Delamotte, J-P Lemoine and De Castellane, controls several other famous wine producers in France. L.P. themselves own only 105 hectares but have contracts with growers covering around 800. The firm is known for its clinically clean plants where oxidation is avoided at all costs. Alain Terrier is the company's head oenologist, a man who is widely praised for his fruity and elegant cuvées. I've never read a negative word about L.P., who have succeeded in creating a house style that suits almost everybody. But that's just what I have against them. For me, L.P.'s champagnes are too contrived and neutral: they are always correct but rarely exciting. Besides, personally I've always had a problem with the unmistakable undertone of amaretto. ***Grand Siècle*** is fabulous though.

L.P. Brut 54
(40% PN, 15% PM, 45% CH)
My friends love to serve this champagne for me blind. So far I've always been able to pinpoint it thanks to the amaretto aroma. Otherwise it's well-made with a good structure and fruit.

L.P. Crémant Brut 59
(33% PN, 33% PM, 34% CH)
Somewhat more exciting than the normal non-vintage champagne, with a hint of chocolate in the nose.

L.P. Ultra Brut 75
(45% PN, 55% CH)
L.P. are pioneers of the completely dry champagne. The wine needs several years aging in the bottle in order to round off a certain harshness and develop its chocolate bouquet.

L.P. Rosé Brut 80
(100% PN)
Skin contact and 100% Pinot grapes together make a successful receipe for rosé. A light colour and a nose which is hard to describe and could only come from a major house. Complexity and finesse but no personality. The mineral-rich flavour is relatively long and pure.

1988 L.P. 82 (Jan 99) 86
(47% PN, 53% CH)
L.P. produce relatively little vintage champagne and the wine follows the house style more than the year. Often the vintage wine is like a slightly richer version of the non-vintage champagne.

1985 L.P. 80 (Nov 94) 87
(50% PN, 50% CH)
The aromas follow the firm's usual pattern, but the concentration and extra richness are very high, which paves the way for a great future. The nose has elements of mint, apples and cinnamon. The flavour is pleasant and harmonious.

1982 L.P. 76 (Jul 93) 82
(60% PN, 40% CH)
An impersonal and surprisingly thin '82. Correct but tame and a trifle toasty.

1979 L.P. 89 (Oct 98) 89
(75% PN, 25% CH)
This vintage almost never disappoints me. L.P.'s contribution isn't one of the stars that shine the brightest, but the champagne is at its peak right now, with a lovely typically-vintage nose of nuts, honey and honeysuckle. The flavour is toffee-like and fresh at the same time.

1978 L.P. 83 (Sep 97) 83
(75% PN, 25% CH)
A mighty wine with low acidity, chocolate aromas and an excess of amaretto flavour.

1976 L.P. 84 (Jan 97) ▼
(75% PN, 25% CH)
Well rounded and smooth, with spicy vanilla, nutmeg and almonds. Flagging a little.

1975 L.P.
(75% PN, 25% CH)
Better kept bottles could still be good. Mine was maderised. Unjudged.

1964 L.P. 70 (Aug 95) ▼
(75% PN, 25% CH)
The '64 has one foot in the grave now but still manages to offer a certain pleasure in its chewy, exotic, fruity style.

1961 L.P. 86 (Aug 95) 86
(75% PN, 25% CH)
This champagne displays a harmonious oneness filled with chocolate, but there's a lack of freshness. The wine probably reached its peak in the early eighties.

1976 L.P. Millésimé Rare 92 (Jan 99) 92
(75% PN, 25% CH)
As the Raré wines are always disgorged after a very long time, they have grown in complexity. The autolytic character really helps this '76. The bread aromas from the yeast smooth out the almond tones in a positive fashion. Very toasty and charming in magnums.

1975 L.P. Millésimé Rare 86 (Dec 92) 89
(75% PN, 25% CH)
Just as with so many 75's, the nose is more developed than the flavour. Milk chocolate dominates the voluptuous bouquet. The excellent attack in the initial taste is of the highest class, but the wine needed a few more years before it developed length in the aftertaste.

1973 L.P. Millésimé Rare 88 (May 90) 88
(75% PN, 25% CH)
The nose is very similar to the '75, with milk chocolate playing the leading role. The flavour is softer and more homogenous. Smoke and earth cellar give character to the sweet, soft whole.

1969 L.P. Millésimé Rare 85 (Aug 93) ▼
(75% PN, 25% CH)
Sadly it's already going downhill! Towards the end of the eighties I gave this wine very high marks, but a couple of years ago maderisation began to creep up on it.

1966 L.P. Millésimé Rare
(75% PN, 25% CH)
L.P. hasn't got a good reputation for making wines for the cellar, and this '66 rather makes that point. Slightly unclear and dull colour with a weak mousse. A broad nose of peas and green peppers which tells tales about the Pinot from '66. The flavour is full and earthy without a trace of maderisation. Unjudged.

1959 L.P. Millésimé Rare
(75% PN, 25% CH)
Once a famous champagne. Today flat and grubby. Unjudged. Should still be lovely direct from the cellar.

Grand Siècle 92
(45% PN, 55% CH)
L.P.'s flagship is made from three vintages which have been stored since blending in the firm's cellar with real corks. This luxurious champagne was first introduced in 1957, and if you have the patience then keep the wine for four or five years, so that you can experience the wonderful vanilla flavour that G.S. develops with time. The mousse is worth a chapter in itself - no other champagne has a more delicate mousse than G.S. The refined and balanced fruit aromas harmonise perfectly with each other, together with a tone of newly-washed sheets.

1990 Grand Siècle 93 (Sep 97) 95
(58% PN, 42% CH)
Wonderfully rich and pure, classically constructed with fantastic elegance. It contains a little extra touch of everything that's found in the non-vintage version.

1988 Grand Siècle 90 (Mar 97) 93
(48% PN, 52% CH)
It seems as if L.P. has given in to pressure and abandoned its conviction regarding the superiority of non-vintage wines. The one-time-only event ***1985 Grand Siècle*** was immediately followed up by the '88. This is a great and aristocratic champagne which should stay in the bottle for a couple more years if it is to do itself justice. The presence of Pinot weighs heavier than in the cuvée.

1985 Grand Siècle 91 (Mar 97) 93
(58% PN, 42% CH)
On the American market G.S. is always a vintage champagne, and in Europe this '85 is the first example. The wine is very much like the non-vintage version with flowers and vanilla as its leading tones. However, there is a greater weight in the '85 which promises well for the future.

1985 Grand Siècle Alexandra Rosé 90 (Oct 97) 92
(80% PN, 20% CH)
A lovely orange fruity and toasty rosé champagne which would grace the finest dinner tables. The colour is appetisingly light and the flavour delightfully sophisticated. This elegant champagne is very like its white sister.

1982 Grand Siècle Alexandra Rosé 82 (Mar 93) 88
(80% PN, 20% CH)
An extremely elegant and delicate prestige rosé which does however lack impact and weight at its base. The wine feels so shy that one wonders if it will ever open up its flowerbud into full bloom.

1975 Laurent-Perrier Wedding Cuvée B. d. B.
(100% CH) 94 (May 97) 94
L.P. joined Veuve Clicquot in making a special cuvée for the wedding of Prince Charles and Lady Diana in 1981. The nose, full of clean sheets and a polished big house style, is clear if a touch shy. The flavour is a firework display of fruit with a delayed action in the mouth. Marvellous!

Chauvet

41 av. de Champagne,
51150 Tours-sur-Marne 03 26 58 92 37
Production: 80,000 bottles.

The company was started in 1848 by Constant Harlin, who at the time used grapes from Bouzy. Later on he bought the Croix Saint Jacques domain in Tours-sur-Marne which had belonged to the Archbishop of Reims, and today the house and wine plant are run by the Chauvet family. The name of Chauvet came from Harlin's nephew Auguste, who successfuly marketed the wines in Paris. In 1946 his daughter Jeanine Chauvet took over, and together with her husband Jean she keeps a loving eye on their two sons Arnaud and Jean-François as they run operations.

Stepping into the family's living room is like moving back in time one hundred years. The walls are filled with stuffed animals, with everything from herons to wild boars. As the family Chauvet collect antique champagne glasses, all the drinks are served in different kinds of glass. Madame Chauvet was very disappointed when I asked to use the same glass to all the champagnes. She also had problems understanding my request for a spitoon at ten o'clock in the morning. She maintains that a little champagne before lunch every day prolongs life, and when you see this incredibly well-kept, stylish, elderly lady you may ask yourself if she may have a point. The firm owns many fine vineyards with an average Cru status of 98%. Four hectares in Bouzy, Ambonnay and Verzenay, and five in Bisseuil. Despite its tiny size, this company has a big reputation, and I too am delighted by its charming and personal wines. Those of you who believe that Frenchmen are boring and introverted should pay a visit to the house of Chauvet.

Chauvet Brut 75
(65% PN, 35% CH)
Chiefly made from Bisseuil grapes. A very nice non-vintage champagne with a nose of red apples and biscuits. Easy to drink and pleasant.

Chauvet B. d. B. 79
(100% CH)
50% Mesnil, 40% Bisseuil and 10% Verzenay. An elusive nose of wettened stones, backed up by toasted bread. The flavour is medium-bodied and dominated at first by grapefruit, before it is finished by a stony, hard and undeveloped tone from Verzenay.

Chauvet Grand Rosé 80
(15% PN, 85% CH)
Still a crémant champagne, although the term is tragically banned today. This is truly a great rosé, despite the high proportion of Chardonnay. The colour is salmon pink, the nose contains all the fruits of the summer and the flavour is an unmistakable buttery Chardonnay.

1985 Chauvet 79 (May 95) 84
(15% PN, 85% CH)
Unusally this wine is dominated by Chardonnay from Verzenay. A great personality with a faintly cheesy nose. The flavour will probably be integrated in a few years' time, but today the Verzenay wine is undeveloped and hard. The aftertaste promises good things with its wealth of minerals.

Lamiable

8 rue de Conde,
51150 Tours-sur-Marne 03 26 58 92 69

Production: 70,000 bottles.

The house was founded in 1950 by Pierre Lamiable and is one of the few in Tours-sur-Marne. 5% of the grapes are bought in and the rest come from the company's six hectares.

Lamiable Grand Cru Brut 75
(75% PN, 25% CH)
Caramel, toast and hawthorn are pleasing elements in the nose. The wine is a little too hollow and short, but enjoyable all the same.

Lamiable Demi-Sec 49
(75% PN, 25% CH)
Clean, frothy and rather elegant dessert champagne.

1988 Lamiable Special Club 80 (May 96) 87
(50% PN, 50% CH)
Creamy and buttery like so many *Special Club* champagnes from various villages. The finish is a little short and diluted, however. Otherwise a fine and elegant champagne rich in minerals.

Other wines: Extra Brut, Vintage, Rosé.

Yves Delporte

12 rue de la Haie du Bois,
51150 Tours-sur-Marne 03 26 58 91 26

Production: 56,000 bottles.

This grower makes loose and rustic wines from three fine villages; Tours-sur-Marne, Bisseuil and Bouzy. The average age of the wines is only 15 years.

Yves Delporte B. d. B. 46
(100% CH)
On paper this is an exciting blend from Bisseuil and Tours-sur-Marne. However, in reality it's a painfully loose effort with a banana aroma.

Yves Delporte Demi-Sec 23
Just look at the marks!

Yves Delporte Rosé 30
Artficial colour and flavour. Eggnog in the nose.

Other wines: Brut, Vintage.

VERZENAY

Puisieulx, Sillery and Beaumont-sur-Vesle have, as I mentioned earlier, received their Grand cru status thanks to their proximity to Verzenay. From its 420 hectares the village produces the blackest grapes in all Champagne. It's one of the wine world's mysteries how northerly slopes from one of the world's northernmost wine villages can produce such rich, peppery and masculine Pinot wines.

Most of the village's so-called northern locations are actually north-easterly and are exposed to the sun's rays for a greater part of the day. Just as in Mailly, the vineyards are warmed by a local hot airstream. Some of the village's most famous vineyards are owned by Bollinger, Mumm, Roederer and Heidsieck & Monopole and lie directly under the historic mill of Moulin de Verzenay. Even the Chardonnay grapes that are grown in the village have had Grand cru status since 1972. Unfortunately more and more growers make blended champagnes instead of concentrating on what they're best at, namely Pinot Noir! Jean-Paul Morel even makes a blanc de blancs from the village. As a Pinot village Verzenay is definitely the star of Montagne-de-Reims. Perhaps the wines from the village don't have the soft aromatic richness of Aÿ's champagnes, but they contain a greater weight with age and are vital as the backbone for major cuvées such as *Bollinger R.D.* and *Roederer Cristal*. The perfume that pure Verzenay champagnes have is very strong and unique. Tones of iron and pepper are mixed with the grape aroma itself. The aftertaste is hard, tough for many years before it softens out to its conclusion. Vin clair from Bollinger and Krug are majestic.

% 100% 90% PN, 10% CH

Bernard Hatté

1 rue de la Petit Fontaine,
51360 Verzenay 03 26 49 40 90

Production: 40,000 bottles.

Bernard Hatté is definitely one of Champagne's best growers. Sadly the Hatté family have recently been influenced by their oenologist, who prefers lighter champagnes with a higher Chardonnay content, vinified in sterile conditions in stainless steel vats. Hatté was one of the last growers in the village to use oak barrels, but on the advice of the oenologist they were replaced by steel tanks after the harvest of 1985. Hatté has the lowest yield in the village and makes storable wines with biting acidity and a youthful harshness.

B. Hatté Brut 73
(70% PN, 30% CH)
A breakfast wine. A nose of apple sauce, cornflakes and toasted bread. Good attack and purity with a recurrent apple aroma in the flavour.

B. Hatté Carte d'Or 75
(50% PN, 30% PM, 20% CH)
The apple aroma is obvious in all the firm's wines but the maturity is clearer here than in the *Réserve*.

B. Hatté Réserve 74
(50% PN, 30% PM, 20% CH)
A pleasing nose of dried fruit and caramel. The flavour is identical to the *Carte d'Or*.

B. Hatté Rosé 84
(100% PN)
It's always exciting to see how this rosé stands against the best Aÿ rosés. The nose is almost burgundy-like, with plums, raspberries and strawberries. The flavour is a little less generous, with green apples and licorice all-sorts that sneak in among the red fruits. One of my fiancée's favourite champagnes.

1990 B. Hatté Special Club 90 (Jan 99) 93
(50% PN, 50% CH)
Full-bodied, distinctly fishy and fruity. Magnificent acidity.

1989 B. Hatté Special Club 87 (Jun 97) 90
(50% PN, 50% CH)
Unfortunately far too much Chardonnay these days, but even so a very fine wine with a nose of minerals and initially a fat, round flavour that has a young, harsh and peppery finish.

1988 B. Hatté Special Club 75 (Jun 93) 90
(40% PN, 60% CH)
Light colour, exemplary mousse and closed nose. Very long undeveloped flavour with a slightly sour extract. Down in the cellar for ten years at least!

1985 B. Hatté Special Club 90 (Mar 93) 94
(100% PN)
The last vintage using oak barrels and exclusively Pinot Noir. A "Rambo champagne" which is almost chewable in its wealth of extracts. Dark colour, a hugely broad nose of cellars, nutcake and bitter chocolate. The champagne feels almost like a red wine with its tannic finish and corpulent structure. One of the most powerful champagne I've ever tasted. An almost indestructible wine which can be stored for decades.

Michel Arnould

28 rue de Mailly, 51360 Verzenay ☎ 03 26 49 40 06
Production: 80,000 bottles.

Patrick Arnould is on to something big. He sold grapes to Bollinger but today he keeps the best ones for his own champagnes. He exchanges grapes with Bonnaire in Cramant and will soon be making vintage wines of the highest class. He and his father Michel control twelve hectares of some of the blackest grapes Champagne can raise. The house style is highly sophisticated with unexpected elegance considering its origins.

M. Arnould Brut 70
(100% PN)
A creamy, easily-drunk champagne with a flavour of cream and ripe apples.

M. Arnould Cuvée Réserve 72
(67% PN, 33% CH)
Somewhat sharper and deeper than the above, but with the same tasteful, sophisticated style.

M. Arnould Cuvée Prestige 79
(100% PN)
One is met by a heavy nose of apple and cinnamon. The flavour is medium-bodied with a delicate honeyed aftertaste.

M. Arnould Rosé 70
(100% PN)
The same wine as *Brut* with 10% still red wine from the village added. The nose is a little more basic but the flavour is even more vinous.

M. Arnould Carte d'Or 84
(50% PN, 50% CH)
Patrick's pride and joy, but half of the wine comes from Bonnaire in Cramant. A voluptuous wine with a sensual, soft nose and caressing flavour. Actually a pure '85.

Jean-Paul Morel

14 rue Chanzy, 51360 Verzenay ☎ 03 26 49 48 01
Production: 70,000 bottles.

This grower runs the production at Langradin along with his own champagne.

J-P Morel Rosé 72
(100% PN)
A dark, red colour and slightly rough mousse, but lovely vinous tones in both nose and flavour. The wine has a piquant spiciness combined with a genuine fruit.

J-P Morel Brut Sélection 77
(80% PN, 20% CH)
A young cuvée de prestige which is a blend of two vintages. Rather light, but already there's plenty of cream and honey in the nose and the wine combines power with elegance in an exceedingly good way.

J-P Morel B. d. B. de Verzenay 74
(100% CH)
A rarity! A very exciting personality where the cru character takes control over the type of grape. Good attack and sharpness with a hard finish. Leave it in the cellar for a while and the mark will rise much higher than I've noted here.

Jean-Claude Mouzon

4 rue des Perthois, 51360 Verzenay ☎ 03 26 49 48 11
Production: 11,000 bottles.

Jean-Claude Mouzon owns 3.5 hectares in Verzenay and sells a great deal of his wine to Moët & Chandon.

Jean-Claude Mouzon Brut 68
(68% PN, 7% PM, 25% CH)
Rich and well-structured with fine vinosity and pleasing apricot aromas. Round, fine finish.

Jean-Claude Mouzon Tradition 69
(68% PN, 7% PM, 25% CH)
Fishy and rooty Pinot nose. Bready aromas dominating the initial palate. Good contrast between fullness of flavour and elegance of style.

Jean-Claude Mouzon Réserve 73
(68% PN, 7% PM, 25% CH)
Firm, lasting and mature. Strong rooty Pinot flavour and a soft finish.

Jean-Claude Mouzon Rosé 80
(80% PN, 7% PM, 13% CH)
What a charmer! Relatively light colour, an appetising nose of mango, strawberry, leather, smoke and stable. Sweet, rounded flavour with plenty of vigour and tones of passion fruit.

Jean-Claude Mouzon Cuvée Fleurie 83
(100% CH)
A rarity - a B. d. B. from Verzenay. A good, fresh champagne with a flowery, perfumed nose of gooseberry and melon. Unexpectedly light flavour and a fruit like nectar.

Jean-Claude Mouzon Grand Cru Verzenay 83
(65% PN, 35% CH)
Surprisingly light and flowery with citrus tones and a faint subtone of banana and flour. Otherwise very easy to drink and tasty.

Landragin

14 rue Chanzy, 51360 Verzenay ☎ 03 26 49 48 01

The Landragin family have been growers here in Verzenay since 1772, and they sold their first-class grapes to the major houses for many years. At the end of the sixties Dominique Langradin decided to make a champagne of his own from his 25 hectares in Verzenay, Sillery, Beaumont-sur-Vesle and Tauxières. The champagne has been made by J-P Morel for the last few years as Landragin himself lives now in Australia, which makes the firm's future extremely uncertain.

Landragin Brut 70
(80% PN, 20% CH)
A pure and clear champagne with a full and rich Pinot character.

Jacques Busin

33 rue Thiers, 51360 Verzenay ☎ 03 26 49 40 36
Production: 100,000 bottles.

A grower who is always much appreciated in French wine guides.

J. Busin Brut Réserve 50
(75% PN, 25% CH)
A very special, spicy hawthorn nose. Despite good acidity and attack I was disturbed by tones of wet wool and potatoes. More unusual than good.

1988 J. Busin 81 (Aug 94) 83
(90% PN, 10% CH)
A strong nose of tequila and burnt sugar. The flavour is very rich, with a compact fat structure and burnt, buttery aromas. Where is the acidity?

Other wines: Carte d'Or, Rosé.

Ludvic Hatté

8 rue Thiers, 51360 Verzenay ☎ 03 26 49 43 94

One of many Hattés in Verzenay. Unfortunately he's following the village trend of using more and more Chardonnay.

1990 Ludvic Hatté 69 (Apr 95) 76
(60% PN, 40% CH)
A creamy champagne that reflects the vintage more than the village character.

Quenardel

Pl. de la Mairie, 51360 Verzenay ☎ 03 26 49 40 63

Quenardel Brut 50
(100% PN)
Dark colour, broad bouquet with spicy elements and a rough taste of aniseed.

Quenardel Rosé 69
(100% PN)
With a more reasonable dosage this rosé would reach greater heights. A faint, gamey Pinot nose where the grapes' fruitiness is more noticeable in the full-bodied flavour.

1985 Quenardel 69 (Jul 91) 83
(100% PN)
Copper colour and indelicately perfumed nose with elements of banana. The concentrated flavour lies in wait with a surprise. Iron and blood are definable tones in the aftertaste.

Michel Henriet

12 rue du Paradis, 51360 Verzenay ☎ 03 26 49 40 42
Production: 30,000 bottles.

The grower owns three hectares in Verzenay and uses modern methods.

1989 Michel Henriet Carte d'Or 76 (Jul 97) 82
(100% PN)
B. d. N. from Verzenay. The colour is so red that it could easily be mistaken for a rosé. The nose has hints of almonds and heavy fruit. The initial flavour is definitely promising but the overall impression is spoiled a little by the lack of finesse.

Other wines: B. d. B., Grande Réserve.

Hugues Godmé

10 rue de Verzy, 51360 Verzenay ☎ 03 26 49 48 70

H. Godmé Brut 25
(100% PN)
A meaty and flat champagne of the very worst kind.

1986 H. Godmé 60 (Jul 92) 69
(100% PN)
The vintage wine was also loose and lacking in acidity. There was however a heavy grape character and a rich candy flavour.

Bovière-Perinet

18 rue Chanzy, 51360 Verzenay ☎ 03 26 49 80 96
Production: 12,000 bottles.

This grower owns three hectares in Verzenay, all of which are planted with Pinot Noir.

Bouvière-Perinet Rosé 66
(100% PN)
A one-track champagne from Verzenay with dark colour, a strong, slightly rough nose and round, sweet flavour. The finish is a touch bitter.

Other wines: Brut, Réserve, Cuvée Spéciale.

Guy Thibaut

7 rue des Perthois, 51360 Verzenay ☎ 03 26 49 41 95
Production: 15,000 bottles.

Claude and Gerard Thibaut own 1.7 hectares in this wonderful Grand cru village. Although the production is small, it's perfectly formed.

Guy Thibaut Brut 63
(80% PN, 20% CH)
There's something gauche about this Verzenay champagne. Elegance and finesse have given way to power and weight.

Other wines: Réserve, Demi-sec.

Godmé Père & Fils

11 rue Werle, 51360 Verzenay ☎ 03 26 49 41 88

Production: 90,000 bottles.

Hugues Godmé's grandfather began the business in 1935, and today Hugues owns ten hectares in Verzenay.

Godmé Brut Réserve 71
(100% PN)
Very light and elegant, considering its origins. A pure apricot tone in the nose gives this refreshing wine a piquant finesse.

Other wines: Rosé, B. d. B., Seduction, Vintage, Extra Brut.

VERZY

The soil in Verzy is Belimnite chalk and two kinds of Micraster chalk. Verzy's cultivations lie alongside the famous vineyards in Verzenay on the north side of Montagne de Reims. The best exposure hits the easterly slopes at a height of 150-200 metres above sea level. Once upon a time Verzy was in fact a Chardonnay village, but nowadays the village is known for its peppery and masculine Pinot wines. Together with Verzenay the black grapes from here supply a strong backbone for the finest cuvées in Champagne. There is often a hint of stones and gunpowder smoke in the aftertaste, just as in Verzenay. The 800,000 bottles that the village produces annually come from 405 hectares. I've tasted some wonderfully well-structured still Verzy wines from Bollinger and Jacquesson, but the most astonishing was a delicious vin clair from Krug which literally exploded in the mouth.

% 100%  80% PN, 20% CH

Ph. Mouzon-Leroux

16 rue Basse des Carrieres,
51380 Verzy ☎ 03 26 97 96 68

Production: 80,000 bottles.

All the wines from Mouzon-Leroux are pure Grand cru champagnes from Verzy.

Ph. Mouzon-Leroux Grande Réserve 61
(70% PN, 30% CH)
Good purity and power, but sadly a little hard and a bitter finish.

Cuvée Mouzon-Juillet 89
(70% PN, 30% CH)
A pure '89 made in oak barrels. This cuvée de prestige is the best I've tasted from Verzy. It's heavy, smoky and nutty with impressive concentration and potential. The ugliest bottle in the history of wine!

Mouzon-Leroux Rosé 69
(100% PN)
A very good rosé that feels a little unripe when recently-disgorged, but which will react well to time in the bottle.

Other wines: Prestige, Demi-sec.

Etienne Lefèvre

Rue de Verzenay, 51380 Verzy ☎ 03 26 97 96 99

Production: 30,000 bottles.

A spontaneous visit took me to the door of this skilful winemaker in Verzy. He sells well-made, mature champagnes at low prices, and if you follow the "Champagne route" it's easy to pop in to a tasting and an uplifting chat with the Lefèvre family.

E. Lefèvre Brut 67
(80% PN, 20% CH)
Mature, nourishing nose and a tight, one-dimensional and long flavour.

E. Lefèvre Demi-Sec 46
(80% PN, 20% CH)
Clean bouquet, very perfumed flavour. Rather well-balanced.

E. Lefèvre Réserve 70
(80% PN, 20% CH)
Nice bouquet of coffee beans. Ripe, clean and dry on the palate.

1985 E. Lefèvre 75 (Jul 92) 85
(80% PN, 20% CH)
Lefèvre makes vintage wines only in very good years, with equal amounts of Verzy and Verzenay. The nose is a bit basic, with a splash of caramel in the musty apple aroma. The flavour is far more fascinating and homogenous, with an oily structure and the aroma of pistachio nuts.

Other wines: Rosé.

Fresnet-Juillet

10 rue de Beaumont, 51380 Verzy ☎ 03 26 97 93 40

Production: 75,000 bottles.

The firm was started in 1954 by Gerard Fresnet, once the Mayor of Verzy. The vineyards cover nine hectares in Mailly and Verzy, planted with 75% PN and 25% CH.

Fresnet-Juillet Brut 55
(80% PN, 20% CH)
A reddish nuance in the colour and large bubbles scare many tasters off. The nose follows the same rough pattern, but the flavour isn't as abrupt. There is a delicious fruit which makes one think of cherries and plums.

Fresnet-Juillet Rosé 51
(50% PN, 50% CH)
The firm has chosen to present a rosé with 50% Chardonnay grapes, which results in a slightly thinner champagne than one expects from this part of Montagne de Reims.

Other wines: B. d. B., Special Club.

Louis de Sacy

6 rue de Verzenay, 51380 Verzy 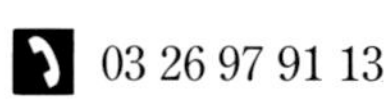 03 26 97 91 13

Production: 240,000 bottles.

When you arrive in the beautiful village of Verzy the overall impression is disrupted by a block of concrete with the giant letters S.A.C.Y. on the wall. The contrast between the ancient Faux de Verzy and this modern complex is marked, to say the least. Sacy is a fast-growing house that owns land in five highly-ranked villages. Only a small amount of Chardonnay is bought in to satisfy the company's grape needs. The Sacy family has a background in wine as far back as the 17th century, but only received house status in 1968. Today the firm goes in for constant new investment, which has yet to show results in the quality of the product.

Louis de Sacy Brut 47
(40% PN, 20% PM, 40% CH)
A remarkable closed nose for such a well-developed, chocolaty and slightly oxidated flavour. The acidity is low and the wine lacks that vital skeleton on which to hang.

Louis de Sacy Rosé 50
(80% PN, 20% PM)
A robust food rosé with a medical element in parallel with tones of boiled vegetables in both nose and mouth.

1983 Louis de Sacy 70 (May 94) 
(30% PN, 30% PM, 40% CH)
Deep, mature colour. The initial nose is rich and promising, but quite soon the wine will collapse and the vegetable aspect will take over. Honey and candy are buried by an earthiness in the full but short flavour.

Other wines: Grand Soir.

Other producers in the Grand cru villages:

Ambonnay

Bernard Brémont 03 26 51 01 65
Serge Demière 03 26 57 07 79
Claude Fauvet 03 26 57 00 39
J. Hulin 03 26 57 01 97
Gérard Payelle 03 26 57 02 57
J-P Pérard 03 26 57 00 96
Roger Croizy 03 26 57 01 52
Robert Fourer 03 26 57 02 68
Roger Gauthier 03 26 57 01 94
Michel Ledru 03 26 57 00 71
Michel Huguet 03 26 57 01 45
C. Millot 03 26 57 07 25
Michel Rodez 03 26 57 00 27
Georges Simon 03 26 57 00 59
Jean Varlot 03 26 57 00 65
Gaston Warin 03 26 57 01 29

Avize

Chapier-Chabonat 03 26 57 51 67
Deregard-Massing 03 26 57 52 92
Gérard Lebrun-Cervenay 03 26 57 52 75
Paveau 03 26 57 93 87
Petit & Fils 03 26 57 51 63

Aÿ

Gabriel Collin 03 26 55 49 04
Julien Massing 03 26 55 20 37
Pierre Leboeuf 03 26 55 21 58
Jean Pol Roger 03 26 54 68 66

Beaumont-sur-Vesle

Virgile Portier 03 26 03 90 15
Maurice Vautier 03 26 03 90 63
Pierre Vautier 03 26 03 90 62

Bouzy

Rémy Galichet 03 26 57 02 94
Pierre Hulin 03 26 57 01 37
Serge Lahaye 03 26 57 00 38
Bernard Ledru 03 26 57 00 04
J.F. Pléner 03 26 57 00 21
E Rémy 03 26 57 08 98

Chouilly

Roland Champion 03 26 55 40 30
David Legras 03 26 54 97 77
C. Gue 03 26 54 50 32
J-J Legras 03 26 55 41 71
Moineaux 03 26 55 40 99
Michel Pouillard 03 26 54 58 58
Voirin-Desmoulins 03 26 54 50 30

Cramant

J-N Crépaux 03 26 57 56 38
Guy Lesage 03 26 57 95 58
C. Petitjean 03 26 57 51 19
Richomme 03 26 57 52 93
Michel Simon 03 26 57 57 37
Coop. de Cramant 03 26 57 50 72

Louvois

André Boever 03 26 57 03 43
Pierre Boever 03 26 57 04 06
Eric Bunel 03 26 57 03 06
Serge Faye 03 26 57 81 66
Cuvelier Pierson 03 26 57 00 75

Mailly

A-M. Barbier	03 26 49 41 34
Bernard Gentil	03 26 49 43 33
Lucien Roguet	03 26 49 41 36
J-P Secondé	03 26 49 44 57
Coop. les Clos	03 26 49 41 47

Le Mesnil-sur-Oger

J-B Pattin	03 26 57 92 30
Michel Rocourt	03 26 57 54 14

Oger

Descotes-Lemaire	03 26 57 53 61
Bernard Dzieciuck	03 26 57 50 49
Coop.Les Côteaux Champ.	03 26 57 53 37
Coop.Les Grappes d´Or	03 26 57 55 79

Verzenay

Pierre Arnould	03 26 49 40 12
Marc Henriet	03 26 49 41 79
Henri Lefèvre	03 26 49 40 18
J-M Namur	03 26 49 40 56
J-M Penet	03 26 49 40 71
G. Rousseaux	03 26 49 40 78
Rousseaux-Pecourt	03 26 49 42 73
Coop. de Verzenay	03 26 49 40 26

Verzy

Cuperly	03 26 70 23 90
J-P Deville	03 26 97 93 50
Pierre Deville	03 26 97 91 75
J-M Faucheron	03 26 97 96 53
J. Hanotin	03 26 97 93 63
Alain Hurier	03 26 97 93 60
Hurier-Jouette	03 26 97 90 87
Pierre Lallement	03 26 97 91 09
J-P Lepreux	03 26 97 95 52
Renoir-Bouy	03 26 97 90 55
Coop. de Verzy	03 26 97 95 12

Premier cru villages

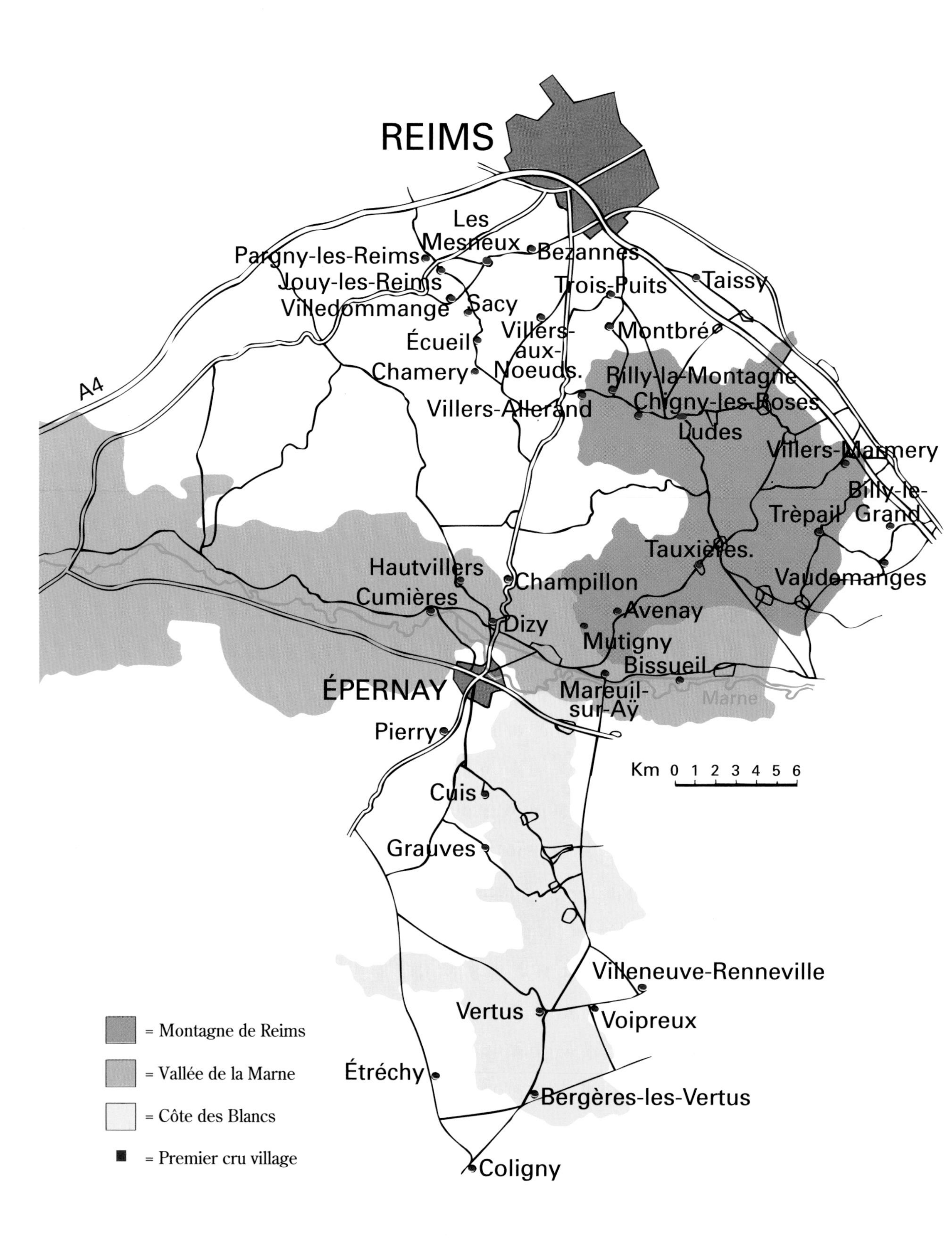

AVENAY

Like many other villages in the Marne valley, the name can be traced to its location in relation to Aÿ. The quality is a very high Premier cru level, particularly a strip of vineyards at a height of between 140 and 180 metres above sea level. The similarities with the round, velvet-smooth Aÿ wines are striking, and this is an important village for the likes of Bollinger, Gosset, Mumm, Henriot, Philipponnat and Pommery.

% 93% 73% PN, 15% PM, 12% CH

Ricciuti-Révolte

18 rue du Lieutenant
de Vaisseau Paris, 51160 Avenay 03 26 52 30 27

Production: 20,000 bottles.

Ricciuti-Révolte is probably the only American grower in Champagne. His grapes come from 3.5 hectares in Avenay and one hectare in Mareuil-sur-Aÿ, and he sells 25% percent of them to Mumm.

Ricciuti-Révolte Brut 70
Always a full, well-made and mature non-vintage champagne with classic breadiness. Soft, uncomplicated Pinot fruit.

Ricciuti-Révolte Brut Rosé 60
A deep red rosé with strawberry aromas in the nose. Unfortunately the full flavour is a touch earthy and unbalanced.

BERGÈRES-LES-VERTUS

This village lies on the southern tip of Côte des Blancs. Just as in Vertus, some of the soil is too rich and fertile, giving wines that are slightly rougher and fruitier. An unexpectedly high proportion of Pinot Noir (5%) is grown here, again as in Vertus. The village lacks well-known producers but the grapes are used by several respected champagne houses.

% 95% CH, 90% PN 5% PN, 95% CH

Robert Adnot

51130 Bergères-les-Vertus 03 26 52 16 57

Robert Adnot B. d. B. 64
(100% CH)
As expected the nose is generous and lacks elegance. Well-made and value for money.

1970 Robert Adnot B. d. B. 79 (Jun 97) 82
(100% CH)
Broad, smoky and mature nose with elements of petroleum. Rich, slightly rough flavour that still has its youth. Somewhat featureless.

Poirot

2 rue Pernet,
51130 Bergères-les-Vertus 03 26 52 02 26

Production: 15,000 bottles.

Alain Poirot is the name of the current owner, the third generation in a company that has existed since 1920. The firm owns three hectares in Bergères-les-Vertus.

Poirot Brut 62
(100% CH)
Light, soft and easy to drink. Aromas of pineapple and pear.

Other wines: B. d. B., Vintage, Tradition, Réserve, Demi-sec.

BEZANNES

A rather unknown village that lies two kilometres south-west of Reims. Only Chardonnay is cultivated in the village's mere twelve hectares, and it is sold to the champagne houses.

% 90% (upgraded 1985) 100% CH

BILLY-LE-GRAND

"Billy the Great" sounds more like a western hero than a Champagne village. Strangely enough, they grow mostly Chardonnay in this Montagne de Reims village. The wine produced here is said to be related to that from the reliable neighbour Vaudemanges. I myself have never tasted a pure champagne from Billy-le-Grand.

% 95% 25% PN, 75% CH

BISSEUIL

East of Mareuil-sur-Aÿ and Avenay lies Bisseuil, an unjustly forgotten village that resembles Hautvillers and Cumières more than the nearby Aÿ and Bouzy. The best way to get to know the rich, uncomplicated, fruity wines produced here is to try the champagnes of the Tours-sur-Marne house Chauvet. They contain a very high proportion of Pinot Noir from the best slopes in Bisseuil. Bollinger also owns vineyards here, as does Charbaut. Cask samples from Bollinger have shown that the acidity in grapes from Bisseuil are lower than those from neighbouring villages.

% 95% 80% PN, 20% CH

Bauchet

Rue de la Crayère, 51150 Bisseuil 03 26 58 92 12

Production: 300,000 bottles.

This relatively unknown property produces quite a healthy quantity of wine from its 37 hectares. The man at the helm is Laurent Bauchet.

Bauchet Brut Sélection 66
(50% PN, 50% CH)
A pale, clear colour and a refreshing nose of tangerine. The uncomplicated flavour is also playing a citrus tune.

Bauchet Brut Réserve 66
(40% PN, 60% CH)
More vinous than the *Sélection*, but still dominated by tangerine and caramel.

Bauchet Rosé 61
(10% PN, 90% CH)
Orange colour and a nose of blueberry, raspberry and woodland. Refreshing, slightly one-paced flavour.

Other wines: Vintage.

CHAMERY

Located to the west of the heart of Montagne de Reims. There aren't any good wines that are produced on this side of the N51 road. Quite simply, there isn't enough sunlight to create grapes so rich in extracts as those on the east side of the road. In 1985's reclassification Chamery was raised from 88% to 90%, and it's a sign of the great variety within Champagne that there are 41 producers in this relatively unknown village.

% 90% 35% PN, 45% PM, 20% CH

Gilbert Bertrand

5 ruelle des Godats, 51500 Chamery 03 26 97 64 57

Gilbert Bertrand Brut 50
A very basic elderflower Pinot Meunier nose. A powerful mousse and a somewhat flat, faintly earthy flavour.

Other wines: Rosé.

Michel Labbé

24 rue du Gluten, 51500 Chamery 03 26 97 65 89

Michel Labbé Rosé Brut 51
An impersonal but pure rosé champagne where everything is nice enough. Just about.

Other wines: Brut.

Bonnet-Ponson

10 rue du Sourd, 51500 Chamery 03 26 97 65 40

Production: 90,000 bottles.

Jules Bonnet controls ten hectares and buys in 5% from elsewhere. Like so many others these days, he's built a champagne museum on his property. Wines not tasted.

Wines: Brut, Vintage, Cuvée Spéciale, Rosé.

CHAMPILLON

The village is best known for the star restaurant "Royal Champagne". It lies on the top of a hill with all of Champillon's supremely beautiful vineyards below. During my hectic travels around the area I've been able to catch my breath on several occasions with a few friends and a bottle of champagne among the vines of Champillon. The panorama over Épernay and the flowing sea of vines has an almost meditative effect on me. Here, if anywhere, you can feel that you're a part of the greater whole. The vines are planted on a height of 120 metres above sea level right up to 250 metres. The grapes that grow here have a southerly to south-easterly exposure and are often among the first to ripen in all of Champagne. They are also of high Premier cru quality level. Sadly they continue to grow far too much Pinot Meunier here. The best locations are owned by Louis Roederer (PN), but Mercier and Oudinot also have vineyards here. Otherwise many companies buy grapes from the village's 44 growers.

% 93% 45% PN, 47% PM, 8% CH

Patrick Visneaux

4 rue Rommes, 51160 Champillon 03 26 59 47 83

Patrick Visneaux Brut 75
I found this grower quite by chance, as his name has never featured in any book that I've read. When you drink this full-blown champagne you wonder how many undiscovered treasures lie hidden in Champagne's top villages. When I tasted this wine blind for the first time I guessed at a vintage champagne from Bouzy. A medium-deep yellow colour, weak but fine mousse, sweet, volatile, flowery Moulin Touchais-like nose and a very long, complex vanilla flavour.

Autreau de Champillon

15 rue Renet Bandet,
51160 Champillon 03 26 59 46 00

Production: 150,000 bottles.

During the ten years that I have travelled around and visited producers in Champagne I have always been struck by the commitment the growers show to their wine. It is very rare that one gets an impression of carelessness or ignorance. Sadly I have to say that Autreau is an exception to that rule. Despite their impressive 21 hectares in Champillon, Aÿ, Dizy and Chouilly, in my opinion they produce sweet and unstructured champagnes.

Autreau Brut 40
(30% PN, 70% PM)
Deep, beautiful golden colour. Large bubbles that disappear quickly in the glass, a mouldy sweet bready nose, and a rich fruit taste of overripe lemons. It finishes ignominiously in the mouth - the dosage is much too high!

1988 Autreau 66 (May 94) 66
(66% PN, 34% CH)
All the Pinot comes from Aÿ, and the Chardonnay grapes from Chouilly. A greenish colour, the nose reeks of almond aromas, the flavour is loose, round and sweet. A tone of honey in the finish lifts the marks a little. Again, too high a dosage!

1988 Cuvée les perles de la Dhuy 72 (May 94) 75
(5% PN, 95% CH)
Even more Chouilly-type almond and honey tones in the nose, an overdeveloped oxidative flavour again wrapped in too much sugar. As with all of Autreau's champagnes the sharp edges are filed down to a soft, slightly mushy mess. This cuvée de prestige, even though it's the firm's top wine, is reminiscent of a similar Chouilly product, Vazart-Coquart. Once again I suspect that older reserve wines have been used in the dosage. The champagne is not bad today, but the lack of acidity and the large amount of sugar involved leads me to doubt any positive development.

1982 Cuvée les perles de la Dhuy 79 (Jul 90) 81
(5% PN, 95% CH)
The same aromas as the '88 but with a faint, pleasant nuance of toasted bread that makes this wine more interesting and fresh.

CHIGNY-LES-ROSES

A magnificent rose garden gave the village its present name around the turn of the century, after it had previously been known simply as Chigny. This is one of the very best Premier cru villages and it's full of excellent winemakers. Its location on the northern side of Montagne de Reims should mean that only Pinot grapes enjoy perfect conditions, but in my opinion it's the only village where Pinot and Chardonnay share the same high class. Neither the green nor the black grapes are of Grand cru level but both are at the top of the Premier crus. This gives the growers the chance to make good cuvées despite them being monocru champagnes. The wines are never as powerful and rich as those from neighbouring Mailly, but when it comes to balance and charm, Chigny has few betters.

% 94% 20% PN, 65% PM, 15% CH

J. Lassalle

Rue des Châtagniers,
51500 Chigny-les-Roses 03 26 03 42 19

Production: 100,000 bottles.

This little pearl is run - like so many others - by a stylish widow and her daughter. Their champagne is marked by a broad, ripe fruit. They are very easy to drink and have few critics. The Chardonnay wine is among the very best outside of Côte-des-Blancs.

Lassalle Brut 75
(60% PN, 40% CH)
Medium-deep colour, impeccable mousse, balanced bready nose. The flavour is soft and uncomplicated with a vanilla aftertaste that is typical of the house.

Lassalle Rosé 70
(70% PN, 30% CH)
Impeccable mousse, soft flavour and a honeyed nose.

1988 Cuvée Angéline 79 (Oct 97) 83
(60% PN, 40% CH)
Softer than the blanc de blancs. A fruity nose of plums and dough. Medium-bodied clean taste.

1987 Cuvée Angéline 75 (Jan 97) 80
(60% PN, 40% CH)
This may be a very good '87, but it's hardly a great wine. The nose hints at vanilla and fresh bread and the flavour plays a similar tune.

1985 Cuvée Angéline 50 (Apr 93) ?
(60% PN, 40% CH)
This is the only champagne from Lassalle that has disappointed me. It has an unpleasant spiciness in the nose and a floury, slightly flat flavour that is absolutely not typical for this firm.

1982 Cuvée Angéline 87 (Apr 93) 89
(60% PN, 40% CH)
A lovely champagne even when it was released, but perhaps more for the revelleer than the analyst. White chocolate, vanilla, butter, honey and candy are there in both flavour and nose. Despite Pinot's greater content it is Chardonnay that dominates proceedings. The acidity is a little too low for the wine to enjoy a really long life.

1992 Special Club 80 (Oct 97) 82
(40% PN, 60% CH)
Very creamy and ripe as always. The wine lacks aging potential but it is quite charming anyhow.

1989 Special Club 85 (May 96) 88
(40% PN, 60% CH)
Lassalle have attracted a lot of attention in the wine press recently. This rich wine has popular appeal and a lovely buttery Chardonnay nose and a fat, full Pinot sweetness.

1985 Special Club 88 (Oct 92) 91
(40% PN, 60% CH)
I wonder if this isn't the best Lassalle I've tasted. It's odd that the *85 Cuvée Angeline* constantly flops while at the same time they did so well with *Special Club*. The nose is typical for the firm with all kinds of pastries and white chocolate. The citrus aroma is stronger than usual and adds yet another dimension. The flavour is marked by an expansive exotic fruit and perfect balance.

1982 Special Club 89 (Aug 96) 89
(40% PN, 60% CH)
Lassalle made a luscious and ripe '82 with great complexity. Fully mature today.

1988 Lassalle B. d. B. 79 (Oct 97) 84
(100% CH)
Still a bit sharp and unpolished. Aromas of grass, gooseberry and mineral. Rather long acidic aftertaste.

1987 Lassalle B. d. B. 80 (Aug 96) 83
(100% CH)
A big, bold nose of daffodils, nectar and honey meets the taster. The flavour is soft and pleasant but lacks the finesse of a B. d. B. from Côte des Blancs.

1985 Lassalle B. d. B. 82 (Aug 94) 82
(100% CH)
This champagne has a very open nose of mature exotic Chardonnay and daffodils. The structure is almost oily, the flavour is rich and creamy and the dosage is just a touch high. The overall impression is more one-dimensional than *Special Club*.

1982 Lassalle B. d. B. 82 (Aug 94) 82
(100% CH)
Amazingly similar to the '85. Here too one discovers the highly personal nose of daffodils. The richness is the same.

Cattier

6 rue Dom Pérignon,
51500 Chigny-les-Roses 03 26 03 42 11

Production: 400,000 bottles.

This family owned vineyards in Chigny as long ago as 1763. At first they sold almost the entire harvest to the major houses, but more recently they established themselves as an independent and respectable champagne house. Today the firm is run by Jean-Louis and Jean-Jacques who took over from their father, unsurprisingly called Jean. Cattier exports as much as 55% of its total product today, and the firm is self-sufficient when it comes to grapes. The house style is made up of charming, well-made and reliable wines at a decent price.

Cattier Brut 67
(40% PN, 35% PM, 25% CH)
A reddish nuance in the colour, large bubbles. The nose is broad but simple, with apple cider and newly-baked bread from Pinot Meunier in the ascendant. Well developed friendly style without fancy trimmings.

Cattier B. d. B. 79
(100% CH)
A completely new product from the house that is non-vintage but made from a base from 1990. It reminds me of ***1990 Deutz Blanc de Blancs*** with its sophisticated style. The nose hints at biscuits, bread and Granny Smith apples, although the flavour is a bit rougher with a relatively sweet, ripe fruitiness.

Cattier Rosé Brut 60
(50% PN, 40% PM, 10% CH)
In my view a little too kind and candy-tasting rosé. Raspberry and banana chews in the nose, cherry and apples in the medium-bodied and somewhat sweet flavour.

1989 Cattier 70 (Feb 95) 79
(35% PN, 30% PM, 35% CH)
The style of a big house. Yeasty and Moët-like, with a flavour that is metallic but correct.

1988 Cattier 75 (Nov 94) 79
(35% PN, 30% PM, 35% CH)
A relative lightweight. Unusually pale colour, slightly unconcentrated with a pleasant whiff of vanilla in the nose its greatest asset.

1985 Cattier 80 (Aug 94) 87
(35% PN, 30% PM, 35% CH)
I've never really found a unified style in Cattier's vintage wines. This example could just as easily have come from Clicquot or Venoge. A classic toasty nose, orange fruit so typical of the vintage, a complex nervy flavour and a harmonious, uplifting finish.

1982 Cattier 75 (Apr 92) 85
(35% PN, 30% PM, 35% CH)
A wine where the nose is far more developed than the flavour. In 1992 the acidity was still hard, and the mineral-rich aftertaste was promising.

1989 Cuvée Renaissance 74 (May 97) 82
(67% PN/PM, 33% CH)
As usual, a well-made and appealing wine with rich, smooth fruit. The aromatic spectrum is dominated by red apples, plums and toffee.

1988 Cuvée Renaissance 80 (Nov 94) 88
(40% PN, 20% PM, 40% CH)
The wines made under this label are very similar to ***Clos du Moulin***. A honeyed creaminess is there already. Balanced, pure acidity.

1983 Cuvée Renaissance 87 (Jun 93) 87
(33% PN, 33% PN, 34% CH)
A deep yellow, developed, gorgeous champagne for early consumption. The nose is like a tropical rainforest with all its exotic flowers. Acacia honey dominates the creamy and soft flavour. It dies in the glass so drink it now.

Clos du Moulin 90
(50% PN, 50% CH)
One of the few champagnes that are allowed to put the Clos sign on their labels. The vineyard covers 2.2 hectares and was once owned by Allart de Maisonneuve, an officer in the army of Louis XV. Jean Cattier bought the land in 1951. The old mill which gave the place its name burned down, but the name stuck. The cuvée is a blend of three vintages and it has an average age of seven or eight years when it comes onto the market. Without doubt it's the firm's finest wine, combining the honey and cream aromas typical of the house with a mineral freshness. The mousse is something I rarely comment on as the differences these days are relatively small, but the velvet-smooth firework displays performed by the bubbles in ***Clos du Moulin*** and Laurent Perrier's ***Grand Siècle*** are unique. Develops well in the bottle for up to five years.

Gardet

13 rue Georges Legros,
51500 Chigny-les-Roses ☎ 03 26 03 42 03
Production: 600,000 bottles.

Charles Gardet founded the house in 1895 in Épernay, but his son George moved it to Chigny, where it is now run by Pierre Gardet. Gardet has no vineyards of its own but is instead forced to buy in all its grapes. Many wine journalists are very enthusiastic about the quality of Gardet's champagnes, but to call them "mini-Krugs" is going a bit too far, I think. There are no oak casks or any other special vinification methods. Gardet's wines are quite simply well-made and good, but it's certainly not in the top league.

Gardet Brut 70
(70% PN, 30% CH)
Every time I've tasted this wine I've been confused by the difference between the nose and the flavour. The nose is nutty with elements of digestive biscuits but the flavour, on the other hand, is a bit thin.

Gardet Rosé 75
(100% PN)
This rosé is made with skin contact which gives it a rather dark red colour. The nose is overwhelming and musty, and the wine has an unambiguous grape character and maturity in the flavour. This is a typical food champagne which may not please everyone, but I must admit I'm quite enchanted by the Pinot character in Gardet's rosé.

1985 Gardet 80 (Jan 95) 87
(50% PN, 50% CH)
A promising undeveloped champagne in January 1995. It reminded me a lot of the '83, but with a somewhat less developed nose.

1983 Gardet 83 (Jul 93) 88
(50% PN, 50% CH)
Superior to the '82! A very fine rose nose combined with the smell of a good bakery. Crystal-clear, pure flavour with perfectly pure acidity and a fruit which lays the foundation for a great future.

1982 Gardet 67 (Jun 92) 75
(50% PN, 50% CH)
The '82 has to be viewed as a major disappointment. Few producers made their worst champagne this year, but Gardet managed the trick. The champagne is impersonal and one-dimensional.

1979 Gardet 92 (Jul 93) 92
(50% PN, 50% CH)
This lovely '79 is a textbook champagne for the vintage. Mature, golden colour, a brilliant Pinot nose with leather, hazelnuts and honey. A fruity revelation in the mouth with a perfectly balanced finish of walnuts. Buy one if you see one!

1976 Gardet 86 (Apr 93) 88
(50% PN, 50% CH)
Unexpectedly light colour for one so old. An extremely broad, wonderful, sweet, exotic nose with elements of bread, chocolate and mint. It feels a little clumsy in the mouth, as do many 76's. The acidity is a trifle too low but it may end up developing like the 59's.

Patrice Leroux.

Hilaire Leroux

12 rue Georges Legros,
51500 Chigny-les-Roses 03 26 03 42 01

Production: 60,000 bottles.

Patrice Leroux makes champagnes that dose not go throw malolactic fermentation. That fact keeps them fresh for a really long time.

Leroux Carte Bleu 65
(33% PN, 33% PM, 34% CH)
Quite a powerful non-vintage champagne with bready nose and a heavy taste.

Leroux Carte Rouge 80
(33% PN, 33% PM, 34% CH)
I've only tasted this wine twice, but I was very impressed by its masculine power. A somewhat subdued, serious Pinot nose and a full, restrained structure. A real "Vin de Garde" that is extremely suitable for storing in the cellar.

Leroux Rosé 81
(60% PN, 20% PM, 20% CH)
Light orange, exotic nose of herbs and flowers. Sold at the great age of ten years.

1989 Leroux 80 (Oct 97) 82
(30% PN, 10% PM, 60% CH)
Very opulent on the nose, but still a good acidity on the palate.

1955 Leroux 88 (Oct 97) 90
(20% PN, 50% PM, 30% CH)
Extremely fresh, light colour and a bit closed at first. Opens up nicely in the glass with aromas of nougat, tar and bread. Tough and acidic. Would have been even better if normaly disgorged.

Jacky Dumangin

3 rue de Rilly,
51500 Chigny-les-Roses 03 26 03 46 34

Production: 60,000 bottles.

Acknowledged as the best of the bewildering number of Dumangins. The Dumangin family have been growers in the village since the beginning of the century. Jacky Dumangin controls 5.2 hectares in Montagne de Reims.

Dumangin Brut 70
(25% PN, 50% PM, 25% CH)
A champagne suitable for keeping, with good concentration and hard acidity. One-dimensional but potent.

Dumangin Grande Réserve 65
(25% PN, 50% PM, 25% CH)
Older and more developed than *Brut*. Not as focused.

Dumangin Rosé 58
(60% PN, 20% PM, 20% CH)
Dumangin's house style is marked by stringency and mineral-rich elegance. The style is wrapped up in a strong flavour of red berries.

1991 Dumangin 81 (Mar 96) 86
(47% PN, 53% CH)
A superb '91! The nose is delightfully perfumed and flowery and the citrus flavour is long and crispy.

Lassalle-Hanin

2 rue des Vignes,
51500 Chigny-les-Roses 03 26 03 40 96

Production: 30 000 bottles.

The cousin of J.Lassalle.

Lassalle-Hanin Réserve 50
(33% PN, 33% PM, 34% CH)
Riesling-like and full of apple aroma. Somewhat flat and uninteresting.

Lassalle-Hanin B. d. B. 60
(100% CH)
A typical blanc de blancs from Pinot country. Aromatic and sturdy, but lacking in elegance.

Lassalle-Hanin Rosé 48
(50% PN, 30% PM, 20% CH)
A simple rosé to drink out of a woman's slippers.

1989 Lassalle-Hanin 82 (Oct 97) 83
(50% PN, 50% CH)
Only 2000 bottles produced of this prestige champagne. Rounded, honeyed and mature.

1988 Lassalle-Hanin 86 (Oct 97) 90
(50% PN, 50% CH)
Superb biscuity and minty bouquet and a concentrated, almost fat feeling on the palate.

Fred Leroux

4 rue du Moulin,
51500 Chigny-les-Roses 03 26 03 42 35

Production: 25 000 bottles.

Strong connections with Ed. Brun in Aÿ. The vintage is made in oak casks.

Fred Leroux Carte d'Argent 64
(60% PM, 40% CH)
Opulent nose of pear and candy. More citrus in the taste.

Fred Leroux Carte d'Or 67
(20% PN, 40% PM, 40% CH)
Better structure and more serious rooty Pinot aroma.

Fred Leroux Rosé 61
(20% PN, 40% PM, 20% CH)
Very similar to *Carte d'Or*, with an added hint of raspberry.

1992 Fred Leroux 79 (Oct 97) 84
(50% PN, 50% CH)
Very good considering the vintage. Good structure and a nice woody taste.

1988 Fred Leroux 82 (Oct 97) 86
(50% PN, 50% CH)
Woody, acidic, dry and storeable. Very good value for money.

1975 Fred Leroux 89 (Sep 98) 89
(50% PN, 50% CH)
I bought a case of this rich and chewable champagne directly from the producer at a bargain price. This is a champagne for all to like, with chocolaty aromas.

Maurice Philippart

16 rue de Rilly,
51500 Chigny-les-Roses ☎ 03 26 03 42 44

Production: 30 000 bottles.

Maurice Philippart Brut 66
(10% PN, 80% PM, 10% CH)
Pure nose of butterscotch and fruit. Good balance.

Maurice Philippart Demi-Sec 30
(10% PN, 80% PM, 10% CH)
The same wine with a lot of sugar.

Maurice Philippart Rosé 64
(20% PN, 80% PM)
Tight and focused as are all wines from this producer.

1986 Maurice Philippart 75 (Oct 97) 75
(10% PN, 80% PM, 10% CH)
Only produced in magnums. Mature and simple aromas.

1989 Maurice Philippart Prestige 75 (Oct 97) 80
(10% PN, 90% CH)
A faint nose, but a long and powerful taste of marzipan.

Guy Tixier

12 rue Jobert,
51500 Chigny-les-Roses ☎ 03 26 03 42 51

Production: 30,000 bottles.

Guy Tixier founded his company in 1960, and the current owner is Olivier Tixier. With the help of the cooperatives in Chigny and Chouilly they vinify champagne that is made from grapes from five hectares in Chigny.

Guy Tixier Cuvée Réserve 58
(40% PN, 40% PM, 20% CH)
Strong nose hinting at banana and pear. Somewhat one-dimensional taste.

Guy Tixier Sélection 76
(60% PN, 40% CH)
A pure 1990 champagne, with great depth and aromas of almonds and grapefruit.

Guy Tixier Rosé 62
(50% PN, 20% PM, 30% CH)
Faint nose of black currants and strawberries. Again a one-dimensional, short taste.

Gilles Menu

1 rue Jobert,
51500 Chigny-les-Roses ☎ 03 26 03 43 35

Production: 30,000 bottles.

Gilles Menu Brut 66
(25% PN, 50% PM, 25% CH)
Very pure and straight forward grower champagne. Obviously quite good Pinot Meunier.

Gilles Menu Grande Réserve 68
(25% PN, 25% PM, 50% CH)
A lot more maturity and nice aromas of honey and almonds.

Gilles Menu Rosé 60
(25% PN, 25% PM, 50% CH)
Not as pure as *Grande Réserve*, but the same mature aromas of honey and almonds.

Bertand Rafflin

4 rue des Carrières,
51500 Chigny-les-Roses ☎ 03 26 03 48 47

Production: 7,000 bottles.

Bertand Rafflin Brut 63
(33% PN, 34% PM, 33% CH)
Much more maturity than the rosé. Nose of almonds and honey. Fresh and rather complex on the palate.

Bertand Rafflin Sec 48
(33% PN, 34% PM, 33% CH)
The same wine with a touch of sugar.

Bertand Rafflin Demi-Sec 38
(33% PN, 34% PM, 33% CH)
The same wine with a lot of sugar.

Bertand Rafflin Rosé 51
(40% PN, 30% PM, 30% CH)
Rather one-dimensional raspberry nose. Light aperitif style.

Cuvée St Vincent 74
(70% PN, 30% CH)
Rounded and soft, gentle mousse and a fruity finish.

Dumangin-Rafflin

42 rue Georges Legros,
51500 Chigny-les-Roses ☎ 03 26 03 48 21

Production: 30,000 bottles.

Dumangin-Rafflin Brut 53
(25% PN, 50% PM, 25% CH)
A bit untidy on the nose, but the fruity taste is correct.

Dumangin-Rafflin Rosé 55
(30% PN, 45% PM, 25% CH)
Full-bodied and a bit clumsy.

Paul Tixier

8 rue Jobert, 51500 Chigny-les-Roses ☎ 03 26 03 42 45

Production: 23,000 bottles.

Paul Tixier Brut 37
(20% PN, 60% PM, 20% CH)
Both nose and taste are fruity and simple. Aromas of pear and banana. Short and uninteresting.

Paul Tixier Demi-Sec 27
(20% PN, 60% PM, 40% CH)
Just look at the marks!

Paul Tixier Grande Année 40
(20% PN, 60% PM, 20% CH)
A very perfumed and soapy champagne. Better on the palate, but still very basic.

COLIGNY

Southwest of Côte des Blancs there lies this unknown village. The vineyards are mostly on the flat and should not have been upgraded to a Premier cru in 1985.

% 90% CH, 87% PN 10% PN, 90% CH

CUIS

Northwest of Cramant lies this excellent Premier cru village. Reserve wines from Bollinger show that Cuis' best locations can give wines of very great elegance. The best vines are at a height of 160-200 metres above sea level, and in general it can be said that the wines from Cuis are a little more powerful than those from Cramant, but with a less refined bouquet. Bollinger owns the best locations, along with Pol Roger and Moët. Among the smaller producers Larmandier and Gimonnet are the most important.

% 95% 1% PN, 9% PM, 90% CH

Guy Vallois

2 rue de'l Egalité, 51530 Cuis 03 26 51 78 99

Unfortunately I've never visited this well-known grower in Cuis, but his family connections with Diebolt-Vallois in Cramant promise well, as does the only wine I've come across.

Guy Vallois B. d. B. 77
(100% CH)
Not unlike Diebolt's young, rich fruitiness. Pears and gooseberry aromas in the nose and a crystal-clear, acidic flavour. Although it's not a vintage champagne this wine should be seen as an embryo which can be stored for between ten and fifteen years without problems.

Pierre Gimonnet

1 rue de la République, 51530 Cuis 03 26 59 78 70

Production: 165,000 bottles.

Gimonnet's prices are a long way under those of the major firms' non-vintage champagnes, even though their quality is higher. When you drive through Côte des Blancs, Gimonnet's house can be seen beside the road and it's easy to creep in for a spontaneous visit and maybe even an improvised tasting. Gimonnet owns 25 hectares of Chardonnay vineyards in Cuis, Chouilly and Cramant. The firm produces some very well-made blanc de blancs at low prices, but they rarely hit the real heights.

Gimmonet B. d. B. 70
(100% CH)
A beautiful green/yellow colour with a very lively mousse. The champagne is a little cumbersome with its yeasty aroma and musty apple cider nose. The flavour is much better, with a mature rustic tone and a long fresh aftertaste.

1989 Gimonnet 83 (Feb 96) 87
(100% CH)
A champagne that already displays a broad spectrum of sun-ripened tastes. Lemon, butter and pineapple are there in both nose and flavour. An extra plus mark for the long, creamy aftertaste.

1988 Gimonnet 74 (Mar 94) 83
(100% CH)
The '88 doesn't really have the body of the '89, but the acidity is higher which should give it an equally long life. Nor is the fruit as expansive and exotic as the '89.

1985 Gimonnet 69 (Mar 94) 75
(100% CH)
An unexpected failure in this wonderful year. The butteriness so typical of the vintage is on the verge of caramels and berry jam. The structure is loose and the aftertaste disappointingly short. Much better in magnums.

1982 Gimonnet 90 (May 93) 91
(100% CH)
A wine of exceptional quality. The nose makes me think of *Taittinger Comtes de Champagne* from the same year. Butterscotch, vanilla and flowers of the fields are blended with passion fruit and citrus aromas. The flavour is extremely pleasing, with a soft, delicate, honeyed aftertaste.

Paul Michel

20 Grande rue, 51530 Cuis 03 26 59 79 77

Production: 140,000 bottles.

A house of considerable size that owns 18 hectares in Cuis, Chouilly, Pierry, Moussy, Avenay and Mancy. 5% is bought in from Bouzy. Wines not tasted.

Wines: B. d. B., Rosé, Vintage.

Coop. de Blémond

Route de Cramant, 51530 Cuis 03 26 59 78 30

Production: 80,000 bottles.

A relatively small cooperative, managed by Christian Deliege, that runs forty hectares in Cuis, Cramant and Chouilly. Wines not tasted.

Wines: Brut, Vintage, Grande Réserve.

CUMIÈRES

The village has a very good reputation for its red coteaux champenois, which in my view often outclasses the Bouzy rouge. Cumières could well have been a Grand cru village were it not for the high number of Pinot Meunier vines. The southerly slopes give the fastest-ripening grapes in all of Champagne. Pascal Leclerc at Leclerc-Briant in Épernay is one of those winemakers who have grasped Cumières' greatness and he makes three fantastic clos wines with lovely personality from this village. In general one can say that the best grapes grow at a height of 50-150 metres above sea level and give fruity, well-structured wines that beat many a Grand cru champagne. Houses that own vineyards, besides Leclerc-Briant, are Joseph Perrier, Moët and Roederer.

% 93% 47% PN, 39% PM, 14% CH

René Geoffroy

150 rue Bois des Jots,
51480 Cumières 03 26 55 32 31

Production: 100,000 bottles.

The Geoffroy family were winemakers as long ago as the 17th century and have kept the property within the family since then. Besides Cumières they own vineyards

in Damery, Hautvillers and Dizy. They aim for the highest possible quality and ferment the wines in oak casks for their *Cuvée Sélectionnée* and *Brut Prestige*. The wines don't go through malolactic fermentation, which gives them the nerve and aging potential that most Cumières champagnes lack. When you talk to the well-educated young Jean-Baptiste Geoffroy you understand that this is a family passionately in love with wine.

Geoffroy Carte Blanche Brut 50
(50% PN, 50% PM)
With a bottle age of only 2.5 years and 50% "second pressing", it isn't so strange that this champagne is at its best when nice and uncomplicated.

Geoffroy Cuvée de Réserve Brut 75
(50% PN, 40% PM, 10% CH)
Always a blend of two vintages that are stored for four years - and only the cuvées. A big step up in quality from *Carte Blanche*. Here we have a lovely rich, fruity nose and an impressive full flavour that's full of freshness thanks to the malic acids.

Geoffroy Rosé 60
(60% PN, 40% PM)
The deep colour has come about after adding only 3% of Cumières rouge. The nose is very strong and precocious, and the flavour is full with a powerful, almost tannic red wine aftertaste. Idiosyncratic but hardly elegant.

Geoffroy Cuvée Sélectionnée Brut 80
(66% PN, 34% CH)
Vinified in oak casks and always from one vintage only. It lies for five years in contact with the yeast and develops a thoroughly full autolytic character. The nose is weak but impressively complex, and the flavour expresses a cannonade of ripe fruit aromas. This champagne will probably cope extremely well with a few years in the cellar.

Geoffroy Brut 77
(34% PN, 66% CH)
The same vinification as the *Cuvée Sélectionnée*, but more contact with the yeast sediment. The firm themselves are proudest of this wine, but I prefer the Pinot-dominated version. Here too the explosive fruit is impressive, but the concentration isn't quite the same.

Geoffroy Prestige 70
(33% PN, 67% CH)
Bright colour, fine mousse and a nose of brioche.

1979 Geoffroy 92 (May 94) 92
(70% PN, 30% CH)
Naturally they save some bottles of their best vintages to open on suitable occasions. I considered it an honour when I was asked to share this wonderful '79 with the family in May of 1994. The colour was almost bronze, the nose was delightfully broad and impressive, with elements of coffee and leather, and the flavour reminded me of an old burgundy with clear aromas of boiled vegetables and earth. An extremely long and smoky aftertaste.

Yves Mignon

166 rue de Dizy, 51480 Cumières 03 26 55 31 21

Yves Mignon Brut 73
Tasted just once. It is very reminiscent of *Geoffroy Cuvée de Réserve* with its full and fruity Pinot flavour.

Denois Père & Fils

Sadly this firm has ceased to exist following a divorce. Love creates its own problems, even in Champagne! If you find a bottle left over somewhere, don't hesitate to buy it. I myself have only tasted two wines but I've heard several reports of their stunning quality.

Denois Carte Blanche 75
More elegant and lighter than Geoffroy but with the same rich fruitiness.

Denois Crémant Rosé 75
Unexpectedly light with ultra fine bubbles, a delicate strawberry nose and lovely initial attack in the mouth that develops into a fruity finish.

Vadin-Plateau

12 rue de la Coopérative,
51480 Cumières 03 26 55 23 36
Production: 50,000 bottles.

Alphonse Perrin, grandfather of the current owner, J.-L Vadin, founded this company, which now owns six hectares of land. 5% of the grapes are bought in. Wines not tasted.

Wines: Carte Blanche, Carte Noire, Vintage, Rosé.

DIZY

The village with the intoxicating name lies in the heart of the Marne valley, where it borders on to the king of Pinot, Aÿ, with which it shares many characteristics. The vines grow at 100-200 metres above sea level and are exposed to the southwest, and the best locations are those closest to Aÿ. One of my favourite Premier cru villages.

% 95% 32% PN, 34% PM, 34% CH

Jacquesson & Fils

68 rue du Colonel Fabien,
51530 Dizy 03 26 55 68 11
Production: 350,000 bottles.

Jacquesson was one of the very first champagne houses when it was founded in 1798 in Châlons-sur-Marne. It didn't take long before they also became one of the most famous, and their reputation wasn't exactly harmed by Napoleon's gift of a gold medal when he visited their beautiful cellars. Their top export market became the United States, where they recently found old bottles of Jacquesson aboard a wreck called the Niantic, a ship that was forgotten after it sank during the great fire of San Francisco in 1851. The first bottle was opened with great pomp and ceremony, and the disappointment must have been acute when they took the first gulp of sea water! As early as in 1867 Jacquesson sold a million bottles, but after the death of Adolphe Jacquesson the firm hit a downward trend. Leon Tassigny took over 1920 and bought the excellent vineyards the company still owns today in Avize, Aÿ, Dizy and Hautvillers, but even so, the quality didn't reach the heights achieved in the 19th century. The firm played second fiddle right up until Jean Chiquet bought the house in 1974, and today it is run by his two purposeful sons Laurent (the winemaker) and Jean-Hervé (the businessman). When I first met Jean-Hervé in 1990 he told me they were aiming at the very top, and new investments were made with the goal of raising quality. The second pressing was sold, the proportion of reserve wine and oak casks were increased and a greater amount of Grand cru grapes were bought in. Today that expensive outlay is beginning to bear fruit. The non-vintage champagne *Perfection* is in my opinion the best from the champagne houses, while the cuvée de prestige *Signature* is among the top flight each year. In their *1975 D.T.* they also have one of the oldest commercially-available champagnes. Jacquesson has to be seen as one of the best bargains in Champagne.

Jacquesson Perfection 82
(33% PN, 35% PM, 32% CH)
One of the secrets behind the dramatic rise in quality of this champagne in recent years is that a quarter is vinified in oak casks. Compare it with Bollinger, who previously made an oak-influenced non-vintage champagne (now only 12%). Another explanation is that all the Chardonnay comes from the Grand cru village of Avize. This champagne combines seriousness with charm in a marvellous manner. The fruity nose is backed up by a creamy Chardonnay aroma, the flavour is perfectly balanced and there's a nutty oak tone in the finish.

Jacquesson Perfection Rosé 73
(31% PN, 36% PM, 33% CH)
9% red wine from Dizy has given this champagne its relatively light colour. This is the wine from Jacquesson that has impressed me the least: the rosé is more full and nourishing than its white sister, but the elegant Chardonnay finesse is not as prominent.

Jacquesson B. d. B. 78
(100% CH)
This pure Avize champagne has long been a favourite of the critics. For instance, Tom Stevenson, the great English expert, believes that this is one of the most elegant blanc de blancs there is. Personally I'm not so impressed as the bottle variation has been too great. Of course it does have that spicy nose so typical of the house and a creamy Chardonnay flavour, but the concentration isn't on a par with the company's best wines.

1990 Jacquesson B. d. B. 88 (Mar 98) 92
(100% CH)
Their first vintage blanc de blancs was released in October 1994, replacing the much-praised non-vintage version with a lot of fuss and bother. I don't know if this remarkable vintage was the reason for the huge jump in quality, but it is clear that this is a much broader and richer champagne. The mousse melts in the mouth like the finest caviar, the nose is rich in bread aromas and Granny Smith apples, the flavour is soft and harmonious with a long, buttery burgundy-like aftertaste.

1985 Jacquesson B. d. B. 92 (Mar 98) 95
(100% CH)
The Chiquet brothers made only 200 magnums of this wonderful wine. It's easy to be fooled by the wine's charming qualities now, but the '85 needs at least ten more years in the bottle before it's reached its full maturity. In June 1997 it was a quite delicious, buttery and classical B.d.B. with Signature-like aromas and an astonishing length.

1990 Perfection 80 (Feb 97) 84
(40% PN, 20% PM, 40% CH)
In my opinion this wine is far too similar to the non-vintage *Perfection*. The Meunier grapes make their presence felt and the fruit is quite ordinary. A disappointment.

1988 Perfection 80 (Oct 94) 84
(40% PN, 20% PM, 40% CH)
This champagne is among those species threatened with extinction. Vintage *Perfection* is no longer sold but is now part of the house's non-vintage champagne of the same name. The '88 has a great deal of the firm's typical spiciness in the nose, while the flavour is young, balanced and fruity.

1987 Perfection 75 (Jul 95) 83
(40% PN, 30% PM, 40% CH)
A wine the brothers regret they never sold. Surprisingly fresh and worth storing.

1986 Perfection 78 (May 94) 80
(40% PN, 20% PM, 40% CH)
Much more developed and charmingly vanilla-like than the more restrained '88. The flavour is uplifting with its tones of lemon and pineapple. This ready-to-drink wine is lighter and less concentrated than either the '85 or '88.

1985 Perfection 74 (Jul 92) 84
(40% PN, 20% PM, 40% CH)
Impersonal and neutral, but with a promising structure.

1979 Perfection 92 (Oct 97) 93
(35% PN, 36% PM, 29% CH)
Superb elegance and rich in glycerol. Clean and lingering on the palate.

1966 Perfection 89 (Oct 97) 89
(32% PN, 36% PM, 32% CH)
Deep golden colour, nose of leather, truffles, sauternes and roasted almonds. A bit tired despite its young appearance. The aftertaste suggests figs.

1953 Perfection 94 (Apr 96) 94
(40% PN, 25% PM, 35% CH)
Pale colour and a shy, multi-faceted, flowery nose. A super-elegant flavour similar to that of the '69. Kiwi and melon work together with a layer of creamy butteriness.

1952 Perfection 92 (Apr 96) 92
(40% PN, 25% PM, 35% CH)
Quite light, fine mousse and wonderfully toasty nose of meat, coffee and bread. The flavour is less good, but has impressive young acidity.

1928 Perfection 95 (Oct 97) 95
The two bottles I had the honour to drink were unfortunately without mousse. The structure and the honeyed taste is majestic. This yquem-copy is probably one of the greatest champagnes ever made.

1990 Signature Non Dosé 90 (Jan 99) 94
(50% PN, 50% CH)
The grapes come from Mailly, Dizy, Aÿ and Avize. This is a wonderful wine that combines the power of the '89 with a good deal of the 88's finesse. The nose is dominated by honey and licorice and the flavour is tremendously focused.

1989 Signature 91 (Oct 98) 92
(50% PN, 50% CH)
An unmistakable *Signature* in which maturity has arrived quicker than expected. The bouquet is broad and elegant with elements of coffee and red fruit. The flavour is puffed-up and soft as honey with a pleasant burst of almond aromas.

1989 Signature Non Dosé 87 (Mar 98) 92
(50% PN, 50% CH)
The richest *Signature* I've tasted. I'm not fully convinced of its longevity, but it's a delightful cuvée de prestige with excellent roundness and a sweet finish.

1988 Signature 92 (Mar 98) 95
(50% PN, 50% CH)
Jacquesson use their very best grapes in their *Signature* and let them ferment in large oak casks (75 hl). At the pressing they do something unique. They aren't satisfied with just using the cuvée but take only the best part, the "coeur de cuvée". All the Chardonnay comes from Avize, while the Pinot grapes come from Aÿ with a small amount from Dizy. The '88 is just as much a classic as the '85. It combines the power of the Pinot grapes with the buttery, soft Avize Chardonnay in a fantastic manner. The awesomely long aftertaste is worth a chapter all to itself.

1988 Signature Non Dosé 91 (Feb 97) 95
(50% PN, 50% CH)
Every time I taste the '88 I become more and more impressed. The wine has outstanding elegance and clear similarities with *1969 D. T.* The nose is full of lilies, nut chocolate and cream. The flavour is like a symphony by Mozart.

1985 Signature 92 (Jun 98) 94
(50% PN, 50% CH)
A gorgeous champagne! It flashes and sparks in golden hues, and the nose has a complete spectrum of tones. Sometimes it's dominated by the fruity and exotic elements, sometimes the deeper aromas of Brazil nuts, smoke, licorice and wood take over. The acidity is very high and will keep this champagne alive for at least another thirty years, although it will reach its peak around the year 2000. Unfortunately some bottle variation.

1983 Signature 92 (Mar 98) 92
(50% PN, 50% CH)
The same craftsmanlike personality as the '88 and '85. The nose has a more developed biscuitiness with elements of orchid. The oak is more noticeable than in other vintages, and the acidity is still very lively.

1982 Signature 80 (Feb 98) 
(50% PN, 50% CH)
When I tasted the '82 in 1990 I was very impressed. However, it hasn't developed as expected, but has instead taken on some odd berry aromas and tones of gingerbread and sherry.

1981 Signature 90 (Jul 95) 90
(50% PN, 50% CH)
Despite the oak aromas it's a more delicate wine than the other *Signature* vintages. The nose is pleasantly romantic, with hawthorn and honeysuckle. The flavour is fresh as a mountain stream with plenty of mineral tones.

1990 Signature Rosé 92 (Oct 98) 94
(54% PN, 46% CH)
Jacquesson's latest product on the market is a hit! It goes straight into my top ten list of best rosé champagnes. Almost all the best rosés have a powerful element of velvet-smooth Aÿ Pinot, and very few are vinified in oak casks. The result is a hedonistic experience far beyond the ordinary. When I tasted this wine for the first time the brothers hadn't decided what dosage they were going to use. I can guarantee that whatever they decide, this will be a hit. A wonderful rosé nose and a deep, oak-influenced, focused flavour.

1989 Signature Rosé 91 (Oct 98) 93
(54% PN, 46% CH)
This rosé is more full and has a lower acidity than the white *Signature*. The nose is reminiscent of *Cristal Rosé* - hazelnuts and candy drowned in strawberry liqueur. The palate is covered with a layer of soft red fruit. The aftertaste is phenomenal!

1985 Dégorgement Tardif 84 (Feb 98) 87
(40% PN, 20% PM, 40% CH)
The same wine as *Perfection*. Unexpectedly young and undeveloped. Those who are used to *75 D. T.* will certainly be displeased with this correct but rather charmless wine.

1978 Dégorgement Tardif 91 (Feb 98) 91
(100% CH)
This wine has never been available on the market, which is a shame. It has a wonderful autolytic character in perfect harmony with an intensely fruity flavour. A hit for this difficult year.

1976 Dégorgement Tardif 93 (Feb 98) 93
(100% CH)
Similar to the '75 with a slightly fatter character and greater power. Fully mature but plenty of life left in it yet.

1975 Dégorgement Tardif 93 (Feb 98) 93
(100% CH)
In 1997 Jacquesson still sold this champagne which is disgorged on demand. As with all recently-disgorged champagnes, there is a great deal of bottle variation. I've drunk the '75 on around 40 occasions, and on five of them it was too old and sherry-like, while just as often it's been too young and closed in the nose. Usually it's tasted best around fifteen months after being disgorged, when the wine has recovered from the shock of being recorked so late in life. The mousse should always be ultra-fine. At its best the nose is superbly toasty and buttery with a great autolytic character that is often confused with oak character. The flavour can contain such diverse tones as truffles, goat's cheese, port, butter and dried fruit. The aftertaste is extremely long. A very controversial wine with a style you either love or hate.

1974/1973 Dégorgement Tardif 85 (Jul 95) 85
(100% CH)
An experimental wine containing 85% of 1974 grapes. The champagne has the scent of a summer's night landscape when the dew hits the vineyards and meadows. The nose resembles tea and wet hay, but with time tones of sauternes arrive. The flavour is light and appetising.

1973 Dégorgement Tardif 93 (Apr 95) 93
(50% PN, 50% CH)
A lot like the '75, despite its high Pinot content. A nose of banana, honey and lemon, while the flavour has even more tones of newly melted butter than the '75, if that's possible. Sometimes there's a faint sherry tone in the very long aftertaste.

1973 Dégorgement Tardif 93 (Feb 98) 94
(100% CH)
This wine gives a much younger impression than the blended '73 or '75. The colour is a light green/yellow, the mousse is almost aggressive and the nose is like a firework display of flower aromas. When aired in the glass the sun ripened dwarf bananas come out, together with fresh-cut hay. The flavour is surprisingly light. Very elegant and youthful.

1970 Dégorgement Tardif 92 (May 97) 92
(35% PN, 25% PM, 40% CH)
The date of dégorgement seems to be critical when it comes to this wine's ability to express its beauty. The recently-disgorged version has a lovely chocolaty, truffle nose and a unified, concentrated flavour.

1969 Dégorgement Tardif 98 (Feb 98) 98
(100% CH)
At first Jacquesson were very unhappy with this vintage and decided to use it as the "liqueur d'expédition" in the non-vintage champagne. Many years later they discovered that it had changed dramatically. Unfortunately there are now only a few bottles left, as the brothers now rank this as the best champagne made by Jacquesson since World War II. I've twice had the honour of tasting this rarity when recently-disgorged. The colour is light green/yellow and the nose is indescribably elegant. Yellow roses, lily of the valley and lime float around in both nose and flavour, along with a faint toasty element. The oily aftertaste is among the longest I've experienced. A superb blanc de blancs with unique finesse!

1961 Dégorgement Tardif 94 (Feb 98) 94
(40% PN, 25% PM, 35% CH)
Majestic and impressive wine of great weight. Plenty of truffle aromas and splendid vigour. A champagne for a classic meal!

Gaston Chiquet

912 av. du Général-Leclerc,
51530 Dizy ☎ 03 26 55 22 02

Production: 120,000 bottles.

Nicolas Chiquet planted his first vines in 1746, and since then eight generations have tilled Dizy's soil. Gaston Chiquet registered the company in 1935 and expanded the property with land in Aÿ, Cumières and Hautvillers. The current owner, Claude Chiquet, controls more than 22 hectares, which he runs together with his two sons. They are best known for making the only blanc de blancs from the Pinot village of Aÿ.

Gaston Chiquet Tradition Brut 66
(20% PN, 45% PM, 35% CH)
A somewhat one-dimensional but well-made, robust non-vintage champagne.

Gaston Chiquet B. d. B. d'Aÿ 78
(100% CH)
100% Aÿ Chardonnay! Always a product from one single year even though it's not called a vintage wine. It is disgorged after four years in contact with the yeast. The aromas are definitely full of Chardonnay but the structure is Pinot-like. This wine shows the importance of the soil.

1988 Gaston Chiquet B. d. B. d'Aÿ 85 (Feb 98) 91
(100% CH)
The company's pride and joy. In really good years they separate out their best Chardonnay grapes and bottle a handful of magnums. They're at least nine years old when they go on sale. Superb elegance and lovely Chardonnay aromas.

1982 Gaston Chiquet B. d. B. d'Aÿ 89 (May 94) 91
(100% CH)
The '82 is very lively and shares the paradoxical character of the non-vintage version. Once again the nose speaks of ripe Chardonnay, but the roundness and full nature whispers of its true origins.

1970 Gaston Chiquet B. d. B. d'Aÿ 90 (Nov 94) 91
(100% CH)
Drunk newly-disgorged "à la minute", without additional sugar, of course. A deep, greenish colour. A medium broad nose of coffee and toasted bread. The flavour is very elegant and rich in minerals with the classic Chardonnay tones of hazelnuts and lime. This could easily have been a blanc de blancs from one of the major plantations in Côte des Blancs.

1989 Gaston Chiquet 70 (Dec 94) 78
(60% PN, 40% CH)
Full, round and aromatic. Perfect with food.

1989 Gaston Chiquet Special Club 80 (Jun 94) 85
(30% PN, 70% CH)
An agreeable wine with a bready nose and a clear whiff of digestive biscuit. The flavour is medium-bodied and charming with a fruity pineapple finish on the palate.

Paul Berthelot

889 av. du Général-Leclerc,
51530 Dizy ☎ 03 26 55 23 83

Production: 150,000 bottles.

The family owns 20 hectares in the Marne valley.

Paul Berthelot Brut Réserve 69
A deep, mature colour and intense nose of leather and mushrooms. One-dimensional, full, soft Pinot flavour with good length.

Other wines: Rosé Brut, Cuvée de Centenaire.

Vautrain-Paulet

195 rue du Colonel Fabien,
51530 Dizy ☎ 03 26 55 24 16

Production: 60,000 bottles.

A neighbour of Jacquesson, Vautrain-Paulet is run by Arnaud Vautrain and owns eight hectares in Dizy and Aÿ.

Vautrain-Paulet Carte Blanche 60
(50% PN, 20% PM, 30% CH)
Reddish copper colour, young Aÿ nose, slightly one-dimensional but complex sweet fruit flavour. Acidic apple aftertaste.

Other wines: Blanc de Blancs, Grande Réserve.

Raymond Bourdelois

737 av. du Général Leclerc,
51530 Dizy ☎ 03 26 55 23 34

Raymond Bourdelois has found a niche - he alone makes a blanc de blancs from Dizy. The champagne is more of a curiousity than a great wine.

Raymond Bourdelois Brut 41
(70% PN, 30% CH)
A basic nose with earthy elements. Good attack but short.

Raymond Bourdelois B. d. B. 60
(100% CH)
A strong terroir nose with earthy elements that air themselves in the glass and move on to become pineapple and grapefruit. The flavour has a good attack but a hard, almost harsh finish of disharmony.

ÉCUEIL

This Pinot village lies seven km southwest of Reims. More important in terms of its history than its current production.

% 90% 85% PN, 5% PM, 10% CH

Brochet-Hervieux

28 rue de Villers-aux-Noeuds
51500 Écueil ☎ 03 26 49 74 10

Production: 60,000 bottles.

The grower has access to 9.4 hectares of Pinot Noir and 1.6 hectares of Chardonnay from Écueil.

Brochet-Hervieux Extra Brut 61
(60% PN, 40% CH)
A pleasant surprise with a fine Pinot aroma in the nose and a rich flavour of ripe apples.

1989 Brochet-Hervieux 68 (Jul 95) 75
(60% PN, 40% CH)
Vigorous and fresh with apple aromas and a slightly short aftertaste.

1983 Brochet-Hervieux Special Club 68 (Jul 90) 75
(60% PN, 40% CH)
A pleasing yeasty and brioche-like nose. Full flavour.

Other wines: Rosé.

Allouchery-Perseval

11 rue de l'Eglise, 51500 Écueil ☎ 03 26 49 74 61

Production: 60,000 bottles.

This house owns 7,3 hectares in Écueil. Wines not tasted.

ETRECHY

Situated 30 km south of Épernay outside Côte des Blancs. This is smallest of all the Premier crus. No pure Etrechy champagnes are produced.

% 90% 100% CH

GRAUVES

A very nice Chardonnay village situated west of Avize. The best slopes lie at a height of 220 metres above sea level with easterly exposure. The village has a reputation for making the heaviest and most full-bodied Chardonnay wines in all of Côte des Blancs. The most important landowner is Bollinger, harvesting Chardonnay grapes that are well suited to their masculine style. Other houses that own land in Grauves are Moët and Pol Roger.

% 95% CH, 90% PN/PM 1% PN, 15% PM, 84% CH

HAUTVILLERS

Northwest of Cumières lies what might be called the cradle of Champagne, Hautvillers. The beautiful abbey in which Dom Pérignon worked is still there, giving the entire village a special historical atmosphere. The vine yards slope down from the village towards different points of the compass and the quality varies. The reputation comes of course from Dom Pérignon's wines, but in truth he made wines from many different villages. I've tasted Hautvillers as still wine from casks many times, but rarely a pure Hautvillers champagne. The wines don't reach the high levels achieved by neighbouring Cumières and Dizy.

% 93% 34% PN, 53% PM, 13% CH

Locret-Lauchaud

40 rue Saint Vincent,
51160 Hautvillers ☎ 03 26 59 40 20

Production: 100,000 bottles.

A company that came into being only recently, but this family of growers have worked in Champagne since 1620. That even predates their neighbour Dom Pérignon! Eric and Philippe Locret make fruity and pure champagnes from their 13 hectares.

Locret-Lachaud Brut 63
(40% PN, 20% PM, 40% CH)
A fruity, smooth and easy-to-drink champagne with excellent freshness and aromas of pear and guava.

Locret-Lachaud Demi-Sec 32
(33% PN, 33% PM, 34% CH)
Sweet, cloying and heavy. Not my cup of tea!

Locret-Lachaud Rosé 56
(33% PN, 33% PM, 34% CH)
A salmon-pink rosé, with flavours of pear and caramel.

Other wines: Abbatiale.

J. M. Gobillard

38 rue de l'Eglise, 51160 Hautvillers ☎ 03 26 51 00 24

Production: 250,000 bottles.

The Gobillard family settled in Hautvillers in 1945. Today Thierry Gobillard runs the company, which owns 25 hectares of vineyards and buys in 30% of its grapes.

J.M. Gobillard Tradition 59
(35% PN, 35% PM, 30% CH)
Surprisingly light and week. Fruity, sweet taste, with a nice incessant stream of pin-head bubbles.

J.M. Gobillard B. d. B. 64
(100% CH)
Discreet flowery nose and a medium-bodied taste.

J.M.Gobillard Grande Réserve 64
(25% PN, 25% PM, 50% CH)
A nose of vanilla and fruity Pinot Meunier. Smooth, easy to drink and charming flavour with an echo of Chardonnay.

J.M. Gobillard Rosé 61
(60% PN, 40% CH)
Well formed mousse of small persistant bubbles. Opulent nose, fruity and sound. A somewhat steely aftertaste.

Other wines: Prestige.

JOUY-LES-REIMS

Southerly slopes by Villedommange which received Premier cru status in 1985.

 90% 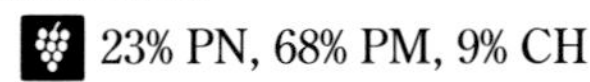 23% PN, 68% PM, 9% CH

LUDES

In the middle of Mailly and Chigny-les-Roses can be found this rather flat-lying cru. When you travel the "Champagne road" you see an enormous concrete block thrown up amidst the vineyards. That is Canard-Duchêne's modern plant in this Montagne de Reims village. The vines face north for the most part. The wines are of average Premier cru level and lend a backbone and body to many cuvées.

% 94% 30% PN, 50% PM, 20% CH

Blondel

B.P. 12, 51500 Ludes 03 26 03 43 92

Production: 35,000 bottles.

A very well-run house that owns ten hectares (50% PN, 50% CH) in the village and makes highly enjoyable and tasty champagnes in a public-pleasing style.

Blondel Carte d'Or 64
(75% PN, 25% CH)
Oxidative, pleasant nose of sweet licorice. This tasty, obliging champagne is full of sweet, generous aromas.

Blondel Rosé 74
(80% PN, 20% CH)
A very broad and polished rosé champagne with tones of Danish pastry and raspberry.

1990 Blondel B. d. B. 80 (Aug 95) 84
(100% CH)
Tones of vanilla and butterscotch dominate this round, rich and delicious blanc de blancs.

1985 Blondel Vieux Millésime 85 (Aug 97) 85
Wonderful nose of digestive biscuits. Long, mature taste.

Ployez-Jacquemart

8 rue Astoin, 51500 Ludes, 03 26 61 11 87

Production: 82,000 bottles.

The house was founded in Ludes in 1930 by Marcel Ployez. After his death it was taken over by his widow until their son Gérard was old enough to take up the reins, which he has done to this day. Ployez-Jacquemart own 1.8 hectares in Mailly and Ludes but buy in 85% of their grapes from fine vineyards in the Marne valley and Côte des Blancs. The cuvée de prestige *Liesse d'Harbonville* is fermented in oak casks.

Ployez-Jacquemart Brut 45
(55% PN, 15% PM, 30% CH)
A boring non-vintage champagne with too much apple cider aroma. Decent structure but a short aftertaste.

1988 Ployez-Jacquemart B. d. B. 68 (Apr 93) 74
(100% CH)
Despite a large proportion of imported Côte des Blancs grapes it feels like the Chardonnay from Pinot villages dominates this wine. A soft, tropical, fruity nose and sweet, rounded vanilla flavour.

1985 Cuvée Liesse d'Harbonville 84 (May 95) 88
(100% CH)
A robust, vinous blanc de blancs with good depth and personality. The cask character is perhaps a little too tangible in relation to the fruit.

Forget-Brimont

51500 Craon de Ludes 03 26 61 10 45

Production: 100,000 bottles.

Eugène Forget began selling champagne in 1920. The current owner Michel Forget runs eight hectares in Ludes, Chigny, Mailly and Verzenay.

Forget-Brimont Carte Blanche 55
(60% PN, 20% PM, 20% CH)
Soft and uncomplicated with a stony aftertaste from the Verzenay grapes.

Forget-Brimont Rosé 50
(75% PN, 12% PM, 13% CH)
A nose of raspberry and strawberry, with a flavour of red berries. Sharp aftertaste.

Canard-Duchêne

1 rue Edmond Canard,
51500 Ludes 03 26 61 10 96

Production: 4 million bottles.

Canard-Duchêne was formed in 1868 by Victor Canard and is owned today by the powerful Louis Vuitton group. Clicquot is a previous owner. Canard-Duchêne's own vineyards supply only 5% of the annual production, and the rest is bought in, with 40% of the grapes coming from the more basic locations in Aube. The firm is definitely one of those that go for quantity instead of quality.

Canard-Duchêne Brut 47
(35% PN, 42% PM, 23% CH)
In most French Super-Marchées you can buy this basic non-vintage champagne for a minimal sum. Aube grapes, not much time in the cellar, second pressing wine together create an earthy and simple champagne.

Canard-Duchêne Demi-Sec 30
(38% PN, 40% PM, 22% CH)
Well, I guess it's ok if you like sweet champagnes. As you may have worked out, I'm not much for this sort of drink.

Canard-Duchêne Rosé 41
(46% PN, 30% PM, 24% CH)
This is pretty much the same wine as the non-vintage variety, with just a little still red wine added. Yeast, earth, wild strawberry and apple can be found if you look properly in this uninteresting wine.

1990 Canard-Duchêne 77 (Oct 96) 84
(46% PN, 24% PM, 30% CH)
An extremely personal and perfectly-scented champagne that hides a great deal of beauty behind its exotic, fruity facade.

1988 Canard-Duchêne 79 (Dec 94) 84
(44% PN, 22% PM, 34% CH)
The vintage wine is of quite another class than the non-vintage champagne, with its lush Pinot nose and charming, rich fruit.

1976 Canard-Duchêne 83 (Feb 96) 83
(66% PN/PM, 34% CH)
Creamy and crusty, but already showing age.

1975 Canard-Duchêne 81 (Feb 96) 81
(66% PN/PM, 34% CH)
A faint bouquet and a nice common taste of chocolate.

1955 Canard-Duchêne
(44% PN, 22% PM, 34% CH)
The bottle I tasted was maderised. My English contacts tell me that some bottles are still in top form. Unjudged.

Charles VII 84
(53% PN, 9% PM, 38% CH)
A very elegant champagne of true refinement and class, but which needs a better backbone if it is to develop into something great.

Gaidoz-Forget

1 rue Carnot, 51500 Ludes ☎ 03 26 61 13 03
Production: 65,000 bottles.

This nine-hectare grower in the heart of Montagne de Reims is attracting more and more attention with his fruity and complex champagnes.

Gaidoz-Forget Réserve 70
(25% PN, 50% PM, 25% CH)
Fruity and complex bouquet with a faint roasted element. The flavour matches the nose well, with a rich, ripe fruit.

Gaidoz-Forget Carte d'Or 60
(25% PN, 50% PM, 25% CH)
Bright young appearence, soft lingering taste, but a simple nose.

Gaidoz-Forget Rosé 59
(30% PN, 70% PM)
The spicy style makes another appearance here, albeit in a sticky sort of way. A full and heavy champagne which needs food.

Other wines: Quintessence.

Georgeton-Rafflin

25 rue Victor Hugo, 51500 Ludes ☎ 03 26 61 13 14
Production: 7,000 bottles.

Georgeton-Rafflin Brut 39
(33% PN, 33% PM, 34% CH)
Deep colour, fishy nose. Dry, boring and short.

Georgeton-Rafflin Demi-Sec 26
(33% PN, 33% PM, 34% CH)
The same boring wine, totally destroyed with a spoon full of sugar.

Georgeton-Rafflin Rosé 46
(33% PN, 33% PM, 34% CH)
One of the reddest champagnes I've ever seen. Lambrusco, declared one taster. The nose leads you back on the right track again, even though the candy aromas are a touch too obvious. The flavour is reminiscent of certain rosés from Aube. Elegance is conspicuous by its absence and the fruit is abrupt and rough.

Monmarthe & Fils

38 rue Victor Hugo, 51500 Ludes ☎ 03 26 61 10 99
Production: 100,000 bottles.

M.Monmarthe owns 15 hectares in Montagne de Reims.

MAREUIL-SUR-AŸ

Directly to the east of Aÿ lies Mareuil-sur-Aÿ, a picturesque village where almost all of the 1,200 inhabitants work with wine. The area by the Marne river is extremely beautiful, but the village is best known for its exceptional location - Clos des Goisses - which are owned by Philipponnat. Mareuil certainly ought to be a Grand cru village, and most of the vineyards are of comparable quality to those in Aÿ. In the wine's youth one can tell the difference between Mareuil and Aÿ by a hawthorn-like floweriness in the nose, but after a while they are almost impossible to tell apart. Clos des Goisses' unusually steep slopes down to the river give the location the highest average temperature of all vineyards in Champagne, which means the wine produced here also has the highest potential alcohol content.

% 99% 82% PN, 9% PM, 9% CH

Billecart-Salmon

40 rue Carnot,
51160 Mareuil-sur-Aÿ ☎ 03 26 52 60 22
Production: 600,000 bottles.

It's a real pleasure for any wine enthusiast to visit the small, well-run house in Mareuil-sur-Aÿ. The firm, which is very much "in" at the moment, makes elegant, sporty wines which match "La nouvelle cuisine" perfectly. The company was formed in 1818 and has always concentrated on quality champagne in quite a light style. Billecart has a very innovative attitude towards winemaking. They are pioneers of cold stabilisation, which entails sinking the wine's temperature to 5°C for two days and then adding dried yeast to the fermentation taking place in stainless steel vats for three weeks. The slow fermentation is made possible by keeping the vat's temperature at around 12°. The wine then must be heated up to 18° so that the malolactic fermentation can take place. The philosophy of the house is to avoid oxidation at all costs: the flavour should come from the grape itself as far as possible, and not from secondary aromas from the vinification. Billecart buy in 95% of their grapes from 27 top-rate vineyards, and their own grapes are Pinot Noir from the home village. They have agreements with many respected growers from Grand cru villages Avize, Cramant and Le Mesnil. I've never tasted a poor wine from Billecart. They always maintain a constant high class, and quite recently they've given me some of those religious wine experiences.

Billecart-Salmon Brut 79
(35% PN, 30% PM, 35% CH)
This is the creation of the son, Antoine Billecart. I'd claim that this is the best non-vintage champagne of the extremely fruity school. The nose is lively and fresh as a spring morning, the flavour is light and citrus-fresh with a long, balanced aftertaste of Granny Smith apples.

Billecart-Salmon Rosé 86
(40% PN, 20% PM, 40% CH)
As opposed to many other wine writers I do not believe that this wine should be drunk in its infancy! After five or six years more years in the bottle the salmon-pink colour gains an orange tone. the elegant, fruity nose gets deeper and nuttier, the flavour more serious and prolonged. A half bottle with a cork straight as a dye at the "Tour d'Argent" restaurant in Paris in 1993 was outstanding.

1989 Billecart- Salmon B. d. B. 83 (Feb 98) 91
(100% CH)
This wine is a clear favourite among many other firms. Billecart's reputation in Champagne is untouchable. So far I'm a little disappointed myself with what is a pure but somewhat shy wine. Give this steely, grassy and mineral-rich wine plenty of years in the cellar.

1988 Billecart-Salmon B. d. B. 81 (Mar 97) 89
(100% CH)
The first time I tasted this wine it was served far too cold. At the right temperature the wine exudes subtle aromas of grass, hawthorn, hay and minerals. A wine to keep for a while.

1986 Billecart-Salmon B. d. B. 77 (Jan 97) 84
(100% CH)
Perhaps rather on the light side for my taste, but otherwise definitely pure and elegant.

1985 Billecart-Salmon B. d. B. 70 (Mar 93) 85
(100% CH)
From the best villages in Côte des Blancs only. A pure style and fruity but a touch naked and impersonal. A disappointment considering the vintage. Needs keeping!

1983 Billecart-Salmon B. d. B. 70 (Jul 90) 80
(100% CH)
Almost water-coloured with an ample mousse. Elements of hay and grass in the nose, and a thin flavour with hard acidity.

1976 Billecart-Salmon B. d. B. 90 (Jan 96) 90
(100% CH)
The rich vintage character suits what is normally a shy wine very well.

1973 Billecart-Salmon B. d. B. 94 (Jan 99) 94
(100% CH)
At the age of 17 it was still very youthful, with a light green hue in the faint golden colour. The mousse was superb, the nose a discreet chocolate affair, backed up by lime and white flowers. The flavour wasn't completely developed but very fine and rich in minerals. Lovely now.

1990 Cuvée N.F. Billecart 90 (Feb 98) 94
(60% PN, 40% CH)
Obviously a wonderful vintage for Billecart. Extraordinary nose of lemon peel, lime, dough and white chocolate. Superb acidity and structure combined with a lovely wealth of crunchy aromas.

1989 Cuvée N.F. Billecart 87 (Jul 98) 91
(60% PN, 40% CH)
A wonderful balance, freshness and charm. Sophisticated and almost impossible to tell apart from the '88.

1988 Cuvée N.F. Billecart 88 (Jun 97) 92
(60% PN, 40% CH)
A delightful, fresh champagne with a superb exotic fruit. By no means a powerful wine but a masterwork of balance.

1986 Cuvée N.F. Billecart 85 (Feb 94) 89
(60% PN, 40% CH)
A buttery, slightly muffled, high-class nose of vanilla. Multi-dimensional and harmonically balanced flavour.

1985 Cuvée N.F. Billecart 92 (Oct 98) 93
(40% PN, 60% CH)
N.F. has always had a brilliant golden colour with an extremely fine mousse - a symphonic masterpiece in a relatively light style. An aristocratic nose, full of finesse, and a feminine Chardonnay flavour wrapped around a backbone of first-class Pinot Noir. Very toasty today.

1983 Cuvée N.F. Billecart 86 (Sep 98) 86
(45% PN, 55% CH)
The '83 is beginning to show its age. The nose is fully mature, toasty but with an undertone of rubber. The flavour is less rich than other vintages. Drink now.

1982 Cuvée N.F. Billecart 82 (Jun 88) 91
(55% PN, 45% CH)
Unfortunately it's been a long time since I drank this promising wine, but my impression from 1988 was very positive. The nose was closed but the champagne's flavour was creamily polished and long.

1975 Cuvée N. F. Billecart 92 (Nov 96) 92
(60% PN, 40% CH)
Initially they had probably gone for a light, fruity approach. Today this wine has some lovely secondary aromas that bear up the charming apple element. Layers of chocolate and vanilla fill a wine that has become very complex.

1982 Billecart-Salmon Grande Cuvée 90 (Feb 97) 92
(40% PN, 60% CH)
A young appearance and unexpectedly mean nose. The true sensation only arrives with the bold, toffee-like flavour. The fruit is explosive and crispy with toasty, nutty undertones.

1990 Billecart-Salmon Rosé Cuvée Elisabeth
(45% PN, 55% CH) 91 (Oct 97) 94
A great rosé champagne with marvellous crispy aromas of fruit and minerals. Perfect length and balance. A wine for the cellar, or for immediate consumption.

1989 Billecart-Salmon Rosé Cuvée Elisabeth
(45% PN, 55% CH) 87 (Jul 98) 92
Billecart are the masters of rosé champagnes. Great elegance, good grip and the year's richness are all there without taking over. A very exciting wine to follow in the future.

Other wines: Cuvée Columbus.

Philipponnat

13 rue du Pont,
51160 Mareuil-sur-Aÿ ☎ 03 26 56 93 00

Production: 500,000 bottles.

The house was founded in 1910 by Pierre Philipponnat, and in 1935 he bought the jewel in the company crown, the 5.5 hectare vineyard Clos des Goisses. In 1987 Philipponnat became part of the Brizard group. They buy in 75% of the grapes from some highly-ranked vineyards (97% on average), with the rest coming from Mareuil-sur-Aÿ. Until quite recently the firm was run purposefully by the sporting and golf-mad Paul Couvreur. He managed the excellent grapes in a praiseworthy manner, and the wines share his charm and personality. All of them are intensely fruity with a characteristically youthful tone of gooseberry in the nose. Philipponnat is now sold to Bruno Paillard. With *Clos des Goisses* it's hard to foul up, but I wonder how good the wine would be in the hands of a magician like Anselme Selosse?

Philipponnat Brut 69
(55% PN, 15% PM, 30% CH)
The wine is disgorged after only two and a half years, but is backed up by 20% reserve wines which make the generous champagne full-bodied. The nose is dominated by gooseberries and rhubarb, while in the mouth it's very lively and fresh, but finishes somewhat abruptly.

Philipponnat Rosé 66
(55% PN, 10% PM, 35% CH)
A champagne in the same fruity style as the non-vintage champagne, with a somewhat more neutral and softer approach.

Le Reflet 80
(50% PN, 50% CH)
Clos des Goisses' second wine, in principle. Those grapes that don't really meet the high demands are included instead in *Le Reflet*, together with Chardonnay from Côte des Blancs. A lovely, generous young fruit that takes one's thoughts to gooseberries and Williams pears. The flavour too is strikingly fruity and easily drunk, and it will develop well for many years despite its immediate charm.

1989 Philipponnat 80 (Aug 97) 83
(65% PN, 35% CH)
A rich, mighty champagne with tremendous maturity. Already one notices tones of mint chocolate and raisins. Most remarkable is a personal tone of the health-bringing flower Enchinacea. Good but not great.

1988 Philipponnat 70 (Oct 94) 75
(65% PN, 35% CH)
Not as charming as *Le Reflet*! The house style dominates the year. The non-vintage is a better buy.

1985 Philipponnat 87 (Apr 96) 89
(65% PN, 35% CH)
A very successful vintage for this firm. There's something lightweight and relaxed about this wine that attracts me. The nose is lightly toasty and very creamy, a feature which is repeated and expanded in the mouth.

1988 Grand Blanc 68 (Oct 94) 73
(100% CH)
A little rough and strong blanc de blancs. I think it's matured too fast and lost some finesse along the way. Uncomplicatedly good in its one-dimensional way.

1980 Grand Blanc 83 (Oct 97) 83
(100% CH)
Pale, delicate, lightly toasty nose. Perfect maturity right now, lacking extract for long aging.

1988 Clos des Goisses 90 (Mar 99) 94 ?
(70% PN, 30% CH)
I'll never understand how *Clos des Goisses* behaves as a young wine. Experience shows that each vintage becomes a power-pack with age. The '88 isn't as undeveloped and grassy as the '82 was at the same age, but is instead quite full and delicate with bready and toasty aromas and a fine, crispy fruit. What will happen next?

1986 Clos des Goisses 94 (Mar 99) 94
(70% PN, 30% CH)
During a lunch at the company Paul Couvreur really convinced me that certain champagnes win by being decanted. An undecanted and a decanted glass of the '86 were amazingly dissimilar. The nose from the decanted glass resembled *Bollinger R.D.* and had a broad, smoky, nutty classical young Pinot bouquet. The flavour was extremely concentrated and rich. A cannonade of hazelnuts and chocolate met my palate, and the aftertaste was aristocratic. The wine easily coped with its company, a steak in morel sauce. A great wine!

1985 Clos des Goisses 94 (Mar 99) 96
(70% PN, 30% CH)
Henrik Arve, my closest friend among wine tasters, claims this is one of the greatest wines he has ever tasted in the middle-aged phase it is currently enjoying. I too am very impressed by the amazingly creamy fruit and the complex, intertwined, subtle spectrum of all clear champagne aromas.

1983 Clos des Goisses 92 (Mar 99) 95
(70% PN, 30% CH)
A fascinating wine where the nose hints at old champagne while the flavour is still very young. The bouquet is rich in chocolate, smoky and nutty. On the palate the attack is fresh and the fruit is youth itself. Long, long aftertaste.

1982 Clos des Goisses 91 (Mar 99) 94
(70% PN, 30% CH)
The first times I tasted the '82 made me doubt the location's greatness, as the wine was flowery and shy for many years before it opened up its peacock's tail of flavours. At a large horizontal tasting of the twenty best 82's, *Clos des Goisses* and *Salon* were clearly the least developed wines. However, the long aftertaste was

prominent from the start. I'm already longing for the next bottle to see if it has begun to develop its gorgeous chocolate style.

1979 Clos des Goisses 95 (Mar 99) 96
(70% PN, 30% CH)
What a brilliant wine! The nose is extremely broad, with a flowery, youthful element and a nutty, older, more serious style. As it warms up in the glass it is dominated by hazelnuts and honeysuckle. The flavour is deep as the ocean floor and thrillingly invigorating.

1978 Clos des Goisses 94 (Dec 96) 94
(70% PN, 30% CH)
Even in such a poor year this unique creation is excellent. Completely developed, with great fruitiness and overflowing with toasty aromas. Is there a better '78 outside Vosne-Romanée?

1975 Clos des Goisses 94 (Mar 99) 96
(70% PN, 30% CH)
Clos des Goisses is the champagne that has taken me the longest time to get to know. This wine is a kind of key as all the mature and great elements are already quite obvious, while the young, sometimes odd aromas are still around. The '75 is to a large extent like the '85, which confirms it as one of those wines destined for a long stay in the cellar.

1959 Clos des Goisses 99 (Dec 96) 99
(70% PN, 30% CH)
This bottle is among the greatest wines I've ever tasted. Even though Pinot Noir is the dominant grape there are strong similarities with the *59 Salon*. I tasted it blind beside five old cuvée champagnes from major houses and it was so apparent that this was a monocru, with all the advantages that implies in terms of power, intensity and personality. This is a creamy and youthful creation with an almost narcotically seductive nose. The flavour is so very full and creamy with citrus tones. Once the wine has stood in the glass for a while there came the special youthful grass and gooseberry nose. A wine that is a long voyage through the pleasures of champagne.

Abel Lepitre

13 rue du Pont,
51160 Mareuil-sur-Aÿ ☎ 03 26 56 93 11

Production: 500,000 bottles.

Founded in 1924 in Ludes. Abel Lepitre was a relatively poor young man who succeeded thanks to his knowledge and stubbornness, selling 100,000 bottles as early as 1939. Hitler put a stop to the success of the young Jew and Abel Lepitre died a tragic death in one of the nazi concentration camps. Fortunately, Abel's son was also ambitious. He managed to get the firm to expand still further by buying a huge house with its own chalk cellar in Reims in 1955. In 1960 Abel Lepitre ceased to be an independent champagne house when it merged with two others of similar size. Today Abel Lepitre is closely linked to Philipponnat, which is run by the same man, Bruno Paillard. This company is hard to get a grip on as they often change the name of their cuvées, they lack any vineyards of their own and have few permanent contracts with growers. This means that the quality has been quite inconsistent over the years, but when Paul Couvreur was at the helm the company found a style all its own.

Abel Lepitre Brut 68
(60% PN, 15% PM, 25% CH)
Tremendously inconsistent from year to year. The latest bottle I tasted was one of the better examples, with a distinct Pinot nose of fish and gunpowder smoke and a restrained and pure flavour.

Cuvée 134 75
(100% CH)
This is really the crémant champagne that has given the firm its good name. Almost colourless, with a fine, soft mousse, discreet Chardonnay nose and a light, appetising flavour.

1988 Abel Lepitre Rosé 81 (Jul 95) 89
(70% PN, 30% CH)
A real surprise, with a lovely tight structure and a sensual nose of peach and vanilla. Balanced and full of nuances.

1988 Abel Lepitre 70 (Jul 95) 83
(60% PN, 40% CH)
A lot like the non-vintage champagne with a slightly acrid, flowery nose backed up by gunpowder smoke and oyster shell. Young, medium-bodied and restrained flavour.

1990 Réserve C. 81 (Jul 95) 90
(100% CH)
A sparkling, youthful champagne full of hawthorn and gooseberry aromas with a perfectly pure, vigorous aftertaste of grapefruit.

1985 Cuvée Réservée 78 (Jul 95) 82
(35% PN, 65% CH)
Surprisingly developed '85 with an oxidative nose of sweet licorice. The flavour is creamy and good if somewhat artificial.

1983 Abel Lepitre B. d. B. 80 (Jun 90) 88
(100% CH)
Intensely perfumed and hawthorn-scented. Very vigorous and fresh. A joker in the pack.

Clos des Goisses becomes a bottle when reflected in the water.

Marc Hébrart

18 rue du Pont,
51160 Mareuil-sur-Aÿ ☎ 03 26 52 60 75

Production: 80,000 bottles.

Marc Hébrart and his son Jean-Paul are the most famous growers in the village. Apart from Pinot grapes from Mareuil they have access to Chardonnay from Chouilly and Oiry with vines averaging 28 years old. It is always a pleasure to visit Jean-Paul on his beautiful property by the Marne river. He is one of the new type of well-educated and quality-minded winemakers, and a grower to keep an eye on.

M. Hébrart Réserve 69
(80% PN, 20% CH)
Hawthorn and red apples back up a personal tone of coconut. The flavour is more basic but still correct.

Sélection Jean-Paul Hébrart 75
(70% PN, 30% CH)
Greater seriousness than in the *Réserve*, and quite another elegance.

Sélection Marc Hébrart 76
(70% PN, 30% CH)
The difference between this wine and the previous one is so small that bottle variation could be the explanation.

Hébrart Rosé 78
(70% PN, 30% CH)
Strong, meaty aromas stream up out of the glass and the mouth is filled with a rich strawberry fruit.

1989 Hébrart Prestige 70 (Apr 95) 79
(60% PN, 40% CH)
Unexpectedly light and elegant wine with an exquisite nose of Williams pears. The flavour is dominated by the characteristic almond aroma from Chouilly.

1990 Hébrart Special Club 76 (May 95) 83
(50% PN, 50% CH)
Deep, almost orange colour. A broad nose of vanilla and ripe apples. A rich young flavour of cheesecake.

Other wines: Brut Réserve, Sélection, Blanc de Blancs.

LES MESNEAUX

Situated very close to Reims on land that is quite flat. Doesn't deserve Premier cru status. Mercier owns most of the vineyards.

% 90% 50% PM, 50% CH

MONTBRÉ

Here too the vineyards are on flat ground without any particularly good conditions for top-quality vine cultivation. The village has no producers of its own.

% 94% 30% PN, 40% PM, 30% CH

MUTIGNY

Just below the village there are some fantastic slopes, but sadly for Mutigny they belong to Mareuil-sur-Aÿ. The 75 hectares that lie within Mutigny's boundaries are of medium Premier cru quality. The village is a good example of how superior Pinot Noir is to the other types of grape on the north side of the Marne river.

% 93% 65% PN, 30% PM, 5% CH

PARGNY-LES-REIMS

Unexpectedly upgraded to Premier cru status in 1985. This tiny village with its very nice restaurant called "Le Pargny" is just north of Jouy-les-Reims. In the village you will find Médot's Clos des Chaulins.

% 90% 25% PN, 65% PM, 10% CH

PIERRY

The monk called Dom Oudart, a contemporary of Dom Pérignon, carried out his work in this suburb of Épernay. Today the village is perhaps best known for the castle La Marquetterie which is owned by Taittinger. The view from Pierry's vineyards is awesome. Behind you there is a forest full of birds and game, to the left you see the towns of Épernay and Champillon, below lies Pierry with Taittinger's magnificent castle and on the other side of the road is the wonderful stone church of Chavot. On the far horizon you can see the heart of Côte des Blancs, with its pearls Cramant and Avize. Pierry's vineyards rest on a bed of chalk earth with elements of flint stone. Several winemakers from the major houses say that Pierry has a clear tone of flint in the flavour.

% 90% 20% PN, 65% PM, 15% CH

Bouché Père & Fils

10 rue Général de Gaulle,
51530 Pierry 03 26 54 12 44
Production: 500,000 bottles.

The firm owns 30 hectares of vineyards in ten villages, of which four are Grand cru (Chouilly, Verzy, Verzenay and Puisieulx), and exports half of its production. Bouché use only the first pressing in all their wines.

Bouché Brut 70
(30% PN, 20% PM, 50% CH)
An extremely tasty, round and mature non-vintage champagne with cheesy undertones and juicy aromas.

Bouché Rosé 67
(60% PN, 30% PM, 10% CH)
Fat and fruit sweet in a festive, crowd-pleasing style. The aftertaste is exquisite, with tones of summer berries.

Bouché B. d. B. 70
(100% CH)
Chardonnay from Chouilly and Tauxières. An open, exotic style with clear tones of passion fruit. Easily drunk and mature with an aftertaste of ice cream.

1988 Bouché 74 (Aug 95) 82
(35% PN, 20% PM, 45% CH)
A pure Grand cru champagne which is marked by heavy Pinot. Meaty and dark aromas.

H. Mandois

66 rue de Général de Gaulle,
51530 Pierry 03 26 54 03 18

A new, pleasant acquaintance for me from Pierry.

Mandois Cuvée Réserve 50
(20% PN, 40% PM, 40% CH)
Faint earthy nose with basic fruitiness. Aggressive attack.

1990 Mandois B. d. B. 82 (Jul 95) 89
(100% CH)
Aromas of peach peel and passion fruit can be traced in the relatively closed and tight nose. Medium-bodied, faintly buttery revelation with good potential and an exciting burgundy-like aftertaste.

1990 Mandois 60 (Aug 95) 62
(70% PN, 30% CH)
The champagne loses a lot in the glass but has initially a nice bread tone in the nose and a tutti-frutti flavour.

Gobillard

Château de Pierry, 51530 Pierry 03 26 54 05 11
Production: 150,000 bottles.

The Gobillard family have been winemakers in Pierry since 1836, but the house wasn't started up until 1941. Founder Paul Gobillard has been followed by his widow and his son Jean-Paul, who now is in charge of the firm.

Gobillard Brut Réserve 60
(70% PN, 30% CH)
A very mature champagne with true bottle maturity. The nose is white cheese and chocolate and has a somewhat fat and full flavour with some length.

Gobillard Rosé 49
Not as developed as the non-vintage champagne, but with some pleasing flower aromas like roses and hyacinth. The flavour is sprawling and unbalanced.

Other wines: Cuvée Régence.

Vollereaux

Rue Léon-Bourgeois, 51530 Pierry ☎ 03 26 54 03 05
Production: 400,000 bottles.

The company owns forty hectares in the Marne valley and makes low price champagnes for the French market. Only 20% is exported.

Vollereaux Brut 51
(33% PN, 33% PM, 34% CH)
A young and fruity champagne which would be improved by staying in contact with the yeast sediment a while longer.

Vollereaux Rosé 35
(100% PN)
A very indelicate style. The champagne is spicy and artifical with elements of cherry and saffron.

1991 Vollereaux B. d. B. 50 (Jul 95) 60
(100% CH)
Moët-like, with aromas of mushroom paste and yeast. A mature flavour but a hard finish. An untypical B. d. B.

1989 Vollereaux 65 (Aug 95) 78
(50% PN, 10% PM, 40% CH)
The nose is already hinting at an oily and fat structure. The wine possesses a high concentration of relatively basic, meaty aromas.

1975 Vollereaux 83 (Jul 95) 84
(30% PN, 30% PM, 40% CH)
Unashamedly fresh and young twenty year-old with beautiful green/yellow colour and a youthful nose of lemon peel, hay and popcorn. A sparkling mousse and a light, lime, crispy finish.

1993 Cuvée Marguerite 70 (Mar 97) 84
(25% PN, 75% CH)
A very young and fresh champagne where the subdued nose has a flowery side, and the promising flavour is full of young acidity.

Vincent d'Astrée

Rue Léon Bourgeois, 51530 Pierry ☎ 03 26 54 03 23

The Pierry cooperative was founded in 1956 and today boasts 140 members with a cultivated area of sixty hectares.

Vincent d'Astrée Brut 52
(80% PM, 20% CH)
A rather soft and round champagne with good purity.

Vincent d'Astrée Cuvée Réserve 55
(40% PN, 60% CH)
Flowery and Chardonnay-influenced with elements of lime and vanilla.

Vincent d'Astrée Rosé 69
(50% PN, 50% CH)
Grapes from Cumières and Chouilly. Pure nose and a faint toasty flavour with superb elegance and unexpected distinction.

Other wines: Cuvée Jean Gabin.

G. Billiard

78 rue de Général de Gaulle,
51530 Pierry ☎ 03 26 54 02 96
Production: 80,000 bottles.

The house was founded in 1935 and controls two hectares in Pierry. 85% of the grapes are bought in, and this producer is one of few that don't have reserve wines.

G Billiard Cachet Rouge 25
(40% PN, 40% PM, 20% CH)
Basic, apple and candy-like, with a touch of flour in the nose. A Muscat sweet raisin flavour.

Other wines: Blanc de Blancs, Rosé, Vintage.

Guy Michel

54 rue León Bourgeois, 51530 Pierry ☎ 03 26 54 67 12

1973 Guy Michel 75 (Jul 95) 75
Well-kept with a fine mousse and plenty of vigour. On the other hand an elementary basic wine without any greater complexity or personality.

RILLY-LA-MONTAGNE

The best vines grow at 140-200 metres above sea level. Exposure varies within the village, but most of the vineyards face the northeast. The wines are much like those from neighbouring Chigny-les-Roses, and in Rilly too the Chardonnay grapes are of high class. The village is full of interesting winemakers to explore.

% 94% 40% PN, 30% PM, 30% CH

Vilmart

4 rue de la république, 51500 Rilly ☎ 03 26 03 40 01
Production: 100,000 bottles.

Vilmart has quickly established cult status only topped among growers by J.Selosse. The firm was started in 1890 in Rilly and is now run by René and Laurent Champs. The grapes are of mere Premier cru level but the vinification is exceptional. Vilmart is one of the few growers that cultivate their grapes biodynamically and have most of the grape juice ferment in large oak casks (foudres). The perfectly pure champagnes that Vilmart produce all have a high, fine acidity as the malolactic fermentation is avoided.

Grand Cellier 80
(30% PN, 70% CH)
In previous versions of this wine I found a lot of oak and heavy aromas. Today Vilmart has hit on a chablis-like

romantic flower-scented, first class, non-vintage champagne. The flavour is pure and elegant.

1989 Grand Cellier d'Or 81 (Apr 95) 85
(30% PN, 70% CH)
In the glass one is met by heavy, smoky, slightly stale aromas. The flavour is a lot better, with the exotic passion fruits leading on to a pure and long finish.

1990 Couer de Cuvée 88 (May 97) 93
(20% PN, 80% CH)
Oaky and dry, with chewy denseness. Rich, ripe fruit on nose and palate. Truly a classic.

1989 Couer de Cuvée 88 (Apr 95) 93
(30% PN, 70% CH)
A wonderfully elegant wine that resembles ***1985 Gosset Grand Millésime*** with its multi-faceted nose and crystal-clear flavour. One of the few 89's that have enough acidity to age well.

Other wines: Grande Réserve, Rubis Brut, Grand Cellier Rubis, Cuvée Création, B. d. B.

Daniel Dumont

11 rue Gambetta, 51500 Rilly 03 26 03 40 67

Production: 50,000 bottles.

Daniel Dumont is one of Champagne's 25 "pépinières" who sell 200,000 selected, grafted vines every year to the growers in the area. He combines his plant farm with a quality-minded champagne production. In his 9-degree church-like cellar the champagnes are stored for at least five years before being sold. Dumont owns ten hectares in seven villages: Sézanne, Villers-Allerand, Villers-Marmery, Ludes, Rilly-la-Montagne, Chigny-les-Roses and Dormans. He produces medium-bodied and well-made wines in a style that is similar to many of the big houses.

D. Dumont Brut 61
(34% PN, 33% PM, 33% CH)
This is a very gentle, easy to drink non-vintage champagne that shouldn't be kept for too long. Muffled bready nose and a smooth flavour with cocoa aromas.

1990 D. Dumont 81 (May 97) 90
(40% PN, 30% PM, 30% CH)
Broad red fruit dominate the nose, which also has an element of toffee and hawthorn. Full-bodied muscular champagne with plenty of potential.

1989 Cuvée d'Exellence 83 (Apr 95) 87
(50% PN, 50% CH)
A typical '89! Sweet and rich nose of honey and red fruits, with a generous, rich, creamy and mature flavour of strawberries.

1970 D. Dumont 80 (Apr 95) 83
(40% PN, 30% PM, 30% CH)
This is the oldest wine in Dumont's archives, but at the age of 25 it was still very young and fresh. Otherwise though the wine's quality is by no means impressive. The nose is a trifle mean, with a weak biscuity element and a steely, hard and somewhat thin flavour. Above all, the aftertaste is too short.

Other wines: Rosé.

Binet

31 rue de Reims, 51500 Rilly 03 26 03 49 18

Production: 300,000 bottles.

Founder Léon Binet's great gift to the world was cold disgorging (dégorgement à la glace). He was head of the house from 1849 to 1893. The house was almost completely destroyed by the Germans' bombs during the first World War, and in order to be able to continue Binet linked up with Piper-Heidsieck. After the second World War it was Germain's turn to take over Binet, and today both Germain and Binet are owned by the Frey group. Hervé Ladouce is the cellar master for both houses and it's no secret that the best grapes end up in the Binet bottles.

Binet Brut Elite 62
(40% PN, 20% PM, 40% CH)
The nose is tame, with a light toasty basic tone and mineral elements. The flavour is citrus fresh but neutral.

1988 Binet B. d. B. 78 (Apr 95) 83
(100% CH)
The character of this champagne is definitely influenced by grapes from the Marne valley and Montagne de Reims. I don't find any finesse or freshness, but the flavour is robust and rich with a long finish.

1979 Binet B. d. B. 84 (Apr 96) 84
(100% CH)
Toasty and nice, without impact.

Binet Sélection 79
(65% PN, 35% CH)
Binet's cuvée de prestige is musty, cheesy and bushy in the nose with a little loose but rich flavour of almonds. Resembles more Germain's house style.

1945 Binet
Totally maderised in 1997. Unjudged.

Other wines: Rosé.

H. Germain

Ch. de Rilly, 51500 Rilly 03 26 03 49 18

Production: 1.6 million bottles.

Germain was founded in Ludes in 1898 but moved to Rilly and is today closely connected to Binet. Henri-Louis Germain's memory was recently honoured with the new cuvée de prestige champagne Cuvée Président. Henri-Louis was for many years president of the town's sporting pride and joy, the Reims football team.

Germain Brut 40
(50% PN, 35% PM, 15% CH)
A basic non-vintage champagne with clear elements of white cheese in the nose and a little bitterness in the aftertaste.

Germain Rosé 50
(10% PN, 10% PM, 80% CH)
A highly unusual collection of grapes in a rosé. Nor is the result particularly impressive. A "white" taste with freshness as its major asset.

1990 Germain 77 (Aug 96) 86
(60% PN, 40% CH)
A sweet, fruity, generous champagne with clear tones of gooseberry, mango and passion fruit in both nose and flavour. However, my fiancée was decidedly less positive when we drank this wine at the Moulin de Mougins outside Cannes.

1988 Germain 70 (May 95) 79
(60% PN, 15% PM, 25% CH)
Pure and fruity with a faint tone of licorice. Rather light.

1979 Germain B. d. B. 88 (Mar 96) 88
(100% CH)
Very positive green-tinged yellow with a stream of small bubbles. Faint nose and fair length.

1986 Germain Président 80 (Apr 95) 86
(20% PN, 80% CH)
It's as if the prestige cuvées of Binet and Germain have exchanged labels. The wine has Binet's slightly more restrained Chardonnay style. The nose is sauternes-like and the flavour is restrained with hints of ginger, gingerbread and strawberries.

1979 Cuvée Venus 89 (Jan 96) 89
(60% PN, 40% CH)
Lighter and more refined than the fleshy '76.

1976 Cuvée Venus 89 (Jan 96) 89
(60% PN, 40% CH)
Yellow colour, minty nose and a fleshy, firm mouth-filling flavour.

1971 Cuvée Venus 87 (Jul 95) 87
(60% PN, 40% CH)
Very well-kept cuvée de prestige with the fine acidity of the vintage and a mature nose of gorgonzola and Danish pastries.

Adam Garnotel

17 rue de Chigny, 51500 Rilly ☎ 03 26 03 40 22
Production: 300,000 bottles.

When you take the "Champagne road" through Rilly it's easy to drive straight into Adam's well-signposted plant. It's much harder to find his champagnes. It was only on my third attempt that I succeeded in finding someone in authority who could supply me with the firm's elixir of life. The firm was founded in 1899 by Louis Adam, and now runs ten hectares in Rilly, having rapidly expanded production since the end of the seventies.

Daniel Adam Brut 61
(33% PN, 33% PM, 34% CH)
Pure but one-dimensional fruit flavour with elements of mineral and yeast.

1990 Cuvée Louis-Adam 85 (Jul 97) 89
(30% PN, 70% CH)
The company's new cuvée de prestige is a pure '90. There's a very tight, concentrated fruit with a creamy feel. It resembles the *Special Club* from several top class growers in Côte des Blancs.

Other wines: Rosé.

Veuve Maurice Lepitre

26 rue de Reims, 51500 Rilly ☎ 03 26 03 40 27
Production: 40,000 bottles.

Maurice Lepitre started his company in 1905, and today his creation owns seven hectares in Rilly-la-Montagne. M. and Mme. Millex are very proud of their chalk cellar.

Maurice Lepitre Brut 60
(33% PN, 33% PM, 34% CH)
Sound and well balanced, but without personality. Clean, dry finish.

Maurice Lepitre Rosé 57
(33% PN, 33% PM, 34% CH)
Raspberry, wild cherries on the nose and strong meaty flavours on the palate.

Cuvée Héritage 81
(100% CH)
A pure B. d. B. from Maurice Lepitre in Rilly-la-Montagne. Clear grape character if somewhat more full-bodied than its equivalent from Côte des Blancs. The fruit is in harmony with tropical elements.

Other wines: Rilly, Vintage.

Lemoine

Rue de Chigny B.P. 7,
51500 Rilly ☎ 03 26 03 40 25
Production: 325,000 bottles.

Owned by Laurent-Perrier. Wines not tasted.

Hubert Paulet

55 rue de Chigny, 51500 Rilly ☎ 03 26 03 40 68
Production: 20,000 bottles.

Pinot Meunier, Pinot Noir and Chardonnay are all used in their cuvées. Paulet owns eight hectares. Wines not tasted.

SACY

There isn't a single vineyard in Petit Montagne that produces really high-class grapes. However, Sacy has the best reputation along with neighbouring Villedommange. Just as with Les Mesneaux, the giant concern Mercier owns most of the vineyards.

% 90% 55% PN, 35% PM, 10% CH

TAISSY

Apart from a southerly sloping hill called Mont Ferré most of the village's vineyards are on flat ground. An overrated village where Moët & Chandon are the largest single landowners.

% 94% 23% PN, 45% PM, 32% CH

TAUXIÈRES

One of the two villages that are just 1% away from achieving Grand cru status, but as opposed to Mareuil-sur-Aÿ, Tauxières is graded far too high. The wines are of low Premier cru quality and are used chiefly in cuvées. As usual Bollinger owns the oldest vines and the best slopes in the village. Other important landowners are Moët and Mercier.

% 99% 80% PN, 5% PM, 15% CH

Yves Louvet

21 rue du Poncet, 51150 Tauxières 03 26 57 03 27

Production: 35,000 bottles.

This producer owns 6,5 hectares in Bouzy and Tauxières.

Yves Louvet Brut 69
(75% PN, 25% CH)
Well-balanced, focused and tight. A good wine for the cellar.

Yves Louvet Réserve 72
(75% PN, 25% CH)
The same impressions with a tiny bit more maturity.

Yves Louvet Rosé 59
(80% PN, 20% CH)
Closed nose, deep colour, medium-bodied and neutral.

1991 Yves Louvet 73 (Oct 97) 78
(75% PN, 25% CH)
Bready, harmonious and surprisingly focused '91.

Other wines: Sélection, B.d.B.

TRÉPAIL

Just to the northeast of Bouzy and Ambonnay lies Trépail, and the village has a lot in common with its neighbours. The best locations with a southeasterly exposure are 160-200 metres above sea level, and as with Bouzy you have to be careful about where within the village the grapes actually come from. Definitely a village to explore further. Surprisingly much Chardonnay.

% 95% 13% PN, 87% CH

Claude Beaufort

5 rue des Neigettes, 51380 Trépail 03 26 57 05 63

Yet another grower from the Bouzy family of Beaufort.

C. Beaufort Brut 65
The same rich, fat style as Herbert Beaufort in Bouzy, with a heavy chocolate flavour. A champagne that is much more at home at the dinner table than some opening day party.

TROIS-PUITS

Now almost a suburb of Reims. The cultivated soil is on flat land and is close to the built-up area. The quality here doesn't have the best of reputations.

% 94% 25% PN, 68% PM, 7% CH

VAUDEMANGE

In practice it is the well-known Reims company of George Goulet that has its headquarters here. Together with Billy-le-Grand, Vaudemange forms the easternmost point of Montagne de Reims. Here we have yet another village that stubbornly grows the kind of grapes it's not best suited for. Of course Vaudemange ought to be a Pinot-dominated village! Mumm now owns most of the Pinot vines.

% 95% 20% PN, 80% CH

VERTUS

Vertus is the largest of all the Premier cru villages in terms of land area, and it's also the southernmost of the top quality villages. In historical terms, strangely enough, the village is probably better known for its Pinot grapes than its Chardonnay. The numerous vin clairs that I have tasted of the Pinot Noir from Vertus have not impressed me, despite the fact that the vines come from pre-phylloxera vines from Beaune. In my opinion the Chardonnay grapes are much more interesting. Although they aren't in the same league as the Grand cru villages, their rich and fruity style puts them atop the second division. Many famous champagne houses buy grapes from here and quite a few of them have their own vineyards in the village. Duval-Leroy and Louis Roederer are the largest individual landowners, with 22 hectares apiece, but Moët, Henriot and Larmandier also control large estates. Few of the growers make pure Vertus champagnes - most are cuvées from various Chardonnay crus.

% 95% 12% PN, 88% CH

Larmandier-Bernier

43 rue du 28 Août, 51130 Vertus 03 26 52 13 24

Production: 85,000 bottles.

The firm owns 9.5 hectares in Bèrgeres-les-Vertus, Chouilly, Cramant and Vertus. Pierre Larmandier, who also chairs the young winemakers association, makes some of the purest Chardonnay champagnes around today. This relaxed and intellectual 35 year-old works in tandem with his mother, who took over after her husband. With his father's death coming so suddenly, it took time before Pierre felt ready to take on the controlling role in the company, and he tells openly of the differing tastes he and his mother have. Pierre loves acidic, restrained champagnes while his mother enjoys more accessible, fruity wines. Fortunately Pierre's taste is taking over more and more. The family has owned a few hectares of extremely old Chardonnay vines in Cramant for a long time, and during the 1990 harvest Pierre decided to make an exclusive champagne from these 80 year-old vines alone. The result is a champagne that will be legendary through into the early 2000's. All his wines gain from keeping for ten years - or maybe even more in a good cellar!

Larmandier-Bernier Tradition 69
(20% PN, 80% CH)
Pure and light aperitif champagne with a young and flowery nose, aggressive attack and a spicy initial taste that develops into a finish full of apples.

Larmandier-Bernier B. d. B. 76
(100% CH)
Chardonnay from the company's four villages. Here too a restrained and light style, more elegant than ***Tradition***, with a creamy finish.

1989 Larmandier-Bernier 84 (Aug 97) 87
(100% CH)
Always refreshing, with an almost chablisien nose. Dry, clean mid-palate and an acidic finish.

1988 Larmandier-Bernier Special Club 80 (Nov 94) 89
(100% CH)
Almost exclusively Cramant grapes in the cuvée. Very similar to the ***88 Bonnaire***, with its butterscotch nose and chablis-like Chardonnay fruit.

1979 Larmandier-Bernier Special Club 91 (Aug 96) 91
(100% CH)
A crisp wine, with citrus flavours and nutty nuances. Dry, classic finish.

1975 Larmandier-Bernier Special Club 93 (Nov 95) 94
(100% CH)
It's always a pleasure to drink an older blanc de blancs straight from the producer himself. The '75 is the firm's first vintage, and it resisted for many years before it eventually found itself. Today it is a wonderfully harmonious champagne, so classical and restrained with all of Chardonnay's mature tones like coffee, toasted bread, butterscotch and popcorn. Perfectly pure acidity, like a great ***Salon***.

1990 Larmandier-Bernier Grand Cru Cramant
(100% CH) 90 (Jun 95) 95
I believe that all the great wines in the world have something in common: a superior intensity in the nose that comes from their unique soil. This Cramant champagne is such a wine. The nose is incredibly elusive, with an explosive, indescribably floweriness. Even though it is a little shy now, it's lying there under the surface, waiting to explode in all its beauty. The flavour is extremely long, tight and focused. Buy all the bottles you can get your hands on and put them away for your grandchildren!

Guy Larmandier

30 rue du Général Koenig,
51130 Vertus ☎ 03 26 52 12 41
Production: 65,000 bottles.

This small company, which was started in Vertus in 1977, has built up a good reputation since Robert Parker boosted their wines. Personally, I think that Côte des Blancs has a great number of more interesting growers, and every wine I've tasted from this property has been well-made but a bit closed in the nose. Guy Larmandier, who left Larmandier in Cramant, is most proud of his four hectares in Cramant, besides his three hectares in Vertus, half a hectare in Cuis and two in Chouilly. The wines are put through malolactic fermentation and cold stabilisation, the vines in Cramant are almost thirty years old and should give more exciting champagnes than they do today. The vintage wine always comes from two Cramant locations: Gros Mont and Fond du Bateaux.

Guy Larmandier Premier Cru 68
(5% PN, 95% CH)
A champagne made entirely from Vertus grapes. Faint, pure nose and a flavour that is just as pure and neutral.

1992 Guy Larmandier 79 (Jul 97) 83
(100% CH)
One of the better champagnes from this vintage. The wine is already showing a friendly attitude, with a rich nose of apple and pear. The flavour is rather sweet and mature with a richness that's unusual among 92's.

1989 Guy Larmandier Grand Cru 81 (Apr 95) 87
(100% CH)
Very pale colour, faint nose with elements of cream candies and white flowers. Creamy, sweet flavour of good purity.

1982 Guy Larmandier Grand Cru 84 (Apr 95) 87
(100% CH)
Once again a shy, closed nose. Those tones that one can make out are high-class and the flavour is restrained and full of finesse, but not so generous for an '82.

Other wines: Rosé, Cuvée Perlée.

Severin-Doublet

10 rue des Falloises, 51130 Vertus ☎ 03 26 52 10 57
Production: 50,000 bottles.

The property in Vertus has one of the best names in Côte des Blancs, but the reputation comes chiefly from their vintage champagnes, which aren't commercially available.

Severin-Doublet B. d. B. 70
(100% CH)
Pin-head bubbles stream out of the green/yellow wine, together with a faint nose of vanilla cake and lemon. The chalk is clearly felt on the palate, but the champagne lacks stamina on the final straight.

Veuve Fourny

5 rue du Mesnil, 51130 Vertus ☎ 03 26 52 16 30
Production: 70,000 bottles.

Since 1955 the Fourny family have made their own champagne, and today Monique Fourny makes some delicious champagnes from her 6.5 hectares.

Fourny Réserve 78
(20% PN, 10% PM, 80% CH)
Pure Chardonnay aroma with excellent mineral and citrus tones. A moreish champagne.

Fourny B. d. B. 59
(100% CH)
Confusingly, this is simpler and looser than the restrained ***Réserve***. The aromas veer more towards red fruit and a clear hint of saffron.

Robert Doyard

61 av. de Bammental, 51130 Vertus ☎ 03 26 52 14 74
Production: 50,000 bottles.

Yannick Doyard is the fourth generation after Maurice Doyard, who was one of the founders of the C.I.V.C. Doyard is one of the few who make a Vertus Rouge.

Robert Doyard Demi-Sec 50
(100% CH)
A not so terribly sweet champagne, with nice fruit aroma.

Robert Doyard B. d. B. 72
(100% CH)
Rather a robust and square B. d. B. with the right tightness and some potential for development. On the other hand that gossamer-thin elegance is lacking.

Robert Doyard Extra Brut 72
(100% CH)
Same as *B. d. B.*, Without any dosage.

Other wines: Rosé, Vintage.

Paul Goerg

4 pl. du Mont Chenil, 51130 Vertus ☎ 03 26 52 15 31
Production: 600,000 bottles.

Paul Georg is the brand from the La Goutte d'Or cooperative, which owns 115 hectares in Vertus, Chouilly and Mesnil. La Goutte d'Or has for many years supplied the major houses with first-class "vin clair" Chardonnay. In 1982 they decided to launch their own label, using only Premier and Grand cru Chardonnay, and only the first pressing is considered good enough. The non-vintage champagne is first sold after three or four years and the vintage after five.

Paul Goerg Brut Tradition 68
(40% PN, 60% CH)
A really elegant non-vintage champagne with a lightly toasty Chardonnay nose and a soft, accessible flavour.

Paul Goerg B. d. B. 71
(100% CH)
A pure nose of apples and sun-warmed rocks. A full flavour with undertones of grapefruit. Dry and unified.

1990 Paul Goerg 80 (Oct 97) 85
(100% CH)
Powerful and elegant at the same time.

1988 Paul Goerg 74 (Apr 95) 82
(100% CH)
This wine is made in the same style as their non-vintage blanc de blancs, but with greater concentration and better length.

Other wines: Rosé, Brut Absolut, Cuvée de Centenaire.

Duval-Leroy

69 av. de Bammental, 51130 Vertus ☎ 03 26 52 10 75
Production: 5 million bottles (2 million as Duval-Leroy).

Seventy percent of the bottles the firm sells go under other names or labels ordered by the buyer. Duval-Leroy is in fact the largest actor on this market, and the company harvests from 48 villages and uses all the grapes from the second pressing. The company, which was founded in 1859 is something of a mixed bag today - some of the worst champagnes I've drunk are second-labeled Duval-Leroy wines. On the other hand those champagnes that carry Duval-Leroy's own name are certainly pure and very good value for money. the owners of the house are very serious and quality-conscious.

E. Michel Brut 24
Is this really champagne? The colour is reddish. A moldy Chenin Blanc nose, and the flavour is definitely earthy. An insult to the district.

P. Vertay Brut 30
The same reddish colour. A more perfumed, basic nose and a somewhat sweeter and slightly less earthy flavour.

Veuve Morant 19
At home I have a whole cupboard full of empty champagne bottles. They are arranged in order of rank. Right now bottle number 100 is of very high quality, but the last bottle in the cupboard - Veuve Morant - is there for quite a different reason. The champagne is, in fact, the worst of any I've tasted that hasn't actually been defective. Reddish colour, rubber and elderflower in a spumante nose. A flavour of apple wrapped up in earth and rusty steel. The mousse foamed like a cheap soda drink. The same impression every time I taste it!

Duval-Leroy Tradition 50
(25% PN, 60% PM, 15% CH)
A light colour, fine mouse, sour nose of unripe apples. The fruit and softness in the aftertaste is, however, very pleasant. Drink it cold, as a candy-like simplicity is revealed when aired.

Fleur de Champagne 70
(25% PN, 75% CH)
An untrustworthy rogue! Sometimes it beats the major houses' non-vintage champagnes while on other occasions it is of more modest quality. At its best it's a lively, mineral-rich light aperitif champagne with pure acidity.

Duval-Leroy B. d. B. 70
(100% CH)
Another champagne with troublesome bottle variation. Quite clearly it demands time in the bottle, and when young there is a disturbing earthiness about it. This taste is rounded off in time and becomes a biscuity, full flavour.

1990 Duval-Leroy B. d. B. 73 (Feb 96) 86
(100% CH)
Typical of the vintage and restrained. This very reasonably-priced champagne hardly expresses any village character, but is instead a good example of a Chardonnay cuvée.

1988 Duval-Leroy Fleur de Champagne 80 (Feb 97) 84
(100% CH)
A little sweet, but a pleasing almond flavour and good grape character.

1986 Fleur de Champagne 68 (Nov 93) 75
(30% PN, 70% CH)
A lively revelation with a nose of hawthorn and green apples. Hardly exciting, but a pure flavour and an undeveloped finish.

1986 Cuvée des Roys 82 (Feb 95) 87
(5% PN, 95% CH)
This champagne lives more on its power than its elegance even though it's almost a full blanc de blancs. Heavy, spicy nose with an undertone of freesia. A strong, bready flavour with a crispy lime finish.

Other wines: Cuvée des Roys Rosé, Fleur Rosé de Saignée.

Douquet-Jeanmaire

44 Chemin du Moulin, 51130 Vertus ☎ 03 26 52 16 50
Production: 100,000 bottles.

This grower owns 13 hectares of Chardonnay in Vertus and has specialised in producing vintage wines during those years when no-one else does. The older vintages remain in contact with the yeast for up to twenty years. This is an initiative worthy of praise, although the wines are more interesting as curios than a source of any great pleasure. The prices are reasonable so if you see an older vintage, snap it up.

Douquet-Jeanmaire B. d. B. 64
(100% CH)
Incredibly light, almost like mineral water. Probably

disgorged as early as after two years. Subtle and delicate but diluted and bordering on thin.

1982 Douquet-Jeanmaire 81 (Dec 96) 81
(100% CH)
Dark, developed colour and a delightfully exotic nose. Sadly the aftertaste contains some oxidation tones.

1977 Douquet-Jeanmaire 70 (May 94) 70
(100% CH)
The nose is complete and classical, but the poor year comes out in the flavour. Diluted with a weak aroma of tea leaves.

1974 Douquet-Jeanmaire 85 (Jan 93) 86
(100% CH)
Strong autolytic character, with hazelnut and wood aromas. The flavour is also surprisingly full of extracts and is concentrated. Vertus produced the best grapes in this mediocre year.

1970 Douquet-Jeanmaire 65 (Apr 94) ▼
(100% CH)
Despite a good mousse and golden colour, the nose was a touch impure. Not only did the wine have the appearance of beer, but the nose had tendencies towards malt and beeswax. The wine collapsed in the mouth as the building bricks had been flattened out into a vague, soft and loose whole. Sherry tones in the aftertaste.

Colin

48 av. Louis Lenoir, 51130 Vertus ☎ 03 26 58 86 32
Production: 20,000 bottles.

Philippe Colin currently has access to eleven hectares in Vertus, Bergères-les-Vertus, Cramant, Oiry and Sézanne. Pierre Radt founded the business in 1890.

Collin B. d. B. 58
(100% CH)
A certain butteriness in the nose gives a lift to what is rather a rustic wine.

Other wines: Alliance, Vintage, Rosé, Cuvée Bacchus.

Charles-Lafitte

"Le Pavé", 51130 Vertus ☎ 03 26 53 33 40
Production: 1.6 million bottles.

Paul François Vranken took over the company in 1983 and this has to be seen as Demoiselle's second firm. Thierry Gomerieux, who is responsible for the blending, sees Lafitte as a classic blended champagne but uses his best grapes in Barancourt and Demoiselle.

Charles-Lafitte Brut 50
(40% PN, 20% PM, 40% CH)
A little, slim wine with apple aromas and green flavour.

Charles-Lafitte Rosé 42
(40% PN, 60% CH)
An unpretentious rosé champagne which at its best can be described as refreshing.

Charles-Lafitte Grand Prestige 79
(100% CH)
A lovely champagne with mature tones of English butterscotch in the nose and a soft, slender creaminess in the mouth. However, the aftertaste is faintly oxidated.

Other wines: Brut Prestige, Vintage.

Napoleon (A.Prieur)

2 rue de Villers-aux-Bois, 51130 Vertus ☎ 03 26 52 11 74
Production: 150,000 bottles.

The firm was founded in 1825 by Jean-Louis Prieur and since then has stayed within the family. They took the name Napoleon in order to conquer the Russian market, which was something they succeeded in doing, and today the firm is led by the very pleasant and committed Vincent Prieur. Napoleon have no vineyards of their own and are forced to buy in all of their grapes. Many wine journalists praise the quality of Prieur's champagne, but although I am loath to admit it I'm afraid I cannot join in singing those praises. The champagnes are dominated by an untypical tone of ginger which has proved to be easy to spot at blind tastings.

Napoleon Carte Vert 39
(8% PN, 66% PM, 26% CH)
A nose of ginger and hawthorn. An aggressive, sharp flavour with no signs of maturity.

Napoleon Traditon Carte d'Or 45
(56% PN, 44% CH)
Once again that nose of ginger and cinnamon. The flavour is a touch more rounded here, but still far too sharp and green.

Napoleon Rosé 48
(60% PN, 40% CH)
The colour is a gorgeous salmon pink, the mousse is fine, but the nose and flavour are peculiar in an otherwise decent structure.

1981 Napoleon 60 (Jul 90) 70
(60% PN, 40% CH)
A wine much praised by the critics, which I have never understood. There is a hint of Chardonnay fruit but the firm's personal spicy tone slammed down the lid on the wine's otherwise good qualities.

Doyard-Mahé

Le Moulin d'Argensol
che Sept Moulins,
51130 Vertus ☎ 03 26 52 23 85

Doyard-Mahé Carte d'Or 49
(100% CH)
This wine from Vertus has, sadly, a faint tone of unclean cellar. Otherwise the fruit is strong, with tones of banana and pineapple juice.

J-P. Boulonnais

14 rue de l'Abbaye, 51130 Vertus ☎ 03 26 52 23 41
Production: 50,000 bottles.

The property was founded in 1970 and today covers five hectares. Wines not tasted.

Wines: B. d. B.

VILLEDOMMANGE

Alongside Sacy this is the best village in Petit Montagne. The wines are planted at heights of 115-240 metres above sea level and are spread throughout the entire village. Clicquot and Oudinot are major landowners here.

% 90%   30% PN, 65% PM, 5% CH

Philippe Bergeroneaux

10 rue Aurore,
51390 Villedommange   03 26 49 24 18

One of the best growers in Petit Montagne.

Philippe Bergeroneaux Brut 60
(30% PN, 50% PM, 20% CH)
Very young and pure fruit. Winter apples and pears are backed up by good acidity and an aftertaste of almonds.

VILLENEUVE-RENNEVILLE

Situated east of Côte des Blancs centre on flat land. The wines from here are very pure and elegant but hardly rate their high rank. A thin strip connects with the lowest hills of Le Mesnil and give the village's best Chardonnay grapes. Henriot is the only champagne house that owns vineyards here, and there are no producers in the village.

% 95%   100% CH

VILLERS-ALLERAND

Despite its northerly location, the village's vineyards are exposed to the light for a sufficient number of hours per day for the grapes to ripen. Of the village's annual production of 50,000 the champagne houses take some 38%, while the other 31,000 bottles are sold by two families: Prévot and Stroebel. The champagnes they sell are blanc de noirs, chiefly made from Pinot Meunier.

% 90%   27% PN, 55% PM, 18% CH

VILLERS-MARMERY

Lying between Verzy and Trépail on the eastern side of Montagne de Reims, this village grows a special clone of grapes that is highly controversial. After talking to several winemakers I've concluded that you either hate or love the wines from Villers-Marmery. One interesting detail is that Deutz uses 5-10% of Chardonnay from Villers-Marmery for its excellent blanc de blancs. it's obvious that the wines have a very clearly defined personality, good potential alcohol content and fine acidity.

% 95%    5% PN, 95% CH

Margaine

3 av. de Champagne,
51380 Villers-Marmery   03 26 97 92 13

Production: 64,000 bottles.

All the wines produced by the company are monocru champagnes. They own seven hectares.

Margaine Traditionelle 67
(12% PN, 88% CH)
Very distinctive Chardonnay-influenced wine with good power and pleasing grape-like fruit.

1989 Margaine Special Club 70 (Jul 95) 86
(100% CH)
The wine hasn't gone through malolactic fermentation and is undeveloped and hard. The flavour is restrained but very long. Hide somewhere in the cellar!

Henriet-Bazin

9 rue Dom Pérignon,
51380 Villers-Marmery   03 26 97 96 81

Production: 60,000 bottles.

The firm owns six hectares in Villers-Marmery, Verzy and Verzenay. It is owned by Daniel Henriet and Marie-Noëlle Henriet.

D. Henriet-Bazin B. d. B. 72
(100% CH)
Tropical, spicy and restrained. I wonder how good the cuvée de prestige is?

D. Henriet-Bazin Rosé 68
(100% PN)
A discreet rosé which should be enjoyed as an aperitif, despite its grape content. Buttery, light flavour.

Other wines: Vintage, N-M Henriet.

Boutillez-Guer

38 rue Pasteur,
51380 Villers-Marmery   03 26 97 91 38

Production: 80,000 bottles.

Chardonnay from Villers-Marmery and Pinot Noir from Verzenay.

Boutillez-Guer Brut 55
(30% PN, 70% CH)
More full-bodied than the blanc de blancs. Otherwise the same perfumed style.

Boutillez-Guer B. d. B. 54
(100% CH)
Nose of tutti-frutti and perfume. Soft, creamy texture and a very fruity taste.

Other wines: Tradition.

Sadi Malot

35 rue Pasteur,
51380 Villers-Marmery   03 26 97 90 48

Production: 80,000 bottles.

This producer owns ten hectares in Montagne de Reims. Wines not tasted.

VILLERS-AUX-NOEUDS

Yet another village outside the central area that was upgraded in 1985.

% 90%

VOIPREUX

An unknown village outside Côte des Blancs, but some slopes border on Vertus and Villeneuve-Renneville and give excellent Chardonnay grapes. Not as excellent as their ranking gives them credit for, however.

% 95%   100% CH

Other producers in the Premier cru area:

Avenay

Jean-Paul Augustin	03 26 52 31 20
François Marniquet	03 26 52 32 36
Pierre Morlet	03 26 52 32 32
Picart-Thiout	03 26 52 31 71
Jean-Pierre Remion	03 26 52 31 05
William Vatel-Fouquy	03 26 52 30 09
Coop. d'Avenay Val d'Or	03 26 52 31 24

Bergères-les-Vertus

Serge Milliat	03 26 52 20 42
Coop. "le Mont Aime"	03 26 52 02 15

Billy-le-Grand

Jean-Claude Bocart	03 26 67 95 67
Roger Lapin	03 26 65 57 83

Bisseuil

Clos-Babot	03 26 58 92 12

Chamery

Michel André	03 26 97 64 66
Roger Bonnet	03 26 97 64 48
Thierry Bonnet	03 26 97 65 40
Michel Delespierre	03 26 97 65 02
Daniel Feneuil	03 26 97 62 35
Philippe Hanon	03 26 97 65 60
Claude Lallement	03 26 97 64 04
Henri Maillart	03 26 97 63 27
Gérard Parmantier	03 26 97 63 15
Coop. de Chamery	03 26 97 64 67

Champillon

Gilles Boucher	03 26 59 48 17
Bertrand Devavry	03 26 59 46 21
Fernand Gelin	03 26 59 46 26
Georges Josseaux	03 26 59 46 70
Jean-Loup Méa	03 26 59 47 50
André Roualet	03 26 59 46 45

Chigny-les-Roses

Jacky Broggini	03 26 03 44 77
Michel Cossy	03 26 03 44 28
Geneviève Duchesne	03 26 03 42 76
Guy Dumangin	03 26 03 46 25
Jean Dumangin	03 26 03 42 17
Dumenil	03 26 03 44 48
Perthois Gerlier	03 26 03 48 20
François Lepitre	03 26 03 42 05
Michel Thoumy	03 26 03 44 58
Coop. de Chigny-les-Roses	03 26 03 44 30

Cuis

Jean Gimonnet	03 26 59 78 39
Pierre Lebrun	03 26 59 78 51
Coop. Vinicole de Cuis	03 26 59 78 30

Cumières

Pierre Bertrand	03 26 55 24 41
Blosseville-Maniquet	03 26 55 25 47
Jeannine Delabaye	03 26 51 63 81
Dominique Denois	03 26 55 42 45
Jean- Marie Etienne	03 26 51 66 62
Madeleine Gaillot	03 26 55 24 80
Philippe Gaillot	03 26 55 66 12
André Itasse	03 26 54 84 51
Alain Laval	03 26 51 61 83
Maitre Geoffroy	03 26 55 29 87
Poittevin	03 26 51 69 86
Guy Vadin	03 26 55 23 36

Dizy

Alain Bernard	03 26 55 24 78
J-L Bernard	03 26 51 23 34
Charbonnier	03 26 51 55 60
Paul Léfuvée	03 26 55 46 82
Francis Tarillon	03 26 55 33 93
Jean Tarillon	03 26 55 33 68
Gérard Leclère	03 26 55 23 09

Écueil

Alain Allouchery	03 26 49 77 48
Daniel Allouchery	03 26 49 71 61
Jean-Pierre Allouchery	03 26 49 74 19
Marie-Rose Bernardon	03 26 49 77 66
Alain Brochet	03 26 49 77 44
Jean-Louis Brochet	03 26 49 74 23
Marc Brugnon	03 26 49 77 59
Marie-F. Godbillon	03 26 49 77 12
Jean-Guy Lacourte	03 26 49 74 75
T. Leclère-Brochet	03 26 49 77 56
Michel Maillart	03 26 49 77 89
Jean-Louis Piontillart	03 26 49 77 24
Philippe Piontillart	03 26 49 74 95
Daniel Savart	03 26 49 77 07
Michelle Varry	03 26 49 77 34
Yves Vely	03 26 49 74 52
Coop. d'Écueil	03 26 49 77 09

Grauves

Pierre Domi	03 26 59 71 03
Jacques Driant	03 26 59 72 26
Bertrand Gaspard	03 26 59 72 46
Philippe Gaspard	03 26 59 75 41
Godard	03 26 59 71 19
Michel Mathieu	03 26 59 71 31
Bernard Populus	03 26 59 71 34
Coop. Royal Coteau	03 26 59 71 12

Hautvillers

L'Altavilloise	03 26 59 40 18
J-P Bosser	03 26 59 41 56
Gobillard	03 26 51 00 24
Fernand Lemaire	03 26 59 40 44
Lopez-Martin	03 26 59 42 17
Louis Nicaise	03 26 59 40 21
G. Tribaut	03 26 59 40 57

Jouy-les-Reims

Jean Aubry	03 26 49 20 12
Aubry & Fils	03 26 49 20 07
Crinque Bonnet	03 26 49 20 07
Francis Cossy	03 26 49 75 56
J-J Perseval	03 26 49 21 25
Julien Perseval	03 26 49 78 42
J-P Tual	03 26 49 21 27
Coop. Rurale et Vinicole	03 26 49 20 20

Ludes

Bérèche & Fils	03 26 61 13 28
Forget-Chauvet	03 26 61 11 73
Forget-Chemin	03 26 61 12 17
Jean-Claude Francois	03 26 61 12 97
Huré	03 26 61 11 20
Francis Janisson	03 26 61 13 23
Gilles Menu	03 26 61 10 77
Monmarthe	03 26 61 10 99
Jean Quartresols	03 26 61 10 57
Serge Raffin	03 26 61 12 84
Coop. de Ludes	03 26 61 10 63

Mareuil-sur-Aÿ

Bénard-Pitois	03 26 50 60 28
Roland Bénard	03 26 50 60 36
André Danteny	03 26 52 60 30
James Pouillon	03 26 52 60 08

Les Mesneaux

Jacquinet & Fils	03 26 36 25 25
Michel Jacquinet	03 26 36 23 04
Maurice Leroy-Bertin	03 26 36 23 60
Jackie Trousset	03 26 36 22 95

Mutigny

Serge Humbert	03 26 52 31 02
Raymond Thibaut	03 26 52 32 92

Pargny-les-Reims

Pascal Cossy	03 26 49 21 05
Denis Jackowiak	03 26 49 20 26

Pierry

Bagnost & Fils	03 26 54 04 22
Michel Lenique	03 26 54 03 65
Michel-Mortier	03 26 54 67 12
Richard Sélèque	03 26 54 02 55

Rilly-la-Montagne

Claude Allemandou	03 26 03 40 40
J-M Beurton	03 26 03 46 27
Michel Bouxin	03 26 03 40 35
Henri Chauvet	03 26 03 42 54
Marc Chauvet	03 26 03 42 71
Robert Chauvet	03 26 03 41 54
Couvreur-Deglaire	03 26 03 44 54
Couvreur-Fondeur	03 26 03 41 14
Jaques Couvreur	03 26 03 40 05
Yves Couvreur	03 26 03 47 04
André Delaunois	03 26 03 41 77
Delaunois Pere & Fils	03 26 03 40 53
Joseph Fagot	03 26 03 40 60
Michel Fagot	03 26 03 40 03
Didier Herbert	03 26 03 41 53
Maurice Manceaux	03 26 03 42 57
Claude Pacque	03 26 03 41 62
Gérard Pacque	03 26 03 42 53
Philbert Père & Fils	03 26 03 42 58
Jean Regnault	03 26 03 40 18
Franck Vilmart	03 26 03 41 57

Sacy

Jean-Luc Chemin	03 26 49 22 42
Damien Degenne	03 26 49 75 92
Degesne-Ronseaux	03 26 49 22 33
Goulin-Roualet	03 26 49 22 77
J-C Grill	03 26 49 23 04
Hervieux-Dumes	03 26 49 22 02
Ponsart-Brochet	03 26 49 75 85
Jany Poret	03 26 49 22 45
Denis Robert	03 26 49 22 65
J-L Valentin	03 26 49 22 51
B Wafflart	03 26 49 22 41
J Wafflart	03 26 49 22 32
Coop. de Sacy	03 26 49 22 90

Taissy

Oliver Brochet	03 26 05 78 67

Tauxières

Cochut	03 26 59 45 15
F. Mahé	03 26 57 03 76
Coop. de Louvois et Tauxières	03 26 57 03 22

Trépail

Claude Carré	03 26 57 06 04
Carré Guébels	03 26 57 05 02
Carré-Herbin	03 26 57 05 74
J-C Dupont	03 26 57 05 59
Pierre Gabriel	03 26 57 05 46
Gilbert Guébels	03 26 57 05 58
Guy Guébels	03 26 57 05 65
Georges Maizières	03 26 57 05 04
Gilbert Petiau	03 26 57 05 48

Vaudemange

Chaudron	03 26 66 44 88
Rochet-Bocart	03 26 97 99 15
Coop. Vaudemange	03 26 69 10 98

Vertus

Daniel Bonnet	03 26 52 22 46
René Bonnet	03 26 52 23 95
Alain Bourgeois	03 26 52 16 94
Paul Charpentier	03 26 52 23 57
Geoffroy	03 26 52 28 69
Guy Moreaux	
	03 26 52 25 84
Pascal Perrot	03 26 52 12 96
Charles Pougeoise	03 26 52 26 63
Michel Rogue	03 26 52 15 68
Rutat	03 26 52 14 79
Coop. Henri Augustin	03 26 52 13 41
Coop. La Vigneronne	03 26 52 20 31
Coop. de Vertus	03 26 52 14 53

Villedommange

Bardoux	03 26 49 25 35
Daniel Camus	03 26 49 25 29
René Chardonnet	03 26 49 25 21
Jaques Charlier	03 26 49 25 19
Guy Froux	03 26 49 25 14
Denis Poret	03 26 49 25 23
J-M. Serurrier	03 26 49 24 10
Coop. Villedommange	03 26 49 24 41
Coop. V. D. C.	03 26 49 26 76

Villers-Allerand

Claude Prévot	03 26 97 66 85
René Prévot	03 26 97 61 16
Stroebel Frères	03 26 97 60 12
Marcel Stroebel	03 26 97 60 40

Villers-Marmery

Pascal Adnet	03 26 97 93 46
Gérard Boutillez	03 26 97 95 87
Emile Brassart	03 26 97 90 23
Loncle	03 26 97 91 73
Jackie Simonet	03 26 97 92 41
Coop. de Villers-Marmery	03 26 97 91 51

Other villages

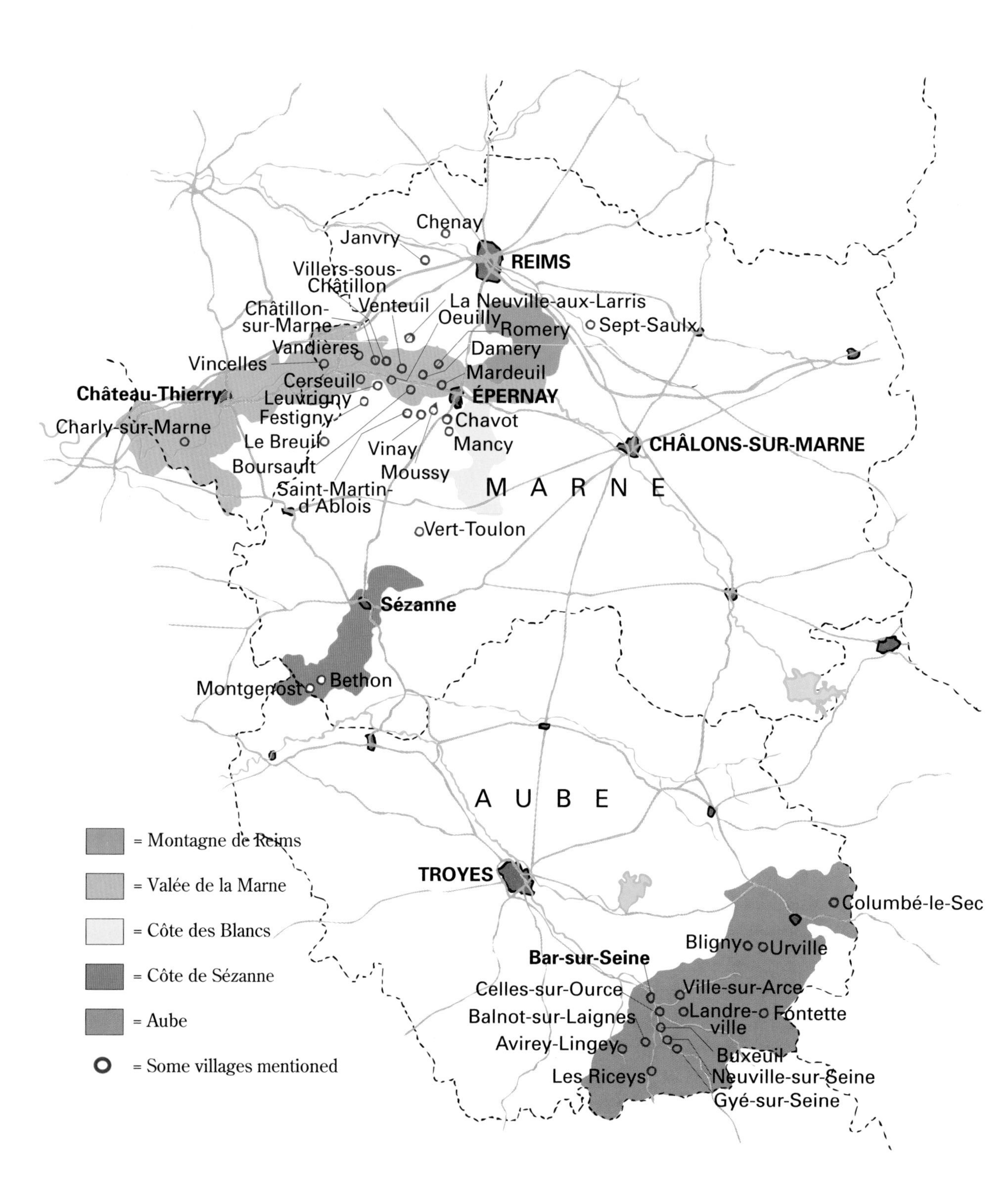

ARCONVILLE

% 80% 90% PN, 5% PM, 5% CH

A fifty-hectare cru that lies 10 km south of Bar-sur-Aube.

Bernard Gaucher

10200 Arconville ☎ 03 25 27 87 31

Production: 50,000 bottles.

Bernard Gaucher has twelve hectares in Côte des Bars. Wines not tasted.

Wines: Carte d'Or, Réserve, Brut.

AVIREY-LINGEY

The village lies in the southeastern Aube district, northwest of Les Riceys.

% 80% 94% PN, 6% CH

Serge Mathieu

Route d'Avirey à Lingey, 10340 ☎ 03 25 29 32 58

Production: 90,000 bottles.

Serge Mathieu is one of Aube's most-praised producers. He owns nine hectares in the surroundings of Avirey-Lingey. A very serious winemaker who would be even better using grapes from Marne.

Serge Mathieu Tradition 47
(90% PN, 10% CH)
Rough and earthy with elements of melon.

Serge Mathieu Prestige 48
(75% PN, 25% CH)
Basic fruit and a touch coarse. Lacking elegance.

Serge Mathieu Blanc de Noirs 62
(100% PN)
Great richness and melon-scented fruitiness, with an earthy tone.

Serge Mathieu Rosé 55
(100% PN)
A broad and aromatic rosé with a clear flavour of cherries and redcurrants.

1989 Serge Mathieu 64 (Aug 95) 75
(75% PN, 25% CH)
A compact champagne with a broad flavour of strawberries and sun-heated butter. Somewhat one-dimensional.

1988 Serge Mathieu 66 (Nov 94) 75
(75% PN, 25% CH)
Surprisingly enough the vintage wine felt lighter than the non-vintage version, although certainly possessing greater acidity and a greater potential for keeping.

Serge Mathieu Cuvée Select 66
(50% PN, 50% CH)
Straw coloured and very fine mousse. Faintly toasty with elements of tropical fruit. A well-balanced surprise from Aube.

BAGNEUX-LA-FOSSE

% 80% 99% PN, 1% CH

Five growers in this Aube village produce 69 000 bottles from 129 hectares.

Michel Beaujean

10340 Bagneaux-la-Fosse ☎ 03 25 29 37 44

Production: 100,000 bottles.

Founded in 1886 and today run by M. and Mme Beau La Mansardiére.

BALNOT-SUR-LAIGNES

34 km southwest of Bar-sur-Aube lies this village (80% on the cru scale) where most of the people are involved in one way or another with the local champagne house Gremillet.

% 80% 90% PN, 10% CH

J.M. Gremillet

1 chemin des Fleurs, Sauvages,
10110 Balnot-sur-Laignes ☎ 03 25 29 37 91

Production: 100,000 bottles.

Extremely low prices are the trademark of this Aube house, which owns 12 hectares in the area.

Gremillet Grande Réserve 40
(50% PN, 50% CH)
Despite being disgorged after four years this is a sprawling champagne with an aggressive, slightly earthy flavour. It lacks the finesse that made champagne famous.

Gremillet Rosé 50
(100% PN)
A deep colour, like some strawberry-flavoured soft drink. This wine's assets are its rich strawberry nose and full caramel flavour.

1989 Gremillet Chardonnay 60 (Aug 97) 65
(100% CH)
A rich and fat blanc de blancs that lacks elegance.

Other wines: Brut Sélection, Brut Prestige.

BAR-SUR-SEINE

All the growers in the village are swallowed up in the cooperative Union Auboise (Devaux). Bar-sur-Seine is the second-largest town in Aube.

% 80% 68% PN, 3% PM, 29% CH

A. Devaux

Domaine de Villeneuve,
10110 Bar-sur-Seine ☎ 03 25 38 30 65

Production: 2.5 million bottles.

The whole thing started in 1967 when the area's eleven cooperatives merged, and now Devaux has 800 member-growers who together control 1,400 hectares in Côte des Bars. This is now the leading company in the Aube district, and everything is impeccably run. The modern facilities where they make the wine are clinically clean, the production methods are serious, with a large amount of reserve wines stored in large oak barrels à la Roederer. All the wines are well-stored and handled in a traditional manner, and the firm will surely improve as they gain access to more grapes from Côte des Blancs. My only complaint is the high prices.

Devaux Grande Réserve 74
(75% PN, 25% CH)
Now made with a dash of Chardonnay from Chouilly. A broad, mature nose of chocolate, and a meaty Pinot structure with a light, toasty, spicy tone. If the acidity hadn't been so low this could have been confused with a non-vintage champagne from Bollinger.

Devaux Rosé 61
(75% PN, 25% CH)
A good rosé from Aube. Opulent and well-structured but with a neutral, pure flavour.

1990 Devaux 40 (Oct 97) 45
(100% CH)
Peculiar aromas of elder and soap. Spumante-like taste that lacks elegance.

1990 Distinction 84 (Oct 97) 86
(50% PN, 50% CH)
Obvious notes of wood and vanilla. Full-bodied and complex, but marks lowered by a somewhat foamy mousse.

Other wines: Distinction Rosé.

BETHON

A highly-ranked village in the Sézanne district, and viewed by many as the best in the area. It is dominated almost completely by the Le Brun de Neuville cooperative.

% 85% PN, 87% CH   20% PN, 80% CH

Le Brun de Neuville

Route de Chantemerle,
51260 Bethon   03 26 80 48 43

Production: 400,000 bottles.

In 1963 the cooperative "La Crayère" was formed, and changed to its present name ten years later. Most of the firm's champagnes are dominated almost completely by Chardonnay.

Le Brun de Neuville Sélection 65
(30% PN, 70% CH)
A very delicate and refreshing champagne with fresh and toasty Chardonnay tones.

Le Brun de Neuville B. d. B. 52
(100% CH)
Rounded nose of grapefruit and pineapple. Soft and pleasantly refreshing, but far too short.

Le Brun de Neuville Rosé 52
(80% PN, 20% CH)
A light and refreshing rosé champagne that fits the house style well. The aftertaste is remarkably short.

1988 Le Brun de Neuville 48 (May 96) ?
(8% PN, 92% CH)
A strange wine that offers overripe aromas of cheese and eggnog. There's nothing wrong with the power here, but what happened to the stringency and the uplifting acidity?

Cuvée du Roi Clovis 83
(50% PN, 50% CH)
The firm's cuvée de prestige is their best wine, as indeed it should be. A multi-vintage with delightfully mature Chardonnay fruit and roundness. Not to be stored.

Triolet

22 rue Pressoirs, 51260 Bethon   03 26 80 48 24

Production: 45,000 bottles.

The grower owns nine hectares in Bethon, Montgenost and Villenauxe-la-Grande. Triolet is one of the winemakers with the best reputation in Sézanne.

Triolet Brut 67
(10% PN, 10% PM, 80% CH)
A champagne with good maturity and grapefruit aromas.

Other wines: Vintage.

André Jarry

25 Grande rue, 51260 Bethon   03 26 80 48 04

Production: 50,000 bottles.

Jarry owns 12 hectares of Chardonnay vineyards in Sézanne and makes a widely-praised cuvée de prestige from 40 year-old vines that I have yet to taste.

André Jarry Brut 66
(100% CH)
Exotic and exciting with a clear terroir character.

BLIGNY

A village in Aube which is known for one of Champagne's most beautiful castles.

% 80%   81% PN, 5% PM, 14% CH

Château de Bligny

Lorin Frère, 10200 Bar-sur-Aube   03 25 27 40 11

One of two castle-bedecked champagnes.

Château de Bligny Brut 59
(50% PN, 50% CH)
A monocru wine from a 6.5 hectare large vineyard with equal proportoins of Pinot and Chardonnay vines. The nose hints at grass and honey. In the mouth one is struck by its dryness and young mousse more than by any vegetable aromas.

1982 Château de Bligny B. d. B. 70 (May 91) 78
(100% CH)
A mineral-rich blanc de blancs with good potential in years to come.

BOUILLY

% 86%   18% PN, 72% PM, 10% CH

Guy Wafflart

6 rue Saint Caprais, 51390 Bouilly   03 26 49 21 01

Guy Wafflart Réserve 48
(100% PM)
Simple and straight up-and-down petrol pump bubbly. A rough nose of earth, marzipan and chocolate. Mature, sweet, one-dimensional flavour.

Guy Wafflart Rosé 45
(100% PM)
Much less ripe than the ***Réserve***, with a seedy, short, slightly sour flavour.

BOURSAULT

The town is best known for the exquisite Château de Boursault. It's a real fairy-tale castle similar to the Château d'Ussé in the Loire valley. The castle was once owned by the widow Clicquot.

% 84%   26% PN, 67% PM, 7% CH

Château de Boursault

51480 Boursault   03 26 58 42 21

Production: 60,000 bottles.

The second of two champagnes named after a castle, this independent company was once owned by Veuve Clicquot. The company doesn't make vintage wines, and in fact probably has the smallest production of any house, even though the proportions of the building itself are impressive.

Château de Boursault Brut 65
(35% PN, 35% PM, 30% CH)
A very pale colour, fine mousse, and a faint nose of green apples and violets. The flavour has a smoky complexity that is very agreeable.

Château de Boursault Rosé 62
(50% PN, 50% PM)
The rosé is also dominated by apple aromas with a hint of violet.

Château de Boursault.

Jacques Bérat

8 rue Saint Roch, 51480 Boursault 03 26 58 42 45

Production: 100,000 bottles.

The Bérat family have cultivated grapes in Champagne since the 18th century, but only in 1950 did Jacques Bérat begin to sell his own champagne. The firm's twelve hectares are in Oeuilly and Boursault, and the current owners are Isabelle and Vincent Bérat.

Jacques Bérat Special Cuvée 59
(50% PN, 25% PM, 25% CH)
A crispy champagne with fine mousse and fruity nose. Pleasant and reasonably priced.

Jacques Bérat Rosé 60
(5% PN, 95% CH)
A certain elegance despite a rather kindly style. Aperitif wine!

Other wines: Vintage, Carte Perle, Carte Blanche.

Lucien Dagonet

7 rue Maurice Gilbert,
51480 Boursault 03 26 58 41 29

Production: 60,000 bottles.

The firm was founded in 1929. Jacques Dagonet is one of the few producers in Champagne that use oak barrels for the first fermentation. 5% of the grapes are bought in while the rest come from the company's six hectares of Pinot Noir. Wines not tasted.

Wines: Brut, Sélection, Rosé, Prestige, Sec, Demi-sec.

LE BREUIL

Within the boundaries of Le Breuil there is one of the western Marne valley's biggest firms, Jean Moutardier. Like most of the villages in Aisne they grow the hardy Meunier grape for the most part. Le Breuil lies beside a tributary of the Marne called the Surmelin.

% 83% 10% PN, 87% PM, 3% CH

Jean Moutardier

Route d'Orbais, 51210 Le Breuil 03 26 59 21 09

Production: 180,000 bottles.

Despite a long growing tradition in the Moutardier family, this house wasn't actually founded until 1920. Jean owns 16 hectares in the Marne valley, which supplies 86% of his production needs. Englishman Jonathan Saxby is beginning to take over more and more of his father-in-law's workload, having given up a brilliant career in the British business world in order to study champagne at the oenology school in Avize. There are differing opinions about whether the Leuvrigny cooperative or Jean Moutardier produce the finest Meunier grapes outside of the Premier and Grand cru villages. Jacques Peters, cellar master at Veuve Clicquot, always uses Moutardier's Meunier grapes as his yardstick.

Jean Moutardier Carte d'Or 39
(90% PM, 10% CH)
A wine for rapid consumption. All the Meunier grapes come from Breuil. The colour has a touch of bronze and the nose hints at fresh-baked bread, while the flavour is vapid and unstructured. Needs retasting.

Jean Moutardier Rosé 42
(100% PM)
Quite a promising fruity nose is dragged down by an earthy Meunier taste. Needs retasting.

Other wines: Sélection, Centenaire.

BUXEUIL

In the middle of Aube you will find Buxeuil with its beautiful stone church. The village contains nine grower producers and one champagne house.

% 80% 90% PN, 1% PM, 9% CH

Moutard-Diligent

10110 Buxeuil 03 25 38 50 73

Production: 400,000 bottles.

The firm was founded in 1927 by François Diligent and is run today by his daughter and her husband François Moutard. The house makes wines under two labels: François Diligent and Moutard Père & Fils.

Moutard Diligent Brut 60
(100% CH)
Unremarkable nose, but good spicy and biscuity taste with a nice acidity in the aftertaste.

Moutard-Diligent Extra Brut 60
(100% CH)
Balanced and harmonious dry champagne, with aromas of pineapple, grapefruit and bread.

1983 Moutard-Diligent 83 (Oct 97) 83
(100% CH)
Lovely biscuity nose, medium-bodied balanced flavour and a rather short aftertaste.

CELLES-SUR-OURCE

An important Aube village with as many as fifty producers! You can find it 29 km southeast of Bar-sur-Aube.

% 85% 85% PN, 10% PM, 5% CH

Michel Furdyna

13 rue du Trot,
10110 Celles-sur-Ource 03 25 38 54 20

Production: 60,000 bottles.

Started by the owner of the same name in 1974, this company's vineyards lie in Celles-sur-Ource, Loches-sur-Ource, Neuville and Landreville.

Michel Furdyna Rosé 62
(100% PN)
This is a rosé of quite a different weight from the *Brut*. The nose is enchanting and fruity, and the flavour is both refreshing and balanced with a decent aftertaste.

1988 Furdyna Cuvée Prestige 80 (Mar 96) 83
(66% PN, 34% CH)
A lovely flowery nose with elements of lime and mint. Creamy, voluptuous flavour that lacks a little acidity.

Marcel Vézien

68 Grande rue,
10110 Celles-sur-Ource 03 25 38 50 22

Production: 150,000 bottles.

Marcel Vézien is mayor of Celles-sur-Ource and makes heavy Pinot-influenced champagne.

Marcel Vézien Brut 55
(80% PN, 20% CH)
I feel a little divided about this wine. It is full-bodied and rich enough to impress me, but there are obvious similarities with a slightly clumsy crémant de Bourgogne.

Richard Cheurlin

18 rue des Huguenots,
10110 Celles-sur-Ource 03 25 38 55 04

Production: 40,000 bottles.

The grower pronounces his name almost as the French pronounce mine. The Cheurlin family originally come from Landreville but have settled in Celles-sur-Ource in force. At least four producers bear this name. Richard is the most famous and he produces two champagnes from all three varieties.

Richard Cheurlin Brut 55
(50% PN, 30% PM, 20% CH)
Rich, full-bodied, slightly rough style with good maturity and tar-like aroma.

Arnaud de Cheurlin

58 Grande rue,
10110 Celles-sur-Ource 03 25 38 53 90

Production: 45,000 bottles.

Mr and Mrs Eisenträger-Cheurlin own six hectares in Aube.

Arnaud de Cheurlin Réserve 59
(70% PN, 30% CH)
Quite refreshing and uplifting acidity. Aromas of apple peel.

Arnaud de Cheurlin Prestige 68
(50% PN, 50% CH)
An added creamieness and sophistication. Otherwise the same aromas of apple peel. Long and acidic.

Other wines: Rosé.

Jean Arnoult

100 Grande rue,
10110 Celles-sur-Ource 03 25 38 56 49

Production: 150,000 bottles.

When the firm was started in 1919 by Jean Arnoult it became the Aube district's first champagne house. Today it is run by Alain Cheurlin, who aims for quality.

Jean Arnoult Brut Réserve 48
(80% PN, 10% PM, 10% CH)
The wine is relatively well-made but fails to avoid Aube's clumsiness and lack of finesse. Bread aromas and a full candy flavour are not enough to impress me.

Other wines: Carte Noir Brut, Rosé, Brut Prestige.

Emmanuel Tassin

13 Grande rue,
10110 Celles-sur-Ource 03 25 38 59 44

Production: 15,000 bottles.

The firm was started by the owner of the same name as recently as 1988. Like many others in Aube, Pinot Noir now stands for 85% of production from the 3.5 hectares.

E. Tassin Cuvée de Réserve 40
(80% PN, 20% CH)
In my opinion a flat and truly boring champagne, without freshness. The aromas are weak and neutral.

Other wines: Prestige, Demi-sec, Tradition, Vintage.

Laurent

12 rue des Huguenots,
10110 Celles-sur-Ource 03 25 38 50 10

Production: 55,000 bottles.

Jean Laurent has a reputation of making Pinot-dominated champagnes at a reasonable price. He is one of few Aube growers who sell older vintage wines. If you're interested in how Aube champagnes develop then Laurent is probably worth a visit. As for myself, I've never tasted any of his wines.

André Fays

94 Grande rue,
10110 Celles-sur-Ource 03 25 38 51 47

Production: 10,000 bottles.

From his 4.3 hectares Philippe Fays makes respected budget champagnes that partly ferment in oak casks. 85% of the production is made from Pinot Noir and the rest from Chardonnay. Wines not tasted.

Wines: Tradition, Brut Réserve.

Eric Legrand

39 Grande rue,
10110 Celles-sur-Ource 03 25 38 55 07

Production: 70,000 bottles.

Eric Legrand started up in 1982 and today controls eight hectares. Wines not tasted.

Wines: Brut, Rosé, Demi-sec, Prestige.

CERSEUIL

The village isn't classified and doesn't have any vineyards of its own, but does have one champagne house - S.A. Dehours - which is owned by the Frey group.

S.A. Dehours

2 rue Chapelle, 51700 Cerseuil ☎ 03 26 52 71 75

Production: 1 million bottles.
The house was founded in 1930 by L. Ludovic. Today it is run by Jérôme Dehours.

Dehours Grande Réserve 65
(33% PN, 33% PM, 34% CH)
Discreet but fine nose, and a pure, flowery flavour.

Other wines: L.D., Rosé, Millésime

Comte de Lantage

20 rue Chapelle, 51700 Cerseuil ☎ 03 26 51 11 39

The current owners, Michèle and Alain Mandois, come from a family with deep roots in Champagne. Victor Mandois founded the house towards the end of the 19th century, and it was later inherited by his grandson, Henri. Up to the stock market crash of the thirties the house concentrated on merely cultivating grapes, but afterwards it became a Récoltant-manipulant, gaining house status in 1987. On the Mandois property there is a house that was earlier used as a hunting lodge by the Comte de Lantage himself. Non-vintage wines are kept for three years before being disgorged.

Comte de Lantage Brut 59
(20% PN, 25% PM, 55% CH)
When tasted blind I guessed this was from the neighbouring village of Leuvrigny, but with a large dose of Chardonnay. A typical Marne valley champagne then, with a rustic fruit and a hint of breadiness.

CHARLY-SUR-MARNE

Situated 13 km southeast of Château-Thierry on the Marne valley's west side.

% 80% 5% PN, 85% PM, 10% CH

Baron Albert

Grand-Porteron,
02310 Charly-sur-Marne ☎ 03 23 82 02 65

Production: 500,000 bottles.

The Baron family has lived in Charly since 1677. Today Claude, Gilbert and Gervais make champagne from their 30 hectares. In the firm's best wines they use a small number of oak barrels to give weight and vanilla aromas.

Baron Albert Carte d'Or 52
(35% PN, 35% PM, 30% CH)
The colour is green/yellow and the mousse is very fine. The nose is a little prickly, with pears and apple peel and a hint of yeast and fresh-baked bread. The flavour is medium-bodied with lots of acidity and cider-like aromas.

CHÂTEAU-THIERRY

Château-Thierry is the capital of the western Marne valley. It lies almost halfway to Paris from Reims, so the 16,000 inhabitants are cut off from Champagne's main area. The town goes back to Roman times and was hard hit by both World Wars.

% 80% 14% PN, 78% PM, 8% CH

Coop. Pannier

23 rue Roger Catillon,
02400 Château-Thierry ☎ 03 23 69 51 30

Production: 1.9 million bottles.

What is now the largest firm in Aisne was founded by Louis-Eugène Pannier in Dizy in 1899, but in 1937 it moved to Château-Thierry. In 1971 the house became a cooperative and expanded rapidly, with 215 growers now involved in the care of 415 hectares in 40 nearby villages. Earlier I was quite indifferent towards Pannier's champagnes, but the most recent vintages show they are on the right track.

Pannier Tradition 45
(19% PN, 40% PM, 41% CH)
The taste of earthy Pinot Meunier is giving an aggressive overall impression.

Pannier Rosé 49
(25% PN, 38% PM, 37% CH)
Basic, robust but correct rosé champagne.

Louis-Eugène Pannier 84
(28% PN, 38% PM, 40% CH)
Very similar to Laurent-Perrier and the almond and amaretto aromas that are so often found in their wines. Strong, but a little overpowering and stale if you drink more than one glass.

1990 Pannier 82 (Jan 97) 86
(20% PN, 46% PM, 34% CH)
The young vintage wines from Pannier have impressed me. The '90 is pure and fruity with toasty aromas and a soft, well-balanced big house style.

1988 Pannier 77 (Oct 95) 84
(20% PN, 46% PM, 34% CH)
Bready and faintly toasty with impressive class and structure despite the high proportion of Pinot Meunier.

1988 Egérie 80 (Oct 95) 84
(25% PN, 33% PM, 42% CH)
Steely and ascetic, but with a superb attack and fresh acidity. The clear aftertaste hints at oranges. The company has obviously gone in for raising its quality with this vintage.

1985 Egérie 78 (Jan 85) 83
(25% PN, 33% PM, 42% CH)
Good weight and backbone, even so, it fails to match the 1985 vintage champagnes from the better houses.

CHÂTILLON-SUR-MARNE

18 kilometres northwest of Épernay lies this little village which has 13 growers sharing 250 hectares of cultivated land.

% 83%

Jackie Charlier

4 rue Pervenches,
51700 Châtillon-sur-Marne ☎ 03 26 58 35 18

Production: 100,000 bottles.

The grapes come from Châtillon, Montigny, Jonquery and Oeuilly. All the wines ferment and are stored in large oak barrels and go through malolactic fermentation. The rosé wine is made using the Saignée method. One of the new dark horses in the area. Lots of attention in the international wine press for their oak-fermented champagnes.

J. Charlier Carte Noir 75
(20% PN, 60% PM, 20% CH)
Deep colour, faintly oaky and oxidative nose. A deep honeyed, buttery and good non-vintage champagne.

J. Charlier Rosé 76
(30% PN, 70% PM)
Oak casks and the Saignée method make for a rare combination, which in this case gives a soft and charming wine for quick consumption while the Meunier grapes are at their vigorous best.

1990 J. Charlier 85 (May 96) 88
(30% PN, 40% PM, 30% CH)
Juicier, purer and more classical than the extravagant *89 Special Club*. The wine is filled with fine nutty and leathery tones.

1989 J. Charlier Special Club 84 (Jun 96) 86
(20% PN, 30% PM, 50% CH)
Wow, what concentration and oily weight! The first gulps slip down much easier than the last, when the champagne becomes almost too much of a good thing. There's a slight lack of elegance, but this honey and toffee-filled wine is certainly impressive.

Heucq

6 rue Eugène Moussé,
51700 Châtillon-sur-Marne ☎ 03 26 58 10 08

Production: 35,000 bottles.

The house was founded in 1920. Today André Heucq is in charge of an area wich is 6,5 hectares large.

CHAUMUZY

This village lies 18 km north of Épernay and covers some 77 hectares. Besides the local cooperative there are 15 growers who work almost exclusively with Pinot Meunier.

% 83% 1% PN, 98% PM, 1% CH

Michel Salmon

21 rue Capit Chesnais,
51170 Chaumuzy ☎ 03 26 61 81 38

Moulin Tochais in Loire have case after case of this grower's champagne in their cellar. I hope they haven't confused it with Billecart-Salmon!!

Michel Salmon Brut Sélection 55
(100% PM)
Creamy and concentrated, with simple candy and fruit aromas. Lacking in minerals and elegance.

CHAVOT

South of Pierry lies Chavot. When you sit in the top restaurant "La Briqueterie" in Vinay outside Épernay the lovely stone church in Chavot rises up dramatically from amongst the vineyards. Everybody in the area knows about the church, but few know much about the village's champagnes.

% 88% 5% PN, 65% PM, 30% CH

Lagache-Lecourt

29 rue du Maréchal Juin,
51530 Chavot ☎ 03 26 54 86 79

Production: 60,000 bottles.

The company owns vineyards in Chavot, Épernay, Mousy and Vinay.

Lagache Sélection 60
(30% PN, 40% PM, 30% CH)
A rich and oxidative aroma of faintly overripe apples and plums means this champagne is quite an enjoyable experience.

Lagache B. d. B. 46
(100% CH)
Heavy rustic and oxidative nose with an even rougher Pinot-like flavour of licorice.

Other wines: Rosé, Cuvée Chambecy.

CHENAY

North of Reims there are no good vineyards, but as they are constantly striving to produce more champagne the cultivation area is expanding the whole time. A century ago the villages north of Reims produced only a negligible amount, but today the quantity from here is considerable. Chenay's fame focuses on the charismatic Count Audoin de Dampierre, who has his mansion and champagne house here.

% 84%

Comte Audoin de Dampierre

5 Grande rue, 51140 Chenay ☎ 03 26 03 11 13

Production: 90,000 bottles.

Counts from the Dampierre family have lived in Chenay for over 700 years. Champagne production started as late as in 1880, and the house run by this Count is one of the newest in Champagne. He lives, together with his wife and dogs, in the lovely mansion in this charming village. Count Audoin has no vineyards of his own but instead buys in all his grapes from Premier and Grand cru villages. They are vinified in Avize, where they are stored for at least four years. I've had the impression that the champagne production is a passionate hobby for the Count. He loves good champagne and classic cars, and the connection between these outwardly seperate things is something he exploits regularly. He has produced a Champagne set for Aston Martin and usually poses in front of his house with his private collection of sports cars and a glass of champagne in his hand. I'll never forget a ride in his black Alvis from 1935. Audoin makes me think of Roger Moore in the old TV series "The Persuaders". Luckily the feeling of frivolity and luxuriousness is not just an image. His champagnes are wines worthy of counts and barons with their aristocratic style. And the Count himself is one of the most charismatic and light-hearted of people in all of Champagne.

Dampierre Grande Cuvée 75
(50% PN, 50% CH)
Despite the name, this is the firm's non-vintage champagne. The grapes come from reputable vineyards: Bouzy, Ambonnay and Cumières are home to the black grapes and the top names of Avize, Cramant and Le Mesnil supply the Chardonnay content. The wine has a suppressed nose of smoke, vanilla and hawthorn and a fresh, balanced crispy lime flavour.

Cuvée de Ambassadeurs 80
(50% PN, 50% CH)
The champagne has a nose of apple blossom and hawthorn with a whiff of white chocolate and lime peel. A tremendously elegant citrus flavour with crystal clear acidity and good length.

1990 Comte Audoin de Dampierre 84 (Apr 96) 90
(65% PN, 35% CH)
Broad, bold, elegant Pinot-dominated fruit with promising structure.

1988 Dampierre Grande Année 86 (Jun 97) 90
(70% PN, 30% CH)
Lovely Pinot bursting in the nose with clear elements of leather, mushrooms and plums. The vanilla flavour that seems to be one of the company's trademarks is present on the palate, in harmony with the Roederer-like fruit.

1985 Dampierre P. G. C. 85 (Jun 98) 89
(100% CH)
The cork is fastened with string instead of a halter. What won't people do to be different? A classical, crispy, equilibristic blanc de blancs with all the aristocratic posture you may expect from the Count's top wine.

1980 Dampierre P. G. C. 92 (Apr 95) 93
(100% CH)
A wine made from equal proportions of Avize, Cramant and Le Mesnil. One of the best champagnes I've drunk from this forgotten vintage. A classical nose in which petroleum and citrus fruits struggle for supremacy. The nuts and toasty aromas are toned down but are present in the wings. The flavour is very fresh and flowery in its fat, almost oily viscosity.

Other wines: Rosé Oeil-de-Pedrix.

COLUMBÉ-LE-SEC

Situated 8 km northeast of Bar-sur-Aube with a cultivated area of 120 hectares.

% 80% 75% PN, 15% PM, 10% CH

Coop. Charles Clement

10200 Colombé-le-Sec 03 25 92 50 70
Production: 100,000 bottles.

This cooperative has been a talking point in many areas recently. It owns 190 hectares in unknown villages like Colombé-le-sec, Colombé-la-Fosse, Saulcy, Rouvres-les-Vignes, Lignol, Argentolles etc.
Wines not tasted.

Wines: Charles Clément Brut, Rosé, Cercle d'Or, Gustave d'Or, Gustave Belon, Cuvée Spéciale.

DAMERY

Damery should certainly be upgraded to Premier cru status. Just like its even better neighbour Cumières, the village has suffered from having most of its cultivated area taken up by Pinot Meunier. Some of the 352 hectares are on steep slopes that give sun-ripened, masculine Pinot grapes. Damery is actually an important Champagne centre which contains 92 growers and eleven champagne houses.

% 89% 19% PN, 72% PM, 9% CH

J. de Telmont

1 av. de Champagne, 51480 Damery ☎ 03 26 58 40 33

Production: 1.5 million bottles.

Henri Lhopital began selling champagne in 1920 but first achieved house status in 1952, and his family still runs the company. In 1989 they carried out major renovations, such as building a luxurious reception room. The Monsieur Lhopital of today reminds one of Gérard Depardieu and produces far better wines than the great actor does in Anjou. The firm owns 28 hectares in Cumières, Damery, Romery and Fleury, but buys in most of its grapes.

Telmont Grande Réserve 68
(34% PN, 35% PM, 31% CH)
Nice herbal nose and layers of fruit flavours on the palate.

Telmont Rosé 65
(100% PN)
A nice bouquet of caramel and raspberry. Ripe, round, forward cherry taste.

1988 Telmont 82 (Apr 95) 85
(35% PN, 34% PM, 31% CH)
A very personal champagne dominated by a nose of lilac and a round, soft peach flavour. Already quite a mature champagne with acidity a touch low.

1988 Telmont B. d. B. 73 (Apr 95) 76
(100% CH)
There's nothing wrong with the nose, with its buttery, developed tones. The flavour, on the other hand, isn't completely pure, with soap and onions affecting the grape aromas.

1985 Grand Couronnement 90 (Feb 97) 92
(100% CH)
This wine has an explosive perfume of toasty vanilla and ripe, exotic fruit. Superb richness and a silky, smooth texture.

1983 Grand Couronnement 83 (Jun 95) 83
(10% PN, 90% CH)
A gamey, mouldy nose that turns many off. The flavour is oily and concentrated, however.

Other wines: Brut.

A.R. Lenoble

35 rue Paul Douce, 51480 Damery ☎ 03 26 58 42 60

Production: 300,000 bottles.

Lenoble was started in 1920 but the house was destroyed in the first World War and Leon de Tassigny from Jacquesson fixed some buildings in Damery for his friend A.R. Lenoble. Today the firm is run by Jean-Marie Malassagne, who controls 18 hectares in Chouilly and Bisseuil.

Lenoble Réserve 45
(33% PN, 33% PM, 34% CH)
A basic elderflower nose in a sour champagne.

Lenoble B. d. B. 60
(100% CH)
Grapes from Chouilly alone. An exciting and remarkable nose of candlewax and medicine, and an interesting personal flavour of flint stone.

Lenoble Rosé 54
(15% PN, 85% CH)
Rich and full-blooded with a far more Pinot-influenced style than the grape content suggests. The aftertaste is spicy.

1988 Lenoble 67 (Aug 95) 80
(60% PN, 40% CH)
When champagne bursts with life and vigour like this '88, you expect young, flowery aromas. Here it is accompanied instead by the restrained, acidic flavour of a sweaty, slightly mouldy touch.

1988 Gentilhomme 86 (Aug 97) 90
(100% CH)
A stylish blanc de blancs from Côte des Blancs. Very pure and elegant, with aromas of lime and butterscotch.

Jeeper

8 rue Georges Clemenceau,
51480 Damery ☎ 03 26 58 41 23

Production: 400,000 bottles.

M. Goutorbe, who is of course related to the Aÿ brothers, runs this house. His father, who was handicapped, always used to drive around in a Jeep, which explains the somewhat unlikely name. Dom Grossard is the name of the monk who took over from Dom Pérignon in Hautvillers.

Jeeper Ducale 50
(40% PN, 40% PM, 20% CH)
Uncomplicated and fruity, with a slightly bitter subtone in the aftertaste.

Jeeper Grande Réserve 62
(100% CH)
Chardonnay from forty villages. Some lime and grape aromas but uninteresting and short.

Jeeper Rosé 39
(90% PN, 10% CH)
Bluish young colour. Mouldy nose and aggressive, disharmonious flavour.

1991 Jeeper 66 (May 96) 70
(100% CH)
Also a blend from forty villages. The same style as G. R., but somewhat rounder despite its fresh acidity.

1989 Dom Grossard 74 (May 96) 80
(40% PN, 60% CH)
Grapes from the vicinity of Damery. The wine resembles ***Piper Brut Sauvage***, with the nose dominated by crispbread, dark chocolate and licorice. The flavour has a nice line in cocoa.

Claude Lemaire

19 rue Pasteur, 51200 Damery ☎ 03 26 58 41 31
Production: 60,000 bottles.

The Lemaires sell 95% of their wine directly to customers at their property. The company was started in 1924. Wines not tasted.

Wines: Réserve, Brut, Extra Dry, Demi-sec, Rosé, Vintage.

ÉTOGES

Situated 25 km south of Épernay, with 86 hectares of vineyards.

% 85% 7% PN, 72% PM, 21% CH

Les Hautes Caves

51270 Étoges ☎ 03 26 59 35 90
Production: 100,000 bottles.

Alain Bergere runs this champagne house with vineyards in Ferebrianges and Étoges. Only certain wines go through malolactic fermentation. Wines not tasted.

Wines: Réserve, B. d. B., Sélection.

FESTIGNY

Why almost all the wine journalists forget this village I don't know, but its style is definitely reminiscent of neighbouring Leuvrigny.

% 84% 4% PN, 95% PM, 1% CH

Michel Loriot

13 rue de Bell Air, 51700 Festigny ☎ 03 26 58 33 44
Production: 300,000 bottles.

Founded in 1931 after having supplied Moët with grapes since the turn of the century. Today they control 14 hectares in Festigny and three neighbouring villages.

M. Loriot Carte Blanche 58
(100% PM)
An exciting nose of violets and mint. Dry and fine, well-balanced flavour with a certain depth.

M. Loriot Demi-Sec 35
(100% PM)
Cloying and boring, with a sour finish.

M. Loriot Rosé 54
(100% PM)
Pure and pleasant aperitif rosé.

1989 M. Loriot 76 (Oct 97) 81
(100% PM)
A scented violets bouquet, good mid-palate and a dry, frothy end.

1990 Le Loriot 78 (Aug 95) 86
(100% PM)
The firm's prestige wine boasts my favourite bird - the Golden Oriole. The champagne itself is impressive with a nose of hay and vanilla. The flavour is concentrated and citrus fresh. Excellent Pinot Meunier.

FONTETTE

In the middle of the Aube district we find Fontette, a village with just two producers - one small grower and one house, Cristian Senez.

% 80% 80% PN, 20% CH

Cristian Senez

6 Grande rue, 10360 Fontette ☎ 03 25 29 60 62
Production: 200,000 bottles.

After many years as a grower Crisitan Senez decided in 1985 to become a négiociant (house) with license to buy grapes. He sells his champagnes under his own name and as ***Cuvée Angélique***. The firm exports 30% of its product and uses modern vinification methods.

Cuvée Angélique 44
(52% PN, 48% CH)
A very basic elderflower and pear nose with a grassy Riesling-like flavour. All quite nicely turned out.

Senez Grande Réserve 67
(90% PN, 10% CH)
A clear yellow colour, a flowery nose of apricot marmelade. A very nice, slightly unusual flavour that tastes like sweet anchovies.

1988 Senez Rosé 43 (Apr 95) 43
(82% PN, 18% CH)
A dark red champagne where the nose is tight but basic in a candy-like way. A flat flavour of dark chocolate.

1988 Senez Millésime 59 (May 95) 64
(30% PN, 70% CH)
I don't really understand the company's style. Here you are met by a flowery nose with elements of violets, while in the mouth it leaves a more rustic impression.

1973 Senez Millésime 83 (May 95) 83
(50% PN, 50% CH)
A very successful vintage for the company, and one which they still sell. A dark, developed colour and a one-dimensional wine that does possess a lovely rich chocolate aroma in both nose and flavour.

GYÉ-SUR-SEINE

Lying next to Buxeuil in southern Aube, this village has a cultivated area of 202 hectares, filled with Pinot. Of the 350,000 bottles which the village churns out each year, two-thirds come from the big four champagne houses. The rest is split between 16 grower/producers.

% 80% 94% PN, 2% PM, 4% CH

Hérard & Fluteau

Route Nationale, 10250 Gyé-sur-Seine ☎ 03 25 38 20 02
Production: 70,000 bottles.

Founded by Georges Fluteau and Émile Hérard in 1935, the firm now owns five hectares in Aube and buys in most of its grapes. The current manager is Bernard Fluteau. Wines untasted.

Wines: Cuvée Réservée, Rosé, Vintage.

Marie Demets

10250 Gye-sur-Seine ☎ 03 25 38 23 30

Marie Demets Brut 58
A bready nose with good autolytic character and surprisingly fruity flavour of orange and berries.
A praiseworthy Aube bubbly.

JANVRY

Janvry lies north of Petit Montagne.

% 85% 20% PN, 75% PM, 5% CH

Coop. de Germigny-Janvry-Rosnay

51390 Janvry 03 26 03 63 40

Production: 400,000 bottles.

Another company that I haven't managed to reach during my work on this book.

Wines: Ch. del Auche, Nectar de St Rémi, Prestige de Sacres, Rosé, Cuvée du Chapitre.

LANDREVILLE

An Aube village that is dominated by the Dufour family.

% 80% 80% PN, 20% CH

Robert Dufour

4 rue de la Croix Malot,
10110 Landreville 03 25 29 66 19

R. Dufour Sélection 50
(50% PN, 50% CH)
Broad, smoky and licorice-soaked nose. A vigorous fruit completes the weight of the flavour.

R. Dufour B. d. B. 25
(100% CH)
Blanc de blancs from Aube are rarities - thankfully. This wine has a mouldy vegetable aroma and untypically stale flavour.

René Jolly

10 rue de la Gare, 10110 Landreville 03 25 38 50 91

Production: 20,000 bottles.

Founded in 1863 and today run by Hervé Jolly. Wines not tasted.

LEUVRIGNY

A magical village on the shaded side of the Marne valley. The magic comes from being an important part of Krug's majestic champagnes. The special clone that is grown here undeniably gives a Pinot Meunier wine with a unique nose and the ability to age well. The aromas from the village's grapes lead one to think of apricot and violet. As the vineyards have a northerly exposure it takes the grapes longer to ripen, which in turn means the acidity levels are higher and the aging potential increased. However, it should be noted that those grapes used by Krug are carefully selected and come from extremely old vines. The special treatment they receive in oak casks and the fact that malolactic fermentation is avoided also contribute to the unique quality. Other still wines I've tasted from this village haven't had the same exceptional character.

% 84% 8% PN, 90% PM, 2% CH

Cave Coop. de Leuvrigny

51700 Leuvrigny 03 26 58 30 75

This cooperative is best know for selling their prime grapes to Krug and Veuve Clicquot.

Coop. de Leuvrigny Brut 65
(100% PM)
Slightly reddish tone and a young, bready nose. If you make an effort you can detect Krug's violet tones hidden in a seaside rock aroma. A soft, balanced flavour.

MANCY

In between Chavot and Grauves lies Mancy, beautifully situated high up with a view over Côte des Blancs. The village ought to replant their vineyards with as much Chardonnay as possible, as with a higher proportion of white wine grapes the village would probably have received Premier cru status in 1985.

% 88% 5% PN, 55% PM, 40% CH

MARDEUIL

I don't know a whole lot about Mardeuil's wines but I know every hill and dale in the area after lots of jogging trips in the wonderful landscape west of Épernay. In 1985 the village was upgraded by 2% from the original 82%, and the village is now dominated by the Beaumont des Crayères cooperative.

% 84% 30% PN, 60% PM, 10% CH

Coop. Vinicole de Mardeuil

64 rue de la Liberté, 51530 Mardeuil 03 26 55 29 40

Production: 350,000 bottles.

This wine is better known under the name ***Beaumont des Crayères***. The second wine is called ***Charles Leprince***. The firm was started in 1955 and now has 200 members. The cooperative's cellar master J-P. Bertus has a very good reputation. He keeps a stern eye on his members and aims for perfectly ripe grapes from some relatively old vines. The firm has really pulled its socks up recently, but although they make very priceworthy wines, I'm not so impressed with their handiwork.

Beaumont des Crayères Cuvée de Réserve 52
(20% PN, 55% PM, 25% CH)
Popular with many people but not one of my favourites. A well-made but impersonal champagne with a slightly yeasty style.

Beaumont des Crayères Rosé Privilége 50
(20% PN, 50% PM, 30% CH)
The rosé is similar to the ***Cuvée de Réserve*** in the nose but has a more powerful flavour which is remarkably short.

Beaumont des Crayères Prestige 78
(40% PN, 15% PM, 45% CH)
A broad, heavy, old-fashioned champagne that demands to be enjoyed with food.

1987 Cuvée Spéciale Nostalgie 78 (Apr 95) 83
(30% PN, 70% CH)
It was an odd decision to produce a cuvée de prestige in this mediocre year. The nose is vigorous and pure but the flavour has an immature metallic tone that is typical of that vintage.

MERREY-SUR-ARCE

% 80% 85% PN, 10% PM, 5% CH

Situated in Aube. Total production is 147,000 bottles from 116 hectares.

Jacob Père & Fils

10110 Merrey-sur-Arce 03 25 29 83 74

Production: 80,000 bottles.

Robert Jacob founded this property in 1960. The manager today is Daniel Jacob. Wines not tasted.

MONTGENOST

Together with Bethon, this is the best village in Sézanne. The Chardonnay grapes from here have a chablis-like wealth of minerals which makes them intensely exciting.

% 85% PN/PM, 87% CH   6% PN, 3% PM, 91% CH

Jacques Copinet

11 rue Ormeau, 51260 Montgenost   03 25 80 49 14
Production: 80,000 bottles.

Jacques Copinet Brut 51
(100% CH)
This is a mineral-rich and extremely personal blanc de blancs with an almost stony aftertaste.

Other wines: Rosé, Cuvée Marie Etienne.

MOUSSY

Situated 7 km south of Épernay with vineyards covering 133 hectares. Home village of the wonderful José Michel.

% 89%   4% PN, 76% PM, 20% CH

Jan Netterberg and José Michel.

José Michel

14 rue Prélot, 51530 Moussy   03 26 54 04 69
Production: 160,000 bottles.

José Michel is one of my latest discoveries. On one single tour I was told on three separate occasions that the best truly old champagnes ever made were pure Pinot Meunier champagnes from José Michel. The winemakers at Deutz and Legras were unanimous. Although they themselves work with Grand cru Chardonnay, the real cellar wines, they confirmed, were Pinot Meunier. Could this really be true?

Krug's wonderful older vintage wines are what I've always seen as the exception that proves the rule, but the fact is that José Michel's receipe is exactly the same. Extremely old vines, no malolactic fermentation and fermentation in oak barrels. The grapes that make up *Special Club* come from vines planted in 1929! The company has been owned by the family for four generations since 1847, and José himself started out in 1955. Today he controls 21 hectares in Moussy, Pierry and Chavot. José's collection of normally-disgorged older vintages is remarkable. There may only be four or five bottles of each vintage, but every year going back to 1912 is represented. 1914, 1928, 1947 and above all 1921 are his own favourites. I'll be back, José!

José Michel Extra Brut 74
(60% PM, 40% CH)
As the grower's ordinary brut has such a minimal dosage there's remarkably little difference between these two wines. There's a flowery element in the brut which is almost metallic. Nice acidity and potential.

José Michel Carte Blanche 74
(60% PN, 40% CH)
A broad and concentrated champagne with tough acidity and a powerful structure. Should be kept in the cellar for a while.

José Michel B. d. B. 79
(100% CH)
A very clear pear aroma, but the wine lacks stringency. As so often when you leave Côte des Blancs, the Chardonnay wines grow more full-bodied and less elegant. The flavour is finished with a clear toffee tone.

José Michel Rosé 72
(50% PN, 50% PM)
The company's least interesting wine, with an unusually sweet charming candy-like base. Undoubtedly a pleasant wine for uncomplicated drinking.

1990 José Michel Special Club 87 (May 98) 92
(50% PM, 50% CH)
It's amazing that all club wines are like one another whether they're made from Pinot or Chardonnay. The creaminess and concentration are reminiscent of Bonnaire in Cramant. Of course, there's a personal tone of spices and fresia, but the creamy citrus-fresh Chardonnay dominates the overall impression.

1989 José Michel 89 (Aug 97) 91
(30% PM, 70% CH)
A sensational wine with a wonderful nose of gunpowder smoke, bread and coffee. The nose resembles a top-class Pinot Noir and the flavour is elegant, with aromas that bring *Cuvée Sir Winston Churchill* to mind.

1986 José Michel 88 (Aug 97) 89
(40% PM, 60% CH)
I can't quite understand the style of the grower's current range, but as they're all so enjoyable it doesn't really matter. this wine is very close to *Krug Grande Cuvée* with its nutty, honeyed, deep nose and flavour.

1982 José Michel 88 (Apr 98) 93
(70% PM, 30% CH)
An outstanding, broad nose of mushroom and meat grilled over a wood fire. A broad, tough, impressive, rasping flavour of great power. Cellar!

1973 José Michel 90 (Jun 97) 93
(50% PM, 50% CH)
An elegant, flowery nose with a strong perfumed tone of musk, violet and dwarf banana. Fresh, steely and well-structured flavour with an extremely long and acidic aftertaste here too.

1965 José Michel 93 (Jun 97) 93
(100% PM)
Wow! A tremendous nose of lilac, plum and violet. Initially fat and oily, once again with impressive acidity. A long, vinous flavour that resembles a great chablis vinified in oak barrels.

1961 José Michel 93 (Aug 97) 94
(100% PM)
Much lighter and more elegant than the '59, with an irresistible, appetising peach nose. The mousse is youthful and the flavour full of finesse, just like a '66. Only the aftertaste needs to be a little longer, and that should be achieved after a couple of years in the bottle.

1959 José Michel 95 (Aug 97) 95
(100% PM)
I can't help returning to comparisons with Krug - in this case the remarkable '61. Well, Michel doesn't quite reach those heights, but the aromatic spectrum is very similar to Krug's. Tar, smoke, wood, tobacco and dark aromas of forest and undergrowth are the associations made by myself and my friends.

1955 José Michel 95 (Jun 97) 96
(100% PM)
Youthful colour with a beautiful golden hue. An extravagant, majestic, warm nose of smoke, nut, tar, nougat and tobacco. The flavour is fruitier than the nose, with a perfect balance of freshness that typifies the vintage.

1921 José Michel 97 (Jun 97) 97
(100% PM)
Probably the best wine ever made from Pinot Meunier. A deep amber colour, faint, prolonged mousse, a toffee-like, gigantic Yquem-like nose and flavour that I've only come across in ***1926 Krug*** and ***1914 Pol Roger***. The depth was even greater here, even if the finesse of the Pol Roger was superior. Sadly there are only four bottles left in José Michel's cellar. I hope he saves a couple for generations to come as archeological milestones of the history of wine.

1990 Clos des Plants de Chênes 87 (Aug 97) 92
(100% CH)
This is a unique clos wine close to Michel's house in Moussy. You feel how much effort has gone into giving the champagne as much concentration as possible. There's plenty of fruit which mostly resembles pear, but there's also a sort of smoky complexity that's lacking in José's other B. d. B.'s.

R. Renaudin

Domaine des Conardins,
51530 Moussy ☎ 03 26 54 03 41

Production: 230,000 bottles.

This is the firm that produces Taillevent (see "Buyers' own brand") and owns 24 hectares around Moussy and Pierry. Dominique Tellier began making kosher champagne in 1990, and has since received a great deal of attention in the British wine press.

Renaudin Brut Réserve 54
(70% PM, 30% CH)
A slightly strange nose of ginger and gingerbread dough. A much more pleasant flavour with good structure and dark fruit.

Renaudin Grande Réserve 57
(25% PN, 20% PM, 55% CH)
Once again a peculiar nose. This time the gingerbread dough is supported by juniper wood. Well-structured and personal flavour.

Other wines: Rosé, Vintage, C.D.

LA NEUVILLE-AUX-LARRIS

Cast out to the north of what is really the Marne valley, west of the Reims forest. The plantations lie north of a tributary of the Marne called the Belval. At the classification of 1945 the village's 81% was upgraded to 84%, and this is another village that has contributed to Pinot Meunier having been the most commonly-grown grape in Champagne for a long time.

% 84% 5% PN, 90% PM, 5% CH

Raymond Boulard

Rue Tambour,
51480 La Neuville-aux-Larris ☎ 03 26 58 12 08

Production: 90,000 bottles.

Raymond Boulard is one of the newest companies in Champagne, having first seen the light of day in 1952. The house is still wholly under the control of the Boulard family, owning vineyards in seven villages: Neuville-aux-Larris, Cuchery, Belval, Paradis, Hermonville and Cauroy-les-Hermonville. All of them are low-ranked villages north of Reims or on the outskirts of the Marne valley. The only high-ranking vineyards owned by the firm lie in the Grand cru village of Mailly. The cuvée de prestige is disgorged à la volée and the average age of the vines is 35 years.

Raymond Boulard Réserve 48
(25% PN, 50% PM, 25% CH)
A foamy mousse and weakly toasty nose. The flavour displays a certain maturity and a lightly smoked aftertaste.

Raymond Boulard B. d. B. 50
(100% CH)
Chardonnay from Montagne de Reims and the Marne valley seldom makes elegant wines, and Boulard's example is no exception. There are rough, tutti-frutti-like aromas that resemble wines from Màconnais.

Cuvée Tradition Symphonie 51
(20% PN, 30% PM, 50% CH)
French wine journalists consistently heap praise upon this wine. It is made from the best of the first pressing and is one of the firm's pride and joys. I was not impressed by either the basic candy aromas or the pear-like fruit. A certain concentration in the flavour will probably enable this champagne to develop in the bottle.

Raymond Boulard Mailly Grand Cru 70
(90% PN, 10% CH)
Made purely from grapes from the harvest of 1990 - this wine looks promising. Drink it in the beginning of the 21st century when its inner power will probably have developed further. In May 1995 the champagne was already a deep bronze colour and had an impressive nose of chocolate and licorice. The flavour was still quite hard and undeveloped.

1986 L'Année de la Comète 80 (May 95) 80
(25% PN, 25% PM, 50% CH)
Fortunately the contents were far more stylish than the bottle. The firm's cuvée de prestige, which received the Guide Hachette's medal of honour "Coupe de Coeur" in 1995, is made from grapes that come from very old vines. At the age of nine it was already fully mature. Without being either particularly concentrated or refined, it's very good, with a broad nose of banana, dried fruit, leather and honey. The flavour is as soft and mature as a champagne from the seventies, but it finishes abruptly in the mouth. Drink within a couple of years!

Other wines: Vintage, Rosé, Vintage rosé.

NEUVILLE-SUR-SEINE

One of Aube's major centres. Almost all the grapes that are harvested in this relatively flat agricultural landscape belong to the local cooperative, Clérambault.

% 80% 90% PN, 5% PN, 5% CH

Clérambault

Grande rue, 10250 Neuville-sur-Seine 03 25 38 38 60

Production: 150,000 bottles.

As with most cooperatives, this one started off supplying the major houses with grape juice, but now the best grapes go to their own champagne production. Clérambault get consistent good reviews in the French press, which I don't really understand.

Clérambault Tradition 48
(100% PN)
A square wine with no finesse, and which gains from being served well chilled. On airing the champagne feels flat and clumsy.

Clérambault Carte Noir 52
(60% PN, 20% PM, 20% CH)
Somewhat tighter than the *Tradition*. The wine has a faint burnt tone in the nose and a fruity but short flavour.

1985 Clérambault Rosé 70 (Feb 95) 70
(100% PN)
The one time I drank this rosé I was struck by how much it was improved by being together with food. Fried breast of chicken in red wine sauce gave the champagne a tremendous lift. Otherwise this too is one-dimensional with low acidity.

1985 Clérambault B. d. B. 69 (Feb 95) 73
(100% CH)
Pure and delicate, but without concentration.

Other wine: Grande Époque.

Paul Herard

31 Grande rue,
10250 Neuville-sur-Seine 03 25 38 20 14

Production: 180,000 bottles.

Paul Herard Blanc de Noirs 52
(100% PN)
Light, with tones of licorice, cheese and fresh vegetables. A pure, unripe flavour.

Paul Herard Réserve 58
(100% PN)
This wine is slightly more complex than the B. d. N. without ever impressing me. Both nose and flavour are pure and fruity, with a leaning toward apples.

OEUILLY

Oeuilly lies 10 km west of Épernay in the Marne valley.

% 84% 27% PN, 53% PM, 20% CH

Tarlant

51480 Oeuilly 03 26 58 30 60

Production: 100,000 bottles.

A family property of 12 hectares in Oeuilly and Boursault. Unusually they use new oak casks from the Vosges for their cuvée de prestige, *Cuvée Louis*. The company, which started life in 1687, is currently run by Jean-Mary Tarlant, who also owns a little hotel and wine museum on the estate.

Tarlant Réserve 58
(33% PN, 34% PM, 33% CH)
Good structure and pure fruit with an overtone of fresh green apples.

Tarlant Tradition 62
(50% PN, 20% PM, 30% CH)
Similar impressions to the wine above, but a somewhat better backbone and possibilities to develop, thanks to the Pinot Noir.

Tarlant Rosé 53
(20% PN, 80% CH)
As all the firm's wines: perfect balance and dosage, but a somewhat neutral fruit.

1988 Tarlant 77 (Jul 95) 81
(40% PN, 60% CH)
Open, pleasant nose of honey and marzipan. Rich, rounded flavour with the same aromas as in the nose.

Cuvée Louis 82
(50% PN, 50% CH)
One of two champagnes completely vinified in new oak casks. The chief reason for the balance of the wine is that it is only in contact with the oak for three weeks. Another explanation is that the malolactic fermentation is avoided and that the oak from the Vosges gives a mild oak tone. Only a couple of thousand bottles of this unique wine from 30 year-old vines are produced. The nose is broad, smoky and influenced by the cask. Full-bodied and muscular, this champagne is definitely suitable to have with white meat.

Other wines: Blanc de Blancs, Vintage rosé.

PROUILLY

% 85% 20% PN, 75% PM, 5% CH

Alain Couvreur

18 Grande rue, 51140 Prouilly 03 26 48 58 95

Production: 35,000 bottles.

Alain Couvreur belongs to the fifth generation of a vine growing family. The grower owns five hectares planted with 40% PN, 20% PM and 40% CH. Wines not tasted.

Wines: Cuvée Réserve, B. d. B., Vintage, Rosé.

ROMERY

Romery, which lies northwest of Hautvillers, was boosted from 83% to 85% in the reclassification of 1985. Half of the cultivated land is owned by champagne houses, the rest by growers who sell most of their harvest.

% 85% 20% PN, 60% PM, 20% CH

Tribaut

21 rue St Vincent, 51480 Romery — 03 26 58 64 21

I don't know if it's just bad luck, but of the four bottles of Tribaut that I've tasted, three had sustained cork damage! Two were bought in the USA and the other in France.

Tribaut Carte Blanche
The only fresh bottle I've had the pleasure of was greatly helped by the quality of the surroundings. My fiancée and I had no problems consuming the wine in a subtropical eucalyptus park in San Fransisco. It flowed like nectar down our throats to the tones of Antonin Dvorák's "New World", played by the San Fransisco Symphony Orchestra. In order to judge it more professionally I've bought Tribaut every time I've seen a bottle, but had to pour it out untouched on each occasion. Unjudged.

LES RICEYS

Without doubt Les Riceys is the most famous village in Aube. The main reason is of course that the unique rosé wine called rosé des Riceys is made here. Several innovative winemakers have found their way here because of that wine and many a fine champagne has been created in its wake. The fact that writer Tom Stevenson and others have paid the village's growers so much attention hasn't done it much harm either.

Bonnet, Horiot, Gallimard and Laurenti are becoming cult producers in Paris and London. I believe that the fuss around the village's champagnes is a grave exaggeration of their worth, but I agree it's Aube's best and most interesting village. The rosé wine is the most distinguished in the world, together with Tavel of the Rhône Valley. The Les Riceys area is the only in Champagne that holds the rights to three different appellations: Champagne, rosé les Riceys and coteaux champenois. Something few people know is that Les Riceys actually includes three small villages with the right to the appellation (Haut, Haut-Rive and Bas).

% 80% — 96% PN, 2% PM, 2% CH

Alexandre Bonnet

138 rue de Général de Gaulle,
10340 Riceys Haut — 03 25 29 30 93

Production: 650,000 bottles.

Bonnet is for me the only grower in the village who almost deserves his cult status. It would be interesting to see what this grower could achieve with Pinot grapes from Aÿ or Verzenay. His rosé des Riceys has a seductive nose and his coteaux champenois is Aube's best. The champagnes are also influenced by an intense grape aroma that lifts them above the wines of his neighbours.

A. Bonnet Cuvée Tradition 68
(100% PN)
Surprisingly fresh and apple-flavoured, considering its origin. The taste can be compared with biting into an unripe apple.

A. Bonnet Rosé 76
(100% PN)
The same personal nose of violets and cherries, backed up by a deep strawberry fruitiness. Once again the flavour is smoky and classical.

Other wines: Blanc de Blancs, Prestige.

Gallimard

18 rue du Magny, 10340 Riceys-Haut — 03 25 29 32 44

Production: 70,000 bottles.

The grower is represented at many of France's top restaurants. Jean and Didier Gallimard own 8 hectares.

Gallimard Cuvée Réserve 67
(100% PN)
Very similar in many ways to Bonnet's non-vintage champagne, but less concentrated.

Gallimard Rosé 72
(100% PN)
A fine grape character where the nose is often greater than Bonnet's, but the fruit aromas limit themselves to strawberry and apple. The flavour has less draw and weight, but it's absolutely a worthwhile rosé champagne.

1990 Gallimard Prestige 75 (Mar 96) 80
(100% PN)
Reddish and pear-scented. A kind, full flavour of Cox's Orange apples.

Laurenti Père & Fils

Rue de la Contrescarpe, Haute Rive,
10340 Les Riceys — 03 25 29 32 32

Production: 100,000 bottles.

This family firm is now run by Dominique and Bruno Laurenti. The 14 hectares they control are planted with 90% Pinot Noir and 10% Chardonnay.

Laurenti Rosé 60
(100% PN)
I've had two very different impressions of the two bottles I've tasted. My guess is that the wine ages very rapidly and should be consumed with its primary fruit intact. A bit of a wild and naughty style with some complexity.

Other wines: Grande Cuvée.

Horiot Père & Fils

11 rue de la Curé, 10340 Riceys-Bas — 03 25 29 32 21

Horiot Brut 50
(50% PN, 50% CH)
Perhaps it's because the Chardonnay grapes in the village don't have Pinot's class that this champagne feels so diluted and neutral compared with the best from the village.

Guy de Forez

32 rue du Général Leclerc,
10340 Les Riceys — 03 25 29 98 73

Production: 20,000 bottles.

This firm started out in 1987, founded by Roland Spagnesi and now run by Sylvie Wenner. Besides champagne they make a respected rosé des Riceys from their eight hectares.

Wines: Brut.

R. Bauser

Route de Tonnerre, 10340 Les Riceys — 03 25 29 32 92

Production: 80,000 bottles.

Yet another grower from Les Riceys with a good reputation. Wines not tasted.

Wines: Brut, Réserve, Rosé, Grande Réserve.

N.B. Morel Père & Fils make no champagne, but instead have specialised with success in rosé des Riceys.

SAINT-MARTIN-D'ABLOIS

Situated on the westernmost point of the strip that includes Pierry and Vinay.

% 86% — 5% PN, 85% PM, 10% CH

Jamart

13 rue Marcel Soyeux
51530 Saint-Martin-d'Ablois — 03 26 59 92 78

Production: 70,000 bottles.

The house was founded in 1936 by Emilien Jamart, and was taken over in 1954 by his son, Robert. Today the firm uses modern vinification methods.

Wines: Carte Blanche, Cuvée de Réserve, Rosé, Blanc de Blancs.

SAULCHERY

A small village in Aisne situated 10 km from Château-Thierry. 16 growers share 110 hectares.

% 80% — 3% PN, 95% PM, 2% CH

Bernard Figuet

144 route Nationale, 02310 Saulchery — 03 23 70 16 32

Production: 80,000 bottles.

Bernard and Eric Figuet control more than eleven hectares in Aisne planted with a majority of Pinot Meunier vines. The company was started in 1946, straight after the war. Their champagnes are remarkably cheap. Personally, I've yet to taste them.

Wines: Réserve, Spéciale, Symphonie, Rosé.

SEPT-SAULX

The village lies outside Champagne's cultivation area but has one of the region's best restaurants, "Cheval Blanc".

Lefévre-Chauffert

Once a well-reputed firm that no longer exists.

1973 Lefévre-Chauffert 87 (Aug 95) 87
This producer was an unknown quantity for me when I was confronted with this well-kept '73. The nose was closed with a gamey touch. The flavour is polished and stylish, with an undertone of vanilla.

SERMIERS

157 hectares and 14 growers.

% 89% — 20% PN, 75% PM, 5% CH

Lacuisse Frères

5 route de Damery, 51500 Sermiers — 03 26 97 64 97

Production: 40,000 bottles.

Philippe Griffon owns 15 hectares in Montagne de Reims. Wines not tasted.

SERZY-ET-PRIN

Seven growers and one cooperative are based in this village.

% 86% — 5% PN 93% PM 2% CH

Yves Delozanne

67 rue de Savigny,
51170 Serzy-et-Prin — 03 26 97 40 18

Production: 50,000 bottles.

Wines not tasted.

TRIGNY

38 growers produce 600,000 bottles from 168 hectares.

% 84% — 25% PN, 69% PM, 6% CH

J.C. Malot

5 route d'Hermonville, 51140 Trigny — 03 26 03 11 81

Production: 60,000 bottles.

Wines not tasted.

URVILLE

Ten kilometres south of Bar-sur-Aube we find Urville, home of well-known company Drappier.

% 80% — 70% PN, 20% PM, 10% CH

Drappier

Grande rue, 10200 Urville — 03 25 27 40 15

Production: 600,000 bottles.

The question is whether Drappier would enjoy the position it does today if president de Gaulle hadn't loved Champagne Drappier so much. This quality-minded firm was started in 1808. Today André Drappier is helped by his oenology-educated son Michel in maintaining the good name of the house. Drappier extract a remarkably low yield from their 35 hectares.

The firm conducts cold fermentation in order to avoid secondary aromas from the fermentation process, and they add minimal amounts of sulphur in order to keep the wine as natural as possible. In 1991 Drappier bought a cellar in Reims where their vintage and prestige cuvées are now stored. That investment may seem a bit odd when they alrea-

dy have a fantastic cellar from the 12th century, built by the monks of the Clairvaux monastery. Drappier's wines are very rich and well-made. With the experimentally-minded and knowledgable Michel at the helm we can expect more positive surprises from Drappier.

Drappier Carte d'Or 50
(90% PN, 5% PM, 5% CH)
Always a lovely classical autolytic nose with fine bread aromas, but sadly a rough mousse that overflows in the mouth.

Drappier Extra Dry 62
(100% PN)
Here the nose is more creamy and restrained, with a pure, elegant fruit flavour. Here too, however, the mousse pulls the marks down.

Rosé Val des Demoiselles 50
(100% PN)
A powerful wine with a cherry nose and clear flavour of chocolate. However, the champagne lacks class in its typically Aube style.

Drappier B. d. B. 60
(100% CH)
Very young and lively. A taste of pears and apples. A bit short.

1988 Grande Sandrée 75 (Apr 95) 78
(55% PN, 45% CH)
Many people say this is Aube's best champagne. Grande Sandrée is a special plot that Drappier is very proud of. The nose is often very pleasant with delicate fruit and a typical "big house style". The mousse is superb and the champagne is soft and easy to drink, but the concentration in the flavour and aftertaste is less than impressive.

Other wines: Charles de Gaulle, Vintage, Blanc de Blancs.

VANDIÈRES

Twenty kilometres northwest of Épernay lies Vandières. I've never tasted any wines from here, nor have I read about anyone else doing so. Even though there are fifty producers in the village!

% 86% 8% PN, 85% PM, 7% CH

VENTEUIL

The village went from 85% to 89% on the cru scale in 1985. A few southerly slopes deserve Premier cru status, but most of the village is average. Venteuil borders on Damery on the north side of Marne.

% 89% 35% PN, 55% PM, 10% CH

J-P. Marniquet

8 rue des Crayères, 51480 Venteuil 03 26 58 48 99

J-P Marniquet Brut 58
Broad, cheesy developed Pinot Noir character in the nose. Unexpectedly fresh and full of berries flavourwise, and decent length.

Maurice Grumier

13 route d'Arty, 51480 Venteuil 03 26 58 48 10

Production: 45,000 bottles.

Guy Grumier controls 6.5 hectares in the Marne valley, chiefly filled with Chardonnay vines. The company started business in that classic year for champagne, 1928. Wines not tasted.

Wines: B. d. B., Sélection, Réserve, Rosé, Vintage.

VERT-TOULON

Lying southwest of Côte des Blancs and twenty km north of Sézanne, almost all of the village's 30 growers have their grapes vinified by the La Grappe d'Or cooperative.

% 85% 10% PN, 14% PM, 76% CH

Raymond Leherle

3 rue des Marais de St-Gond,
51130 Vert-Toulon 03 26 52 26 94

Production: 100,000 bottles.

The firms' wines are made partially by the village cooperative, thus the cheap prices. Leherle also sells grapes to Moët and Clicquot. Similarities with the half-sweet "Yellow Widow" can't be missed.

Raymond Leherle Brut 66
(34% PN, 33% PM, 33% CH)
Sweet, soft nose of red apples and new-baked bread. The flavour is too sweet but satisfactory.

Raymond Leherle Rosé 67
This budget producer continues to surprise in a positive way. The rosé is elegant, fruity, sophisticated and very easy to drink.

VILLE-SUR-ARCE

East of Bar-sur-Seine runs a tributary of the Seine called the Arce. The only champagne village of any quality that graces its banks is Ville-sur-Arce. The cultivated land is quite large - 192 hectares which produce half a million bottles.

% 80% 93% PN, 3% PM, 4% CH

VILLERS-SOUS-CHÂTILLON

In 1971 the village's grade was raised to 85% from its original 83%, and in 1976 they reached their current rank of 86%. Even though the wine cultivation area extends tens of kilometres out west, we're already a long way out in terms of quality. The soil is dominated by clay and sandstone and loose combinations of calcium. The village lies in a frost-sensitive belt, which means the growers prefer the tough Pinot Meunier ahead of the more noble types of grape. Almost a million bottles are churned out annually from the village's twenty hectares. Talk about a high yield!

% 86% 4% PN, 95% PM, 1% CH

J. Charpentier

88 rue de Reuil,
51700 Villers-sous-Châtillon ☎ 03 26 58 05 78

Production: 90,000 bottles.

Pinot Meunier fills most of the property's ten hectares. The location is extremely beautiful, lying at the foot of the village's magnificent papal statue. Wines not tasted.

Wines: Réserve, Rosé, Tradition, Prestige, Comte de Chenizot.

VILLEVENARD

Half a million bottles are produced each year from 120 hectares.

% 85% 3% PN, 70% PM, 27% CH

Roger Barnier

1 rue du Marais de Saint-Gond,
51270 Villevenard ☎ 03 26 52 82 77

Production: 50,000 bottles.

The house was founded in 1932. Frédéric Berthelot owns seven hectares.

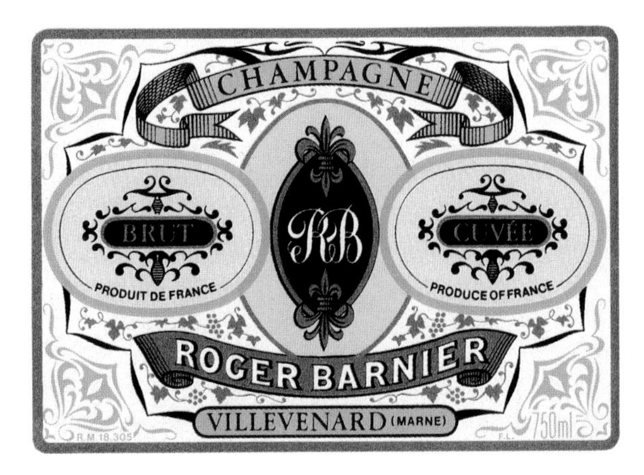

Roger Barnier Carte Noire 48
(20% PN, 40% PM, 40% CH)
Rather full-bodied and rustic. A champagne to drink with food.

Roger Barnier Rosé 50
(50% PN, 5% PM, 45% CH)
Simple and rather sweet rosé. Needs more years in the bottle.

1991 Roger Barnier 73 (Oct 97) 76
(45% PN, 5% PM, 50% CH)
Clear, fruity aroma of grapefruit. Short on the palate.

VINCELLES

Halfway to Château-Thierry from Épernay along the Marne valley lies Vincelles. On relatively flat ground they grow grapes that give charming wines for early consumption.

% 86% 25% PN, 60% PM, 15% CH

H. Blin

5 rue de Verdun, 51700 Vincelles ☎ 03 26 58 20 04

Production: 500,000 bottles.

This Marne cooperative was formed in Vincelles in 1947. The 96 members control more than 90 hectares, and today 30% of the harvest is exported and the grapes come from ten villages in the valley. I've been positively surprised by Blin's charming champagnes. They're no classics but offer a lot for your money with their mature, personal style. In all the wines I found aromas of orange chocolate and nougat.

H. Blin Tradition 51
(5% PN, 95% PM)
Young, slightly elderflower Meunier character but with a touch of orange chocolate and nougat. The flavour is uninteresting but surprisingly mature.

H. Blin Brut Réserve 68
(80% PN, 20% CH)
Plenty of orange chocolate - a good wine for the hedonist, but the aftertaste may be a touch short.

H. Blin Rosé 50
(50% PN, 50% PM)
Dark colour, slightly rough nose with elements of licorice and strawberry ice cream. Sweet and rich but a basic candy flavour.

H. Blin Chardonnay 65
(100% CH)
The nose contains the firm's usual trait, orange chocolate, although not as strongly as in *Réserve*. The structure is sprawling and hollow.

1988 H. Blin 71 (Apr 95) 79
(50% PN, 50% CH)
A champagne typical of the house, with aromas of nougat and orange chocolate. More restrained than the two non-vintage champagnes, with a dry, fine aftertaste.

1979 H. Blin 83 (Feb 96) 83
(70% PM, 30% CH)
Golden yellow, toasty nose and a fine round long aftertaste.

VINAY

Geologically this village has the same origin as Pierry, but with a larger cultivated area and far too high yields. The village is best known for its exquisite restaurant "La Briqueterie", with its unbeatable duck liver terrine.

% 86% 11% PN, 71% PM, 18% CH

VRIGNY

Situated eight km from Reims. 24 growers share 83 hectares.

% 89% 20% PN, 40% PM, 40% CH

Roger Coulon

12 rue Vigne du Roy, 51390 Vrigny ☎ 03 25 03 61 65

Roger Coulon 65
A positive surprise with a fine toasty nose and generous fruity flavour.

The buyer's own brand

There is an incalculable number of M.A. champagnes under different brand labels. Who actually makes the wine varies from year to year. Here are some of the best-known.

Baron Donat

Hudson and Hill Ltd, Albert Bridgehouse London SW2

1961 Baron Donat 87 (Feb 95) 87

Absolutely not a great wine but in perfect condition and with the lovely chocolate tones of aged champagne in both nose and flavour. The concentration and length left a great deal to be desired.

Lechere

21410 Le Noyer en Ouche

Lechere Brut 70

The champagne of the Orient Express often appears in wine magazines all over the world, winning good reviews. I was also impressed by the biscuity, balanced non-vintage champagne.

Eugene Laroche

Harrods Ltd, Knightsbridge, London Swix

1985 Eugene Laroche 69 (Jul 93) 78

Medium light, medium broad and medium long. Quite a boring but perfect description of a champagne that had one asset in its faint toasty tone.

Taillevent

15 rue Lamennais, 5008 Paris

The top Paris restaurant of the same name has this wine as its house champagne. Just as with other M.A. champagnes the producer varies from year to year, but Renaudin from Moussy is often the secret behind the label.

Taillevent Brut 38

A champagne of the very worst sort! A nose of candy and soap. Sweet unstructured flavour with a secondary tone of flour. Not tasted for several years - probably better now.

1985 Taillevent B. d. B. 50 (Feb 93) 60
(100% CH)

The same secondary tone of flour in the flavour. The nose is better: although hardly classical it is correct with hawthorn and mineral tones.

Other producers:

Balnot-sur-Laignes

Gérard Fontaine	03 25 29 31 87
Coop. de Balnot-sur-Laignes	03 25 29 35 15

Bethon

Guy Petit	03 26 80 48 31
André Vandier	03 26 80 48 17
Coop. U.V.C.B.	03 26 80 48 61

Bligny

Gérard Demilly	03 25 27 44 81
J-C Moutaux	03 25 27 40 25

Le Breuil

Jean Depit	03 26 59 21 22
Roger Depit	03 26 59 22 99
Philippe Mignon	03 26 59 24 99
Pierre Mignon	03 26 59 22 03

Buxeuil

Pierre Diligent	03 25 38 51 79
Claude Gruet	03 25 38 54 94
Noël Leblond-Lenoir	03 25 38 53 33
Pascal Leblond-Lenoir	03 25 38 54 04
René Lenoir	03 25 38 50 72

Celles-sur-Ource

Jacqueline Baroni	03 25 38 52 44
J-C Bouchard	03 25 38 55 62
J-P Bouchard	03 25 38 55 73
Michel Brocard	03 25 38 51 43
Pierre Brocard	03 25 38 55 05
Christiane Cheurlin	03 25 38 50 26
Daniel Cheurlin	03 25 38 51 34
Cheurlin-Dangin	03 25 38 50 26
Paul Dangin	03 25 38 50 27
M. Delot	03 25 38 50 12
Pierre Gerbais	03 25 38 51 29
Michel Patour	03 25 38 51 32
Jean Sandrin	03 25 38 57 04

Châtillon-sur-Marne

Q. Billet	03 26 58 36 23
Charlot	03 26 58 34 72
Perrin	03 26 58 34 31
Henri Plekhoff	03 26 58 34 77
Hervé Plekhoff	03 26 58 34 34
Coop. "La Grappe"	03 26 58 34 54
Coop. de Châtillon	03 26 58 35 33

Chavot

Charles Demarest	03 26 55 24 55
Roger Desbordes	03 26 54 31 94
René Jacquesson	03 26 54 32 13
Roland Laherte	03 26 54 31 91
Robert Lebeau	03 26 54 32 52
Lucien Leblond	03 26 54 32 56
André Tissier	03 26 54 32 16
Coop. de Chavot	03 26 54 31 89

Columbé-le-Sec

René Dosne	03 25 27 02 14
C.F Paradis	03 25 27 02 12

Damery

Jean Billiard	03 26 58 42 58
Daniel Caillez	03 26 58 46 02
Grosjean Caillez	03 26 58 42 02
Caillez-Lemaire	03 26 58 41 85
Vincent Casters	03 26 58 41 50
Paul Gonet	03 26 58 42 67
André Goutorbe	03 26 58 43 47
Roland Guyot	03 26 58 46 55
Philippe Haton	03 26 58 41 11
J.N Haton	03 26 58 40 45
Michel Henry	03 26 58 45 10
Joseph Lefebvre	03 26 58 42 76
Michel Lemaire	03 26 58 41 47
Philippe Lète	03 26 58 44 50
Pierre Lète	03 26 58 41 37
Dominique Moinier	03 26 58 63 84
Bernard Namur	03 26 58 41 18
J.C Namur	03 26 58 40 57
Guy Niziolek	03 26 58 61 96
Claude Pajon	03 26 58 46 18
Dominique Papleux	03 26 58 47 43

Fontette

René Lhuillier	03 25 29 61 80

Gyé-sur-Seine

J-C Bartnicki	03 25 38 24 53
Cheurlin	03 25 38 20 27
Claude Cousin	03 25 38 21 67
Jean Josselin	03 25 38 21 48

Janvry

Armand Blin	03 26 03 64 15
Paul Delagarde	03 26 03 63 45
René Lamblot	03 26 03 63 11

Landreville

Chaussin-Vetraino	03 25 38 52 61
Jacques Dufour	03 25 38 52 23
Daniel Lardoux	03 25 38 52 87
Rouer Père & Fils	03 25 38 52 16

Leuvrigny

Michel Brateau	03 26 58 31 20
F. Lasnier	03 26 58 31 88
Mangin	03 26 58 01 18
A. Rodier	03 26 58 39 52
C. Rodier	03 26 58 30 03

Mancy

José Desbordes	03 26 59 71 79
Bernard Girardin	03 26 59 71 65
Pernet-Lebrun	03 26 59 71 63

Mardeuil

Eric Albert	03 26 51 61 66
Charles Barbier	03 26 51 58 38
Gérard Bénard	03 26 55 56 21
Pol Briaux	03 26 51 55 76
François Gamet	03 26 55 25 46
Marcel Garnier	03 26 51 58 25
Emile Leclère	03 26 55 24 45
Lenique	03 26 55 23 27
Jacques Tanneux	03 26 55 24 57

Montgenost

Michel Cocteaux	03 26 80 49 09

La Neuville-aux-Larris

Simone Claisse	03 26 58 12 29
Coop. l'Entraide	03 26 58 12 18

Neuville-sur-Seine

Lucette Charasse	03 25 38 21 40

Les Riceys

Michel Clergeot	03 25 29 36 68
Daniel Lamoreaux	03 25 29 33 41
Georges Lamoreaux	03 25 29 30 75
Guy Lamoreaux	03 25 29 34 39
Michel Noirot	03 25 29 38 46
Gaetan Pehu	03 25 29 39 25
Coop. des Riceys	03 25 29 33 29

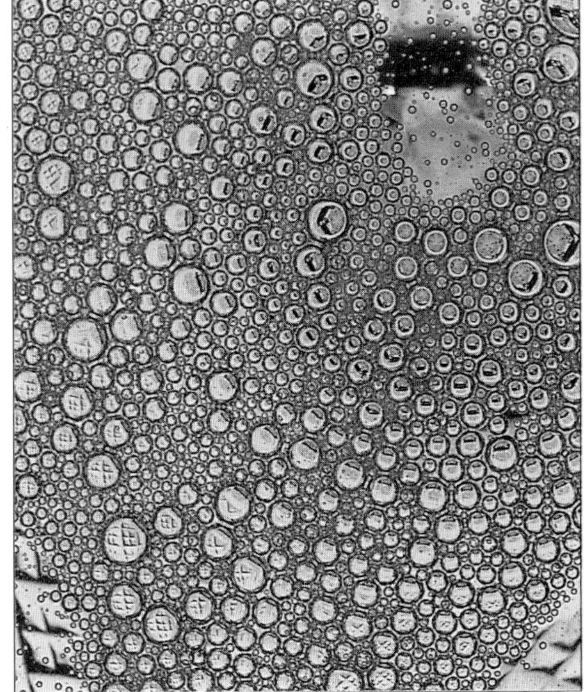

Saint-Martin-d'Ablois

Jean Cez	03 26 59 93 54
Desmoulins	03 26 59 93 10
Christophe Didier	03 26 59 93 94
Coop. St-Martin-d'Ablois	03 26 59 34 39

Urville

Daniel Biliette	03 25 27 40 09
Daniel Labbé	03 25 27 46 80
Daniel Perrin	03 25 27 40 36
Coop. d'Urville	03 25 26 40 14

Vandières

José Ardinat	03 26 58 36 07
Bertrand Delouvin	03 26 58 07 96
Gérard Delouvin	03 26 58 04 17
Serge Faust	03 26 58 02 12
Bernard Nowack	03 26 58 02 69
Denis Salomon	03 26 58 05 77
Coop. Vinicole l'Union	03 26 58 04 20

Venteuil

Autréau-Lasnot	03 26 58 49 35
François Drot	03 26 58 48 69
Claude Dubois	03 26 58 48 37
Michel Guerre	03 26 58 62 72
J-F Launay	03 26 58 48 54
Liébart & Fils	03 26 58 48 09
Marx-Barbier	03 26 58 48 39
Boulard Mignon	03 26 58 60 79
Gérard Mignon	03 26 58 49 57
Mignon Père & Fils	03 26 58 48 90
Thierry Mignon	03 26 58 61 62
Coop. de Venteuil	03 26 58 48 46

Ville-sur-Arce

Régis Barbe	03 25 38 78 47
Alain Coessens	03 25 38 77 07
J-M Féviés	03 25 38 74 13
J-N Féviés	03 25 38 76 49
D. Massin	03 25 38 74 97
R. Massin	03 25 38 74 09
Y. Massin	03 25 38 75 20
Philippe Thévenin	03 25 38 78 04
Raymond Thévenin	03 25 38 75 21
Coop. Chassenay d'Arce	03 25 38 30 10

Villers-sous-Châtillon

Claude Allait	03 26 58 33 29
Château de Villers	03 26 58 33 01
Bérnard Clouet	03 26 58 01 13
José Guérin	03 26 58 00 76
Luc Guérin	03 26 58 36 27
Hubert Père & Fils	03 26 58 33 11
Eric Loriot	03 26 58 36 26
Roger Loriot	03 26 58 33 42
Xavier Loriot	03 26 58 08 28
Alain Marle	03 26 58 07 03
Régis Robert	03 26 58 37 23
Gilles Tournant	03 26 58 36 79
Coop.Villers-sous-Châtillon	03 26 58 33 26

Vincelles

Jacki Durdon	03 26 58 24 26
Christian Hu	03 26 58 85 16
Nicholas Sévilland	03 26 58 23 88

Vinay

René Arrois	03 26 59 90 12
Lecomte Père & Fils	03 26 59 90 79
Pierre Mignon	03 26 59 90 58
Coop. P. Decarrier	03 26 59 90 09

Evaluation of champagnes in the producers' section

The judgement on which these lists are based is only intended to cover the potential maximum points score of the wine. No reference has been made to the wine's drinkability today.

Please note that these lists are updated in february 1999. Therefore some of the listed wines are not included in the producers section earlier in the book.

NON-VINTAGE

1.	Chèvres Pierreuses	86
2.	Paillard Chardonnay	86
3.	Clos des Champions	85
4.	Les Crayères	84
5.	Selosse Extra Brut	84
6.	Selosse Vieux Réserve	83
7.	Guy Charlemagne	83
8.	M. Turgy	83
9.	Clouet Silver Brut	83
10.	Brice Aÿ	83

NON-VINTAGE ROSÉ

1.	Krug Rosé	92
2.	P. Laurain Rosé	88
3.	Fliniaux Rosé	88
4.	Billecart Rosé	86
5.	A. Clouet Rosé	85
6.	B. Hatté Rosé	84
7.	P. Bara Rosé	84
8.	Selosse Rosé	84
9.	Blason de France Rosé	82
10.	Hilaire Leroux Rosé	81

DEMI-SEC

1.	1990 Veuve Clicquot	83
2.	1990 Delamotte	83
3.	1989 Veuve Clicquot	78
4.	1990 Deutz	75
5.	1988 Veuve Clicquot	75
6.	Pol Roger	55
7.	Veuve Clicquot	55
8.	Moët & Chandon Dry	54
9.	Deutz	52
10.	P. Laurain	52

NON-VINTAGE PRESTIGE

1.	Krug Private Cuvée	94
2.	Krug Grande Cuvée	93
3.	Selosse Origine	93
4.	l'Exclusive Ruinart	92
5.	Grand Siècle	92
6.	Diebolt Prestige	91
7.	Clos du Moulin	90
8.	Cent Cinquantenaire	90
9.	A. Robert Vieux Dosé	90
10.	Cuvée Mouzon-Juillet	89

VINTAGE ROSÉ

1.	1988 Cristal Rosé	98
2.	1985 Cristal Rosé	96
3.	1982 Cristal Rosé	96
4.	1989 Cristal Rosé	96
5.	1990 William Deutz Rosé	96
6.	1952 Roederer Rosé	96
7.	1985 Dom Pérignon Rosé	96
8.	1959 Mumm Rosé	96
9.	1982 William Deutz Rosé	96
10.	1985 Belle Epoque Rosé	95
11.	1982 Belle Epoque Rosé	95
12.	1989 Belle Epoque Rosé	95
13.	1979 Belle Epoque Rosé	94
14.	1966 Roederer Rosé	94
15.	1973 Comtes de Champ. Rosé	94
16.	1981 Cristal Rosé	94
17.	1983 Cristal Rosé	94
18.	1990 Signature Rosé	94
19.	1990 Elisabeth Salmon Rosé	94
20.	1988 La Grande Dame Rosé	94

1990

1.	Bollinger Vieilles Vignes	97-99
2.	Salon	98
3.	Selosse "N"	96-97
4.	Cristal	96
5.	William Deutz Rosé	96
6.	Peters Cuvée Spéciale	96
7.	La Grande Dame	96
8.	William Deutz	95
9.	Comtes de Champagne	95
10.	Roederer B. d. B.	95

Top Ten of the Eighties

1.	1985 Bollinger Vieilles Vignes	99
2.	1985 Krug Clos du Mesnil	99
3.	1982 Krug	98
4.	1989 Bollinger Vieilles Vignes	98
5.	1988 Cristal Rosé	98
6.	1989 Krug Clos du Mesnil	98
7.	1988 Bollinger Vieilles Vignes	97
8.	1989 Krug	97
9.	1982 Krug Clos du Mesnil	97
10.	1982 Bollinger Vieilles Vignes	97

1989

1.	Krug Clos du Mesnil	98
2.	Bollinger Vieilles Vignes	98
3.	Krug	97
4.	Cristal	96
5.	Cristal Rosé	96
6.	Selosse "N"	96
7.	Clos des Goisses	96
8.	Diebolt	95
9.	Belle Epoque	95
10.	Belle Epoque Rosé	95

1988

1.	Cristal Rosé	98
2.	Bollinger Vieilles Vignes	97
3.	Salon	96
4.	Winston Churchill	96
5.	William Deutz	95
6.	Dom Ruinart	95
7.	P.R.	95
8.	Charlemagne Mesnillesime	95
9.	Signature	95
10.	Launois Special Club	95

1987

1.	Selosse Origine	90
2.	Bonnaire	90

1986

1.	Selosse	97
2.	Bollinger Vieilles Vignes	95
3.	Clos des Goisses	94
4.	Bonnaire Special Club	93
5.	Belle Epoque Rosé	93
6.	Winston Churchill	92
7.	Comtes de Champagne	91
8.	P.R.	91

Top Ten of the Seventies

1.	1979 Krug Clos du Mesnil	99
2.	1970 Bollinger Vieilles Vignes	98
3.	1979 Krug Collection	97
4.	1979 Krug	97
5.	1975 Winston Churchill	97
6.	1975 Bollinger Vieilles Vignes	97
7.	1979 Launois Special Club	97
8.	1975 Deutz Aÿ	97
9.	1973 Peters	96
10.	1971 Krug Collection	96

1985

1.	Bollinger Vieilles Vignes	99
2.	Krug Clos du Mesnil	99
3.	Comtes de Champagne	97
4.	Cristal Rosé	96
5.	Clos des Goisses	96
6.	Dom Pérignon Rosé	96
7.	Salon	96
8.	Peters Cuvée Spéciale	96
9.	Winston Churchill	96
10.	Belle Epoque Rosé	95

1983

1.	Krug Clos du Mesnil	96
2.	Clos des Goisses	95
3.	Comtes de Champagne	94
4.	Salon	94
5.	Cristal Rosé	94
6.	Cristal	93
7.	Bonnaire Special Club	93
8.	Bonnaire	93
9.	Gratien	92
10.	Bollinger	92

1982

1.	Krug	98
2.	Krug Clos du Mesnil	97
3.	Bollinger Vieilles Vignes	97
4.	Cristal Rosé	96
5.	Salon	96
6.	William Deutz Rosé	96
7.	Cristal	95
8.	Selosse	95
9.	Belle Epoque Rosé	94
10.	Josephine	94

1981

1.	Bollinger Vieilles Vignes	96
2.	Krug Clos du Mesnil	95
3.	Krug	95
4.	Launois Special Club	95
5.	Bonnaire Special Club	95
6.	Cristal Rosé	94
7.	Cristal	94
8.	Cuvée Liberté	93
9.	Lanson Cuvée"225"	93
10.	Comtes de Champagne	92

1980

1.	Bollinger Vieilles Vignes	95
2.	Audoin de Dampierre	93
3.	Cuvée Liberté	92
4.	Dom Pérignon Rosé	92
5.	Dom Pérignon	90

1979

1.	Krug Clos du Mesnil	99
2.	Krug Collection	97
3.	Krug	97
4.	Launois Special Club	97
5.	Clos des Goisses	96
6.	Salon	95
7.	Comtes de Champagne	95
8.	Sugot-Feneuil	95
9.	Peters	95
10.	La Grande Dame	95

1978

1.	Clos des Goisses	94
2.	Cristal	93
3.	Dom Ruinart Rosé	93
4.	Bonnaire Special Club	92
5.	Peters	91
6.	Jacquesson D.T.	91
7.	P. Bara Special Club	90
8.	Dom Ruinart	90
9.	Coutier	90
10.	Launois Special Club	90

1977

1.	Cristal	93

1976

1.	Cristal	96
2.	Comtes de Champagne	96
3.	Des Princes	96
4.	Blason de France	95
5.	Salon	95
6.	Diamant Bleu	94
7.	Comtes de Champagne Rosé	94
8.	Krug	94
9.	Henriot	94
10.	Dom Ruinart Rosé	93

1975

1.	Winston Churchill	97
2.	Bollinger Vieilles Vignes	97
3.	Deutz Aÿ	97
4.	La Grande Dame	95
5.	Bollinger R.D.	95
6.	Bollinger R.D. Année Rare	95
7.	Clos des Goisses	95
8.	Krug	95
9.	Clicquot Wedding Cuvée	94
10.	Bollinger	94

POMMERY
VEUVE
BILLECART

1974

1.	Cristal	91

1973

1.	Peters	96
2.	Dom Pérignon	96
3.	Belle Epoque	95
4.	Krug Collection	95
5.	Krug	95
6.	Comtes de Champagne Rosé	94
7.	Dom Ruinart Anniversary	94
8.	Dom Ruinart	94
9.	Billecart B. d. B.	94
10.	Bonnaire	94

1971

1.	Krug Collection	96
2.	Krug	96
3.	Comtes de Champagne	95
4.	Dom Pérignon	94
5.	Launois	94
6.	Gosset	93
7.	Florens-Louis	93

1970

1.	Bollinger Vieilles Vignes	98
2.	Bollinger R.D. Année Rare	94
3.	Bollinger R.D.	94
4.	Bollinger	93
5.	Comtes de Champagne Rosé	93

Top Ten of the Sixties

1.	1966 Krug	98
2.	1969 Jacquesson D.T.	98
3.	1964 Cristal	98
4.	1961 Krug Collection	98
5.	1961 Krug	98
6.	1966 Bollinger	98
7.	1964 Dom Pérignon	98
8.	1966 Cristal	98
9.	1969 Bollinger Vieilles Vignes	97
10.	1966 Salon	97

1969

1.	Jacquesson D.T.	98
2.	Bollinger Vieilles Vignes	97
3.	Cristal	97
4.	Salon	97
5.	Florens-Louis	96
6.	Bollinger R.D.	95
7.	Bollinger	95
8.	Legras	95
9.	Dom Pérignon	95
10.	Krug Collection	95

1967

1.	Cristal	93

1966

1.	Krug	98
2.	Bollinger	98
3.	Cristal	98
4.	Salon	97
5.	Launois	97
6.	Florens-Louis	97
7.	Dom Pérignon	96
8.	La Royale	96
9.	Louis Roederer	95
10.	Blason de France	95

1964

1.	Cristal	98
2.	Dom Pérignon	98
3.	Diamant Bleu	97
4.	Bollinger R.D.	97
5.	Comtes de Champagne	97
6.	Salon	97
7.	Pol Roger B. d. B.	96
8.	Launois	96
9.	Des Princes	96
10.	Bollinger	96

1962

1.	Bollinger	95
2.	Krug Collection	94
3.	Krug	94
4.	Dom Pérignon	94

1961

1.	Krug Collection	98
2.	Krug	98
3.	Billecart N.F.	97
4.	Diebolt	97
5.	Clicquot	97
6.	Comtes de Champagne	97
7.	Dom Pérignon	95
8.	William Deutz	94
9.	Pol Roger	94
10.	Jacquesson D.T.	94

Top Ten of the Fifties

1.	1959 Clos des Goisses	99
2.	1959 Cristal	99
3.	1953 Salon	98
4.	1955 Salon	98
5.	1955 Clicquot	98
6.	1953 Diebolt	98
7.	1959 Billecart N.F.	98
8.	1959 Krug Collection	98
9.	1955 Gratien	98
10.	1959 Salon	98

Top Ten of the Fourties

1.	1947 Salon	98
2.	1949 Cristal	98
3.	1949 Salon	97
4.	1947 Launois	97
5.	1949 Roederer	96
6.	1949 Krug	96
7.	1945 Roederer	96
8.	1945 Bollinger	96
9.	1949 Pol Roger	96
10.	1947 Pol Roger	96

1959

1. Clos des Goisses 99
2. Cristal 99
3. Billecart N.F. 98
4. Krug Collection 98
5. Salon 98
6. Krug 97
7. Bollinger 97
8. Pol Roger 97
9. P. Bara 96
10. Mumm Rosé 96

1955

1. Salon 98
2. Clicquot 98
3. Gratien 98
4. Krug 97
5. Roederer B. d. B. 96
6. Piper-Heidsieck 96
7. Roederer 96
8. José Michel 96
9. Dom Pérignon 95
10. Pol Roger 95

1953

1. Salon 98
2. Diebolt 98
3. Krug 96
4. Moët & Chandon 95
5. Cristal 94
6. Bollinger 94
7. Jacquesson Perfection 93
8. Clicquot 93
9. Perrier-Jouët 93
10. Pommery 93

1952

1. Roederer Rosé 96
2. Pommery 95
3. Dom Pérignon 95
4. Heidsieck & Monopole 94
5. José Michel 94
6. Gosset 93
7. Pol Roger 93
8. Jacquesson Perfection 92
9. Krug Collection 92

1951

1. Salon 93

1949

1. Cristal 98
2. Salon 97
3. Roederer 96
4. Krug 96
5. Pol Roger 96
6. Clicquot 95
7. Pommery 95
8. Charles Heidsieck 94
9. Mumm 94

1947

1. Salon 98
2. Launois 97
3. Pol Roger 96
4. Krug 94
5. Moët & Chandon 94

1945

1. Roederer 96
2. Bollinger 96
3. Clicquot 96
4. Pol Roger 94
5. Delbeck 94
6. Boizel 94

1943

1. José Michel 96
2. Krug 95
3. Irroy 94
4. Moët Coronation Cuvée 94
5. Dom Pérignon 94
6. Perrier-Jouët 93

EVEN OLDER

1. 1938 Krug 99
2. 1914 Pol Roger 97
3. 1911 Pol Roger 97
4. 1921 José Michel 97
5. 1928 Roederer 97
6. 1921 Pol Roger 97
7. 1914 Moët & Chandon 97
8. 1921 Heidsieck & Monopole 96
9. 1928 Jacquesson Perfection 95
10. 1929 Pommery 95
11. 1926 Krug 95
12. 1937 Krug 95
13. 1919 Clicquot 95
14. 1928 Irroy 95

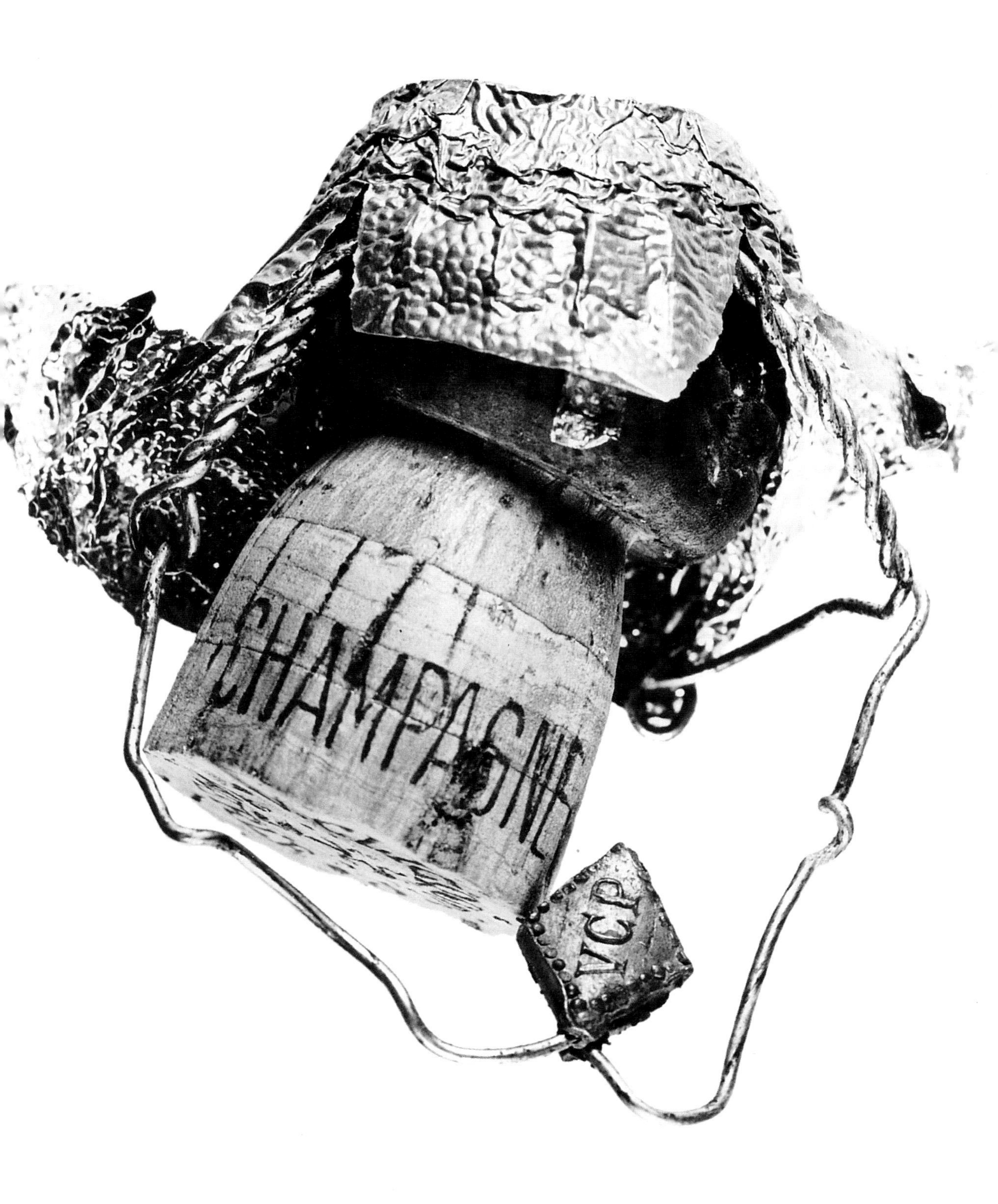
CHAMPAGNE
VCP

Top Hundred

1.	1938 Krug	99	51.	1969 Cristal	97
2.	1959 Clos des Goisses	99	52.	1975 Bollinger Vieilles Vignes	97
3.	1959 Cristal	99	53.	1989 Krug	97
4.	1985 Bollinger Vieilles Vignes	99	54.	1928 Roederer	97
5.	1985 Krug Clos du Mesnil	99	55.	1982 Krug Clos du Mesnil	97
6.	1979 Krug Clos du Mesnil	99	56.	1982 Bollinger Vieilles Vignes	97
7.	1990 Bollinger Vieilles Vignes	99	57.	1986 Selosse	97
8.	1947 Salon	98	58.	1959 Pol Roger	97
9.	1953 Salon	98	59.	1921 Pol Roger	97
10.	1955 Salon	98	60.	1964 Comtes de Champagne	97
11.	1955 Clicquot	98	61.	1979 Launois Special Club	97
12.	1953 Diebolt	98	62.	1985 Comtes de Champagne	97
13.	1966 Krug	98	63.	1961 Diebolt	97
14.	1949 Cristal	98	64.	1975 Deutz Aÿ	97
15.	1969 Jacquesson D.T.	98	65.	1964 Salon	97
16.	1959 Billecart N.F.	98	66.	1961 Comtes de Champagne	97
17.	1982 Krug	98	67.	1969 Salon	97
18.	1964 Cristal	98	68.	1961 Clicquot	97
19.	1988 Cristal Rosé	98	69.	1914 Moët & Chandon	97
20.	1961 Krug Collection	98	70.	1990 Selosse "N"	97
21.	1961 Krug	98	71.	1985 Cristal Rosé	96
22.	1966 Bollinger	98	72.	1973 Peters	96
23.	1959 Krug Collection	98	73.	1982 Cristal Rosé	96
24.	1955 Gratien	98	74.	1949 Roederer	96
25.	1989 Krug Clos du Mesnil	98	75.	1949 Krug	96
26.	1959 Salon	98	76.	1945 Roederer	96
27.	1989 Bollinger Vieilles Vignes	98	77.	1945 Bollinger	96
28.	1970 Bollinger Vieilles Vignes	98	78.	1949 Pol Roger	96
29.	1964 Dom Pérignon	98	79.	1947 Pol Roger	96
30.	1966 Cristal	98	80.	1971 Krug Collection	96
31.	1990 Salon	98	81.	1971 Krug	96
32.	1959 Krug	97	82.	1964 Pol Roger B. d. B.	96
33.	1914 Pol Roger	97	83.	1964 Launois	96
34.	1969 Bollinger Vieilles Vignes	97	84.	1989 Cristal Rosé	96
35.	1911 Pol Roger	97	85.	1945 Clicquot	96
36.	1921 José Michel	97	86.	1990 Cristal	96
37.	1949 Salon	97	87.	1990 William Deutz Rosé	96
38.	1966 Salon	97	88.	1989 Cristal	96
39.	1988 Bollinger Vieilles Vignes	97	89.	1964 Des Princes	96
40.	1959 Bollinger	97	90.	1989 Selosse "N"	96
41.	1964 Diamant Bleu	97	91.	1985 Clos des Goisses	96
42.	1961 Billecart N.F.	97	92.	1985 Dom Pérignon Rosé	96
43.	1955 Krug	97	93.	1990 Peters Cuvée Spéciale	96
44.	1979 Krug Collection	97	94.	1985 Peters Cuvée Spéciale	96
45.	1947 Launois	97	95.	1985 Winston Churchill	96
46.	1979 Krug	97	96.	1921 Heidsieck & Monopole	96
47.	1975 Winston Churchill	97	97.	1976 Cristal	96
48.	1966 Launois	97	98.	1953 Krug	96
49.	1966 Florens-Louis	97	99.	1952 Roederer Rosé	96
50.	1964 Bollinger R.D.	97	100.	1964 Bollinger	96

The author's personal grading of villages

Chardonnay

Grand cru 100 %
1 Le Mesnil
2 Cramant
3 Avize
4 Oger
5 Chouilly

Premier cru 95 %
6 Cuis
7 Grauves
8 Vertus
9 Aÿ

Premier cru 93 %
10 Oiry
11 Bergères-les-Vertus
12 Verzenay
13 Ambonnay
14 Bouzy

Premier cru 90 %
15 Chigny-les-Roses
16 Dizy
17 Mareuil-sur-Aÿ
18 Villers-Marmery
19 Sillery
20 Verzy
21 Louvois
22 Cumières
23 Mailly
24 Rilly-la-Montagne

85 %
Other current Grand cru and Premier cru villages.

80 %
All other villages.

Pinot Noir

Grand cru 100 %
1 Aÿ
2 Verzenay
3 Ambonnay
4 Bouzy
5 Mareuil-sur-Aÿ
6 Verzy
7 Cumières

Premier cru 95 %
8 Mailly
9 Sillery
10 Dizy
11 Louvois

Premier cru 90 %
12 Tours-sur-Marne
13 Trépail
14 Chigny-les-Roses
15 Champillon
16 Hautvillers
17 Damery
18 Ludes
19 Villers-Marmery
20 Mutigny
21 Tauxières
22 Bisseuil
23 Beaumont-sur-Vesle

85 %
Other current Grand cru and Premier cru villages.

80 %
All other villages.

Champagne statistics

– Total sales 1996: **255.8 million bottles.**

– Sales distribution 1996:

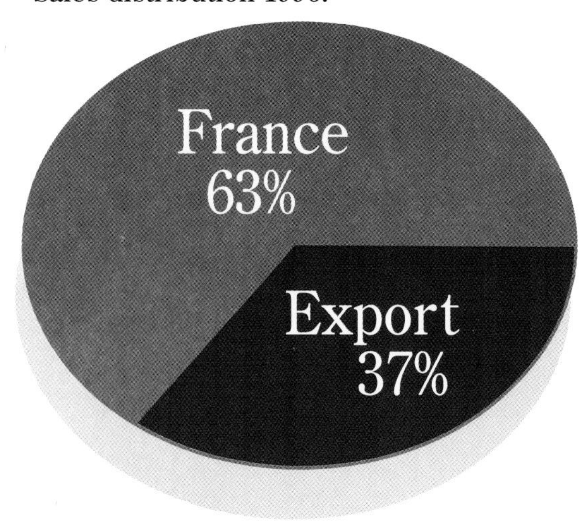

– Total sales in the last twelve years:

1984: 188 million bottles.
1985: 195 million bottles.
1986: 205 million bottles.
1987: 218 million bottles.
1988: 237 million bottles.
1989: 249 million bottles.
1990: 232 million bottles.
1991: 214 million bottles.
1992: 214 million bottles.
1993: 229 million bottles.
1994: 242 million bottles.
1995: 247 million bottles.

– Export share of total sales:

1984: 33%
1985: 37%
1986: 37%
1987: 37%
1988: 38%
1989: 38%
1990: 36%
1991: 35%
1992: 34%
1993: 33%
1994: 35%
1995: 35%

– Global distribution of exports:

Europe	74,0 %
America	17,6 %
Asia	4,7 %
Oceania	1,3 %
Africa	1,4 %

– On 31.07.1996, Champagne maintained a store of **980 million bottles.**

– The total cultivated area of **30,717** hectares is divided up among the following areas:

22,781 hectares in Marne
2,045 hectares in Aisne
18 hectares in Seine et Marne
5,854 hectares in Aube
19 hectares in Haute Marne

– 1995 there were **5,461** champagne producers in the region. That figure is made up of:

5,152 growers
44 cooperatives
265 champagne houses

– Of 1993's total sales, champagne houses answered for **71.4** %.

– Of 1994's total sales, champagne houses answered for **72.6** %.

– Of 1995's total sales, champagne houses answered for **73.3** %.

– Of 1996's total sales, champagne houses answered for **71.8** %.

– Grape varieties 1996:

Pinot Noir	37.9 %
Pinot Meunier	35.2 %
Chardonnay	26.9 %

– 1996's sales in countries outside France:

1. UK	18,844,853 bottles
2. Germany	17,021,214 bottles
3. USA	11,992,414 bottles
4. Belgium	7,524,137 bottles
5. Switzerland	6,616,110 bottles
6. Italy	6,552,579 bottles
7. Japan	2,387,240 bottles
8. Netherlands	2,133,062 bottles
9. Spain	1,155,177 bottles
10. Australia	873,691 bottles
11. Canada	852,631 bottles
12. Denmark	750,567 bottles
13. Austria	687,699 bottles
14. Luxemburg	653,917 bottles
15. Singapore	492,336 bottles
16. Hong-Kong	480,254 bottles
17. Sweden	439,144 bottles

– Sales in some French possessions:

Guadeloupe	2,266,777 bottles
Réunion	535,328 bottles
Martinique	201,065 bottles

– Annual consumption per capita:

1. Guadeloupe	6.67 bottles
2. France	2.70 bottles
3. Switzerland	1.00 bottles
4. Réunion	0.92 bottles
5. Belgien	0.70 bottles
6. Martinique	0.61 bottles
7. UK	0.34 bottles
8. Germany	0.23 bottles
9. Denmark	0.15 bottles
10. Netherlands	0.14 bottles
11. Italy	0.11 bottles
12. Australia	0.05 bottles
13. USA	0.05 bottles
14. Sweden	0.05 bottles
15. Canada	0.03 bottles

– The share of champagne among worldwide sparkling wines, is estimated at about **13%**.

A little champagne dictionary

À la glace
– mechanical dégorgement involving freezing the bottle neck.

Adding sulphur
- a method of preventing oxidation or interrupting fermentation.

Agrafe
- the metal clip that secures the cork.

Alcohol
- in the context of wine, ethyl alcohol that builds up during fermentation.

AOC Appellation d'Origine Contrôlée
- the original system for quality french wines.

Appellation
- original designation.

Assemblage
- base wines that are blended into a cuvée.

Autolysis
- the breaking down of the yeast cells by enzymes. This is a necessary biochemical process which gives champagne its own special flavour.

Belemnite chalk, Belemnita quadrata
- champagne soil.

Blanc de blancs
- white wine from white grapes.

Blanc de noirs
- white wine from black grapes.

Body
- an important quality of wine with a high extract content, giving weight.

Botrytis
- rot.

Boues de ville
- refuse from the town which is spread in the vineyards to act as fertilizer and warm up the soil.

Brut Absolut, Brut Intégral, Brut non Dosé, Brut Zero
- sugar-free champagne.

Cave
- cellar.

Cendres noires
- the black, energy-rich soil used as fertilizer in the region.

Chaptalisation
- the addition of sugar to the juice or must before fermentation in order to achieve a greater alcohol content.

Chef de caves
- cellarmaster.

Clone
- a plant which, through the use of asexual propagation, retains the genetic qualities of the original plant.

Comité Interprofessionel du Vin de Champagne C.I.V.C.
- the leading body of Champagne.

Coopérativ-manipulant
- a cooperative that makes champagne under its own label.

Crayères
- gallo-roman chalk pit used as champagne cellar.

Crown-cap
- the cap used for the prise de mousse.

Cru
- place of growth.

Cuvée
- the blend or the first pressing.

Débourbage
- purging or cleaning.

Dégorgement
- the removal of the sediment.

Demi-muid
- 600 litre wooden cask.

Demi-sec
- semi-sweet.

Deuxième taille
- the third pressing, now forbidden.

Dosage
- sugar additive.

Doux
- sweet champagne.

Échelle des crus
- ranking of areas of cultivation.

Epinettes
- secateurs used at harvest time.

Esters
- sweet-smelling components formed during fermentation and the wine's maturing process.

Extract
- all the ingredients remaining after the evaporation of water and alcohol.

Les Falaises
- the hills of Champagne.

Fermentation
- quite simply, the conversion of grape juice into wine. The yeast feeds off the sugar in the grapes, setting off a chain of chemical reactions.

Filtering
- the removal of yeast particles etc. prior to bottling.

Fining
- the process that separates certain particles from the wine, either by filtration or adding gelatine which attracts particles on its way to the bottom of the vat.

Foudre
- large oak cask.

en Foule
- old-fashioned method of cultivating vines.

Grand cru
- the 17 highest-ranking villages.

Lees
- sediment.

Legs (or "tears")
- lines of liquid along the sides of the glass. These indicate a high content of glycerol, sugar or alcohol.

Liqueur d'expédition
- sugar additive.

Liqueur de tirage
- addition of yeast and sugar before the second fermentation in the bottle.

Macération
- the process in which the grape juice extracts colour and tannin from the skin.

Maderised
- a quality of old wines. Creates a dark colour and flavour of sherry, overripe apples and plums.

Malolactic fermentation
- the process which turns the hard malic acid into soft lactic acid.

Marque Auxiliaire (M.A.)
- buyer's own brand.

Micraster
- A chalk widespread on the plains, but also in the hills, of champagne, particularly to the north of Montagne de Reims.

Millésime
- vintage.

Monocru
- wine from one village.

Mousse
- the bubbles and effervescence formed by the carbon dioxide in the wine.

Négociant-manipulant
- champagne house.

Premier cru
- wine villages or communes ranked one level under Grand cru. 90-99% on the cru scale.

Pupitre
- large wooden racks for remuage.

Racking
- the process of draining a wine from one cask to another.

R.D.
- recently disgorged.

Recolté-manipulant (R.M.)
- grower who sells his own champagne.

Remuage
- the bottles are turned in different stages to collect the sediment before dégorgement.

Remueur
- the person who carries out remuage.

Reserve wines
- older wines that are used to give non-vintage champagne a more mature flavour.

Sommelier
- wine waiter.

Sur lattes
- the horizontal position of the bottles when stored in the cellar.

Taille
- the grape juice that follows the cuvée.

Tannin
- tannic acid.

Terroir
- soil.

Transvasage
- transferring wine to a different-sized bottle.

Vin clair
- still wines before blending the cuvée.

Vintage
- year of production.

Important addresses in Champagne

Tourist bureaus etc.

Reims tourist bureau
2 rue Guillaume de Mauchault
51100 Reims
tel 03 26 47 25 69

Épernay tourist bureau
7 av. de Champagne
51200 Épernay
tel 03 26 55 33 00

Bar-sur-Aube tourist bureau
Place del Hôtel de Ville
10200 Bar-sur-Aube
tel 03 27 24 25

Bar-sur-Seine tourist bureau
154 Grande rue de la Resistance
10110 Bar-sur-Seine
tel 03 25 29 94 43

Château-Thierry tourist bureau
11 rue Vallée
02400 Château-Thierry
tel 03 23 83 10 14

Charly-sur-Marne tourist bureau
20 Place du Général de Gaulle
02310 Charly-sur-Marne
tel 03 23 82 07 49

Institut du Champagne
5 rue des Marmouzels
51100 Reims
tel 03 26 50 62 10

Comité departemental du tourisme del Aube
34 quai Dampierre
1000 Troyes
tel 03 25 42 50 50

Comité departemental du tourisme de la Marne
2 boulevard Vaubecourt
51000 Châlons-en-Champagne
tel 03 26 68 37 52

Syndicat General des Vigne-rons
44 rue Jean Jaures
51200 Épernay
tel 03 26 59 55 00

Syndicat des Grandes Mar-ques
1 rue Marie Stuart
51100 Reims
tel 03 26 47 90 58

Comité Interprofessionnel du Vin de Champagne
5 rue Henri Martin
51200 Épernay
tel 03 26 51 19 30

Restaurants

(H) – also hotel

Ambonnay
Auberge Saint-Vincent
tel 03 26 57 01 98

Aÿ
La Petite Chaumière
tel 03 26 55 43 20

Au Vieux Pressoir
tel 03 26 55 43 31

Bar-sur-Aube
La Chaumière
tel 03 25 27 91 02

Moulin du Landion
tel 03 25 27 92 17 (H)

Bar-sur-Seine
Le Cérès
tel 03 25 29 86 65 (H)

Le Barséquanais
tel 03 25 29 82 75 (H)

Le Parc de Villeneuve
tel 03 25 29 16 80

Bergères-les-Vertus
Hostellerie du Mont-Aime
tel 03 26 52 21 31 (H)

Berry-au-Bac
La Côte 108
tel 03 23 79 95 04

Champigny-sur-Vesle
La Garenne
tel 03 26 08 26 62

Champillon
Royal Champagne
tel 03 26 52 87 11 (H)

Châlons-en-Champagne
Angleterre
tel 03 26 68 21 51 (H)

Le Pré Saint-Alpin
tel 03 26 70 20 26

Château-Thierry
Ile de France
tel 03 23 69 10 12 (H)

Courcelles-sur-Vesle
Château de Courcelles
tel 03 23 74 06 41

L'Epine
Aux Armes de Champagne
tel 03 26 69 30 30 (H)

Fère-en -Tardenois
Château de Fère
tel 23 82 21 13 84 28

Épernay
Les Berceaux
tel 03 26 55 28 84 (H)

Au Petit Comptoir
tel 03 26 51 53 51

La Cave a Champagne
tel 03 26 55 50 70

La Flambée
tel 03 26 51 76 48

Taverne Alsacienne
tel 03 26 59 45 57

La Brigueterie
tel 03 26 59 99 99

Etoges
Le Château d'Etoges
tel 03 26 59 30 08

La Ferté-sous-Jouarre
Auberge de Condé
tel 03 60 22 00 07

Hautvillers
l'Abbeye
tel 03 26 59 44 79

Le Mesnil
Le Mesnil
tel 03 26 57 95 57

Sept-Saulx
Cheval Blanc
tel 03 26 59 10 03 (H)

Reuilly-Sauvigny
Le Relais
tel 03 23 70 35 36 (H)

Les Riceys
Le Magny
tel 03 25 29 38 39 (H)

Reims
Les Crayères
tel 03 26 82 80 80 (H)

Orphée
tel 03 26 88 63 74

Univers
tel 03 26 88 68 08 (H)

Volnelly-Gambetta
tel 03 26 47 41 64 (H)

Au Petit Bachus
tel 03 26 47 10 05

Au Petit Comptoir
tel 03 26 40 58 58

Brasserie du Boulingrin
tel 03 26 40 96 22

Le Chardonnay
tel 03 26 06 08 60

Le Continental
tel 03 26 47 01 47

Le Foch
tel 03 26 47 48 22

Le Vigneron
tel 03 26 47 00 71

l'Assiette Champenois
tel 03 26 84 64 64 (H)

Tours-sur-Marne

La Touraine Champenoise
tel 03 26 58 91 93 (H)

Troyes

La Poste
tel 03 25 73 05 05 (H)

Le Clos Juillet
tel 03 25 73 31 32

Vertus

La Reine Blanche
tel 03 26 52 26 76 (H)

La Touraine Champenoise.

Other hotels

Chalons-en-Champagne

Ibis
tel 03 26 68 31 88

Pasteur
tel 03 26 21 51 09

Pot d'Etain
tel 03 26 68 09 09

Sainte-Croix
tel 03 26 67 50 40

Bon Accueil
tel 03 26 68 09 48

Épernay

Hôtel de la Cloche
tel 03 26 55 24 05

Ibis
tel 03 26 55 41 72

Climat de France
tel 03 26 54 17 39

Reims

Hôtel de la Paix
tel 03 26 40 04 08

Les Templiers
tel 03 26 88 55 08

Les Consuls
tel 03 26 88 46 10

Grand Hôtel Continental
tel 03 26 40 39 35

Holiday Inn
tel 03 26 47 56 00

Le Jeroboam
tel 03 26 84 49 49

New Hôtel Europe
tel 03 26 40 14 37

Porte Mars
tel 03 26 40 28 35

Quality Hôtel
tel 03 26 40 01 08

Les Crayères.

List of producers (with page numbers)

Clos des Goisses
CHAMPAGNE
BRUT
Clos des Goisses
1959
PHILIPPONNAT
MAREUIL-SUR-AY

Sources of information and inspiration:

John Arlott: Krug, House of Champagne, 1976.
Michel Dovaz: l'Encyclopédie des vins de Champagne, 1983.
Hubrecht Duijker: The Wines of the Loire, Alsace and Champagne, 1983.
Dussert-Gerber: The best French wines, 1989.
Colin Fenton: Salon le Mesnil, 1981.
Patrick Forbes: The Wine, the Land and the People, 1967.
André Garcia: Grandes Marques & Maisons de Champagne, 1982.
Gilbert & Gaillard: Le Guide des meilleurs Champagnes, 1996.
Cyril Ray: Bollinger, 1971.
André Simon: The History of Champagne, 1962.
Pamela Vandyke Price: The Wines of Champagne, 1984.
Tom Stevenson: Champagne, 1986.
Michael Edwards: The Champagne Companion, 1994.
Jane MacQuitty: Pocketguide to Champagne and sparkling Wines, 1986.
Jean-Marie Curien: Guide Curien de la Champagne, 1993, 1994, 1995.
Don Hewitson: The Glory of Champagne, 1989.
Nicholas Faith: The Story of Champagne, 1988.
Serena Sutcliffe: A Celebration of Champagne, 1988.
Steven Spurrier, Michel Dovaz: Académie du Vin Wine Course, 1990.
Aimé Adnet: Le Mesnil sur Oger, 1985.
Rosmary George: The Wine Dictionary, 1989.
Michael Broadbent: The Great Vintage Winebook II, 1991.
Jancis Robinson: Vines, Grapes and Wines, 1986.

Picture sources:

All the photographs and illustrations in this book have been taken or created by Pelle Bergentz unless otherwise stated below.

Pål Allan; page 18, 42-43, 48, 49, 78, 79, 85, 87, 94-95, 103, 105, 108-109, 123, 128, 133, 170, 173, 178, 187, 206, 209, 227, 228, 266, 277, 279, 308, 322, 326, 327, 330, 332-333, 342, 343 and cover photos.

Claes Löfgren; page 53, 144, 205 and 286.

Pictures on loan:
Ayala; page 22 and 23.
Boizel; page 179.
C.I.V.C; page 39, 50, 55, 57(x 2), 59 and 244.
Demoiselle; page 184.
Jacquesson & Fils; page 17, 283 and 284.
Gosset; 233.
Hôtel d'Angleterre; page 130.
Krug; page 45 and 62.
Marc Hébrart; page 291.
Mercier; page 25(x 2), 145 and 181.
Moët & Chandon; page 18, 20, 24(x 2), 51, 55(x 2), 61 and 70.
Palmer; page 63 and 213.
Perrier-Jouët; page 25.
Philipponnat; page 290.
Pommery; page 71.
Reims tourist bureau; page 60, 144 and 188.
Roederer; page 37 and 193.
Ruinart; page 203.
Veuve Clicquot; page 62 and 198.

My thanks to all the above companies and organisations.